CW01401810

Identity and Intercultural Communication

Identity and Intercultural Communication

Edited by

Nicoleta Corbu, Dana Popescu-Jourdy
and Tudor Vlad

Identity and Intercultural Communication,
Edited by Nicoleta Corbu, Dana Popescu-Jourdy and Tudor Vlad

This book first published 2014

Cambridge Scholars Publishing

12 Back Chapman Street, Newcastle upon Tyne, NE6 2XX, UK

British Library Cataloguing in Publication Data
A catalogue record for this book is available from the British Library

ISBN (10): 1-4438-6397-1, ISBN (13): 978-1-4438-6397-1

TABLE OF CONTENTS

Introduction: Redefining Identity in Intercultural Context 1
Nicoleta Corbu, Dana Popescu-Jourdy and Tudor Vlad

Part One: In Search of a European Identity

Promoting European Identity: The Construction and Reconstruction of European Union Identity Myths, Israel vs. Romania 6
Mira Moshe and Nicoleta Corbu

Bridging the Gap through Europeanized Media: A Content Analysis of National and Transnational EurActiv News Portals.............................. 34
Adina Marincea

In Search of a European Identity: The Romanian Perspective 63
Valeriu Frunzaru and Mădălina Boţan

Visibility of the EU through EU-funded Programmes and Projects: What about an Instrumental European Identity? 75
Roxana Maria Dascalu

Building the "Eurosphere" under External Pressure? The Arab Crisis Seen by www.euronews.net... 97
Loredana Radu

Développement de la dimension européenne et de la compétence interculturelle à travers les Programmes d'Assistanat Comenius de l'Enseignement Tout au long de la Vie dans l'Enseignement Secondaire 117
Christina Ene, Argyris Kyridis and Ifigenia Vamvakidou

Is Europe the Problem or the Solution? An Analysis of Euroscepticism in Romania 135
Paul Dobrescu, Flavia Durach and Alina Bârgăoanu

European Cultural Identity and Its Challenges in Intercultural Context: An Empirical Approach 158
Nicoleta Corbu and Georgiana Udrea

Local Identity vs. European Identity in Romanian Advertising 175
Mădălina Moraru

Reading between the Headlines: How Media Framed the Postponement of Romania's Accession to the Schengen Area 199
Elenea Negrea

Towards a Europeanized Romanian Public Sphere? Media Framing of Romania's Accession to the Schengen Area of Free Movement........ 211
Flavia Durach and Oana Ştefăniţă

Part Two: Identity, Intercultural Communication: National Perspectives

A President in the Headlines: President Dalia Itzik as Reflected in the Israeli Media 238
Dalia Liran Alper

A New Solidarity among Ultra-Orthodox Women in Israel 265
Orly Tsarfaty and Dalia Liran-Alper

Crise de l'identité collectiviste des jeunes employés chinois dans les entreprises à capitaux étrangers 296
Xi Jiang

Communion: An Approach towards (Re)Defining Community: The Romanian Case 314
Adrian Lesenciuc, Ion Teofil Creţu and Viana Popică

Communication interculturelle provoquee: entre identité et recadrage presentiel 330
Christian Agbobli and Oumar Kane

L'image des acteurs humanitaires auprès des haïtiens: sauveurs ou colonisateurs ? 349
Colette Nguemedyam Djadeu

Anxiety and Uncertainty in Expatriate Everyday Life: Identity Boundary Regulation within Estonian Online Communities.................. 360
Kristel Kaljund and Anne-Liis Peterson

Raising Public Issues in Romanian Media: Visibility Patterns and Deliberative Practices in Debating Professional Migration Impact.. 379
Mălina Ciocea

Stéréotypes croisés et identités : Une étude empirique menée en contexte universitaire multiculturel 394
Anne-Marie Codrescu

Defining Romanian Cultural Identity: Guidelines for an Intercultural History of a Theoretical Quest.. 414
Grigore Georgiu and Alexandru Cârlan

Percevoir l'altérité, se sentir autre l'alterite a travers trois philosophes Français: Michel Foucault, Emmanuel Levinas, Paul Ricoeur 430
Odile Riondet

Encounter between the Western Gaze and the Picturesque Other in the Tourist Culture... 449
Simona Bucşa

Patterns of Communication in Public Space in Romania 470
Corina Daba Buzoianu and Cristina Cîrtiţă-Buzoianu

Part Three: Professional Identities and Networks

Déprofessionnalisation du journalisme ou retour aux sources ?............. 488
Arnaud Noblet

Factuality as a Crisis Communication Tool—Case Study: Roşia Montană Gold Corporation.. 504
George David and Ion Chiciudean

The Impact of the New Technologies on the Journalist's Status and on Mass Communication Education 535
Tudor Vlad and Lee B. Becker

Les contours d'une communauté imaginée : Le thème-évenement Europe à l'intérieur des journaux télévisés français (1951–2009) 547
Jean-Claude Soulages

The Use of Social Networks for Building Political Brands: A Comparative Perspective 563
Diana Maria Cismaru

OS de là, la transcendance des environnements informatiques 577
Vincent Mabillot

Nonverbal Sensitivity and Network Centrality: Using Our Abilities to Interpret Emotions and Become Popular 595
Loredana Ivan

Le discours de solidarité internationale: l'identité de l'autre à travers les pratiques des ONG 616
Dana Popescu Jourdy and Elisabeth Vercher

Explorative Pilot Study regarding the Role of Negative Affect in Performing Emotional Labour 630
Dan Florin Stanescu and Elena Madalina Iorga

ICT, Migrant Networks and Transnational Identity 652
Rita Sever

INTRODUCTION: REDEFINING IDENTITY IN INTERCULTURAL CONTEXT

NICOLETA CORBU, DANA POPESCU-JOURDY AND TUDOR VLAD

The search for identity is a continuous challenge in the academic field, a much-discussed topic and a point of junction of different research fields. Placing the topic against an intercultural background, with a focus on communication, opens a three-fold perspective that is addressed in this book.

The first chapter focuses on the European dimension of identity, questioning the very concept of "European identity", from both theoretical and empirical points of view.

The concept of European identity was coined at the European Community summit in Copenhagen, in 1973, after the first enlargement. It marked a step forward in the European construction, as a reaction to the lack of identity visible in the interpretative framework existent at the time. The Declaration on European identity, or Declaration of Copenhagen, signed by the then nine European Community member states, marks a period of constant academic inquiry about the new concept.

The debates on European identity are nowadays focused on two main approaches. On the one hand, many scholars agree that European identity is a rather theoretical construct, a form lacking content, an empty shell, a desired ideal, far from being achieved. On the other hand some scholars argue that European identity is a well-established presence, a new layer of one's identity, just as real as national identity.

A lot of research has been done with regard to the possible construction of a European public sphere, and a common European agenda, within which the European identity is constantly questioned and analysed. In this context, the Europeanization of national public spheres and of national media raises the problem of a fragmented and rather inconsistent identity. The role played by the media in the Europeanization process and in the construction of a European public sphere is another rich field of constant academic attention.

In this regard, the first chapter addresses issues related to European identity myths, the Europeanization of national media, the European public sphere, intercultural communication within the EU, Euroscepticism and the media framing of European topics, as well as specific national perspectives on European identity.

The second chapter of the book discusses the concept of identity in national and intercultural contexts. The question of identity can be placed at the crossroads of different fields of study: sociology (social and/or professional identities), anthropology (behaviours, rituals, ways of life), political science (identity trough institutional structures) etc. Thus, the academic discussion about identity takes place in the general framework of intercultural communication and gives the concept of "communication" its entire disciplinary importance, referring to those academic and professional works that structure communication as scientific knowledge. Specifically, authors discuss the possible relationships among communication, culture and identity during the encounter with the Other.

The representation of otherness is mostly developed by media discourse. Included in the logic of expression of our own identity, "our" media provide us with specific definitions of the difference to the Other, inside a dynamic news discourse.

Researchers often speak of the ideological dimension of culture. On the one hand, this dimension can create, in an intercultural context, a specific connection between identity and commitment. On the other hand, it can contribute, in certain cases, to specific strategies of argumentation or persuasion, according to a hierarchy of values or assimilation logics.

This general background helps build an academic debate about national identity and related concepts: cultural stereotypes, diasporic identities, communities, intercultural communication etc.

The third chapter, Professional Identities, repositions the concept of identity in the context of professional life: journalism, political communication, information technology, organizational communication etc.

The sharp downturn in the world economy, the collapse of the economic model for media industries in the country and the strong impact of new communication technologies at the end of the first decade of the new century have had a dramatic impact on the media job market and on the professional communicators' status. The turmoil was not limited to the entry-level segment of the job market. Television, radio and news magazines trimmed their staffs, often by eliminating positions at the top. Perhaps what is more important, the journalists continuing to work in the established media and those who have gone out on their own have found themselves in competition with another group of individuals, often labelled "citizen" journalists.

The turmoil has affected other communication occupations as well. The professional identity of various fields has gone through a process of redefinition and repositioning in recent years. In the same time, any deprofessionalization of an occupation raises questions about the necessity for and components of the educational paths that lead to it.

Some specific situations develop today professional practices of intercultural communication, which contribute to the definition of identity: geographical mobility, cohabitation (personnel, "communities"), cooperation between organizations in an international context.

In this context, the third chapter gather together papers focused on deprofessionalization, impact of new technologies on various aspects of professional identities, professional stereotypes, organizational communication etc.

The internal consistency of this book resides in the authors' constant inquiry about redefining identity in intercultural context, at the crossroad of different perspectives: political, social, cultural, professional.

PART ONE:

IN SEARCH OF A EUROPEAN IDENTITY

Promoting European Identity: The Construction and Reconstruction of European Union Identity Myths, Israel vs. Romania

Mira Moshe and Nicoleta Corbu

Abstract

Academic investigation of European identity has been constantly challenged in recent decades. While the pessimistic approach ("doom and gloom") is based upon the widespread Euroscepticism which criticizes the enlargement process, the optimistic path portrays European identity as a promising entity, strengthened by pro-European life-saving migration, television without frontiers etc. In this context, the present study aims to identify the way in which the online press promotes the European identity through the construction and reconstruction of myths that appear in Israeli and Romanian online media. Juxtaposing these cultural spaces offers the benefit of diversified perspectives, based on each nation's political position vis-à-vis the European Union: Israel, a member of the Mediterranean European initiative, and Romania, a newly integrated member state of the EU. These dual analytical economic and political contexts have revealed "insider" and "outsider" insights with regard to promoting an optimistic versus a pessimistic mythical perception of European identity. Moreover, both Romania and the EU have been undergoing some of their most challenging times in recent months. The struggles of Romania are connected to the postponement of Schengen Area integration (postponed in December 2010), while the struggles of the EU comprise the most difficult economic and political period in its existence. These circumstances present a unique opportunity to confront identity construction during the massive and ongoing crises that have arisen. Hence, we examined all EU-related news from the most prominent online news sites in Israel and Romania immediately after the postponement of Romania's Schengen integration for a period of two months, January and February 2011. Framing analysis was employed to identify and compare the ways in which media coverage of the EU has created and shaped mythological narratives regarding European identity. The research population included 452 news items identified on the Israeli news sites Ha'aretz and Ynet, and 289 news reports from the Romanian news sites Hotnews and Ziare.com. Findings showed a dialectical approach to the European identity. On the one hand, Israeli online media have fostered the myth of the EU as a powerful and united geopolitical player, based on a narrative of the foundation and fortification of the European Union, viewed as a saviour from both an economic and a political point of view. On the other hand, Romanian media have constructed a much more fragmented and disruptive image of the EU and its identity. They have indicated internal inequities, as well as political and economic disputes. Both sites discuss the imbalance between "old" and "new" member states, as well as the constant loss of Euroenthusiasm, which occurred in newly integrated countries soon after their admission into the EU. In conclusion, the promotion by the media of the EU as a political myth is dually represented by various reportage patterns x-raying heterogeneous positions regarding one of the most prominent actors in the political arena nowadays: the "outsider" view of the EU as a saviour and the disenchanted "insider" perspective of the EU myth.

Key words: European Union identity, myths, political myths and media

Introduction

The preoccupation of media research with the European Union has been coming to terms with the Union's attempt to generate a "new" European identity with the purpose to replace local national identities (Henry, 2001; Marciniak, 2009). On the one hand, it is clear that the legitimacy of the EU rests on a collective agreement regarding the symbols, values and narratives created by the Union, past and present (Bruter, 2009). But on the other hand, in order to create that same consensus (which relies on a common identity, whether real or imaginary), it is vital for the European Union to create, promote and establish appropriate values, symbols and myths (Hardt-Mautner, 1995). This task is made especially difficult by numerous challenging voices asking: "Is a unified European identity myth or reality?" (Blokker, 2008; Maguire, Poulton & Possamai, 1999).

This dual attitude towards the ability of EU institutions to generate a European identity having mythological meaning is also evident in mass media. As far as the media are concerned, research shows that in the long run (Bruter, 2007), news has an important impact on European identity; it shapes people's understanding of the world and their place within it; and it "contributes to our understanding of what it means to belong to a cultural and political collective such as Europe" (Inthorn, 2006, p. 72).

Little attention has been paid so far to the new media, mainly because they are fragmented, difficult to investigate, less policy driven, and led by the elite (Trandafoiu, 2006, p. 96). Central to the present article is the question of how the press promotes European identity. In other words, does the public arena, as represented by the press, present mythical reportage of EU institutions? How are journalists in various countries promoting a united European identity, and what kind of mythological frameworks are they employing to do so? In the present article, an attempt will be made to answer these questions based on two case studies: press coverage of the EU in Israel (a member of the Mediterranean European initiative) compared to that of Romania (a member state since 2007).

Myths and Identity

The attitude towards mythology has changed considerably in the past hundred years. From having been regarded as a mystical tale of a pagan or religious nature describing impossible events, myth has become a significant social tool that is clearly relevant to the structure of any given society and the changes taking place in it. Thus, perceiving myth as a pre-scientific naturalist theory gave way in the twentieth century to a wide range of new conceptions and approaches (Honko, 1984; Kirk, 1984, Rogerson et al., 1984). In daily parlance, the term "myth" refers to beliefs that lack factual basis, a fabrication or illusion that is the product of fantasy (Tudor, 1972). To a great extent, the myth is the most basic form of holiness performed by the human race (Cassirer, 1971). It appears in the form of a personal, symbolic story that starts out dramatically and describes unusual events that are of vital importance to the community. This story is not necessarily true in the sense of an objective description of reality or historical fact. The truth of the myth does not derive from external proof, but is intrinsic to the myth itself and the social truth that it represents and transmits. Accordingly, it is not surprising to discover that from time immemorial mythology has had a strong impact on the formation of the national, political and economic identity of individuals and collectives (Hedeager, 1998; Quispel, 1999; Judaken, 1999; Gerstle, 2000; Buchanan, 2002; Roof, 2009). Cultural myths, like political ones, provide the imaginative impetus necessary for adopting frameworks and characteristics of identity (Sarbin, 1997). At times, the identity-shaping mythical story draws on sources celebrating the optimistic, hopeful and resilient human spirit (Girardelli, 2004; Buchanan, 2002). Especially in cases of tales of bravery that reinforce collective identity, such myths are translated into legal or behavioural codes (Davis, 2000); at other times myths derive from sources describing fear and insecurity in the face of cruel human behaviour (McDonald-Walker, 1998). In such cases, especially regarding tragic reality, the myths become the basis for tragic identification (Nyusztay, 2002). At times the mythical story turns to technology in order to promote the shaping of identity; at other times, the mythical tale depicts science and technology as the enemy, arousing primeval fear and trembling (Caeton, 2007).

To a large extent, the powerful influence of the mythological story deviates from the physical space we inhabit and penetrates the cultural space that surrounds us (Josephs, 2002; Light, 2009).

The various media make it possible for myths to extend their influence to individuals who are no longer living in their country of national origin (Isabella, 2006). However, myths are capable of breaking through not only spatial boundaries, but also temporal ones. That is, on the one hand, modern nation states make it possible to bridge the gap between modernity and religious mythology (Rahman, 2003; Rosen & Rosen, 2000; Nygren, 1998). But on the other hand, the nation state facilitates jumping ahead in time, minimizing the importance of the past, the old myth, in favour of building a new ethos for a better future (Dos Santos, 2003; Martel, 2003). In such cases, myth represents a form of interpretation, a point of view that possesses internal cohesion and spiritual topography. It constitutes a firm permanent basis for culture and identity. It is created by culture, while it also creates a culture of its own.

Political Myths

As stated above, myths play an integral role in daily life and in preserving identity (Arruda, 1996). In cases where myths justify customs, a common past or hope for the future, communities will cling to their mythical beliefs and reject information that challenges them (Flowerdew, 1997). Over the years, Sorel's (1999) view that political myths spur us on to action by means of an appeal to our irrational inner worlds has prevailed in one form or another. Cassirer (1971), for example, claimed that in everything related to political action, people tend to forget what they've learned in the course of their intellectual development and return to the earliest stages of human culture. In this context, myth departs from an empirical perception of reality. This leads people to political action inspired by the emotional, passionate manipulation characteristic of irrational thinking. This can lead to a potentially dangerous situation. As Spinoza claimed, all societies are aided to one degree or another by mythological political imagination as the basis for cooperation and identification. This does not mean, however, that every society is capable of subjecting its imaginary mythical dimension to critical ethical discourse (Duff, 1903; McShea, 1968).

The political myth, then, is a fantasy or illusion regarding political matters (Tudor, 1972), but it is more than just a fantasy or an illusion. According to Tudor, those who generate myths also play a central role in setting them in motion; the inner structure of such myths will reflect the political motivations of their creators, as well as the roles and needs they are meant to fill. Furthermore, political myths will retain their validity as long as they serve a particular world order, while in the modern era the creation and fading of myths is an integral part of the dynamic struggle for cultural-political hegemony in a society. For example,

> The clash of two economic systems generates the contradiction of the political myth of a state in perpetual waiting and in opposition to it. (Boer, 2009, p. 4)

Accordingly, it is only natural to discover that the human difficulty in coping with phenomena that carry critical implications for our period has turned the political myth into a factor imparting significance to events or processes by means of developing a compatible narrative. Namely,

> the concept of political myth points to the fact that this imaginary mediation can also take the form of a narrative that coagulates and reproduces significance, that is, it creates the form of a myth. (Bottici, 2007, p. 132)

However, what narrative is being discussed?

> [M]odern political myths are narratives of past, present, or predicted political events which their tellers seek to make intelligible and meaningful to their audience. (Flood, 2002, p. 41)

Hence, we should

> understand political myth as the continual process of work on a common narrative by which the members of a social group can provide significance to their political conditions and experience. (Bottici & Challand, 2006, p. 315)

At the same time, the meaning created by political myths is closely tied to cultural and political contexts, which provide the conditions that allow the birth of these myths. It is no less true that today the ability to create and circulate any particular political myth depends on the cooperation of the mass media.

POLITICAL MYTHS AND THE MEDIA

Dominant ideology, cultural climate and economic structures are greatly assisted by the mediating ability of various media to circulate myths (Winslow, 2010; Ivie & Giner, 2009). Furthermore, government administrations create a rhetoric that includes mythical elements in order to justify power decisions and actions, especially in times of security crises and military instability (Williamson, 2010). It also seems that broadcasting companies and news agencies find it difficult to create an objective framework for controversial topics, turning instead to mythological media coverage. Such coverage can place a specific aspect of the conflict at its centre (Lacy, 2010; Ivie, 2009) or alternatively turn to the film industry in order to seek support for a particular myth (Blum, 2010). Even when the media attempt to uncover, mock or denigrate mythological coverage, it is still perceived to be an effective propaganda tool (Hollander, 2010).

It is rather surprising, then, that mythological media coverage diverges from areas of political security, also dealing with matters related to the politics of technology, i.e., the penetration of the Internet into third world countries and weaker populations (Eko, 2010) and other groups and an awareness of the abilities inherent in the new media (Couldry, 2010); with the use of myth in the politics of language and rights (Jones, 2009); with the politics of gender, romance and heterosexual love (Smith, 2009); and with the politics of music and the mythical creation of meaning through music (Wolfe, Loy & Chidester, 2009; Kistler & Lee, 2010). The modern media are capable of creating or supporting political myths by selecting heroes (Sealey-Morris, 2009) that can be glorified by the use of reportage frameworks parallel to the symbolic world which they inhabit (for example, the Kennedy family [O'Rourke, 2009]). Politicians also use various media in order to create, support or disseminate myths of a more general or pragmatic nature, such as the "myth of the small city" (that served Jimmy Carter in his 1976 presidential campaign [Lee, 1995]), the "myth of the West" and the "birth of a nation myth" (connecting the Western myth with the birth of the nation myth as was done by Barry Goldwater in 1964 and Ronald Reagan in his 1980 presidential campaign [Moore, 1991). Incidentally, one of the myths common to many United

States leaders is the "public faith" myth that is deeply engrained in the American civil religion myth (Roof, 2009).

Newspapers and reporters make use of mythological coverage in a number of ways. It may be of a coercive "top-down" nature, as in the case of Goebbels and Nazi Germany, where the regime demanded the use of mythological newspaper coverage for propaganda purposes (Gibbs, 2008). However, reporters can use mythological coverage also as a result of the influences of the cultural milieu in which they are active, and not necessarily due to political coercion (Ehrlich, 2006). Among other things, this can be seen, for instance, in the media structures of the community and local press (Berry, 2008). The creation of myths by means of newspaper coverage may be effected by a combination of printed journalism and television (Johnson, 2008); by the use of iconic newspaper photography (Spratt, 2008); by creating news headlines that generate a textual mythological story (Weinblatt, 2008); by including human interest stories (Mason, 2007) and by other techniques. A mythical news analysis can be performed by content analysis of news items and reports (Parkinson, 2007); and of course through an analysis of recontextualization of newspaper publications (Erjavec & Volcic, 2007). It seems, however, that the importance of the political myth is in fact derived more from the nature of the media world than from that of the political world. In such a reality, it would not be surprising to discover that political figures pay court to the various media in order to disseminate their ideas.

METHODOLOGY

It indeed seems that the European Union utilizes different media channels and employs a variety of convincing strategies in order to disseminate its ideas, values and symbols (Bruter, 2009; Olausson, 2010). Among other methods, this is done by appealing to children (the EU Kids Online Project [Hasebrink, Olafsson & Stetka, 2010; Taraszow et al., 2010]); by shaping media policy while presenting a new European media agenda and encouraging digital broadcasting as a tool for disseminating information (D'Arma, 2009); by determining a European public space by means of media regulation despite the fact that the level of dialogue being conducted in this cultural space is still inadequate (Bruggemann, 2010); by encouraging journalists who work in Brussels to adopt a unique newspaper style, one that will better explain the goals of the organization and its decision-making process (at times at the expense of press criticism [Lecheler & Hinrichsen, 2010]), and more. All the techniques described above can be categorized as "top-down" pressure to shape a European identity. One may ask, however, if and how such an identity will be shaped by means of "bottom-up" media pressure. Accordingly, the research questions for the present study are as follows: What are the characteristics of the media structure of the European Union? Does EU newspaper coverage create a mythological narrative? What are the mythical elements of this coverage? Does the coverage with these characteristics traverse national borders and identities?

In order to answer the questions regarding the press portrayal of the EU myth, two case studies were performed involving newspaper coverage of the European Union on Romanian Internet news sites and EU coverage on Israeli Internet news sites. That is, the research population includes all Internet press reports that appeared on two leading Romanian sites – one of which leans in the direction of the party in power and the other in the direction of the opposition party. Similarly, press publications were examined on two leading Israeli news sites – one (the Y-Net site) in favour of the party in power and the other (the Ha'aretz site) in favour of the left-wing Israeli elite and the opposition parties.

The time frame set for the research was January and February 2011, since that period was a dramatic one in Romania's process of joining the European Union. In March 2011, Romania was supposed to be accepted as part of the Schengen Area, after a period of technical preparation prior to its integration (securing its borders to European standards and dealing with internal problems, such as corruption and the justice system). On 21 December 2010, the French and German Ministers of the Interior sent a letter in which they notified the European Commissioner for Justice and Interior Affairs about their proposal to delay the inclusion of Romania and Bulgaria in the Schengen Area. The Romanian officials' reactions to the letter, as well as the responses of both internal and external actors to the French and German positions, were widely covered and commented upon in the news during January 2011.

The research method used was framing analysis. The concept of framing was introduced by Goffman (1974), who proposed a method of structuring meanings by organizing the process of interpreting events. But it was not until the early 1990s that Entman (1991) and Snow and Benford (1992) gave framing theory its most significant development, defining framing as

> an interpretive schemata that signifies and condenses the "world out there" by selectively punctuating and encoding objects, situations, events, experiences, and sequences of action in one's present or past environment. (Snow & Benford, 1992, p. 137)

In addition, they argued that there is a "master frame" – a relatively stable configuration of ideas, elements, and symbols that act as a kind of grammar through which collective action is elucidated. Framing is analysed, then, by describing the process of creating meanings and elements of persuasion vital to both collective action and cognitive processes (Benford, 1997). The basic premise of these analyses is that the media construct various frames for covering events; the main rationale for the premise being that reporters' attitudes and values influence the way they write (Parenti, 1986; Hess, 1996; Shoemaker & Reese, 1996; Wolfsfeld, 1997).

THE CASE STUDIES

Romania and the European Union[1]

The fifth wave of EU expansion began in 2004 and ended in 2007 with the entry of Romania and Bulgaria to the European Union. The relationship between Romania (the first Eastern European country to have official relations with the EU) and the EU started back in 1974, with a Treaty that included Romania in the Community's Generalized System of Preferences. After the Romanian Revolution in 1989 and the fall of communism, accession to the Union became one of the main goals of every government, especially after 1995, when Romania submitted an official application for membership.

After official intergovernmental negotiations began in 2000 (together with Malta, Slovakia, Latvia, Lithuania and Bulgaria), Romania initiated a series of reforms to prepare for its entry into the EU. On 13 April 2005, the European Parliament approved Romania's and Bulgaria's accession to the EU, and on 1 January 2007 Romania officially became a member of the European Union.

Inclusion in the Schengen Area of Free Movement was considered a further step in European integration, although non-member states are also included in this Area, along with most of the European Union countries. Romania's negotiations for inclusion in the Schengen Area started in 2001, soon after the commencement of official negotiations for joining the European Union. At the end of 2007, Romania and Bulgaria were both officially accepted for the Schengen Area and preparations were intended to be complete by March 2011. However, on 21 December 2010 the

---

[1] Official background information for this section was retrieved from www.europa.eu.

French and German Ministers of the Interior notified the European Commissioner for Justice and Interior Affairs of their proposal to delay the inclusion of Romania and Bulgaria in the Schengen Area.

Presently, as these lines are written, Romania is still in process of integration into the Schengen Area of Free Movement, but a final date for this has not yet been determined.

Israel and the European Union

> In 1964 an agreement was signed between Israel and member nations of the European Community. This treaty was the first in a series signed by the two parties, which in 1975 finally led to establishing a free trade zone. This treaty determined that apart from a small number of exceptions there would be trade restrictions on all sides. Despite the fact that both parties succeeded in reaching an agreement regarding a free market between Israel and the EU, cooperation between the parties did not expand to other areas. An opportunity to change this situation presented itself in 1995 as a result of an EU decision to launch a European-Mediterranean joint initiative, generally known as the "Barcelona Process". The participants in this initiative included the fifteen members of the European Union together with the twelve Mediterranean nations (Algeria, Tunisia, Turkey, Jordan, Israel, Lebanon, Malta, Egypt, Syria, Cyprus, the Palestinian Authority, and Libya as an observer). The idea that guided the initiators of the Barcelona Process was to reproduce the European model in order to achieve stability and encourage development in the region. An additional development regarding Israel and the European Union took place as a result of Israel becoming a part of the EU framework plan for technical research and development in 1996, and again in 2003. Since March 2003 there has been cooperation between Israel and the European Union in the framework of the European Neighbours policy intended to allow neighbouring countries that are not members of the EU to become part of the European Free Trade Zone. In 2008, the EU and Israel decided on an additional upgrade of their relations. According to this agreement, Israel joined the programmes of the European Union in various fields, while a communal work group was set up with the goal of including Israel in the EU Single Market. ("A milestone in Israel's relations with the European Union: the Union upgrades its ties with Israel", Israel Foreign Office Website, accessed 16 June 2008)

As we write these lines, an official delegation of the European Union Commission has been established in Israel, while in Brussels there is a resident Israeli Ambassador to the European Union and a diplomatic corps.

FINDINGS

The Israeli Case

In January 2011 and February 2011, 342 news items and articles were published on the *Ha'aretz* website – the website of the elite Israeli newspaper identified with the Israeli Left – concerning the European Union. Similarly, on the opposite side of the arena, 110 news items and articles were published on the *Ynet* site (the website of the most popular Israeli newspaper identified with the Israeli Right). Despite the obvious differences between the two websites, both are making their contribution towards creating the myth of a powerful European Union – or, to be more specific, the myth of recreation. Not only is the EU gaining power, it is recreating a new European and a new global order by organizing a new balance of power and status in today's and tomorrow's world in accordance with principles of global stratification.

For years now we have been witnessing fundamental changes in the socio-economic fragmentation of societies (Standing, 2002) and the interconnection between nations. A key aspect of those European and global changes is attributed to the EU, which has established itself as a major player with a significant role in this process (Bartle, 2005). It is therefore not surprising to discover that the narrative of the foundation and fortification of the European Union has been related in past years by means of the various media, using dramatic reportage structures to create a mythical construction of the Union. The preliminary feature of the European Union mythological notion is the saviour – the EU as an economic, political and environmental redeemer. It offers: a) economic salvation to countries such as Ireland and Portugal "that had a particularly bad year and needed EU economic rescue plans" (News Agencies A., 1.1.11); b) it is a political saviour of countries such as Greece which has been aided "by a quick intervention force at its borders of about 175 armed guards from 25 member countries of the EU who patrol the border in order to keep out illegal immigrants and ease the pressure on Greece" (Herman, 4.1.11); c) and it is a lifesaver that forbids the marketing of hundreds of dangerous substances that cause "serious side effects and poisoning as a result of herbal remedies" (Gal, 1.1.11).

In the case of Israel, however, the salvation narrative takes on the nature of self-redemption. The European Union is offering the Israelis and the Palestinians, who are having difficulties rescuing themselves and solving the Israeli-Palestinian dispute, intervention. In January 2011 EU representatives in Jerusalem and Ramallah prepared a scathing report that "determines that the Union must increase its protest measures against Israel and act as though East Jerusalem is the capital of Palestine" (Hason, 10.1.11).

The functionaries even requested that European officials act to further their interests with the Israeli Government. The fact that both right-wing and left-wing news sources were dedicated to this issue and published 12 news items and articles in two days (7 on the *Ynet* site and 5 on that of *Ha'aretz*) only emphasizes the mythological role of the European Union as an agent that helps deal with difficult human situations. Inspired by Armstrong (2005), we suggest that while handling ideological disputes, the European Union attempts to help Palestinians and Israelis find their place in the world and give them new hope. Furthermore, Armstrong claims that myths always derive from a near-death experience and the fear of extinction. In the second millennium Israel's fear of death and extinction is represented by Iran. The leader of the Israeli opposition, Tsipi Livni, for example, reassures readers that:

> As stated in a meeting with the Foreign Minister of the EU, Catherine Ashton, "Europe's stand against Iran must be firm so that Iran understands that the world will not accept any more dragging of feet and marking time in an attempt to obtain nuclear weapons. This is definitely in Europe's best interest and must be stated clearly and harshly, especially now. (Shumpelby, 5.1.11)

The request for help presented to the Foreign Minister of the EU runs parallel with the traditional ability of mythology to extricate us from problematic, destructive, human situations. It seems that by means of an appeal to the European Union, Israelis hope to be able to cope more effectively with future threats and dangers:

> The Iranians are hard bargainers and their aim is to create a schism among the (six nations) and see if they can negotiate concessions . . . the Foreign Minister of the European Union, Catherine Ashton, stood firm in the negotiations (and) did not fall into a single one of their traps. (ibid.)

This further emphasizes the mythical power of the EU as an agent that is likely to save the Israelis from annihilation, from a second holocaust. The EU representatives understand and respect the deep Israeli fear of destruction and they are prepared to stand by Israel – as was evident on International Holocaust Day, when "The EU Parliament is convening in commemoration" (Magnezi, 25.1.11).

To a large extent, the preoccupation with generating hope is anchored in and constructed from the creation myth, specifically the *re-creation* myth. The significance and value of acts does not depend on physical data alone, but rather on the ability to reconstruct an act of genesis, to reiterate a mythical model. Thus, the myth of salvation is firmly grounded in the myth of re-creation. The act of creation realizes the transition from non-appearance to appearance, the transition from chaos to cosmos. In general, a mythical, symbolic outlook attributes much importance to transitional moments, the most significant of which is no doubt celebrating the New Year (Eliade, 1989). New Year celebrations in Europe illustrate the transformation of the European Union into a creative force to which one prays in time of need (News Agencies, A. 1.1.11).

The Eurobloc, if so, is a kind of centre with a prestigious and honourable status. According to Eliade (1989), the creation myth views the centre as holy. The creation, to its full extent, takes place at the centre of the world by means of sanctifying the area, making it holy and then ratifying the act by offering a godly sacrifice. The recreation is accompanied by a difficult path that must be travelled on the way to the centre, a road full of dangers that stand for the transitional ceremony from the profane to the sacred, from the imaginary and the fleeting to the real and the eternal, from death to life (AFP, 7.1.11; AP, 15.1.11). That is, the approach to the centre, i.e., the Eurobloc, represents the transition to a new, different existence, one that is more moral, efficient and lasting. Re-creation is assured only after a hard struggle among different agents.

Accordingly, at the foundation of the mythological recreation story rests the drama, the conflict among figures, circumstances and attitudes. The construction of the European Union myth in Israel includes two dramatic foci: a) a particular state's internal affairs; b) the internal conflicts among Union nations. An example of the drama of a state's internal affairs is Israel's coverage of France's attitude towards the European Union. On the one hand, the French president is represented as defending the EU:

> The President of France said that it is his intention to oppose with all his power those that try to put an end to the Euro. "Europe was strong and Europe defended us," he stated in a speech to the nation on New Year's Eve. (News Agencies B. 1.1.11).

On the other hand, the leader of the extreme right opposition in France, Marine Le Pen, clarifies that

> We were the first to object to transferring rights of national sovereignty to the institutions of the European Union. (Primor, 7.1.11)

Newspaper coverage of the internal French conflict between the government and the opposition, between left and right, also embodies a media conflict between the left-wing press in Israel (which in fact represents the French right-wing stance) and the right-wing Israeli press (which in fact represents the left-wing Israeli position). What we have here are parallel patterns of conflict, right versus left, government versus opposition, in an effort to spur to action because, in order to nourish a determination to act, a myth has to stage a dramatic performance, or rather, has to be perceived as a drama (Bottici, 2007).

An example of an internal European drama (an internal conflict among the Union nations) may be found in the news report that:

> From the Wikileaks documents it appears that in opposition to France and the other member states, Berlin and Washington are working towards especially accurate spy satellite networks, which are expected to come into use shortly. The project was camouflaged as an environmental trade initiative, but is being run by the intelligence agencies. (AP, 3.1.11)

While Paris did everything in its power to stop the project, officials in Berlin were quoted as claiming that they were sick of being manipulated by France. Of course, the importance of the current internal European conflict goes beyond issues in the here and now, symbolizing conflict pertaining to the future of these nations. This might be understood in light of Tudor (1996), who claims that every current political struggle is just a preview, an introduction, to future battles.

It seems, then, that the mythological narrative relates to drama as action. "The myth is the continuation of the dialogue, but the dialogue itself is a mythical tribunal" (Strauss et al., 1993/2004).

Since we are discussing the press, it is clear that the main part of the mythical action is a dialogue that is reproduced in the ongoing discourse of the present moment. This means that the dramatic newspaper text that constructs the myth of the European Union is grounded on a dialogue where each of the speakers sets out an intention as part of a dialogue or a symposium. For instance, while the morning headlines on the Ynet website announced that the foreign minister of the EU, Catherine Ashton, "arrives in Israel and states 'there is no replacement for negotiations'" (Shumpelby, 5.1.11), the evening headlines had already reported the reply of the Israel foreign minister, Avigdor Lieberman, who promised that "when the smuggling of arms to Gaza ceases, the embargo will be lifted" (Medzini, 5.1.11).

There are those like North (1977) who claim that the myth of the European Union has been constructed by means of the technique of dialogue, but it is clear that a real dialogue between Israel and the European Union has not come into existence. One way or another, it is clear that dialogue is central to the myth of re-creation.

The Romanian Case

During the month of January 2011, 279 news items covering topics related to the European Union were published on major news sites in Romania, 123 on Hotnews.ro (this site generally perceived as supportive of the incumbent party), and 156 on Ziare.com (this site generally considered to be supportive of the opposition). About 205 news items covered "the Schengen case"[2] and 74 presented other EU-related news, such as external political subjects, internal decisions related to the financial crisis, different events regarding European member states, institutions or people, etc. The analysis showed no important differences in coverage between the two sites, both sites showing a rather fractured image of EU identity regarding the deconstruction and reconstruction of two myths. On the one hand, the myth of the saviour, constantly present in the Romanian media before and immediately after the Romanian integration into the EU (January 2007), was about to be replaced by the myth of the punisher, a Europe that punishes Romania, whether justly or not, for its problems connected to corruption, the Roma population, or justice etc. On the other hand, the general myth of a united and coherent European Union has partially been replaced by the myth of a stratified Europe, which is driven by political, socio-economic and integration issues.

Turbulent times such as the current economic global crisis favour the deconstruction of myths and the construction of new ones, just as times of economic and political stability favour the consolidation of myths (Girling, 1993, p. 62). Myths related to European identity are no exception to this rule. The insider perspective offered by the Romanian media shows a transition period dominated by frequently opposing ideas or stereotypes related to the European Union as a whole, a fractured paradigm within which can identify the serious changes facing European identity currently. One of the recurrent depictions of the European Union in the Romanian

[2] Although in March 2011, Romania was supposed to have been accepted to the Schengen Area, on 21 December 2010 the French and the Germans notified the European Commissioner for Justice and Interior Affairs of their proposal to delay the affixation of Romania and Bulgaria to the Schengen Area. As a result, the Romanian media have paid increased attention to what it called "the Schengen case".

media at the beginning of 2011 is that of a supreme force which punishes Romania and Romanians. This appears as the myth of a *punisher* who checks to see if Romania has done its homework and has fulfilled its obligation, without really caring about preserving its rights. During the period analysed, the face of the European Union was not composed of its representatives (rarely present in the news), but rather of its most prominent geopolitical actors, the countries that are perceived to be "the engine of the EU", "the core of the EU", namely France and Germany. That is the reason why, symbolically, the letter sent by the French and German Ministers of the Interior was considered "a European position".

Most of the time, France and Germany appeared in the Romanian media as the forces punishing and deciding Romania's fate within the European Union.

> France and Germany's objections regarding the adhesion were received with indignation by the Romanian officials; President Băsescu stated that we are being discriminated against. (21.01.2011, Ziare.com)

The general perception of Romania's penalization is highlighted by the dominant frame of Schengen-related news: the powerlessness frame. Romanians are depicted as humble, incapable of managing the situation, discriminated against, isolated beggars, spineless worms etc. At the same time, we find voices calling out the injustice of the European Union's decision regarding the postponement of Romanian integration into the Schengen Area, thus the labels of "discrimination", lack of respect, etc.:

> President Traian Băsescu stated that Romania asks that its adhesion to the Schengen Area be accomplished following the rules agreed upon by the EU treaties, and that Romania should not be treated in a discriminatory way. (28.01.11, Ziare.com)

> This constitutes discrimination against Romania. We are now forced to wait like worms, as they recommend; 22 million Romanians have the right to be respected. (06.01.11, Ziare.com)

However, the general perception is that Romanians deserve their fate; they deserve to be punished due to their consistently humble attitude on the one hand, and the real problems Romania is facing today on the other:

> Our problem is that when we should have preserved our dignity and negotiated integration into the EU far more honorably, when we should not have been so desperate to obtain a place that we did not deserve, we were humble, we kept our heads down, worms with no claims of their own. And

> now, when we should put our irritated tone and hurt pride aside and admit that we are too dirty and ill-mannered to enter once more into a clean house with our boots full of mud, now we get hysterical and cry that "it is not acceptable to be treated like this" (07.01.11, Ziare.com)

The idea of powerlessness has often been used in past years to represent external Romanian politics in respect of its "lack of professionalism in promoting Romania's interests abroad" (03.01.11, Ziare.com) and the low self-esteem of the Romanian mentality:

> We have very low self-esteem. Every day the TV channels and the media generally repeat all these things so obsessively that we have come to believe that we are powerless. They have their reasons. . . . In the "Golden Era" (i.e., the Ceauşescu regime), we thought we were the center of the world; now we believe we are dust on the ground. We are neither; just an unbalanced society, with its good and bad elements." (Ciucu, 07.01.11, Hotnews.ro)

Overall, the EU is portrayed as a punisher, the general saviour myth created before and immediately after the Romanian integration into the EU being replaced by the myth of an all-powerful Europe symbolically represented by France and Germany, which is in a position to "dictate" the rules inside the EU.

In addition, this new European Union identity has changed the myth of a united Europe, inside which countries have equal positions and commonly decide upon the well-being of European citizens. The Romanian media have depicted a fractured Union, divided by spheres of influence and unequal power centres. The original member states are viewed as the central European Union, and they decide upon the fate of newly integrated countries. They are referred to as "the A-Team", comprising Germany, France, Austria, the Netherlands and Luxemburg, an "exclusive elite", "the saviours of the European retained students" (Mixich, Hotnews.ro, 21.01.11).

In this context, Romania is depicted as a "small county at the mercy of world powers, a 'casualty' in the battle for power within the EU or France" (Ziare.com, 24.01.11).

Romania is often viewed as a victim of France's power game within the EU or of France's internal political games. Headlines such as "The French knife stuck in Romania's back. Possible victim: the European Union" (Mixich, Hotnews.ro, 17.01.11) bring to the forefront the weak and powerless position of Romania in the European "chess game".

To sum up, the Romanian media have deconstructed two major myths regarding the European Union: the myth of the saviour, largely present in the media before and immediately after the Romanian integration into the EU in 2007, and the myth of a Europe that is united, fair and balanced, a Europe for all its citizens. Instead, a new myth began its ascent, depicting a Europe divided by power games and interests into spheres of influence, the EU as a punisher who decides the fate of its weaker members. The tone of EU-related news not referring to Romania's adhesion to the Schengen Area is much more neutral. The EU is seen either as an important external partner or player, helping other countries (such as Tunisia) solve some specific problems, deciding upon potential candidates for integration (Serbia), or debating various issues with external actors (such as Russia, China, Iran etc.). The general tone is neutral; facts are presented, at times accompanied by political or strategic explanations.

Discussion

The enlargement of the European Union in past years has brought new countries into the European arena, whose citizens have entered into the new social order with disproportionate illusions of future prosperity and well-being. These structural notions or desires for belonging and succeeding might be linked to historical events and elite cultures, but most importantly, since myths are bound up with popular culture and everyday life, they influence each and every Romanian and Israeli. However, since myth is a narrative that can preserve or alter social and political structures by its authoritative iteration under appropriate conditions (Stigliano, 1994), in both the Israeli and the Romanian media, political leaders motivate the construction and deconstruction of myths. Therefore, it is not surprising to find that, as on other occasions (Degenaar, 2007), European myth operates in the service of power.

Furthermore, Sowa (1984, p. 23) states that "mythologies generally revolve around major life crises . . . each mythology in its own way tries to bring order to human experience of crises". Accordingly, the processes of recounting myths constitute acts of interpretation that allow their writers to include or omit whatever they believe to be relevant or irrelevant in the major or minor details of each myth. These acts of inclusion or omission result in different readings or versions of the myth which add to, or distort, its meaning. This becomes important when we recall that our initial understanding of myths often comes from entries found in various kinds of reference works (Ullyatt, 2009). Moreover, following Girling's idea that "crisis and stress evoke the power of myth, which remains latent during periods of routine and order" (1996, p. 62), we offer a general media background related to the European Union identity myths from two perspectives: one of the "insider", based on Romanian online news regarding the EU, and one of the "outsider", based on the Israeli media. The inside perspective has shown a fractured and troubled picture of the European Union, a disrupted image of internal inequities, political and economic disputes, and an imbalance between "old" and "new" member states. The myth of the saviour, which dominated the Romanian media before and immediately after its integration into the EU in 2007, was replaced by the myth of the punisher. The "old" European Union, the "A-Team" composed of the old member states appear as the authority which decides the fate of the new member states, sometimes ignoring what was stipulated by previous treaties. Using the powerlessness frame, Romanian authorities and citizens are portrayed as discriminated against and weak, incapable of defending themselves and at the mercy of the great powers, Germany and France. Thus, a disenchantment myth is in the making: people are disillusioned, deprived of their hopes of well-being and European prosperity. On the other hand, regarding the general image of the EU, the old myth of a Europe that is unified and fair for all its members has lost its power, leaving room for a new, divided Europe based on political strategies, economic inequities and different levels of integration. A fragmented European Union is born, in which old member states, economically prosperous and balanced, form an elite core around which other "strata" are situated, based on levels of general power-influence within the EU.

The outsider perspective still preserves the general myth of the saviour: the European Union brings economic or political salvation (to countries affected by the economic crisis in the last few years), the European Union takes the role of the mediator ready to intervene in the Israeli-Palestinian dispute. Following Sowa's (1984, p. 23) notion that "mythologies generally revolve around the great life crises . . . each mythology in its own way tries to bring order to human experience of the crises".

Acting as a saviour allows the EU to construct, according to the Israeli media, a re-creation myth. By adopting a symbolic framing of the earliest beginnings, of the ideal world in which we want to live, the Israeli media nourish a fundamental trust in the union. To a large extent, they describe the ordering of an Israeli cosmos. Connecting the two perspectives, the European Union appears to have a two-faced identity, simultaneously showing strengths and weaknesses. Seen from the outside, the EU raises the myth of the savior built upon the recreation myth. From the inside, from the perspective of a newly integrated country, such as Romania, the EU image is constructed on the disenchantment myth, as a punisher who decides the fate of weaker countries. At the same time, the outsider looks favorably at a myth of unity and democratic values, while the insider sees the EU as fractured, stratified and unequal in these times of crisis. To conclude, we estimate that European Union identity myths are still in the making; the EU image has constantly and rather brutally changed in recent years, in the context of the global economic crisis. At any rate, whether today's myths will become dominant features portraying the EU is a question to be decided by future history.

References

Armstrong, K (2005). *A Short History of Myth*, Edinburgh, Scotland: Canongate Books.

Arruda, R S V (1996). Rikbaktsa Myths: History, Society and Nature Mitos Rikbakrsa: historia, sociedade e natureza. *MARGEM,* 5, 31–57.

Bartle, I (2005). *Globalization and EU Policy-making: The Neo-liberal Transformation of Telecommunications and Electricity*, Manchester, UK: Manchester University Press.

Benford, R D (1997). An Insider's Critique of the Social Movement Framing Perspective. *Sociological Inquiry* 6(4), 409–430.

Berger, A A (2010). The Myth Model. *Myth & Symbol*, 6(2), 2–7.

Berry, D (2008). The South Wales Argus and Cultural Representations of Gwent Journalism Studies. *Journalism Studies*, 9(1), 105–116.

Blokker, P (2008). Europe "United in Diversity": From a Central European Identity to Post-Nationality? *European Journal of Social Theory,* 11(2), 257–274.

Blum, R H (2010). Anxious Latitudes: Heterotopias, Subduction Zones, and the Historico-spatial Configurations within Dead Man. *Critical Studies in Media Communication,* 27(1), 55–66.

Boer, R (2009). *Political Myth: on the Use and Abuse of Biblical Themes*, Durham, NC: Duke University Press.

Bottici, C (2007). *A Philosophy of Political Myth*, Cambridge, UK and New York, NY: Cambridge University Press.

Bottici, C, & Challand (2006). Rethinking Political Myth: The Clash of Civilizations as a Self-Fulfilling Prophecy. *European Journal of Social Theory*, 9(3), 315–336.

Bruggemann, M (2010). Information Policy and the Public Sphere: EU Communications and the Promises of Dialogue and Transparency. *Javnost – The Public,* 17(1), 5–22.

Bruter, M (2007). Symbols, Media, And The Emergence Of A Mass European Identity In Six Democracies. Paper Presented at the

American Political Science Association Annual Meeting 2007 in Chicago, 1–38.
—. (2009). Time Bomb?: The Dynamic Effect of News and Symbols on the Political Identity of European Citizens. *Comparative Political Studies,* 42(12), 1498–1536.
Buchanan, B (2002). “An Anthropomorphic Insolence of Short Duration”: Oedipus, Masculinity, and the Death of “Man” in the Work of Samuel Beckett. *Men and Masculinities,* 4(4), 357–367.
Caeton, D A (2007). The Cultural Phenomenon of Identity Theft and the Domestication of the World Wide Web. *Bulletin of Science, Technology & Society*, 27(1), 11–23.
Cassirer, E (1971) *The Myth of the State,* New Haven and London: Yale University Press.
Couldry, N (2010). Does “the Media” Have a Future? *European Journal of Communication,* 24(4), 437–449.
D’Arma, A (2009). Broadcasting policy in Italy’s “Second Republic”: National Politics and European Influences. *Media, Culture & Society,* 31(5), 769–786.
Davis, E B (2000). *Myth and Identity in the Epic of Imperial Spain,* Columbia, Missouri: University of Missouri Press.
Degenaar, J (2007). Discourses on Myth. *Myth & Symbol,* 4(1), 1–14.
Dos Santos, M S, & Sepúlveda, M (2003). Museums without a Past: The Brazilian Case. *International Journal of Cultural Studies,* 6(2), 180–201.
Duff, R A (1903). *Spinoza’s Political and Ethical Philosophy*, Glasgow: James Maclehose.
Ehrlich, M C (2006). Facts, Truth and Bad Journalists in the Movies. *Journalism*, 7(4) 501–519.
Eko, L (2010). New Technologies, Ancient Archetypes: The Boston Globe’s Discursive Construction of Internet Connectivity in Africa. *Howard Journal of Communications,* 21(2), 182–198.
Eliade, M (1989). *Le Mythe de l’éternal retour*, Paris, France: Gallimard.
Entman, R M (1991). Framing U.S. Coverage of International News: Contrasts in Narratives of the KAL and Iran Air Incidents. *Journal of Communication*, 41(4), 6–27.
Erjavec, K, & Volcic, Z (2007). The Kosovo Battle: Media’s Recontextualization of the Serbian Nationalistic Discourses. *Harvard International Journal of Press Politics*, 12(3), 67–86.
Flood, C G (2002). *Political Myth*, New York, NY: Routledge.

Flowerdew, J (1997). The Discourse of Colonial Withdrawal: A Case Study in the Creation of Myth Discourse. *Discourse and Society,* 8(4), 453–478.

Gerstle, G (2000). American Freedom, American Coercion: Immigrant Journeys in the "Promised Land". *Social Compass,* 47(1), 63–76.

Gibbs, J (2008). The Berlin Newspaper Der Panzerbar, April 1945. *Media History*, 14(2), 205–221.

Girardelli, D (2004). Commodified Identities: The Myth of Italian Food in the United States. *Journal of Communication Inquiry*, 28(4), 307–324.

Girling, J (1993). Myths and Politics in Western Societies: Evaluating the Crisis of Modernity in the United States, Germany and Great Britain, New Brunswick, New Jersey: Transaction Publishers.

Goffman, E (1974). *Frame Analysis: An Essay on the Organization of Experience*, New York: Harper and Row.

Hardt-Mautner, G (1995). How does One Become a Good European?: The British Press and European Integration. *Discourse & Society,* 6(2), 177–205.

Hasebrink, U, Olafsson, K, & Stetka, V (2010). Commonalities and Differences: How to Learn from International Comparisons of Children's Online Behavior. *International Journal of Media and Cultural Politics,* 6(1), 9–24.

Hedeager, L (1998). Cosmological Endurance: Pagan Identities in Early Christian Europe. *European Journal of Archaeology*, 1(3), 382–396.

Henry, B (2001). The Role of Symbols for European Political Identity: Political Identity as Myth? In F. Cerutti & E. Rudolph (eds). *A Soul for Europe*, Vol. 2, *On the Cultural and Political Identity of the Europeans. An Essay Collection* (pp. 49-70), Louvain, Peeters.

Hess, S (1996). *News and Newsmaking*, Washington, DC, The Brookings Institution.

Hollander, B A (2010). Persistence in the Perception of Barack Obama as a Muslim in the 2008 Presidential Campaign. *Journal of Media and Religion,* 9(2), 55–66.

Honko, L (1984). The Problem of Defining Myth. In A. Dundes (ed.). *Sacred Narrative, Readings in the Theory of Myth,* (pp. 41–52), California, University of California Press.

Inthorn, S (2006). What Does It Mean to Be an EU Citizen? How News Media Construct Civic and Cultural Concepts of Europe. *Westminster Papers in Communication and Culture*, 3(3), 71–90.

Isabella, M (2006). Exile and Nationalism: The Case of the Risorgimento. *European History Quarterly*, 36(4), 493–520.

Ivie, R L (2009). Breaking the Spell of War: Peace Journalism's Democratic Prospect. *Javnost – The Public,* 16(4), 5–22.

Ivie, R L, & Giner, O (2009). More Good, Less Evil: Contesting the Mythos of National Insecurity in the 2008 Presidential Primaries. *Rhetoric and Public Affairs,* 12(2), 279–301.

Johnson, V E (2008). *Heartland TV: Prime Time Television and the Struggle for U.S. Identity*, New York: New York University Press.

Jones, P E (2009). From "external speech" to "inner speech" in Vygotsky: A Critical Appraisal and Fresh Perspectives. *Language & Communication,* 29(2), 166–181.

Josephs, I E (2002). Self-Construction in a Nightly Gathering of Culture and Person: Rendezvous or Conflict? *Culture & Psychology*, 8(4), 449–458.

Judaken, J (1999). The Queer Jew: Gender, Sexuality and Jean-Paul Sartre's Anti-Antisemitism. *Patterns of Prejudice,* 33(3), 45–63.

Kirk, G S (1984). On Defining Myths. In A. Dundes (ed.). *Sacred Narrative, Readings in the Theory of Myth* (pp. 53-61). California: University of California Press.

Kistler, M E, & Lee, M J (2010). Does Exposure to Sexual Hip-hop Music Videos Iinfluence the Sexual Attitudes of College Students? *Mass Communication & Society,* 13(1), 67–86.

Lacy, M G (2010). White Innocence Heroes: Recovery, Reversals, Paternalism, and David Duke. *Journal of International and Intercultural Communication*, 3(3), 206–227.

Lecheler, S K, & Hinrichsen, M C (2010). Role Conceptions of Brussels Correspondents from the New Member States. *Javnost – The Public,* 17(1), 73–86.

Lee, R (1995). Electoral Politics and Visions of Community: Jimmy Carter, Virtue, and the Small Town Myth. *Western Journal of Communication*, 59(1), 39–60.

Light, D (2009). Performing Transylvania: Tourism, Fantasy and Play in a Liminal Place. *Tourist Studies*, 9(3), 240–258.

McDonald-Walker, S (1998). Fighting the Legacy: British Bikers in the 1990s. *Sociology,* 32(2), 379–396.

McShea, R J (1968). *The Political Philosophy of Spinoza.* New York, NY: Columbia University Press.

Maguire, J, Poulton, E, & Possamai, C (1999). The War of the Words? Identity Politics in Anglo-German Press Coverage of EURO 96. *European Journal of Communication*, 14(1), 61–89.

Marciniak, K (2009). Post-socialist Hybrids. *European Journal of Cultural Studies,* 12(2), 173–190.

Martel, E (2003). From Mensch to Macho? The Social Construction of a Jewish Masculinity. *Men and Masculinities*, 3(4), 347–369.

Mason, P (2007). Misinformation, Myth and Distortion. *Journalism Studies,* 8(3), 481–496.

Moore, Mark P (1991). A Rhetorical Criticism of Political Myth: From Goldwater Legend to Reagan Mystique. *Communication Studies,* 42(3), 295–308.

North, H (1977). *Interpretations of Plato: A Swarthmore Symposium*, Leiden, The Netherlands: E J Brill.

Nygren, A (1998). Struggle over Meanings: Reconstruction of Indigenous Mythology, Cultural Identity, and Social Representation. *Ethnohistory,* 45(1), 31–63.

Nyusztay, I (2002). *Myth, Telos, Identity: the Tragic Schema in Greek and Shakespearean Drama,* The Netherlands: Rodopi.

Olausson, U (2010). Towards a European Identity? The News Media and the Case of Climate Change. *European Journal of Communication,* 25(2), 18–152.

O'Rourke, S P (2009). Bobby. *Rhetoric & Public Affairs,* 12(4), 635–654.

Parenti, M (1986). *Inventing Reality: The Politics of the Mass Media*, New York: St Martin's Press.

Parkinson, R G (2007). "An Astonishing Account of CIVIL WAR in North Carolina": Rethinking the Newspaper Response to the Battle of Alamance. *Journalism History,* 32(4), 223–230.

Quispel, C (1999). Faithful Servants and Dangerous Beasts: Race, Nationalism and Historical Mythmaking. *Patterns of Prejudice,* 33(3), 29–44.

Rahman, N (2003). The Trial of Heritage and the Legacy of Abraham. *Men and Masculinities*, 5(3), 295–398.

Rogerson, J W (1984). Slippert Words: Myth. In A. Dundes (ed.). *Sacred Narrative: Readings in the Theory of Myth* (pp. 62–71). California: University of California Press.

Roof, W C (2009). American Presidential Rhetoric from Ronald Reagan to George W. Bush: Another Look at Civil Religion. *Social Compass*, 56(2), 286–301.

Rosen, D M, & Rosen V P (2000). New Myths and Meanings in Jewish New Moon Rituals, *Ethnology,* 39(3), 263–277.

Sarbin, T R (1997). The Poetics of Identity, *Theory & Psychology,* 7(1), 67–82.

Sealey-Morris, G (2009). A Cool Drink of Water Before I Die: Four Modern John Henry Songs, *Southern Communication Journal,* 74(4), 406–421.

Shoemaker, P J and Reese, S T (1996). *Mediating the Message*, New York: Longman.

Smith, G D Jr (2009). Love as Redemption: The American Dream Myth and the Celebrity Biopic, *Journal of Communication Inquiry,* 33(3), 222–238.

Snow, D A, & Benford, R D (1992). Master Frames and Cycles of Protest. In A D Morris & C M M Mueller (eds), *Frontiers Controversies* (pp. 133–155). New York: Basic Books.

Sorel, G (1999). *Reflection of Violence*, Cambridge, UK: Cambridge University Press.

Sowa, C A (1984). *Traditional Themes and the Homeric Hymns*, Illinois, USA: Bolchazy-Carducci Publishers.

Spratt, M (2008). When Police Dogs Attacked: Iconic News Photographs and Construction of History, Mythology, and Political Discourse. *American Journalism,* 25(2), 85–105.

Standing, G (2002). *Beyond the New Paternalism: Basic Security as Equality*, London and New York: Verso.

Stigliano, A (1994). Myth as Political and Social Performance, *The Humanistic Psychologist,* 22(2), 134–165.

Strauss, E, Voegelin, P, Emberley, C, & Cooper, B (eds.) (1993/2004). *Faith and Political Philosophy: The Correspondence Between Leo Strauss and Eric Voegelin, 1934–1964*, Missouri, USA: University of Missouri Press, 3–108.

Taraszow, T, Aristodemou, E, Shitta, G, Laouris, Y, & Arsoy, A (2010). Disclosure of Personal and Contact Information by Young People in Social Networking Sites: An Analysis Using Facebook Profiles as an Example, *International Journal of Media and Cultural Politics,* 6(1), 81–102.

Trandafoiu, R (2006). The Whole Greater than the Sum of Its Parts: An Investigation into the Existence of European Identity, Its Unity and Its Divisions, *Westminster Papers in Communication and Culture,* 3(3), 91–108.

Tudor, H (1972). *Political Myth*, London: Macmillan.

Tudor, J (1996). *Remaking the Labour Party: from Gaitskell to Blair*, London: Taylor & Francis.

Ullyatt, T (2009). "Wings, Sails, and the Inevitability of a Boy Drowning": Reference Works as Versions and Variants of the Daedalus and Icarus Myth, *Myth & Symbol,* 5(2), 20–36.

Weinblatt, K T (2008). Fighting for the Story's Life: Non-closure in Journalistic Narrative. *Journalism,* 9(1), 31–51.

Williamson, L A (2010). Bush's Mythic America: A Critique of the Rhetoric of War. *Southern Communication Journal,* 75(3), 215–231.

Winslow, L (2010). Comforting the Comfortable: Extreme Makeover Home Edition's Ideological Conquest. *Critical Studies in Media Communication,* 27(3), 267–290.

Wolfe, A S, Loy, M, & Chidester, P (2009). Mass Communication and Identity Construction: Theory and a Case Study of Song-Recordings by a Popular Musician. *Journalism and Communication Monographs,* 11(1), 67–113.

Wolfsfeld, G (1997). *Constructing News about Peace: The Role of The Israeli Media in the Oslo Peace Process*, Tel-Aviv: The Tami Steinmetz Center for Peace Research.

Media Articles Cited in the Paper

Israeli Media

AP. 3.1.11. Anger in Europe: Germany and the United States are Developing Satellites. (Hebrew) *Ynet*. Retrieved 9.2.11. http://www.ynet.co.il/articles/0,7340,L-4008521,00.html

Gal, I. (1.1.11). Europe Will Prohibit the Marketing of Hundreds of Herbal Medicines.(Hebrew)*Ynet.* Retrieved 9.2.11. http://www.ynet.co.il/articles/0,7340,L-4007335,00.html

Harman, D. (4.1.11). Greece Initiates Construction of a Fence against the Infiltration of Immigrants from Turkey. (Hebrew) *Ha'aretz.* Retrieved 9.2.11. http://www.haaretz.co.il/hasite/spages/1207757.html

Hason, N., Ravid, B., & Yissacharov, A. (11.1.11). Activists against Destruction of Houses in Silwan Request Defense from Europe against Israel. (Hebrew) *Ha'aretz.* Retrieved 9.2.11. http://www.haaretz.co.il/hasite/pages/arch/ArchArticle.jhtml?_DARGS=%2Fhasite%2Fobjects%2Fdata%2FArchiveSearchResults.jhtml.1

Hason, N. (10.1.11). European Consuls Demand Protest Measures against Israel. (Hebrew) *Ha'aretz.* Retrieved 9.2.11. http://www.haaretz.co.il/hasite/spages/1208820.html

Magnesi, R. (5.1.11). Lieberman to Ashton: "When the Smuggling of Arms to Gaza Ceases, the Embargo Will be Lifted". (Hebrew) *Ynet.* Retrieved 9.2.11. http://www.ynet.co.il/articles/0,7340,L-4009620,00.html

§News Agencies, A. (1.1.11). About a Million Partygoers Welcomed 2011 in Times Square. (Hebrew) *Ynet*. Retrieved 9.2.11. http://www.ynet.co.il/articles/0,7340,L-4007301,00.html

News Agencies, B. (1.1.11). Sarkozy: The End of the Euro will also be the End of Europe. (Hebrew) *Ynet.* Retrieved 9.2.11. http://www.ynet.co.il/articles/0,7340,L-4007343,00.html

Primor, A. (7.1.11). The Leader of the Extreme Right-Wing Organizations in France, Marine Le Pen: "Are we Racists? Look in the Mirror. (Hebrew) *Ha'aretz.* Retrieved 9.2.11. http://www.ynet.co.il/articles/0,7340,L-4007343,00.html

Shumpelby, E. (5.1.11). The Foreign Minister of the European Union Arrives in Israel: "There is no substitute for negotiations". (Hebrew) *Ynet*. Retrieved 9.2.11. http://www.ynet.co.il/articles/0,7340,L-4009187,00.html

Romanian Media

*** (03.01.11). Corlăţean: Baconschi's strategy is the strategy of an animal upset with the bag. (Romanian). *Ziare.com*. Retrieved 11.02.11

*** (06.01.11). Băsescu accuse Germany of abuse and says that we will not stay "as worms" in the European Union. (Romanian). *Ziare.com*. Retrieved 11.02.11 http://www.ziare.com/basescu/presedinte/basescu-acuza-franta-si-germania-de-abuz-dar-isi-asuma-esecul-pe-schengen-1066951

*** (07.01.11) The unpleasant worms of Europe. (Romanian). *Ziare.com*. Retrieved 11.02.11 http://www.ziare.com/politica/schengen/ramele-dezagreabile-ale-europei-1066980

*** (21.01.11). Declassification of the reports regarding Schengen adhesion asked in the European Parliament. (Romanian). *Ziare.com*. Retrieved 11.02.11 http://www.ziare.com/politica/schengen/desecretizarea-rapoartelor-privind-aderarea-la-schengen-ceruta-in-pe-1070251

*** (24.01.11). Băsescu, at the edge of the Empire. (Romanian). *Ziare.com*. Retrieved 11.02.11 http://www.ziare.com/europa/franta/basescu-la-marginea-imperiului-1070223

*** (28.01.11). Romania in Schengen. The evaluation group will give an answer on Friday for the technical report. (Romanian). *Ziare.com*. Retrieved 11.02.11 http://www.ziare.com/politica/schengen/romania-in-schengen-grupul-de-evaluare-da-vineri-raspuns-pentru-raportul-tehnic-1071595

Ciucu, C. (07.01.11). How long should we repent?. (Romanian). *Hotnews.ro*. Retrieved 11.02.11 http://www.hotnews.ro/stiri-politic-8188109-cata-cenusa-mai-punem-cap.htm

Mixich, V. (21.01.11). The Dark Year. (Romanian). *Hotnews.ro*. Retrieved 11.02.11 http://www.hotnews.ro/stiri-international-8227676-anul-negru.htm

Mixich, V., Pantazi, C. (17.01.11). The French knife stuck in Romania's back. Possible victim: the European Union. (Romanian). *Hotnews.ro*. Retrieved 11.02.11 http://www.hotnews.ro/stiri-esential-8213738-titul-francez-infipt-spatele-romaniei-victima-posibila-uniunea-europeana.htm

BRIDGING THE GAP THROUGH EUROPEANIZED MEDIA: A CONTENT ANALYSIS OF NATIONAL AND TRANSNATIONAL EURACTIV NEWS PORTALS

ADINA MARINCEA

Abstract

There is little consensus among scholars regarding the emergence of a European public sphere and the theoretical model on which it relies. However, the role that media play in bridging the gap between Brussels and EU citizens has been acknowledged as essential. The paper relies on the concept of a "light" European public sphere, developed through the Europeanization of national mediated public spheres. The emergence of such a public sphere is tested in this article by analyzing the news coverage of European topics on the EurActiv network in two EU countries – Romania and Spain, compared to the Brussels central news portal – euractiv.com. Systematic content analysis is conducted in order to answer questions regarding the predominance of specific EU and national topics in the media, the visibility of EU actors and the types of news prevalent in each country. The analysis is based on a similar study conducted by Hans-Jörg Trenz on national quality newspapers in six EU countries. Thus, the analysis tests the presence of the three types of news that resulted from his study: European articles, Europeanized articles and articles with a European referential frame. Based on the results of the research, this article draws a sketch of the emergent European public sphere, seen as a communicative mediation between EU countries on issues of common relevance.

Key words: European public sphere, Europeanization, European media, the EU's Communication deficit.

Scholars have dedicated their work for more than a decade to tackling the concept of a European public sphere. While there is a wide consensus that the Habermasian normative ideal of a public sphere is rather utopic in today's complex society, an adapted definition for the European public sphere should be guided by at least two functions: it represents a "civic forum" that interpolates political power and thus becomes a mediator between citizens and government institutions/actors.

There is consensus among scholars that a "heavy", supranational European public sphere does not and could not exist. Instead, as Habermas later points out, the solution is rather in the trans-nationalization of national public spheres (Habermas, 2009). Other authors (Machill, Beiler & Fischer, 2006) subscribe to this view of the European public sphere as a network, a "communicative space" (Fossum & Schlesinger, 2007) or a "community of communication" (Steeg & Risse, 2010). Mass-media (national and transnational) play a central role in the Europeanization of national public spheres (a "light" European public sphere), both by "shifting their focus away from the national political arena towards the European level" (Pfetsch et al., 2004, p. 4) and by facilitating the convergence of national news agendas (Meyer, 1999).

In order for a public sphere to exist, a forum is needed to stir or even host a public debate. Due to criteria such as accessibility and large audiences, mass media provide this forum, mediating between the public and politics. However, as Koopmans and Pfetsch point out (2007, 59), mass media should not only be seen as a communication channel serving other actors, but also as a political actor itself, carrying a voice of its own. In this latter function, "media are granted a role as actors in their own right which allows for their own contribution to political agenda-setting and opinion formation" (Pfetsch et al., 2004, p. 6).

There is still a wide debate on defining and conceptualizing Europeanization. In my opinion, this is a long-term process which is shaped through the interactions that take place between the actors involved (political actors and institutions, mass-media, civil society and other non-state actors, both at a national and a European level), rather than follow a pre-defined pattern. It is not within the scope of this paper to define Europeanization. Therefore, I will continue with a more general conceptualization, from the perspective of media studies: Europeanization as "a multi-dimensional and gradual process that in one way or another extends public discourse beyond national spaces" (Brüggemann et al., 2006, p. 4).

Furthermore, this process is specifically related to the EU countries, as Brüggemann and Königslöw (2007, p. 3) highlight: "Europeanization is a form of trans-nationalization limited to the European continent, or more specifically to the member states of the European Union".

Koopmans and Erbe (2003, p. 6) distinguished between three different forms of Europeanization of public communication: the emergence of a supranational European public sphere, characterized by interactions between European institutions and actors on European themes, with the support of European-wide mass media; vertical Europeanization, either "bottom-up" – where national actors address European actors – or "top-down" – "in which European actors intervene in national policies and public debates in the name of regulations and common interests". On the other hand, horizontal Europeanization refers to a mutual observation between different member states and has a weak and a strong dimension.

> In the weak variant, the media in one country cover debates and contestation in another member state, but there is no linkage between the countries in the structure of the claim-making itself. In the stronger variant, actors from one country explicitly address, or refer to actors or policies in another member state. (Koopmans and Erbe, 2007, pp. 6–7)

It is the aim of this paper to study the extent to which each of these three forms of Europeanization is present in the three news websites analysed.

An extension of this typology is provided by Brüggemann and Königslöw (2007, p. 4). The two authors have combined the vertical and horizontal dimensions of Europeanization (according to the values they may take), resulting in four Europeanization patterns: comprehensive Europeanization – high levels of vertical and horizontal Europeanization; segmented Europeanization – vertical, but no horizontal Europeanization; Europeanization aloof from the EU – horizontal without vertical Europeanization and a parochial public sphere – neither vertical, nor horizontal Europeanization. This distinction will also be the topic of this paper. In addition to this typology, the two authors have also operationalized the concepts of vertical and horizontal Europeanization, which will guide the present analysis.

Framing Europe

The European Commission has acknowledged the need to bridge the gap between European citizens and Brussels officials. A solution has been seen in the creation of a European public sphere, an idea formally introduced in the Commission's *White Paper on a European Communication Policy* (COM (2006) 35 final) and extended in *Communicating Europe in*

Partnership (CEP) (COM (2007) 569 final). However, the concept is treated rather superficially in those documents. The EC seems to show a certain lack of understanding regarding how media work, leading to a "no news is good news" policy, as De Vreese notices (2003, 6). According to the author, "a long-term goal of the EU is to communicate – and, in fact, brand and promote – the notion of Europe to its citizens and beyond. This involves a process of strategic, long-term image-building which projects a positive, emotionally appealing European narrative, based on 'European' values (such as democracy, equality, tolerance etc.) and a history of European integration as that of a continent which overcame division and achieved a morally and rationally superior form of coexistence among peoples' (De Vreese, 2003, p. 8).

Scholars (Kunelius & Sparks, 2001; Mihelj, 2007; Michailidou, 2010) have pointed out the faltering communication strategy of the EU, and have even held the "communication deficit" accountable for the "democratic deficit" in Europe. What has often been criticized about EU communication is the high technicality of information, a characteristic that makes the material difficult to digest. In many cases, journalists pass the information from the EC to the public without filtering it or packing it in an accessible form. This practice raises debates regarding the role of journalists in the process of Europeanization of national media public spheres. If a "European narrative" is needed, then certainly informational journalism does not suffice. In order for media to become true "watchdogs" and politically mobilizing agents, actively participating in the creation of a symbolic European public sphere (in a constructivist perspective), a type of "deliberative"/ "interpretative" journalism is needed (Beciu, 2007). On the other hand, Statham (2007, p. 473) notices that "journalists see the 'democratic deficit' as an important topic, but not as a motivator to extend their own political role. On the contrary, they place responsibility for remedying the 'democratic deficit' squarely on the shoulders of elected politicians".

According to De Vreese (2003), a frame-building process can help transform European news in "communicable stories". Frames are a way of "packing" information in different patterns that provide a meaning or interpretation of the issues discussed. For Gitlin (1980, p. 7), frames are "persistent patterns of cognition, interpretation, and presentation, of selection, emphasis and exclusion by which symbol-handlers routinely organize discourse". De Vreese (2005) goes through news-framing related literature and distinguishes between issue-specific and generic frames. While the first category is limited to specific topics or events, generic frames "transcend thematic limitations and can be identified in relation to different topics, some even over time and in different cultural contexts" (De Vreese, 2005, p. 54).

In my analysis I aim to identify six of the generic frames in De Vreese's classification: the episodic frame – issues are limited to events (see Iyengar, 1991) – and the news frames developed by Semetko and Valkenburg (2000): "conflict", "human interest", "attribution of responsibility", "morality", and "economic consequences".

> The conflict frame emphasizes conflict between individuals, groups, institutions or countries. The human interest frame brings a human face, an individual's story, or an emotional angle to the presentation of an event, issue or problem. The responsibility frame presents an issue or problem in such a way as to attribute responsibility for causing or solving the issue to either the government or to an individual or group. The morality frame interprets an event or issue in the context of religious tenets or moral prescriptions. The economic consequences frame presents an event, problem or issue in terms of the economic consequences it will have on an individual, group, institution, region or country. (De Vreese, 2005, p. 56)

In addition, I expect to find the three-dimensional frame model used by Trenz (2004) in his content analysis: interests (instrumental dimension), values (normative dimension) and identity (ethical-identitarian dimension). According to the author (Trenz, 2004, p. 309), "the distinction indicates a further three dimensions of reflexivity, which tell why an issue is relevant for us: because it touches our particular sphere of interests, because it touches a universal sphere of values or because it touches our collective identity". These frames can offer an insight to the way EurActiv journalists approach European issues and the type of perception that is transferred to readers.

Two issue-specific frames are tested in this paper, frames that have been identified in the Romanian media in relation to European issues: "messianic Europe" and "penalizing Europe" (Bârgăoanu, Dobrescu & Marincea, 2010; Bârgăoanu, 2011; Marincea, 2011). The first news frame portrays the image of the EU as Romania's saviour in the context of economic crisis, corruption problems, especially by providing access to EU funds. On the other hand, Europe is referred to as a superior entity that punishes or sanctions Romania for its flaws (Bârgăoanu, 2011, p. 129). Another similar issue-specific frame that emerged from the current analysis sees the EU as an "arbitrator" of conflicts and disputes between member states. It is the purpose of this research to test these frames in order to see if they persist in journalistic practices outside Romania and if they can therefore be validated as issue-specific frames in regard to European topics. The messianic and penalizing Europe issue-specific frames are news frames that imply either positive connotations like "European" opportunities at a national level ("messianic Europe"), or negative connotations brought by the perception of Europe in terms of risks for member states ("penalizing Europe"). Schuck and De Vreese show in their experimental research (2006) that "risk" and "opportunity" are news frames that have a strong impact on public support for EU enlargement, which is why I consider it important to test the presence of the two issue-specific frames previously identified in the news provided by the three EU-oriented and specialized news portals.

According to De Vreese (2003), news frames can be used in order to "translate" the EU messages to the general public. The author pleads for the use of frames such as the conflict frame, human interests, economic consequences, responsibility or the historical context frame in order to make the EU a "communicable story". In support of these recommendations, De Vreese (2003) cites results of different research studies that show, for example, that "the audience of conflict-framed news often reacts in a more reflexive manner to the information, and develops a fairly balanced point of view" (De Vreese, 2003, p. 26) or that "referring to a historical context for a story . . . can evoke some powerful ideals such as peace or shared European values, which, as a result, the EU comes to represent in the minds of the audience" (De Vreese, 2003, p. 24).

After all, newsworthiness is an essential feature that articles must have in order to reach the media agenda and this type of frames can help translate EU politics, "which journalists typically perceive as inaccessible, overly bureaucratic, and abstract" (Meyer, 1999).

Research Methodology

This research attempts to answer questions on who communicates or becomes the subject of communication of European issues, what is communicated (European topics), and how these topics are communicated (news frames). A content analysis is conducted in order to measure the extent to which online national and trans-national media can be considered Europeanized and in order to map the actors and issues that dominate what scholars call the emergent European public sphere.

150 articles on three EurActiv websites have been analyzed in a four-month period (March – June 2011). Due to the large amount of news per day (especially on the Spanish website) and to the purpose of analysing news on a wider variety of EU topics, a random sample of 1 out of 10 articles in each category has been subjected to analysis. In order to increase the comparability of the research results, the variables for the

content analysis have been chosen and coded in accordance with the codebook used by Hans-Jörg Trenz (2004) in his analysis of daily newspapers.

EurActiv is an independent, cross-lingual twelve-country media network entirely dedicated to EU affairs. With an average of 588,847 monthly unique visitors across EurActiv websites (source: Google Analytics April 2009–March 2010, http://www.euractiv.com/en/audience), the EurActiv network is dedicated to "the Community of EU Actors", namely EU decision-makers, journalists, national administrators and multipliers. The declared goal of the network is to deepen EU policy debate, "both within and outside the institutions as well as upstream of decisions", by focusing on "policy positions by EU Actors trying to influence policies already in the pre-legislative phase, before a Commission proposal" (Concept & Objectives, http://www.euractiv.com). In addition, the web portal aims to "develop better-informed policy proposals" and "bring these policy debates to the national capital" (http://www.euractiv.com/en/audience). The strong policy-focus is marked by the news categories on each portal, which follow the main EU policy fields.

The EurActiv portal was chosen for the content analysis due to its declared and assumed role as mediator, "watchdog" and, to a certain extent, political agent. It is within this media network that I expect to find a higher tendency towards the Europeanization of national media public spheres and a more vivid dialogue between Member States and between MS and EU actors. Three websites have been chosen: the Romanian and Spanish versions, on the one hand, and the trans-national, central news portal – euractiv.com, based in Brussels, on the other hand. While the two national portals take up news from euractiv.com, they either give it a "local spin" or produce news of their own, according to their specific national contexts and interests. Consequently, it is expected that differences occur at the level of article content. The analysis also aims to identify the differences that occur between EU coverage in an older member state (Spain) and a newer one (Romania), in comparison to the transnational website, which is expected to embody a more "European" and "Europeanized" approach.

The research also combines deductive and inductive frame analysis, seeking to identify both generic and issue-specific news frames. The goal of the frame analysis is to provide qualitative insight into the "how" of EU communication and descry the journalistic patterns in which European issues are put forward. Twelve news-frames, described in the theoretical section of the paper, have been thought to appear in the articles analysed.

EMPIRICAL FINDINGS

Article Classification

As expected, most of the articles (77%) on the three news portals have a European framework, while the rest of the articles promote either exclusively national (13%) or international (10%) issues. However, different patterns occur between the three online sources regarding the predominance of certain article types.

Three types of European articles were evident in the content analysis, according to the typology identified by Hans-Jörg Trenz (2004): European articles, Europeanized articles and articles with a European referential frame. In the first category (European articles) European topics are dominant and they are treated at a European level, while in the Europeanized articles they are either treated at a national level ("top-down" Europeanization) or appear as a framework for national issues ("bottom-up" Europeanization). The analysis distinguishes between two types of Europeanized articles, based on Koopmans and Erbe's distinction (2003) between vertical and horizontal Europeanization. Vertical Europeanization articles have been defined as the ones where supranational actors (the EU Commission, Parliament or other institutions) either intervene in national policies/debates or address national actors (the government, other institutions) – for "top-down" Europeanization classification – or national actors address European actors ("bottom-up" Europeanization). On the other hand, horizontal Europeanization articles have been defined as ones in which a country different from the country news-portal (Romania or Spain) is the main subject (mutual observation) or, in the case of EurActiv.com, in which relations between different EU countries comprise the topic.

There is a common tendency of the three news sources towards Europeanized articles, with similar frequencies of articles both on the horizontal and on the vertical dimension. A quarter of the articles on the Romanian and Spanish websites and 20% of the ones on euractiv.com fit into the vertical "top-down" Europeanization category, while only 2% (euractiv.com) and 4% (euractiv.es) promote a "bottom-up" perspective, which is entirely absent from the Romanian website. A potential hypothesis to be tested in future studies could be that "bottom-up" vertical Europeanization increases with the duration of a country's membership in the EU.

One fifth of the articles on all three news portals are devoted to issues concerning other countries, mostly Western European countries (France, Germany, also Italy). Greece is also a subject in many articles on all three websites, due to its financial problems which are considered European issues. The results of the analysis prove that, to a certain extent, mutual observation between EU members is a common journalistic practice for the EurActiv network and an indicator of horizontal Europeanization, though mostly in its weak form. The results contradict a study conducted in 2008 (Wessler et al.) on ten online newspapers, according to which mutual observation is less predominant in the case of newer EU member states (such as Romania), which have a weaker EU focus. The difference in findings might rely on the type of newspapers analysed. While the 2008 study was conducted on newspapers (including a Romanian tabloid, *Libertatea*), the types of articles and editorial mission are different from the ones analysed in this paper, EurActiv being an online network specializing in European news.

The results of the analysis show that, though European articles represent over a quarter of the total number of articles, they are distributed unevenly on each news portal. EurActiv.com, the transnational website, focuses on articles with a dominant European topic (42%), while the Romanian and Spanish counterparts place a smaller emphasis on the European dimension of the issues, with only 28%, respectively 14% of the articles. On the other hand, one third of the Spanish articles have an exclusively national approach, while only 10% of the Romanian articles adopt an entirely national framework.

	EurActiv.com	**Romania**	**Spain**	**TOTAL**
Exclusively national	0%	10%	30%	13.33%
European articles	42%	28%	14%	28%
Vertical,“top-down” Europeanization	20%	24%	24%	22.67%
Vertical,“bottom-up” Europeanization	2%	0%	4%	2%
Horizontal Europeanization	22%	20%	20%	20.67%
International	12%	14%	6%	10.67%
European Rhetoric	2%	4%	2%	2.67%

Fig 2-1. Types of articles in relation to the level of the dominant topic

In comparison to the study conducted by Trenz (2004), where one third of the articles were dominated by a European rhetoric, in the analysis of the three EurActiv portals only 2% of the articles refer to "Europe" merely as a rhetorical pretext for other issues. This can be explained in relation to the organizational culture and the editorial mission of EurActiv, on the one hand and, on the other hand, in relation to the audience of the news network: professionals, EU actors, national and European decision-makers or, at least, readers who are familiar with EU topics.

The results of the content analysis show a higher tendency of Romania, one of the newest Member States, to discuss issues in a European and international context, in comparison to Spain. The Spanish news portal focuses more on promoting issues either at an exclusively national level or in a Europeanized manner. This contradicts the findings of Brüggemann and Königslöw's research (2007, p. 23), according to which "newspapers in countries that have long been assimilated in the EU tend to discuss EU politics more often as both journalists and readers have become more used to this subject".

Two types of explanations can be provided. One is related to the specifics of the organizational culture of Romanian journalists (unfortunately not much data is available on this issue). Another possible explanation could come from the recent membership status of Romania (2007) and its above-the-European-average confidence in the EU.

Ten referential frameworks have been identified as a result of the content analysis, consistent with the types of articles identified. Most of the articles on euractiv.com (38%) present the European issues in formal references to European laws, treaties, norms and conventions. The Spanish website has an opposing tendency, with a third of the articles having exclusively national references. Only a quarter of the articles on the Spanish portal contain references to specific European actors, institutions or events and 14% to European laws, treaties and norms. On the other hand, euractiv.ro equally uses (22%) the national framework and the European laws framework, with a similar frequency (20%) of references to European actors, institutions or events. Most of the references in European or Europeanized articles have an institutional dimension, similar to the communication style of the European Commission. Other reference frameworks identified are, in order of their average frequency: reference to EU interests/position in international context, Europe as a generalization in the context of EU issues treated nationally, Europe as a generalization/ Europe's position in the context of non-EU issues, references to conflicts between the EU and the national level, Europe as a framework for comparison between MS, exclusively international references and Europe as a comparison in the context of non-EU issues.

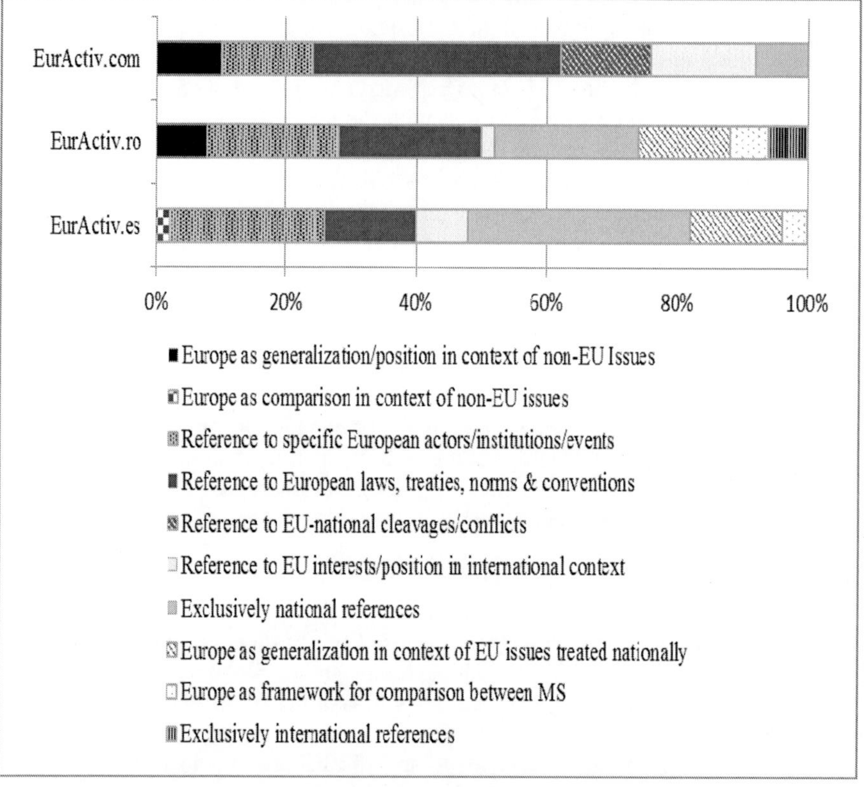

Fig 2-2. Distribution of referential frameworks

Actor Mapping

The analysis tries to identify the main agents of the news articles, focusing both on the level (national, European, international) and on the type of actors mentioned. Almost half of the articles on the trans-national portal (euractiv.com) refer to European supranational actors such as the European Commission, the European Parliament and other EU institutions. These actors are dominant in the European articles, while most of the Europeanized articles focus on different EU Member States (e.g. France, Germany, Italy and Spain) and on bilateral/multilateral relations between European countries. The most frequently mentioned national actors on euractiv.com are either representatives of different governments (ministers, prime-ministers or national governments as a whole), the Parliament and other national institutions (22% of the articles), or different countries (10% of the articles).

In comparison, the Romanian website focuses equally on actors at the supranational and national levels, each present in a third of the articles. The most frequent referrals (a quarter of the articles) point towards countries as a whole, while the European Commission is mentioned less often (12%) than on euractiv.com. The most visible national actors are the Romanian government, the Parliament, or other institutions. The Romanian website has a stronger focus both on other Member States and on countries outside Europe or the EU, in comparison to Spain.

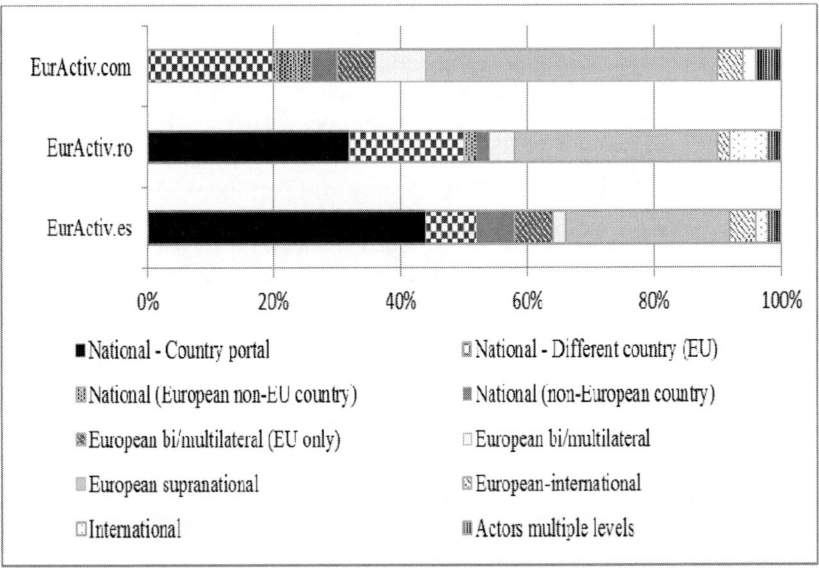

Fig 2-3. Actor level

EurActiv.es stands out for its clear predilection for treating issues at a national level. Almost half of the articles (44%) mention Spanish actors, the most visible being the Spanish government (prime-minister José Luis Rodríguez Zapatero is frequently referenced) or other national or sub-national (regional) institutions. Only one fourth of the articles place EU supranational institutions or representatives in a leading role, and the EC and the EP specifically are mentioned even less frequently. These results are in line with another research study (Peter, 2003 after De Vreese, 2003, p. 18) which found that countries with a shorter membership history (e.g. Romania) have more references to EU representatives than older member states (e.g. Spain).

What is common for all three websites is the variety of actors who dominate the articles. Apart from the aforementioned, other actors such as European or international intergovernmental organizations (e.g. the Organization for Economic Cooperation and Development – OECD, the United Nations Organization, the World Health Organization) parties, federations, NGOs, business actors or other non-state actors. In comparison to the results of Trenz's analysis (2004), civil society representatives are present, though in a small number of articles (under 10%).

When it comes to the actors cited in the articles, actors who may be regarded as sources of information and, at a certain level, agenda-setters, the results confirm the three different patterns adopted by the three websites analysed. The transnational portal, as expected, primarily cites official EU sources (in half of the articles), mostly European Commissioners (in a third of the articles) and members of the European Parliament, while national representatives are cited in only a fourth of the total number of articles. In contrast, the Spanish journalists maintain their national focus, citing national or sub-national actors in a third of the articles, while European actors become official sources of information in fewer articles (a quarter).

The Romanian counterpart is situated in the middle of the tendencies of the two portals, citing both national and European actors with almost the same frequency (with a slight tendency towards European sources). However, the two national websites tend to cite other EU representatives (e.g. the European Central Bank, the European Court of Justice) more often than euractiv.com. The other sources (non-state actors, intergovernmental organizations, business actors) are cited by the three websites with similar frequencies, accounting for an average of 20% of the articles.

The same pattern is reflected in the frequency of the different actors that appear in the images in the articles. EurActiv.com shows a clear predominance of EU actors and symbols (flag, euro), the Spanish website posts more pictures of national actors and symbols while the Romanian one maintains a balance between national and European actors, with a slight inclination towards the latter.

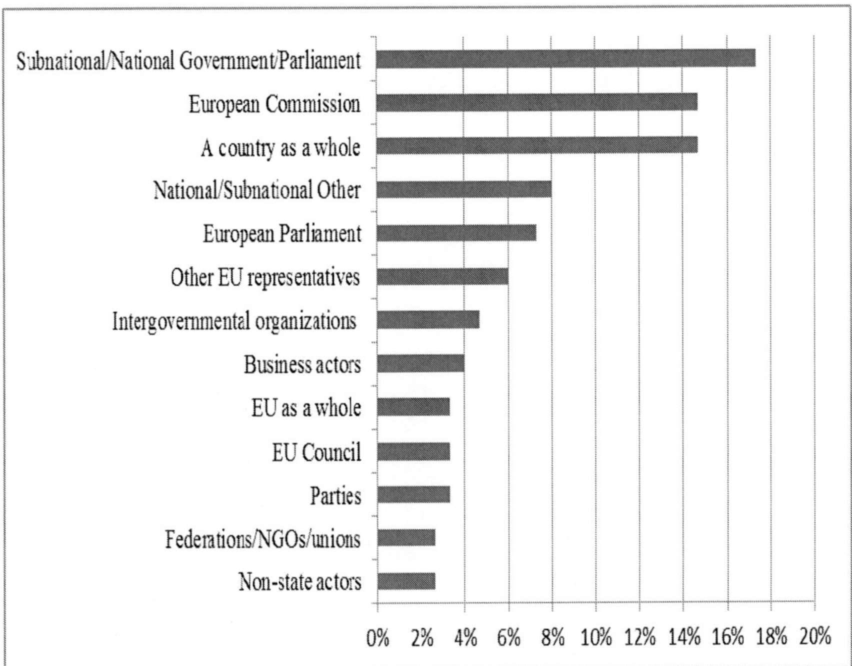

Fig 2-4. Types of actors

The results of the analysis show that the main agenda setters of European topics are EU Commissioners, while national actors who represent the government can be identified as agents of media Europeanization, or agents of the domestication of EU topics. The high visibility of EU Commissioners seems to take into account De Vreese's recommendation of "giving Europe a face" by "making national commissioners key communication agents" (De Vreese, 2003, p. 28).

Governments are not necessarily agenda-setters when it comes to European issues, but they are gatekeepers with a position on European topics that could influence the perception of these issues or of the EU as a whole. Non-state actors are also visible in the media (considerably less so), but they are treated from the perspective of their position on an issue, rather than as agenda-setters.

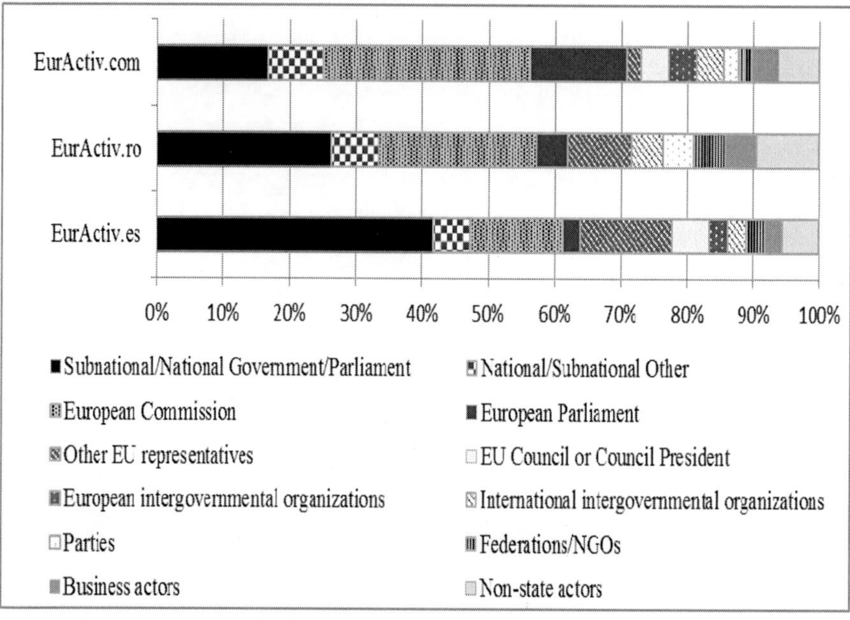

Fig 2-5. Types of actors cited

The analysis also shows that, apart from the visibility of the EC, other important institutions such as the European Parliament or the European Council have a poor media strategy, resulting in reduced visibility. Hans-Jörg Trenz (2004, p. 301) reached the same conclusion regarding the under-representation of these institutions, explaining this result in relation to "the lack of competencies in promoting and monitoring European policies, the absence of centralized media policies, the low impact and visibility of European parliamentarian debates, no collective representation or voice, and the very few VIPs among parliamentarians".

European Topics

The analysis has tried to identify the main issues that emerge on the three sites, in relation to different policy fields. The classification of the policy fields is based on the classification available on the EU Commission official website (http://ec.europa.eu), to which I have added the constitutional and institutional dimensions previously defined by Hans-Jörg Trenz (2004).

The analysis shows that all policy fields are covered by the articles, to a greater or lesser extent. There is also a certain convergence of the distribution of the various policy issues that are topics of the articles on the three websites, though the frequency of certain policy fields is different from one site to another. The two national websites focus on European issues related to economy, finance and tax policy (around a quarter of all articles), while on euractiv.com the economic policy is present in only 14% of all articles. The transnational website is primarily concerned with external relations/foreign affairs (22%) and justice policy (16%). While European foreign affairs are also mentioned in 16% of the Spanish articles, the Romanian counterpart dedicates only a minimal number of articles (6%) to this topic. This result may be due to the relatively recent acceptance of Romania in the EU, which might determine an interest more focused on internal affairs, rather than on external relations of the EU, as the former have a greater and more direct impact on a national level. A hypothesis that could be studied in future analyses is that the interest of member states towards European foreign affairs strengthens over time, proportional to the duration of their membership.

Apart from economic issues, the Romanian website is concerned with institutional issues regarding the EU (e.g. corruption issues – the scandal involving MEPs and journalists from the *Sunday Times*, including a Romanian MEP – Adrian Severin; European Law, subsidies distribution of competences between EU and MS etc.). The interest euractiv.ro shows in EU institutional issues is also connected to the relatively recent membership of Romania, as an effort to get people acquainted with the structures and the functional side of the European construction.

There is a common interest of euractiv.com and euractiv.ro in citizens' rights and home affairs, concentrated around immigration issues. This focus can be explained in relation to the discussions about Romania and Bulgaria's admission to the Schengen area, occurring simultaneously to the articles analysed.

An atypical result is the high frequency (14%) of issues related to agriculture policy in the Spanish articles. This result is also determined by an event that occurred in the period analysed and involved Spain and other EU countries (especially Germany) – the E. coli outburst. The issue is treated as an agricultural subject, rather than from the perspective of the health policy. This is due to the tendency of journalists towards economic consequences framing (more thoroughly discussed in the next section of the paper), more exactly the effects of the "cucumber crisis" on Spanish agriculture incomes.

	EurActiv.com	EurActiv.ro	EurActiv.es	Total
Economy, finance and tax	14%	28%	24%	19.76%
External relations, foreign affairs and security	22%	6%	16%	13.17%
Justice, citizens' rights and home affairs	16%	12%	4%	9.58%
Institutional affairs	8%	16%	4%	8.38%
Environment	10%	10%	4%	7.78%
Science and technology	10%	4%	6%	5.99%
Business (Enterprise & Industry)	8%	2%	8%	5.39%
Agriculture, fisheries and food	0%	2%	14%	4.79%
Health and Consumer Policy	8%	4%	4%	4.79%
Constitutional affairs	6%	4%	2%	3.59%
Employment and social rights	2%	10%	0%	3.59%
Energy and natural resources	8%	4%	0%	3.59%
Transport and travel	2%	4%	4%	2.99%
Climate action (global climate)	4%	2%	0%	1.80%
Cross-cutting policies – Europa 2020	4%	2%	0%	1.80%
Culture, education and youth	0%	2%	4%	1.80%
Regional Policy	2%	0%	2%	1.20%

Fig 2-6. Distribution of articles according to European policy fields

The three news sources analysed are divergent when it comes to topics like employment and social rights which seem to attract the attention of Romanian EurActiv journalists more so than of the other websites (10% of the articles). This is due to the strong concern of Romanian citizens with the European labour market and work migration possibilities.

The distribution of the issues related to the European policy fields shows that there is a general interest in economic issues. On the other hand, the media diverges when it comes to national interests, priorities or events that have repercussions at the national level. Events such as the debate on the Schengen Agreement or the E. coli outburst, though

European in dimension, influence the news coverage in the countries mostly involved or affected and may push certain policies to higher visibility in the public agenda. This leads to a form of Europeanization of events, which, as seen in Statham and Guiraudon's research (2004, p. 16) as well, although creating "common and simultaneous types of debates within the different national public spheres . . . are still viewed through a national lens and the extent to which they are considered important and enter the public sphere is also dependent on national political conditions". In other words, as the analysis shows, Romanian articles regarding the Schengen Agreement and immigration issues are more frequent than the articles on the Spanish website regarding the same topic, similar to Spain's strong interest in the E. coli issue.

A fourth of all articles contain references to events, a tendency more pronounced on the Romanian website. However, the high frequency of events does not necessarily point to episodic framing, as, in most cases, the events are only contextually mentioned and not primary topics of the articles. An exception is the Romanian website, where almost half of the articles containing events use these in order to depict certain issues, without placing them in a larger context (episodic framing). The main reason that could explain this different approach regards the specific editorial features of euractiv.ro. Almost half of the Romanian articles analysed are taken almost verbatim from other online media or media agencies (e.g. hotnews.ro, Mediafax), which might be more inclined towards using episodic framing (as they address the general public). In addition, only three authors have been identified for all the 50 articles analysed, and the author of most of the articles is a journalist from hotnews.ro, an online news portal targeting the general public and not solely dedicated to European issues. This points out a lack of Romanian journalists specializing in European affairs and a rather generalized approach, not very different from other online quality newspapers.

Besides the topics that are dominant in the three media sources, the analysis also points out the absolute absence of certain important issues, or so-called "non-issues", using Trenz's (2004) terminology. There are no references to topics like European identity, the recently adopted EU Constitution, multiculturalism, youth, minority protection or even discussions regarding the advantages or disadvantages of EU membership), among others missing. This shows that there are many relevant European issues which do not make the public/media agenda, even though they are substantially present in other forms of debate (especially academic).

Another tendency that emerges from the analysis and is common for all three news portals is the editorial style or journalists' attitudes towards European news. In 95% of the articles the journalists adopt a neutral, objective tone, keeping to the simple transmission of the information from one level (mostly EU or member states) to another (citizens or different stakeholders). Most articles resemble formal reports where different actors are involved and their statements are presented. This raises serious questions about the role of the journalist as gatekeeper of European information and as facilitator of debates between citizens and national/supranational institutions/actors. On the one hand, it may be argued that objectivity is a desirable feature of quality journalism, though, as Camelia Beciu (2007) observed, pure objectivity is not possible, as the selection of news itself, for instance, is a manifestation of a journalist's preferences. On the other hand, several reasons could be invoked for the need of a more interpretative journalistic attitude. First, the high level of technical, specialized and often hard-to-assimilate information would make a journalistic filter (be it at a semantic/symbolic or at least at a syntactic level) useful for the readers. In addition, in order for journalists to fulfill the role of "watchdogs" and facilitate critical debate on European issues, they themselves should adopt a more critical attitude. As far as I am concerned, the media should opt for "evaluative" journalism, rather than "informational", without, however, falling into the extreme of "speculative journalism" (see Beciu, 2007).

This tendency towards neutrality can explain the "non-issues", or the absence of certain relevant issues (such as the ones previously presented). Most of these "non-issues" (European identity, multiculturalism, instrumentality etc.) involve a strong symbolic or axiological approach, thus they call for debate and interpretation. The analysis shows that there is a clear tendency of EurActiv journalists towards informational content, which is explicitly incorporated in the editorial mission ("neutrality" and "impartiality" are stated as key principles for the EurActiv network). This makes it difficult for journalists to tackle issues like European identity in an informational, reporter-like style. The editorial commitment to "neutrality" also leads, in the case of the three EurActiv portals analysed, to a lack of problematization, a practice considered fundamental in creating a public sphere in habermasian terms (Beciu, 2007).

Returning to policy fields, a significant proportion of the total articles (36%) address policies outside the EU, at a national level (either Spanish or Romanian ones, or other countries' policies). Both euractiv.com and euractiv.es focus on institutional issues in different countries (mostly elections, but also national Parliament activity, reforms etc.) in 41%, respectively 30% of the articles. The Romanian counterpart, on the other hand, is equally preoccupied (13% of the articles) with economic, infrastructure and justice/home affairs issues. With only two exceptions (an article about China and one about the former Serbian leader Ratko Mladici for euractiv.ro and two articles on euractiv.es regarding Greece and Peru), the majority of the articles refer to national (Romanian and Spanish) policy-related issues, while euractiv.com focuses mostly on EU members (Portugal, Bulgaria, Belgium, Greece).

At the content level, the analysis reinforces the results of Trenz's research (2004). Even though there are many policy-related issues, they are treated generally with a low degree of specialization. European policies are only a general framework, not discussed in terms of particularities, but rather referred to implicitly or explicitly. This may help in terms of visibility, but more certainly it maintains citizens' confusion and lack of understanding regarding European policies, and thus has little chance of generating debate among them.

Framing European Issues

The analysis tries to identify the type of frames used by EurActiv journalists when writing about European issues. This gives us insight into the interpretative pattern proposed by journalists at the content level. Based on the distinction made by Trenz (2004) between the instrumental, normative and identitarian dimensions, I have searched for frames regarding interests, values and identity, following the author's line of thought. In addition, it was expected to find other generic news frames validated by several researchers: economic consequences, conflict, responsibility, morality and human interest. These frames have been described in the theoretical section of the paper. In addition to these generic frames, the analysis tested two issue-specific news frames that have been found in previous research studies (Bârgăoanu, Dobrescu & Marincea, 2010; Bârgăoanu, 2011; Marincea, 2011). These are: Messianic Europe and Penalizing Europe. Another similar issue-specific frame emerged from the current analysis, resulting from an inductive approach: "Arbitrator Europe" – the EU seen as an arbitrator for conflicts and disputes between Member States.

The results of the analysis point out a convergence between the three online portals in terms of dominant news frames, but at different intensities. Two frames dominate the media discourse, both pointing to an instrumental dimension: economic consequences and interests (an average of 32%, respectively 24% for all three websites). However, the two frames are far more frequent on eeuractiv.com (in over half of the articles) than on the national counterparts. Almost a third of the Spanish articles are framed in terms of economic consequences, while Romanian journalists are only half as interested in this type of framing. The "interests" frame is even less frequent on both websites (14% for Spain and only 8% for Romania).

EurActiv.com journalists often present EU affairs in the light of the conflicts emerging between different actors (42% of the articles). Other common frames identified in the EurActiv.com news are values, identity, morality, responsibility and human interest. However, except for the values frame, present in 34% of the articles, all others are less frequent (in less than a quarter of the articles), with the human interest frame almost absent. Across the national counterparts, all these frames (except for economic consequences and interests) are scarce (occurring in less than 10% of the articles). Moreover, euractiv.com expressly uses what De Vreese identifies as the "historical context" frame in most of the articles, having a "background" section that gives readers context information for the issues discussed. The only frame that is almost absent in the euractiv.com articles is human interest, due to its emotional dimension, which is not in line with the editorial mission. On the other hand, there is a slight tendency of Romanian journalists towards the human interest and the responsibility frame (in comparison with the other two sites), while on both euractiv.ro and euractiv.es the morality frame is entirely absent.

The transnational website is much more prone to frame the news in comparison to the national portals. An explanation could reside in the profile of journalists (experience, issue/field specialization etc.). Most of the journalists from euractiv.com are either specialists in EU affairs or have experience as correspondents (including Brussels correspondents) for other national or international media channels (e.g. *The Guardian*, *The Economist*, the BBC etc.) or they have worked for different EU institutions. In addition, some of the euractiv.com articles analysed were written in partnership with the Reuters agency, which might increase the frequency of instrumental frames.

EurActiv.com journalists' tendency to frame news shows with pure objectivity is not a realistic concept for the journalistic field and a clear distinction between informational and interpretative journalism is hard to attain (Beciu, 2007). In other words, even though the editorial principles of EurActiv point towards neutrality and the content of the articles is rather informational, consciously or not, journalists integrate some of their own interpretations in the process of frame-building (see De Vreese, 2005).

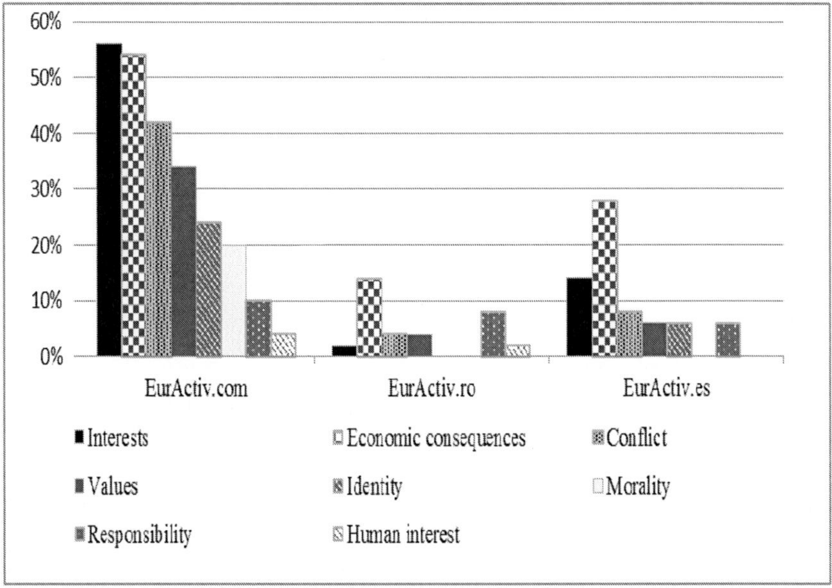

Fig 2-7. The distribution of generic frames

What can be concluded is that, one the one hand, the transnational website is more prone to news framing, while the two national websites are much less inclined towards frame-building (especially euractiv.ro). This difference may reside in the editorial style (articles on euractiv.com are longer, more thorough and elaborate), in journalistic practice, or in the specifics of organizational culture. As Statham (2007, p. 464) shows, "seen as an internalized set of values, this 'organizational culture' shapes journalists' decisions regarding their writing. Most journalists consciously identify with their newspaper's 'editorial line'".

On the other hand, the analysis shows a clear tendency towards an instrumental approach to European issues, whereas normative (values, morality) and identitarian dimensions, along with more subjective (responsibility) or even emotional interpretations (human interest) are less frequent. These results contradict research on German quality newspapers, which "emphasize the collective identities, norms, and values that Europe should stand for" (Koopmans & Pfetsch, 2007, p. 84). This can be explained in relation to the editorial "pledge" for neutrality taken by EurActiv journalists and their inclination towards informational journalism. The editorial tendency of EurActiv towards instrumental framing points to a "cosmopolitan European identity project" based on political citizenship and rights, rather than to a "populist" one, emphasizing social citizenship and cultural authenticity (Udrea & Corbu, 2010, p. 77).

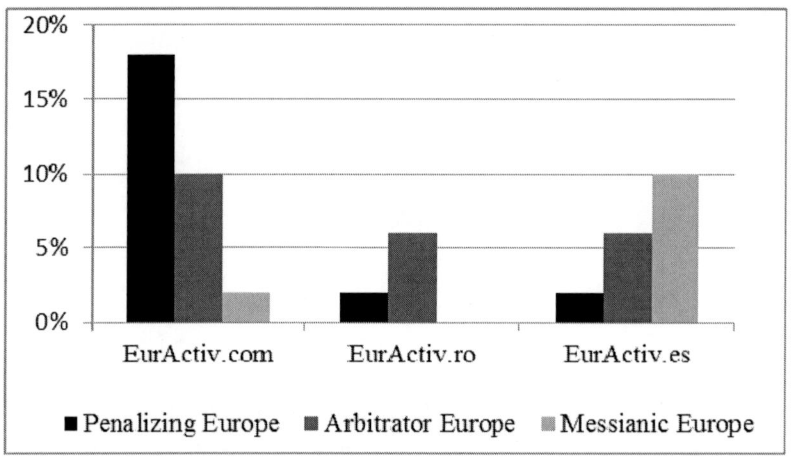

Fig 2-8. The distribution of issue-specific frames

When it comes to framing the EU, the tendencies remain the same as the ones identified above, in terms of frame frequency. The distribution of the three issue-specific frames shows a rather divergent pattern, with the exception of Europe as an arbitrator, which is a common interpretation frame for all three websites, with similar frequencies. The news portals diverge when it comes to the other two frames, which call for interpretation and "national spin". Surprisingly, the transnational news source tends to refer to Europe (the EU) in relation to the sanctions and penalties that it can or does apply to Member States ("Penalizing Europe"), rather than to EU as a benefactor (due to the EU funds, for example). In the case of the Romanian counterpart, the "Messianic" perception of Europe is completely absent. Though a previous study (Bârgăoanu et al., 2010) showed that online quality newspapers are more inclined towards a "penalizing Europe" frame rather than towards "messianic Europe", the absence of this frame is surprising considering that Euroscepticism seems to be higher among older member states (*Eurobarometer*, August 2011) and, on the other hand, that Romania is a beneficiary of European funds. A possible explanation resides in the results of a previous analysis (Marincea, 2011), which show that Romanian news reports on European funds are mainly framed in terms of the sanctions imposed by the EU as a result of Romania's inability to manage the funds and the corruption of the political class. In contrast, Spanish EurActiv journalists have a more optimistic/enthusiastic perspective in regard to the EU. Europe becomes "messianic" in two contexts: rescuing Greece and providing EU funds (e.g. The Seventh Framework Project – FP7).

CONCLUSION

The study shows that there is a high level of Europeanization of the EurActiv media network, according to the quantitative indicators. All three websites have developed a Europeanized news pattern, both in regard to European topics and in regard to European actors. As expected, the Europe-wide news portal EurActiv.com also has a pronounced tendency towards a supranational media public sphere. The Europeanization of media content on EurActiv is significantly higher in comparison to results of similar research conducted on other media sources, either newspapers or TV analyses. This is due to factors such as the organizational culture, the editorial mission and the target audience of the EurActiv network, a media channel specialized in EU affairs.

All three websites analyzed show the characteristics of comprehensive Europeanization, though in the case of the Spanish portal there is also a strong "parochial" tendency. The main European actors and agenda-setters present in the media are the EU Commissioners, while national government representatives are seen as agents of the domestication of EU issues. In comparison to Spain, the Romanian portal has a stronger focus both on EU topics and on European actors, which might be correlated to Romania's more recently attained EU membership.

Though there is a certain convergence of the news coverage, the websites analyzed tend to give a "local" spin, prioritizing issues according to their own interests. While euractiv.com is mainly concerned with foreign affairs, the national counterparts are preoccupied with European issues related to economy, as the EU may be considered, above all, an economic union. The research also shows a tendency towards event Europeanization. Events with a European dimension make the news on all three websites, though their coverage and interpretation may differ from one country to another. The analysis shows that events can change the news agenda, prioritizing or overshadowing certain EU topics.

On the other hand, relevant topics are completely absent from EurActiv news coverage. Debates about Europe in terms of identity, culture, political construction or democratic deficit do not make the news agenda in a standard period of time, but might be discussed around major European events. This could be a direction for future analysis. The lack of these "non-issues" is due to the predominant informational style of EurActiv journalists, similar to reporting on EU issues. This formal, informational journalism is highlighted on the national websites by the lack of news frames. Instrumental frames (interests and economic consequences) have a clear predominance on all three portals, while normative or identitarian dimensions, though present on the supranational portal, to some extent, are almost absent from the national counterparts. This proves that, even though Brussels correspondents might pick up messages in terms of values or identity from EU actors, these messages do not reach the national public spheres, either because there is no interest from the national media, or because they are not communicated properly. Either way, the professionalization of the EurActiv network and the pledge to neutrality is equivalent to a formal, rigid image of Europe, described in terms of interests and economic win or loss, different from the recommendations scholars bring in order to "bridge the gap".

The absence of the responsibility frame on all three websites is also an important result of the analysis, because it points out a lack of accountability, which is often correlated with the democratic deficit of the EU. On the other hand, news is, to some extent, depicted in terms of conflict or controversy (with the exception of the Romanian website). As for the issue-specific frames, journalists' editorial commitment to neutrality takes the shape of a frame portraying the EU as arbitrator, frame identified through an inductive approach. However, journalists' attitudes towards the EU differ from one website to another. While the trans-national portal focuses on sanctions – "penalizing Europe", the Spanish journalists are more inclined towards a "messianic" view (mostly in instrumental terms), whereas the Romanian website describes an "arbitrator" Europe, in the few articles where specific-issue frames could be identified.

The results of the frame analysis show that EurActiv coverage of EU topics is far from transforming Europe into a "communicable story", lacking essential attributes for "newsworthiness". Journalists from all three websites have adopted a formal, rigid communication style similar to the official communication of the Commission. This shows that a quantitative measurement of the formal degree of media Europeanization does not suffice as a condition for the emergence of a European public sphere or for a verdict upon the Europeanization of national public spheres. Qualitative, in-depth analysis should be conducted in order to identify the conditions based on which such a project could rely on and how it could look.

Though EurActiv websites seem to meet the role of a "watchdog", actively reporting on EU policy-issues and the activity of EU actors, it can hardly be considered a "civic forum" or a facilitator of rational/critical debate at the citizen level. The network addresses a rather elitist public, aiming not to build a common, identitarian/symbolic ground, but rather to inform about what happens in Brussels and in other member states. Lacking in problematization practice and interpretative patterns, EurActiv websites might prolong the EU communication deficit. The underlying premise for this type of communication seems to shift from a "no news is good news" perspective to one of "all news is good news".

REFERENCES

Bârgăoanu, A (2011). *Examenul Schengen.* În căutarea sferei publice europene. *[The Schengen Exam. Searching for the European Public Sphere],* Bucharest: Comunicare.ro.

Bârgăoanu, A, Dobrescu, P, & Marincea, A (2010). Does Europe Come to "Save" Us or to "Scold" Us? An Analysis of the Media Discourse on EU Funds. *Globalization and Changing Patterns in the Public Sphere.* Bucharest: Comunicare.ro. Paper presented at the Globalization and Changing Patterns in the Public Sphere Conference, Bucharest.

Beciu, C (2007). Forme mediatice de dezbatare a normelor europene. Redefinirea "misiunii" jurnalistului – elemente analitice (I). [Media Forms of Debating European Norms. Redefining the Journalist's "Mission" – Analytical Elements (I)]. Revista Română de Sociologie [Romanian Review of Sociology], XVIII (3/4).

Brüggemann, M, Sifft, S, Königslöw, K K, Peters, B, & Wimmel, A (2006). Segmented Europeanization. The Transnationalization of Public Spheres in Europe: Trends and Patterns". *TransState Working Papers 37*. Bremen: Sfb 597 Staatlichkeit im Wandel [Transformations of the State].

Brüggemann, M, & Königslöw, K K (2007). Let's talk about Europe. Explaining Vertical and Horizontal Europeanization in the Quality Press. *TransState Working Papers* 60, Bremen: Sfb 597 Staatlichkeit im Wandel [Transformations of the State].

De Vreese C H (2003). *Communicating Europe*, Retrieved July 10, 2011, from fpc.org.uk/fsblob/89.pdf.

—. (2005). News Framing: Theory and Typology. *Information Design Journal + Document Design*, 13(1), 51–62.

European Commission (2006). *White Paper on a European Communication Policy*, COM (2006) 35 final, Brussels, 1 February.

European Commission. (2010). *Communication from the Commission to the European Parliament, the Council, the European Economic and Social Committee and the Committee of the Regions, Communicating Europe in Partnership*, COM (2007) 569 final, Brussels, 3 October.

—. (2011). Eurobaromètre 75. *L'opinion publique dans l'Union européenne [Public Opinion in the European Union]*, European Commission, DG Communication. Retrieved 14 August 2011, from http://ec.europa.eu/public_opinion/archives/eb/eb75/eb75_en.htm

Fossum, J E, & Schlesinger, P (2007). The European Union and The Public Sphere: A Communicative Space in the Making? In Fossum, J E, & Schlesinger, P (eds) *The European Union and The Public Sphere: A Communicative Space in the Making?* (pp. 1–20). New York: Routledge.

Gitlin, T (1980). *The Whole World is Watching*, Berkeley, CA: University of California Press.

Habermas, J (2009). *Europe: The Faltering Project,* trans. C. Cronin. Cambridge: Polity Press.

Iyengar, S (1991). *Is Anyone Responsible? How Television Frames Political Issues*, Chicago: University of Chicago Press.

Koopmans, R, & Pfetsch, B (2007). Towards a Europeanised Public Sphere? Comparing Political Actors and the Media in Germany. In Fossum, J E, Schlesinger, P, & Kværk, G E (eds). *Public Sphere and Civil Society? Transformations of the European Union* (pp. 57–88). ARENA Report No. 02/2007. Oslo: ARENA.

Koopmans, R, & Erbe, J (2003). *Towards a European Public Sphere? – Vertical and Horizontal Dimensions of Europeanised Political Communication*, Paper presented at the conference "The Europeanization of Public Spheres", Science Center Berlin, June 20–22.

Kunelius, R, & Sparks, C (2001). Problems with a European Public Sphere: An Introduction. *The Public (Javnost)*, 8(1), pp. 5–20.

Machill, M, Beiler, M, & Fischer, C (2006). Europe-Topics in Europe's Media: The Debate about the European Public Sphere: A Meta-Analysis of Media Content Analysis. *European Journal of Communication*, 21(1), 57–88.

Marincea, A E (2011). Fondurile europene – pretext pentru europenizare? Analiza ştirilor în media online din România [The European Funds – Pretext for Europeanization? The Analysis of News in the Romanian Online Media]. In A. Bârgăoanu & E. Negrea (eds), Comunicarea în Uniunea Europeană. Modele teoretice şi aspecte practice [Communication in the European Union. *Theoretical Models and Practical Aspects]*. Bucharest: Comunicare.ro.

Meyer, C O (1999). Political Legitimacy and the Invisibility of Politics: Exploring the European Union's Communication Deficit. *Journal of Common Market Studies,* 37(4), 617–639.

Michailidou, A (2010). Vertical Europeanisation of the Online Public Dialogue: EU Public Ccommunication Policy and Online Implementation. In Bee, C, & Bozzini, E (eds), *Mapping the European Public Sphere: Institutions, Media and Civil Society*. Farnham, Surrey: Ashgate Publishers.

Mihelj, S (2007). The European and the National in Communication Research. *European Journal of Communication*, 22(4), 443–459.

Peter, J (2003). *Why European TV News Matters. A Cross-nationally Comparative Analysis of TV News about the European Union and its Effects*. Unpublished PhD dissertation, University of Amsterdam.

Pfetsch, B, collab. Silke, A, Berkel, B, & Medrano, J D (2004). *The Voice of the Media in European Public Sphere: Comparative Analysis of Newspaper Editorials*. Europub Project Report. Retrieved 20 July 2011 from http://europub.wzb.eu/project%20reports.en.htm.

Schuck, A R T, & De Vreese, C H (2006). Between Risk and Opportunity: News Framing and its Effects on Public Support for EU Enlargement. *European Journal of Communication,* 21(1), 5–32.

Semetko, H A, & Valkenburg, P M (2000). Framing European Politics: A Content Analysis of Press and Television News. *Journal of Communication,* 52(2), 93–109.

Statham, P (2007). Journalists as Commentators on European Politics: Educators, Partisans or Ideologues? *European Journal of Communication*, 22(4), 461–477.

Statham, P, & Guiraudon, V (2004). *Different paths of "Europeanization"? Evidence from the Public Debates over Europe in Britain and France*, Paper presented at the Cidel Workshop "One EU – Many Publics?", Stirling.

Steeg, M, & Risse, T (2010). The Emergence of a European Community of Communication. Insights from Empirical Research on the Europeanization of Public Spheres. *KFG Working Paper Series*, 15. Kolleg-Forschergruppe (KFG) "The Transformative Power of Europe", Freie Universität Berlin.

Trenz, H J (2004). Media Coverage on European Governance: Exploring the European Public Sphere in National Quality Newspapers, *European Journal of Communication*, 19(3), 291–319.

Udrea, G, & Corbu, N (2010). The Building of a European Identity and Its Challenges. *Romanian Journal of Communication and Public Relations*, 12, 3(20), 63–83.

Wessler, H, Skorek, M, Königslöw, K K, Held, M, Dobreva, M, & Adolphsen, M (2008). Comparing Media Systems and Media Content: Online Newspapers in Ten Eastern and Western European Countries, *Journal of Global Mass Communication*, 1(3/4), 165–189.

IN SEARCH OF A EUROPEAN IDENTITY: THE ROMANIAN PERSPECTIVE

VALERIU FRUNZARU AND MĂDĂLINA BOȚAN

Abstract

The construction of a community of European citizens presumes a certain shared identity. However, the elaboration of a European identity faces several challenges. The main problem is whether or not and to what extent EU citizens feel not only national but also "European". Based on a survey completed by a sample of the Romanian adult population, this paper shows the important role of socio-demographic variables such as "age", "income" and "education" in developing European identity defined as civic identity. People who consider themselves not only Romanian but also European have visited other member states, have a better knowledge of the EU and consider that Romania's accession to the EU has primarily brought advantages. The respondents who are more likely to identify themselves as Europeans know more about the European Union. Information about EU affairs seems to be an important factor in the attempts of elaboration of a European identity; however reported media consumption cannot be correlated with an increased willingness of citizens to categorize themselves on a cognitive level as Europeans.

Key words: European Union identity, civic identity, Europeanization, European public sphere.

IDENTITY OF EUROPEAN CITIZENS

Over the last two decades, Romania has faced dramatic changes that resulted in joining the European Union and adding the sense of belonging to the EU to the national identity. The construction of the EU identity is a political goal (see the 1973 Copenhagen summit) and an important topic studied by academics, some of whom consider the EU as an "artificial" geographical and political unit, while others see EU as a homogeneous image of a single unified Europe. According to the Eurobarometers, most EU citizens feel they are only nationals, some of them nationals and European, fewer European and nationals, and very few only European. Taking this into consideration, two main questions arise. Who are the people who identify themselves not only as Romanians but also as Europeans? And what is the role of mass media in developing the European identity?

Michel Bruter underlines the fact that identity is very difficult to measure because it is something that should be expressed spontaneously and "is tailored to the assumed expectations of the interlocutor" (Bruter, 2009, p. 1500). If a Londoner is asked "Where are you from?", she would answer "from Britain" if the interlocutor is German, "from London" if the interlocutor is from Britain, and "from Hackney" to a Londoner. In the Eurobarometers, EU citizens are asked if in the near future they see themselves as national and/or European. This question focuses on *civic* identity that regards the identification of the respondent with a political system, in contrast to cultural identity which is an indicator of a citizen's self-identification to a human community (Bruter, 2009, p. 1500). In this paper we will talk about civic identity as a non-exclusive identity. In other words, while cultural identity is based on in-group/out-group relationships, civic identity could deal with two or more groups (political systems). For example, a citizen could identify with the village/city where s/he lives, with the region (or department), with his/her country, and with the European Union. "Unity in diversity", the slogan of the European Union, could be interpreted as describing "the double, national and common identity of Europe which, as recent research emphasizes, should complement each other like 'two sides of the same coin'" (Udrea and Corbu, 2010, p. 76).

The process of shaping the European Union identity was an important research topic for academics even from the beginning of the European Community, when "at the basis of the European Union stood a political project crafted with economical means" (Andreescu and Severin, 2001, p. 31).

In 1961, Ernst B. Haas focused, from a neo-functional perspective, on the role of elites in developing a European polity, which would gradually lead to a transfer of loyalties to the European Union level (Haas, 1961). If Haas's theory explains the building of the European Union identity at the level of the elites, after almost 40 years, Adrian Favel underlines the role of the mobility of Europeans between the Member States, a phenomenon "at the heart of EU Commission efforts to build Europe through dynamic mobility policies" (Favel, 2009, p. 178). Neil Fligstein has a more complex position, pointing out that the beneficiaries of European integration tend to identify more with European Union. Young people, educated, speaking one or more foreign languages, with higher income and the opportunity to travel and interact with similar individuals from other member states, have a higher probability of feeling European (Fligstein, 2009, pp. 133–145).

There is no consensus among scholars regarding the meaning, or even the existence, of the so-called "European identity" and it is not in our intention to criticize or stress the strong points of such theories. Our goal is to determine whether or not there are Romanians who see themselves as Europeans too, and who these individuals are from a socio-demographic point of view. With the theoretic background provided by the authors mentioned above, our goal is to verify whether young, educated individuals, with higher income, who travel within the Member States, and who consider that Romania's accession to the European Union has brought advantages, are more willing to identify themselves as Europeans.

IDENTITY: AN AMBIVALENT NOTION

Exploring the complex question of European identity involves looking back into national backgrounds; nevertheless, identity cannot be defined in a static way, simply as a result of a historic process. As various authors emphasize, for a European public sphere to exist, European identity has to be reinforced and European citizens have to take responsibility for common public matters (Heller & Rényi, 2007, p. 184). But the notion of identity and the divergent criteria of exclusion and inclusion have to be tackled carefully and tolerantly, especially in the context of the pessimistic predictions for the future of a Union that seems to face its most severe crisis in 50 years, jeopardizing the European project started after WWII.

The current economic crisis might lead to a decrease in the willingness of people to identify themselves as Europeans. It is likely that Europe is a common reference point for the majority of EU citizens. However, the degree and form of the Europeanization of national societies is highly disputed (Koopmans & Statham, 2010, p. 3). Regardless of the communication efforts of EU officials, there seems to be a constant gap between structural change and public perception. Several authors maintain that the EU has to overcome the deficit of the lack of a pre-existing sense of collective identity (Fossum & Schlessinger, 2007, p. 29). As there is a lack of collective identity, the prospect for a viable European public sphere is rather bleak. There is no agreement on common interests or values, and different languages and disparate national cultures make the formation of collective opinion impossible.

Public debate can lead to opinion formation, the forging of a process for shaping a common identity. In order to make the European Union an effective institution capable of uniting 27 countries, several conditions have to be met. Political and institutional restructuring is vital, but cognitive and attitudinal aspects have to be taken into account as well (Heller & Rényi, 2007, p. 169). The millions of EU citizens need to forge some kind of common identity. However, some authors argue that a collective "we" is not a natural identity but is constructed from different social categories that unite and divide people (Eriksen, 2007, p. 31). Rather, Eriksen argues that what is needed is a "reflexive identity" that also recognizes differences.

Identities help individuals feel involved and oriented in the world, to acquire a cultural heritage, value systems, as well as a sense of belonging to a group and patterns of behaviour (Heller & Rényi, 2007, p. 169). The notion of identity is also closely related to that of citizenship and for the formation of common European solidarity, diverse patterns of identity formation (national, ethnic, religious, gender or other) have to be examined. Identities are strongly influenced by collective cultural, historical, religious and social traditions, and also by individual cognitive and emotional elements, driven by personal experience (Eriksen, 2007, p. 32). Individual and collective identities are constructions. They are flexible, changing and unstable. Their social role is to define and represent the "self" and its place among others (Heller & Rényi, 2007, p. 171). Identity plays a crucial role in the definition of Europeanness, and national identities are the most important constructions that influence European development.

If the past decades witnessed the awakening of various collective identities (religious, ethnic, national) in the context of European integration, Romania was somehow different, since there has always been – in the past 20 years at least – a valorization of the West. Even the political arena, otherwise extremely divergent, was always consensual regarding EU accession. However, the creation of a European identity is much more controversial although public attitude towards enlargement was overwhelmingly positive.

Methodology

In order to identify whether or not and to what extent Romanian citizens feel not only national but also European and in order to determine the role of mass media in constructing such a collective identity, in May 2011 we conducted a sociological survey on a national representative sample (N=1199) of the Romanian adult population, with a 2.8% sampling error for a 95% confidence level. We used stratified sampling, in three stages, taking into consideration population structure according to the size of localities and development regions.

In order to measure the degree to which Romanian citizens feel Romanian and/or European, we used the scale used by Eurostat surveys where individuals were asked if they feel Romanian only, Romanian and European, European and Romanian, or European only (single choice question). We have opted for this type of measurement because, on one hand, it allows for the comparison of our research results with Eurostat survey findings, and, on the other hand, it constrains respondents to choose one of these categories. An interval level of measurement, i.e. from 1 which means "Romanian only" to 7 which means "European only", would give us more freedom for more statistical operations, but would indicate who considers himself/herself Romanian and/or European.

To measure the degree of knowledge on the European Union, we used the same scale that measured this issue in Eurostat surveys. In order to update the scale, we made small changes to two of the 10 items on the scale. For example, the first item, "The European Union currently consists of 12 Member States", became "The European Union currently consists of 15 Member States". Individuals who got 0 points on this scale did not give a correct answer, and those who got 10 points gave correct answers to all of the questions.

Research Findings

The majority of respondents feel Romanian only (61%), about one third feel Romanian and European (35%), only a few European and Romanian (2%), or only European (0.3%). The percent of people who feel to some extent European in our survey is lower than the European Union average. According to the Eurobarometer conducted in May 2010, 46% of Europeans identified themselves only by their nationality (European Commission, 2010, vol. 2, pp. 113–114). A higher level of identification only by nationality occurred in the United Kingdom (70%), Lithuania (60%), the Czech Republic (59%), Ireland (58%), Slovenia (55%), Latvia (52%), and Bulgaria (51%). It is important to mention that the findings of the May 2010 Eurobarometer show that only 50% of Romanians see themselves as national.

Academic papers and Eurostat reports show the importance of social factors in the way respondents define their identity. In order to know to what extent variables such as "education", "age", and "income" explain the dependent variable "identification with the European Union" we ran a logistic regression. Prior to that, we transformed the dependent variable (a categorical variable) into a dummy variable, coding with "0" the answer "Romanian only" and with "1" "Romanian and European", "European and Romanian", and "European only". We labelled the respondents in situation "1" as "Romanian and European" because there are very few people who see themselves as "European and Romanian", or "European only". In the regression model, we also introduced two additional variables that measure a pragmatic attitude towards the European Union: attitude regarding the Romanian accession to the EU and the visit to another Member State in the last 12 months.

Th e findings confirm the assumptions of Neil Fligstein (2009) and Adrian Favel (2009), and the Eurobarometer findings showing that young, educated people with higher incomes are more prone to identify themselves with the European Union. For example, if age goes up by one year, the chance of feeling both Romanian and European compared to feeling only Romanian decreases by 1.2% (Table 3-1). Due to the fact that people who perceive European Union accession as a positive thing are more willing to identify themselves as European, we can conclude that identification with the European Union has pragmatic reasons, too. If we hold all the other variables constant, a person who visited another Member State in the last 12 months is 1.83 more likely to see him/herself as European compared to a person who did not visit another European Union state within the last 12 months.

The pragmatic identification with the European Union could be depicted in the respondents' answers to the questions regarding what the European Union means to them. For the respondents who reported feeling both Romanian and European compared to those who reported feeling only Romanian, the European Union represents more freedom of travel, study and work anywhere in the Member States, social protection, and economic prosperity. There were significant differences between the two groups in regards to the positive aspects of the European Union (Fig. 3-1). Respondents who identified themselves as only Romanian evaluated the European Union more negatively, pointing out concepts like the waste of money or bureaucracy (Fig. 3-2). There was no significant difference between the two groups regarding other negative aspects.

Table 3-1. Logistic regression explaining Romanian and European identity

	B	S.E.	Wald	df	Sig.	Exp(B)
Joining the EU was a good thing	0.415	0.098	17.886	1	0	1.514
Education	0.111	0.051	4.739	1	0.029	1.117
Income	0.303	0.084	12.871	1	0	1.353
Age	0.012	0.004	7.380	1	0.007	0.988
Have visited other UE country	0.603	0.169	12.678	1	0	1.827
Constant	-0.671	0.443	2.298	1	0.130	0.511

Note. Nagelkerke R Square = 0,14, n=960

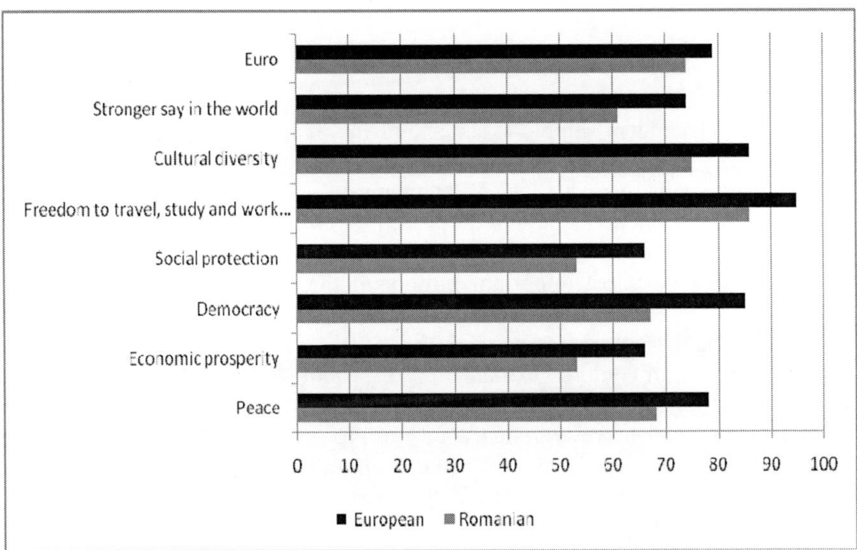

Fig. 3-1. What does the European Union mean to you personally? (Positive aspects)

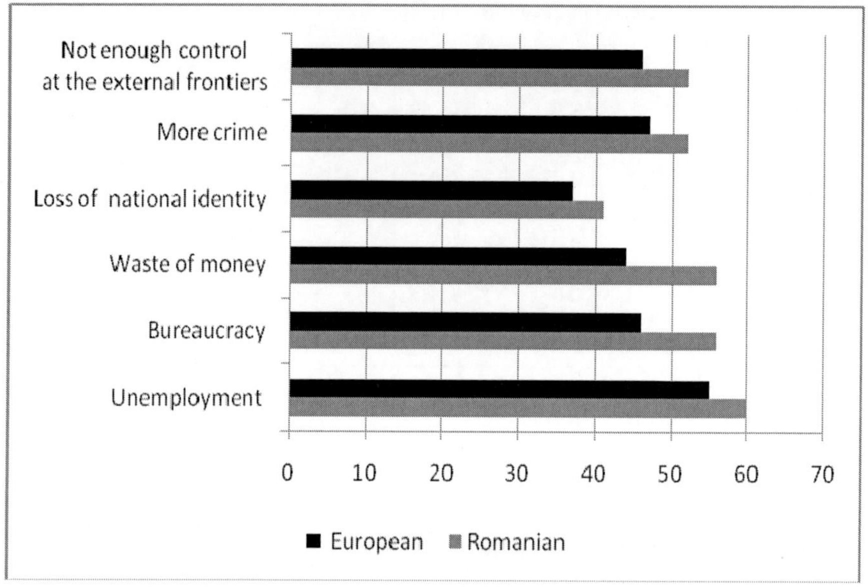

Fig. 3-2. What does the European Union mean to you personally? (Negative aspects)

The independent sample T test shows that respondents who also view themselves as European were more informed about the European Union than the respondents who considered themselves Romanian only (Table 3-2). For all respondents, the highest percent of correct answers occurred for the item "The European flag is blue with yellow stars" (75%). Therefore it is clear that the most important symbol of the European Union is well known among Romanians.

The significant difference in the level of knowledge about the European Union could be explained by the fact that respondents who feel European were more educated. But, beyond the fact that this category of respondents had more experience of visiting other member states, what was the source of information on the European Union? And, in general, what is the role of mass media in informing people about the European Union? Is there a significant difference between these two categories of respondents in how they get and use information from mass media?

Table 3-2. T test to compare the degree of knowledge on the EU, with "European identity" as the grouping variable

	Levene's Test for Equality of Variances		t-test for Equality of Means						
	F	Sig.	t	df	Sig. (2-tailed)	Mean Difference	Std. Error Differ	95% Confidence Interval of the Difference	
								Lower	Upper
Equal variances assumed	7.436	,006	-5.329	1059	0	-0.773	0.145	-1.058	-0.489
Equal variances not assumed			-5.523	932.697	0	-0.773	0.140	-1.048	-0.498

This survey shows that the most important source of information about the European Union is television. Compared to respondents who identified themselves as only Romanian, the respondents who feel Romanian and European obtained information on the European Union less often from television and radio, and more often from newspapers and the internet (Fig. 3-3).

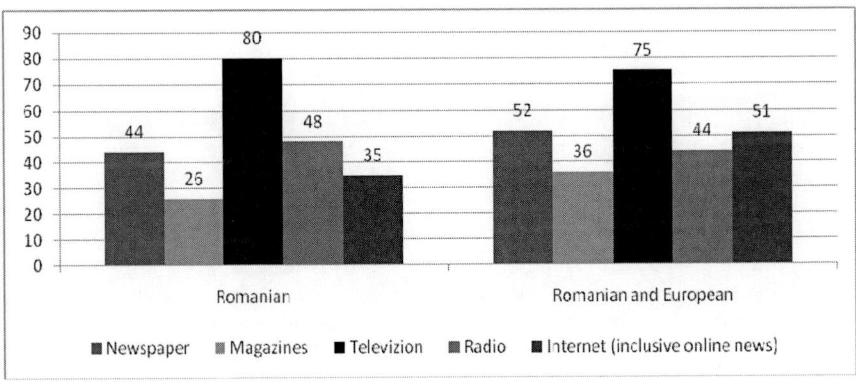

Fig. 3-3. Where are you looking for information about European Union on . . . ? (%)

Table 3-3. Relationship between national/European identity and getting information from TV news

	To what extent do you watch news about the EU on . . . ?			. . . gives you enough information about the EU?			. . . gives you too negative/neutral/too positive information about the EU		
	χ2	A	N	χ2	α	n	χ2	α	n
Antena 1	7.247	0.123	990	1.225	0.542	715	1.233	0.540	670
Pro TV	6.883	0.142	992	0.258	0.879	722	0.078	0.962	659
TVR1	5.986	0.200	991	0.988	0.610	624	1.362	0.506	563
TVR2	11.817	0.019	971	1.689	0.639	563	1.123	0.570	504
TVR3	9.746	0.045	925	3.162	0.206	507	1.471	0.479	451

Note. Watching news on the European Union was measured using a five point likert scale.

In media consumption, there is no significant difference between respondents who also identify themselves with the European Union and respondents who only see themselves as Romanian. The only difference between the two groups is that respondents who also identify with Europe are more prone to look for European information on the two public TV channels, TVR2 and TVR 3. A possible explanation is that people who watch these two channels have a higher level of education, and therefore, would be more likely to identify themselves with the European Union.

There is no difference between the two compared groups regarding their evaluation of the information about the EU on TV (too negative, neutral, or too positive) (see Table 3-3, third item). These findings do not confirm Michel Bruter's conclusions (2009) about the impact of positive and negative news on European Union citizens. This fact could be explained by the methodological differences (in our study, negative and positive news reports are defined as such by respondents), and the impact of information in the long run. According to Bruter, news has a time bomb effect.

Conclusions

Efforts to construct a European identity are enhanced by communication and dedicated information available in every member state. However, the flow of information promoting Europeanness can sometimes lead to a very diffuse idea and practice of European identity. This is one of the main reasons why, when trying to monitor Romanian public opinion on Europe, we chose to leave it up to the respondents to determine what they perceived as a European identity when asked if they felt European. Without limiting it to specific characteristics, this survey mainly tried to monitor this hybrid entity labeled "European identity".

Media consumption remains an important agent of Europeanization, but, regardless of its efficiency, it cannot bind citizens of the European Union to a new collective identity. Our survey confirms that adequate information regarding the EU is a necessary but insufficient condition of shaping the European identity. Over the last 20 years, Romanians have constantly sought to belong to the West. However, regardless of the optimism and benevolence towards the EU, Romanian citizens tend to become more pragmatic when assessing their EU membership.

Our findings show that the creation of a European identity can also be associated with demographic characteristics (age, education and income), and a pragmatic attitude towards the European Union. The strategy of building an open market economy and of encouraging the freedom of travel and of working abroad are not just means of being globally competitive and of decreasing the level of social exclusion. It is also a means of strengthening the European identity and belonging, at least for Romanian citizens. Through specific European rights, and especially through freedom of travel, it appears that a new kind of European solidarity can be generated by appealing to an awareness of opportunities and a sense of a shared European future. Younger, wealthier, more educated, and more dynamic Romanians view themselves as Europeans to a larger extent, contributing to the formation of a civic identity that can provide the social glue necessary for the stability of complex social structures like the European Union.

REFERENCES

Andreescu, G & Severin, A (2001). Un concept românesc al Europei Federale. In R Weber (ed.). *Un concept românesc privind viitorul Uniunii Europene* (pp. 17–54), Iaşi: Editura Polirom.

Bruter, M (2009). Time Bomb? The Dynamic Effect of News and Symbols on the Political Identity of European Citizens. *Comparative Political Studies,* 42(12), 1498–1536.

Collins, R (2002). *Media and Identity in Contemporary Europe*, Bristol: Intellect Books.

Eriksen, E O (2007). Conceptualizing European public spheres: General, Segmented and Strong Publics. In J E Fossum & P Schlessinger (eds). *The European Union and the Public Sphere: A Communicative Space in the Making?* (pp. 23–43). London: Routledge.

European Commission (2010). Eurobarometer 73. *Public Opinion in the European Union*, vol. I and II, from http://ec.europa.eu/public_opinion/archives/eb/eb73/eb73_en.htm.

Favel, A (2009). Immigration, Migration, and Free Movement in the Making of Europe. In J T Checkel & P J Katzenstein (eds). *European Identity* (pp. 167–189), Cambridge: Cambridge University Press.

Fligstein, N (2009). Who Are the Europeans and How Does This Matter for Politics? In J T

Checkel & P J Katzenstein (eds). *European identity* (pp. 132-166). Cambridge:Cambridge University Press.

Fossum, E J & Schlessinger, P (eds) (2007). *The European Union and the Public Sphere,* London: Routledge.

Haas, E B (1961). International Integration: The European and the Universal Process. *International Organization,* 15, 366–392.

Heller, M & Rényi, A (2007). EU Enlargement, Identity and the Public DSphere. In J E Fossum & P Schlesinger (eds). *The European Union and the Public Sphere: A Communicative Space in the Making?* (pp. 169–186). London: Routledge.

Koopmans, R & Statham, P (2010). *The Making of a European Public Sphere,* Cambridge: Cambridge University Press.

Udrea, G & Corbu, N (2010). The Building of a European Identity and its Challenges. *Romanian Journal of Communication and Public Relation,* 12(3), 63–83.

VISIBILITY OF THE EU THROUGH EU-FUNDED PROGRAMMES AND PROJECTS: WHAT ABOUT AN INSTRUMENTAL EUROPEAN IDENTITY?

ROXANA MARIA DASCĂLU[1]

Abstract

The emergences of a European public sphere and of a European identity are the fundamental related processes that decide the shape of the current European polity. Citizens of EU member states should have a European identity, albeit a secondary one, and actively participate in private and public debates concerning EU affairs, policies and common future.

Although there is not yet consensus in literature regarding the existence of a European identity, there are more and more scholars who consider the multiple identities theory to be valid. Therefore, a European identity already exists, in spite of the fact that "country first, but Europe too" is the result of the Eurobarometer. Ruiz Jimenez et al. (2004) bring a fresh perspective to the field, as they consider the nature of the compatibility between the national and European identity to be the different approaches of identity emergence: while national identities are largely "cultural", European identities are primarily "instrumental". The paper argues that the Instrumental European identity, as the identity based on self-interested calculation, is a reality. EU is experimenting new ways to contribute to the emergence of a European identity, trying to promote to its citizens symbols as identity markers once used by nations with the same goal (such as a flag, an anthem, a currency). In the EU context, funding opportunities are also being used to foster European identity

[1] "Beneficiary of the Doctoral Scholarships for a Sustainable Society" project, project co-financed by the European Union through the European Social Fund, Sectorial Operational Programme Human Resources Development 2007–2013.

acquisition through the visibility rules the EU asks to be respected by the beneficiaries of EU-funded programs and projects. Unlike other donors, these EU efforts may well be interpreted as specifically tailored to build a European identity (Sanchez Salgado, 2008). In this theoretical context, a content analysis study is conducted on two online news portals in Romania – www.hotnews.ro and www.ziare.com – for the March-June 2011 time frame in order to answer questions such as: Which are the markers and frames of an instrumental European identity promoted through articles about EU funds posted on the two news portals?; what is the visibility of EU identity markers and frames reflected through news on the management of EU funds and the implementation of EU-funded programs and projects?; what is the predominance of such news?; how do Romanian citizens comment on these news in terms of identity acquisition? This paper shows the relevance of the EU identity markers and specific frames in building an Instrumental European identity.

Moreover, it suggests that, if carefully managed by the EU, these efforts may trigger, in time, the emergence of a civic and even cultural identity for the supranational multilayered structure.

Key words: European identity, European funds, EU-funded programmes and projects, Instrumental European identity

IDENTITY AS "COLLECTIVE IDENTITY"

Identity is a vast topic with great significance in both everyday life and academic research. For the past two decades, the attention given to this concept – both in social science and in the world at large – has continued to rise (Abdelal et al., 2006). Processes of globalization and regionalization and the increasing influence of mass media and other communications have triggered numerous contacts of individuals around the world. These many contacts have led to different approaches on how people construe their identity, in the process of defining and knowing themselves.

The literature reveals two perspectives that illustrate how individuals construe their identities: the individualist and the collectivist perspectives (Grant, 2010). The individualist view claims that "individuals think of themselves as independent of relationships", as "they value autonomy and uniqueness and construe their sense of self separate from the others" (idem), while others see themselves as part of different groups, they define themselves in terms of their relationships with others, by their roles in the groups and situations they face as members of the particular groups (idem). This perspective understands identity as "the relational aspects that qualify subjects in terms of categories such as race, gender, class, nation, sexuality, work and occupation, and thus in terms of acknowledged social relations and affiliations to groups" (Venn in Hollway, 2010). Henri Tajfel claims that social identity involves "both knowing that one belongs to certain social groups and perceiving value and emotional connection related to that membership" (Gaines, 2010).

Social identity theory, developed by Henri Tajfel and John Turner, explains the implications, specific features and motives of collective identity. According to this theory of identity, "individuals strive to achieve or to maintain a positive social identity", which is based on favourable comparisons between one's own group (in-group) and any relevant distinct group (out-group) (Grant, 2010). Once an individual strongly identifies with a group, he/she will do everything possible to ensure that the in-group is better than the out-group(s). However, if one's social identity is unsatisfactory, "individuals may leave their group to join a more positive group, improve the positivity of their group or redefine in-group characteristics as being positive" (idem). The formation and loss of one's identity depends on the relations of the individual with others. If the individual is properly respected or recognized, his/her identity is assured. By contrast, if one "is forced to confront a reduced, demeaning, or contemptible image of himself, one can suffer real psychological damage" (Muldoon, 2010) and reveal negative attitudes towards the in-group. Therefore, collective identity should not be taken for granted, as it might be subject to change, a process known in literature as *identity change*: "One's identity is the product of a continued negotiation among myriad factors, including one's choices, social circumstances, historical background and political institutions" (Davidson, 2010). Individuals construe and become aware of their identity through *identification*, a process which links individuals (who) to social groups (what) (Risse, 2010b). The author makes a relevant distinction between the subjects (who – elites, citizens and so on) and the objects of identification (what – gender, nation, Europe and so on). The process of identification involves "an interaction, between how we identify ourselves and how others categorize us, between self-image and public image" (Jenkins, 2010) and it basically is "a process of classification, drawing on criteria of similarity and difference" (idem), between the characteristics of in-groups and out-groups, known in literature as the 'I–Other dialectic". Stuart Hall argues that entire communities construct their identities in relation to the Other (Baaji, 2010).

The communication theory of identity (CTI) highlights the explicitly acknowledged interdependency between communication and identity, as "identity is formed, maintained, and modified in a communicative process, and communication is a performance of identity" (Hecht & Hopfer, 2010). Communication is internalized as identity "when people place themselves in socially recognizable categories and thereby validate, through social interaction, whether these categories are relevant to them" (idem). Identity is manifested in social interaction through expectations and motivations, which influence the person's communication. Thus, "identity is externalized to social interaction through expectations attached to identities" (Hecht & Hopfer, 2010).

The two theories of identity are relevant to this study, as European identity is a genuine collective identity which is intimately linked to concepts such as the European public sphere. Communication, through the emergence of a communicative space for the citizens of the EU, is the essential condition for the emergence of a European identity and a European polity.

EUROPEAN IDENTITY AS THE MAJOR CARD TO PLAY FOR THE POLITICAL EU

The issue of a common identity that would bind together the citizens of the member states has been one of the major challenges of the EU. While at the EU institutional level there is a strong support for both deepening and enlargement, these processes are not as appreciated by its citizens (Inthorn, 2006). Therefore, as many theoreticians endorse, one of the major issues when debating on the possible emergence of a European identity is the gap between the institutional EU and the feeling of belonging to the EU (Beciu, 2004). Recognition of this problem is not new. Even the founders of the European Communities predicted that the citizens of EU member states would gradually identify themselves more and more with these institutions and less with their own nations – a change of attachment in favor of the new political power (Duchesne & Frognier, 2007). EU officials started to look into the concept of a European identity starting with the 1970s (Stråth in Schlesinger & Foret, 2007). Until then, while a "European consciousness might sometimes have been evoked, identity as such was not a card to play" (Schlesinger & Foret, 2007, p. 127). The economic crisis of 1970s urged the member states to reinforce their global position by deepening the European construction, thus coming across the European identity issue, which became a permanent concern of EU institutions. Therefore, in 1972, a "Declaration on a European Identity" defined European identity based on three pillars: (1) common heritage, interests and special obligations within the community; (2) the "dynamic nature" of European unification; and (3) the extent to which the nine member states are collaborating in relation to the rest of the world (Burgess, 2002, p.479). This beginning of the concept of European identity is based on internal unity and heritage with regard to the rest of the world. Thus, it assumes common features of the nine member states in relation to other international associations and states (Bârgăoanu, Negrea, Dascălu, 2010).

Trenz (2005, p. 9) synthesizes the approaches in analysing the formation of a European collective identity in two main categories: understanding European identity as the degree of support of European citizens towards the EU (by analysing Eurobarometer surveys which, since 1975, have included questions on Europeans' feeling of belonging) and looking at a European collective identity "as a projection that is developed in public discourse". In our opinion, these two approaches have to be integrated in order to determine empirical results in the direction of creating a European identity, and they must be strongly correlated to the public communication of EU institutions and the feedback offered by "EU citizens".

As already announced, the literature reveals European identity as referring to the concept of collective identity. "Collective identities are social constructions which use psychological needs and motives to provide an answer to the questions "who do I belong to?" or "who do we belong to?"(Eder, 2009, p. 431). Therefore, one person is able to have multiple identities, which do not exclude each other. Moreover, one should bear in mind that not all the multiple collective identities of a person are salient at the same time. Which collective identity becomes salient while others remain dormant depends on the specific situation the person faces (Simon & Klandermans, 2001). This is essential because debates on the issue of European identity and the notion of national identity often occur in zero-sum terms: citizens of member states may feel either German, British, Greek etc. or European (belonging to the European Union) and not as having complementary identities. This has been a contested assumption (Bruter, 2004; Risse, 2003; Burgess, 2002), as the Eurobarometer surveys show that "country first, but Europe too" is the dominant outlook in most EU countries and people do not perceive this as contradictory (Risse, 2003). Most of the cases belong to the following scheme when referring to the collective identities related to territorial aspects: a person relates first to their community identity, then to their regional identity, their national identity, their European/Asian (and so on) identity, all to be integrated in a global identity.[2] Another way of conceptualizing the relationship between European and national identities is the "marble cake" model, which is not explicitly discussed in literature (Risse, 2004). This model suggests that the various identities that an individual holds cannot be completely separated on different levels. This classification might only be suitable for academic purposes. Risse (2004, p. 6) claims that "identity components influence each other, mesh and blend into each other"; thus we cannot truly separate a German or Dutch identity from the European identity. Moreover, the author has an interesting position suggesting that "European identity might mean different things to different people" (idem).

We argue that, although the argument of multiple identities is valid, the preeminence of the national identity over the European identity of most of the people living across the EU is a serious matter when it comes to the EU democratic deficit, the lack of an EU polity and a European public sphere (Bârgăoanu, Negrea & Dascălu, 2010). These facts are clearly revealed as true in crisis situations, when different groups, communities or nations feel that their identity and interests are threatened by EU integration, as the Greek crisis in 2010 shows. Basically, national identity is reinforced when any of its components are threatened or if some nations are thought to benefit more from the EU (more resources, for example) than others (Hix, 1998). This happens because people who highly identify with a group are "willing to work for the group and promote action when things go badly" (Scheepers et al., 2003). Therefore, in times of crisis for the EU, European citizens promote action in favour of their countries and relate to their national identity, not their European one, even in cases when people hold their European identity as a secondary one. Creating a strong European identity is compulsory, as many scholars emphasize: "a collective identity above the level of primary groups and a collective we-feeling are needed in order for EU citizens to acknowledge the sacrifices imposed in the name of the European collective goods" (Eriksen, 2007, p. 24). As Eriksen and Fossum (2004, p. 437) put it, "the success of the EU depends upon developing a shared identity and a value basis for integrating different conceptions of the good life, and a diverse range of societal interests". Although "common norms and values are required to motivate collective action" (Eriksen & Fossum, 2004, p. 440), achieving one's goals and interests due to membership of a particular group (e.g. the EU) might be enough for a person (the European citizen) to promote action in favour of the group (European citizens). This could happen if the

[2] At this point, one has to bear in mind the difference between European and EU identity (in this paper European identity equals EU identity), as people might identify with Europe, but not with the EU and vice versa.

EU made efforts to at least develop this instrumental sense of belonging to the EU. And, as we show in this paper, this is already the case.

Moreover, the EU desperately needs strong leadership that defines itself as European. Jacques Delors, one of the most respected leaders of the European Community, clearly highlights this need that the EU faces: "we don't just need firefighters; we need architects too. And there are no architects left – and no visionaries either . . . By 'visionaries' I mean people who will evoke, stimulate or awaken in us that which is best in the human race" (Delors, 2011). Successful leadership depends on building internalized commitment and strong identification with the goals and interests of the community (Gaines, 2010). This is achieved through communication. Once trust is strengthened, "leaders can help shift individual members to align more closely with collective identity" (idem). A strong leadership of the EU should be able to communicate to its citizens their common destiny and fate, because only with the EU's proper communication with its citizens "people are turned into compatriots who are willing to take on new collective action to provide for each other's well-being" (Eriksen & Fossum, 2004, p. 442). And this is what the EU needs.

In our opinion, an additional solution for the emergence of a European identity could be postponing the enlargement process, because a well-defined territory is an essential condition for the construction of a community, since the acknowledgement of the differences that separate "us" from the "others" is a core feature of any collective identity (Fuchs & Klingemann, 2000). The EU's "others" are frequently constructed as territorially defined entities such as America, Russia, Asia and even Turkey (Risse et al., 1999). Nowadays, Turkey is a candidate for membership of the EU, a development that triggers confusion in identifying the specific "other" relative to the EU. This controversy will be resolved once the decision on granting membership or postponing enlargement is made. European leaders have also tried to present the continent's own past of wars and nationalist rivalries as the "other" to the public (idem), a relevant example is the Franco-German reconciliation and the strong relationship between the two since then.

Although a truly consolidated European identity will emerge in centuries rather than decades (Lewis, 2008), if European leaders fail to support this process for themselves and for the European citizens the future of this European identity might be in danger (Bârgăoanu, Negrea & Dascălu, 2010).

WHAT ABOUT AN INSTRUMENTAL EUROPEAN IDENTITY?

We consider one of the most relevant perspectives on European identity in literature to be the theories of the emergence of a European identity (Ruiz Jimenez, Gorniak, Kosic, Kiss & Kandulla, 2004):
a. *a "cultural" theory*, which understands identities being based on ethno-cultural factors generated through a long-term process;
b. *a "civic" theory*, which understands identities as based on agreement over rules for peaceful political co-existence;
c. *an "instrumental" theory*, which conceives identities as being based on self-interested calculation (whether economic or political).

In what concerns the "cultural" theory, scholars argue that if a European identity were to emerge, it would not, and should not, be based on the same identity markers that the nation state promotes, such as language, myths or a common cultural heritage (Ruiz Jimenez et al., 2004). The authors claim that "while it may be possible for a cultural European identity to emerge, this would certainly take a long time and would ultimately lead to the substitution of national identities" (Ruiz Jimenez et al., 2004, p. 2).

From the "civic" perspective on European identity, "the substance of EU membership lies in a commitment to the shared values of the Union as expressed in its constituent documents, a commitment to the duties and rights of a civic society covering specific areas of public life, a commitment to membership of a polity which promotes the direct opposite of classic ethno-nationalism" (Ruiz Jimenez et al., 2004, p. 4). This perspective connects European identity to concepts such as the Habermasian communicative rationality and the European public sphere, which are seen as crucial for the emergence of a European identity.

Other scholars argue that instrumental factors may play an important role in defining and strengthening individuals' sense of identification with the EU. Some premises accepted in literature are that the perception of the potential gains or losses that might result from membership in the EU may influence peoples' identification with the Union and "the better the citizen's evaluation of the results of European policies (compared to the results of policies pursued by national government), the more likely s/he is to feel European" (Ruiz Jimenez et al., 2004, p. 3). Schoen (2008, p. 5) claims that "drawing on Eurobarometer data, the analysis shows that instrumental self-interest and territorial identities contribute considerably to explaining support for common foreign affairs and defense policies". Risse ét al. (1999, p. 157) believe that every type of collective identity has an instrumental component also: "Collective identities define and shape, in the first place, how actors view their perceived instrumental and material interests and which preferences are regarded as legitimate and appropriate for enacting given identities. At the same time, a change in perceived material and instrumental interests might well lead, over time, to changes in collective identities". As Sanchez-Cuenca (2000, p. 168) suggests, "identities, so to speak, do not fall from heaven: they are a consequence of complex economic and political calculations".

Moreover, we find evidence in literature for the existence of different types of European citizens, a finding which is correlated with the typology of the emergence of a European identity. The following classification of European citizens in terms of their support to European integration is relevant: positive Europeans, with Europhiles and instrumental Europeans and Eurosceptics (Haesly, 2001). Europhiles are those who "enthusiastically endorse all aspects of European integration", while instrumental Europeans "support only specific aspects of European integration, as they believe the EU delivers important economic benefits to their communities and to their country" (Haesly, 2001, p. 82). The author's hypothesis, which is validated in the cited study, is that instrumental EU support consistently leads to lower levels of European pride than in the case of the Europhiles, but higher levels than expressed by the Eurosceptics.

In this context, the authors promote an interesting perspective on the multiple identities theory, as they consider the nature of the compatibility between the national and European identity to be the difference in approaches of identity emergence: while national identities are largely "cultural", European identities are primarily "instrumental". We firmly support this theory and claim that the only theory of European identity which has empirical evidence is the instrumental one. People across the EU tend to identify with the supranational structure when they perceive the benefits that the EU brings once the EU becomes real to them. The most relevant and perceivable instruments in developing such an identity across the EU are the financial opportunities that the EU bring to its citizens (Sanchez Salgado, 2008) through the funds it offers under the Regional and Cohesion Policy, the Common Agriculture and Fisheries Policies and the thematic policies. This could be a valid solution for the emergence of a European identity, which could be promoted by a strong leadership of the EU, along with a well communicated vision and mission for the supranational structure. As Jacques Delors (2011) notices, "awareness of shared interests is not sufficiently widespread. And yet, it is through the formulation of shared interests that Europe can exist and can renew itself".

In consolidating national identity, nation states make use of various symbols and instruments ("identity markers") that serve the purpose of reminding citizens that they belong to a national community. Such symbols and instruments are the flag, the anthem, the currency, passports and particular national holidays when relevant moments in the nation's history are commemorated (Risse, 2010a). The EU has followed the national strategy in promoting its own identity markers, such as the EU flag and anthem, the Euro, the EU flag on European citizens' passports, and even holidays, such as 9 May, when every European should celebrate the birth of the Union. As these identity markers don't have the same power as the national ones, the EU has had to be innovative and use other strategies to enforce a sense of belonging to the EU. We believe that the most innovative strategy is represented by the mandatory rules regarding the visual identity of the EU that every institution which manages European funds, and every beneficiary of these funds, must respect and apply.

Moreover, the EU gives great amounts of money for large communication campaigns, which use different media to reach the objective of informing both potential beneficiaries *and the public* of the financial opportunities that the EU offers its citizens to develop their business, the region's infrastructure, their organizations' human resources and so on.

Therefore, all citizens of member states, even those not directly involved, have to know that the EU has a major contribution to making their lives better. We consider this is one of the major strategies that the EU enforces in order to create a sense of belonging to the EU for every European citizen, as it makes the EU real to citizens, just as it is for the European elites. Taken into account that the message of the large communication campaigns and the purpose of the mandatory rules regarding the visual identity of the EU connect more with the instrumental component of one's collective identity than with the cultural or affective components, we consider that both at the EU level (as in strategic objectives) and the empirical level, the emergence of an instrumental European identity is considered the winning card in developing a sense of belonging for EU citizens. This paper focuses on finding the empirical evidence for using identity markers and specific frames in order to develop such an instrumental identity in articles of two online news portals in Romania – www.hotnews.ro and www.ziare.com – in March–June 2011.

RESEARCH INTO MARKERS AND FRAMES OF AN INSTRUMENTAL EUROPEAN IDENTITY IN ROMANIAN ONLINE MEDIA REGARDING EU FUNDS

Methodology

Bearing these arguments in mind, we carried out a content analysis on the extent to which Romanian online media promote markers and frames of an instrumental European identity to the general public, with a high level of education (higher education), mainly in urban areas. The two selected portals, www.hotnews.ro and www.ziare.com, are some of the most visited news portals in Romania that cover the subject of EU funds, their management and the implementation of EU-funded projects and programs.

The research questions were the following:

a. Which are the markers and frames of an instrumental European identity promoted through articles on EU funds posted on the two news portals?
b. What is the visibility of EU identity markers and frames reflected through news on the management of EU funds and the implementation of EU-funded programs and projects?
c. What is the predominance of such news?
d. How do Romanian citizens comment on this news in terms of identity acquisition?

In order to find the answer to these research questions, we first collected data for the application of the content analysis. Therefore, we downloaded all relevant articles published from March to June 2011 on EU funds, EU-funded projects and programmes from the news portals www.hotnews.ro and www.ziare.com. The categories we chose to research for relevant articles were "Economy" for www.hotnews.ro and "Business" for www.ziare.com, as these chapters cover the subject of European funds in the portals' structure – "euROfonduri" for www.hotnews.ro and "Funds" for www.ziare.com.

This search revealed 14 relevant articles on www.hotnews.ro and 19 such articles on the other portal. Both the unit of analysis and the unit of observation consist in the individual article for the first content analysis application (to find answers to questions a–c) and the comment for the second analysis, expected to answer the last research question.

Results and Discussion

The predominance of articles on subjects such as EU funds implementation and management of EU-funded projects and programs in Romania appears to be quite low, as there are only 0.47% articles on these topics in the "Economy" chapter of www.hotnews.ro, in the March-June, 2011 time frame and 0.46% in the "Business" chapter of www.ziare.com, in the same time frame (see Tables 4-1 and 4-2 below).

Therefore, these subjects have similar visibility on the two portals analysed.

Table 4-1. Articles in the "Economy" chapter, www.hotnews.ro, March–June 2011

Month	Articles on EU funds	Articles on other subjects in the "Economy" chapter
March 2011	4	807
April 2011	3	818
May 2011	5	836
June 2011	3	757
Total	15	3218

Although the predominance of news on the subjects mentioned is quite low, we consider it relevant, as there are a significant number of diverse topics debated in the articles of the portals' two chapters. Therefore, the fact that EU funds were the focus of 6 articles in March 2011 (as an example) shows that journalists are interested in the topic and consider it relevant to their readers.

In order to identify the EU identity markers and frames reflected through news on the management of EU funds and the implementation of EU-funded programmes and projects, and to analyse their visibility in the articles mentioned, we applied the following category scheme:

Table 4-2. Category scheme 1

Category*	Subcategory	Frequency of the unit of analysis (individual article)
A. EU identity markers	1. picture of EU flag	1
	2. picture of the Euro symbol	2
	3.picture of European the European currency (Euros)	1
	4. Other	6
	5. None	23
B.	1. EU offers great amounts of money	14
	2. Not mentioned	19
C.	1. EU offers free money	6
	2. Not mentioned	27
D. EU funds absorption rate in Romania	1. Negative	16
	2. Positive	1
	3. Not mentioned	16
E.	1.Beneficiaries of EU funds	20
	2. Not mentioned	13
F.	1. Gains of absorbing EU money	11
	2. Not mentioned	22
G.	1.Disadvantages of absorbing EU money	1
	2. Not mentioned	32

H.	1.Romania mismanages EU funds	17
	2. Not mentioned	16
I.	1. Presence of EU disclaimers**	0
	2. No EU disclaimers	33
J. Presence of EU institutions	1. Active role	7
	2. Passive role	1
	3. No presence	25

* From category B to category J. we refer to frames.
** EU disclaimers are sentences that mention the source that financed the project/programme, more precisely the EU fund and the operational program, e.g.: "Project funded by the EU and the Romanian government through the European Regional Development Fund and the Cohesion Fund"

We have mentioned that the EU has followed the national strategy in promoting its own identity markers, such as the EU flag, the anthem and the euro. Therefore, we searched for such identity markers in the articles on EU fund implementation and management of EU-funded projects and programmes in Romania. We have found that 4 articles from the 33 relevant articles posted on both news portals used photos of the EU flag (1), the euro symbol (2) and European money (1). A relevant fact is that the majority of articles – 23 – did not have any picture at all. Therefore, although we found low visibility of these EU identity markers, their appearance suggests that journalists – authors of the articles – relate to an EU identity and unconsciously promote it to their readers, the Romanian citizens. Moreover, the fact that pictures of the Euro symbol and EU currency appear 3 times compared to just one picture of the EU flag, one might suggest that this is an instance of an instrumental European identity, more than a cultural or civic one (although at a rudimentary level). Another relevant fact is that these results also show that identity markers are not that memorable and as relevant to the EU as to the nation state – even journalists did not insist on these markers. More relevant for the acquisition of EU identity are the frames used in the articles, thus transmitted to the public.

We also tried to determine the frequency of frames that suggest that a common strategy of the EU is to create a sense of belonging for member states through highlighting the benefits and gains created by EU funds in each nation state. We discovered this frequency to be high. Fourteen of 33 articles (9 from www.hotnews.ro and 5 from www.ziare.com) positively promote the idea that the EU offers Romania great amounts of money. Moreover, 6 articles highlight that this is "free money". Although unconsciously used, this frame helps to speed the active and significant role that instrumental factors play in defining and strengthening individuals' sense of identification with the EU.

A commonly used frame is that of the EU funds absorption rate in Romania, which appears to be presented both in a positive, but mostly in a negative light: only 1 article presents the situation as positive, while 16 articles promote the idea that Romania does not perform well at all when it comes to spending EU funds. Despite the fact that one might consider this frame to negatively affect Romanians' identification with the EU, it actually enforces it, as the second analysis will show. The idea unanimously promoted by the articles on both is that the EU gives Romania great amounts of money and if it is not spent, it is Romania's, not the EU's, fault. EU institutions do everything possible to help Romanian authorities to best manage the EU funds, but Romanian institutions are not able to work accordingly, and are even accused of being obstacles to the beneficiaries' using the funds.

Beneficiaries of EU funds are mentioned at least once in 20 of the 33 articles analysed. This frame is one of the most frequently used in highlighting the gains of being a European citizen, which directly connects to our definition of the instrumental European identity. Actually, 11 articles show examples of specific gains Romanian citizens have once they absorb EU money, most of them presenting the end results of different EU-funded projects, while just 1 article (it does not present advantages/gains also) mentions some disadvantages beneficiaries of EU-funded projects face. Therefore, EU funds are presented as significant for Romania's development, sometimes as the only driver for the modernization of different sectors of society. EU funds bring mostly benefits and a few disadvantages. Furthermore, when problems appear, it is the Romanian authorities who are responsible, not the EU.

Another relevant frame used to make the EU visible to its citizens is the presence of EU institutions, mostly the European Commission. Seven articles show EU institutions in active roles, while one article mentions the European Commission as having a passive approach to a specific debated issue. Through the European Commission, the EU acts as an objective judge of the way its rules are respected, using "carrots and sticks" as necessary.

"Romania mismanages EU funds" is another frame that occurs in the selected articles, specifically in 17 of the articles. This helps promote the image of the "good guy" vs. "bad guy" scenario, which, as we will show in the second content analysis, also appears in the comments readers posted in response to the articles. Therefore, as already mentioned, the situation is presented in favour of the EU which gives free money to European citizens – in this case Romanians – and Romania is not able to spend it properly due to corruption, discrimination, incompetence, lack of money for co-funding the projects and so on.

None of the 33 articles contained EU disclaimers, which came as a surprise. Although it is mandatory that EU disclaimers appear on all material and in all campaign communications about EU-funded projects and programmes, they seem not to be included in these articles. Therefore, this research does not offer the opportunity to discuss the effects of the mandatory visual identity rules that every beneficiary of EU-funded projects and institution which manages EU funds must respect and apply. This might be a promising topic of research, but on another corpus (for example press ads, print informative materials and TV spots of EU funded projects and programmes).

In order to find an answer to the fourth research question, we conducted a second content analysis (see Table 4 below).

Table 4-3. Category scheme 2

Category	Subcategory	Frequency of the unit of analysis (comment)
A.	1. The EU offers Romania free money ("good guy")	7
	2. The EU discriminates against Romania ("bad guy")	3
	3. Not mentioned	106
B.	1. Romania mismanages EU money ("bad guy")	51
	2. Romania does everything it can ("good guy")	3
	3. Not mentioned	62

The content analysis shows that Romanians see the EU as affecting their lives in a positive way, as a "good guy" (7 comments) rather than a "bad guy" (3 comments). Moreover, 51 comments suggest Romania is the "bad guy", as its institutions mismanage EU money, while only 3 comments claim that Romanian authorities do everything they can in spending and managing EU money. These findings suggest that well educated Romanians who read online articles identify with the EU in instrumental terms, as they clearly perceive the benefits that the EU brings to their lives. The EU is real to them. Therefore, the EU appears to be "the good guy" in relation to the implementation and spending of EU funds, while Romanian institutions are the ones that make mistake after mistake in helping citizens benefit from EU grants. This is an empirical finding of hypotheses promoted in literature that the better the citizen's evaluation of European policy results, compared to the results of policies pursued by national governments, the more likely s/he is to identify with the EU.

When it comes to the implementation and management of EU funds, Romanian citizens tend to penalize Romanian institutions and relate to the EU in a positive manner. We consider that in this context an interesting hypothesis to test in further studies is that when facing a poor absorption rate and poor management of EU funds, citizens of a member state identify (in instrumental terms) more with the EU than with the member state.

Conclusion

This paper suggests that the citizens of EU member states should have a European identity, albeit a secondary one, to actively participate in private and public debates concerning EU affairs, policies and a common future. The paper argues that the Instrumental European identity, as the identity based on self-interested calculation, is a reality and presents the results of two content analyses conducted on 33 articles and reader comments covering EU fund management and implementation on two Romanian news portals.

The EU cannot make use of the same identity markers that countries promote to reinforce their citizens' identification with the respective countries, as similar EU identity markers don't have the same power as the national ones. This study shows that few articles had pictures of the EU flag or currency, which means that journalists are unconsciously aware of this fact. Therefore, the EU has had to be innovative and use other strategies to enforce a sense of belonging for the citizens of its member states. People across the EU tend to identify with the supranational structure when they perceive the benefits that the EU brings into their lives, when the EU becomes real to them. The most relevant and recognisable instruments in developing such an identity across the EU are the financial opportunities that it bring to its citizens through the funds it offers under the Regional and Cohesion Policy, the Common Agriculture and Fisheries Policies and the thematic policies.

Research results have confirmed the presence, although minimal, of instrumental identity markers in articles posted on the two news portals taken into account, such as the pictures of the euro symbol and European money. Moreover, we have found one frame to be particularly relevant and frequent: the idea that one of the primary strategies used by the EU to create a sense of belonging for its citizens is to highlight the benefits these citizens experience as a result of EU funds allocated to their nation state. The frames that occurred frequently in the 33 selected articles are: "the EU offers great amounts of money", "EU fund absorption rate in Romania is low", "there are actual beneficiaries of EU funds", "gains of absorbing EU money" and "Romania mismanages EU funds". It came as a surprise that none of the 33 articles contained any EU disclaimer. Although EU disclaimers are mandatory in every material and deliverable of communication campaigns of EU-funded projects and programs, they were not promoted by these articles. Therefore, this research does not offer the opportunity to discuss the effects of the mandatory visual identity rules that every beneficiary of EU-funded projects and every institution which manages EU funds must respect and apply. This might be a promising topic of research, but on another corpus (for example press ads, printed information materials and TV coverage of EU-funded projects and programmes).

The findings of the second content analysis, which has as unit of analysis comments of Romanian citizens on the selected articles, suggest that when it comes to the implementation and management of EU funds, Romanians tend to penalize Romanian institutions and relate to the EU in a positive manner, as Romania mismanages EU money, while the EU offers great grants. Therefore, Romanians are aware and believe that the EU delivers important economic benefits to their communities and their country. We consider this to be both a necessary condition for the emergence of an instrumental European identity and an instance of this concept in real life circumstances. Although it is currently only at a rudimentary level, an instrumental European identity exists due to efforts promoted by EU institutions through a strategy of EU funds and their inherent gains and benefits. Moreover, this may be just a first step in consolidating a European identity, as, if carefully managed by the EU, such efforts may gradually trigger the acquisition of different values, customs and other rules promoted at the EU level and the emergence of a civic and even cultural identity for the supranational multilayered structure.

REFERENCES

Abdelal, Rawi, Herrera, Yoshiko M, Johnston, Alastair Iain & McDermott, Rose (2006). Identity as a Variable. *Perspectives on Politics*, 4(4).

Baaji, Murali (2010). I-Other Dialectic. *Encyclopedia of Identity*. SAGE Publications. Retrieved 9 April 2011 from http://www.sage-ereference.com/identity/Article_n143.html.

Bârgăoanu, Alina, Negrea, Elena, Dascălu, Roxana (2010). Communicating the European (Lack of) Union: An Analysis of Greece's Financial Crisis in Communication Terms. *Romanian Journal of Communication and Public Relations*, 12(1).

Beciu, Camelia (2004). Spaţiul public european – Emergenţa unei problematici [European Public Sphere – the Emergence of a Theoretical Concern]. Revista Română de Sociologie [Romanian Journal of Sociology] , VII(4), 287–298.

Bruter, Michael (2004). On What Citizens Mean by Feeling "European": Perceptions of News, Symbols and Borderless-ness. *Journal of Ethnic and Migration Studies,* 30(1), 21–39.

Burgess, J Peter (2002). What's so European about the European Union? Legitimacy between Institution and Identity. *European Journal of Social Theory*, 5(4), 467–481.

Davidson, Maria (2010). Identity Change. *Encyclopedia of Identity*. SAGE Publications. Retrived 9 April 2011 from http://www.sage-ereference.com/identity/Article_n121.html.

Delors, Jacques (2011). In search of Europe: An interview with Jacques Delors, www.eurozine.com

Duchesne, Sophie, & Frognier, Andre-Paul (2007). Why Is It so Difficult to Know if National Pride Leads the Way to European Identity or Prevents It? *Cahiers Européens*, 3.

Eder, Klaus (2009). A Theory of Collective Identity: Making Sense of the Debate on a European Identity. *European Journal of Social Theory*, 12(4), 427–447.

Eriksen, Erik Oddvar. (2007). Conceptualizing European Public Sphere: General, Segmented and Strong Publics. In Fossum, John Erik and Schlesinger, Philip (eds). *The European Union and the Public Sphere.*

A Communicative Space in the Making? London: Routledge, pp. 23–44.

Eriksen, Erik Oddvar, & Fossum, John Erik (2004). Europe in Search of Legitimacy: Strategies of Legitimation Assessed. *International Political Science Review,* 25(4), 435–459.

Fuchs, Dieter, Klingemann, Hans-Dieter (2000). *Eastward Enlargement of the European Union and the Identity of Europe*, Discussion Paper FS III 00-206. *Wissenschaftszentrum Berlin für Sozialforschung*, 1–44.

Gaines, Kathryn (2010). Communication. *Political and Civic Leadership.* Retrived 9 April 2011 from http://www.sage-ereference.com/civicleadership/Article_n102.html.

Grant, Fiona (2010). Collective/Social Identity. *Encyclopedia of Identity*, SAGE Publications. Retrived 09 April 2011 from http://www.sage-ereference.com/identity/Article_n37.html.

Haesly, Richard, (2001). Euroskeptics, Europhiles and Instrumental Europeans: European Attachment in Scotland and Wales. *European Union Politics,* 2.

Hecht, Michael L, and Suellen Hopfer (2010). Communication Theory of Identity. *Encyclopedia of Identity*. SAGE Publications.

Hollway, Wendy (2010). Relationality: The Intersubjective Foundations of Identity. *The Sage Handbook of Identities*. SAGE Publications. Retrived 9 April 2011 from http://www.sage-ereference.com/hdbk_identities/Article_n12.html.

Hix, S (1998). Dimensions and Alignments in European Union Politics: Cognitive Constraints and Partisan Responses. *Working Paper Series in European Studies*, 1(3). Retrieved August 2011 from http://uw-madison-ces.org/files/hix.pdf.

Inthorn, Sanna (2006). What Does It Mean to Be an EU Citizen? How News Media Construct Civic and Cultural Concepts of Europe. *Westminster Papers in Communication and Culture*, 3(3), 71–90.

Jenkins, Richard (2010). Society and Social Identity. *Encyclopedia of Identity*. SAGE Publications. Retrived 9 April 2011 from http://www.sage-ereference.com/identity/Article_n262.html.

Lewis, Richard (2008). *New Europeans, New Identities: Reflections on Europe's Dilemma.* IES Working Paper, No. 01. Brussels: Institute for European Studies.

Muldoon, Paul. Identity. *Encyclopedia of Political Theory*, SAGE Publications. Retrived 9 April 2011 from http://www.sage-ereference.com/politicaltheory/Article_n223.html.

Risse, Thomas (2003). An Emerging European Public Sphere? *Theoretical Clarifications and Empirical Indicators*, 1–11.

—. (2004). Neo-Functionalism, European Identity, and the Puzzles of European Integration. In Tanja Börzel (ed.), *The Disparity of European Integration: Revisiting Neofunctionalism in Honour of Ernst B. Haas*, Special Issue of the *Journal of European Public Policy*.

—. (2010a). Multiple Europes: The Europeanization of Citizens' Identities. In Thomas Risse, *A Community of Europeans? Transnational Identities and Public Spheres*, Ithaca: Cornell University Press.

—. (2010b). Collective Identities: Conceptual and Methodological Questions. In Thomas Risse, *A Community of Europeans? Transnational identities and Public Spheres*, Ithaca: Cornell University Press.

Risse, Thomas, Engelmann-Martin, Daniela, Knopf, Hans-Joachim & Roscher, Klaus (1999).To Euro or Not to Euro? The EMU and Identity Politics in the European Union. *European Journal of International Relations,* 5(2), 147–187.

Ruiz Jimenez, Antonia M, Gorniak, Jaroslaw Jozef, Kosic, Ankika, Kiss, Paszkal & Kandulla, Maren (2004). European and National Identities in EU's Old and New Member States: Ethnic, Civic, Instrumental and Symbolic Components. *European Integration online Papers (EIoP)*, 8(11).

Sanchez-Cuenca, Ignacio (2000). The Political Basis of Support for European Integration. *European Union Politics*, 1.

Sanchez Salgado, Rosa (2008). European Money at Work: Contracting a European Identity? *Les Cahiers européens*, 04.

Scheepers, Daan, Spears, Russell, Doosje, Bertjan & Manstead, Antony S. R. (2003). Two Functions of Verbal Intergroup Discrimination: Identity and Instrumental Motives as a Result of Group Identification and Threat. *Personality and Social Psychology Bulletin,* 29.

Schlesinger, Philip, & Foret, François (2007). Political Roof and Sacred Canopy? Religion and the EU Constitution. In Fossum, John Erik, Schlesinger, Philip Kværk, & Ove, Geir (eds), *ARENA Report No 2*, 113–139.

Schoen, Harald, (2008). Identity, Instrumental Self-Interest and Institutional Evaluations Explaining Public Opinion on Common European Policies in Foreign Affairs and Defence. *European Union Politics*, 9(1), 5–29.

Simon, Bernd, & Klandermans, Bert (2001). Politicized Collective Identity: A Social Psychological Analysis. *American Psychologist*, 56(4), 319–331.

Trenz, Hans-Jorg (2005). Review Essay: The European Public Sphere: Contradictory Findings in a Diverse Research Field. *European Political Science*, 00, 1–14.

BUILDING THE "EUROSPHERE" UNDER EXTERNAL PRESSURE? THE ARAB CRISIS SEEN BY WWW.EURONEWS.NET

LOREDANA RADU

Abstract

The Eurobarometer (EB) survey published in February 2011 shows a decline in the confidence of citizens in the European Union (EU). Over one year (late 2009 vs. late 2010), the perceptions on the benefits of EU membership experienced a negative trend, while opinions on the EU's lack of support for member states gained ground. Compared to 2008, the EU image has seen severe erosion, consisting in the prevalence of rather negative representations in the minds of Europeans, such as the "technocratic Union" or the "ineffective Union". These results are also a consequence of the economic turmoil that the EU is facing. In a nutshell, "amid the economic crisis, people's confidence has decreased, while euroscepticism has increased" (Bârgăoanu et al., 2010, p. 1).

According to some scholars, the emergence of euro-scepticism challenges the idea of a European identity. Empirical studies claim that the lack of a collective European identity is mainly caused by a weak or even absent European public sphere.

While early research provided a pessimistic prognosis for the emergence of a European public sphere, more recent findings (Koopmans, & Erbe, 2004; Van de Steeg, & Risse, 2010) are more optimistic and highlight several established processes that contribute to the formation of an agora of civil society or of the general public, a place for exchange of information, ideas, opinions, a vehicle of contestation, and, thus, an engine of democratization. For example, research points out the emergence of a "transnational community of communication" (Risse, 2003, p. 9), which would eventually leverage the "Eurosphere". The community of communication is built on the proliferation of a vivid European "we" in media discourse, leading to a certain degree of collective identification with each other's' fate. Does this European "we" really exist or is it another chimera fed by Europeans' great expectations?

The paper will examine the extent to which the European "we" is used and promoted by Europe's official news portal www.euronews.net, during a series of violent events that shattered the globe in 2011, now extensively labelled as "the Arab crisis". More specifically, the paper will address two key research questions. On the one hand, it will analyse whether euronews.net uses a European reference point when addressing the "Arab question"; on the other hand, it will seek to identify the main frames used by euronews.net when discussing the current turmoil in Arab countries. The research study is qualitative and analyses a group of articles on the "Arab crisis" published by euronews.net during February–April 2011.

Key words: European "we", Arab crisis, qualitative framing

Introduction

As Hix (2005) has noticed, the erosion of citizen belief in the EU as a panacea of democracy and public participation is a trend that emerged during the process of ratifying the Maastricht Treaty (1992–1993), in referendums held in France, Denmark and Ireland. The opposing views of citizens initiated what is often referred to as a new era, in which Europeans are no longer bound to the so-called "permissive consensus" (Hix, 2005, p. 149), thus being "less likely to blindly follow the positions of their governments" (Hix, 2005, p. 151).

Europeans "grew up" in terms of political judgement. The birth of active citizenship demands constant commitment from two sides: the commitment of the EU to transparency and access to information, on one side, and the commitment of citizens to freely express their opinions in the public arena, on the other side. As we will show below, this twofold commitment premised the creation of the EU communication policy. The most recent documents on EU communication issued by the European Commission seem to confirm what several authors predicted (e.g. Eriksen, 2009) several years ago: the new European citizen should be seen as an active actor in the political scene, who will make herself or himself heard whenever (s)he is granted the opportunity to speak out. The European citizen has been subject to a paradigm shift – from the passive recipient of European political decisions to the active voice that is made more and more audible on the political level.

If we take a close look at the history of the EU, we will observe that EU communication is subject to a paradox. Technically, the crisis of the European governance model has premised the formulation of the European communication policy as a new horizontal policy aimed at bridging the gap between European institutions and European citizens. We will illustrate this assumption by taking a close look at several events that have put a question mark against European cohesion. Such events are mainly related to the referendums organized around key moments: Ireland's refusal to support the Lisbon Treaty in 2007, the vetoes by the Netherlands and France against the European Constitution in 2005, Ireland's lack of support for the Treaty of Nice in 2001. In a nutshell, EU communication policy was formed as a means of coping with Europeans' (negative) attitudes towards the European project. Although these reactions are widely known as "Euroscepticism", we must admit that Euroscepticism is not the only force responsible for attitudes against the European Union. "The image of a mentally lethargic population lagging behind the political elites represents just one side of the icon" (Habermas, 2009, p. 129).

In the theoretical field, there is a strong tendency to explain the lack of cohesion in Europe by entering the rather complex field of European identity studies, which tackle several sensitive subjects, such as the Europeanization of national cultures or the creation of a European public sphere or "Eurosphere". Scholars interested in EU communication argue that the lack of cohesion in Europe or of a collective identity is a result of the European "public sphere deficit" (Ward, 2004), which is seen as a part of a larger democratic deficit. As any theoretical field, EU communication is subject to many controversies and opposing perspectives. Some believe that we cannot speak of a European public sphere in a meaningful way (Baisnée, 2007), whereas others argue that public spheres "are out there waiting to be discovered by analysts" (Risse, 2010, p. 110).

Thus, in order to understand the complex mechanism behind the creation of the European identity, we are going to structure our discussion around the public sphere as a concept in the making and we are going to propose and test a new way of analysing the way in which the European public sphere emerges. We assume that it is possible to configure the European public sphere under the pressure of external, non-European events occurring outside the European Union.

THE PUBLIC SPHERE: THEORETICAL APPROACHES

EU Communication and the Public Sphere

Despite its rather complex and long history, EU communication became a strategic objective of the EC only in 2005. This was the year when, spurred by the votes by France and the Netherlands against the European Constitution, the European Commission issued several key documents aimed at closing the gap between EU institutions and EU citizens. If we take a simple count, we can observe a gap of around 50 years between the creation of the European Community and the formation of a European policy in the field of communication. This gap was filled with rather isolated initiatives in the field of EU communication, such as the establishment of the Press and Information Service (1955) within the High Authority of the European Coal and Steel Community or the creation of the Eurobarometer (1973), which still operates as the European opinion survey tool. Despite the fact that many European documents claim to be premised on the idea that the European citizen has the right of being actively involved in the political life of the European Union, the social and political reality shows something different. Each time Europeans have been granted the opportunity to clearly state their political wishes (e.g. in referendums), the European government has had to cope with complex and problematic situations. There were situations when even those states that are in the "avant-garde" of the European project (e.g. France and the Netherlands) were not able to reach a political consensus. "One explanation for the unpredictability of referenda is that a politically mobilized population can make decisions without concern for politicians' interest in power retention" (Habermas, 2009, p. 129).

During referenda organized on European issues, political interests are irrelevant for the general public, who act and behave according to their own "code of honour", which is mainly leveraged by a feeling of belonging to a common European reality or, more simply, by the "European we-feeling" (Eriksen, 2009). A poor European "we-feeling" translates into a low level of citizen involvement, which may be seen as an indicator of poor communication between the European Union, on one side, and European citizens, on the other side. Since citizens are not informed about high-level European decisions, they cannot make any educated decisions regarding the EU. Furthermore, they will lack the motivation to analyse the actual political context and thus will try to deny or to reject whatever they do not understand. This would be the explanation provided by a communication theorist.

If we analyse this through the lens of the cultural anthropologist, then the situation is perfectly natural and logical.

> In both qualitative and quantitative terms, the development of the European Union represents one of the most sophisticated and mature attempts to construct an intergovernmental, and to a lesser extent, supranational framework for the initiation, implementation and enforcement of a variety of economic, political and public policy objectives. (Ward, 2004, p. 1).

Indeed, the "European project" is one of the most ambitious endeavours in contemporary history. When referring to the European Union, "diversity through unity" appears to be a credible slogan – at least as far as the institutional level is concerned. By building a transnational "state", organized according to its own principles, institutions and laws, the European Union meets most of the formal prerequisites for a functional entity. At an upper institutional level, the European Union appears to be an engine of unity and solidarity. However, history has put its fingerprint on the actual European picture, and nowadays we see many "Europes" in terms of cultures, languages, norms, values, traditions, knowledge, political involvement etc. " The plurality of Europe is more than a diversity of cultures and nations, but extends into its very civilizational nature" (Delanty & Rumford, 2005, p. 35).

If there are several "Europes" – Western, Northern, Southern, Eastern, Latin, Anglo-Saxon, Slav, Catholic, Orthodox, Protestant, etc. – does this mean that the European project is only a chimera fed by the enthusiasm that followed the end of World War II? A thorough analysis of Europe's deeper level can provide a pertinent answer to this question. This deeper level consists of the so-called "public sphere", which creates the premise for "collective identity" or the European "we-feeling" (Eriksen, 2009). Why focus on the public sphere? The public sphere is a prerequisite of collective identity. In brief, "the public sphere plays an important role for the emergence of a common identity" (Risse & Brabowsky, 2008, p. 1).

While early research provided pessimistic prognosis for the emergence of a European public sphere, more recent findings (Van de Steeg, & Risse, 2010) are more optimistic and highlight several established processes that contribute to the formation of an agora of civil society or of the general public, a place for the exchange of information, ideas, opinions, a vehicle of contestation and, thus, an engine of democratization. According to Jurgen Habermas, who is considered the "creator of the public sphere" (Bârgăoanu, 2011, p. 192), the emergence of the public sphere seems to be a fascinating and intriguing process that is mainly leveraged by media and public communication. "Public communication is a force which both stimulates and orients citizen opinions and desires, while at the same time compelling the political system to adapt and become more transparent." (Habermas, 2009, p. 136).

Recent findings emphasize that communication is a key element in configuring the European public sphere:

> Public spheres – whether local, regional, national, or issue-specific – are social constructions in the true sense of the word. They do not pre-exist outside communication, but are created precisely when people speak to one another, be it in interpersonal settings or through the media. Public spheres emerge through the process by which people debate controversial issues in public. " (Risse, 2010, p. 110)

What is the Public Sphere?

The Commission's White Paper on a European Communication Policy, published in February 2006 and aimed at laying the foundation of the EU communication policy, adopts "public sphere" as a "current bureaucratic term of reference" (Schlesinger, 2007, p. 67). This suggests a fruitful convergence of academic and political interests, and, furthermore, proves that the public sphere is not (only) an over-rated and over-theorized notion. Moreover, the 5th and 6th Framework Programs, focused on funding international research projects, listed the public sphere as a specific field of research, implying that the Commission tacitly confirmed that researching the public sphere is a necessity. But what is the public sphere? Or, to paraphrase M. Schudson, we could ask "Was there ever a public sphere? If so, when?" (Calhoun, 1996, p. 143).

At a rather trivial level, "public sphere" is a term used to describe a communicative space populated by citizens who gather together in order to freely express their opinions, to protest, to contest, to debate or to influence political decision. These citizens may act as a common voice, as a volonté générale; they want to make themselves heard. As the public sphere is regarded as a key ingredient in finding the "Eldorado" of the European project, or a European identity shared by all European citizens, the literature in the field of a EU public sphere is abundant and still flourishing.

The concept of a "public sphere" has long been theorized. Historically speaking, the public sphere was born twice, under two paradigms. The American paradigm intimately links the public sphere to the rise of the "public" and "public opinion". In this light, the famous polemic between the philosopher John Dewey and the journalist Walter Lippman is eloquent. In 1927 this polemic became widely known through the publication of two important books: *The Public and Its Problems* by John Dewey and *The Phantom Public* by Walter Lippmann. The dispute was shaped by two opposing attitudes towards the public: Dewey inferred that citizens should continue to participate in public affairs and search for the legitimacy of their opinions, whereas Lippmann concluded that the public cannot lead a nation and that only well-educated and informed people – the so-called "experts" – should be granted the opportunity to make themselves heard in the public space. Both authors based their arguments on the fact that democracy is an effective mechanism of conducting a nation. However, their perspectives on the role of the ordinary citizen in the democratic system are totally different and, to a certain extent, still applicable.

If the American inauguration of the public sphere is strongly influenced by mass media, publicity, and advertising, the European birth of the public sphere is more ideologically grounded. Seyla Benhabib (1996) delineates three different approaches of the public sphere in the European context. The first one is called the "agonistic" approach. Hannah Arendt, its major advocate, views public space as a "republican virtue" or "civic virtue" (Calhoun, 1996, p. 73). The second approach is the "legalistic" model of the public space, which brings into the limelight the notion of "public dialogue". Typical of the liberal tradition, this model was inaugurated by Immanuel Kant. The third and last model is mastered by Jürgen Habermas and is labelled the "discursive public space". The Kantian tradition played a very important role in the configuration of Habermasian theory on the public sphere. Habermas has used the rational and normative perspective, typical of the Kantian system, in order to configure a public sphere which is regulated by the power of public debate and political communication.

However, the concept of "public sphere" has gained considerable popularity in the academic world since the translation to English of Jürgen Habermas's book *Strukturwandel der Öffentlichkeit* (1962), known to English speakers as *The Structural Transformation of the Public Sphere* (1989). "Linguistically, the syntagm 'public sphere' seems to be a recent construction, selected by a translator to find a label for a word that has been in regular use in Germany since the 18th century" (Kleinsteuber, 2001, p. 96). As Habermas himself stated, "the usage of the words 'public' and 'public sphere' betrays a multiplicity of concurrent meanings" (Habermas, 1991, p. 1). The public sphere is

> a realm of our social life in which something approaching public opinion can be formed. Access is guaranteed to all citizens. A portion of the public

> sphere comes into being in every conversation in which private individuals assemble to form a public body. (Habermas, 1974, p. 49).

According to Habermas, the public sphere is a space where private persons assemble to debate matters of public concern. The freedom of publicly expressing one's opinions, ideas and beliefs, of getting involved in a public debate in order to identify the best solution for a collective problem, or of debating political options is a basic feature of modern democracies. Without this freedom, the public sphere is a utopia.

In specialized literature there are many definitions of the public sphere. We will just review the most prominent ones. For Eriksen, the public sphere is "the place where civil society is linked to the power structure of the state" (Eriksen, 2009, p. 120); for Fraser it is "the informally mobilized body of nongovernmental discursive opinion that can serve as a counterweight to the state" (Fraser, 1990, p. 134); Trenz sees it as "the engine of democratization", "an open field of communicative exchange" (Trenz, 2008, p. 2); Risse focuses on an empirical definition of the concept by stating that the public sphere is "a shared community of communication" (Risse, 2003, p. 7). Taylor defined the public sphere as a "metatopical space" (Taylor, 2002) in order to capture the "non-assembly" character of this common space of thoughts, attitudes, and actions. Claes H. de Vreese sums up the different approaches related to the public sphere, by differentiating between the "'public sphere heavy' notion of a singular, pan-European public", and the "'public sphere light' notion of co-existing national public spheres in regard to European politics" (de Vreese, 2007, p. 8).

The concept of a single transnational European public sphere (already widely rejected due to differences imposed by language, religion, access to mass media etc) experienced a short delusive resurrection in 2003, when both Habermas and Derrida saw the empirical birth of the European public sphere in public demonstrations against the US invasion in Iraq. Since these popular reactions did not occur in Europe only, it is reasonable to agree that these events were "rather a manifestation of the 'maturing of global civil society' and not an expression of a European public sphere" (de Vreese, 2007, p. 8).

The most recent interpretations of the public sphere are focused on its communicative character and highlight the fact that public spheres are social constructs that emerge "in the process during which people engage one another and debate issues of common concern in the public. Public spheres and communities of communication come into being when people argue about controversial issues" (Risse, 2010, p. 125). Habermas argues that the public sphere contributes to the legitimation of political discourse "by keeping it active, by steering – and filtering – it" (Habermas, 2009, p. 159). Thus, the public sphere could be understood as

> an intermediary system of mass communication, situated between the formally organized deliberations and negotiations at the centre, and the arranged or informal conversations which take place in civil society at the periphery of the political system. (Habermas, 2009, p. 159)

Recent research on EU communication and the public sphere is starting to surpass the already traditional discourse on the existence or non-existence of a European or Europeanized public sphere. Koopmans and Statham (2010, p. 38) arrive at three different types of Europeanization. The first is the emergence of a supranational European public sphere that consists of interactions "among European-level institutions and collective actors" (Koopmans & Statham, 2010, p. 38); the second is vertical Europeanization, which consists of "communicative linkages between different European countries" (idem); the third is horizontal Europeanization, "which consists of communicative linkages between different European countries". This shows that scholar discourse on EU communication and on the public sphere has matured, along with the acceptance of the idea that "Europe's emergent public sphere is not the final stage of a full post-national and federal democracy" (de Beus, in Koopmans & Statham, 2010, p. 33).

The Role of Mass Media in Broadcasting "Europe's Single Voice"

Euronews.net and "Europe's single voice"

When analysing the role of mass media in the emergence of the public sphere, Europeanization is a matter of adopting a tone and logic focused on "Europe's single voice". Mass media is often referred to as "the infrastructure of the public sphere" (Habermas, 2009, p. 164), which means that its role in the creation of the European identity is well recognized and documented in various studies and research projects (e.g. Risse (2003), Trenz (2008), Koopmans & Statham (2010)). My assumption is that "Europe's single voice" should be more visible and easily quantifiable when analysing the mass media channels that are in close relation with the European Union and the European Commission.

This may seem redundant, as the official goal of media tools funded by the Commission (e.g. euronews.net) is to frame international events from the EU perspective. In the Commission Communication of 9 July 2003, which called for an ad hoc evaluation of Community support for the

EuroNews channel, it is explicitly stated that "EuroNews is clearly relevant to EU objectives" and that "it is efficient as a partner for the Commission compared to comparable alternatives and to industry norms". This is consistent with the Maastricht Treaty (1993), which clearly stipulates that the EU must promote a single unitary image on the international (non-European) stage. This "single image" should be centred on the core values of the European Union, which are related to social and economic cohesion, decisional transparency and respect for cultural diversity.

EuroNews was founded in 1992, following the First Persian Gulf War, during which CNN's position as the preeminent source of 24-hour news programming was cemented. Thus, the European Broadcasting Union decided to establish the channel to present information from a European perspective. Euronews had its first broadcast on 1 January 1993 from Lyon. "By going outside the traditional national or international frameworks within which the journalistic profession functions, the members of the channel came to slowly define what news with a European perspective meant." (Baisnee & Marchetti, 2010, p. 9).

Like most of the television channels that do news, Euronews depends on external sources. It is a so-called channel of post-production (without camera), as it depends on a plurality of sources for footage. This is due to financial constraints, as Olivier Baisnee explains (2010, p. 10). Since 2008, Euronews is available online through the web site euronews.net that broadcasts news related to European and non-European events.

Research Methodology and Background

I have used qualitative framing as a means for exploring how euronews.net approaches the "Arab Spring". The final goal is to understand how the EU is framed in relation to important and very visible non-European events, such as the Arab revolutions. Qualitative framing is also used to see if "Europe's single voice" is promoted by the European news portal.

Qualitative framing was performed on all the news articles related to the Arab revolutions and posted by euronews.net during February, March and April 2011. This entailed a group composed of 42 articles: 18 articles published in February, 19 articles published in March, and 5 articles published in April. Following the political and military tensions, the period between February and April 2011 is rather rich in news and comments focused on the Arab revolutions.

In brief, the "Arab Revolutions" or the "Arab Spring" consisted of a wave of demonstrations and protests occurring in the Arab world. Since 18 December 2010 there have been: revolutions in Tunisia and Egypt; a civil war in Libya resulting in the fall of its regime; civil uprisings in Bahrain, Syria, and Yemen; major protests in Israel, Algeria, Iraq, Jordan, Morocco and Oman; minor protests in Kuwait, Lebanon, Mauritania, Saudi Arabia, Sudan and Western Sahara. Protests peaked in the Spring of 2011, which is why a I chose to analyse the period February–April 2011. During the "Arab Spring", the most violent protests took place in Tunisia, Egypt and Libya, and escalated very rapidly. The Tunisian President fled to Saudi Arabia on 14 January following the Tunisian revolution protests; the Egyptian President resigned on 11 February 2011 after 18 days of massive protests, ending his 30-year presidency; the Libyan leader Muammar al-Gaddafi was overthrown on 23 August 2011 after the National Transitional Council (NTC) took control of Bab al-Azizia.

Research Questions and Key Findings

Research question 1: What are the key factors that influenced the agenda-setting of euronews.net in the Arab conflicts?

Most of the articles covering the Arab revolutions were published by euronews.net during two periods: 1. between 21 and 28 February, and 2. between 10 and 28 March. These two periods account for approximately 70% of the news related to the violent events in Arab countries. In the table below I explain the informational and communicational "thickness" of these periods by making correlations between the number of articles published by euronews.net and the political and military events:

Table 5-1. Correlation between the propensity of news and the actual events around the Arab revolutions

Period	Key events
21–28 February = 13 articles (30% of the total number of articles) Focus: Egypt (36%) and Libya (64%)	10 February : President Mubarak ceded all presidential power to Vice President Omar Suleiman, but soon thereafter announced that he would remain President until the end of his term. 18 February: Human Rights Watch reported 84 deaths in Libya since the beginning of riots. 24 February: the European Union diplomats met to discuss sanctions. These included an EU travel ban, an asset freeze and an arms embargo. US President Barack Obama stated that Gaddafi has "lost the legitimacy to rule" and must leave "now". 26 February: The UN Security Council announced sanctions against Libya.
10–28 March = 17 articles (40% of the total number of articles) Focus: Libya (80%), Tunisia (10%), Egypt (5%), Others (5%)	▪ 11 March: the leaders of the 27 EU countries organized a special summit to discuss Libya. They unanimously stated that Gaddafi must surrender power immediately. ▪ 17 March: the United Nations Security Council Resolution 1973 was adopted, authorizing a no-fly zone over Libya, and "all necessary measures" to protect civilians. Two days later, France, the United States and the United Kingdom intervened in Libya with a bombing campaign against pro-Gaddafi forces.

As shown in Table 5-1, on euronews.net, the most visible Arab country involved in the "Arab Spring" is Libya, followed by Egypt. In February, over 60% of the articles were focused on the Libyan conflict, while in March, euronews.net dedicated its news almost exclusively to the Libyan revolution. Other countries that were mentioned in the news posted on euronews.net were Tunisia and Syria.

By correlating the visibility of the Arab countries affected by turmoil with the international political events taking place during the same period, one can conclude that, between February and April, 2011, the agenda-setting for the "Arab Spring" was influenced by two factors, at least as euronews.net is concerned: 1. the political and military implications of the events for both the EU and the UN, and 2. the geographical proximity to Europe (e.g. Libya, Egypt, Tunisia). Thus, the political implications of an event/an organization/a country and its geographical proximity are key aspects that influenced the way euronews.net set the agenda in this international non-European context.

There were poor or no correlations between the actual gravity of events occurring in the Arab states affected by the revolutions and the agenda set by euronews.net. For example, the Syrian people were subject to the regime's violent reactions, but euronews.net hardly covered these facts. Two articles published in March and one article published in April illustrated the Syrian revolution, but only through a short mention. As it is evident in the following quotes, euronews.net mentioned the facts with no additional explanations:

> "In the Syrian city of Deraa crowds have set fire to a building housing the local headquarters of the ruling Baath party." (21 March)

Noticeably, there is a difference between the way euronews.net comments the conflicts in Libya and Egypt – which are by far the focus of the European news portal –, on the one hand, and the way it addresses the conflicts in other Arab countries, on the other. The news on Libya or Egypt is rather analytical and focused on their relationship with EU or the UN and on specific events, while the news on Syria, Qatar or Tunisia is rather informational, presenting facts in a simple and plain language.

UN involvement had a big stake in establishing how the euronews.net should approach the Arab revolutions. By reviewing all news reports on the Arab spring, one will find that the "UN" was mentioned 29 times, the "US" was mentioned 8 times, and "NATO" was mentioned 30 times – each time in relation to the Libyan revolution. The focus of external non-European authorities was on Libya rather than on other Arab countries that were equally affected by violent events. Thus, one may rightly assume that non-European organizations played an important role in the way euronews.net approached the Arab revolutions. Of course, this assumption should be judged under the limitations which are somehow inherent to any pilot study: the limited period of analysis, the limited number of media channels, and the limited number of articles subject to analysis. Despite these evident limitations, the study shows that the propensity of euronews.net towards certain events is highly influenced by the way external non-EU authorities relate to those events. There is an important difference between the way euronews.net builds its discourse on those countries that are its key focus and which set its agenda (e.g. Libya, Egypt) and the way it approaches other Arab countries. The analytical tone, used by euronews.net in describing the events in "agenda-setting" countries is mainly leveraged by the direct involvement of the EU or UN in peace-setting measures.

Table 5-2: Examples of analytical focus in news about Libya and Egypt versus informational focus of news on Syria, Qatar or Tunisia

Analytical focus	Informational focus
"The turmoil in **Cairo** is felt by Egyptians around the world. In Brussels, crowds of people marched through the streets to lend their support to calls for President Mubarak to step down. 'Mubarak, clear off,' they shouted, while some were even more blunt. EU leaders have urged Egypt to move swiftly towards democracy. But some say the 27-member bloc has been slow to respond to events unfolding in Cairo." (www.euronews.net, 6 February 2011 22:34 CET) "**Libya**'s Muammar Gaddafi now has to reckon with all of NATO. The 28-member military alliance has agreed to be in charge of the UN-backed western-led coalition intervening in Libya. A structure has been worked out to police the skies, enforce the arms embargo and safeguard civilian lives." (www.euronews.net, 28 March 2011 18:11 CET)	"Police in **Tunisia** have fired warning shots and tear gas to disperse crowds of protesters in the center of the capital, Tunis." (www.euronews.net, 26 February 2011 00:44 CET) "The **Tunisian** Prime Minister has announced his resignation following a series of street protests." (www.euronews.net, 27 February 2011 18:13 CET) "At least 88 people were killed in the latest protests in **Syria,** says the human rights organization Sawasia. . . . Tens of thousands took to the streets with killings reported in one Damascus district and six of its suburbs, in the central city of Homs, Latakia, and in Izra'a in the south. Dozens more were injured." (www.euronews.net, 22 April 2011 22:34 CET)

Research question 2: How is the EU framed in relation to the Arab conflict?

In order to answer the second research question, I used qualitative framing. My focus was not on general frames, as the conflict frame would be predominant given the topic of the news. Rather, I tried to identify several specific frames, which are relevant to the EU position relative to the Arab revolutions. I identified two main frames used by euronews.net in order to address the Arab conflicts: “the open, supporting Europe” and “the closed, defensive Europe”.

The “open Europe” reveals the humanitarian side of Europe; www. euronews.net highlights a Europe mainly concerned with the fate of the affected populations. This frame is approached in two ways. First, the EU is framed as a model of democracy for the Arab countries. In an article published on 22 February, euronews.net presents the EU foreign minister’s determination “to provide support to those countries in the grip of unrest” and to “manage their peaceful transition to a peaceful government”. When an EU official frames the EU as a model of democracy, the result is almost apologetic. For example, the British Foreign Secretary William Hague speaks of the EU’s “historic responsibility” to fight the “instability on our frontiers” (22 February 2011). The tone adopted by Jose Manuel Barroso is also very firm: “We must do everything so that the current regime leaves the country and stops its actions against the Libyan people” (2 March 2011). Another article states that “The European Union’s 27 leaders have said unanimously that the Libyan leader Muammar Gaddafi must leave power now” (11 March 2011).

The second way of framing the “open Europe” is by underlining the EU’s humanitarian values and its determination to provide unconditioned support to all those in deep need. For example, www.euronews.net explicitly mentions that the EU is very supportive of the Arab people in need of special assistance:

> The European Union’s foreign policy chief Catherine Ashton, in talks in Tunis, has expressed support for Tunisia’s caretaker administration, as increasing numbers of illegal migrants from that country ask for help from Italy.

Also, Kristalina Georgieva, the European Commissioner for Humanitarian Aid, said:

> In the Benghazi area, we have humanitarian teams already on the ground, and they report that there is a need for medical assistance. Because the Libyan health system had foreigners at its heart and they have left, leaving behind a huge void, which has to be filled. (2 March 2011)

In addition, the President of the EC declares:

> We will step up our cooperation with international humanitarian organizations to alleviate the situation inside Libya and at its borders. We have already freed-up 37 million Euros and deployed teams on the ground. (11 March 2011)

The second frame is "the closed defensive Europe". In this frame, we see a Europe that fears its own stability and who is prepared to act as a military ally in order to avoid further turmoil. The Italian Foreign Minister makes EU officials aware of the dangers resting at the Mediterranean shores:

> Italy is a first destination country for which an enormous number of immigrants could potentially head . . . dozens of people who, due to disasters, chaos or violence could flood on to its shores. (22 February 2011)

or

> I'm extremely concerned about the self-proclamation of this so-called Islamic Emirate of Benghazi. Could you imagine having an Islamic Arab Emirate at the borders of Europe? This would be a very serious threat. (21 February 2011)

Germany's Minister for External Affairs declares that Germany "will not participate with soldiers", which does not mean that Germany is "neutral" or that it has "any sympathy for the dictator Gaddafi". Rather, Germany's non-intervention means that it "sees the risks" and that it has "reasons for concern" (21 March 2011).

However, the predominant frame is the "open Europe". In general, this frame is mainly advocated by EU officials, such as Jose Manuel Barroso or Catherine Ashton, who become very active in promoting the image of the "humanitarian and democratic Europe". The "closed Europe" is mainly leveraged by several key representatives of the member states – i.e. the Foreign Ministers from Italy or Germany. In the Arab context, the tendency of EU officials to position the EU as open and caring is counterbalanced by the need of several Member States to reaffirm their status quo concerning political and military decisions. In their quest for stability, the Member States use NATO as a panacea of military interventions. Thus, one may conclude that the EU is not perceived by its Member States as a military or political construction; rather, it is positioned as a funding institution, which is ready to offer financial assistance to the victims of the Arab conflicts. This dichotomy is coherent with what political analysts and historians observed when analysing the EU role in the Arab Spring. For T. Schumacher, the "EU clearly revealed itself as both an actor and spectator by resorting to both activism and passivism in a seemingly erratic fashion" (Schumacher, 2011, p. 108). Furthermore, the Arab Spring revealed

> regular displays of disunity among EU member states' governments over how best to react and finally led to a policy response that reaffirmed, yet again, the different degrees of importance the EU attaches to the southern Mediterranean and Gulf countries. (Schumacher, 2011, p. 117)

If one takes a closer look at the visibility of the key actors mentioned by www.euronews.net within the period analysed and in relation to the Arab Spring, the dichotomy between the EU and the member state perspectives is striking. Jose Manuel Barroso, the President of the European Commission, is presented as a defender and promoter of humanistic values, his discourse focusing on how the EU could support the Arab people subject to violence and crimes: "We must do everything so that the current regime leaves the country and stops its actions against the Libyan people." Catherine Ashton, the European foreign policy chief, also focused on "the open Europe":

> We are extremely concerned by the events that are unfolding in Libya. We condemn the ongoing repression against demonstrators, and deplore the violence and the death of civilians.

In the case of representatives from Member State governments, Great Britain has the greatest visibility through its Prime-Minister, David Cameron, and its Foreign Minister, William Hague. Interestingly, their focus is on the "closed Europe" rather than the "open Europe". Compared to EU officials, national officials are less concerned with advocating the image of an open, humanistic Europe, and more focused on making a clear point regarding the political and military stability of the EU.

CONCLUSIONS

In relation to the "Arab Spring", the European Union is framed in a dual manner: the "open Europe" vs. the "closed Europe". This duality creates a rather confusing image about the EU. On one hand, EU officials position the EU somewhere between a trustful partner and an advocate of political stability, which is emblematic for the core values of the Union; on the other hand, the member states promote their national logic and build their discourse around a "closed Europe", which is very concerned about its stability and fears the unknown. These frames are also coherent with how political analysts assessed EU foreign policy within the context of the Arab Spring. "Seemingly overwhelmed by the magnitude of developments in its southern neighbourhood, the EU responded with hesitation before it resorted to a rather incoherent mix of activism and passivism" (Schumacher, 2011, p. 117).

Despite this duality, this research study shows that euronews.net adopts a "European we-feeling". Qualitative framing shows that both EU and Member State representatives used the EU as a reference point in their discourse. The members of the national governments calibrated their discourse by referring to a collective or European "we", as if national interest actually overlapped with European interest.

The euronews.net agenda is highly influenced by the position adopted by external non-European authorities in relation to important international events. My research showed that, whenever the US, NATO and the UN are present, euronews.net tends to frame the topic as a priority, thus setting an agenda that is consistent with external non-European "voices".

Despite its obvious limitations, given by the limited number of articles and the rather short period of analysis, we have found sufficient evidence that euronews.net creates a sense of a "European we-feeling", which can be the prerequisite for a community of communication (Risse, 2010). Given the complexity of political and military developments, it is difficult to assess whether the European tone used by both EU and Member States officials can anticipate the emergence of a true "community of communication". However, within the analysed period, one could notice that euronews.net partially fulfills two out of the three empirical indicators set by Thomas Risse to identify the "community of communication". The first indicator is that, as already shown, the actors from member states and the EU are treated as "legitimate speakers in a common discourse" (Risse, 2010, p. 122); the second is that the news promoted a common European perspective on issues of European concern. The issues related to the relationship between the EU and the Arab conflict were discussed "from the common perspective of a community" (Risse, 2010, p. 123), although the national perspectives of certain member states seemed to prevail. The third empirical indicator of a community of communication, the interconnectedness between national media, cannot be validated by this research.

To conclude, from a communicative perspective, one can identify a rather evident "European we-feeling" on euronews.net, that is a common manner of approaching subjects of common interest, which is the prerequisite for the emergence of a European community of communication. This is an interesting and positive trend, even though the emergence of the European public sphere remains a distant target.

REFERENCES

Baisnee, O, & Marchetti, D (2010). *Producing European News: Case of the Pan-European News Channel Euronews*, University of Delhi Working Papers Series.

Baisnee, O (2007). The European Public Sphere Does Not Exist (At Least It's Worth Wondering...). *European Journal of Communication December, 22, 4, 493-503.*

Bârgăoanu, A (2011). Examenul Schengen. În căutarea sferei publice europene, Bucureşti: comunicare.ro.

Bârgăoanu, A., Negrea, E., Dascălu, R. (2010). „Communicating the European (Lack of) Union. An Analysis of Greece's Financial Crisis in Terms of Communication", *Romanian Journal of Communication and Public Relations*, 12 (1), 1-17.

Benhabib, S (1996). Models of Pulbic Space: Hannah Arendt, the Liberal Tradition, adn Jurgen Habermas. In Calhoun, C (ed.). *Habermas and the Public Sphere.* USA: MIT Press.

Calhoun, C (ed.) (1996). *Habermas and the Public Sphere,* USA: MIT Press.

Delanty, G, & Rumford, C (2005). *Rethinking Europe: Social Theory and Implications of Europeanization,* New York: Routledge.

de Vreese, C (2007). The EU as a public sphere. *Living Reviews in European Governance.*

Eriksen, E (2009). *The Unfinished Democratization of Europe*, Oxford: Oxford University Press.

Fraser, N (1990). Rethinking the Public Sphere: A Contribution to the Critique of Actually Existing Democracy Author(s). *Social Text*, 25/26, 56–80.

Habermas, J (1974). The Public Sphere: An Encyclopedia Article (1964), *New German Critique,* 3(autumn), 49–55.

—. (1991). *The Structural Transformation of the Public Sphere. An Inquiry into A Category of Bourgeois Society,* USA: MIT Press.

—. (2009). *Europe: The Faltering Project,* Cambridge: Polity Press.

Hix, S (2005). *The Political System of the European Union.* 2nd ed. New York: Palgrave Macmillan.

Kantner, C (2006). Collective Identity as a Shared Ethical Self-Understanding: The Case of the Emerging European Identity. *European Journal of Social Theory,* 9(4), 501–23.

Kleinsteuber, H (2001). J. Habermas and the Public Sphere: from a German to a European Perspective. *The Public*, 8, 95–108.

Koopmans, R, & Statham, P (eds) (2010). *The Making of a European Public Sphere: Media Discourse and Political Contention,* Cambridge: Cambridge University Press.

Koopmans, R., & Erbe, J. (2004). "Towards a European Public Sphere? Vertical and Horizontal Dimensions of Europeanized Political Communication". *European Journal of Social Science Research.* 17(2), 97–118.

Risse, T (2003). *An Emerging European Public Sphere? Theoretical Clarifications and Empirical Indicators,* http://www.fu-berlin.de

Risse, T, & Brabowsky, J K (2008). *European Identity Formation in the Public Sphere and in Foreign Policy.* RECON Online Working Paper 2008/04. http://www.reconproject.eu/projectweb/portalproject/RECON WorkingPapers.html

Risse, T (2010). *A Community of Europeans? Transnational Identities and Public Spheres,* London: Cornell University Press.

Schlesinger, P (2007). A Cosmopolitan Temptation. *European Journal of Communication,* 22(4): 413–426.

Schumacher, T (2011). The EU and the Arab Spring: Between Spectatorship and Actorness. *Insight Turkey* 13(3), 107–119.

Van de Steeg, M., & Risse, T (2010). "The Emergence of a European Community of Communication. Insights from Empirical Research on the Europeanization of Public Spheres". *KFG Working Paper.*

Taylor, C (2002). *Modern Social Imaginaries.* Durham: Duke University Press.

Trenz, H-J (2008). *In Search of a European Public Sphere. Between Normative Overstretch and Empirical Disenchantment.* RECON Online Working Paper No. 07, May: 1–16.

Ward, D (2004). *The European Union Democratic Deficit and the Public Sphere,* Amsterdam: IOS Press.

DEVELOPPEMENT DE LA DIMENSION EUROPEENNE ET DE LA COMPETENCE INTERCULTURELLE A TRAVERS LES PROGRAMMES D'ASSISTANAT COMENIUS DE L'ENSEIGNEMENT TOUT AU LONG DE LA VIE DANS L'ENSEIGNEMENT SECONDAIRE

CHRISTINA ENE, ARGYRIS KYRIDIS AND IFIGENIA VAMVAKIDOU

Résumé

Cette étude a pour but d'identifier le développement de la compétence interculturelle ainsi que la prise de conscience européenne par des élèves appartenant à des écoles secondaires qui étudient le Français Langue Étrangère à l'aide d'assistants Comenius. L'Assistanat Comenius constitue une action développée et financée par l'Union Européenne visant au renforcement de la dimension européenne dans l'enseignement primaire et secondaire et à la promotion de la coopération des élèves avec des personnes provenant de divers pays de l'Union. Basés sur l'observation de 100 adolescents âgés de 13 à 18 ans, élèves de deux établissements scolaires grecs qui ont accueilli des assistants Comenius pendant six années consécutives. Nous avons utilisé le modèle de la compétence interculturelle de Deardorff pour évaluer l'acquisition de connaissances, compétences et attitudes requises qui permettront aux élèves de devenir les futurs citoyens européens du 21ème siècle.

Mots-clés : Compétence Interculturelle, Assistanat Comenius

À l'époque de l'internationalisation et du mouvement continu d'employés, de cadres, de profs et d'élèves, l'acquisition de la compétence interculturelle par les jeunes constitue un besoin aussi impératif que leur formation professionnelle. Rendre capables les nouvelles générations de vivre et travailler avec succès dans n'importe quel endroit de l'Union Européenne à un certain moment de leur vie et de leur carrière semble un grand défi pour l'école contemporaine. L'orientation interculturelle de l'éducation impose l'intégration du concept de l'apprentissage tout au long de la vie dans toutes les étapes de l'enseignement secondaire à travers : la participation des établissements scolaires aux Programmes Européens, l'enseignement à l'aide de nouvelles technologies, la réalisation de mobilités d'élèves et de stages d'assistanat Comenius et l'enseignement systématique de Langues Étrangères.

La prise de conscience de la citoyenneté européenne et sa perception comme un lien entre les citoyens et l'UE destiné à favoriser l'identification des citoyens à l'UE et le développement d'une opinion publique et d'une identité européennes (Traité de Maastricht art. 9 TUE) constitue une priorité de l'école contemporaine visant au renforcement de l'esprit de tolérance, de coopération, de dialogue et de respect au sein de l'établissement scolaire ainsi qu'à l'extérieur de l'école.

Dans les textes européens, le dialogue interculturel ne renvoie pas uniquement à des valeurs, mais également à une fonction : il devient l'outil d'une éducation aux valeurs sociales et européennes fondatrices et garant d'une continuité. Dans cette perspective, la gestion de la diversité culturelle est conçue comme une source d'enrichissement mutuel, qui doit favoriser non seulement le dialogue interculturel, mais également le dialogue politique et interreligieux, grâce à des actions de coopération ciblées (Foucard & al, 2008)

Pour arriver à la création des futurs Citoyens Européens, l'école doit apprendre aux élèves à illustrer l'interdépendance au moyen d'exemples de leur propre monde, à examiner les intérêts opposés, à voir les positions des différents acteurs et à les comparer, à examiner et à évaluer l'exactitude et l'exhaustivité d'une situation ou d'un évènement, à illustrer le rôle des institutions internationales, à tirer des conclusions sur la malléabilité de la société et sur son propre rôle éventuel, à comprendre qu'il y a différentes visions sur la prospérité et la redistribution de cette prospérité (Association Européenne des Enseignants Programme SOCRATES n° 2001-0928/001-001 SO2 81COMP)

> Le cours de langue constitue un moment privilégié qui permet à l'apprenant de découvrir d'autres perceptions et classifications de la réalité, d'autres valeurs, d'autres modes de vie . . . Bref, apprendre une langue

étrangère, cela signifie entrer en contact avec une nouvelle culture. (Myriam Denis, *Dialogues et cultures* n° 44, 2000, p. 62).

Pourtant, l'évaluation de la compétence interculturelle obtenue par les élèves en classe de langue pendant les cours et après leur participation aux projets européens reste un problème dans le contexte européen où on tend à considérer que la responsabilité de l'intégration des individus incombe de manière prioritaire aux individus eux-mêmes (Abdallah-Pretceille, 1999, pp. 46–52) contrairement à la mise en place de programmes d'éducation multiculturelle dans les établissements scolaires et les universités des États-Unis et "la reconnaissance de l'importance de maintenir et valoriser le patrimoine multiculturel des Canadiens" (Parlement Canadien, 1988, p. 4). La majorité de professeurs responsables se limitent souvent à inventorier les compétences linguistiques acquises par leurs élèves et se déclarent hésitants à approfondir l'évaluation de la compétence interculturelle par manque d'obligation, d'inexistence de programmation et d'absence d'outils officiels. Ainsi, on se rend compte que la compétence interculturelle, probablement la plus essentielle du XXIe siècle se trouve à l'écart du système d'évaluation scolaire qui se limite à mesurer les connaissances requises par le programme disciplinaire.

Ayant comme point de départ cette constatation, nous avons réalisé une recherche sur le degré d'acquisition de la compétence interculturelle par des élèves dont les établissements scolaires organisent régulièrement de Programmes d'Assistanat Comenius en se basant sur des critères qualitatifs généraux résumés sous le binôme engagement – distanciation.

Nous avons d'abord examiné l'existence d'un engagement réel dans le dialogue interculturel qui fonde la base de tout apprentissage (Anquetil, 2006).

L'évaluation descriptive constitue l'essentiel du protocole car la description des compétences est conceptualisée dans le projet particulier mis en œuvre par l'étudiant afin d'en faire apparaître dans toute originalité (Anquetil, 2006).

Reste la nécessité de disposer d'un outil d'évaluation concret, permettant aux compétences interculturelles d'accéder à la reconnaissance académique, ce qui suppose de se plier aux normes de l'évaluation chiffrée avec un seuil d'acceptabilité (Zarate & Gohard, 2004)

Nous avons proposé une solution de compromis entre les contraintes institutionnelles et la prise de distance vis-à-vis de l'idéologisation et adopté comme méthode d'évaluation le modèle interculturel de Darla Deardorff.

LES PROGRAMMES EUROPÉENS D'ASSISTANAT COMENIUS.

Les Actions d'Assistanat Comenius se réalisent dans le cadre des Programmes Européens de l'Enseignement tout au Long de la Vie Comenius(EFLTV). Toute personne se destinant à la carrière d'enseignant ou de formateur, n'ayant jamais exercé et souhaitant poursuivre sa formation initiale peut aller exercer ses classes à l'étranger (dans un pays participant au programme EFLTV) afin d'acquérir ou développer des compétences pédagogiques, linguistiques etc. Une subvention lui est accordée par l'agence nationale de son pays d'origine dans le cadre de cette mobilité, pour une période allant de 13 à 45 semaines Les activités d'un assistant sont les suivantes:

Enseignement de la discipline à laquelle il souhaite se consacrer
Enseignement des langues vivantes qu'il maîtrise
Enseignement de sa langue et de sa culture d'origine
Développement de projets européens ou de partenariats
Soutien des apprenants en travail en groupe et en pédagogie de projet
Soutien des apprenants présentant des besoins éducatifs spécifiques
Informations sur son pays d'origine.
Introduction ou renforcement de la dimension européenne au sein de la structure d'accueil. (Dictionnaire collaboratif de l'Agence 2^{e}2f, 2010)

LA COMPÉTENCE INTERCULTURELLE ET L'APPROCHE DE DARLA DEARDORFF

Dans la recherche de définitions de la compétence interculturelle on constate qu'il y a une vaste problématique environnant ses composantes et son évaluation.

Kim (1992) considère que l'adaptabilité se trouve au cœur de la compétence communicative interculturelle et la définit comme la capacité d'une personne de suspendre ou modifier ses vieilles habitudes culturelles, à en apprendre et adopter de nouvelles aussi bien que de trouver de moyens créatifs pour gérer la dynamique de différences culturelles, du mal à l'aise, du stress qui s'en provoque (p. 377).

Byram (1997) dans son modèle de compétence communicative interculturelle constitué de cinq savoirs met l'accent sur l'importance de la langue et inclue dans sa conceptualisation la notion de l'identité et de la compréhension culturelle.

Selon Bertelsmann « la compétence interculturelle est la capacité d'interagir de manière efficace et appropriée dans des situations interculturelles, à partir de comportements, de connaissances, de compétences et d'une réflexion interculturelle spécifique » (Bertelsmann, 2006, 5).

Pour Paige(1993), 'l'effectivité interculturelle' constitue la question de base de la compétence de communication interculturelle.

On constate que pour tous les experts, la compétence interculturelle inclue les savoirs et les attitudes. La compétence linguistique est la seule qui soit remise en question. De même, il y a un accord général sur sa dynamique et le besoin qu'elle soit continuellement pratiquée.

Le Livre blanc souligne la nécessité de l'apprentissage et de l'enseignement des compétences interculturelles : *« Les compétences nécessaires au dialogue interculturel ne sont pas automatiquement maîtrisées : elles doivent être acquises, pratiquées et entretenues tout au long de la vie.* » (2008, 28)

Le modèle de ce processus d'apprentissage dynamique, selon Darla Deardorff, comporte quatre dimensions majeures de la compétence interculturelle: *les comportements* : la capacité à valoriser la diversité culturelle et à tolérer l'ambiguïté ; *les connaissances et aptitudes interculturelles,* comme *production interne* : la capacité à avoir une réflexion interculturelle et comme *production externe* : l'aptitude à se comporter et à communiquer d'une manière appropriée. On peut supposer que ces quatre dimensions s'influencent entre elles. Le niveau de compétences interculturelles s'accroît avec le nombre de ces dimensions qui sont maîtrisées et la fréquence avec laquelle elles sont sollicitées.

PUBLIC

Notre public se constitue de 100 élèves du 2ème Collège d'Edessa, capitale de la région de Pella dans la Grèce du Nord, et de deux professeurs de Français Langue Étrangère, responsables de programmes d'assistanat Comenius. L'endroit étant une zone agricole, limitrophe de l'Albanie et de la F.Y.R.O.M, les habitants de la région démontrent souvent des sentiments ethnocentriques et xénophobes. Un nombre considérable d'adolescents provenant de villages éloignés et montagneux, loin de se sentir citoyens européens, préfèrent être maîtres de leur microcosme que de s'ouvrir vers le reste du monde. Les ``étrangers`` pour eux ne sont que les immigrants économiques qui travaillent dans les champs et vivent dans des conditions de pauvreté. La langue et la culture grecque constituent le centre de leur univers et ils se méfient souvent de tout ce qui n'est pas grec.

Ainsi, la présence d'un jeune professeur provenant d'un autre pays de l'Union Européenne a d'abord provoqué une grande surprise aux élèves du collège mais aussi à la société locale. Leur étonnement a été encore plus grand quand de jeunes professeurs de couleur de nationalité française y sont arrivés pour enseigner dans leur collège et s'installer dans leur ville.

Les réactions, diverses et ambigües, ont été le début d'un changement de mentalité tant des élèves que de la société locale. Pour réaliser notre étude, nous avons choisi 4 classes que nous avons observées pendant les trois années du collège. Au total, notre échantillon était de 100 élèves âgés au début de notre recherche de 12 ans. Les deux professeurs responsables de programmes d'assistanat Comenius ont participé volontairement à notre recherche. Après avoir étudié le modèle de Deardorff ils se sont mis en accord de l'appliquer pour observer l'évolution de leurs élèves et constater si après trois années de contact continu avec des assistants provenant de France, Lituanie et Pologne, ils avaient développé des compétences interculturelles.

Méthodologie

D'abord, nous avons proposé aux professeurs l'utilisation d'une grille Annexe I, basée sur le modèle de compétence interculturelle Deardorff. Chaque enseignant a préparé des grilles pour tous ses élèves et les a complétées au début de l'étude, vers la fin du mois d'Octobre, pour pouvoir en avoir une image complète. En même temps, ils ont gardé un journal de classe dans lequel ils prenaient des notes sur le comportement des élèves. À la fin de la troisième année de collège, les professeurs ont rempli les mêmes grilles pour contrôler le degré d'acquisition de la compétence interculturelle par les élèves à l'aide aussi du journal de classe qui confirmait ou mettait en doute le rapport final concernant les résultats obtenus.

La grille notait du 1-5 les quatre catégories du modèle Deardorff:

- Les comportements: la capacité à valoriser la diversité culturelle et à tolérer l'ambiguïté
- Les connaissances et aptitudes interculturelles
- La production interne, c'est à dire la capacité à avoir une réflexion interculturelle
- La production externe, c'est à dire l'aptitude à se comporter et à communiquer d'une manière appropriée.

ANALYSE DES RÉSULTATS

Une fois les résultats rassemblés, ils ont été analysés. Les grilles ont été traitées dans une feuille Excel et les données ont été présentées sous forme de diagrammes. Les informations des journaux de classe ont été dépouillées, évaluées et mises en relation avec les diagrammes. Les conclusions ainsi tirées ont été présentées aux professeurs responsables qui ont été invités à donner leur opinion et faire des propositions.
Ainsi, nous avons fait les constatations suivantes :

En ce qui concerne *le comportement et la capacité des élèves à valoriser la diversité culturelle et à tolérer l'ambiguïté,* les élèves ont réalisé un progrès considérable.

Tableau 6-1

Les comportements		
Note	Nombre d'élèves Avant	Nombre d'élèves Après
1	5	
2	35	10
3	47	13
4	13	49
5		28

Au début de l'étude, 40% d'entre eux avait été noté entre 1 et 2 et aucun d'eux n'avait reçu la note maximale tandis que trois années après, 77% avaient été notés entre 4 et 5.

Les comportements

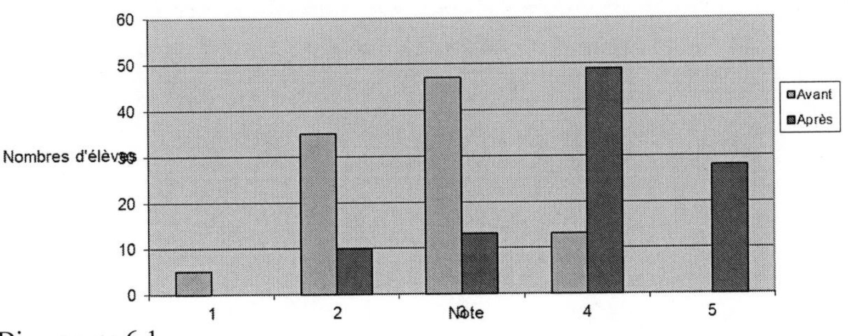

Diagramme 6-1

Selon les professeurs responsables, au début du collège, un nombre considérable d'élèves avait une réticence à collaborer avec le jeune assistant Comenius influencés par des stéréotypes du genre '*les Français sont sales'* , '*ils préfèrent leurs animaux domestiques à leurs enfants'*,'*ils ne mangent que de la viande saignante', 'ils boivent trop de vin'* ou bien des conceptions ethnocentrique comme *'les Européens sont Catholiques et pas Orthodoxes', 'les Français sont nationalistes, ils veulent que tout le monde parle leur langue', 'ils sont snobs', 'ils imposent leur culture aux autres.'* Au fur et à mesure, l'hésitation des élèves vis-à-vis des assistants a été remplacée par la volonté d'en connaitre plus sur leurs vies et leurs pays d'origine. Et l'acceptation du fait que quelqu'un se comporte d'une autre manière ou bien qu'il soit d'une couleur différente, tout en étant à la recherche des points communs, entre leur propre culture et celle des jeunes professeurs. De plus, ils ont commencé à faire des activités typiques des pays d'origine des assistants comme par exemple la canne de combat en France et à l' Île de la Réunion, ils ont appris à préparer des recettes polonaises et lituaniennes, ils se sont ouverts à la musique apportée par les assistants. S'en est suivi la volonté de répandre leurs nouvelles connaissances dans leur milieu familial et dans leur village.

En analysant les résultats sur *les connaissances et les aptitudes interculturelles* des élèves avant et après le programme d'assistanat, on constate que 63% des élèves avaient été initialement notés entre 1 et 2 tandis qu'à la fin de l'étude il n'y avait plus que 30% qui recevaient une notation défavorable.

Tableau 6-2

Les connaissances et aptitudes interculturelles		
Note	Nombre d'élèves Avant	Nombre d'élèves Après
1	25	8
2	38	22
3	32	25
4	5	41
5		4

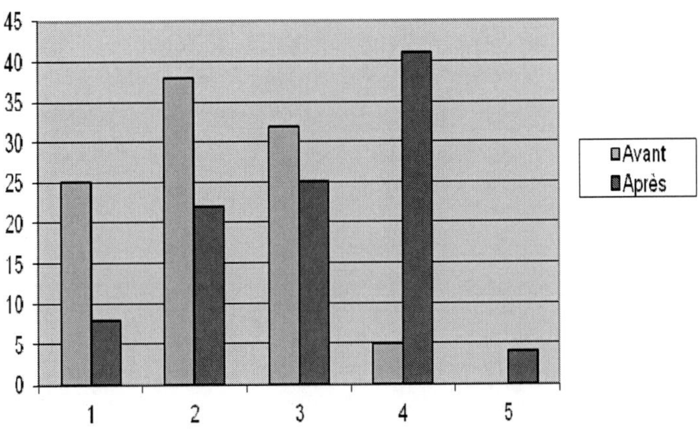

Diagramme 6-2

De plus, 45% finissent le collège avec une note comprise entre 4 et 5, contre 5% au début. Les professeurs impliqués ont constaté que la majorité des élèves a fait preuve d'un vif intérêt concernant les connaissances linguistique, la civilisation et le pays d'origine des assistants. Certains d'entre eux ont même réussi à les utiliser pour améliorer la communication avec leur professeur-assistant en essayant de mieux comprendre sa manière de pensée, ses points de vue, ses attentes et sa façon de voire le monde. Les professeurs titulaires ont pu se rendre compte que les élèves avec un niveau linguistique et d'instruction avancé ont réussi plus facilement à développer des aptitudes interculturelles. Cependant, durant les trois années de participation au programme, même les élèves moins forts mais motivés ont mis en pratique toutes leurs aptitudes (connaissances sur les sports, la musique, le cinéma) pour communiquer avec les assistants.

Production interne - Capacité à avoir une réflexion interculturelle

À ce point on constate un changement considérable chez les adolescents participants aux projets d'assistanat.

Tableau 6-3

Capacité à avoir une réflexion interculturelle		
Note	Nombre d'élèves Avant	Nombre d'élèves Après
1	22	9
2	46	17
3	30	25
4	2	41
5		8

De 68% d'élèves à avoir un niveau très bas de réflexion interculturelle au début du programme, 49% d'entre eux ont évolué en interlocuteurs de haute compétence. On peut donc dire que l'Assistanat Comenius a aidé les jeunes adolescents à s'adapter à une nouvelle réalité, dans laquelle chaque citoyen de l'Union Européenne doit développer une attitude tolérante et ouverte, une envie de comprendre l'autre, une volonté de s'intégrer dans la société européenne et communiquer d'une manière efficace avec ses concitoyens. On constate aussi que la majorité des élèves a réussi à mettre en pratique les connaissances de nature interculturelle qu'ils acquéraient au fur et à mesure du programme d'assistanat en développant une relation d'amitié, de collaboration et compréhension mutuelle avec de personnes provenant de pays, de cultures et de mentalités différentes.

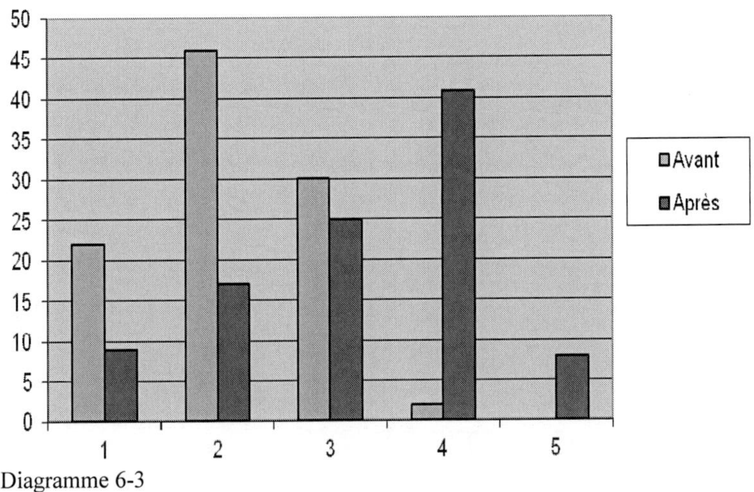

Diagramme 6-3

PRODUCTION EXTERNE - APTITUDE À SE COMPORTER ET À COMMUNIQUER D'UNE MANIÈRE APPROPRIÉE

Le point culminant de la pyramide de Deardorff est constitué de la synthèse des composantes préalables et leur application appropriée qui se reflète dans l'atteinte d'un haut niveau de communication avec de personnes appartenant à des cultures et mentalités différentes. Pendant cette phase finale d'acquisition de la compétence interculturelle, on contrôle à quel degré les élèves sont capables de s'adapter et d'agir dans des conditions socioculturelles, émotionnelles, professionnelles, pédagogiques qui ne coïncident pas avec les leurs. Dans notre cas, le taux élevé d'adolescents d'abord incapables de se comporter d'une manière appropriée avec des personnes appartenant à une autre culture (74%) s'est très fortement atténué (26%) et a été remplacé par 59% ayant un niveau de communication interculturelle moyen et 15% très bon.

Aptitude à se comporter et à communiquer d'une manière appropriée.

Note	Nombre d'élèves Avant	Nombre d'élèves Après
1	34	7
2	40	19
3	20	59
4	6	11
5		4

Tableau 6-4

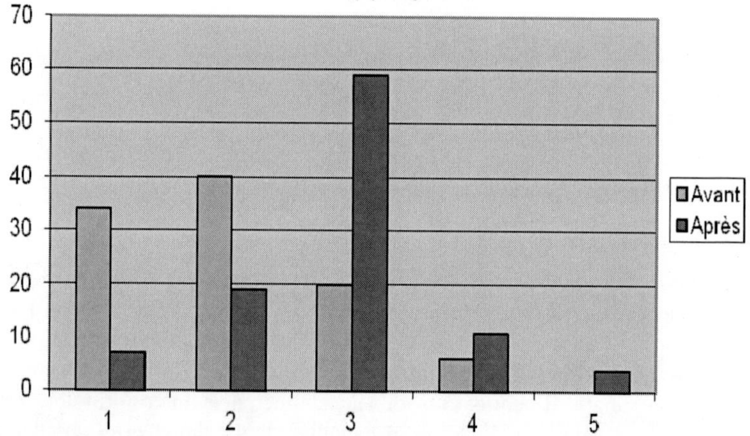

Diagramme 6-4

En interprétant les informations fournies par les journaux de classe, on constate que le comportement des élèves est devenu de plus en plus flexible vis-à-vis des assistants qui arrivaient dans leur école. Ils ont réussi à ne plus être choqués par la différence (que quelqu'un soit noir, musulman, qu'il vienne d'un pays ex communiste ou qu'il ait un serpent comme animal domestique). Et ont apprécié la chance de connaître des personnes différentes et d'en savoir plus sur leur mode de vie, croyances, idées etc. Ils ont également été sensibilisés (et certains adhérer) à de comportements qu'ils ont considérés positifs (respecter la distance personnelle, diner plus tôt, être plus sensibles envers les animaux, pratiquer le recyclage dans la vie quotidienne etc.). Dans un même temps, ils ont mis en évidence leurs propres valeurs culturelles et ont entamé une réflexion sur ce qu'ils considéraient comme une normalité (en Grèce on peut être en retard à un rendez-vous mais c'est normal, les élèves se couchent tard - c'est à cause du climat, on ne porte pas de casque sur la mobylette - s'est plus chic, on brûle souvent le feu rouge - c'est parce qu'ils sont de bons chauffeurs, on fume encore dans les restaurants – les Grecs ne se compromettent jamais etc.). De l'autre, ils ont réussi à bénéficier de la dynamique de la différence en ajustant leur comportement aux attentes et aux besoins de leurs interlocuteurs. Ils ont relativisé leurs propres croyances et points de vue et se sont efforcés de trouver les moyens pour s'approcher de l'assistant et de son univers socioculturel. Cette ouverture les a aidés à mieux comprendre l'autre et à améliorer leur compétence de communication non seulement avec les personnes étrangères mais aussi avec leurs concitoyens. Le bagage culturel acquis à l'occasion du contact de jeunes adolescents avec les assistants a contribué à l'enrichissement de leur microcosme, au renforcement de leur personnalité et à l'amélioration de leur capacité de communication. L'acquisition de connaissances sur l'île de la Réunion a aidé les élèves non seulement à élargir leur horizon culturel mais aussi de mieux communiquer avec l'assistant français (provenant d'une ville aux cascades, les adolescents ont trouvé assez de points commun avec le jeune professeur, l'ont fait visiter les chutes d'eau, lui ont demandé d'initier un projet sur l'eau et sa dynamique. Pareillement, les chansons russes ont constitué un point de départ pour une longue relation d'amitié entre les élèves et l'assistant lithuanienne qui ont organisé un spectacle musical pour leurs amis Comenius de la Belgique. Dans le même esprit, les élèves de classes au profil sportif du collège ont développé une communication effective avec un assistant français qui était sportif et qui désirait entrainer les enfants les après-midis, après l'école. L'amour de l'assistante polonaise pour le cinéma a constitué le début d'une grande amitié entre celle-ci et les élèves qui ont reconnu dans son visage la personne qui leur donnerait la chance de combiner l'apprentissage de la langue étrangère avec leur loisir le plus pratiqué : le cinéma. La faculté d'adaptation a été renforcée chez presque tous les élèves à travers les programmes d'assistanat. Ils ont réussi à pénétrer dans le système de l'Autre et à décoder correctement les messages de l'interlocuteur. Comme mentionné dans les journaux de classe, les élèves se sont rendu compte que la distance personnelle désirée par les assistants était un trait culturel et pas un signe de mécontentement ou bien que la notion du bruit et du volume de la voix est relative et pouvait créer de malentendus en cas d'exc. Ils ont acquis des aptitudes pratiques qui les ont aidés à s'ajuster au contexte culturel d'autrui. Dans les journaux de classe on retrouve les commentaires des enseignants sur la flexibilité des élèves dans des situations subtiles où les assistants font preuve d'ethnocentrisme. Le commentaire d'un assistant français selon lequel 'les Grecs sont les plus grands corrupteurs' a été traité avec sagesse par une élève qui lui a répondu que c'était un sujet intéressant à discuter et a demandé à son professeur d'en organiser un débat. À ce point, il faudrait mentionner que les réactions habituelles des élèves dans de cas pareils étaient du genre 'Et bien, si vous n'aimez pas la Grèce, allez-vous-en!' ou 'Êtes-vous vraiment meilleurs?' ou 'Nous ne voulons pas changer. Nous sommes comme ça, nous menons une vie libre et vous en êtes jaloux!'

Conclusion

En faisant le bilan de notre recherche, nous nous sommes efforcés de répondre aux questions suivantes :

- Est-ce que les professeurs ont été facilités par l'utilisation du modèle de Deardorff pour mesurer la compétence interculturelle de leurs élèves?
- Est-ce que les programmes d'Assistanat Comenius ont aidé les élèves participants à devenir inter-culturellement compétents?
- Quels sont les propositions des professeurs responsables de programmes européens pour que les élèves développent la compétence interculturelle?

Utilisation du modèle Deardorff

Le choix du modèle Deardorff a été fait après une longue recherche bibliographique. Nous avons décidé de l'utiliser parce qu'il constituait un outil flexible qui pouvait être ajusté aux besoins particuliers de publics différents. Sa structure dynamique, le passage de l'évaluation de traits concrets (comportements, capacité de faire face à la diversité culturelle, connaissances et aptitudes interculturelles,) à des notions plus complexes (production interne, réflexion interculturelle, production externe, communication et comportement approprié) ont démontré que le modèle de Deardorff constitue un instrument pratique et exploitable par tous ceux qui travaillent dans l'enseignement interculturel.

La création des grilles n'a pas posé de problèmes particuliers aux enseignants. D'abord, ils se sont mis en accord sur les éléments à évaluer pendant chaque étape Ensuite, ils les ont conçues et distribuées aux élèves, une fois au début du collège et une autre à la fin de leurs études.

Dans le même esprit, ils ont complété leur observation en remplissant un journal de classe pour noter tout changement d'attitude des élèves, incident ou évènement dans la classe ou dehors les cours qui pourrait enluminer le progrès des élèves sur le plan interculturel. L'ajournement était systématique et se faisait régulièrement au moins une fois par semaine.

La suite des étapes du modèle de Deardorff a facilité le dépouillement des grilles et des journaux de classe.

Les professeurs qui ont participé à l'étude ont décidé de le réutiliser pour évaluer la compétence interculturelle de leurs élèves même sous d'autres formes (questionnaires et journaux de bord remplis par les élèves, interview avec certains d'entre eux, interviews avec les assistants pour observer l'impact de la compétence interculturelle acquise par les élèves sur le public cible.

Les Programmes d'Assistanat dans l'enseignement secondaire

Notre étude a démontré l'impact et l'importance des programmes d'Assistanat Comenius dans l'enseignement secondaire sur le plan interculturel. Le contact des élèves avec de jeunes professeurs provenant d'autres pays de l'Union Européenne les a aidés considérablement à s'ouvrir vers le reste du monde, se débarrasser des sentiments ethnocentriques et redéfinir leurs attitudes et croyances sur la citoyenneté européenne. L'analyse des grilles a démontré que tous les élèves ont été favorisés par leur collaboration avec les assistants. Plus concrètement, tandis qu'au début du programme, 20 élèves seulement recevaient une note de 3 pour leur capacité à se comporter et communiquer d'une manière appropriée, à la fin de l'étude ils y en avait 59.

La réussite des programmes d'assistanat sur le plan interculturel devient encore plus évidente si on prend en considération les relations amicales développées entre les élèves et les assistants et entretenues jusqu'à présent, la volonté des membres de la communauté scolaire de visiter les pays d'origine de jeunes professeurs, le changement du comportement, de la mentalité et de la personnalité des élèves (acquisition d'empathie, tolérance, compréhension vers l'Autre, acceptation de la différence, volonté de vivre et collaborer avec des personnes d'origine et culture différente, désir continuel d'acquérir de nouvelles connaissances)

Propositions des professeurs responsables

Après leur longue expérience de mentorat, les professeurs responsables ont exprimé unanimement leur volonté de continuer à organiser ce genre de programmes en mettant l'accent sur les bénéfices qui en résultent tant pour les élèves que pour les établissements scolaires Le développement de la compétence interculturelle, question de base pour tous les futurs citoyens européens est étroitement liée à l'ouverture de l'école vers la société européenne. Ainsi, la réalisation de stages d'assistanat, l'organisation de programmes d'échanges et la formation des professeurs à travers de séminaires pour l'insertion des innovations dans le curriculum scolaire constituent des actions financées par le Conseil de l'Europe qui visent à l'atteinte de plus hauts buts pédagogiques et interculturels aussi bien qu'à la promotion de la Dimension Européenne dans l'Enseignement Secondaire. On peut donc dire que :

Les Programmes d'Assistanat Comenius devraient se réaliser dans toutes les écoles, surtout dans celles évoluant en zones moins favorisées. La présence d'un assistant au milieu scolaire permet l'intégration de nouvelles méthodes pédagogiques dans le curriculum classique (pédagogie différenciée, introduction de nouvelles technologies en classe de langue, enseignement interculturel, organisation de classes d'immersion etc.)

Les programme d'assistanat devraient être appliqués parallèlement aux autres Actions Comenius (Projets Multilatéraux et Linguistiques, travail sur la plateforme E-twinning, stages de formation de professeurs). Faisant part du Programme d'Apprentissage tout au Long de la Vie, ils doivent être abordés par les professeurs – mentors comme un processus dynamique de formation de jeunes professeurs, d'application du concept de la pédagogie du projet dans la classe de langue, d'acquisition de la compétence interculturelle par tous les élèves de l'établissement scolaire, de création de nouvelles générations de citoyens européens.

Dans tous les cas, l'évaluation de la compétence interculturelle acquise par les élèves devrait être évaluée systématiquement avec soin en utilisant de méthodes testées et adaptables selon les conditions spécifiques de chaque école. Utiliser plusieurs types d'évaluation (formative, sommative, holistique, auto-évaluation) du début jusqu'à l'accomplissement des programmes semble la solution la plus valable pour contrôler le degré de réussite, redéfinir les buts, planifier de nouvelles activités, dépister et analyser les fautes commises, réduire les inconvénients et atteindre le maximum de rentabilité sur le plan pédagogique et interculturel

Le plus grand défi de l'École du 21ème siècle constitue sans doute la création de nouvelles générations d'élèves pour lesquels l'Altérité représente une source d'inspiration, une occasion de création d'une voie commune de coexistence et collaboration dans un milieu géographique, social et productif commun : l'Europe.

Dans sa pièce «Huis clos», Jean-Paul Sartre montre que l'homme ne se connaît lui-même que grâce à l'existence des Autres. Il nous faut un Autre pour pouvoir nous regarder dans ses yeux comme dans un miroir. C'est le fameux effet de miroir: sans l'existence des Autres, nous ne pourrions pas prendre conscience de notre propre identité, de notre propre culture, nous ne saurions pas qui nous sommes. C'est justement ce processus en miroir qui donne lieu à l'espace interculturel. Car la tolérance ou plutôt l'acceptation d'autres cultures passe par la prise de conscience de notre propre identité culturelle.

BIBLIOGRAPHIE

Abdallah-Pretceille, M., 1999. *L'éducation interculturelle*. Paris : PUF, Que sais-je?

Anquetil M., 2006. *Mobilité Erasmus et communication interculturelle*. Bern: Peter Lang

Byram, M. (1997). *Teaching and assessing intercultural communicative competence*.

Clevedon: Multilingual Matters.

Foucard M., Lawes S., Niclot D., 2008 *Un outil pour préparer les futures enseignants en formation à la dimension interculturelle de la mobilité internationale* dans *Échanges et mobilités académiques – Quel bilan ?* Paris : L'Harmattan

Livre blanc sur le dialogue interculturel du Conseil de l'Europe « Vivre ensemble dans l'égale dignité ». Lancé par les ministres des Affaires étrangères du Conseil de l'Europe à leur 118e réunion ministérielle (Strasbourg, 7 mai 2008). Strasbourg : Éditions du Conseil de l'Europe.

Kim, Y.Y., & Ruben, B. D. (1992). Intercultural transformation. In W.B. Gudykunst & Y.Y. Kim (Eds.), *Readings on communicating with strangers: An approach to intercultural communication* (pp. 401-414). New York: McGraw-Hill.

Paige, R. M. (Ed.). (1993). *Education for the intercultural experience*. Yarmouth, ME: Intercultural Press.

Twentieth Century French Texts, Jean-Paul Sartre, Huis Clos, Pièce en un acte (1976) Keith Gore. Oxford

Zarate G., & Gohard-Radenkovic, A. 2004. *La reconnaissance des compétences interculturelles : de la grille à la carte*. Sèvres : Cahiers du CIEP.

Articles en Revues

Denis, M. (2000) Dialogues et cultures n° 44,p. 62

Articles de conférences

Conseil de l'Europe – Rencontre des 29 et 30 juin 2009 Schreiner , P. « La formation à la compréhension du fait religieux et des convictions non religieuses : fondements et pistes d'action pour une coexistence citoyenne.

Citations Web

Association Européenne des Enseignants Programme SOCRATES n° 2001-0928/001-001 SO2 81COMP) http://www.aede.eu/fileadmin/docs/news/citeuract_fr.pdf

Bertelsmann Foundation (Hg) (2006): *Intercultural Competence – The key competence for the 21st century?* http://www.bertelsmann-stiftung.de/cps/rde/xchg/SID-2E1CD0C4-2AFD6F77/bst/hs.xsl/11187.htm

Deardorff, D. (2006). "Identification and assessment of intercultural competence as a student outcome of internationalization". *Journal of Studies in International Education* 10 (3), 241266.

Dictionnaire collaboratif de l'Agence 2e2f ,2010) http://www.europe-education-formation.fr/comenius-assistants.php

Parlement Canadien, 1988 : 4 http://www.parl.gc.ca/Content/LOP/ResearchPublications/prb0920-e.pdf

Traité de Maastricht art. 9 TUE http://www.vie-publique.fr/decouverte-institutions/union-europeenne/ue-citoyennete/citoyennete-europeenne/qui-est-citoyen-europeen.html

IS EUROPE THE PROBLEM OR THE SOLUTION? AN ANALYSIS OF EUROSCEPTICISM IN ROMANIA

PAUL DOBRESCU, FLAVIA DURACH AND ALINA BÂRGĂOANU

Abstract

This paper addresses the level of Euroscepticism in Romanian society in a particular context: the request made by the French and German Ministers of Internal Affairs on 21 December to delay Romania's accession to the Schengen area. The issue was hotly debated in Romanian society. We tested the influence of this topic on Euroscepticism and the way Romanian citizens relate to the European Union in general by conducting a survey between 14 and 19 January 2011. The results show a decrease in the level of Euroenthusiasm, compared to the moment of EU accession in 2007, as citizen contact with the real EU deepened. Nevertheless, the level of trust in the European Union remains rather high and is associated with high levels of education and income. The survey showed that the higher the interest in the Schengen issue, the higher the trust in the EU, due to an increased level of knowledge about the EU in general. Despite such encouraging results, the majority of Romanians do not feel they share a European identity, suggesting the process of integration has not gone much further beyond actual accession. The first section of our paper is dedicated to the existing literature on Euroscepticism: conceptualization, causes and explanatory mechanisms. The results of the survey are presented in the second half of this paper, together with some analysis of the trends shown in Eurobarometers.

Key words: Euroenthusiasm, Euroscepticism, Romania's accession to the Schengen Area, European identity, European Union

THE CONCEPT OF "EUROSCEPTICISM"

In a statement made by the Council for the Future of Europe, in September 2011, the members of the committee openly admitted that the European Union is standing at a crossroad (Europe is the solution, not the problem, 6 September 2011). The statement explicitly describes citizens as "disconnected and alienated from the abstract processes in Brussels" (Europe is the solution, not the problem, 6 September 2011, p. 2) and warns European leaders about the difficulty of engaging the doubts and anxieties of European citizens. The vision of Europe that will succeed, according to the document, is that which "inspires the commitment of its citizens whose faith in a European future is shaken" (*ibid.*). We have chosen to open our discussion with this particular quote because it sheds light on the current meanings of Euroscepticism. In a European Union shaken by the crisis and uncertain of what its future, feelings of Euroscepticism can ruin the very delicate balance of public opinion.

The problem is, to some extent, related to the current economic and financial crisis, but the phenomenon itself is not new. The origins of the term "Euroscepticism" can be traced back in the British political discourse, which is traditionally associated with a strong opposition to the process of European integration. It became a significant political force in French and especially in the Danish referenda on Maastricht, which opened up both political elite and academic discourses on the importance of public opinion in the process of integration (Milner, 2000, in Taggart & Szczerbiak, 2008, p. 4).

The literature on Euroscepticism has developed under the influence of several factors. First of all, there has been a decline of permissive consensus (starting with difficulties in ratifying the Maastricht treaty). Second, the tendency to resort to referendums to ratify treaties has turned into an opportunity for citizens to express their feelings of discontent or scepticism. The most visible expression of the phenomenon took place in the summer of 2005, when France and Holland firmly rejected the project of the Constitutional Treaty. Third, the enlargement of the EU and the crisis led to new patterns of politics and ways of perceiving and debating the European issue (Taggart & Szczerbiak, 2008, p. 3). The arguments of Eurosceptics are numerous, but they all gravitate around the following: European institutions are too strong and lack transparency, the European super-state has become distant from its citizens, the EU supports unpopular politics, the sovereignty of the national state is threatened, European requirements are not fully applicable to developing economies in Central and Eastern Europe (Bârgăoanu, 2011, pp. 42–43).

From the various definitions of the term "Euroscepticism" suggested in literature, probably the most cited is that of Paul Taggart: Euroscepticism is conceptualized as "contingent or a qualified opposition, as well as incorporating outright and unqualified opposition to the process of European integration" (Taggart & Szerbiak, 2008, p. 7). The author also distinguishes between the "hard" and "soft" expressions of Euroscepticism. "Hard Euroskepticism is a principled opposition to the EU and European integration and therefore can be seen in parties who think that their countries should withdraw from membership, or whose policies toward the EU are tantamount to being opposed to the whole project of European integration." Party-based soft Euroscepticism is characterized by opposition not to European integration or to EU membership, but to one or many policies which indicate "a sense that national interest is currently at odds with the EU trajectory" (Taggart & Szczerbiak, 2003: 2).

Many scholars have focused on the conceptualization of Euroscepticism, with notable results. We have mentioned Taggart's distinction between soft and hard Euroskepticism. Petr Kopecky & Cas Mudde (2002) responded to the initial hard and soft distinction with a critique that emphasized the difference between underlying attitudes regarding European integration or the EU, and came up with a fourfold distinction between Euroenthusiasts, Eurorejects, Eurosceptics, and Europragmatists (Kopecky & Mudde, 2002, p. 303).

Abts and Krouwel (2007) suggest that Eurosceptics may differ in intensity and in their arguments for opposing the European Union (EU), by focusing their critiques on different political targets and/or aspects of Europeanization. These authors try to expand upon existing research on popular Euroscepticism by developing a two-dimensional conceptualization that allows them to simultaneously investigate the targets *and* the degree of popular discontent towards the EU and the European integration. By combining targets and the degree of discontent, the structure of European attitudes can be described as a sliding scale of political attitudes ranging from confidence and scepticism to distrust, cynicism and alienation.

Another conceptualization of contemporary Euroscepticism integrates existing theoretical insights with public opinion and legitimacy with targeted empirical indicators, establishing four categories: economic, sovereignty-based, democratic and social Euroscepticism. Each type assumes a distinct degree of intensity (Sørensen, 2008, p. 87).

EUROSCEPTICISM: SOURCES, CAUSES AND EXPLANATIONS

The debate has also expanded into another area: identifying the sources, causes and possible explanations for Euroskepticism. Gabel (1998) describes and tests the validity of five theories and explains why public support varies. The first theory (cognitive mobilization) involves the relationship between the citizens' cognitive skills and their attitudes toward European integration. Ronald Inglehart (1970, in Gabel, 1998, p. 335), who first investigated this relationship, argued that high cognitive mobilization, characterized by a high level of political awareness and well developed skills in political communication, enables citizens to identify with a supranational political community. As a citizen's cognitive mobilization increases, (s)he is more familiar with and less threatened by the topic of European integration.

The second theory, political values, posits that support for European integration is associated with values economic and political issues. According to the theory, citizens' political attitudes are shaped by the socioeconomic conditions surrounding their formative or pre-adult years, when the person adheres to certain values and attitudes. Citizens with post materialist values should be more supportive of European integration than those with materialist values (Gabel, 1998, p. 336).

The utilitarian model of public support for European integration first proposed by Gabel & Palmer (1995, in Gabel, 1998, p. 336) argued that EU citizens in different socioeconomic situations experience different costs and benefits from integrative policy; that these differences in economic welfare shape their attitudes toward integration; and consequently, that citizen support of integration is positively related to their welfare gains from integrative policy. The utilitarian theory is improved by the concept of "political allegiance", formally defined as

> the willingness of a national public to approve of and to support the decisions made by a government, in return for a more or less immediate and straightforward reward or benefit to which the public feels entitled on the basis of it having rendered approval and support. (van Kersbergen & Netjes, 2005, p. 11)

The support for European integration translates into the evaluation of citizens of the extent to which supranational institutions allow national political elites to provide political, social, psychological and economic security and well-being.

The fourth theory is related to class partisanship: citizens adopt attitudes towards integration that reflect the position of the party they support (Gabel, 1998, p. 338). Another group of scholars posits that parties play a different role in shaping public support for integration. Several studies by Franklin and other scholars argued that voters tie their support for integration to their support for their government (the presidency in France) (Gabel, 1998, p. 339). After empirically testing the five theories, Gabel concludes that the utilitarian theory and the class partisanship theory provide a robust explanation for variation in support for integration. The political values and cognitive mobilization theories only clearly provide valid explanations for citizens in the original EU member states.

Other research focuses on the formation of opinions in the public sphere and the role played by the media. The work of Trenz et. al. (2010) shifts attention from diffuse, non-articulated and isolated attitudes on European integration to targeted, publically articulated and frequently justified statements as elements of the ongoing discourse on EU public legitimacy. By analysing online media during the European Parliament elections, the authors approach Euroscepticism as part of "existential debates" contesting the EU or European integration in terms of polity. The authors found that the democratic function of European Parliamentary elections is met to a limited extent only. Online campaigning reinforces the electoral disconnect between EU citizens and the EU policy-making process by focusing either on domestic campaigns or on existential issues concerning the legitimacy of the EU. Euroskepticism is a form of opposition that relies on media infrastructures for salience or amplification (Trenz et al., 2010, p. 17).

Claes de Vreese (2005) analysed how the media influence the variation of public support for European integration. Cynicism at the level of the political debate and political elites may help to understand why citizens do not support or even reject specific policy proposals, such as those proposed by referenda. More precisely, exposure to strategic news (news that focuses on winning and losing and is driven by "war and games" language) leads to Euro-cynicism. However, this effect is conditional upon two factors: the pervasiveness of strategically framed news reporting and characteristics of individuals, such as the degree of political sophistication (de Vreese, 2005, pp. 12–13).

Whatever explanatory mechanisms scholars can find for Euroscepticism, one solid fact remains: the level of popular enthusiasm has dropped severely in recent years, thus questioning both the efficacy of the European institutions and their communication with regular citizens.

THE ECONOMIC CRISIS: RESHAPING EUROPE

Recently, criticism and contestation of the integration process and the European Union have intensified. The political consensus over European integration has constantly eroded. In Britain, for example, anti-EU sentiment is deepening with the European financial crisis rumbling on. Two polls — one by YouGov for PoliticsHome (www.politicshome.com, 13 July 2011) and the other by Angus Reid (http://www.angus-reid.com, 12 July 2011) – show that 50% of the public would vote for Britain to leave the EU in the case of a referendum. And for the first time in history, the suggestion of a referendum to decide whether or not Great Britain should leave the EU has been subjected to a vote in the national Parliament, but failed to gather the necessary number of votes (BBC News website, 25 October 2011).

Analysts say that, a decade after swapping the mighty Deutschmark for the euro, the once fiercely pro-euro Germans are becoming more Eurosceptic. A poll by the German Marshall Fund published in September 2011 found that 76% of Germans were in favour of the European Union, but support dropped to to 48% when asked about the monetary union (www.eubusiness.com, 18 September 2011).

Germany is not the only Eurosceptic country, of course. But due to its size and the special role it played in European integration, "its Eurosceptic shift has greater consequences for Europe as a whole than that of some other member states" (Leonard & Guérot, 2011: 4). Leonard & Guérot (2011) talk about a new Germany, more assertive and more nationalist. German elites tend to see the German economic and monetary model as the *only* solution for overcoming the euro crisis. Germany's economic base has also shifted away from Europe towards the so-called BRICs. As a result of these long-term changes in Germany since reunification, Euroskepticism has become more socially acceptable, if not chic. Germany's temptation to "go it alone" has led to coalitions of member states against and in favor of Germany (idem, 7). In the authors' opinion, the other member states should develop "incentives for Germany to play a more positive role within the EU": a new deal on economic governance within the EU, a new approach to regional security, and a vision for a global Europe that advances the interests of all member states in dealings with rising powers such as China.

Beyond Germany, the crisis has amplified the hostility towards the European project and the process of European integration all across the continent. Just before his country took the 6-month presidency of the EU, the Polish prime-minister Donald Tusk pointed to France and Italy in his criticism of fresh border restrictions in the passport-free Schengen zone after Tunisian migrants began crossing the Mediterranean en masse and warned at an event in Warsaw on 1 July 2011 that:

> The union is going through one of the most difficult and complicated moments in its history. When I speak of a new Euroskepticism, I am not talking about traditional Euroskepticism as in [the UK] . . . I am talking about the birth of a phenomenon which does not declare itself. I mean the behavior of politicians who say they support the EU and integration but at the same time take steps that weaken the union. (euobserver.com, 1 July 2011)

The economic problems that the Union faces are expected to divide member states. But even the recovery solutions have the same wicked effect. In his recent work, Jürgen Habermas (2011, pp. 83–89) emphasized that the measures intended to correct the flawed design of the euro zone will only continue to alienate European citizens. Referring to the intergovernmental agreement on economic policies, the author explains:

> As long as European citizens only see their national governments as actors on the European stage, they will continue to see the decision-making processes as zero-sum games in which they simply have to stand their ground. Their national heroes line up against the "others", who are to blame for everything imposed on or demanded from "them" by the Brussels monster. Only by seeing the parliament in Strasbourg as made up of parties rather than nations will European citizens ever come to see the task of economic governance as a common challenge. (Habermas, 2011, p. 85)

The political elites of Europe are worried about the effects of the crisis on the European Union. The crisis has led to a paradox: the revival of individualism and nationalism in politics, but also a high level of concern with policy design in this new context. It seems that Europe will never be the same again.

Euroscepticism in Romania

Up to this point of our paper, we have discussed the main theoretical approaches to Euroskepticism and the practical implications of the financial and economic crisis on the degree of support towards the EU. An assessment of the degree of Euroscepticism in Romania follows below.

Context

The research on the degree of Euroscepticism among Romanian citizens, as presented in this paper, is part of a larger research project carried out between 10 January and 22 March 2011 by the Centre of Research in Communication, at the College of Communication and Public Relations (The National School of Administrative and Political Studies, Bucharest). The project took advantage of a particular context in Romania: the negotiations for the country's accession to the Schengen area of free movement and the letter publicized by the French and German Ministers of Internal Affairs on 21 December 2010 in which the two officials requested a delay in Romania's and Bulgaria's accession to the Schengen area, originally intended for the spring of 2011.

The research project covered the following areas: the coverage of the Schengen subject in mass-media in France, Germany, Great Britain, Bulgaria and Hungary, media coverage and framing in Romania (news and talk-shows on TV and articles published by news websites), the public perception on the matter and the opinion of ten Romanian high-profile actors involved in EU affairs. The public perception on Romania's accession was measured through a survey that shows interesting results concerning the public knowledge and attitudes regarding the EU and the degree of Euroscepticism.

Methodology

This paper addresses two major areas:

1. The evolution of Euroscepticism in Romania and in the European Union, as recorded by Eurobarometers between spring 2007 and spring 2011 (with an emphasis on the influence of the financial and economic crisis)

and

2. The level of Euroscepticism in Romania, in the context of the Schengen issue.

The first issue is addressed by using secondary data analysis of Eurobarometers. In the case of the second issue, data analyzed result from a phone survey conducted on a national sample of 1168 individuals, with a margin of error of +/-2,9%, between 14 and 19 January 2011.

Romania's level of Euroscepticism – Eurobarometer results

In this section of the paper we will compare results from standard Eurobarometers during 2007–2011, in order to depict the evolution of Euroskepticism and to find out which are the current trends. We will take into consideration 5 indicators of degree of Euroenthusiasm (or its opposite – Euroscepticism): trust in the EU versus trust in national institutions, the estimation regarding the right/wrong direction, the perceived benefits of EU membership, the support for EU policies, the attitude towards the future of the EU. Eurobarometers indicate a constant decrease in trust in the European Union, both at the European level and in Romania.

In the fall of 2007, less than a year after Romania's accession to the EU, 68% of Romanians stated that they trust the EU, 20% above the European average. In comparison, the survey conducted in the neighbor state, Bulgaria, indicated that only 58% of citizens admitted trusting the EU. Nevertheless, Romanians' degree of trust has decreased constantly since 2007, with the only exception in 2009, as shown in the chart below. The lowest trust was recorded in 2010, when only 54% of respondents answered they trust the EU. But even then, the degree of trust was 10% above the European average of 42% in the spring of 2010 and 43% in the fall of the same year.

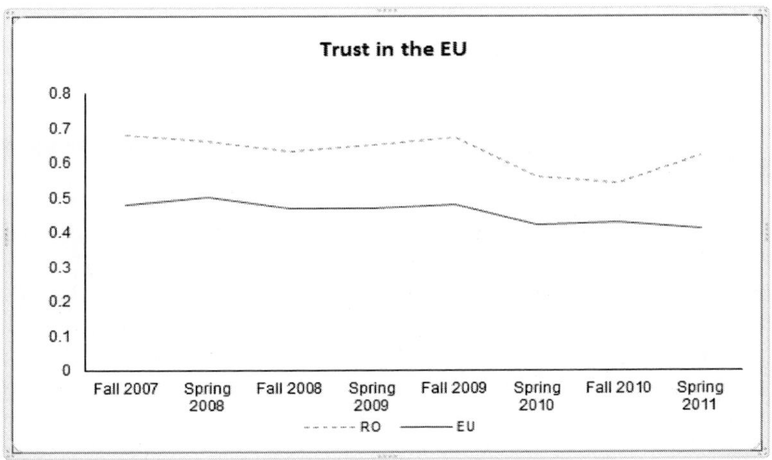

Fig 7-1. Evolution of trust in the EU: Romania vs the European average

Nevertheless, Romania is still above the European average when it comes to trusting the EU. The two founding states, France and Germany, show significantly lower levels of trust: starting from 51% and 56% in spring 2007 (EB 67), constantly declining to 39 and 36% in 2010 (EB 74), to a historical low of 39% and 35% in spring 2011 (EB 75). In the most recent Eurobarometer (EB 75, spring 2011), trust in the EU prevails in 16 countries and stands more higher than 50% in 14 member states, with the highest levels in Romania (62%), Estonia (61%), Slovakia (61%) and Belgium (61%). Trust is under 50% in 10 member states (compared to 6 member states in the previous survey), including the UK (23%), France (39%) and Germany (35%). Overall, the EU27 average of trust is 41%, two points lower than in 2010.

There is a significant increase in trust in the European Union in Romania (+8 points), Austria (+6 points), Cyprus (+5 points), Ireland (+5 points), the United Kingdom (+4 points) and Finland (+4 points). In contrast, there is a clearly noticeable deterioration of trust in Slovakia (−10 points), Lithuania (−9 points), Latvia (−8 points), Hungary (−8 points), Poland (−6 points) and Portugal (−6 points).

EB75 (spring 2011) indicates that the perceptions of Europeans are in line with the actual economic situation (as indicators evaluating the national and European economic situation record a positive trend). Despite these facts, improvement of economic indicators does not equal to an improvement in the opinion on EU institutions, as support for common policies is experiencing a slight decline and confidence in the national government is on the rise. Although in minority, there is a slight increase of trust in the national Government (32%, +4p, EU27 average) and in the national Parliament (33%, +2p, EU27 average). The evolution of trust in the national institutions (Romania versus EU27 average) is depicted in the chart below.

Results can be correlated to another question in the standard Eurobarometer, regarding the direction in which things are going in the European Union. Romanians prove themselves once again to be very optimistic, as the general opinion agrees that the EU is heading in the right direction. It is worth mentioning that, despite a positive attitude towards the future of the Union, opinions stating that the EU is heading in the a wrong direction have increased constantly since 2007. The average results in the EU27 member states are, once again, below the results in Romania. In the EB75 (spring 2011), the majority of Europeans continue to think that things are going in the wrong direction in the European Union (40%, +1).

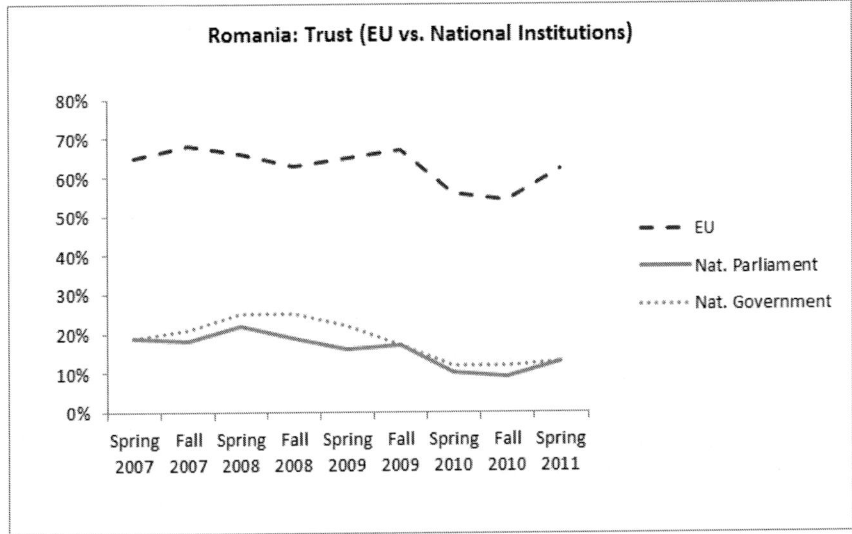

Fig 7-2. Romania: level of trust in the EU vs. the national institutions

There are more positive than negative opinions about the direction taken by the European Union in nine Member States (and opinion is evenly divided in four additional countries). The most positive respondents are in Bulgaria (54% think that things are going in the right direction), Lithuania (54%), Romania (52%) and Estonia (51%). Positive outnumber negative opinions in Poland (47%), Slovakia (45%), Latvia (40%), Hungary (36%), and Ireland (32%). The most critical countries are Greece (55%), Finland (53%) and France (52%). The impression that things are going in the right direction in the European Union is increasing especially in Romania (52%, +9) and Spain (32%, +8). It is declining in the Netherlands (21%, −10) and Slovakia (45%, −9).

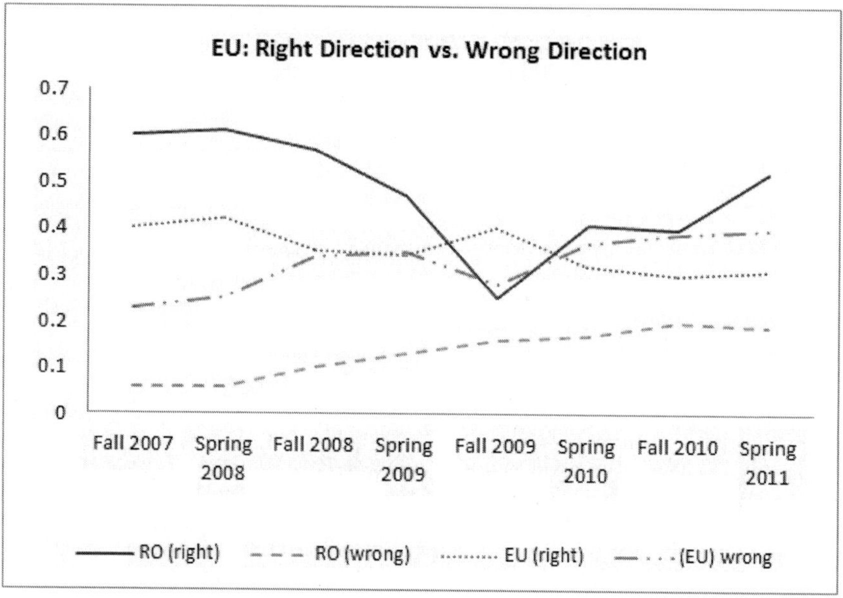

Fig 7-3. EU: right direction/ wrong direction

Some previously mentioned theories state that Euroskepticism fluctuates according to the perception of personal benefits deriving from EU membership. From this perspective, the results on the perceived benefits of EU membership included in the standard Eurobarometers become highly relevant to our discussion. To the question "Would you say that your country has benefited or not from being part of the EU?" the most recent answers (EB75, spring 2011) are encouraging. After the deteriorations recorded in spring 2010 (EB73) and autumn 2010 (EB74), opinions of the benefits of European membership have improved slightly in the spring 2011 survey: 52% of Europeans today think that their country has benefited from membership, a two-point increase since the autumn 2010 survey. The contradictory opinion, of the country not benefiting from membership, has declined slightly (37%, –2 points). There are 22 Member States where a majority says that European membership is beneficial. This belief is particularly strong in Ireland (78%), Poland (73%), Luxembourg (73%), Slovakia (72%), and Denmark (70%). Conversely this is the minority view in four countries: the United Kingdom (35% versus 54%), Hungary (40% versus 49%), Greece (47% versus 50%), and Austria (44% versus 46%). In Latvia respondents are evenly divided (47% versus 47%).

Since the year of accession, most Romanians have believed that their country has benefited from membership, with the highest percentage in spring 2007 (69%) and the lowest value in 2010 (56%). Results suggest, once again, that Romanians relate to the EU in a positive manner.

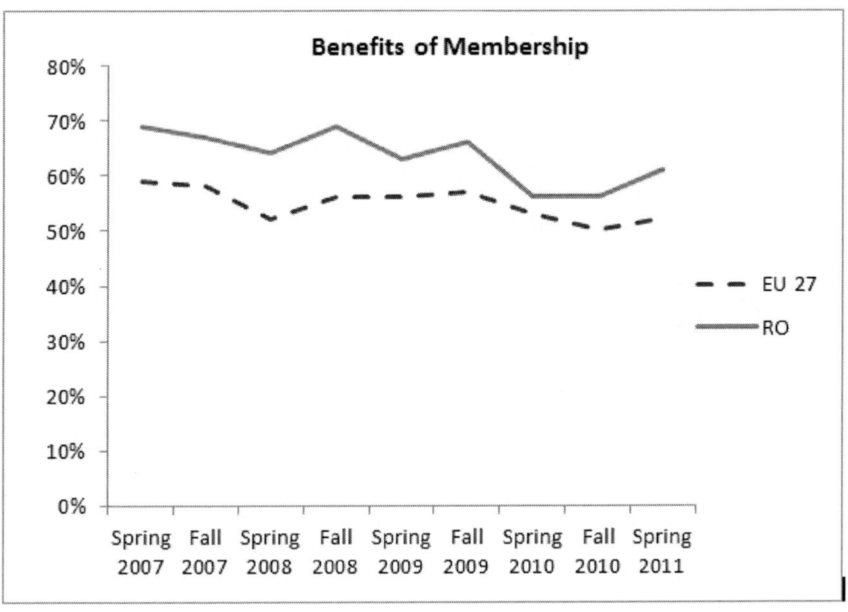

Fig 7-4. Benefits of EU membership

The economic and financial crisis has triggered a vivid debate on the future steps to be taken in the European Union. This issue is linked to actual support of current policies, with emphasis on the single currency policy and the enlargement subject.

In spring 2011 (EB75) a majority support the European economic and monetary union with a single currency, the euro, but there has been a two-point fall in this (56% against
37%, +2). There is majority support for an economic and monetary union and the euro in 22Member States. On the other hand, the majority of Europeans outside the euro zone are opposed to it (54% against, +2). The two most recent Eurobarometers (EB 74 and EB75) do not provide explicit data on the subject in the case of Romania, but we can trace the evolution of support for the euro back to 2007, as depicted in the chart below.

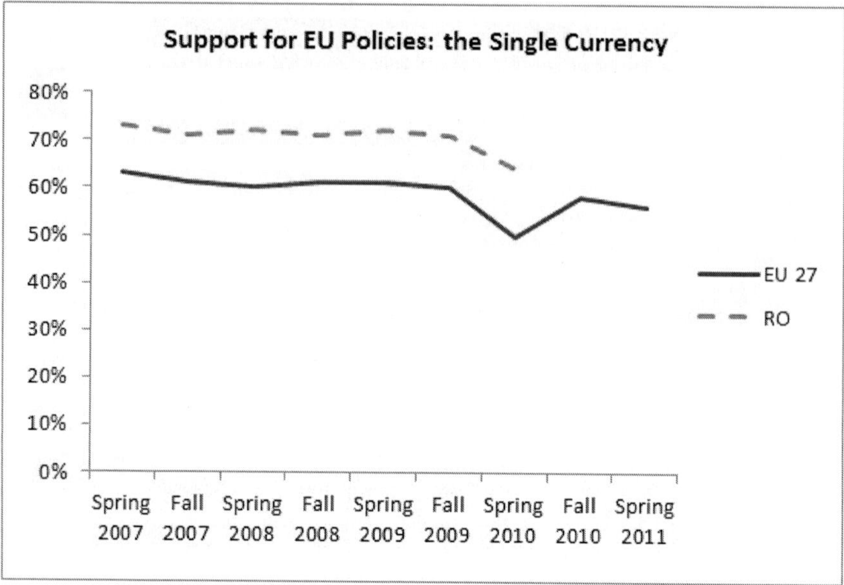

Fig 7-5. Support for EU policies: the single currency

Overall, optimism remains the majority opinion: the EB75 (spring 2011) recorded that 58% of Europeans believe in a bright future of the Union and only 36% believed the opposite. The most enthusiastic are Denmark (75% optimistic, −1), Romania (72%, +4), Belgium (70%, +4) and Poland (70%, −4). The most pessimistic are Greece (57%,+3), Portugal (48%, stable), and the United Kingdom (48%, +2), where the majority are pessimistic. In France there are also many pessimists (47%, +4), even if optimism remains stronger (48%, −4).

Differences between socio-demographic categories are significant for this issue: young

Europeans (aged 15 to 24) are more optimistic than the older generations with regard to the Union's future (68% compared to 52% for the over-55s). The more educated (those who continued their education until 20+) are also clearly more confident in the Union's future (66% compared to 46% for those who left education before 16), along with those Europeans who place themselves at the top of the social scale (68% compared to 45% of those who place themselves at the bottom).

The evolution of positive opinion on the future of the EU is shown in the chart below.

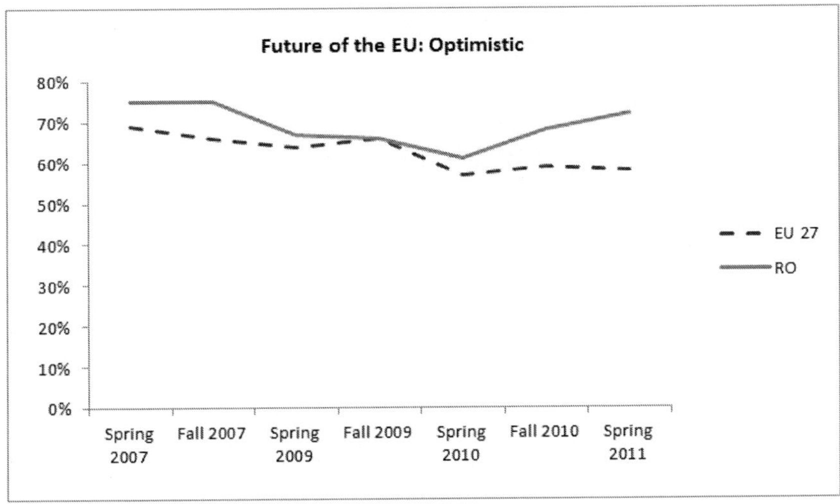

Fig 7-6. Future of the EU: Optimistic

On this particular subject, the values recorded in Romania are relatively close to the average opinion in EU27. Since spring 2010, Romanian citizens have felt more optimistic about the future of the European Union, which suggests that the current economic situation has not shattered Romania's faith in the Union.

The European Citizens and the Crisis: Pessimism or Blind Faith?

In spring 2011, a relative majority of Europeans thought that the consequences of the economic crisis for employment had not been fully felt yet and that "the worst is still to come" (47). It is worth mentioning that the results from spring 2011 have remained stable when compared to autumn 2010, but there has been a clear strengthening of this result since 2009 (+15 points since May-June 2009). Some countries are more optimistic than in the autumn of 2010, in particular Romania (42% believed the crisis already reached its peak, +13 points), Denmark (68%, +12 points) and Ireland (31%, +10 points) (Eurobarometer 75, 2011a).

One interesting fact is that the European Union is still perceived as the most effective player to respond to the impact of the crisis (22%), ahead of the national government (20%). The European Union is mentioned first in Greece, Poland and Luxembourg (34% each) and Bulgaria (33%). The

European Union is also at the top in 13 other Member States: Belgium (29%), Italy (28%), Estonia (28%), Slovakia (28%), Romania (27%), Ireland (26%), Lithuania (26%), Spain (25%), Hungary (25%), Portugal (25%), Cyprus (24%), Austria (23%) and Slovenia (23%).

The chart below compares Romania to three major European powers according to the perceived role of the European Union in dealing with the effects of the crisis. The UK has the lowest levels of trust in the EU as an effective player; these results are consistent with British opinion on all the indicators considered in this paper. The UK can undoubtedly be considered one of the most Eurosceptic countries in the EU, whereas Romania is one of the most Euroenthusiastic, even during the economic crisis.

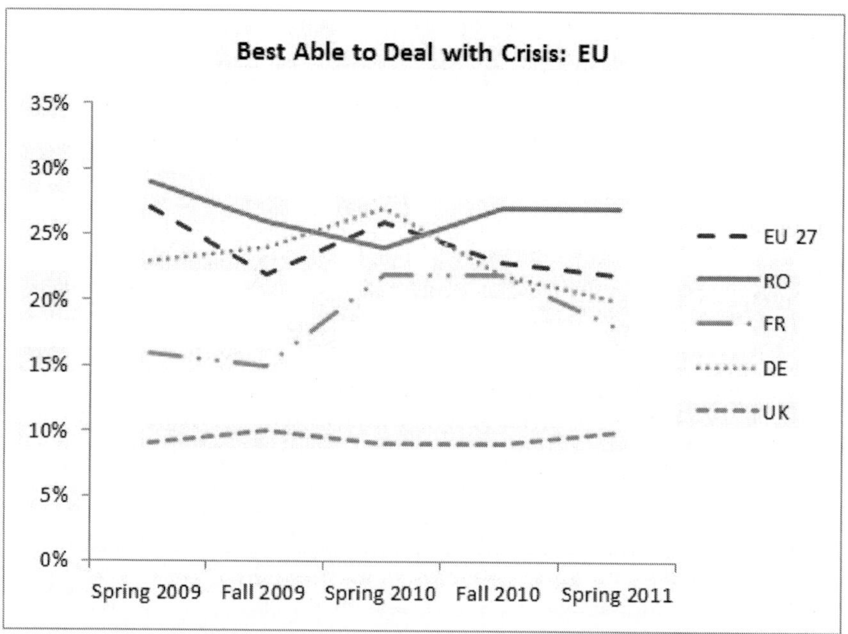

Fig 7-7. Best able to deal with the economic crisis – answer: the EU

Overall, the most recent Eurobarometer (spring 2011) showed that Europeans gave credit to the European Union for its strategy to emerge from the crisis and face new challenges: a majority of them believed that the European Union was going in the right direction (46%, unchanged since autumn 2010). Less than a quarter held the opposite opinion (23%, stable), while 20% spontaneously answered "neither one nor the other" (Eurobarometer 75, 2011).

In this context, it is reasonable to question whether Euroskeptic feelings belong to certain political parties and to some mass media channels or whether they actually express the beliefs of the population. Based on the results of the Eurobarometers, it can be argued that Euroscepticism is significant, but not as dominant as portrayed. The figures in the Eurobarometers speak for themselves, yet they do not convey the whole story, which may be even more complicated. At least three points can be raised in this context. First, Eurobarometers measure popular Euroscepticism; to this, elite Euroscepticism must be added, which is also growing (Leonard & Guérot, 2011). Second, Euroscepticism – both popular and elite – must also be explained along national lines; one can talk about German Euroscepticism, a Danish or a French one etc., each with its symbolism and significance. Third, other surveys containing questions different from those included in the Eurobarometers, reveal even higher levels of distrust. For example, according to a recent poll, two thirds of EU citizens believe that the single market has benefited only large corporations" (Strohschneider, 2011).

Romanians and Euroscepticism

In an attempt to gather more data on the phenomenon of Euroscepticism in Romania, we conducted a survey to measure the influence of the delay in the country's accession to the Schengen area on the way citizens relate to the EU. The results are presented in the next section of the paper.

In order to determine if the interest for the Schengen issue is linked to the problem of Euroscepticism and to identify the main predictors of trust in the European Union, we conducted two linear regressions ("trust in the EU" as a dependent variable). The predictors taken into consideration are those related to socio-demographic characteristics; in addition: the subjects' exposure to media news in general, the degree of knowledge on the EU, the extent to which respondents feel they are European. In the case of the second regression, the predictor "interest in the Schengen issue" has been added.

From a statistical point of view, only sex and education are significant predictors, whereas age, income and residence are not. The age represents a significant predictor only when interests towards the Schengen subject are not taken into consideration. Looking at contextual factors, the European identity is not a significant predictor, and neither is the exposure to media.

There is little hierarchical difference between the significant predictors, with a slight prominence of the degree of education (β=0.135), followed by the knowledge about the EU (β=-0.118), then age (β=0,096) and genre (β=0.086). The explicative value for the model is 5.2% (R square=0.052).

Table 7-1. Linear regression (to predict trust in the EU)

	First model (B)	First model (β)	Second model (B)	Second model (β)
Age	1.830*	0.096	0.003	0.047
Sex	0.005*	0.086	0.137*	0.071
Education	0.165**	0.135	0.045*	0.089
Revenue	0.068	−0.017	0	0
Residence	−0.004	−0.008	−0.012	−0.027
TV news usage	−0.004	−0.014	−0.036	−0.029
Internet news usage	−0.018	0.003	−0.008	−0.014
European identity	0.002	0.031	0.101	0.025
Knowledge about the EU	0.125**	−0.118	−0.174**	−0.090

Interest in Schengen			0.134**	0.205
Constant	1.830**		1.796**	
R Squared	0.052		0.087	

*significant at p<.05
**significant at p<.01

When the predictor "interest in the Schengen subject" is added, the explicative value of the model increases to 8.7% (R square=0.087). From the four predictors already mentioned, three remain significant (with the exception of age). The newly added predictor has a significantly greater explicative power (β=0.205 compared to β=-0.090 for the degree of knowledge about the EU, β=0.089 in the case of education, β=0.071 for genre).

Generally speaking, the interest in the Schengen case is an important predictor, increasing the explicative power of the model by 0.025%, and representing the most powerful predictor of the model. The more interested people are in the Schengen case, the more they trust the EU in general.

Discussions and Conclusions

When evaluating the degree of popular Euroscepticism, we took into consideration 5 main indicators: the trust in the EU versus the trust in national institutions, the perception of the right/wrong direction, the perceived benefits of EU membership, the support for EU policies, and the attitude towards the future of the EU.

Overall, Romania has a very positive perception of the EU, according to Eurobarometer results. The country is situated above the EU 27 average on all indicators, although it is experiencing a declining trend in the values recorded. Compared to 2010, the spring of 2011 (EB75) indicates a slight improvement in results, both in the case of Romania and the of European average. Romania has one of the highest levels of trust in the EU and has recorded a significant increase in 2011 (+8 points).

There is only one area where the country is situated below the European average: the degree of trust in national institutions, but with slight improvement in spring 2011. The highest levels of trust were recorded a short time after accession (2008). Romanian citizens have significantly more trust in the EU than in national institutions.

There is a majority in Romania that thinks the EU is heading in the right direction, although the opposing answer is steadily gaining support. Romania is among the 9 member states where there are more positive than negative opinions on the subject.

Even though the indicators of trust in the EU in general are in decline, there are no signs of deterioration in the global image of the Union – and Romania is the best example of this. Additionally, 58% of Europeans are optimistic about the future of the EU.

The majority still supports important common policies: the single currency and the enlargement, but the trend is declining. The single currency is supported by the majority of eurozone countries, while the majority of Europeans outside the Eurozone opposes it.

The latest Eurobarometer shows a very interesting result: the EU is still considered to be the most effective player in responding to the economic crisis, ahead of the national government. The EU is mentioned first in 17 member states, Romania included. Nine out of ten Europeans favor greater cooperation to combat the crisis – an encouraging result for the future of the European project.

Our research on the Schengen affair suggests that from all socio-demographic characteristics taken into consideration, sex and education are significant in influencing the degree of trust in the EU. Men generally tend to have more trust in the Union than women do. The higher the degree of education, the higher the degree of trust in the EU.

A high degree of knowledge about the European Union is associated with the degree of trust. In other words, opinions that result from a good informational background are more likely to be positive, showing optimism towards the European project. In this particular case, the interest in the Schengen subject proved to be the strongest predictor in the regression equation and also improved the explanatory power of the model. The higher the interest in the Schengen issue, the higher the trust in the EU. This apparently surprising result is explained by the degree of knowledge. The interest shown inRomania's accession to Schengen is probably extended to EU news in general, thus enhancing the information on the European Union and, by consequence, resulting in higher levels of trust.

There can be several explanations for the constant decrease in enthusiasm identified by our research. Each reason deserves thorough examination in future research. First of all, we must emphasize that Romanians' Euroenthusiasm at the moment of EU accession was, undoubtedly, excessive. That kind of euphoria has been possible mainly due to an information gap regarding actual rights and obligations of a member state. As citizen contact with EU reality deepened, the euphoria started to fade and the enthusiasm decreased below the excessive initial degrees.

Secondly, there is a very thin line between being disappointed with the EU and being negatively influenced by the difficulties the Romanian society faces today; some people may confuse the two issues and extend their dissatisfactions from a national to a European level.

Thirdly, the media could be responsible for the decrease of Euroenthusiasm. Recent findings (Bârgăoanu, 2011, pp. 129–137) show that the media have abandoned the "messianic Europe" frame and started focusing more on the penalties and conditions that EU policies impose on member states. Europe is now depicted as an inflexible agent, designed to apply sanctions for every deficiency Romania has. To conclude, we must ask ourselves whether or not the arguably emerging Romanian Euroskepticism is a consequence of disappointment or of a fresh dose of reality.

References

Abts, Koen & Krouwel, André (2007). Varieties of Euroscepticism and Populist Mobilization: Transforming Attitudes from Mild Euroskepticism to Harsh Eurocynicism. *Acta Politica: Tijdschrift voor politicologie,* 42(2/3), 252–270.

Bârgăoanu, Alina (2011). Examenul Schengen. În căutarea sferei publice europene, [The Schengen Exam. In Search of the European public Sphere]. Bucharest: Comunicare.ro

De Vreese, Claes (2005). *Euro-cynicism: The conditional nature of media effects on public cynicism about European integration,* Paper prepared for the international conference on Euro-skepticism, Amsterdam, July 1–2, 2005.

Gabel, Matthew (1998). Public Support for European Integration: An Empirical Test of Five Theories. *Journal of Politics*, 60(2), 333–354.

Habermas, Jürgen (2011). A Pact for or against Europe? In Guérot, Ulrike & Hénard, Jaqueline (eds), *What Does Germany Think about Europe?* London: European Council on Foreign Relations, pp. 83–93.

Kopecky, Petr & Mudde, Cas (2002). The Two Sides of Euroskepticism: Party Positions on European Integration in East Central Europe. *European Union Politics*, 3, 297–326.

Leonard, Mark & Guérot, Ulrike (2011). *The New German Question: How Europe Can Get the Germany It Needs* (policy brief). London: European Council on Foreign Relations. Available at: http://www.ecfr.eu/page

Sørensen, Catharina (2008). *Danish Euroskepticism: Unique or Part of Broader Patterns?,* Available at http://www.diis.dk/graphics/Publications/Books2008/Yearbook08/Yearbook_2008_Danish_Euroskepticism.pdf

Strohschneider, Tom (2011). Beware the Saviors of Europe. *Der Freitag,* 5 October, available at http://www.presseurop.eu/en/content/author/1023971-tom-strohschneider

Taggart, Paul & Szczerbiak, Aleks (2008). Introduction: Opposing Europe? The Politics of Euroskepticism in Europe. In *Opposing Europe? The Comparative Party Politics of Euroskepticism*, Volume 1, Oxford: Oxford University Press, pp. 1–15.

Taggart, Paul & Szczerbiak, Aleks (2003). *Theorising Party-Based Eurocepticism: Problems of Definition, Measurement and Causality,* Paper prepared for presentation at the 8th Biannual International Conference, Nashville, 2003.

Trenz, Hans-Jörg, de Wilde, Pieter & Michailidu, Asimina (2010). *Contesting EU Legitimacy. The Proeminence, Content and Justification of Euroskepticism during 2009 EP Election Campaigns,* RECON online working paper, 2010/22 www.reconproject.eu/projectweb/portalproject/RECONWorkingPapers.html.

van Kersbergen, Kees & Netjes Catherine (2005). *Interests, Identity and Political Allegiance in the European Union,* paper prepared for Euroskepticism conference, 1–2 July, Amsterdam.

Online sources

www.angus-reid.com. (2011). *Half of Britons Would Vote to Leave the European Union in a Referendum.* http://www.angus-reid.com/polls/43951/half-of-britons-would-vote-to-leave-the-european-union-in-a-referendum/

www.bbc.co.uk. (25th of October 2011). *EU referendum: Rebels lose vote in Commons*. Available at http://www.bbc.co.uk/news/uk-politics-15425256

www.eubusiness.com. (2011). *Euroskepticism rises in crisis-weary Germany.* http://www.eubusiness.com/news-eu/finance-economy.ca8

euobserver.com. (2011). *Polish leader raises alarm about 'new' Euroskepticism.* http://euobserver.com/18/32578

—. *Europe is not the problem, is the solution. Statement by the Council for the Future of Europe.* (2011). Available at http://berggruen.org/files/press/future_of_europe_statement_090511.pdf

—. *Eurobarometer 67.* (2007). Public Opinion in the European Union, Brussels: European Commission. Available at http://ec.europa.eu/public_opinion/archives/eb/eb67/eb67_en.htm

—. *Eurobarometer 68.* (2007). Public Opinion in the European Union, Brussels: European Commission. Available at http://ec.europa.eu/public_opinion/archives/eb/eb68/eb68_en.htm

—. *Eurobarometer 69.* (2008). Public Opinion in the European Union, Brussels: European Commission. Available at http://ec.europa.eu/public_opinion/archives/eb/eb69/eb69_en.htm

—. *Eurobarometer 70.* (2008). Public Opinion in the European Union, Brussels: European Commission. Available at http://ec.europa.eu/public_opinion/archives/eb/eb70/eb70_en.htm

—. *Eurobarometer 71.* (2009). Public Opinion in the European Union, Brussels: European Commission. Available at http://ec.europa.eu/public_opinion/archives/eb/eb71/eb71_en.htm

—. *Eurobarometer 72.* (2009). Public Opinion in the European Union, Brussels: European Commission. Available at http://ec.europa.eu/public_opinion/archives/eb/eb72/eb72_en.htm

—. *Eurobarometer 73.* (2010). Public Opinion in the European Union, Brussels: European Commission. Available at http://ec.europa.eu/public_opinion/archives/eb/eb73/eb73_en.htm

—. *Eurobarometer 74.* (2010). Public Opinion in the European Union, Brussels: European Commission. Available at http://ec.europa.eu/public_opinion/archives/eb/eb74/eb74_en.htm

—. *Eurobarometer 75.* (2011). Public Opinion in the European Union, Brussels: European Commission. Available at http://ec.europa.eu/public_opinion/archives/eb/eb75/eb75_publ_en.pdf

—. *Eurobarometer 75. Europeans, the European union and the Crisis.* (2011a). Public Opinion in the European Union, Brussels: European Commission. Available at http://ec.europa.eu/public_opinion/archives/eb/eb75/eb75_cri_en.pdf

www.politicshome.com. (2011). *Euro crisis turns public against EU membership.* http://www.politicshome.com/uk/article/31822/euro_crisis_turning_public_against_eu_membership.html

European Cultural Identity and Its Challenges in Intercultural Context: An Empirical Approach

Nicoleta Corbu and Georgiana Udrea

Abstract

In the context of the construction and enlargement of the European Union, what could theoretically be called European identity has become a constant source of inquiry and empirical investigation. Literature in the field explores the attributes of a European identity and its complex relationships with national, local, ethnic or cultural identities. However, little is known about actualizations of European identity in cultural European environments, especially for EU citizens from the new member states, such as Romania.

This paper evaluates the relationship between national and European identities in intercultural contexts. By means of qualitative analysis (21 in-depth semi-structured interviews) we explored how identities are activated in short-term sojourns of young people in different national cultural environments. The focus of the study was on the situation of Romanian Erasmus students who studied abroad and spent, in the last two years, between 5 and 8 months in a culture different from their native one.

We aimed to identify if, how and to what extent Romanian students perceived themselves as Europeans in a European cultural environment, other than their own. Findings showed that students actualized more than one layer of identity. The most powerful one was the national identity, Romanian identity being perceived as the main identity during their sojourn. European identity was rarely mentioned alone, but often as a secondary aspect, brought to light especially in specific contexts. In addition, the status of international Erasmus students added a third layer to the analysis, a group identity that helped them deal with the challenges of adapting to a new environment. Overall, we found out that European identity is rarely perceived and experienced as such by Romanian students studying abroad in a European country. Possible explanations are related to the status of Romania as a newly integrated country into the European Union, and thus not allowing time for its citizens to appropriate a common European identity, as well as the lack of consistency of a rather theoretical concept, yet to be filled with meaning, along with the political, social, and cultural changes that the EU will bring in the future.

Key words: European identity, national identity, intercultural context, short-term sojourners.

INTRODUCTION

The problem of cultural identity has long been discussed in the recent decades, especially in a European context. This happens due to the need of legitimizing the European cultural identity as a common ground for European citizens and as a unifying principle of a great variety of cultural heritages. Today, the people within Europe are confronted with an ever increasing need of redefining their identity as well as their position, in the process of reconfiguration of the political, social and economic surrounding.

Starting with theoretical considerations of "cultural identity", this paper looks at the relationship between National and European identities in intercultural contexts. More specifically, how identities are activated in short-term sojourns of young people in different national cultural environments. We argue that cultural identity reacts to changes in the environment. As long as an individual stays in his/her cultural environment, cultural identity changes slowly, as to incorporate new information into old patterns. However, when individuals find themselves in intercultural contexts, cultural identity is challenged by new patterns, and demands a considerable adaptive effort.

At present, little is known about how people experience European cultural identity in intercultural contexts. Do people experience a sense of being European or of being citizens of their country? Does the European dimension of one's identity facilitate in any way the adaptive efforts to a new cultural environment? These were the main questions that guided our research and that were answered in 21 in-depth interviews with Romanian Erasmus students, studying abroad in the last 2 years.

CULTURAL IDENTITY. THEORETICAL PERSPECTIVES

Cultural identity has been defined as a particular aspect of identity, which is commonly thought of as "a socio-cultural construct that affects how people behave and communicate" (Shin & Jackson, 2003, p. 212). Identity is a key concept in culture related theories and covers a large variety of things. For the purpose of this paper, though, identity will be understood as a perception of self in relation to the others. In literature, there are plenty of writings dedicated to otherness as a source of identity construction (Shore, 1993; Jenkins, [1996] 2000; Arts & Halman, 2006; Tiryaki, 2006; Staszak, 2008; Wintle, 2008; Checkel & Katzenstein, 2009). Although each author insists on different aspects of "identity", a common point in all these writings is that identity can be viewed as a process of classification, involving boundaries of inclusion and exclusion. Identity provides the necessary delimitation between the self and the others, between the group and the out-groups. In essence, it is "a dualistic concept: in order to define 'us', there must be a corresponding 'them', against which we come to recognize ourselves as different" (Shore, 1993, p. 782). In other words, "identity" construction very often involves a process of "othering". And this "othering" process, or the construction of identity by defining alterity, implies noticing either real or imagined differences between "us" and "them", "presented as a motive of discrimination" (Staszak, 2008, p. 2).

Culture is also a concept based on the dichotomy "us"/ "others", including everything that is specific to "us" as opposed to what is not "us" or "ours", but belongs to "strangers", to "foreigners", to "others". As scholars put it, collectivities, nations and even continents identify themselves both by defining their characteristics, and by defining those which they do not share. That is to say, the sense of community among members of a social group is accentuated by a sense of distinctiveness with regard to "other" social groups. Identity is then the unit that explains the sense of self, and the sense of belonging to a group. And cultural identity is one of the most specific sources of equilibrium of the human being as it assures the global background of the individual, inside which he manifests his other "layers" of (self) identity.

Cultural identity, as defined by Kim (2007a, p. 238) "is employed broadly to include related concepts such as sub-cultural, national, ethno-linguistic, and racial identity. Cultural identity also designates both a sociological or demographic classification, as well as an individual's psychological identification with a particular group. Both sociological and psychological meanings of cultural identity are regarded as two inseparable correlates of the same phenomenon". Therefore, the term is interchangeable with other terms commonly used, such as "national", "ethnic", "racial", "ethno-linguistic", etc. (Kim, 2007b). Cultural identity is based on identification with a group that has shared systems of symbols, meanings and norms of conduct (Collier, 1997; Shin & Jackson, 2003). From a psychological point of view, cultural identity is defined in terms of "the subjective orientation of an individual toward his/her ethnic origin" (Alba, in Kim, 2007a, p. 241). Although aware of the different layers of cultural identity, most commonly in their research, scholars consider cultural identity as mainly related to a particular ethnic group (which sometimes is superposed with a national group) (Hatcher, 2001; Ojha, 2003; Aldridge, 2004; Urban & Orbe, 2007).

In the context of the construction of the European Union, and the progressive integration of the European states, cultural identity has added a new layer to its multiple facets. In the same context, the cultural identity of Romanians acquired a new dimension, a superposition that can become the dominant layer in various circumstances. We argue that even with a relatively short amount of time spent in a different culture, the cultural identity of a person changes, as a transitory process of adaptation, as to be less of a "stranger" and more fit to the host culture. Therefore the person develops, for the time of his/her sojourn in the new country, an "intercultural identity" (Kim, 2007b) – a broader, more universal identity, combining and assimilating elements of multiple cultures – which will re-adapt and become once again the original cultural identity after returning to the "native" cultural environment.

MULTIPLE IDENTITIES

As research shows (Smith, 1992, 1993; Straubhaar, 2008), people articulate local, regional, national or supra-national and (even) global senses of self, as well as social, religious or ethnic, linguistic, professional senses of self that define different but co-existing identities (local or national identity, social class identity, religious, professional, educational identity etc.). All these specific facets of cultural identity intersect with each other and coexist in a sort of equilibrium. They are highlighted in different contexts, based on the situation in which identity becomes visible and important.

In the postmodern times of industrial capitalism and bureaucracy, of globalization and mass communications, the number of possible cultural identities has significantly increased. Gender, age, class and religious loyalties continue to be influential, while "professional, civic and ethnic allegiances have proliferated, involving ever larger populations across the globe" (Smith, 1992, p. 58). People accumulate many allegiances in today's world; they hold "multiple identities" (Smith, 1992, 1993; Christiansen, Jørgensen & Wiener, 2001; Wintle, 2005; Arts & Halman, 2006; Dufek,

2009), and can move between these identities according to context and situation. Or, as Brubaker and Cooper put it, "self- and other-identification are fundamentally situational and contextual" (2000, p. 14). That is to say, the various situations in which the individuals find themselves are relevant in the process of identification.

Identities are not fixed or static entities, but processes open to change, processes of constant negotiation with those around us, products of agreement and disagreement (Jenkins, [1996] 2000). Being more convergent than conflicting, human identities are said to be "fluid" and "flexible" because, nowadays, more and more people are exposed to various situations as a direct consequence of travelling, mass communication, increased social interaction etc.

Today, multiculturalism is highly recognized as a "new chapter in Europe's evolution" (Katzenstein & Checkel, 2009, pp. 224–225). Research shows that individuals possess several identities. Depending on the specific context and the various roles that they play, individuals invoke different elements of their social identity in different situations. Thus, they can be members of both, a nation, and a wider European Union. New empirical findings centered on Europe with the EU at its core suggested that people are proud to be citizens of their countries and to be European, at the same time. That is to say, "identities do not wax or wane at each other's expense" (Checkel & Katzenstein, 2009, pp. 9–10); one can be French or Romanian and European at one time. Put differently, European identity can be defined as a "multilevel identity" which "does not exclude other "identities", other "loyalties", whether these are local or national, or "Western" or "Atlantic" (Varsori & Petricioli, 2004, p. 90).

NATIONAL VERSUS EUROPEAN IDENTITY

The research studies on national and European identity are many and extremely varied. Therefore, in what follows, we will only highlight some of the most common interpretations of these powerful forces in modern life and politics.

National identity is defined as "a collective cultural phenomenon", "a multidimensional concept, extended to include a specific language, sentiments and symbolism" (Smith, 1991, p. vii). According to the same author, national identification transcends all other loyalties, in scope and power, becoming the "cultural and political norm" (Smith, 1992, p. 58). In other words, the ethnic and national levels of identification take priority and remain much more vivid and accessible to the mass population than more abstract identities like that of Europe (Smith, 1993, Risse, 2001).

National identity can never be induced in a population by artificial means. It is a complex construct, composed of interrelated components – ethnic, cultural, territorial, economic and legal-political, coexisting in varying degrees and different forms, and signifying bonds of solidarity among community members. These interrelated elements provide people with a sense of common identity and belonging. National identity "provides a powerful means of defining and locating individual selves in the world" (Smith, 1991, p. 17). The author also stresses that through a shared, unique culture, people are enabled to know who they are in the world. By rediscovering that culture, they rediscover themselves. This process of self-definition is considered to be the key to national identity.

European identity has been in a construction and reconstruction process throughout history, but during the last two decades, the debate around this concept has generated growing interest and research in various academic disciplines. The construction of the EU and the progressive integration of the European states have questioned the existence of a distinctive supra-national common identity, which is frequently perceived as the ideal of the European project.

Is there such a thing as a European identity? Current literature on this subject brings into full light several competing claims regarding the existence of a European identity. On the one hand, it is perceived as a continuous process, a real entity, its existence proven and supported by different phenomena such as migration (in search of a job, an education or a better lifestyle) or media coverage of European issues (Trandafoiu, 2006). On the other hand, some scholars argue that a sense of European identity has begun to develop and that more Europeans identify themselves in one way or another with Europe and the European community (Baycroft, 2004; Wintle 2005). Using Risse's words, we can say that, at present, a significant percentage of European citizens "incorporate Europe into their sense of identity" (2010, p. 6); this is to say, they hold "Europeanized national identities, if only as a secondary identity" (*ibid.*). At the same time, many academics affirm that European identity is rather a theoretical construction, a form lacking content, an empty shell (Kamphausen, 2006; Ferencová, 2006). Finally, and most recently, many scholars agree that the intellectual debate should focus on "European identities" that exist in plurality. It seems that "there is not one European identity, just as there is not one Europe" (Checkel & Katzenstein, 2009, p. 213).

European identities today are open to multiple interpretations. As scholars underline (Bruter, 2005; Wintle, 2005), they may refer to citizens' sense of belonging to the EU (with reference to its values) or to citizens' sense of belonging to Europe (with reference to common cultural characteristics). They are "neither defined primordially from within, nor simply imposed politically from the exterior" (Checkel & Katzenstein, 2009, p. 226).

Certainly, they can be understood, academics prove, as both a social process and a political project, involving publics and elites (Checkel & Katzenstein, 2009). In their words, ongoing social processes (like discourses, daily practice, institutions), related to the real experiences of Europeans (shopping in supermarket chains, meeting via Europe-wide social and business networks, participating in shared sporting occasions) as well as the elites and their political projects play key-roles in crafting Europe's identities. Thus, entrepreneurs and elites working in Brussels, Strasbourg and other national settings, together with anti-globalization Euro-skeptics or acerbic critics of the enlargement process, pro-European academics, politicians and journalists, xenophobic nationalists, and the wide European public, are all involved in shaping European identities which are "in a constant process of modernization and updating" (Trandafoiu, 2006, p. 92).

There are at least two trends identified in discussing the relationship between national and European identities. On the one hand, there are people who perceive "European identity" as a threat to their national allegiance. In this case, European identity is seen as fundamentally opposed to, and designed to undermine, people's national loyalties. On the other hand, as recent research shows, there are more and more Europeans who claim to have some kind of European identity, often alongside a national identity. This is the case when feelings of Europeanness are not necessarily incompatible with national loyalties. Very often, as already mentioned, one level of loyalty within an identity may be stronger than another, depending on the context and situation, but this doesn't mean that the weaker levels are entirely eclipsed. Instead, people's primary loyalties can be to their nations and, at the same time, to supranational institutions, to global regions or continents.

At this point, a logical question is why, across Europe, some people are likely to adopt a European identity while others are not? The initial answers to this question were enriched by new meanings added through the European integration process. Focusing on EU member states, recent studies (Favell, 2009; Fligstein, 2009) have pointed to social interaction, as a main source of such an identity. European integration has changed the patterns of interpersonal interaction, and today, large numbers of people travel across borders every year, either for business, for working abroad, for school, or for a good time. By means of traveling and contact with foreigners, people learned that they have many things in common with their counterparts in other countries. The positive interactions have caused some people to identify themselves as Europeans. Their number is not representative yet, but it is increasing as the year progresses. Another appropriate question is why, after more than half a century of European integration, only small numbers of people around Europe have developed a European sense of belonging? Neil Fligstein argues, in one of his most recent articles (2009), that integration, which has acted unevenly in bringing individuals together, is the right answer. He explains that the main beneficiaries of European integration have been people from the privileged strata of society, who speak one or more foreign languages, benefit from higher incomes or the opportunity to travel and interact with similar individuals across borders. Being especially young, highly cultured and educated , and sharing common interests with their counterparts around Europe, the people who tend to think of themselves as Europeans are managers, owners of businesses, professionals, white-collar workers (Fligstein, 2009, pp. 133–145). Therefore, a new sense of what it means to have a European identity is slowly emerging, and men, the young and non-religious, those with higher income and higher education "identify with a broader geographical unit" (Arts & Halman, 2006, p. 179). By contrast, the older individuals, the less educated, and those with few or no possibilities to travel abroad are prouder of their country or region, and seldom or never think of themselves as European. In general, this second category of people perceives European identity as a threat to their national sense of belonging.

To summarize, feelings of European identity, and their consequences, do not need to compete directly with national identity. In the contemporary world, people accumulate many loyalties which are not necessarily opposed or in conflict. These loyalties are all very important, and one does not necessarily exclude the others. As scholars have argued for decades now, identity is a multilevel construction, a continuous process that changes over time and place. There are contexts in which one's national identity becomes prominent, as well as contexts and situations when one's European identity may be highlighted. At any rate, national identity and European identity are not mutually incompatible, but rather different levels of individual identification, accentuated or left in the shadow according to place, time or situation.

METHODOLOGY

Starting with the premise that people, in general, possess multiple identities (including a European one, if they are citizens of Europe), the empirical research carried out in this paper analysed 21 Romanian Erasmus students who studied abroad for at least 5 months and returned home in the last two years. Using the in-depth semi-structured interview method, the purpose of our research was to capture whether the "alleged" secondary European identity that every European citizen should possess to different degrees (as numerous studies emphasize), especially the young and educated, highly cultured people – provides students with a common heritage (traditions, symbols, myths, knowledge, stereotypes and norms) with the role to facilitate their adaptation to a foreign culture. In other words, if European identity is more than a theoretical concept, Romanians or any other individuals who have a national identity within Europe do feel at ease in any European country, in any cultural environment? The research questions that guided our analysis were: Do short-time sojourners in a European cultural environment (other than their own) experience a sense of being European or rather of being citizens of their own country? How does European identity (if experienced) function in relation to other identities (especially the national one)? Does the European dimension of one's identity facilitate in any way the efforts of adapting to a new cultural environment?

The interviews were conducted with young Romanian individuals, between 20 and 24, with higher education completed or in progress. 21 students of The National School of Political Studies and Public Administration and of The Academy of Economic Studies in Bucharest, Romania, who studied abroad at universities in Italy, Germany, Belgium, France, The Netherlands or Spain, accepted to participate in this study. The interviews, which lasted between 35 and 65 minutes, were conducted in the interval between January and March 2011.

FINDINGS

The analysis of our results highlights the layers of (self) identity as experienced by these students in a European cultural environment (other than their native one). The analysis also focuses on how national identity works in relation to other identities (especially the European one). At the same time, it addresses the European dimension of the Romanian students' identity (if experienced) and its role in facilitating their efforts to integrate (for a short time) in a foreign culture. Our research showed that 18 of the

21 respondents mentioned the Romanian identity as the primary identity. Most of them perceived a European identity as second or third nature, and only in certain circumstances: "I felt Romanian in the first place, I was Livia from Romania" (Livia, Italy); "I felt Romanian first and foremost. I remember an exercise about this. We had to write down quickly, off the top of our minds, words to describe us, and for me it was something like "Romanian", "student"; I would have never thought of "European", and neither did anybody else; from what I can remember, everybody mentioned his/her nationality" (Silvia, Belgium); "I always feel more Romanian and I am proud of my nationality no matter where I go" (Radu, Spain). Most of the respondents said that, during their sojourn abroad, they identified with their homeland in the first place, despite the negative image associated with Romania. Moreover, they were proud of their origins and tried, whenever possible, to promote (especially through personal example) another facet of their country – Romania as a state that, in recent years, has made remarkable progress economically, culturally, academically, etc., Romania as more than the country reduced to the same few stereotypes presented in movies and believed by many foreigners. Moreover, for most respondents, the Romanian identity was very visible in intercultural contexts, when sharing cultural experiences with other international students and/or with local students: "There were a lot of questions about who we are, about life in Romania, about our values, our traditions and I felt like I had a lot of things to share with them" (Anca, Germany).

Research also showed that more than half of the respondents distinguished between a group identity (they were Erasmus students, different and somewhat foreign to the locals) and an individual identity experienced differently, depending on context and situation. That is, the majority of the interviewed students mentioned actualizations of both identity layers (national and European), specifying different contexts in which one of the two facets of their identity became prominent: "I felt European during my interactions with non-European colleagues from Korea or the USA, who had great expectations of us, the Europeans. They expected us to have solid general knowledge, to know things they didn't know etc."(Raluca E., Netherlands); "When relating to other Erasmus students I felt more Romanian; when interacting with neighbours or people I met on the street I was a European citizen" (Irina, Belgium); "I felt European and different as opposed to my colleagues from other continents; I was also curious and eager to learn as much as possible about them, because I knew there were lots of cultural differences between us" (Miruna, Italy). During their interactions with students from other continents, most of the respondents said they felt European in the first place, since at this level, cultural differences between the European countries fade away compared to those between continents. All the students who had the opportunity to interact with their counterparts from Asia, USA, South Africa etc. pointed to significant cultural differences which sometimes made communication and interaction difficult: "With the Chinese there was absolutely no connection, no tie, for they are completely "locked" in their community; they do not go out much, and if they party they do it by themselves; there were many Chinese students on Campus, but one could not see any who came to a club or to eat in the cafeteria, with the rest of us" (Raluca, Germany); "It was a lot more difficult for us to identify with people from outside of Europe… there were the students from China or Africa with whom we did not have much to do… They only stayed with each other" (Mihaela, Germany).

On the other hand, interacting with their European colleagues made respondents realize that they shared many things which had not been obvious before. Thus, they spoke about the common market of which they became aware when they discovered familiar products in the supermarkets in the host country. Respondents also mentioned that certain holidays and traditions they considered to be Romanian are also celebrated in other parts of Europe but on different dates and under different names (Dragobetele, All Saints). Finally, they found out that European cuisine includes many dishes that are common to different countries within Europe and, although they carry different names, their preparation and taste are very similar.

A European identity was felt more strongly when these students traveled freely from one country to another without many formalities: "I felt European when I traveled. When I went from Germany to France I had no border, no check points, it was the Schengen area, and then I felt that there are benefits in all of this" (Mihaela, Germany); "The fact that I could travel freely around Europe, without a visa, made me feel European. I realized then that joining the EU was a positive thing, because I visited France and England and the Netherlands as if I had gone from Bucharest to Focşani" (Roxana, Belgium).

At the same time, short visits to the European Parliament represented another context when the students' European identity was emphasized. Three students mentioned these occasions as relevant for their identification with Europe and the European community: "I felt European in Belgium, when they brought us to Brussels in order to visit the European Parliament and the European Commission" (Ana S., Belgium); "I felt European from time to time. I had school trips to Brussels and visited the European Parliament and then I had the feeling that we are part of this big thing. I don't think I would have felt the same elsewhere" (Armina, Belgium).

Besides the identification with their country of origin and with Europe (which were emphasized contextually and situationally), many Romanian students talked about a group identity – their identity as Erasmus students. Although they came from various parts of the world and carried different cultural backgrounds, the fact that they all shared the same status – that of international students, of "foreigners" in a new cultural environment – helped students adapt more easily. In other words, the Erasmus identity was a driver of the adaptation process for most of these students.

Other layers of identity brought into discussion only sporadically included the regional and the local identities: "Maybe more than Romanian I felt East European, because our Western colleagues treated us (their Eastern counterparts) in the same way" (Ana S., Belgium); "The overall national identity was followed, in my case, by the regional identity, the Transylvanian identity. I mean, I felt some cultural differences between me and my colleagues from Constanţa" (Bogdan, Germany).

When it comes to the European dimension of these students' identity and its role in the process of adaptation, the results of this empirical research showed that this specific layer of identity played a minor role in the students' integration. Rather, our research discovered two primary ways of dealing with the various challenges raised by being the foreigner in the host country: the friendship with other Romanians and the Erasmus group identity: "While trying to adapt, it was very important that I left with two other Romanians I already knew, and I became friends with another Romanian I met there. If it wasn't for them, things would have surely been different" (Raluca E., Netherlands); "I adapted easily to the new environment because I left Romania with two other colleagues, and also because I met other Romanian students who were already there upon my arrival" (Sorana, Germany).

The European identity was rarely mentioned as a form of support or comfort in this context. Only two respondents considered that the European layer of their identity had a role in facilitating their adaptation to the host country: "I think I related more easily to students from Europe, but it probably was a matter of context, because there were more people from Europe in the home where I lived" (Miruna, Italy); "I think it mattered that we were European in that we had some common understanding of things… Take for example religion, nobody was very religious, but whether we were Orthodox, Catholic or Protestant, we had the same God, while our colleagues from China or Africa were totally different" (Mihaela, Germany).

In most cases, the Erasmus identity proved to help students integrate more easily in the foreign culture: "I don't think that the fact of being European made us interact better…. Usually we became friends with the people we understood better; we became friends because we were Erasmus students" (Anca, Spain); "Europe was not a bridge between us; we became friends because we were all students from other countries" (Bogdan, Germany).

The Erasmus identity was strengthened by the various formal and informal events that the host university provided to all international students, by the fact that the foreign students lived together in most cases and by them feeling similar, united and close to each other just by being Erasmus: "We never felt excluded, but it is true, we were hanging out with other Erasmus students all the time" (Raluca I., Belgium); "I was always an Erasmus student there; we were different, we looked different, everybody treated you differently (not in a negative sense), I mean they were always very nice to us, we tried to speak Dutch, they answered back in English, etc." (Roxana, Belgium).

Discussion and Conclusions

Erasmus students who lived abroad for 5–8 months experienced more than one layer of their identities. Discussing the various contexts that highlighted or overshadowed different facets of their identity, respondents talked mostly about the Romanian identity as their main identity during their exchange study. However, they also mentioned group, local, regional or European identities that were actualized at a specific time, depending strictly on the context of interaction.

All participants in this study perceived their national identity as the most strongly manifested during their short-term sojourn in a European cultural environment other than their own. The European identity was often mentioned as a second or third loyalty and was emphasized especially in specific circumstances. The context that was most frequently mentioned in relation to the assuming of a European sense of belonging referred to the "dissolution of borders" across Europe, which facilitated to a great extent students' free travels within the continent, in the absence of the usual passport or visa control formalities. This achievement made them feel part of the larger European community. Other contexts that highlighted the European dimension of students' identity included the interactions with people from outside the campus (*e.g.* the locals) or the intercultural encounters with fellow students from other continents. The group identity ("Erasmus" or "international student" identity in respondents' own words) was spontaneously discussed especially when they recalled specific events or joint activities, both academic and interpersonal.

The adaptive process everyone experienced abroad emphasized the Romanian identity through the strong support of Romanian colleagues or friends. The group identity was also an important element in helping students adapt to various situations. This is to say that both national and group identities (in this particular case, Romanian and Erasmus identities) were often perceived as important patterns of adaptation to the host culture. Furthermore, the communication and friendships with other exchange students, good English (or/ and a good knowledge of the host language), the constant support they received from tutors and professors, the intercultural parties, and the fact that some of them have travelled or even lived abroad before the Erasmus experience were also emphasized as very important factors that helped Romanian interviewees cope more easily with the new socio-cultural settings. Regional identity seldom proved to be equally relevant from the same point of view. More precisely, the East European identity was mentioned very few times in relation to the ease of the relocation experience.

In conclusion, this research shows that the role of European identity in facilitating students' adaptive process to a foreign European culture was minor. Additionally, the European dimension of students' identity was never mentioned spontaneously as an important means of adaptation abroad in none of the 21 cases analyzed in this paper. As mentioned before, for the Romanian interviewees, there were two other ways of dealing with the various challenges raised by the experience of being the "foreigner": their increased interaction and friendship with co-nationals and the Erasmus group identity. European identity (even when experienced) was not necessarily enumerated among the main factors that helped students diminish their adaptive efforts and integrate abroad.

References

Aldridge, G M (2004). "What Is the Basis of American Culture?" In F E Jandt (ed), *Intercultural Communication. A Global Reader* (pp. 84–98). Thousand Oaks: Sage Publications.

Arts, W & Halman, L (2006). "Identity: The case of the European Union", *Journal of Civil Society*. 2(3), 179–198.

Baycroft, T (2004). “European Identity”. In G Taylor & S Spencer (eds), *Social Identities: Multidisciplinary Approaches* (pp. 145–161), New-York: Routledge.

Brubaker, R & Cooper, F (2000). “Beyond ‘Identity’”. *Theory and Society*. 29(1), 1–47.

Bruter, M (2005). *Citizens of Europe? The Emergence of a Mass European Identity*. Palgrave: Macmillan.

Checkel, J T & Katzenstein, P J (2009). “The Politicization of European Identities”. In J T Checkel & P J Katzenstein (eds), *European Identity* (pp. 1–25), Cambridge: Cambridge University Press.

Christiansen, T, Jørgensen, K E & Wiener, A (eds) (2001). *The Social Construction of Europe*. Thousand Oaks: Sage Publications.

Collier, M J (1997). “Cultural Identity and Intercultural Communication”. In L A Samovar & R E Porter (ed), *Intercultural Communication. A Reader* (pp. 36-44). New York: Wadsworth Publishing.

Dufek, P (2009). “Fortress Europe or Pace-Setter? Identity and Values in an Integrating Europe”. *Czech Journal of Political Science*. 1, 44–62.

Favell, A (2009). “Immigration, Migration, and Free Movement in the Making of Europe”. In J T Checkel & P J Katzenstein (eds). *European Identity* (pp. 167–189), Cambridge: Cambridge University Press.

Ferencová, M (2006). “Reframing Identities: Some Theoretical Remarks on ‘European Identity’ Building”. *International Issues & Slovak Foreign Policy Affairs*. 1, 4–17.

Fligstein, N (2009). “Who Are the Europeans and How Does This Matter for Politics?”. In J T Checkel & P J Katzenstein (eds). *European Identity* (pp. 132–166). Cambridge: Cambridge University Press.

Hatcher, C (2001). “Cultural Identity: Past, Present, and Future”. *World Communication*, 30(1), 12–16.

Jenkins, R ([1996] 2000). *Ide*ntitatea Socială (Social Identity), trans. Alex Butucelea. Bucharest: Univers.

Kamphausen, G (2006). “European Integration and European Identity: Towards a Politics of Difference?”. *International Issues & Slovak Foreign Policy Affairs*. 1, 24–31.

Katzenstein, P J & Checkel, J T (2009). “Conclusion – European Identity in Context”. In J T Checkel & P J Katzenstein (eds), *European Identity* (pp. 213–227). Cambridge: Cambridge University Press.

Kim, Y Y (2007a). “Ideology, Identity, and Intercultural Communication: An Analysis of Differing Academic Conceptions of Cultural Identity”. *Journal of Intercultural Communication Research* 36(3), 237–253.

—. (2007b). "Intercultural Personhood: Globalization and a Way of Being". Conference Papers – International Communication Association, Annual Meeting.

Ojha, A K (2003). "Humos: A Distinctive Way of Speaking That Can Create Cultural Identity". *Journal of Intercultural Communication Research* 32(3), 161–174.

Risse, T (2001). "A European identity? Europeanization and the Evolution of Nation-State Identities". In M Green Cowles, J Caporaso & T Risse (eds). *Transforming Europe: Europeanization and Domestic Change* (pp. 198–216). New - York: Cornell University Press.

—. (2010). *A Community of Europeans?* London: Cornell University Press.

Shin, C I & Jackson, R L (2003). "A Review of Identity Research in Communication Theory. Reconceptualizing Cultural Identity". In W J Starosta & G M Chen (eds), *Ferment in the Intercultural Field. Axiology/Value/Praxis International and Intercultural Communication Annual*. XXVI, Sage, Thousand Oaks, 211–242.

Shore, C (1993). "Inventing the 'People's Europe': Critical Approaches to European Community 'Cultural Policy'". *Man*. New Series 28(4), 779–800.

Smith, A D (1991). *National identity*. London: Penguin Books.

—. (1992). "National Identity and the Idea of European Unity". *International Affairs* (Royal Institute of International Affairs) 68(1), 55–76.

—. (1993). "A Europe of Nations. Or the Nation of Europe?" *Journal of Peace Research* 30(2), 129–135.

Staszak, J F (2008). "Other/Otherness". Retrieved 31 May 2008 from: http://www.unige.ch/ses/geo/collaborateurs/publicationsJFS/OtherOtherness.pdf

Straubhaar, J D (2008). "Global, Hybrid or Multiple? Cultural Identities in the Age of Satellite TV and the Internet". *NORDICOM Review* 29(2), 11–29.

Trandafoiu, R (2006). "The Whole Greater than the Sum of Its Parts: An Investigation into the Existence of European Identity, Its Unity and Its Divisions". *Westminster Papers in Communication and Culture* 3(3), 91–108.

Tiryaki, S (2006). "European Identity 2006". *International Issues & Slovak Foreign Policy Affairs* 15(1), 41–52.

Urban, E & Orbe, M P (2007). "The Syndrome of the Boiled Frog: Exploring International Students on US Campuses as Co-Cultural

Group Members". *Journal of Intercultural Communication Research* 36(2), 117–138.

Varsori, A & Petricioli, M (2004). "Europe, Its Borders and the Others". In R Frank (ed). *Les identités européenes au XX siècle: diversités, convergences et solidarités* (pp. 81–99), Paris: Publications de la Sorbonne.

Wintle, M J (2005). "European Identity: A Threat to the Nation?" *Europe's Journal of Psychology*. Retrieved 15 February 2011 from: http://www.ejop.org/archives/2006/02/communication_a.html.

Wintle, M J (ed) (2008). "Imagining Europe. Europe and European Civilization as Seen from its Margins and by the Rest of the World, in the Nineteenth and Twentieth Centuries". Brussels: P I E Peter Lang.

LOCAL IDENTITY VS. EUROPEAN IDENTITY IN ROMANIAN ADVERTISING*

MĂDĂLINA MORARU

Abstract

Romanian advertising tried to fill the political gap that left it behind Europe after the Communist era, and accomplished this by means of importing external models and reconstructing the image of old surviving brands. The political integration into the European Union was a good start for changes in Romanian advertising, which had become less local due to globalization. The difference between global and local features depends on the consumer, whose age and experience demand specific values. Given this image translation, Romanian commercials may be easily classified as traditional commercials, imported models and a mixture of both (resembling a metaphorical centaur). Globalization obviously appropriates the last two types, based on building some common brand image patterns and their creative strategy.

The present research focuses on identifying local features in order to make a comparison with global characteristics. The research method will be the content analysis applied on a sample of 100 commercials of brands belonging to the following categories: the traditional perspective, the innovative perspective, and the combined model. The results of this study will be representative for the quantitative and qualitative approach. We are going to organize this article according to research variables regarding aspects such as product categories, traditional/innovative elements, national vs. European identity (cultural, linguistic and political identity), positioning strategy (for example, the one based on time is specific to traditional commercials), brand identity.

---

* Acknowledgement: This work was supported by the strategic grant POSDRU/89/1.5/S/62259, Project "Applied social, human and political sciences. Postdoctoral training and postdoctoral fellowships in social, human and political sciences" cofinanced by the European Social Fund within the Sectorial Operational Program Human Resources Development 2007–2013.

Our main hypothesis is to identify the European impact on Romanian advertising, and we will support it by analyzing different brands (international and local) belonging to the same product categories. Thus, similarities and distinctions will be more obvious, justifying the contamination of local values by European features. Additionally, this research aims to identify some patterns for preserving national identity in local commercials either for European brands or for Romanian ones, from different points of view such as topic, linguistic tools, narrative structures, and personalities. At the end of this study, we will focus on the advantages and disadvantages of creating a chameleonic identity for the brands by importing external values.

The main challenge of this research is to prove that national identity has been equally developed in commercials broadcast not only for local brands, but for global brands as well, due to consumer needs and insight. Moreover, another issue this study will answer regards the way European brands are perceived by consumers in local commercials on the Romanian market. Establishing the relationship between European and Romanian advertising implies answering the following questions: Do European brands emphasize the values of their country of origin, or are they similar to other global brands? Can we really talk about a Romanian identity in this context of assimilation of European values and lifestyles?

Key words: national, European, identity, Romanian, advertising.

The Theoretical Framework

The European Macro-Identity vs National Micro-Identity

When it comes to globalization, researchers cannot forget the role of advertising in promoting not only a well-known fast-food product (McDonalds), but also a lifestyle, in recommending not a simple drink at Christmas, but a Santa's symbol. McDonaldization and Cocalization are two examples of how global brands reach their target all over the world by exporting few values. How is it possible to sell a hamburger in the Arab world, where the restrictions are very harsh and people very conservative? By giving up some global features of the brand and adapting it to the target that may like to eat quickly and on the go.

Scholte dedicated an entire chapter to the paradox between globalization and nationalism, finding some solutions to cope with this incompatible transition (2005, pp. 224–255). In his opinion, "globalization has encouraged the growth of national identities on scales other than the state, in respect of sub-state, macro-regional and trans-world spheres" (Scholte, 2005, p. 224). The immediate consequence of both world wars was the construction of a European identity of macro-nations, pretty much accelerated by globalization. In the beginning, this union worked for the powerful states, but since the Communist failure, the identity of East European countries has been shaped according to these first models to politically integrate them into the European Union. Beside the political actions, the Council of Europe focuses on extending the market and educating people for EU citizenship. This macro-regionalization has been very much helped by the globalization wave and one of the first reactions of the new integrated states was to invest more in their identity, and Scholte named this "supra-state identities like region-nations" (Scholte, 2005, p. 237). Globalization definitely consists in improving the nation-states' identities and transforming them into region-nations, but this phenomenon cannot change the national identity that relies on the cultural, traditional, and historical background.

Advertising anticipated very well these trans-world nations by supporting the global mobility of brands and, given their power, by creating target categories that transcended any kind of borders. The opening of the nation border is actually related to the European wars, when American soldiers brought Coca-Cola to the continent and Volkswagen reached the American market. In time, national brands tend to externalize their values and products, and some of them became non-territorial identities. But they have always been interacting with local brands and tried to rebuild their identity according to the cultural differences in each country.

Hybridization makes things happen!

There is no way to ignore or get over so many cultural differences, no matter the brand power or any history it has. The intention to standardize the political system, consumerism, family needs and income brought to light national differences whose role is to preserve the national character or identity. Pieterse approaches this relationship between globalization and culture, synthesizing three paradigms that explain perspectives on cultural differences: "cultural differentiation or lasting difference, cultural convergence or growing sameness, and cultural hybridization or ongoing mixing" (Pieterse, 2009, p. 44) All these perspectives are actually historical stages in understanding cultural differences according to diverse criteria such as: religious features, anthropological roots, popular culture aspects. For example, the first view regards the oldest way to understand immutable cultural differences. Second, the cultural convergence expresses very well the universalism, as in the world religions. The last perspective, hybridization, "refers to a postmodern sensibility of traveling culture" (Pieterse, 2009, p. 44) that can reveal the connection between global and local in many fields, including advertising. Cultural representations in advertising are often linked with brand symbols that were created according to the country of origin.

By establishing a connection between all these views on cultural differences and advertising, we are going to point out some models of creating advertising that reflect the global and local strategies. According to Moriarty, Mitchell and Wells, there are three approaches focusing on the balance between standardization, localization and combination (Moriarty et al., 2009, pp. 548–568). The easiest model to identify is standardization that focuses on consumer similarities from all over the world, without any specific issue. Localization, sometimes named adaptation, consists in considering many other important coordinates of each market such as: lifestyles, cultural, economic and political particularities. Combination is nothing else than finding a middle way to amalgamate both previous directions in order to produce a more effective advertising by preserving general brand strategies and translating them for local customers. There is a new concept that very well describes this advertising hybridization, namely glocalization.

Coming back to the identity issue, we think glocalization not only provides the mixing of global with local features, but helps the micro-market integrate into regional markets and encourages the sense of belonging. The glocalization phenomenon works according to some important aspects whose role is to respect the brand identity and the consumer insight:

- Encouraging local identities to accept global brands;
- Adapting product features to the cultural restrictions of local market;
- Developing campaigns based on "global mélange", a concept that belongs to Pieterse (2009);
- Using syncretism as a way to preserve brand identity, and the consumer identity as well;
- Recovering the gap between diversity and homogeneity, making those two worlds cohabit without losing the sense of identity;
- Weaving the cultural needs of consumers with brand attraction, to integrate them into a transnational target.

Brand Identity

In the early years of advertising, brands were specifically associated with their country of origin, because they represented a general overview of the nation. Therefore, the reputation of a brand reflected a country's reputation and no confusion was possible. Meanwhile, advertising became a channel to communicate similar values by buying and using the same brands. Preoccupied by conceptualizing national identity, Anderson (1991) argues that nations are "imagined communities", and advertising encourages the construction and deconstruction of identities. In his opinion, in all the media, advertising is a way of creating "unified fields of exchange and communication" (Anderson, 1991, p. 44).

Therefore, commercials, no matter whether promoting global or local products, reflect not only brand reputation but market values as well. Defending a brand reputation involves managing its qualities and capital that supports these important features: authenticity, credibility and reliability. Sicco van Gelder broadly developed this concept of brand reputation, identifying three types of reputation qualities (2010, pp. 107–108): contextual, intrinsic and associative. The first type refers to the brand's rights given by birth, its past, its founder and creator. The intrinsic reputation consists in developing the brand's qualities over the years, while the last category is based on the association between brand and personalities, other brands or consumers. Further, the author identifies six types of brand reputation very well represented in Table 9-1 (Van Gelder, 2010, p. 108).

Table 9-1. The six types of brand reputation according to Sicco van Gelder

	Qualities		
Relation	Contextual	Intrinsic	Associative
Category specific	Pedigree brands	Quality brands	Endorsed brands
Category transcendent	Origin brands	Promise brands	Personality brands

According to the purpose of this research, the contextual reputation provides information about brand identity and its connection with the advertising dedicated to it. Pedigree brands are related to a particular context, a region, a language, the founder, and make the brand unique. Considering this aspect of authenticity, Van Gelder believes that "A true pedigree brand is formed by an emphasis on its roots, the unique qualities it inherits from its founder, those that are bestowed on it by their birthplace" (2010, p. 11).

This means that advertisers should be careful when ranking the authentic "pedigree" signs. We may briefly say that historical, cultural values and symbols belong to a brand pedigree. International campaigns for mega brands should obviously express their message from two perspectives: first, the brand reputation and, second, the consumer's needs.

Origin brands represent another way to come back to the brand reputation, using other indices, such as naming, or connecting with the genuine city of the founder. The airlines provide the best example in this case, by including the country name in the brand name: British Airlines, American Airlines, Air France, TAROM (Romanian airlines). In some cases, even if the brand becomes part of an international company, its name reminds the consumer of its origin. Romtelecom is the national phone company, which has become part of a Greek and German trust since 1998. The name has been preserved and Romanian consumers still consider it a national brand. Of course, another issue is called into question here: what is an origin brand? From the economic point of view, we may consider it a brand completely supported by its country. From the brand history, we may consider a national brand one that was born and developed in a specific country, even if it is associated with other brands like Dacia-Renault. This research carries on according to the second criterion: brand history, name, and main consumer. Powerful companies embrace a new strategy to enter a specific market, by creating or overtaking regional brands. The Heineken "Kingdom" built its portfolio in this way, and beers like Bucegi, Ciucaş, Ciuc, Gambrinus, and Silva sound very Romanian, but they are no longer supported by Romanian financing. Most of the consumers do not think about Heineken when they drink one of these beers, whose history was quite rich before being overtaken by the international mammoth. Their names are directly connected with geographical details (Bucegi, one of the Carpathian mountains), Silva (the word comes from old Latin and means forest). One of the most important aspects of the brand reputation is the variety of its perceptions according to the market specificity. Amine, Chao and Arnold (2005) consider that sound familiarity influences the loyalty towards a brand very much, and, for this reason, they recommended using local-sounding brand names. The previous discussion about the Heineken strategy illustrates this concerning on adapting a global brand to local features.

Moreover, the country of origin represents a background that allows the brand a better position in the consumer's mind. Everyone knows that German cars reflect very well the German style: technical, serious and competent. Champagne and wine along with Chanel fragrance remind the consumer of the French style. Italy is synonymous with fashion for many of us, everyone connecting this country with brands like Gucci, Dolce & Gabana, Versace. For ages, Switzerland has been and remains the king of watch manufacturing, reaching the highest performance in the world by producing Rolex, Tissot and Omega.

The most European trusted brands

The way cultural differences affect the European advertising and marketing arises from a very good segmentation of national markets, consumptions patterns, consumer behaviour, family structure and factors of decision making. According to Bennett, culture influences advertising given to such issues as:

- How local consumers perceive the market positions of various products;
- How the female form may be used in advertisements;
- The acceptability of nudity and/or what parts of the human body may be shown;
- The extent of an advertisement's display or physical contact between people (of the same or of differing sexes);
- The degree of elegance, quality, urbanity expected from advertisements (Bennett, 1993, p. 142).

All of these aspects may be synthetically called lifestyles and they are more or less developed due to the national media. Bennett pays attention to the battle between the standardization and customization of advertisements, this time related to the European campaigns only. He believes standardization relies on considering the European market as a very homogenous one, ignoring national differences and emphasizing on consumers with the same attitude. In terms of customization, Bennett understands the European market according to hybridization rules and to media situation as well. Even if we speak about a brand distributed in the whole of Europe, its campaigns and market positioning may be very differently promoted. What seems to be very interesting in his research is the separation between nationalistic and non-nationalistic states, considering this feeling to be roused more in Eastern Europe due to the communist failure. Obviously, advertising has to deal with a young market, still confused and childish, dominated by nostalgia and restrictions. But, even in this case, consumer attitude varies despite the similar experience. Lwin, Stanaland and Williams (2010) highlight the importance of two consumer characteristics towards foreign products and brands, namely ethnocentrism and country-specificity. These theories explicitly reflect why consumers are very selective when buying outside brands over inside ones, influenced by the origin of some products. The ethnocentrism "refers to consumer beliefs regarding the morality of buying foreign-made goods with the general belief that doing so is unpatriotic and harmful to the domestic economy" (Lwin et al., 2010, p. 249). This concept relates to specific feelings such as responsibility, patriotism, conservative behaviour and rejection of new opportunities. It means that you buy a national brand not because you like it or appreciate it, but because it is right to consume what you produce.

Klein, Ettenson and Morris (1998) add to this theory the country-specific animosity that justifies the rejection of any product that may carry negative connotations from the past or the present, related not to the product but to the producers. The authors define this concept "as the remnants of antipathy related to previous or ongoing military, political or economic events" (Klein et al., 1998, p. 90). Those brands are a mirror of some bad experiences in different fields and the consumer relives this feeling forever. The comparison between two concepts regards the way local and global brands are affected. In the first case, only global brands are rejected, while, in the second one, both brand categories may be treated this way. The country of origin could be an advantage or, on the contrary, a real burden that may destroy the brand reputation.

Analysing European consumers' perception of common brands, local and global, provides a lot of information that may explain both theories discussed earlier. Reader's Digest publishes each year a trusted brand survey that tests the brand affiliation in many countries integrated into the European Union. In 2011, the research was conducted using on-line and postal questionnaires in 16 countries, including Romania. It chose 20 common brands to be judged by the respondents in order to establish a top list of the most trusted European brands. Each country decided on which brand was more representative for those common categories. Respondents were asked to rate each brand based on four criteria – quality, excellent value, strong image, understands customer needs. Each had a maximum

Table 9-2. The trusted brands: Comparison of winning brands over 5 years in Romania

Product category	2011	2010	2009	2008	2007
Automotive	Dacia	Dacia	Dacia	Mercedes	Mercedes
Kitchen appliances	Philips	Philips	Philips	Philips	Arctic
Personal computers	Dell	Dell	Dell	IBM	IBM
Internet service provider	RCS&RDS	RCS&RDS	RCS&RDS	RCS&RDS	RDS
Mobile phone handset	Nokia	Nokia	Nokia	Nokia	Nokia
Mobile phone service provider	Orange	Vodafone	Vodafone	Vodafone	Vodafone/ Orange
Camera	Sony	Canon	Sony	Sony	Sony
Holiday company	Paralela 45	Paralela 45	Paralela 45	Paralela 45	Paralela 45
Banks/Building Societies	BCR	BCR	BRD	BCR	BCR
Credit card	Visa	Visa	Visa	Visa	Visa
Insurance company	ASIROM	ASIROM	ING	ASIROM	ASIROM
Petrol retailer	Petrom	Petrom	Petrom	Petrom	Petrom
Cough/cold remedy	Nurofen	Nurofen	Nurofen	Nurofen	Nurofen
Analgesic/ Pain relief	Algocalmin	Algocalmin	Algocalmin	Algocalmin	Algocalmin
Vitamins	Eurovita	Eurovita	Eurovita	Eurovita	Eurovita
Hair care product	Head & Shoulders	Head & Shoulders	Head & Shoulders	Head & Shoulders	Head & Shoulders
Cosmetics	Nivea	Nivea	Nivea	Avon	Avon
Skin care	Nivea	Nivea	Nivea	Nivea	Nivea
Washing powder	Ariel	Ariel	Ariel	Ariel	Ariel
Breakfast cereal	Nestlé	Nestlé	Nestlé	Nestlé	Nestlé

score of 5. This study answers a few questions about some important issues, such as the relationship between the global and the local, the credibility of national brands, the loyalty and the impact of local campaigns regarding national or European brands. Table 9-2 shows us what has been the Romanian respondents' opinion in the last 5 years, comparing the results and showing the stability/instability of the market. We are very interested to see how many Romanian brands were trusted in comparison with the European ones.

As you can see, only 7 local brands (those brands in italic and bold formatted in the chart) out of 20 are at the top in their category, and they may be classified according to their history as old surviving brands created before 1990 (Dacia, Algocalmin, ASIROM), while new brands (so called "democratic brands") came up on the market after the Revolution (RCS&RDS, BCR, Petrom, Paralela 45). All these brands are easily recognizable as their names indicate their Romanian roots. In addition to these common choices, each country had the option to include a number of product categories that tend to be relevant to some countries and not to others, or where the range of brands available is most likely to be local and not known outside the country. Romania included 9 local categories and 9 represented by global brands. What is very interesting is that Romanian people considered trusted brands those used daily – bakery products, dairy products, mineral water, cooking oil, meat products and mass media – which is quite representative of the traditional lifestyle. This means that we can identify a kind of consumer ethnocentrism in this area of foods. Even though Dacia was the most popular Romanian car brand during the communist period, and it was a real personal victory to buy one, the repositioning and the association with Renault improved its image a lot, and externalized its values. Dacia recorded huge sales in many European countries during the last two years, and its celebrity went back up very quickly in Romania. Returning to the comparison between countries and brands within the same market, we may say that Romanian consumers trust their national car manufacturer as much as German, French, Swedish and Czech consumers do. This is why the previous chart does not bring to light any kind of country-specific animosity in the case of Romanian consumers.

RESEARCH METHOD

The research method is the content analysis applied on a sample of 100 TV commercials broadcast on the Romanian market, equally made up of European and local brands and of different product categories. The product categories we choose to exemplify (the national identity versus Romanian identity) are very diverse, as you can see in Table 9-3.

Table 9-3: Product categories included in the research sample

Product categories	Romanian Brands		European Brands		Total ads number
	Brand names	Ads number	Brand names	Ads number	
Mobile phone service provider	Romtelecom	5	Orange, Cosmote	6	11
Cars	Dacia Logan	5	Mercedes Renault	5	10
Dairy	Napolact, Covalact	5	Hochland, Milli	4	9
Salami and sausages	Banat bun, Pate Ardealul, Scandia	3	Caroli, Rio Mare, Gourmet	3	6
Chocolate and coffee	Rom	6	Milka, Kinder, Poiana, Jakobs	4	10
Biscuits and bakery products	Eugenia, Măgura	2	Joe, Oreo	2	4
Banks and insurance company	Banca Transilvania	5	Raiffeisen, Millennium Bank, Alpha Bank, BRD	4	9
Nonalcoholic drinks	Frutti Fresh, Adria, Giusto, Fruttia	5	Granini, Tedi	2	7

Alcoholic drinks (bier, vine, vodka, cognac)	Timişoreana, Ursus, Murfatlar, Domeniile Sâmbureşti, Lacrima lui Ovidiu	7	Bucegi, Golden Brau, Tuborg, Alexandrion, Stalinskaya	9	16
Medicines	Algocalmin, Carmol	2	Eurovita, Memo Plus	2	4
Soap powder	Dero	1	Bonux, Ariel	2	3
Cosmetics	Gerovital	1	Nivea, Avon	2	3
Electronic appliances	Arctic, Altex	2	Beko	1	3
Mineral water	Izvorul Minunilor, Biborţeni	2		0	2
Spicy		0	Fuchs, Maggy, Tomi	3	3

The principle we followed during the quantitative research was to look for identical elements in commercials broadcast on the Romanian market, for each product category. The selection of commercials involves the application of a few criteria in order to check our hypothesis such as:

- Establishing a balance between European and local commercials dedicated to each brand category;
- Choosing TV commercials only for two reasons: the visual richness helps watchers get the meaning easier and second, there is always a relationship between denotation and connotation noticeable from different stages of reading;
- Trying to find product categories represented by both European and Romanian brands, except mineral water and condiments, to make a real comparison between brand identities;
- Each selected commercials were produced on the Romanian market by local agencies, so we did not use adaptation or translation of

European campaigns distributed at an international level to underline the approach of identity in advertising.

The aspects we are concerned about in the quantitative analysis refer to verbal and visual identity, features of Romanian and European identity, brand reputation and positioning strategies.

The main hypothesis is that Romanian advertising has obviously been developed in the following directions: first, the commercials focusing on local identity arisen from tradition and local life-styles (models of localization); second, on borrowing, preserving and encouraging European values (model of standardization), and on a double identity consisting in local and European values (model of hybridization or glocalization). This research intends to reveal first, what kind of European influences are more often absorbed by the local ads in a very creative manner, not as a simple mimesis, and, second, what is the substance of the brand identity on the local market.

Results

All quantitative results will be explained in a qualitative way to answer some questions about identity in Romanian advertising.

What is the balance between visual and verbal identity in promoting brands on the Romanian market?

First of all, recognizing a brand identity is a very complex process that implies paying attention to both visual and verbal messages. The way the concept of identity has been applied here regards brand history, connection to the origin country, and connotation of national and European values. Sometimes verbal indices emphasize brand identities, or visual indices open the consumer's eyes, sometimes both of them are relevant or irrelevant. We are very interested to see if there is any connection between product categories and brands belonging to the national or European field. Figure 9-1 answers the main question debated in this research:

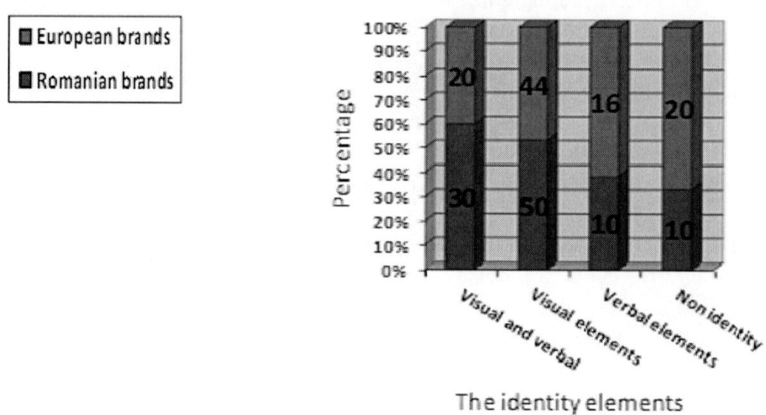

Fig 9-1. Visual and verbal identity of brands

This figure reveals a double comparison: first, between verbal and visual aspects within local and European brands analyzed individually, and, second, between each aspect mentioned before but regarding Romanian and European brands. In the case of Romanian brands visual identity is best represented from two points of view: the product categories and the ads number. The sample includes 25 Romanian commercials dedicated to cars, mobile phones, dairy, banks, non-alcoholic drinks, alcoholic drinks, and mineral water, detergent, chocolate (9 categories of 15) that visually emphasize brand identity. Visual and verbal indices have been noticed in fewer situations, only 15 commercials, regarding non-alcoholic and alcoholic drinks, salami and sausages, electronic appliances. Verbal identity and non-identity are equally represented in the Romanian sample, each of them with 5 commercials. Taking a look at the European brands, it is easy to observe almost the same distribution between verbal and visual elements, except non-identity indices that cover 20 per cent of the entire corpus. Basically, the product categories seem to be almost the same in the case of visual representation, except spices and cosmetics that come up as new elements. A different situation arises from visual and verbal indices in the case of European brands, according to new product categories such as: mobile phones, banks, spices and biscuits. The same aspect emphasizes verbal elements by underlining other product categories in comparison to the Romanian sample such as coffee, medicines and cars. The non-identity elements are those that do not present any connection to the brand history or home country, maybe because they are very well known and used, and have crossed the production borders for a long time. This is the case for brands like Granini, Renault, Hochland, Nivea, Eurovita and Beko.

To sum up, the balance between verbal and local features of brand identity highlights similar aspects regardless the local and global belonging. The previous analysis does not bring to light what kind of identity, local or European, the commercials reveal, but only the presence of brand identity, generally speaking.

Which is the specificity of identity in the entire research corpus?

Answering this question implies extending the previous conclusion about the brand identity that rose from the commercials included in the research corpus. The main purpose of this aspect consists in researching the way Romanian and European brands focus on general or particular issues of their identity on local market. In our opinion, local market and consumers request a special approach regarding the perception of European or international brands. According to Marieke de Mooij, consumer behaviour cannot be easily changed by global product perception in other markets: "There may be global products, but there are no global people. They may be global brands, but there are no global motivations for buying those brands" (2010, p. 5).

Therefore, Figure 9-2 presents the quantitative results of identity by considering the market characteristics and local consumers as very important factors for creating a persuasive message. The variables this research looks for are very simple: double influence (local and European), country of origin aspects and no clues that may indicate affiliation to the European or Romanian space.

The first category that emerged from the previous chart is the double identity that includes commercials developing Romanian and European cultural, social and historical features regardless the production country. It is relevant that this type is dominant in the Romanian sample, covering 58% of the national corpus and 42% of the entire sample. Almost all product categories lead to this result by encouraging this strategy of positioning a brand of the local market. From the European point of view, the most important product categories that this double identity is concerned about are mobile phones service, cars, beer (alcoholic drinks), chocolate and banks. There is no doubt that beer and chocolate consumers and mobile phone users should identify with the commercials broadcast on local market, given the high levels of sales. Moreover, the local market is not so well represented on these levels by local brands, at least when it comes to mobile phones, chocolates and cars. This is the main reason why only a few product categories are highly represented in our corpus in comparison to other types of products.

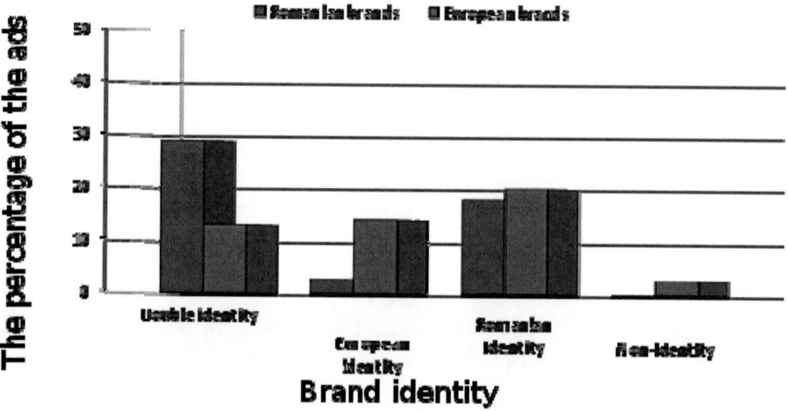

Fig. 9-2. Brand identity

The European identity is sometimes associated with global identity, as in a Romtelecom ad (Tarzan is the hero) or with cultural issues ("The Golden Fish" by the Brothers Grimm, "The Snow Queen" by Hans Christian Andersen). It is understandable that this issue is rarely met in the research sample without being woven into local aspects. When analyzing the European brands, the exclusively European identity should be more present, but not dominant, considering the profile of local consumers. Cultural features do not specifically have to do with the country of origin of brands. For example, Cosmote, which is a very successful Greek mobile phone network in Romania, appeals to Shakespeare's story of Romeo and Juliet in promoting its values. Sometimes, English or French is the language of the verbal message, even if the commercials were created for Romanian customers. This proves the importance of the globalization phenomena and the role of international communication, as most of the words used in the ads are English. We may say that there is no immediate connection between the production country and the foreign language used in advertising "pedigree brands". The best example this corpus offers is a commercial created for Jacobs Krönung where a young man tries to introduce himself to a young and beautiful woman who is his new next-door neighbour. The lady seems to be completely unfriendly, but the next day the aroma of a very good coffee lures her. She knocks on his door and she asks for a coffee in Spanish. What do we have here? A Romanian man named George drinking a German quality coffee and being desired by a beautiful Spanish woman.

The Romanian identity occupies a higher level in the hierarchy of the European brand in comparison with the local ones. There is no doubt that local brands are concerned about local consumers. The product categories included into this type are diverse and local features the same. The Romanian identity consists in local Christmas songs, Bucharest pictures, countryside landscapes, specific architectures, specific Romanian last names (Ionescu and Popescu), local personalities (most of them artists and sport players), school uniform and specific gastronomy. In the Romanian sample, the features are very similar, but also enriched by historical aspects (Nicolae Ceauşescu's image, the colour of the national flag, one of Romania's old hymns (Hora Unirii), popular costumes, old and new life styles, rituals, natural medicine and art aspects. All of these aspects are details very well understood by local consumers and acting as clues to national identity. Global brands used some of them in their campaigns, but not with a particular meaning; they are used for the products, not only for the consumers.

The ads classified as non-identity examples are completely absent from the Romanian corpus, while in the other sample they are present in only three cases that are not significant for the present research. The first question we answered in this study regarded brand identity, but this time the study follows any kind of indices that suggest a connection with Romanian or European identity not a special connection with the brand. This is the difference between brand image and connection with cultures and spaces from Europe. The first ad presents a conversation between fruits in a very exotic place (the brand is Granini), the second ad, for Tomi, describes an imaginative scene from Hell, and the last example regards the ritual of eating Oreo biscuits in a family. Nothing specific, everything is available for consumers all over the world.

To sum up the answers to this question, the double approach of identity dominates the Romanian sample, while the Romanian identity represents the winner in the case of the corpus made up of ads dedicated to European brands. We may say that the situation reaches a kind of similar level, but in the opposite direction. If we discuss the results from a general perspective, referring to all commercials included in the research corpus at the same time, the first place would belong to the double identity again, by adding up the individual results.

What does the brand reputation consist in?

Brand reputation is another concept very well connected with identity, because it is based on three different qualities that justify the relationship between external and internal brand features. This discussion has been earlier started in the theoretical part of this paper, by presenting the six types of brand reputation according to Sicco van Gelder (Table 9-1). At that time of the research, we only explained the types determined by the advertising context, namely pedigree brands and origin brands. Given the purpose of the present study, we searched for all these 6 types of brand reputation within the research sample, organizing the analysis again on two coordinates: first, individually identifying the types of brand reputation for local and European commercials, and, second, comparing the results. This is actually the main idea that carries on throughout this paper all the time. Figure 9-3 presents the results by including both dimensions of this research: brand reputation and the comparison between local and global issues.

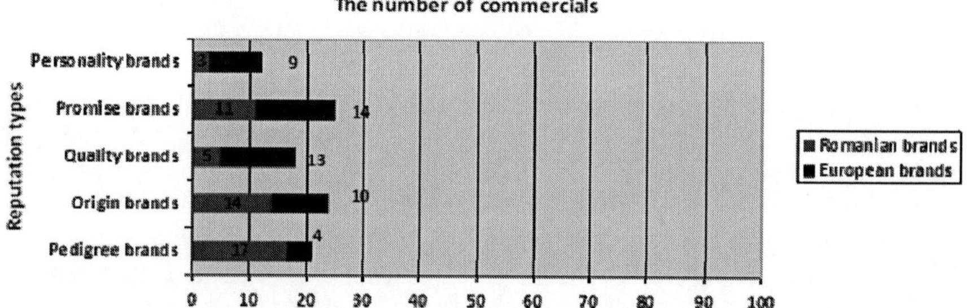

Fig. 9-3. Brand reputation

What is obvious at first sight is the absence of any of the associative brand categories, namely the endorsed brands that were not noticed in the sample. This type consists in supporting a brand image by using a specialist (doctor, engineer, mechanic) to explain how efficient a product is. The other type of distribution shows us a very diverse hierarchy, comparing national brands with the European ones. Pedigree brands deserve special attention in both cases, representing 21% of the entire corpus, and 17 ads only in the corpus made up by local brands. Emphasis on the brand roots and inheritance are more relevant for the Romanian sample, to increase product authority and credibility. Most of the ads focus on history and use a specific verbal message that derives from the word

"Romania" to remind consumers that these brands belong to their life. The local categories refer to dairy, chocolate, non-alcoholic and alcoholic drinks, mineral water and sausages and they are always associated with Romanian art and a style of producing something unique and precious. For example, a commercial for the Rom chocolate created a message describing the way Romanian people perceive love, not for Valentine's day, but for Dragobete, the old traditional celebration with a similar meaning: "You really show your love in a Romanian style during Dragobete." Another ad dedicated to a dairy brand makes a strong connection with the place of production, suggested very well by the name of the brand, Napolact, and the message points out its nobility: "So, healthy as you may be at 20 you will only stay if you eat what mother nature gives you and what is worked out by hand: Napolact milk, as only people living in Ardeal know how to do it". A good example for European brands belongs to the cognac Alexandrion whose commercial on the Romanian market celebrates the product's birth in mythical Greece, reminds the consumer about legendary culture and mythology: "There is a place in Greece where gods and people made a deal".

The brand origin associates its attributes with the country lifestyle and native features of that nation, such as Germany with technique and reliability, France with romanticism, Spain for passion, Italy representing style and sophistication. According to this research, features may be synthesized by a couple of keywords such as: fidelity, nostalgia, sense of humour, natural and traditional food, old wine and traditional behaviour. Nature and traditions often become synonymous with Romanian lifestyle according to the examples provided by the research sample: German resistance for Mercedes, the healthful taste of the Alps milk for Hochland and the Italian salami indicate European brand reputation. However, this sample brought to light some ads where the origin identity was confused, indicating many local aspects, so that they may be perceived as Romanian brands. This is the case with Caroli (salami) "that keeps Romanian folks on the move" or for Germanos (a mobile phone provider) that describes how Romanian children sang Christmas songs in the past and how they still do it now.

According to Sicco Van Gelder (2010, p. 114), "Quality brands derive their reputation from the appreciation of consumers towards their product or service excellence, and subsequent consumer loyalty." Figure 9-3 does not emphasize the quality reputation of Romanian brands as much as it does for European brands. This is quite understandable, given the authority of those brands all over the world. The commercials are aimed at

Romanian consumers, but the product qualities are available everywhere they can be used.

The promising brands make dreams come true based on the consumers' insight, on their expectations and values. These are not especially connected with local or global values, but they give the feeling of "the dream land". The chart indicates this type as the winner in the hierarchy, without any specific connection with Romanian or European identity. The promise lies in improving life, experimenting and trying new challenges, offering the consumer a comparative perspective: the one without this brand and the other one offering something better and, maybe, more challenging.

The last type identified by van Gelder's classification develops brand reputation through relying on different celebrities who do not support the product specifically but can transfer their aura to it. These personalities usually work in areas of interest such as art, sport, film or science and everyone knows and appreciates them. In the Romanian research sample, we identified only three ads that rely on this strategy: the first is linked to Romtelecom, the second to CEC (the oldest Romanian savings bank) and the third to a traditional wine, Murfatlar. In all these situations, personalities are not specific to the local market or to the Romanian culture, but are selected for their global attraction: Tarzan and Jane for Romtelecom, Elvis Presley for CEC and the Roman poet Ovid for Ovid's Tear (a wine produced by Murfatlar-originally named Lacrima lui Ovidiu). The only local connection established here is between Ovid, who was exiled to Tomis on the Black Sea shore, and the old vineyards cultivated close by. The European brands use both global and local personalities, which proves how much they are concerned about the local consumer and his cultural background. The famous tennis player Ilie Năstase is the image of a bank, the Romanian actress Magda Catone represents the detergent Bonux, Ceauşescu proves the history of Bucegi beer (produced by Heineken), and Romeo and Juliet remind the Romanian users of Cosmote mobile phone service how important communication is. Here we obviously face the opposite strategy of adapting a brand image either to a market of aspiration (Europe), speaking about local products, or to a market of product distribution (Romania), as in the case of European brands.

In partial conclusion, pedigree and origin brands focus on Romanian brands that recover or build their history in this way, while promise and quality brands characterize better the emergence of European brands into the local market.

Which are the main positioning strategies used by the brands under discussion?

Positioning concept is the easiest way to check whether a brand is selected in the consumers' mind and gets to the top, by winning the "battle" with other attractive brands, according to Ries and Trout (2001). In 1996, Jack Trout (with Steve Rivkin as co-author this time) reviewed his theoretical approach on the concept, in a book whose title is suggestive of its purpose: The New Positioning: The Latest on the World's #1 Business Strategy. The first chapter, called "Things are getting worse", made the connection with Trout's first book, because it came back to the features of the human being who determines brand retention. The authors specified five important elements in the positioning process: "1. Minds are limited 2. Minds hate confusion 3. Minds are insecure 4. Minds don't change 5. Minds can lose focus"(Trout & Rivkin, 1996, p. 8). For each element, the writers identified different types of positioning, thus extending the first list presented by Trout and Ries. They spotlighted positioning according to some important strategies. For example, positioning based on analogies corresponds to commercials created as "slices of life". Another type is the positioning developed following the "Bandwagon" effect, and this effect is the struggle to be always the first in your domain.

Table 9-4 provides information about positioning types identified in the research sample, extending the concept to some particular features. The main purpose of this question is to find a connection between brand reputation and positioning strategies, to better explain the Romanian identity vs. European identity in the selected ads.

For both categories of brands, positioning based on consumer needs reveals the top results in different proportion, which suggests the predominance of promise brand, especially for European brands. Product quality is the second important classification alongside positioning which, by using the product and based on price, justifies the reputation of quality brands. The next important types are those relying on time and tradition (or brand history) alongside symbolic elements, because they certify the origin and pedigree brands that may also be metaphorically described as "nobility ads". Leader authority refers to a kind of origin brand, given to the message of Gerovital cosmetics that emphasized the market supremacy of the Romanian products: "The best seller brand in Romania". The other examples of positioning categories do not reflect a direct correspondence with a single type of brand reputation, because the message is very flexible and every time changes the image of the brand reputation. Opposition and comparison describe the qualities of a banking service (Transilvania Bank) by suggesting a comparison with other credit providers that demands time and patience from the consumers. Another ad created for an important mobile phone service (Cosmote) underlines the competition between other brands from the same category by using cultural personality, Romeo and Juliet.

Table 9-4. Positioning types identified for European and Romanian brands

Positioning types	European brands	Romanian brands	Total ads
Based on consumer needs	13	11	24
By product qualities	13	8	21
Symbolical elements	11	9	20
Based on time and tradition	0	11	11
Busing the product	7	2	9
By niche	3	3	6
By opposition and comparison	3	3	6
Based on relationship between price and quality	0	2	2
Based on leader authority	0	1	1

This correspondence briefly points out that pedigree and origin brands build their image with concern for consumer insight and their representations, regarding values and credibility provided by some products.

Conclusions

Local brands strongly develop their identity regarding some product categories, such as dairy, banks, sausages, alcoholic drinks (especially wine and beer), by promoting them as pedigree or origin brands. At the same time, European brands respect the local identity of consumers and organize their campaigns by paying attention to the Romanian culture and values. The adaptation strategies to the local market are very diverse and consist in several issues such as: naming local brands of European companies according to the consumer insight, using Romanian personalities to get more credibility, looking for visual symbols and not emphasizing the origin brands so much.

On the contrary, Romanian brands tend to externalize their values and get closer to the European perception of quality by importing some patterns of creative strategy. The word that best describes this opening to other countries' identity is hybridization. This aim is quite understandable for two reasons: first, the necessity to let out some products and brands on the European market to improve the economic situation in Romania, and, second, the wish to adapt to the regional market, to be part of it, by dissolving the difference created by the communist ages.

In our opinion, answering the questions this research put forward in the abstract ("Do European brands emphasize the values of their country of origin?" or "Are they similar to other global brands?" "Can we really talk about a Romanian identity in this context of assimilation of European values and lifestyles?") involves the acceptance of a paradox. European brands do not emphasize their genuine values so much (according to Figure 9-3), at least not explicitly and it is difficult to establish their specificity, except cars, beers, cosmetics and alcoholic drinks. Romanian brands play cards on both sides: traditional and old brands develop double campaigns, for local and global consumers, while new brands try to be very much associated with European brands. The local identity is differently expressed according to the consumers: everyday products are more traditional and symbolic, while expensive products (like cars, electronics, banks) tend to be positioned based on quality and consumer needs. Therefore, Romanian advertising works on identity in a very chameleonic way, and, sometimes, the same brand uses both perspectives to emphasize the transition from local to global. On the one side, the verbal message of commercials intensively uses the lexical family of the word "Romania", to make consumers aware and proud of their identity, on the other side they mix all cultural influences to give consumers the feeling of belonging to Europe.

In conclusion, this research definitively points out the Romanian advertising preoccupation for building and rebuilding its identity according to local consumers and brand history, in a decided effort to get out on the European market.

References

Amine, L S, Chao, M & Arnold, M J (2005). Executive Insights: Exploring the Practical Effects of Country of Origin, Animosity, and Price-Quality Issues: Two Case Studies of Taiwan and Acer in China. Journal of International Marketing, 13(2), 114–124.

Anderson, B (1991). Imagined Communities, London: Verso.

Bennett, R (1993). The Handbook of European Advertising: Media Planning, Marketing Analysis and Country-by-country Profiles, London: Kogan Page.

De Mooij, M (2010). Global Marketing and Advertising: Understanding Cultural Paradoxes, 2nd edition. London: Sage.

Klein, J G, Ettenson, R & Morris, M D (1998). The Animosity Model of Foreign Product Purchase: An Empirical Test in the People's Republic of China. Journal of Marketing, 62 (January), 89–100.

Lwin, M O, Stanaland, A J S & Williams, J D (2010). Exporting America: Usage of Symbols in Iinternational Advertising under Conditions of Consumer Ethnocentrism and US-focused Animosity. International Journal of Advertising. 29 (2), 245–277.

Moriarty, S, Mitchell, N & Wells, W (2009). Advertising: Principles & Practice, 8th edition, New Jersey: Pearson Education.

Pieterse, J N (2009). Globalization and Culture: Global Mélange, 2nd edition, Maryland: The Rowman & Littlefield Publishing Group.

Ries, A & Trout, J (2001). Positioning: The Battle for Your Mind, 20th anniversary edition, New York: McGraw-Hill.

Scholte, J A (2005). Globalization: A Critical Introduction, 2nd edition. New York: Palgrave Macmillan.

Trout, J, & Rivkin, S (1996). The New Positioning: The Latest on the World's #1 Business Strategy, New York: McGraw-Hill.

Van Gelder, S (2010). Global Brand Strategy: Unlocking Brand Potential across Countries, Cultures and Markets, London: Kogan Page.

Electronic references

Reader' Digest, www.rdtrustedbrands.com accessed 18 July 2011 http://www.rdtrustedbrands.com/tables/Europe%2520Wide%2520Winners.country.Romania.shtml

Europe Wide Winners accessed 15 July 2011 http://www.rdtrustedbrands.com/tables/Influence%2520on%2520brand%2520choice.country.Romania.shtml-Influence

READING BETWEEN THE HEADLINES: HOW MEDIA FRAMED THE POSTPONEMENT OF ROMANIA'S ACCESSION TO THE SCHENGEN AREA

ELENEA NEGREA

Abstract

This paper examines the role of conceptual metaphors in the representation of the postponement of Romania's accession to the Schengen Area and the connection between the metaphoric interpretation and the news frames used to present this issue. The units of analysis are the headlines of TV news broadcasts from 21 December 2010 to 21 January 2011 on three major Romanian channels. The article focuses on the metaphors of war, sports and family, which are used to interpret Romania's failure to accede to the Schengen Area. Furthermore, the paper attempts to shed some light on the link between the metaphoric headlines and the frames used to present the issue in the news.

Key words: headlines, conceptual metaphor, news frames, emotional discourse

WHAT STORY DO THE HEADLINES TELL US?

From a journalistic perspective, headlines are viewed as distinct units linked to the content of the news they introduce. Their role in the economy of the news article is twofold: on the one hand, headlines act as summaries of the full text (van Dijk, 1988), while, on the other hand, they are used to attract the reader's attention. In this paper, both dimensions of headlines will be examined: broadcast news headlines aimed at providing a summary of TV news on a particular topic – Romania's accession to the Schengen Area – will be assessed against the content of the news, the frames identified in the news, and the pragmatic and rhetorical roles of conceptual metaphors embedded in the analysed headlines.

Whether we consider them as "proxies used to locate and represent media content" (Althaus et al., 2001, p. 708), "media-generated shortcuts" (Andrew, 2007) or "relevance optimizers" (Dor, 2003), it is widely accepted in the literature that headlines are a separate meaningful unit of the news they lead. Usually, the information they contain has a high news value. Perhaps more important than informing about the content of the news article is their role of persuading the reader to go through the whole text and thus gain the full meaning of the story it describes. It is known that readers first pay attention to the headline and then read the article or watch the news. Therefore, the catchier the headline and the more intriguing its formulation, the more motivated is the reader to continue reading the whole news item. However, despite their function of providing an attractive, "eye-catching" summary, the content of news headlines may reveal distinct information from the full text that they introduce. Research on news headlines content has shown that the information conveyed by the headlines is not always consistent with the rest of the text (Althaus et al., 2001; Andrew, 2007). The under-representation or over-representation – actually, misrepresentation – of news stories that they introduce to the readers may explain the powerful impact that headlines have on people's perception of the topic of the news report, especially if this is a politics-related topic. From his investigation of the media coverage of the 2004 Canadian election campaign, Andrew (2007) found that the content of campaign news headlines differed substantively from the content of the full-text reports. Drawing on the low-information rationality theory (Lau & Redlawsk, 2001), the author concludes that Canadian readers seem not to have improved their knowledge about politics since "scanning election headlines was not a close substitute for paying more attention" (Andrew, 2007, p. 25).

The lack of consistency between the content of headlines and that of the news reports they represent may be a consequence of the dash to get more readers and viewers. The objectivity imperative has been slowly replaced by the market or economic imperative. News reports currently show great concern for audience-winning (Schudson, 1978) at the expense of taking an objective stance towards the issue presented. News headlines have also evolved in this direction; they are not only media-generated shortcuts, but also market-driven tools for "selling the news". The newsworthiness of a story is measured in terms of its potential to "make the headlines". Headlines are very important for news consumers, and the observed incongruence between the information supplied by the story and the one held by the headline used to introduce it seems to be less disturbing for them than expected.

INTERPRETING THE FIGURATIVE LANGUAGE OF HEADLINES

The primary focus of a reader when confronted with a newspaper article or televised news is on the headline. This is why the interpretation of the news depends on decoding and interpreting the headline first of all. The interpretation of the headline is no different from the interpretation of any other sentence (Dijk, 1998). In order to facilitate this process, it is recommended that headlines be composed of relatively short sentences, that active verbs be used and that their content be clear and unambiguous. The use of information supposedly already known by the readers also helps them to easily determine the meaning of the headlines and pursue the interpretation of the full story. Despite these general recommendations, cultural references, figurative language (e.g. use of metaphor, metonymy, irony, puns, humour) or implied meaning are widely used in news headlines. Studies have demonstrated that figurative language is more appealing to readers when interpreting the headlines (Ifantidou, 2009) and that metaphors and metonymies guide headline interpretation by deriving pragmatic inferences from the text, which ultimately contributes to the fulfilling of the role of attracting readers' attention (Shie, 2011). Furthermore, for the subjects participating in a study on headline interpretation, the mismatch between the content of the headline and the meaning of the article has no significant impact on the effectiveness of the headline as such. This finding is consistent with the view that headlines should be treated as autonomous texts and interpreted as such (Ifantidou, 2009).

The use of figurative language in headlines, especially of metaphors, metonymies and irony, stems from the news reporters' constant and urgent need to grab readers' attention. The news discourse contained by metaphorical, metonymic or ironic headlines guides the reader through the whole text. The metaphors and other forms of figurative language used in headlines provide the target reader with a "suggested" or "preferred" interpretative schema of the news report. Reading the headline and skimming the text sometimes suffice for a reader to determine whether he is interested in the news and to retrieve a preferred interpretation of the content presented to him.

While significant work examining instances of figurative language in newspaper articles or in televised debates has been done (Burnes, 2011; Kimmel, 2010; Negrea, 2010; Musolff, 2004; Musolff, 2006; Kovecses,

2005; El Refaie, 2005), little attention has been paid to the analysis of metaphors and metonymies in broadcast news, and even less to the examination of figurative language in TV news headlines. This paper attempts to provide an inventory of conceptual metaphors in the headlines of TV news and to highlight the connection between the interpretation favoured by the metaphors and the frames that the media used to portray the postponement of Romania's accession to the Schengen Area, at the beginning of 2011.

THE ANALYSIS OF TV NEWS ON THE "SCHENGEN AFFAIR"

On 21 December 2010, a letter sent by the French and German Ministers of Interior concerning the postponement of Romania and Bulgaria's accession to the Schengen Area (planned for March 2011) excited Romanian public opinion. It was the start of what has been called the "Schengen Affair" by a research team from the Centre for Research in Communication (www.centrucomunicare.ro) in Bucharest. The topic has been investigated using a three-pronged approach: public perception, media coverage and elite opinion. While the main findings of the research project have been published elsewhere (Bârgăoanu, 2011), this paper only tackles some of the results of the content analysis of TV news carried out during a 1-month period (21 December 2010 – 21 January 2011). The analysis comprised all prime time news broadcast on three Romanian channels – TVR 1 (the publicly-funded TV channel), Pro TV and Antena 1 (two private channels). The content analysis of the "Schengen Affair" in TV and online news sought to assess the visibility of the topic, its prominence and the visibility of political actors involved. Ten students from the Department of Communication and Public Relations (National School of Political Studies and Public Administration, Bucharest, Romania) coded the news items. The inter-coder reliability, which was measured using Holsti's formula, is situated between 0.72 and 0.92 (Bârgăoanu, 2011).

A total of 2,408 news items were content analysed, out of which only 59 (i.e., 2%) dealt with the "Schengen Affair", our research's main focus. Needless to say, this is sufficient proof for researchers to infer that the "Schengen Affair" did not set the media agenda during the 1-month period of the analysis. On a more subtle note, both the content analysis used to determine media coverage of the topic and the survey used to assess the public perception have produced substantive evidence that, despite the impression that the "Schengen Affair" ranked highly on media and public agendas, in reality it lacked visibility and public interest (Bârgăoanu, 2011).

This paper aims at analysing the headlines of the 59 news articles on Schengen and at determining the metaphors used to convey their meaning. Five pieces of news were excluded from the analysis due to their lack of headline (3) and to their belonging to a predefined category of the TVR 1 newscast (2), which is called Tema zilei [The topic of the day]. Furthermore, the article seeks to map the metaphoric interpretation of the examined news headlines with the frames used by the media to portray the postponement of Romania's accession to the Schengen Area. The idea underlying this endeavour is that the favoured metaphoric interpretation of headlines combined with the excessive use of the conflict frame have triggered and, at the same time, have amplified the emotional discourse on the topic (based on the dichotomy "us/them") at the expense of a technical and expert approach.

"THEY DON'T WANT US": CONCEPTUAL METAPHORS IN NEWS HEADLINES

Media discourse is abundant in metaphors and other types of figurative language. Newspaper articles, talk shows or televised debates are filled with metaphors, metonymies and irony, which makes meaning-grasping and interpretation a challenge for many readers and viewers. News reports have been considered until recently the last outpost of literal interpretation in media discourse, the genre of journalism most likely not to be affected by journalists' and the readers' need to assign different meanings to what is said and, thus, make the interpretation of the text a more complex process. Although there is not (yet) sufficient data to support this claim, it seems that headlines are predisposed to invite to a metaphoric, metonymic, ironic or even humorous interpretation of the story they foreground.

The headlines of the 54 news articles on the "Schengen Affair" will be analysed in terms of the metaphorical mappings across domains. According to the conceptual metaphor theory (Lakoff & Johnson, 1980), metaphors can be conceptualised as correspondences between source domains and target domains, the latter being understood in terms of the former. More than half of the headlines analysed (29 out of 59) contain linguistic expressions of conceptual metaphors in which war, sports or family are source domains. Here are some examples of how Romania's accession to the Schengen Area was conceptually related to the three broad domains:

(1) Schengen – o bătălie pierdută
Schengen – a lost fight politics (accession) is war
(Antena 1, 7 January 2011)

(2) Armele secrete ale României
Romania's secret weapons politics (accession) is war
(Pro TV, 4 January 2011)

(3) Franţa şi Germania nu ne vor
France and Germany don't want usnation (europe) is a family
(Pro TV, 21 December 2010)

(4) Nici Finlanda nu ne vrea
Finland doesn't want us either nation (europe) is a family
(Pro TV, 21 January 2011)

(5) Schengen, ultima turnantă
Schengen, the final lap politics (accession) is sports
(TVR 1, 28 December 2010)

The examples above show how abstract target domains – the accession to the Schengen Area, Romania's status in the European Union or, more comprising, the politics of Romania as a Member State – are mapped to concrete source domains – war, family, sports – in order to facilitate the interpretation. The less tangible areas of experience – state politics, for instance – are associated with or conceptualized into more familiar areas. This conceptualization is motivated by the viewers' search for understanding. In (1) and (2), the conceptual metaphor used is one of the most frequently used in political discourse: politics is war. The postponement of Romania's accession is the consequence of a lost fight with more powerful adversaries (France and Germany). The headline that contains this metaphor accompanies a news item referring to the opinion of a Brussels official who said that Romania would not accede to the Schengen Area at a different date than Bulgaria, and that Bulgaria faced serious security issues at the borders with Turkey (1). Fourteen of the 29 metaphoric headlines contain expressions of the conceptual metaphor politics is war. Conceptualizing the accession and the postponement of the accession in terms of war between different parties (Romania, on the one hand, and France, Germany, Finland and the European Union, on the other hand) is consistent with the preference of media for the conflict frame, as this paper will further show.

Although used to a lesser extent than the "war" metaphor, politics is sports is another way of conceptually representing the target domain (the politics of the accession) by means of a concrete, more familiar source domain – sports. Not only is the sports domain tangible for the majority of viewers, but also it is also suitable for emphasising the conflict dimension of cross-domain mapping. Romania's accession to the Schengen Area is understood in terms of compliance (5 and 6) with the rules of the game or in terms of failure to meet the required criteria for the players (7).

(6) Pregătiţi pentru Schengen
Ready for Schengen
(TVR 1, 17 January 2011)

(7) Avertismente europene
European warnings
(TVR 1, 8 January 2011)

The sports metaphor invites the viewers to have partisan feelings and divides the public in supporters of one or other of the teams involved in a sports competition. This scenario or schema of interpretation amplifies the emotional touch of media discourse on the postponement of Romania's accession to the Schengen Area.

Finally, the headlines used in the TV newscasts to introduce the information materials on the "Schengen Affair" contain linguistic expressions of the conceptual metaphor nation is a family, which provides the viewers with a frame of reference for interpreting the abstract concept of "nation" in terms of what family means to them, of what they know about family relations. The "family" metaphors that appear in the news headlines analysed here do not target a single nation state (as, for instance, in the examples provided by Lakoff & Johnson, 1980), but an assembly of nation states that form the European Union (EU).

There is no doubt that conflict is a powerful component of family relationships. However, more important than conflict relationships, people seem to value family in terms of belonging to it or not. The identity feeling that belonging to a family (a source domain used to target a nation state) gives to people is the foundation of national identity. The reproduction of the national feeling is made manifest and "flagged" by a nation's "political discourse, cultural products or event in the structuring of newspapers" (Billig, 1995, p. 8).

What about "flagging" the European identity? In spite of the crucial importance of a common European identity for the future of the EU, the results of the European public opinion surveys and the findings of research work in the field of identity (Marcussen et al., 2001; McLaren, 2004) have shown that the issue of Europeanization and identity is more delicate than expected. The European identity is constantly undermined by national identity; moreover, the mere idea of “national identity” is deemed irreconcilable with the sense of “Europeanness” that the EU struggles to instil in citizens of its member states. For what it is worth, it seems so far that no notable success has been achieved. On the contrary, the gap between national and European identities has deepened. Events such as the postponement of Romania’s accession to the Schengen Area are triggers of emotional and identity-based evaluation of the EU and EU membership.

The “family” metaphor was found in 8 of the 29 metaphoric headlines investigated. Despite its more modest presence compared with the recurrences of the “war” metaphor, the emotional impact of the metaphoric interpretation of the postponement in terms of being rejected by the “European family” is far greater than the conflict representation. This interpretation has amplified the national frustration and has enforced feelings of national identity that are based on the dichotomy “us vs them” (see examples (3) and (4) above and (8) below).

(8) Oficial, nu ne vor în Schengen
Officially, they don’t want us in Schengen
(Antena 1, 21 December 2010)

The headlines examined have revealed another interesting fact about the “family” metaphor used to represent Romania’s failure to accede to the Schengen Area. Together with the “us vs them” pattern, there is another interpretation scenario favoured by the eu as a family conceptual metaphor: rejection from the “European family” has also made manifest the longing to be accepted as a member of this family.

(9) Cum ar fi fost în Schengen
How Schengen membership would have been
(TVR 1, 8 January 2011)

All these scenario-based presuppositions used to analyse the headlines of the TV news on the “Schengen Affair” are needed to grasp and interpret the meaning of the text of the headline and of the news it introduces, too. Moreover, these scenarios offer a valuable explanation for the emotional touch of the Romanian media discourse on the “Schengen Affair”.

HEADLINES, METAPHORS AND FRAMES

Extensive research on metaphors and their role in discourse has shown that they are a powerful tool to frame social and political issues. This section of the paper seeks to underscore the connection between the conceptual metaphors used in headlines and the frames identified in the TV news that they introduce. What is interesting about this approach is the fact that it attempts at bridging the analysis of conceptual metaphors and framings used in the news. Entman (1993) noted that the role of framing is "to offer a way to describe the power of a communicative text" (p. 51). While framing the news helps the viewers evaluate and interpret the issue presented, conceptualizing metaphorically the categories involved in the communication of the issue allows them to grasp the meaning and organize their understanding of the world (Lakoff & Johnson, 1980; Johnson, 1987).

Why choose headlines to highlight this connection? Because they are framing mechanisms that can be used to identify and measure news frames (de Vreese, 2005). A deductive approach was used in the framing analysis of TV news on the "Schengen Affair"; five types of frames defined prior to the analysis have been used. Three out of the five were generic news frames such as conflict, attribution of responsibility and economic consequences (de Vreese, 2005). The other two were issue-specific frames – the costs-benefits frame and the powerlessness frame. The 29 metaphoric headlines were examined in order to highlight how accurately they combined with the types of frames identified in the TV news that they led. Put differently, the aim of this investigation was to demonstrate to what extent the metaphorical interpretation of the headline is consistent with the news frame used to present the content of the news. The results are presented in Table 10-1.

Not surprisingly, the use of the "war" metaphor in headlines is followed by the presentation of the issue in terms of conflict. More interesting is the fact that the frame of attribution of responsibility is equally identified in pieces of news that were introduced by headlines containing linguistic expression of the "war" metaphor. The powerlessness frame is also present in the news introduced by this type of metaphoric headlines, which support the interpretation of a conflict between two uneven adversaries. This frequency pattern is valid for the "sports" metaphor headlines, too. Since sports competitions also involve opposing parties, the conflict frame is used in news introduced by these headlines. However, the attribution of responsibility is easier to pinpoint in this type of headlines; in sports, the responsibility for losing usually lies with the less prepared participant. In the case of Romania's failure to accede to the Schengen Area, the less prepared participant seemed to be the country itself; therefore, the responsibility was most frequently attributed to Romanian authorities. As far as the "family" metaphor is concerned, the high presence of the conflict frame may be explained by the fact that the relationship Romania – EU is conceived of in terms of "us vs them", which invites to an interpretation based on clashing interests and opposition. This is another piece of evidence supporting the idea that the media's approach to the topic of Romania's accession to Schengen was intensely emotional.

Table 10-1. Frequency of news frames in items introduced by metaphoric headlines

News frame / Type of metaphor	Conflict frame	Attribution of responsibility frame	Economic consequences frame	Costs/ benefits frame	Powerlessness frame
war (n=14)	12	12	1	4	11
sports (n=6)	3	5	-	3	4
family (n=8)	7	7	1	2	4

Conclusions

News headlines are one of the most interesting features of media discourse. Their examination may reveal exciting facts to the researcher preoccupied with the analysis of the way in which media frame newsworthy issues. This paper aimed at investigating news headlines in terms of their metaphoric potential and with respect to their relationship with the rest of the information. As literature suggested, there is significant evidence pertaining to the fact that headlines do not accurately represent the story that they introduce. Whereas this may be true, this paper shows that, the content of the headlines is at least consistent with the news frames used to present it. Furthermore, it has been indicated here that the conceptual metaphors contained by the news headlines analysed, combined with the news frames used to present the information to viewers, determined the intense emotional approach to the issue of the postponement of Romania's accession to the Schengen Area.

The analysis indicated that Romania's failure to accede to the Schengen Area has been conceptualized as a war that the country lost, a sports competition in which it has been defeated and as a family that rejected it. Conceiving the event in these terms triggered an emotional approach in media discourse. This may also offer an explanation for the lack of visibility of the topic in TV news. Since an expert discourse filled with technical details is of little interest to news reporters, only the conflict-driven peaks of the "Schengen Affair" were extensively covered in newscasts, namely the moments when France and Germany's decision to postpone the accession was made public and later sustained by other member states as well. Due to the limitations of the small corpus of headlines analysed in this paper, it is not possible to draw significant conclusions about the difference between the use of metaphorical headlines on the one hand and non-metaphorical headlines on the other to favour an emotional interpretation of the topic. Further investigation of the headlines of online news on the "Schengen Affair" may prove to be more insightful in this direction.

References

Althaus, S L, Edy, A J & Phalen, P F (2001). Using Substitutes for Full-text News Stories in Content Analysis: Which Text Is Best? American Journal of Political Science 45(3), 707–23.

Andrew, B C (2007). Media-generated Shortcuts: Do Newspaper Headlines Present Another Roadblock for Low-information Rationality? Harvard International Journal of Press/Politics 12(2), 24–43.

Bârgăoanu, A (2011). Examenul Schengen. În căutarea sferei publice europene, Bucureşti: comunicare.ro.

Billig, M (1995). Banal nationalism, London: Sage Publications.

Burnes, S (2011). Metaphors in press reports of elections: Obama walked on water, but Musharraf was beaten by a knockout. Journal of Pragmatics, 43(8), 2160–2175.

de Vreese, C H (2005). News framing: Theory and Typology. Information Design Journal + Document Design 13(1), 51–62.

Dijk, T A van (1988). News as Discourse, Hillsdale, NJ: Lawrence Erlbaum Associates.

Dor, D (2003). On Newspaper Headlines as Relevance Optimizers. Journal of Pragmatics 35, 695–721.

El Refaie, E (2005). "Our Purebred Ethnic Compatriots": Irony in Newspaper Journalism. Journal of Pragmatics, 37(6), 781–797.

Entman, R M (1993). Framing: Toward Clarification of a Fractured Paradigm. Journal of Communication 43(4), 51–58.

Ifantidou, E (2009). Newspaper Headlines and Relevance: Ad hoc Concepts in Ad hoc Contexts. Journal of Pragmatics 41, 699–720.

Johnson, M (1987). The Body in the Mind, Chicago and London: University of Chicago Press.

Kimmel, M (2010). Why We Mix Metaphors (and Mix Them Well): Discourse Coherence, Conceptual Metaphor, and Beyond. Journal of Pragmatics, 42(1), 97–115.

Kovecses, Z (2005). Metaphor in Culture: Universality and Variation, Cambridge: Cambridge University Press.

Lakoff, G, & Johnson, M (1980). Metaphors We Live By, Chicago and London: University of Chicago Press.

Lau, R R, & Redlawsk, D P (2001). Advantages and Disadvantages of Cognitive Heuristics in Political Decision Making. American Journal of Political Science 45(October), 951–971.

McLaren, L M (2004). Opposition to European Integration and Fear of Loss of National Identity: Debunking a Basic Assumption Regarding Hostility to the Integration Project. European Journal of Political Research, 43, 895–911.

Marcussen, M, Risse, T, Engelmann-Martin, D, Knopf, H J, & Roscher, K (2001).Constructing Europe? The Evolution of Nation-State Identities. I Thomas Christiansen, Knud Erik Jørgensen and Antje Wiener (eds), The Social Construction of Europe, Sage Publications, 101–120.

Musolff, A (2004). Metaphor and Political Discourse: Analogical Reasoning in Debates about Europe, Basingstoke, Hampshire: Palgrave Macmillan.

—. (2006). Metaphor Scenarios in Public Discourse. Metaphor and Symbol, 21(1), 23–38.

Negrea, E (2010). Pragmatica ironiei. Studiu asupra ironiei in presa scrisa romaneasca, Bucuresti: Tritonic.

Shie, J-S (2011). Metaphors and Metonymies in New York Times and Times Supplement News Headlines. Journal of Pragmatics 43, 1318–1334.

Schudson, M (1978). Discovering the News: A Social History of American Newspapers, NY: Basic Books.

TOWARDS A EUROPEANIZED ROMANIAN PUBLIC SPHERE? MEDIA FRAMING OF ROMANIA'S ACCESSION TO THE SCHENGEN AREA OF FREE MOVEMENT*

FLAVIA DURACH AND OANA ŞTEFĂNIŢĂ

Abstract

This paper analyses the possibility of the existence of a Europeanized public sphere in Romania by carrying out research on media discourse regarding Romania's accession to the Schengen area of free movement.

The starting point is the concept of public sphere introduced by Jürgen Habermas and its contemporary developments.

Within the research carried out in this area, three main models have been suggested. The first model endorses the idea of a unique supranational European public sphere, while the second introduces the concept of Europeanized national public spheres characterized by mutual sensitivity among member states (horizontal Europeanization) and a greater presence of European policies in national public debates. The third model emphasizes the formation of transnational elite groups temporarily aggregated around European issues.

The present paper is conceived within the framework of the second model in which mass media play the fundamental role in creating mutual sensitivity of national spheres of member states by presenting European issues to the public and by offering information on European policies, which is of relevance in a national context.

* This article is the result of the research grant *Romania's Accession to the Schengen Area (2011): Social Perception, Media Coverage and Public Debate*, financed and implemented by the Centre for Research in Communication, National School of Political Studies and Public Administration (Bucharest).

In order to test the existence of a Romanian Europeanized public sphere, we focus our research on a particular context – the proposal to delay Romania's accession to Schengen – and the way in which that was covered by national mass media. The research covers a period of one month, starting with 21 December 2010, when the German and French ministers of internal affairs formally made that proposal. Our qualitative research is driven by the following questions: what kind of actors, national or European, were present in the media, what were their opinions on Romania's accession to the Schengen area, and how was the subject framed by different media? In order to answer the research questions, we chose two online media sources and two TV channels. The online corpus consisted of 194 news items, whereas the TV corpus consisted of nine talk shows dedicated to the subject. The research method is text analysis with predefined key categories. Data is structured around several aspects: topics and subjects, main frames, actors involved and the perspective on the European Union.

The results obtained so far suggest that the issue of postponing Romania's accession to Schengen sparked a lot of public interest. At the same time, that interest was accompanied by a simplistic and somehow contradictory perspective: Romania's attempt to become a member of the Schengen area was an instance of an utter (internal) failure and a proof of its internal deficiencies, but the European Union's decision was unfair. The public discourse on the subject is driven by emotional, identity-related elements and is characterized by a local perspective, instead of a European one. The prevalence of national actors in the public sphere at the expense of European ones and the tendency to transform the Schengen subject in a mere rhetorical framework in which to discuss internal political matters suggests a weak level of connectivity of the Romanian public sphere to topics of European interest.

Key words: public sphere, Europeanized national public spheres, media framing, Schengen.

INTRODUCTION

Romania's accession to the Schengen area of free movement was a hot issue for journalists, members of the government and the general public between the end of 2010 and the beginning of 2011, due to the letter signed and made public on 21 December by the French and German Ministers of Internal Affairs. The two officials requested that the European Commission and the Belgian and Hungarian presidents of the European

Union delay Romania and Bulgaria's accession to the Schengen area, which was intended for the year 2011.

Taking advantage of this particular context, the Centre of Research in Communication, at the Faculty of Communication and Public Relations (The National School of Administrative and Political Studies, Bucharest) tested the recent concept of a "European public sphere" in Romanian society, by means of a research project conducted between 10 January and 22 March 2011. The project covered the following areas: the coverage of the Schengen subject by mass media in France, Germany, Great Britain, Bulgaria and Hungary, media coverage and framing in Romania (news and talk-shows on TV and articles published by news websites), the public perception on the matter and the opinion of ten Romanian important public actors.

The present paper is dedicated to the results of the qualitative research within the project. It focuses mainly on the frames used by journalists working both for news websites and news television channels and has the secondary objective of investigating the existence of a Europeanized public sphere in Romania.

THEORETICAL BACKGROUND

In the context of European integration, concepts such as European identity, European public sphere or Europeanization become more frequent in everyday speech, especially regarding the media's role in spreading the feeling of affiliation to a European family. Therefore, when we deal with subjects of European importance we wonder if mass media frame the facts in a national or a European perspective, if the public finds out more about European officials' statements than national politicians' views and if the audience is informed about other EU countries and their leaders' positions or just about Brussels officials' declarations. Can we speak about a European public sphere or of a Europeanized national public sphere? In order to approach these questions we focused on inquiries and research regarding such essential concepts as the public sphere, Europeanization and the European public sphere.

The concept of the public sphere as a space for the generation of public opinion was introduced by Jürgen Habermas (1964). The transformation of the concept is related to the transformation of the state and the evolution of economy and society. The public sphere originated in Germany at the end of the eighteenth century, initially constituted around book readers and then encountered structural transformations as a consequence of the interplay of state with society and afterwards, due to media evolution.

Habermas distinguishes between a literary public sphere and a political public sphere, both having the same subject – the public as an entity that carries public opinion. The bourgeois public sphere was first perceived as a sphere of private persons reunited as a public, a sphere that developed in a context of tension between the state and the society (Habermas, 2005). The public sphere is defined in Habermas' perspective as a dispersed, discursive network within which citizens, connected by means of mass communication, form currents of opinion in their attempt to find ways that best resolve common problems (idem). By public sphere is understood a realm of social life in which something close to public opinion can be formed. All citizens have access to it and a part of this public sphere can be found in every conversations in which private individuals assemble to form a public body. This involves freedom of assembly and association and the freedom to express their opinions regarding matters of general interest. It also requires specific means for transmitting information and influencing those who receive it, and media contributing to the creation of a public sphere (Habermas, 1964). The concept of a public sphere as formulated by Habermas encountered several critiques and determined discussions on the concept. For example Gordon Finlayson (2005) states that the concept of the public sphere as a space where subjects participate as equals in rational discussions in pursuit of the common good is an illusion as communication and freedom of expression are restricted in various ways, and uneducated people are often excluded. Additionally, the public sphere in the nineteenth and twentieth centuries became an arena in which public opinion could be stage-managed and manipulated as newspapers acquired a mass circulation, became affiliated to capitalist corporations and thus operated in the private interests of a few powerful individuals. In these conditions, public opinion lost its autonomy and its critical function. The main interest was to win public acclaim and support. "This support consisted, however, in the private opinions of servile, uncritical, and economically dependent consumers, rather than a healthy public opinion forged through reasoned public debate" (Finlayson, 2005, p. 13).

Nowadays, media have great influence in setting the agenda, in inducing opinions and framing subjects, in directing public debates in accordance with their promoted perspectives, in determining the public opinion, the future trends in debates and the whole flow of communication within public spheres.

In order to approach the concept of a European public sphere or of Europeanized national public spheres we have to determine the way in which media are involved in the process of Europeanization, in creating a European identity and in promoting and framing European news.

The process of Europeanization suggests a "top-down diffusion of common political rules, norms and practices in Europe" (Hughes, Sasse & Gordon, 2005, p. 27). The process is associated with the pressure of being an EU member and thus having to synchronize along with other members, and it involves the spreading of European-wide norms. It has an essential role in assuring the convergence of institutions and policies, and in constructing a European identity (Hughes, Sasse & Gordon, 2005). Europeanization can also be understood as a societal interpenetration since European societies become more and more convergent and mixed as a result of the common currency, migration, multiculturalism, common norms, educational exchanges and media broadcasts with European distribution (Delanty & Rumford, 2005). The phenomenon of Europeanization can be defined as a set of two interconnected processes. While the first represents the way in which national political, social and economic forces is giving birth to a new supranational European political and institutional dimension, the second consists in the way EU political, social and economic dynamics are becoming an important part of the domestic political system. These two processes thus represent the construction and then the diffusion of European institutions and policies within EU members (Graziano, 2003).

The concept of Europeanization includes all transformations that take place at the level of nation-states in order to increase the convergence process developed under the idea of spreading common European values and perspectives and thus amplifying a common European identity. National media have a major role in distributing information and news regarding EU as a whole, EU institutions, policies, official declarations, positions of the member states regarding important decisions and evolutions. The Europeanization process can be developed by an increase in reporting and broadcasting European topics in national media and some indicators of the process can be that EU official protagonists enter into debate with protagonists from other places, different actors from EU member states take part in debates on common issues and agree upon solutions, similar topics are discussed simultaneously in the media of several EU states, EU protagonists from different states interact through national media inquiries and Brussels' policies are present on news agendas from EU member states (Machill, Beiler & Fischer, 2006; Trenz & Eder, 2004).

Regarding the significant media role in the process of Europeanization, there have been some differentiations in the way that European subjects are dealt with and two models thus resulted: vertical Europeanization and horizontal Europeanization. While within the first model, media pay more attention to Brussels' policies, positions and statements, to EU issues or European actors, in the second one, they focus on events, actors and statements of officials in other EU member states (Koopmans & Erbe, 2004).

Mixing these two dimensions of Europeanization can result in four other forms of the process:

1. Comprehensive Europeanization: both levels – vertical and horizontal Europeanization are present.
2. Segmented Europeanization: focuses on the vertical level, meaning an increased attention paid to EU as an entity, and not to member states.
3. Europeanization aloof from the EU: focuses on the horizontal level, on communicative exchanges among member states.
4. A parochial public sphere: in this case neither a vertical, nor a horizontal Europeanization in the national media can be identified (Brüggemann & Kleinen-von Königslöw, 2009). While the first type is desirable for the amplification of Europeanization, there are still difficulties in offering mere EU information at national levels and give a face to Europe as a singular entity.

Therefore, a Europeanized communication system cannot be matched by a mere increase in reporting of European topics in national media especially if the news is meant for a national public and remains attached to national viewpoints and communication specifics. A European public (and a European public sphere) cannot be created simply by distributing more news about the EU (Van de Steeg, 2002).

The Europeanization process is modeled by media as they choose to include European subjects on debating agendas and by the way they lean upon EU institutions, European policies or upon other countries within the EU and their officials, on both EU as a singular entity and as dispersed member states, or on subjects that are considered from a national impact perspective. The media can have a decisive contribution in spreading the European identity elements and in increasing the Europeanization process. The manner in which the media frame important European subjects can also give us a clue to the level of Europeanization within certain countries, a perspective regarding the way in which a country gives, or does not give, credit to Europe as a union, a measure of the European level of dealing with policies detrimental to a national one (Semetko, de Vreese & Peter,

2000). However, limits to the process of Europeanization in terms of expansion can be found in the lack of interest regarding European subjects among people, and in the domination of national approaches to EU issues. The European public sphere holds a premise that the public does not usually become interested in European issues that have an impact at national levels or which are initiated by scandals and political campaigns, but on general basis has a frequent need for information (Lauristin, 2007).

Considering the level of Europeanization three main models have been suggested – the pan-European public sphere, the Europeanized national public spheres and the segmented transnational public spheres (de Vreese, 2007).

The European public sphere is mainly considered in research literature as being unlikely to materialize in the near future, as there is neither a strong European identity at the level of EU member states nor a common language or significant common communication space. From a historical view, the public sphere is affiliated to the concept of state, of citizens of a territory that share social and cultural characteristics. The EU mechanisms have not yet overcome either national perspectives detrimental to a supranational one, or national identities and cultures detrimental to a European identification. No real common interests of states, lack of political identification, different languages, disparate national cultures, no significant European media – these make the process of opinion formation extremely difficult (Eriksen, 2005; Kevin, 2004). Thus, a common public debate through a communication network that enables citizens to argue on common issues based on the same premises is not yet achievable at a large scale; consequently, a European public sphere is not really achievable either. Although the infrastructure of a general public sphere in the EU is not completely missing and English can substitute for a common language, it seems insufficient to determine that feeling of collective identity. Thus, "a single overarching communicative space accessible for all, in which proponents and opponents can voice and justify opinions and claims, and mobilize support in order to sluice them into the decision-making units via social movements and political parties, is lacking" (Eriksen, 2005, p. 355). Instead, we can say that there is a tendency for Europeanized national public debates to be conducted through media discourse.

We can speak of a European public sphere when people debate the same issues, at the same period of time, using the same criteria in evaluating and forming opinions and being mutually aware of each others' views (Risse, 2003). Both a European public sphere and Europeanized national public spheres depend on the level of Europeanization transcending the media frames used when promoting actors and issues regarding the EU. Media can frame subjects from a national angle (national news, sources, perspectives and national interests are privileged over others), a European (European sources, perspectives and interests are asserted over national or global interests) or a global perspective (global sources, views and interests are presented as paramount) (Downey & Koenig, 2006). Only by having a European perspective can a European identity and Europeanized national public spheres be constructed, let alone a single European public sphere.

Hans-Jörg Trenz and Klaus Eder (2004) state that a European public space emerges at the intersection of two elements: a self-justificatory resonance of institutional actors and an external public resonance addressing these actors and institutions. Additionally, there are two mechanisms that help to support the self-constituting of a European public sphere: an increase in communication within European political institutions or within enlarged institutional environments (institutional actors, experts and representatives of civil society) and the increase in the level of attention/interest paid by audiences and in the level of awareness regarding European political communication related to governance at the supranational, national or local dimension. The EU needs a European public sphere to achieve its political dimension and reduce the democratic deficit and for this it addresses its public mainly through national media of the member states. The construct of a single public sphere is perceived as unlikely since EU's public is sectoral and highly socially selective; it might also include actors that are not located within EU official borders (Baisnée, 2007). Moreover, an individualized European public is scarcely recognized to exist. Most often we deal with a public related to the EU, formed by professionals within EU institutions, commissioners or civil servants, and not to ordinary people of the member states who are usually not interested in issues discussed at the EU level (Negrea, 2010). Therefore, without the existence of a European public it becomes irrelevant to speak about a European public sphere as these two concepts are interconnected.

Claes de Vreese (2007) distinguishes between a utopian model, an elitist and a realist one. The utopian model consists in a singular, supra-national, pan-European public sphere as a communicative space, which requires a shared identity, a transnational media system and a common language. The elitist model defines the segmented transnational public spheres, which are based on communicative spaces at national levels on a specific subject, determined by media with global or European outreach, and thus involving mainly elites in the politic or economic fields. The realist model promotes the Europeanization of national public spheres and includes an increased coverage of European subjects and an evaluation of those issues that transcend the interests of one country.

Three main forms of a European public sphere have also been identified : 1. Heavy public sphere, 2. Light public sphere, 3. Ad hoc public sphere (Bârgăoanu, 2011). The heavy public sphere is the utopian model in De Vreese's classification and is that controversial unique European public sphere at a supranational level. Critiques raised against this model, for example Schlesinger (1999), emphasized the lack of a significant number of European media consumers, organized in common audiences at a transnational level, this aspect being essential for the existence of a singular public sphere at a European level. However, Schlesinger argues that, despite predominant national interests, elements of a European civil society have begun to emerge, particularly within political and business elites, thus indicating how it might develop into a complex sphere of connected national publics. The light public sphere is considered the most plausible one and refers to the process of Europeanization of national public spheres, especially through media news and debates. The third model, the ad hoc public sphere, is a result of an aggregation of opinions around topics and common European interests, resembling the concept of issue communities and implying the involvement of elites, of publics that have some specialization and interest regarding the core issues (Bârgăoanu, 2011).

The most realistic approach regards the light public sphere, as it is utterly premature to state that we can distinguish a European public sphere and an individualized European public. The Europeanization of national public spheres is the process most likely to evolve in the near future, to develop at the level of mass perception within member states. Media are the main factor in amplifying this phenomenon, although other elements as mentioned above are necessary. However, as media have an essential contribution to Europeanization and to the creation of a European identity, we chose to focus our research on this aspect by analysing how media framed the subject – the proposal to delay Romania's accession to Schengen – and thus determine if we can speak about a Europeanized Romanian public sphere.

METHODOLOGY

The research investigated, with a qualitative approach, the media discourse and coverage of one subject in particular: Romania's accession to the Schengen area of free movement. We took into consideration two types of media: online media (Romanian news portals) and Romanian television channels, focusing on the following research questions:

Q1: How is Romania's accession to the Schengen area covered by the selected media in terms of editorial format, editorial tone and information sources?
Q2: What types of actors (national or European) are present in the news and what are their opinions on the subject?
Q3: How is the subject of Romania's accession to the Schengen area framed in the selected media?

In order to answer these questions, we selected two news portals (www.hotnews.ro and www.ziare.com) and two news television channels (Realitatea TV and Antena3), which were monitored from 21 December 2010 to 21 January 2011. The first date represents the moment when France and Germany officially requested a delay in Romania and Bulgaria's accession to the Schengen area. Within a month, numerous public statements were made on the subject, offering consisting research material.

We included all the news articles related to the Schengen subject, resulting in a total of 79 articles on Hotnews.ro and 115 articles on Ziare.com. In respect of television, we analysed the following talk shows: on Realitatea TV – "Ora de foc" (21 December 2010, 5 January 2011 and 6 January 2011), "Ultima ora" (21 December 2010); on Antena3 – "La ordinea zilei" (21 December 2010, 6 January 2011) and "Sinteza zilei" (21 December 2010, 22 December 2010, 5 January 2011).

The results were analysed with text analysis without a preexistent grid. Instead, we chose a list of categories to focus upon: editorial format, information sources (other media, Romanian officials, foreign officials, anonymous), subjects, frames (meaning interpretation schemas delivered by journalists and public actors willingly or unwillingly, resulting in a quick and easy way of mentally understanding an event), actors (European actors – members of the European Parliament, European Commissioners, others; Romanian actors – journalists, analysts, experts, political actors, members of the government, Secretaries of State, members of the Parliament, the Romanian President), the perspective on the European Union.

DATA ANALYSIS

Editorial tone and editorial format

In the case of television channels, the talk show format is very popular and represents a valuable information source for public opinion. Furthermore, the analysis conducted on the online news indicates that journalists use the statements made by talk show guests as a starting point for writing news articles on the subject of the Schengen area.

On TV, Romania's accession to the Schengen area was presented as an important issue on 21 and 22 December 2010 and 5 and 6 January 2011, following developments in the situation. The subject was approached in a distinct section of the talk show (in 7 cases) and even exclusively in 2 cases. Producers dedicated a generous amount of time to the Schengen issue, ranging between 30 minutes and an hour, thus proving the perceived significance of the events.

The tone of voice of the talk shows is rather acid. The headlines on the screen are suggestive:

> Băsescu made knockout by Merkel and Sarkozy (Ora de foc, 21 December 2010)
>
> Romania fails with Băsescu in command (Ora de foc, 5 January 2011)
>
> 21 years after the Revolution, we are rejected by Europe (Sinteza zilei, 22 December 2010)
>
> The Schengen scandal: Left out (La ordinea zilei, 6 January 2011).

In order to ensure the desired number of viewers, the talk show producers and hosts exploit the controversies surrounding the delay of Romania's accession. The journalists take advantage of the public interest in scandal and conflict by covering the subject in terms of soon-to-be failure, claims of discrimination, the political class's errors of judgement, and flaws in the Romanian foreign affairs strategy. The headlines explicitly name the responsible for this failure – the Head of State, president Traian Băsescu.

By analysing the editors' approach, we can identify some frames that give an a priori orientation to the viewer. These frames are: Romania's accession is a failure, the Government is responsible for the negative developments of the situation, and Romania is isolated from an international point of view. These frames are embraced and developed further by the guests of the talk shows, thus annulling the possibility of alternative interpretations.

In the case of online news, interest in the subject is also high. By monitoring the selected news websites between 21 December 2010 and 21 January 2011, we found a total of 115 news articles on Ziare.com (an average of 3.6 articles/day) and 79 results on Hotnews (average 2.4 articles/day). Ziare.com grants the Schengen subject with greater significance, as it dedicates a whole section of the website to collecting news related to Schengen. This is not the case of Hotnews, which includes the subject in the regular sections (such as Foreign affairs or Politics).

Another difference between the two news sites is related to the writing styles. On Hotnews, the articles are shorter, favoring the essential information and some concise public statements on the matter. Ziare.com publishes broader articles that not only present information, but also contextualization, additional details, technicalities. Both news sources have a neutral approach, which is very different from the obvious bias of the TV talk shows described above. Editorials make the exception by expressing the personal beliefs of the journalist writing them.

The analysis identified three types of editorial formats: news articles, editorials and press reviews. Ziare.com gathered the highest number of articles (94), in comparison to Hotnews (only 68). The former is more interested in providing interpretation to the readers. 20 editorials were dedicated to the Schengen subject, whereas Hotnews published only 9. In both cases, the editorials discuss the following subjects: who is responsible for Romania's failure, how does the country present itself to the European Union, what is the EU's position, whether the political class has an adequate reaction and what needs to be done in the future.

Information sources

In order to see how rigorous journalists are in covering the Schengen subject, an analysis of their sources of information is necessary. In the case of the TV talk shows, the information sources quoted are scarce. Traian Băsescu's statements are used most frequently (he is quoted in 8 out of 9 talk shows). This leads to a great visibility of the Head of State. Nevertheless, the president's exposure is mainly negative, as he is criticized both by the hosts and the guests of the TV shows. Alternative information sources are: other media (in 2 cases) and foreign officials – the French Minister of European Affairs, Laurent Wauquiez (in 2 cases).

In the case of the online media, the news sources are much more diverse. The main information sources are other media (used in 93 cases on Ziare.com and 69 cases on Hotnews). Official information is used less frequently: 14 news on Ziare.com and 8 articles on Hotnews quote Romanian officials, and only 3 news on Ziare.com and 1 news article on Hotnews quote foreign officials.

These results prove that, at least in this particular case, journalists base their writings on too little reliable sources, as officials of the EU and members of the government would be. They use secondary sources instead, such as press agencies and other media. The risk is to provide the public with incorrect, incomplete or biased information due to the multiple filters of selection involved. Multiple framing occurs: one made by the original source of information, the second one by the first journalist and then other frames introduced by those journalists who base their articles on pieces of information provided by their colleagues. The risk of distortion increases.

Subjects

Inside the broader subject of Romania's accession to Schengen, multiple other issues can be identified. In the case of the talk shows analysed, we can reduce the apparent variety of subjects to some major themes: the failure in the process of accession, criticism addressed to the Government, efforts to name those responsible, evaluation of the political class. The news articles can be grouped around three major themes: the significance of the accession, the position of the EU and its member states (mainly France and Germany), the reaction of the Romanian political class.

Inside each theme mentioned above, certain frames should be deducted. These frames provide specific interpretation of the events and influence the public opinion accordingly.

Frames identified in the TV talk shows

As talk shows are, by definition, opportunities for public debate and for expressing personal opinions, they can also be a source of bias and controversy. For example, when discussing whether the delay of Romania's accession to Schengen is or is not Romania's fault, the guests fail to reach agreement. One side argues that Romania is responsible for its own faith. The negative development of the situation is a consequence of a bad strategy:

> We have seen today the consequences of Romania's foreign policy. (Bogdan Chiriac, Ora de foc, 6 January 2011)

Romania has some deficiencies that cannot be hidden, such as corruption and a dysfunctional justice system and fails in terms of political criteria.

> We did not do our job in the justice system, we did not do our job in what concerns the borders. (Moderator, Ultima oră, 21 December 2010)

The opposite opinion states that Romania fulfilled all the technical requirements and cannot be held responsible. It was expressed in 6 situations (3 times on Realitatea TV, 3 times on Antena 1).

Related to Romania's responsibility is the problem of the motives behind the rejection. This subject is vividly discussed in the talk shows; some arguing that behind the refusal stand political arguments. The latter allegedly include the unsolved problem of the Roma community or the bribery imposed to some French and German companies. Another frame favors the interpretation that Europe fears for its security if Romania adheres to the Schengen area.

> If they trusted us we would be able to prevent contraband goods from Russia and Asia from entering the EU, we would not have any problems, no matter how we would behave in Europe. (Magor Csibi, Ultima oră, 21 December 2010)

This leads to another important point: what the true significance of the accession is. The debate revolves around the idea that Romania's accession is a very important national project. In seven out of nine talk shows, guests agree that this is a crucial objective. Titus Corlăţean argues that Romania's position, profile and importance in Europe are at stake (Ora de foc, 21 December 2010).

> Everybody wins if Romania adheres to Schengen, everybody loses if it doesn't. (Mircea Geoană, Sinteza zilei, 21 December 2010)

There are serious economic consequences, mostly in the area of commercial transport and foreign investments.

Another theme of discussion relates to the positions of France and Germany in particular and the EU in general. The frame "EU is fair in its decision to postpone Romania's accession" is present in five out of nine talk shows, but the majority of opinions argues that Romania is a victim of discrimination. France and Germany are accused of taking an arbitrary decision.

> The two Ministers discriminate Romania and the Romanian people in what concerns their rights as members of the European Union, as they have the right to be part of the Schengen area. (Traian Băsescu, La ordinea zilei, 21 December 2010)

Concerning the reactions of the political class to the problem of a postponed accession, the most frequent ones are less diplomatic: rejection of the accusations, repeated attacks made by politicians who feel offended.

> They have no explicit reproaches, nothing measurable when they mention corruption. This accusation hides something else and is completely immoral. (Adrian Severin, La ordinea zilei, 6 January 2011)

This attitude attracts criticism:

> [Traian Băsescu] started to yell at the first two political powers in Europe. (Cornel Nistorescu, Sinteza zilei, 21 December 2010)

The use of framing in the 9 talk shows analyzed indicates that the leaders of opinion are pessimistic in what concerns Romania's odds of success. The members of the Government are held responsible for failure and are permanently criticized. Their aggressive reactions are characterized as inappropriate. The dilemma "Discrimination or not?" remains unsolved.

Frames identified in the online news articles

Data resulting from the analysis of online news articles indicate similarities to the TV talk shows in terms of themes and frames.

As in the case of the talk shows, the news articles discuss whether Romania is or is not responsible for the delay in its accession process. Most of them exonerate Romania, arguing that the country has met all the technical criteria requested (34 articles on Ziare.com and 34 articles on Hotnews). Romanian officials are quoted as an argument:

> We have done our homework and the degree in which we are prepared has been confirmed by 7 evaluation missions. I would say that, de facto, Romania is already in the Schengen area. (Teodor Baconschi; Hotnews: Teodor Baconschi despre aderarea la Schengen: Credibilitatea UE e în pericol dacă statele membre nu sunt tratate conform acelorlaşi reguli, vrem să evităm tentaţia euroscepticismului, Alina Neagu, 17 January 2011)

Significantly, few articles hold Romania responsible – on Hotnews, this interpretation is basically absent (only 4 articles), and on Ziare.com it can be read in 19 articles. When the articles state that the delay is Romania's fault, the members of the Government are blamed for the situation.

The reasons for rejection, as presented in the online media, are mainly related to security flaws and technical aspects (29 articles on Ziare.com and 19 articles in Hotnews).

> France and Germany believe that Bulgaria's and Romania's access to the Schengen area is premature and expect guarantees that the two countries have finished with corruption, organized crime and have well protected borders, as Laurent Wauquiez recently explained. (Hotnews: Preşedinţia ungară a UE: Căutăm o soluţie de compromis pentru aderarea României, care şi-a îndeplinit obligaţiile, şi a Bulgariei la zona Schengen, R.M., 10 January 2011)

A few articles (5 on Ziare.com and 7 on Hotnews) suggest that Romania is rejected based on political grounds or as a strategy to gain popularity before the elections (in the case of France).

Nevertheless, the majority of online journalists believe that Romania's accession is an essential national objective – 11 articles on Ziare.com and 6 articles on Hotnews, compared to only 4 articles on Ziare.com and 1 article on Hotnews expressing the idea that Romania's accession is overrated. Those in favour of the accession argue that the whole political class should unite to reach this goal.

> The head of the Romanian diplomacy urged once again the political actors in Romania to realize that the accession to Schengen is an objective of national importance, not the objective a specific parties. (Teodor Baconschi; Ziare.com: Baconschi: România are nevoie de mai mult timp pentru aderarea la Schengen, 11 January 2011)

The online news articles subjected to the analysis strongly support the idea that Romania is discriminated. The EU appears to be changing the rules during the game – this idea is expressed in 36 articles on Ziare.com and 26 articles on Hotnews. Furthermore, France and Germany's hostility is emphasized in 21 articles on Ziare.com and 11 articles on Hotnews. These countries are depicted as members of an exclusive club in which Romania is failing to be accepted.

> Welcome to Schengen turns into "You have nothing to do in this exclusive area." "Unity in diversity" becomes "primus inter pares". (Hotnews: Vlad

> Mixich, Cristian Pantazi, Cuţitul francez înfipt în spatele României. Victima posibilă: Uniunea Europeană, 17 January 2011)

The most vivid depiction of the situation is the title of one editorial:

> The French Knife in Romania's Back. Potential Victim: the European Union. (Hotnews: Vlad Mixich, Cristian Pantazi, 17 January 2011)

Almost all news articles focus on the reactions of the political class when faced with the delay in Romania's accession to Schengen.

Some articles mention moderate positions, such as advocating compromise (accession in stages), encouraging the EU to follow the rules, or suggesting international lobby to gain support from EU member states. Other articles choose to describe the more aggressive actions, such as firm rejection of the accusations (12 articles on Ziare.com and 15 articles on Hotnews) and even rough verbal attacks on France, Germany or the EU as a whole (27 articles on Ziare.com and 14 articles on Hotnews).

> Any delay is a discrimination against Romania. Should we stay here, like boneless worms, as some suggest we should, or should we fight for the rights of the 22 million Romanian citizens who deserve respect? (Traian Băsescu, President; Hotnews: Daily Mail: Temeri legate de imigranţi în Marea Britanie, după ce preşedintele României a spus că nu poate garanta securitatea graniţelor, R.M., 7 January 2011)

Most journalists agree that these reactions are a mistake (29 articles on Ziare.com and 12 articles on Hotnews).

Actors

Another section of the research is dedicated to the actors involved. The talk shows gathered a broad spectrum of actors, from leaders of the political parties to members of the Government and the Parliament, analysts, experts and journalists. The distribution favours the Romanian actors. European voices, such as members of the EP or officials from other member states are quoted in the debate on only 5 occasions. Representatives of the local public scene are much more numerous: journalists/experts/analysts are recorded 16 times, followed by members of the Parliament (15 times), leaders of the political parties (9 times), the President (7 times), former ministers (5 times), ministers (3 times).

As guests of the talk shows, each group of actors favors specific interpretation frames. For example, the officials from the member states (e.g. the French Minister for European Affairs) emphasize Romania's security flaws:

> We must feel sure of our borders in the first place. (Sinteza zilei, 21 December 2010)

In reaction, Romanian members of the EP insist that Romania has met all the technical requirements, although they admit the country's problem with corruption. From their point of view, the rejection is an abuse.

Romanian political actors are divided into two sides: members of the party in government and members of the opposition, each with a biased discourse. The members of the Government tend to find excuses: Romania fulfilled all technical requirements and is rejected due to unrelated issues, the EU is unfair and France and Germany are subjective. A potential failure in the process of accession is a consequence of the activity of the political class as a whole.

Members of the opposition take advantage of the moment to name those responsible:

> To make it very clear, this is a personal failure of the Romanian President in the light of his attributions in conducting the foreign affairs of the Minister of Foreign Affairs, Mr. Baconschi, and it is a failure of the Liberal-Democrat Party, the political majority that rules. (Crin Antonescu, La ordinea zilei, 21 December 2010)

Furthermore, the opposition denounces the lack of strategy and the inappropriate reactions of the Romanian officials. The journalists, analysts and experts have a similar opinion. They consider the accession process a huge failure and accuse the political rulers of escaping responsibility.

When analysing the distribution of actors quoted in the online news articles, the prevalence of the Romanian actors becomes visible. They are quoted 122 times, whereas the European actors are mentioned only 72 times. The Romanian president and the members of the Government appear most frequently in the news, whereas experts or political analysts are almost never quoted, resulting in a worrying absence of authorized points of view.

The European officials insist that they follow all the rules as they reject Romania due to serious security threats. The Romanian members of the EP make rather moderate statements. According to them, the political class must admit deficiencies related to the reinforcement of law and corruption, thus have to take immediate action to correct them. Other voices are radical:

> The strategic partnership with France is dead. (Adrian Severin, member of the EP; Hotnews: Adrian Severin la RFI: Franţa ar trebui exclusă din Schengen, dacă vorbim de criteriul corupţiei, RFI, 6 January 2011)

The reactions of the Romanian actors cover a broad spectrum: from verbal attacks against an inequitable Europe to rather moderate positions. The latter emphasize the fulfillment of all technical requirements. In this line of thinking, Romania must use all diplomatic channels to gain international support. The less usual points of view argue that this failure will work as an incentive for fighting against corruption and the flaws in the system.

The distinction between the members of the party in government and the members of the opposition is visible as in the case of television talk shows. The opposition accuses, while the Government rejects all accusations in a dignified manner:

> I find the letter of the two ministers an act of discrimination against Romania. At the last reunion of the European Council we proved that Romania is ready, in what concerns the technical requirements. (Traian Băsescu, President of Roamnia; Hotnews: Traian Băsescu despre Schengen: Nu vom accepta o discriminare din partea nimănui, fie ea şi din partea celor mai puternice state ale UE, 21 December 2010)

The perspective on the European Union

One last element taken into consideration by the present research is the Romanian perspective on the European Union as a whole. At this point, there are two possible interpretations. The first one supports the image of a "Messianic Europe" – a saviour from all the structural problems Romania faces. The second one is centred on the image of a "Punishing Europe", which applies sanctions for Romania's deficiencies. Only the latter is present both in the online news articles and the television talk shows analysed.

Media framing on this subject depicts Europe as the supreme judge of Romania's failures and Romania as an outsider, waiting at the periphery of Europe. For example, in all the nine talk shows, the guests argue that Europe is punishing Romania for many reasons, but mostly due to lack of trust in Romania's capacity to solve its own problems:

> They tell us one more thing: we don't trust you, we don't trust your political and administrative systems, we don't trust you can manage efficiently your Eastern borders, that you can fight corruption, because you are corrupted. (Titus Corlăţean, Ora de foc, 5 January 2011)

Europe is no longer a myth of redemption, but a mechanism designed to apply sanctions. Romania suffers from lack of influence and prestige on the European scene. As a consequence, a situation without precedent occurs: the accent shifts from technical requirements to political issues, a totally new criterion, proving the failure of Romanian diplomacy (Mircea Geoană, Sinteza zilei, 21 December 2010). In contrast to Romania's peripheral position, the European Union is depicted as an exclusive club:

> Europeans see us as we really are, not as the Government tries to prove we are, in theory and in statistics. In essence, they see us as we are: unprepared. More than this, we are not only unprepared, but also irritating. (Bogdan Ciucă, Sinteza zilei, 5 January 2011)

The tone of voice is pessimistic and very drastic in terms of self-image. Romanians cannot compare themselves to Great Britain or France, as they are inferior. Romania is currently in the second league and will soon fall in the third league, Victor Ponta argues (Ora de foc, 21 December 2010).

In essence, the online news analysed describes the relationship between Romania and the European Union in similar terms. The frame "Europe is punishing us" was identified in 40 articles, with a distinction between fair sanctions (7 articles) and unfair sanctions (a majority of 20 articles). In one article, Europe preserves some of its image as a saviour, initially projected by the Romanian citizens onto the EU:

> The future is in the European Union and this has to be the priority of the Romanian politics. (Hotnews: UE, Schengen şi corectitudinea politică, Theophyle, 22 December 2010)

Some articles argue that the European Union has the right to make the rules and to apply them, whereas Romania faces major problems, but refuses to accept the truth. Corruption is a reality in Romania and Europe has no obligation to expose itself to it. Some radical points of view see a benefit in the Europeans' intransigence:

> Romania is not ready to adhere to the Schengen area and it is for our own good to maintain pressure from the outside. (Hotnews: Franţa, centralele nucleare şi aderarea la Schengen. Faţa nevăzută a unei afaceri", Dan Tapalagă, 22 December 2010).

Other articles express the opposite: a strong European Union uses its powers based on subjective arguments, chooses to change the rules during the game and applies double standards (Ziare.com: Sophia Eco: Băsescu dă înapoi în polemica pe Schegen, 7 January 2011). The EU humbles

Romania. The former does not seem to be aware that in a world centered on Brussels, one cannot remain local in mentalities, behavior and way of thinking. Romania's actions led to its inferior position:

> Our problem is that we acted as worms when we begged at the gates of the most important European powers to welcome us too. (Ziare.com, Opinii: Râmele dezagreabile ale Europei, 7 January 2011)

The majority of articles draw the unpleasant conclusion that Romania is not wanted in Europe, due to valid arguments. Romanian citizens put their fate in the hands of the great European powers with little hope for improvement.

Discussion

In this section we will discuss the main differences and similarities between the results of both analyses (talk shows and online news articles).

Both online media and news TV channels showed great interest in the Schengen subject during the research period. As of online news articles, this interest is proven by the frequency of appearance of news related to Schengen – between 2 and 3 news items per day. The subject is present on the agenda of the talk show host; furthermore, a significant amount of broadcasting time is dedicated to discussing the Schengen issue – between 30 minutes and an hour in the case of a two-hour talk show. The political class, the journalists and political analysts respond to the media interest by expressing opinions, by giving statements and by taking sides.

In what concerns the information sources used, we must highlight the fact that in the news articles more diverse sources are used than in the case of talk shows. The latter turn to other media institutions (press agencies, newspapers, television channels) for new pieces of information. Online journalists base their articles on official statements instead, thus increasing the accuracy of their writings. They also use the talk shows as a valuable source of statements made by Romanian politicians. As a consequence, the information that is originally presented by the television is then included in news articles on the two web sites monitored. The articles on Hotnews.ro and Ziare.ro are filled with the frames generated by the television debates; the journalists writing the news conduct another selection, with a greater risk of distortions.

There are many similarities regarding the frames identified. In the case of the news articles and the political talk shows, the accession to Schengen is described as an important objective that the Romanian political class failed to reach. Although the existence of the current deficiencies is admitted, the EU is depicted as unfair, basing decisions on political arguments instead of the objective technical criteria that Romania already met. The argumentation is full of contradictions: "it is unfair, but we deserve it". The authorities' reactions, a combination of denials, excessive pride and aggressive public statements, are characterized as diplomatic faux pas.

In terms of differences, the majority of news articles state that Romania is not responsible for this failure, while the opinions expressed during talk shows are balanced: one side argues that Romania has fulfilled all requirements and the other fraction believes that Romania is, indeed, corrupted. The guests of the talk shows express their opinions in a very direct manner to the extent that a debate can turn into fight. By definition, the news articles have to maintain an objective style and are moderated in covering the subject. The only subjective parts of the news articles are those quoting the statements of important national and European public figures.

One important observation is that in both cases, Romanian actors are obviously more visible than the European voices. This situation can be partially explained due to the increased availability of Romanian officials comparing to EU officials. Nevertheless, these results suggest that journalist have a limited, local approach of the Schengen subject. The issue is turned into an internal political fight; a broader perspective is forever lost. The political class has a biased discourse addressed to its own voters. The two fractions – members of the party in government and members of the opposition – produce two sets of sterile arguments that keep the debate in the grey area of internal race to political power.

Journalists, analysts, politicians relate to the EU in a negative manner. The image promoted is the one of an unmerciful Europe that applies sanctions. The EU is no longer the saviour, but the exclusive club of states which rejects a humbled Romania from the "big league". This shift in perception can be partially explained by the natural decrease in enthusiasm after Romania's accession to the EU. Confronted with the new standard, the Romanian citizens start to realize that being part of the European project involves both privileges and responsibilities; some resentment is not unlikely.

The results of the research also indicate that Romanians' image about Romania is negative. Romania is labelled as a peripheral country ignored by the powerful players on the European scene. The general view is that pessimistic Romania is responsible for its own sad fate. In other words, Romanians themselves reject the feeling of a European identity, making the birth of the Europeanized public sphere a remote expectation.

CONCLUSIONS

The research is focused on the concepts of public sphere, Europeanization and European public sphere, as defined in the existent literature. Our work is based on the model of the light European public sphere, in which mass media play the fundamental role in creating mutual sensitivity of national spheres of member states by presenting European issues of relevance in a national context. The light public sphere refers to the process of Europeanization of the national public spheres, especially through media news and debates.

Media influences Europeanization by setting the agenda, by inducing opinions and framing subjects, by directing public debates in accordance with their promoted perspectives. It has a large impact in determining the public opinion, the future trends in debates and the whole flow of communication within public spheres.

Europeanization is associated with the pressure of being a EU member and thus having to synchronize along with other members, and it involves the spreading of European-wide norms. It has an essential role in assuring the convergence of institutions and policies, and in constructing a European identity. The manner in which the media frame values European subjects can give a clue on the level of Europeanization within certain countries, a perspective regarding the way in which a country gives credit to Europe as a unique project or not, a measure of the European level of dealing with policies detrimental to a national one.

The results obtained so far suggest that the issue of postponing Romania's accession to Schengen has sparked a lot of public interest. The main problem is that this interest is driven by a local agenda, rather than a real interest to European problems. The media discourse is dominated by controversy and scandal, in an attempt to appeal to a broader audience. What appear to matter the most are the internal political fights. The news articles and the talk shows bring together two fractions: representatives of the party in government and members of the opposition. The debate turns rapidly into efforts to gain the sympathy of the electorate by accusing the opposite party of irresponsibility.

The media discourse is full of contradictions, such as "it is true that Romania has serious deficiencies and does not deserve to stand alongside the great European powers, but the EU's decision to postpone the accession to Schengen is unfair". These inconsistencies suggest a shallow perspective on the European project, lack of official information and superficial documentation from the part of the journalists. The media discourse failed to explain what Europe has to gain from Romania's accession to Schengen or to analyze the events from a European point of view.

The public discourse on the subject is driven by emotional, identity-related elements and is characterized by a local perspective, instead of a European one. The prevalence of national actors in the public sphere at the expense of European ones and the tendency to transform the Schengen subject in a mere rhetorical framework in which to discuss internal political matters suggest a weak level of connectivity of the Romanian public sphere to topics of European interest. In addition, we must emphasize that the Romanian perspective on the European Union is marked with resentment. Media framing leads to the image of a vindictive European Union, which is designed to sanction Romania for its problems, instead of solving them. As a consequence, the dichotomy between Romania and the European Union drives away the possibility of a true connection with other national public spheres or with the European policies and issues.

In conclusion, the Romanian public sphere is not yet connected and receptive to European issue. The research indicated interest in the Schengen subject, but its real importance is under-evaluated. The media coverage, contextualization and framing, the actors involved in the public debate, the problems discussed have all been subjected to the same local, limited perspective. Our national public sphere has failed to connect to European problems, as the Schengen subject was included to an internal agenda. The Schengen accession has worked as a pretext to debate local problems, such as political fights or corruption. The presence of a Europeanized public sphere in Romania does not support the empirical evidence presented in this paper.

References

Baisnée, O (2007). "The European Public Sphere Does Not Exist (At Least It's Worth Wondering...). European Journal of Communication, 22(4), 493–503.

Bârgăoanu, A (2001). Examenul Schengen. În căutarea sferei publice europene [The Schengen Exam. In search of the European Public Sphere], Bucharest: Comunicare.ro.

Brüggemann, M & Kleinen-von Königslöw, K (2009)."Let's Talk about Europe": Why Europeanization Shows a Different Face in Different Newspapers. European Journal of Communication, 24(1), 27–48.

Delanty, G & Rumford, C (2005). Rethinking Europe: Social Theory and the Implications of Europeanization, London: Routledge.

De Vreese, C (2007). The EU as a public sphere. Retrieved 29 July 2011 from http://europeangovernance.livingreviews.org/Articles/lreg-2007-3/

Downey, J & Koenig T (2006). Is There a European Public Sphere? The Berlusconi & Schulz Case. European Journal of Communication, 21(2), 165–187.

Eriksen, E O (2005). An Emerging European Public Sphere. European Journal of Social Theory, 8(3), 341–363.

Finlayson, G J (2005). Habermas: A Very Short Introduction, New York: Oxford University Press.

Graziano, P (2003). Europeanization or Globalization? A Framework for Empirical Research (with Some Evidence from the Italian Case). Global Social Policy, 3(2), 173–194.

Habermas, J (1964). The Public Sphere: An Encyclopedia Article 1964, originally in Fischer Lexicon, Staat und Politik, new edition (Frankfurt am Main, 1964), pp. 220–226. Retrieved 30 July 2011, from http://www.propertyistheft.com/courses/social-web-media/readings/habermas-1964-the-public-sphere.pdf

—. (2005). Sfera publică şi transformarea ei structurală. Studiu asupra unei categorii a societăţii burgheze [Structural Transformation of the Public Sphere: An Investigation of a Category of Bourgeois Society], Bucharest: Comunicare.ro

Hughes, J, Sasse, G & Gordon, C (2005). *Europeanization and Regionalization in the EU's Enlargement to Central and Eastern Europe, The Myth of Conditionality*, London: Palgrave Macmillan.

Kevin, D. (2004). Europe in the media: A comparison of reporting, representation and rhetoric in national media systems in Europe. New Jersey / London: Lawrence Erlbaum Associates.

Koopmans, R & Erbe, J (2004). "Towards a European Public Sphere? Vertical and Horizontal Dimensions of Europeanized Political Communication", The European Journal of Social Science Research. 17(2), 97–118.

Lauristin, M (2007). "The European Public Sphere and the Social Imaginary of the 'New Europe'", European Journal of Communication. 22(4), 397–412.

Machill, M, Beiler, M & Fischer, C (2006). "Europe-Topics in Europe's Media: The Debate about the European Public Sphere: A Meta-Analysis of Media Content Analyses", European Journal of Communication. 21(1), 57–88.

Negrea, E (2010). What Makes the European Public Sphere Still a Prospective Project?, Paper presented at the International Conference –

Globalization and Changing patterns in the Public Sphere, November 12-13, Bucharest, Romania.
Risse, T (2003). An Emerging European Public Sphere? Theoretical Clarifications and Empirical Indicators, Paper presented at the Annual Meeting of the European Union Studies Association (EUSA), Nashville, TN, 27–30 March. Retrieved July 29, 2011, from http://userpage.fu-berlin.de/~atasp/texte/030322_europe_public.pdf.
Schlessinger, P (1999). Changing Spaces of Political Communication: The Case of the European Union, Political Communication 16, 276-277.
Semetko, H., de Vreese, C. & Peter, J. (2000). Europeanised politics – Europeanised media? European integration and political communication, West European Politics 23 (4), 121–141.
Trenz, H J & Eder, K (2004). "The Democratizing Dynamics of a European Public Sphere: Towards a Theory of Democratic Functionalism", European Journal of Social Theory. 7(1), 5–25.
Van de Steeg, M (2002). "Rethinking the Conditions for a Public Sphere in the European Union", European Journal of Social Theory. 5(4), 499–519.

PART TWO:

IDENTITY, INTERCULTURAL COMMUNICATION: NATIONAL PERSPECTIVES

A President in the Headlines: President Dalia Itzik as Reflected in the Israeli Media

Dalia Liran Alper

Abstract

The study comprising a review and analysis of the media image of Knesset Member Dalia Itzik, who served as acting president of the State of Israel from January to July 2007. Qualitative content analyses were conducted on all the reports and articles (360) published in the Israeli dailies Ha'aretz, Yedioth Ahronoth and Ma'ariv during this period. Letters to the editor, editorials, and reader "talkbacks" published in response to these articles were also analysed.

Research in the field indicates that although female politicians occasionally gained greater prominence than their male rivals, they were frequently depicted as odd figures, unfeminine in their conduct and appearance, and generally as a "novelty" (Liran-Alper, 1994). Women are presented as trespassers when they enter the political arena. The success of this minority in the public arena reinforces the image according to which this is not an appropriate place for women. Their coverage is emphasized in sections intended for the female readership and in women's magazines, and the greatest emphasis is placed on their femininity and being "first of all a woman".

Like other female politicians in many countries, Itzik suffered particularly critical treatment by means of "exclusionary representation" strategies – emphasis on aspects irrelevant to the office, such as appearance, traits that undermine suitability for a leadership role, such as over-emotionality ("a woman's heart"), on dependent relationships with men in the political system, and emphasis on her achievements in secondary spheres perceived as "feminine" (remodelling the residence).

The media's propensity to relate political stories in masculine terms of power, struggle and conflict (Trimble, 2005) establishes gendered framing. In this symbolic world, women – and femininity – are perceived as out of the ordinary and unsuitable. The coverage of women leaders, even when they hold a state leadership office, marks them as outsiders. The present study combines with a wave of recently conducted studies showing that the gendered framing of female politicians is no longer merely simple or crude monolithic stereotyping, but more "multifaceted" and refined.

Key words: female politicians, gender framing, gender stereotypes

INTRODUCTION[1]

In recent years we have witnessed a growing trend of women attaining senior political office, with some even elected or appointed heads of state. Prominent among them is German Chancellor Angela Merkel, Prime Minister of New Zealand Helen Clark, President of the Philippines Gloria. Macapagal-Arroyo, President of Chile Michelle Bachelet, President of Argentina Cristina Fernández de Kirchner, and even one of the African states, Liberia, elected a woman as president, Ellen Johnson-Sirleaf.[2]

In Israel too, in 2007, for the first time a woman served as acting president of the State of Israel for a period of six months.[3] Israel is a parliamentary democracy in which the parliament serves as the legislative authority; it is the source of power and appoints the executive authority. The president of the State of Israel is the head of state and the functions of the office include receiving reports from cabinet meetings, attending official ceremonies and official visits in Israel and abroad as the representative of the state, receiving credentials from foreign ambassadors, and recommending pardons or reduced sentences for prisoners.[4]

---

[1] My deepest gratitude to my colleague Dr Amit Kama, who read a preliminary version of this article and offered illuminating remarks.

[2] Nobel Peace Prize Laureate, 2011.

[3] Dalia Itzik was born in Jerusalem in 1952. She graduated from a teacher training college and holds a BA in literature, history and law. She served as chair of the Israel Teachers Union. She has been a Knesset member since 1992 (13th to 18th Knessets) on behalf of the Labor Party and then Kadima. In the Knesset she served as chair of the Labor-Meimad parliamentary faction and as coordinator of the opposition parliamentary factions, as chair of the Science and Technology Committee and of the Education, Culture and Sport Committee. She served in ministerial positions as Minister of Communications, Minister of the Environment, and Minister of Industry and Trade. Dalia Itzik is married and the mother of three (www.wikipedia.org/wiki).

[4] The functions of the President of the State of Israel also include opening the first session of a new Knesset, consulting with the parliamentary factions elected to the Knesset, and assigning the task of forming a new government to the head of the parliamentary faction with the best chances of forming a government (www.knesset.gov.il/president/eng/presidency_frame_eng.htm).

Dalia Itzik replaced the eighth president of the State of Israel Moshe Katzav when he announced his incapacity to continue his office in light of the intention of the Attorney General to file charges against him (based on allegations of sexual harassment). In accordance with the law, in her capacity as Speaker of the Knesset, Itzik was appointed acting president (effective from 25 January 25 2007). On 1 July 2007, Katzav's resignation came into effect and Itzik continued serving as acting president for about two weeks until Shimon Peres was sworn in and took office.

The increase in the number of women entering the centre of public space, i.e., the political arena, has been attended by a lively media discourse. In accordance with the role of the media in democratic societies, the media expose and cover the candidates for political office and examine the functioning of those who are elected. Female leaders who have been elected to high political office, and certain heads of state, gain a high level of visibility and media prominence.

In the Age of the Internet new forms of discourse are constantly emerging alongside the traditional press that intertwine with and influence the culture of discourse. Internet talkbacks constitute a meeting point between the virtual texts and Internet users, and allow them to express their opinion and respond instantly and spontaneously to journalistic articles (Bernstein & Mandelzis, 2008).

At the centre of the present paper is an exploration and analysis of the media discourse that took place in the electronic media, and the public discourse as it was expressed in talkbacks during MK Dalia Itzik's term of office as president of the State of Israel. How did the public discourse, i.e., talkbacks, integrate with the media narrative? What can be deduced from an analysis of this unique case? Have changes occurred in the characteristics of the discourse, the representative framing, and images attending the activities of women in politics?

THEORETICAL BACKGROUND

The theoretical background will focus on two aspects: the media image of female politicians around the world, with emphasis on research in Israel, and Media Framing Theory.

The Media Image of Female Politicians in Israel and Around the World

A wide range of studies conducted in recent years in the United States (Norris, 1997b; Falk, 2008), the United Kingdom (Sereberny-Mohammadi

& Ross, 1996), Germany (Holtz-Bacha & Koch, 2008), Australia (Van Acker, 1999), Canada (Gidengil & Everitt, 1999; Trimble, 2005) and New Zealand (Fountaine & McGregor, 2003) have addressed the "encounter" between women, the media and politics, with some focusing on the representation of women who ran for and attained high political office (Ross, 2002; Norris, 1997b; Braden, 1996; Leidenberger, 2008). In previous studies that addressed printed and broadcast media and focused on the news genre, it has been argued that women are invisible in media coverage (Kahn & Goldenberg, 1991). Women's representation (or rather, the lack of it) has been frequently described and analysed in these studies by means of the theoretical concept of "symbolic annihilation" (Tuchman, 1978) outlined by Gerbner and Gross (1976), which refers to the absence of various minority groups in media discourse, and their trivialization and condemnation. Symbolic annihilation is manifested in the avoidance of presenting the "weak" on the media stage.

> This argument can be formulated in quantitative/numerical terms: many strong vs. few "weak", but symbolic annihilation is also effected by means of sophisticated mechanisms that are attained latently and implicitly – in other words, qualitative symbolic annihilation. (Kama, 2004: 448–449).

Gidengil and Everitt (1999) identified three phases in the evolution of studies on women, the media and politics. The first is the issue of visibility/invisibility, as observed by Tuchman (1978); in the second phase attention shifted to the narrow focus in coverage of female politicians; and finally, in the third phase, a transition to studies indicating a more subtle bias, i.e., applying conventional political frames more rigorously to female politicians (Fountaine & McGregor, 2003: 49). It should be noted, however, that Tuchman's concepts of omission, trivialization and condemnation remain key reference points for numerous studies in this field (e.g., Lemish & Tidhar, 1999).

Notable among studies that attempted to investigate the media coverage of female politicians over a long period is the study conducted by Maria Braden (1996), who presents the stories of several dozen women who have made their mark on the political scene in the United States, from Jeanette Rankin, the first woman elected to Congress, to Geraldine Ferraro, the 1984 Democratic candidate for vice-president, and Christine Todd Whitman, New Jersey's Republican governor. Braden raises a number of questions regarding the scepticism among journalists concerning the ability of female politicians to make tough decisions, the complex relationship between female politicians and female journalists, and the consistency with which political women are penalized for their marital status. One ray of light noted by Braden is that television has vastly increased women's visibility in the public arena. She also argues that despite the current situation, with the number of women serving in high political office in Washington higher than ever before, the media treats them as a novelty and an anomaly, and consequently the public perceives them as "bench warmers" rather than an integral part of government (see also Falk, 2008).

Karen Ross (2002) conducted interviews with female politicians in the United States, Great Britain, Australia and South Africa, and found substantial similarities in the media's attitude toward women in the different countries. Her main conclusion is that the media ignore female endeavour in the spheres of welfare, education and health policy. Additionally, the media give considerably more coverage to male politicians and issues in masculine formats, such as aggressive "round table" debate programmes. Like other researchers, Ross too contends that in its excessive preoccupation with female politicians' appearance and their status as wives and mothers, and the recurring question (according to the interviewees) of how they manage to balance family obligations with their career, the media diminish their contribution. They are generally presented as women first and only later as politicians. According to Ross, the media adversely impact democracy by failing to encourage female participation in the political arena.

The growing number of women running for political office at the beginning of the twenty-first century has been accompanied by research on the media and female politicians broadening and extending to other countries. A study comparing the representation in the French and German press of Marie-Ségolène Royal, the French Socialist Party's presidential candidate in 2007, with that of the male candidates, Sarkozy and Bayrou, found a quantitative difference. In other words, Royal gained less coverage, but her appearance held greater interest for the media than that of her male counterparts (Leidenberger, 2008). The importance of an attractive appearance was also found in another study that dealt with the representation of Angela Merkel in photographs published in the press during the 2005 election campaign for German chancellor (Holtz-Bacha & Koch, 2008). Another study examined the attitude of the Argentine and German media to Eva Perón and Cristina Kirchner. Content analysis corroborated the emphasis placed by the media on the appearance of the female politician (or first lady), and the tendency to compare and draw a connection between female contenders and celebrities in different countries, and consequently they are not "politicians" but "women politicians" (Rodriguez, 2008). Yet another study addressed the press coverage of the race between Belinda Stronach, Stephen Harper and Tony Clement for leadership of the Canadian Conservative Party. Quantitative and qualitative content analyses of all the reports, editorials and op-eds published in the three major Canadian newspapers were conducted. The findings showed that it was the female contender who gained the most prominence and visibility, but a third of the reports and articles discussed her appearance. Furthermore, expressions of mockery were found in the media concerning her aspirations as well as misgivings regarding her suitability for high political office. Whereas her rivals were presented as players and their action strategies were discussed, Stronach was portrayed as an outsider, although she had already served as a high-ranking member of parliament (Trimble, 2005).

Various studies conducted in recent years focus on the image of women in the Israeli media discourse (see, inter alia, Lemish, 2007, 1997; Lavie, 2000; Lachover, 2000 Lahav, 2006; First, 2000; Lemish & Drob, 2002; Ariel, 1988), but only a few address the image of women in political office. In her study on women in local politics in Israel, Herzog (1994) found that journalists (male and female alike) tend to adopt exclusionary and inclusionary[5] practices toward women in politics. Such practices promote the image construction of women engaged in politics as trying to attain the impossible and as a unique, marginal group, a "ghetto" of women in politics. The success of the few women in the public arena reinforces the image that it is not an appropriate place for women, and they are presented as interlopers when they enter the political arena. Their coverage is emphasized in sections intended for a female readership and in women's magazines, and the greatest emphasis is placed on their femininity and being "first and foremost a woman". In her quantitative and qualitative content analysis study, Liran-Alper (1994) examined the press coverage of female Knesset members in Israel in the early 1990s. The coverage of female Knesset members was compared with that of their male counterparts, and the study found that women received less coverage than men. Moreover, aspects irrelevant to the office were emphasized in the coverage of women, such as appearance and marital status, and traits of emotionality on the one hand and belligerence on the other were underscored. According to the media narrative, these women expressed greater interest and engaged more in social issues than foreign affairs, security and the economy, contrary to their actual activities as manifested in the Knesset committees and plenum. They were depicted as odd figures,

[5] "Exclusion" in terms of separation and exclusion from the whole, and "inclusion" in terms of concentration and reference to a group as a discrete and distinct sector – "ghettoization".

unfeminine in their conduct and appearance, and generally as a "novelty". Various findings in another study examining the media representation of male and female politicians in women's magazines in Israel show that women gained extensive coverage and less stereotypical representation. This anomalous phenomenon is explained by the unique characteristics of the target audience – women (Cohen-Avigdor, 2000).

Liran-Alper (2003) also found that women candidates gained prominence in the media coverage of the 2002 primaries, but the media framed them in an image of "female wrestlers" – an image that functions as inclusionary and exclusionary, and incorporates the characteristics of power and impulsive violence that are attributed to politics with a feminine-erotic flavour (see also Shenkar-Shreck, 2000). Additionally, an analysis of the televised election campaign broadcasts in Israel in 1996 and 1998 conducted by Lemish and Tidhar (1999) found unequal coverage patterns of men and women. The women who appeared in the broadcasts were younger than the men and were represented as more emotional. They were frequently presented in dependent roles as the "girlfriend of . . ." or "daughter of . . .". In the 1996 campaign the female politicians received relatively little exposure and expressed positions in areas that are considered an extension of the private domain – education, health and welfare. Particularly prominent in the 1996 campaign was the "motherhood strategy", with their role as mothers constituting justification for their appearance and their message regarding the future and peace. Even Limor Livnat, a veteran politician and member of the Likud Party leadership, addressed the electorate as a mother of two sons (see also Weimann & Cohen, 2000).

A summary of the research background reveals that changes are taking place in the media representation of female politicians. There are contradictory findings concerning the prominence of the media representation of female politicians. According to some studies women receive less media coverage than men, whereas others indicate an equal amount of coverage, or even that women receive more coverage than men. The majority of studies, however, indicate that inclusionary and exclusionary representation frames are adopted toward women.

Framing Theory

"Framing" is the term employed in media studies that refers to the principles of selecting material and content with the aim of organizing social experience and knowledge.

> Framing news material is a normative and accepted process of coding texts in a way that also constructs the ways it is deciphered by different audiences. (Limor, Adoni, & Mann, 2007: 330)

The questions preoccupying many media researchers are how subjects are structured, how discourse is structured, and how meanings develop (Gamson, 1989).

The term "frame/framing" alludes to an active process as well as to an outcome, and refers to a frame the media imposes on reality, as well as to a tool for media and culture researchers to deconstruct the discourse and meanings each community accords to its narratives (Neiger, 2007).[6] A variety of definitions have been proposed for the term "framing", for example,

> To frame is to select some aspects of a perceived reality and make them more salient in a communicating text, in such a way as to promote a particular problem definition, causal interpretation, moral evaluation, and/or treatment recommendation for the item described. (Entman, 1993: 52)

A longstanding and widely accepted definition is the one proposed by Gitlin (1980: 7) who views media frames as "patterns of cognition, interpretation, and presentation, of selection, emphasis, and exclusion, by which symbol-handlers routinely organize discourse, whether verbal or visual".

According to the new and expanded definition offered by Tankard (2001), "news frames" are ongoing patterns of selection, interpretation, and presentation processes that create order and meaning in complex issues, processes, and events. Media frames efficiently process and organize the components of reality for journalists and their audiences alike. The media frames events in processes that include selection (what to publish) and editing (how to publish), how it presents these events and the figures participating in them, proposes an explanation and establishes context that create the meaning of the events (Tankard, 2001).

In his study, Reese (2001, p. 11) argues that "Frames are organizing principles that are socially shared and persistent over time, that work symbolically to meaningfully structure the social world". This definition comprises six elements:

[6] The Israel Communication Association even chose to name its journal, which has been published since 2007, *Media Frames*.

Organizing: Framing varies in how successfully, comprehensively, or completely it organizes information. It often does so by appealing to basic psychological biases and emphasizing positive or negative aspects, and frequently employs stories embedded in a particular cultural environment.

Principles: The frame is based on abstract principles that function by means of "schemata" of interpretation and which are manifested in the discourse.

Shared: The frame must be shared on some level for it to be significant and communicable.

Persistent: The significance of frames lies in their durability, their persistent and routine use over time, resembling the habitual character noted by Gitlin that causes the framing to be perceived as self-evident and "natural" (Gitlin, 1980).

Symbolically: The frame is revealed in symbolic forms of expression.

Structure: Media frames structure meaning by means of the pattern they impose on the social world. Employing a minimalist definition, it could be argued that frames call attention to certain aspects of reality by means of exclusion and inclusion.

Framing theory provides a theoretical organizing tool to analyse and understand the functioning of the media – which is of particular relevance to gender, political, and media research. Norris argues that "gendered framing" delineates the mainstream media discourse in the United States (Norris, 1997a). The issue she positions at the centre of her book is: "does the media frame gender politics 'with a different eye', which hinders and diminishes women's participation in public life, and if so, how?" (p. 11).

Her criticism focuses on the degree of stereotyping in the representation of women, neglecting issues that are important to women and diminishing their achievements. Gendered framing is created due the propensity to relate political stories in masculine terms of power, struggle and conflict. The coverage of female leaders, even when they are heads of state, treats them as outsiders, as "pioneers" and agents of change. News information frequently focuses on women's contribution to politics primarily in issues traditionally perceived as women's rather than general issues that affect all the citizens of the state.

In the present study the theoretical concepts of qualitative symbolic annihilation-omission, trivialization and condemnation (Tuchman, 1978) have been combined with media framing theory (Reese, 2001; Tankard, 2001; Gamson, 1989; Gitlin, 1980). In the wake of the accumulated research in various countries, including Israel, on the media representation of central women in politics, the present study seeks to examine the "media frames" that attended the activities of Acting President of the State of Israel Dalia Itzik. Questions addressed include: Was there a different and unique perspective on a "woman president" in Israel in 2007? Was gendered framing (Norris, 1997a) applied, and what are its component parts?

RESEARCH QUESTIONS AND METHODOLOGY

The questions at the basis of the present study are: can distinct gender-based media frames be identified in the media coverage and public discourse of a female political leader in Israel at the start of the twenty-first century as they were manifested in talkbacks? And, what can be learned from this individual case; is there a unique narrative in the Israeli media and public discourse that presents women leaders, and if so, what are its component parts?[7]

The study reviews and analyses the media image of Speaker of the Knesset Dalia Itzik during a period in which she also served as acting president of the State of Israel, from January to July 2007. The study examined all the reports and articles that mentioned Itzik that were published during this period in the online versions of the three major Israeli dailies Haaretz, Ynet (Yedioth Ahronoth) and nrg (Maariv). A total of 360 reports and articles were found in the online newspapers (Haaretz – 15; Ynet – 62; nrg – 148). It should be noted that only online newspapers were reviewed and no comparison was conducted between online and printed newspapers (on online newspapers, see Caspi, 2007).[8] The reports, articles and reader talkbacks published in response to these articles and

[7] "Domineering dowagers and scheming concubines" was the prevalent narrative concerning the depiction of women leaders since Antiquity and up to the beginning of the twentieth century. In *Stereotypes of Women in Power: Historical Perspectives and Revisionist Views* (1992), Saxonhouse compiled studies on female leaders, from Lysistrata in Ancient Greece to the twentieth century. According to Saxonhouse, the distinction between "masculine is public" and "feminine is private" continues throughout history, according primacy to the public arena. Women who crossed the lines into the public sphere crossed "the threshold out of the darkness of silence into the light of speech" (p. 5). They were portrayed as "domineering dowagers and scheming concubines" (p. 11) and as a contradiction to "good women".

[8] The study only additionally refers to a concluding profile published at the end of Itzik's term of office as president, in the printed issue of *Haaretz* (Naama Lanski, "Itzik Days", *Haaretz* Weekend Supplement, 12.09.07, pp. 18–26).

reports were analysed employing a qualitative methodology in accordance with the elements of Framing Theory (Reese, 2001). Only the texts that appeared in the published reports, articles and headlines were included in the analysis (not images).

The study belongs to the large corpus of content analysis studies in the field, but its uniqueness lies in the combination of the two intertwined discourse types: the media discourse that appeared in the online newspapers, and the talkbacks that emerged following publication of the articles and reports. The media and public discourse that attends female politicians will be examined as a sophisticated game of media frames, with emphasis on components of the principles of organization, structure, and symbolism (Reese, 2001).

Talkbacks

Letters to the editor in the printed press have been an element of public discourse since the very beginnings of newspapers, and were typified by their dialogic character in which writers often referred to previous articles (Morrison & Love, 1996). Amit Kama examined the letters section in the Israeli daily *Haaretz*, and concluded that the letters published in this elitist newspaper constitute part of a discourse of the elites – in terms of content and language (for radio talkbacks, see Hacohen in Kohn & Neiger, 2007). Linking feedback to the virtual press creates a center of public discourse on the Internet. Talkbacks are a fascinating new arena that invites an attempt to ponder the relationship between the journalistic article and the responses. Unlike letters in traditional media channels where responses are screened, mediated, or moderated, in this new medium interactivity between readers and the news desk is enhanced, and mediation – so it is claimed – is minimal, although there is growing evidence of censorship and editing in this medium as well.[9] In a ground breaking study on the rhetoric of talkbacks, Kohn and Neiger (2007) claim that in this discourse too, writers often react to the arguments of the journalist. They contend that the knowledge that one can react spontaneously without the presence of a guiding hand or ideology-based instructions "endows the responses with their quality as a primary cultural act representing linguistic and social innovations alike" (Kohn & Neiger, 2007: 327).

---

[9] An interview with editor of *Ynet* Yon Feder, he said that approximately half of the reactions received are screened out: www.themarker.com/tmc/article.jhtml?log=tag&Elementld=skira20060909_760371.

They further note that in the Israeli context this discourse is particularly confrontational and violent, possessing discourse attributes defined by Tamar Katriel (1999) as *dugri* and *laredet kassach* (straight, no-holds-barred talking).

The present study will examine the contention that the journalistic story as it is expressed in the media discourse plays a role in framing the story and constructing images in a narrative context from which the component parts of the talkbacks develop, and media frames formulated in the media discourse frequently resonate in the "spontaneous" public discourse, as illustrated in the following example: in a report covering the speech delivered in the Knesset by the president of the European Parliament, Arik Bender wrote about Acting President and Knesset Speaker Itzik's aggressive response,

> And if that weren't enough, Itzik recalled the good old days when she was a **teacher** and sent the German guest off to do his homework. . . . She should arm herself with a little information. (nrg, 31 May 2007)

From the ensuing talkbacks: "You know what, Dalia Itzik isn't doing such a bad job at all". "Like a schoolteacher, what's she got beside that?" "She's nothing more than a blabbermouth." The journalist described Itzik's conduct when hosting the German politician by framing her activity under the familiar professional label, "teacher". Attaching the label of "teacher" constitutes a media frame that charges the event with meaning and context and leads the ensuing public discourse on the Internet in the wake of the journalistic article.

Analysis and Discussion – Frames and Strategies of Exclusionary Representation

In her capacity as acting president of the State of Israel, Dalia Itzik gained extensive media coverage, hence quantitative symbolic annihilation cannot be claimed (Tuchman, 1978). In feminist research the term "exclusionary representation" is used to describe the framing of events as "men's matters" in a way that accords legitimacy to the marginality of women (Lahav, 2008). Various "gendered framing" strategies were identified in the analysis of the media coverage Itzik received in her role as acting president, as well as the talkbacks posted in the wake of news reports and articles.

Similar to previous studies examining the media coverage of female politicians, the present study found that the media frames Itzik's representation with a "different eye" that conceals and diminishes her activity in the high-ranking office of President of the State of Israel. A selection of exclusionary representation patterns yielded a variety of misgivings and reasons for her being unsuited to the office. From aspects irrelevant to the office such as family status and appearance, through attributing her political success to a male patron, to diverting the debate to assertions concerning her lack of qualifications to fill the office and accusing her of weaknesses originating in her being overly or insufficiently "feminine".

The online newspapers and talkbacks extensively discussed aspects that are irrelevant to the office of acting president. The framing in the media and public discourse was created in processes of persistent structuring over time (Reese, 2001), diverting attention from relevant endeavor to marginal, personal, and stereotypically women's characteristics:

Appearance and Hairstyle. Journalists and talk backers alike frequently discussed the suits Dalia Itzik wore to various events and the changes she made in her hairstyle, and were not averse to making sexist and malicious remarks. An example from the press:

> Unless Dalia Itzik is planning a second career as a NASA water girl, we have no other explanation for the white space suit and the long-range spikes she went to all the trouble to adorn herself with for Shimon Peres's swearing-in ceremony as president. (Rotem Rosenthal and Gabi Bar-Haim, nrg Fashion Section, 6 February 2007)

Examples from the ensuing talkbacks:

> If Dalia Itzik didn't have "spikes" in her hair and a décolletage, who'd be paying her any attention? (Ynet, Talkback 43, 25 January 2007)

> Isn't she related to Kermit the Frog? Her physiognomy fits. (nrg, Talkback 3, 24 January 2007)

> Dalia, you showed up for the festivities in just-off-the-boat fashion that was appropriate 59 years ago, the office is not for you, it mandates an elegant appearance. (On the Independence Day torch-lighting ceremony, Ynet, Talkback 175, 24 July 2007)

The excessive preoccupation with appearance and hairstyle, which went beyond what is generally accepted for female politicians, was frequently a substitute for appropriate public debate. The clothes Acting President Dalia Itzik chose to wear, or her coiffure, were described in detail and drew amused, derisory or even maliciously critical remarks. These findings are consistent with Falk's assertion that the coverage of female candidates in the US presidential campaigns focused disproportionately on feminine subjects such as appearance, wardrobe and family status (Falk, 2008), like the German media's attitude toward Angela Merkel (Holtz-Bacha & Koch, 2008), the French media's attitude toward Marie-Ségolène Royal (Leidenberger, 2008), and the Argentine media's attitude toward Eva Perón and Cristina Kirchner (Rodriguez, 2008). Content analysis studies have corroborated the emphasis the media places on a female politician's appearance. With cynical humour O'Brien (1996) notes "in politics, a woman loses credibility if she has the wrong hairdo". Beyond all the amusing and derisory examples, it would be fitting to adopt the important argument made by Ross that the media's preoccupation with female politicians' appearance diminishes women's contributions in the public and political arena (Ross, 2002).

Family Status. The cumulative corpus of research indicates that the media tends to make extensive reference to the family status of women running for political office. In the studied period no extensive references to Dalia Itzik's family status were identified. Nevertheless, her motherhood was enlisted to the general gendered framing of her political conduct, as demonstrated for example by the choice of headline "The Housemother", and in the article itself:

> *Speaker of the Knesset Dalia Itzik is still acting president, which doesn't stop her behaving like a political* activist and vote contractor . . . which she does over private luncheons. (Bender, nrg, 28 June 2007)

The media frame constructs Itzik's image as a mother, emphasizing motherly tasks such as lunch. In a talkback which, as we have seen, in the Israeli context excels in belligerence and sometimes vulgarity, the expression is more direct and simplistic: "Stay at home" (Ynet, Talkback 15, 8 January 2007).

It should be noted that the two types of discourse discussed in the present article treat Itzik's family status as significant and relevant to the discussion about her, and indeed despite her extensive seniority in political activity Itzik is known as someone who managed to balance family with a career and was not accused of pursuing a political career at her family's expense. This contrasts with other female politicians who are consistently penalized for their family status (Braden, 1996; see also the media's attitude toward MK Ora Namir, in Liran-Alper, 1994). Motherhood became a central issue in New Zealand's general election (Fountaine &

McGregor, 2003). In her comparative study of female politicians in four different countries, Ross, too, notes that the media frequently engaged with their status as wives and mothers, as well as the recurring question, according to the interviewees, of how they manage to balance family obligations and a career. Lemish and Tidhar (1999) emphasize the "motherhood strategy", which served to accord legitimacy to statements made by female politicians as part of the election campaign on Israel Television on important issues such as security.

Accusations of being overly or insufficiently "feminine" are a common exclusionary representation strategy that was employed in the media and public discourse on Dalia Itzik when she served as acting president of the state. This can be viewed as a principle (Reese, 2001) that creates the typical framing for women's representation.

Overly Feminine

Women in general, and hence women in politics, are described as less rational and more emotional than men (Liran-Alper, 1994; Lemish & Tidhar, 1999). Journalists express misgivings concerning the ability of female politicians to make tough decisions and they are liable, heaven forefend, to burst into tears in moments of crisis (Braden, 1996).[10] Itzik's qualifications to make considered and rational decisions were also criticized and called into question. An example of this are her decisions on pardons, one of the president's most central and perhaps most powerful function. Her functioning in the process of granting pardons drew accusations of being overly softhearted, whether in the media discourse, where it was stated that,

> Among others, she signed a pardon for a single mother experiencing hardship. (*Ynet*, Subhead, 14 March 2007)

or the public discourse:

> A woman's heart. (Ynet, Talkback 10, 14 March 2007)

[10] Braden analyses news reports and interviews some of the most prominent women, such as Dianne Feinstein who was captured on camera struggling to hold back her tears during her campaign to be elected Mayor of San Francisco. On this Feinstein is quoted as saying that a woman should never cry because a man can cry and somehow it doesn't bother anybody, but if a woman cries it is devastating and everybody will remember it.

Itzik's conduct during the process of granting pardons is framed in the phrase "a woman's heart", a metaphor for traits of over-emotionality attributed to women. The journalistic wording implies that it was her soft-heartedness toward a single mother that determined her decision. Kind heartedness, which is "typical" of women, is presented as a thinly disguised argument for Itzik's inability to apply the rational consideration and judgement required to address requests for pardons, and calls into question her competence to fulfill this important function.

Additionally, the above example also illustrates the power of the journalistic article in creating the talkbacks that develop in its wake. The professional element frames the activity of granting pardons by selecting and emphasizing a specific case – "a single mother". This is a media frame designed to create a particular way of thinking to which the media consumer adapts him- or herself and continues with a blunt verbal attack: "A woman's heart".

The media offer a narrative that binds the lack of independence and resolve of female politicians with the tendency to develop dependent relationships of political patronage with a male politician, and using him to attain office and climb up the political ladder (Liran-Alper, 1994; Lemish & Tidhar, 1999). In Itzik's case, Shimon Peres has been depicted as her patron throughout her entire career, and his name was repeatedly mentioned in the context of her role as acting president:

> Dalia Itzik is Peres's protégé. (Haaretz, Mazal Mualem, 29 January 2007)

> This is how a protégé repays her godfather. (Ynet, Talkback 32, 9 May 2007)

Manipulativeness and Intrigue. These social skills are attributed to women more than to men, being portrayed frequently as "overly feminine" traits and presented negatively, i.e., as intrigue and manipulative behaviour in which female politicians excel. The routine fulfilment of the tasks of office is framed in a way that evokes negative emotions and creates a repulsive, manipulative image. Furthermore, manipulative conduct and power games are legitimate means in political behaviour, yet Dalia Itzik was condemned for her conduct as a politician. For example:

> Dalia? She capitalizes on everything that falls into her hands . . . go run a campaign when Dalia is being photographed receiving ambassadors at the president's residence and entertaining soldiers on Holy Days. (Haaretz, Mazal Mualem, 29 January 2007)

During her term of office as acting president, Itzik acquired another classic feminine metaphor when the media enlisted the image of the "princess" to create an interesting media story around her high-level meeting with the British crown prince during his visit to Israel. Thus for example in the title of a report on the subject:

> When the Prince Met Mrs. President (Dafna Vardi, nrg, 7 July 2007)

> The frog is a frog and the prince a prince, nothing's changed (nrg, Talkback 30, 7 July 2007)

Employing the age-old "princess" metaphor that is deeply rooted in contemporary popular culture evokes connotations of a pretty, delicate and especially passive feminine figure – an image that runs completely counter to the characteristics of taking action and initiative required from a figure in a leadership role. In this instance, too, the journalists offer the symbolic description and the talk backers relate to it and develop the story in their reactions to the article.

Another appellation and feminine metaphor employed to describe Itzik is "teacher", which was first used by a journalist and frequently appeared among talk backers as well. It can be argued that "teacher" is not only an allusion to the profession, but a rich, well-grounded metaphor in Israeli culture. More often than not teachers are women, and a wide variety of images and negative behavioural norms are attached to this status, from punctilious behavior and enforcing discipline to fussiness, meticulousness and a preaching tone of voice. In any case, it is not an appropriate image for a leader, and attaching it to Itzik in her capacity as acting president is another example of media framing that is designed to exclude by ridicule, and also an example of how the language employed by the media frequently alludes to the unsuitability of a woman for the office (Falk, 2008).

Insufficiently Feminine

The principle of "femininity" enlisted to examine the functioning of a female politician can lead to the opposite conclusion, which also evokes negative emotions – insufficient or absence of "femininity" (i.e., employing the same exclusionary representation frame, but in reverse). Several statements pertaining to this issue were found, all by talk backers, according to which Itzik is not a "real" or "proper" woman, and that she in fact suffers from a "lack of femininity", hence her appointment to a leadership office or her success as a leader does not in any way attest to the possible suitability of women to the political arena. For example:

> Even if Itzik submits her candidacy it still doesn't change the fact that only men are appointed to this office; the girl's quite a man. (Ynet, Talkback 30, 25 January 2007)

Another possible interpretation is that if Dalia Itzik is aspiring to the office, then she is insufficiently feminine, since by its very nature femininity runs counter to ambition and aspirations to political power centres. Itzik is accused of being overly masculine, the "Iron Lady", or an aggressive teacher.

In literature, the female politician is described as aggressive and lacking emotion, the "bitch" that trampled everybody, men and women alike, on her way up. The women are portrayed as being overly belligerent, which is manifested in aggressiveness. In their study on the 1993 Canadian election campaign, Gidengil and Everitt claim that competitiveness, which

> is perceived – positively – to be combative in a man may be judged – negatively – to be aggressive in a woman. (Gidengil & Everitt, 1999, p. 62)

Another exclusionary representation strategy is the framing of (the absence of) traits and skills as the female politician's personal and "reasoned" unsuitability: Dalia Itzik's unsuitability for the office of acting president of the State of Israel is explained by and justified with a wide variety of critical reasons. Accusations of her unsuitability are justified first and foremost by her lack of security experience, but also by her lack of essential skills for the office (insufficient fluency in English).

The day before her appointment as acting president, Haaretz published the headline: "Madam President to be Briefed by the Chief of Staff" (Haaretz, Alon, 24 January 2007). Evident in the choice of headline, which gains prominence beyond what is expressed in the article itself, is the power of the media in framing events in reality. In our view, this ostensibly purely factual headline can easily be understood as the media's misgivings about a situation whereby Itzik will be fed security information by the chief of staff, her subordinate, while she herself lacks knowledge and experience in an area so crucial to the existence of the State of Israel.[11]

---

[11] When Tzipi Livni ran in the primaries for leadership of the Kadima party against former chief of the general staff Shaul Mofaz (2008), the issue of her qualifications for the office due to her lack of security experience was discussed in the public discourse by means of the question: Who's going to pick up the phone at 3 a.m.?

The veteran politician and Speaker of the Knesset drew criticism for being insufficiently skilled to fill the high public office of president. Her knowledge of foreign languages was scrutinized with a meticulous eye, as expressed in the remark about Itzik lacking fluency in English. For example:

> Just not Dalia Itzik. She doesn't speak English either. (Ynet, Talkback 46, 24 January 2007)

The argument of a female candidate's unsuitability constitutes a media frame and paves the way for subtle and complex gender bias (Norris, 1997; Fountaine & McGregor, 2003). The media places emphasis on inexperience and lack of essential skills for success in the office. Trimble (2005) describes the derisory expressions that prevailed in the Canadian media concerning Stronach's obvious unsuitability for the high-level office, while joking about her excessive aspirations to leadership of the Conservative Party. Thus the media frequently allude to the woman's unsuitability for the aspired-to office, as well as to the slim probability of her being elected. Sexism continues to influence politics, in which the media plays a key role when it portrays women not as "candidates" but as "women candidates" (Falk, 2008).

Another exclusionary representation strategy focuses on diminishing the value of female politicians' endeavour and disparaging the spheres of their activity: Itzik's activities in hosting receptions and organizing (and participating in) official ceremonies gained considerable prominence in the media discourse and a broad and relatively favourable discussion. For example:

> Dalia Itzik's speech was amazing, ten levels above any other politician in Israel. (Following the Remembrance Day ceremony on Mt Herzl, Ynet, Talkback 58, 28 April 2007)

She was depicted as being good at "social hospitality" activities, in accordance with and as expected within the stereotypical frame of women. Her involvement in the design and remodelling of the Knesset building complex can be similarly explained as stereotypically feminine spheres of interest, which are considered extremely marginal in national terms. For example:

> Parliament has undergone a substantial facelift and Itzik is proud to present the country's display window. (Haaretz, Lansky, 12 September 2007)

During the period in which she served as president of the State of Israel, Itzik also continued to serve as Speaker of the Knesset who is charged, inter alia, with maintenance of the Knesset building complex. When she took office, Itzik devoted a certain amount of time to the interior design of the complex, which the media frequently derided. Aesthetics, design, and care for the surroundings are perceived as befitting the private domain with which women are charged. When a woman directs her energies to the public domain, e.g., the political arena, the media tend to continue framing her activities in terms drawn from feminine preoccupations in the private domain. This media framing aims to minimize and diminish the value of the female politician's endeavour. The media tend to accentuate women's engagement in "feminine" spheres, and women are presented as being primarily active in areas perceived as an extension of the private domain, such as education, culture, welfare, and health, which are traditionally considered to be less prestigious and meaningful in the political arena and society in general (Lemish & Tidhar, 1999; Norris, 1997), even in cases where female politicians actually engaged extensively in the economic or security spheres (Liran-Alper, 1994).

We found frequent amused or derisory descriptions of Dalia Itzik's activities:

> The tea lady is handing out pardons. (Ynet, Talkback 31, 16 Febraury 2007)

Although this talkbacker's attitude can be viewed as part of the belligerent nature of Israeli Internet talkbacks (Kohn & Neiger, 2007), it could also indicate the deep-rooted and ongoing meanings embedded in the cultural environment of scornful expressions of this kind.

Exclusion through ridicule is a trend of qualitative symbolic annihilation effected by means of sophisticated mechanisms that are commonly attained latently and implicitly. This mode of representation is achieved in devious, cunning and problematic ways. The problematic nature of this mode of representation stems primarily from the way in which it is coded (i.e., coding that appears natural or hidden from view): the way in which the figure is presented and in which her identity is constructed are liable to be the product of general exclusion processes, for the ridiculous representation does not indicate equitable participation in the media discourse. This symbolic annihilation is therefore carried out not only by the omission or annihilation of people, but in setting up their identity as a target for ridicule and a patronizing attitude by participants in media processes (Liran-Alper & Kama, 2007; Kama, 2005).

Summary and Conclusions

The discussion on the media coverage of Dalia Itzik as acting president of the State of Israel corroborates the assertion that it is the status of being a woman that constitutes the focus of media visibility and the discourse on leadership patterns when dealing with a woman leader. The vague statements about being overly or insufficiently "feminine" are a feeble attempt to disguise opposition stemming from the figure's gender status, i.e., being a woman. Supportive or complimentary expressions on a good speech she delivered, or a ceremony she conducted with decorum can be construed as expressions of surprise that Itzik managed not to fail in her office (!). The latent expectation that a woman is prone to failure when she expresses excessive ambition and aspires to a powerful political office constitutes a gender obstacle placed by the media before female politicians. This is consistent with Heith's (2001) assertion that the American media vigorously engaged in the stages of and reasons for Geraldine Ferraro bowing out of the 1984 presidential race for vice-president of the United States.[12]

Acting President of the State of Israel Dalia Itzik is depicted as a woman, a political leader, assiduous yet ruthless and manipulative, and a subject of ridicule and derision over her appearance. Analysis of the talkbacks illuminates possible explanations. Itzik is presented as a ridiculous/amusing novelty due to her activity in a place where she does not belong, a woman who has pushed herself into the centre of the public space, over the fence and beyond gender boundaries.[13] The attitude toward Dalia Itzik reinforces Braden's assertions concerning female politicians in the United States who are treated by the media as a novelty and an anomaly. The media's propensity to relate political stories in masculine terms of power, struggle and conflict (Trimble, 2005) establishes gendered

---

[12] About a year after Dalia Itzik's term of office as president, another woman gained prominence in the Israeli political arena, Tzipi Livni, and she, too, received "special" treatment at the hands of the media. "Will she or won't she succeed? Like spectators in a gladiatorial arena, the public is waiting to see whether Tzipi Livni succeeds in building a coalition" (Barel, Z., "Let Her Lead", *Haaretz*, 28 August 2008, p. 16).

[13] "You wouldn't believe what a grueling year Dalia Itzik has had. She had to reupholster the Knesset members' seats, ship the Chagall tapestries to Paris for cleaning, educate employees to stop coming to work in jeans, step into President Katzav's dirty shoes, inspire the nation on Independence Day, work on her romance with Olmert . . . and take to task all the unsympathetic journalists trying to rob her of her success story." (Lanski, N., *Haaretz* Weekend Supplement, 12 August 2007, subhead, p. 18)

framing. In this symbolic world women – and femininity – are perceived as out of the ordinary and unsuitable. The coverage of women leaders, even when they hold a state leadership office, marks them as outsiders (Norris, 1997), and they are not "politicians" but "female politicians" (Rodriguez, 2008; Falk, 2008).

The present study combines with a wave of recently conducted studies showing that the gendered framing of female politicians is no longer merely simple or crude monolithic stereotyping, but more "multifaceted" and refined (Fountaine & McGregor, 2003). However, the different facets of media frames and representation strategies employed to describe female politicians continue to create a system of negative images and condemnation. When the Western media critically scrutinize the few women who dare aspire to leadership at the pinnacle of the political arena, it engenders a message that these women are acting in a social field unsuited to the female gender.

In the present study the application of framing theory concepts has been expanded beyond the boundaries of media discourse to the public discourse created in the wake of journalistic articles in the form of Internet talkbacks. The study examined the meeting point between the virtual text and the immediate reaction of Internet users. Despite the unique characteristics of talkbacks, including the spontaneity and verbal attacks typifying it (Kohn & Neiger, 2007), the present study suggests – with the caution appropriate to an initial study – that the media frames outline to a considerable degree the messages produced in the talkbacks as well. The cultural environment shared by professional writers and laypeople can provide a partial explanation for a phenomenon that requires further research. The organizing principles, symbols, and construction are defined in the media text (Reese, 2001), and frequently resonate in the reactions of talk backers, hence the continued importance of the framing created by the media.

A dangerous outcome of exclusionary representation media framing is that it reinforces perceptions of women as outsiders, not as an integral part of the political establishment, or figures worthy of leadership (Braden, 1996). Thus, the media is liable to deter additional women from trying to run for political office and playing an active role in public power centres. Emerging from the present study, which focused on a single figure over a limited period, is that despite the opportunity to cover a woman in a powerful position and form a new narrative of a female leader, the Israeli media at the beginning of the twenty-first century reverts to reinforcing the gender social order and the traditional division of roles, which assigns administration of the public space solely to men.

Finally, the accumulated corpus of knowledge on the research of female politicians in the media and public discourse is still scant. Consequently, our recommendation is to continue studying the media discourse that attends the activities of women in the public arena, in leadership roles – especially those who attain the pinnacle and are elected to the office of head of state. The relationship formed between the media discourse and the talkbacks certainly mandates further research, with reference to the diverse communication channels emerging in the new media platforms. Moreover, it is essential and important to continue researching the development of the representation of female politicians in the media and public discourse throughout their career. A worthy platform for discussion of this subject and a comparison between Israeli and other societies can only be created by means of future research that will engage in different countries and diverse cultural environments.

References

Ariel, M (1988). Female and Male Stereotypes in Israeli Literature and Media: Evidence from Introductory Patterns. *Languages and Communication* 8(1), 43–68.

Bernstein, A & Mandelzis, L (2008). *New Media – New Discourse? Talkbacks, Football, Minorities and National Identity in Israel*, A paper presented at the IAMCR Conference in Stockholm, July 20–25.

Braden, M (1996). *Women Politicians and the Media*, Lexington: University Press of Kentucky.

Caspi, D (2007). Online Newspapers in Israel. In T. Schwartz-Altshuler (Ed.), *Journalism Dot.Com – Online Newspapers in Israel*, Jerusalem: Israel Democracy Institute and Hubert Burda Center for Innovative Communications at Ben Gurion University of the Negev, 31–50 (Hebrew).

Cohen-Avigdor, N (2000). Women Politicians (Compared to Men) in Israeli Women's Magazines: The Way They Were Portrayed During the Knesset Election Years 1959, 1977, 1996. *PATUACH* 4, 75–99 (Hebrew).

Entman, R (1993). Framing: Toward Clarification of a Fractured Paradigm. *Journal of Communication*, 43(4), 51–58.

Falk E (2008). *Women for President: Media Bias in Eight Campaigns*, University of Illinois Press.

First, A (2000). Nothing New in Israel?! Men's and Women's Images in Printed Advertising in Israel. *PATUACH* 4, 127–156 (Hebrew).

Fountaine, S & McGregor, J (2003). Reconstructing Gender for the 21st Century: New Media Framing of Political Women in New Zealand. www.bond.edu.au/hss/communication/ANZCA/.

Gamson, W (1989). News as Framing. *American Behavioral Scientist*, 33(2), 157–161.

Gerbner, G & Gross, L (1976). Living with Television: The Violence Profile. *Journal of Communication*, 26(2), 173–199.

Gidengil, E & Everitt, J (1999). Metaphors and Misrepresentations: Gendered Mediation in News Coverage of the 1993 Canadian Leaders' Debates. *Harvard International Journal of Press/Politics* 4(1), 48–65.

Gitlin, T (1980). *The Whole World is Watching*, Berkeley, CA: University of California Press.

Heith, D (2001). Footwear, Lipstick and an Orthodox Sabbath: Media Coverage of Nontraditional Candidates (Geraldine Ferraro, Elizabeth Dole and Joseph Lieberman). *White House Studies* 1(3), 335–349.

Herzog, H (1994). *Realistic Women – Women in Israeli Local Politics*, Jerusalem: The Jerusalem Institute for Israel Studies (Hebrew).

Holtz-Bacha, C & Koch, T (2008). *Appearance Counts: The Visual Portrayal of Angela Merkel in the German Print Media During the Election Year 2005*, A paper presented at the IAMCR Conference, Stockholm, July 20–25, 2008.

Kahn, K F & Goldenberg, E N (1991). Women Candidates in the News: An Examination of Gender Differences in the U.S. Senate Campaign Coverage. *Public Opinion Quarterly,* 55(2), 180–199.

Kama, A (2004). Active Reading, Multiculturalism and the Constraints of Hegemonic Discourse. In T. Liebes, A. Kama, M. Talmon, & D. Levin (Eds.), *Communication as Culture*, 2:12. Tel Aviv: The Open University (Hebrew).

—. (2005). *Letters-to-the-Editor as a Site for Civil Participation and Group Identity Construction: An Israeli Test Case*. Tel Aviv: Chaim Herzog Institute for Media, Politics and Society at Tel Aviv University (Hebrew).

Katriel, T (1999). *Keywords: Patterns of Culture and Communication in Israel*, Tel Aviv: University of Haifa and Zmora Bitan (Hebrew).

Kohn, A & Neiger, M (2007). To Talk and To Talkback: The Rhetoric of the Talk-Back in Israeli Online Newspapers. In T. Altshuler (ed.), *Journalism Dot Com: Online Newspapers in Israel*. Jerusalem: Israel Democracy Institute and Hubert Burda Center for Innovative Communications at Ben Gurion University of the Negev, Jerusalem, pp. 321–352 (Hebrew).

Lachover, E (2000). Women Journalists in the Israeli Press, *Kesher* 28, 63–74 (Hebrew).

Lahav, H (2006). *Transparent – Patriarchy and Editing in Journalistic Text: A Case-study of the Coverage of Sexual Violence in the Israeli Press* (PhD Dissertation, Tel Aviv University) (Hebrew).

—. (2008). *A Gendered View of Israeli Television Coverage of the 2006 Lebanon War*. The 12th Annual Conference of the Israeli Association of Communication, Tel Aviv, 13 April 2008 (Hebrew).

Lavie, A. (2000). News is News – It Has no Gender. *PATUACH* 4, 45–74. (Hebrew).

Leidenberger, J (2008). *The Portrayal of Ségolène Royal in French and German Print Media During the 2007 Presidential Election Campaign*, A paper presented at the IAMCR Conference, Stockholm, July 20–25, 2008.

Lemish, D (1997). Equal Communication Rights: A Feminist Perspective on Israeli Media. In D. Caspi (Ed.), *Media and Democracy in Israel.* Jerusalem and Tel Aviv: Van-Leer Jerusalem Institute and Hakibbutz Hameuchad pp. 119–139 (Hebrew).

—. (2007). The Politics of Exclusion: Representations of Women and Violence Against Them. In D. Caspi (ed.), *Communications and Politics in Israel.* Jerusalem and Tel Aviv: Van-Leer Jerusalem Institute and Hakibbutz Hameuchad pp. 185–207 (Hebrew).

Lemish, D, & Drob, G (2002). "All the Time His Wife": Portrayals of First Ladies in the Israeli Press. *Parliamentary Affairs* 55(1), 129–142.

Lemish, D & Tidhar, C E, (1999). Still Marginal: Women in Israel's 1996 Television Election Campaign. *Sex Roles*, 41, 389–412.

Limor, Y, Adoni, C, & Mann, R (2007). *Communication Lexicon*, Tel-Aviv: Miskal.

Liran-Alper, D (1994). *Media Representation of Women in Politics: Are They Still "Domineering Dowagers and Scheming Concubines"?* (Masters thesis, Hebrew University Department of Communications) (Hebrew).

Liran-Alper, D (2003). Mud Wrestlers: The Media Image of Women Contending for Internal Party Elections in Israel in 2002. *Matzav HaInyanim* 20, Beit Berl Academic College. (Hebrew).

Liran-Alper, D & Kama, A (2007). *Body Design and Identity Building in Commercial Television.* Tel Aviv: Chaim Herzog Institute for Media, Politics and Society, Tel-Aviv University (Hebrew).

Morrison, A & Love, A (1996). A Discourse of Disillusionment: Letters to the Editor in Two Zimbabwean Magazines 10 Years after Independence. *Discourse & Society*, 7(1), 39–75.

Neiger, M (Ed.). *Media Frames: Israeli Journal of Communication*, The Israel Communication Association. Netanya, 1:H (Hebrew)

Norris, P (ed.) (1997a). *Women, Media and Politics*, New York: Oxford University Press.

Norris, P (1997b). World Leaders Worldwide: A Splasah of Color in the Photo Op. In P. Norris (ed.), *Women, Media and Politics* (pp. 149–165), New York: Oxford University Press.

O'Brien, P (1996). Women Politicians and the Media. *Columbia Journalism Review* 35(3), 60–63.

Reese, S D (2001). Prologue – Framing Public Life: A Bridging Model for Media Research. In S D Reese, O H Gandy & A E Grant (eds), *Framing Public Life: Perspectives on Media and Our Understanding of the Social World* (pp. 7–31), Mahwah, NJ: Lawrence Erlbaum.

Rodriguez, H (2008). *Resembling Evita or Hillary? Cristina Kirchner and the Argentine Electoral Campaign for the Presidency in the Argentine and the German Press*, A paper presented at the IAMCR Conference, Stockholm, July 20–25, 2008.

Ross, K (2002). *Women, Politics, Media: Uneasy Relations in Comparative Perspectives*, Cresskill, NJ: Hampton Press.

Saxonhouse, A W (ed.) (1992). Introduction, *Stereotypes of Women in Power: Historical Perspectives and Revisionist Views*. New York: Greenwood.

Shenkar-Shreck, D (2000). Media Representation and Political Marketing of Women in the Age of the Primaries, *PATUACH* 4, 100–126 (Hebrew).

Sereberny-Mohammadi, A & Ross, K (1996). Women MPs and the Media: Representing the Body Politic. *Parliamentary Affairs*, 49(1), 103–116.

Tankard, J W (2001). The Empirical Approach to the Study of Media Framing. In S D Reese, O H Gandy & A E Grant (eds), *Framing Public Life: Perspectives on Media and Our Understanding of the Social World* (pp. 95–106). Mahwah, NJ: Lawrence Erlbaum.

Trimble, L (2005). *Who Framed Belinda Stronach? National Newspaper Coverage of the Conservative Party in Canada's 2004 Leadership Race*, Paper presented to the Canadian Political Association Conference, London, Ontario, 4 June 2005.

Tuchman, G (Ed.) (1978). *Hearth and Home: Images of Women and the Media*. New York: Oxford University Press.

Van Acker, E (1999). *Different Voices: Gender and Politics in Australia*, South Yarra, Australia: Macmillan Education.

Weimann, G & Cohen, J (2000). A Disappearing World? Women in TV Election Campaigns in Israel. *Kesher*, 28, 53–62 (Hebrew).

A New Solidarity among Ultra-Orthodox Women in Israel[1]

Orly Tsarfaty and Dalia Liran-Alper

Abstract

The Haredi (Jewish ultra-Orthodox) society in Israel views itself as upholding traditional European Judaism that preceded the external influences of modernism. The desire to preserve the framework of religious-Jewish life in the Zionist-secular State of Israel reinforced the need for geographical and cultural isolation from the secular society. The last two decades have seen significant, far-reaching changes in Haredi society, which include changes in Haredi women's status.

Jewish thinking, as well as a religious way of life and ritual, is based on clear gender distinction that perpetuates a hierarchic social structure. With few exceptions, women are excluded from the centres of leadership and public power and are relegated to the limited inner domestic sphere. For the most part, women are presented with reference to their stereotypical feminine attributes.

The study focuses on a thematic textual analysis of the feminine-media discourse published in the commercial Haredi magazine Mishpacha Tova (A Good Family), and in the Betoch Hamishpacha (In the Family) supplement of the Mishpacha (Family) magazine.

The models of femininity presented in the commercial Haredi magazines indicate processes of change taking place among Haredi women in Israel.

Commercial magazines are "sphericules", that contribute to the development of a new women's discourse. It is our contention that these magazines constitute a site for creating and reinforcing women's solidarity. They create and reflect a discrete women's community. Hence, the changes occurring in Haredi women's status, their involvement in new

[1] The authors express gratitude to the Research Fund of the Research Authority of the College of Management Academic Studies, Rishon Lezion, Israel, for the financial support provided for this research.

spheres of interest, the combination between their traditional roles in the home and self-fulfilment and diverse social interactions outside the family, are manifested in journalistic content as presented in the reviewed examples.

To a great extent, commercial Haredi women's magazines represent the dramatic processes taking place in Haredi society, in which forces of change – economic, ideological, and structural – struggle with forces of preservation and tradition.

Key words: feminine media discourse, solidarity, stereotyopes

Introduction

Haredi (Jewish ultra-Orthodox) society in Israel views itself as upholding traditional European Judaism that preceded the external influences of modernism, education, secularism and national ideology. Whether this perception is faithful to historical developments or not, one of its outcomes is the cultural ideal guiding the preservation of the traditional religious way of life in the Jewish communities (Katz, 1978; Ravitzky, 1993; Ravitzky 2006, pp. 1–20; Salmon, 2006, pp. 367–380; Salmon, Ravitzky, & Ferziger 2006). The desire to preserve the framework of Jewish religious life in the secular Zionist State of Israel reinforced the need for geographical and cultural isolation from secular society's adoption of modern values and its alienation from the Jewish religion (Friedman, 1991). This ideological stand of voluntarily "building a wall" and rejecting modernity, including avoiding innovations ("the Torah forbids the new"), enabled Haredi society, up to the end of the 1980s, to exist as a "cultural enclave" (Sivan, 1990, pp. 45–97) relatively resistant to the external influences of secular society in Israel. The last two decades have seen significant, far-reaching changes in Haredi society, some of which originated from external influences and others from internal processes of change, which include changes in Haredi women's status. The present study seeks to examine manifestations of change in Haredi women's status by analysing media texts whose target audience is women.

The study focuses on the following questions: Can we identify a nascent feminist discourse in Haredi family commercial magazines adopting the characteristics of a women's magazine style? Do they replicate the model of traditional femininity or construct more complex models of femininity?

Women's magazines provide fertile ground for a study awaiting its researchers (Herzog, 2000, pp. 43–52). To focus on the popular press is appropriate for cultural studies, which define culture as the meaning we give to our day-to-day experiences in a specific social context. The importance of studying women's magazines lay in that they are cultural texts generating ideologies on women and femininity. Furthermore, the feminist opinion is critical of investigative processes based solely on dominant establishment sources, and seeks to locate knowledge in spheres that are traditionally perceived as marginal, such as women's magazines (Brown, 1989, pp. 161–164). Research on women's magazines in Israel is scant and limited (Cohen, Z., 1971; Rubin, 1987; Cohen-Avigdor, 1998; Herzog (2000); Leiden 2000; Lachover 2010).

The study focuses on a thematic textual analysis[2] of the feminine-media discourse published in the commercial Haredi magazine *Mishpacha Tova* (A Good Family),[3] and in the "Betoch Hamishpacha" (In the Family) supplement of *Mishpacha* (Family) magazine.[4] These

---

[2] The thematic categories are: marital relations; running the household; raising children and education; beauty and grooming; women's social network; work; volunteering, contributing to the community, and self-fulfillment. The corpus of the study includes the letters to the editor section, personal columns, and articles. The reading of the texts is polysemic and any interpretation proposed is merely one of many.

[3] *Mishpacha Tova* was a monthly magazine for religious and Haredi families. Founded in 1999, circulation figures were unavailable. The editor is Esti Reider-Reichman, who is supervised by a committee of rabbis. The magazine defines itself as such: "No politics, no gossip, but everything a mother raising fine children needs to know from every sphere of life: education, health, psychology, family communication, the Jewish home, consumerism, grooming, design, and leisure". Some of the magazine's contents appear on the ifeel website. The magazine was published by SBC, publisher of a group of (secular) magazines. Due to financial difficulties the magazine closed down in April 2009.

[4] *Mishpacha* is a weekly magazine for the Haredi sector, which was founded in 1987 by Asher Zuckerman and Eli Paley; up to Issue 84 it appeared monthly. It is considered to have the widest circulation in the Haredi sector, and is published in Hebrew and English under the supervision of a spiritual committee. Its circulation is estimated at some 25,000 copies, mainly subscriptions. The magazine's exposure to Haredi society is at least four times that of its circulation. The editor in chief is Rabbi Moshe Grylak, and deputy editors are appointed for the supplements. The magazine comprises a main part and supplements: "Betoch Hamishpacha", for women; "Yeladim" (Children), a children's magazine; "Kulmos", a monthly supplement on Jewish matters; and "Te'itmot" (Tastes), a food supplement. From 1994 a separate news section was added – "Hadashot Mishpacha" (Family News). In the present study we shall examine only the "Betoch Hamishpacha" supplement, "The *Mishpacha* magazine for parents", edited by Henia Shachar. An online edition also exists: www.mishpacha.com.

magazines were chosen since they address all women in the Haredi community, as opposed to those magazines that address defined sub-groups in Haredi society.

"Blessed art thou, who made me according to His will": Women's status in Haredi society

A comprehensive and exhaustive discussion of women's status in Haredi society is beyond the purview of this article. We shall, however, seek to indicate the main outline of several reciprocal processes of change influencing the representation of women's discourse in the Haredi press.[5]

The ideological view

Jewish thinking, as well as being a religious way of life and ritual, is also based on clear gender distinction that perpetuates a hierarchic social structure. (Azmon, 1995; Azmon, 2001, pp. 17–26; Buber-Agassi, 1982; Friedman 1991).

Ancient biblical texts established the gendered structure texts and canonical post-biblical texts consolidated through the generations. Biblical texts, as the seminal texts of Jewish (and Western) culture, situate men, who were created in God's image, in a position of superiority over women ("She shall be called Woman, because she was taken out of Man", Genesis 2:23). This superiority is manifested in men's positions of control, e.g., in political, military and religious leadership, and is attended by unique legal rights that reinforce and perpetuate it. With few exceptions, women are excluded from the centres of leadership and public power and are relegated to the limited inner domestic space. For the most part, women are presented according to their stereotypical feminine attributes: they are considered manipulative and devious, leading to sin, they are sexually seductive and are restricted to the role of mother and wife. The cultural post-biblical texts created by and for men too became established as the spiritual-religious assets of the Jewish people (the Talmud, Midrashic literature and legend, religious literature). Women were excluded to such an extent that "Rather should the words of Torah be burnt than entrusted to women". (Tractate Sota 83:4) Several limitations set by men throughout

[5] Due to differences between the various groups in Haredi society (Lithuanians, Hasidic dynasties that also possess unique characteristics, Ashkenazi, Sephardi, and repentant Jews), the present paper describes general processes without individual reference to specific changes taking place in the subgroups.

the generations were designed to exclude women from the centre of religious ritual and from their involvement in the religious texts through various assertions aimed at diminishing their mental capacity, e.g., "Women are simple-minded [or frivolous]", (Tractate Shabbat 33:72) or "A woman has no learning except about the spindle" (Tractate Yoma 66:72).

Concurrently with women's exclusion from the public space, an image of the ideal woman developed, whereby a woman's primary purpose is to be a man's "helpmeet". The inequality in the duty of observance contributed to gender distinction as well.

Nevertheless, the attitude toward women described above is not as radical in all the sources. Alongside statements diminishing the value of women, there are also statements that accord women honour and respect.[6] Rachel Elior (2001) argues that the attitude toward women in traditional Jewish culture draws from three central and interwoven sources: the sanctified written tradition, the traditional patriarchal order and traditional cultural conventions.

Like other traditional patriarchal societies, there are two defined spaces in Jewish society, which are characterized by gendered division whereby the external-public space is a masculine domain. Men's life comprises the religious school, study, religious authority, public institutions and politics. Women do not take part in these spheres and thus are excluded from the centres of public power. "The Woman's respect depends on the traditional acceptation of her absence from the public domain" (Elior, 2001). The inner-private space, namely the home, is the feminine domain, as expressed in a verse frequently quoted as a model of behaviour: "All glorious is the king's daughter within the palace" (Psalms 45:14). This space is limited and defined both geographically and in terms of the activities conducted within it, and is subject to constant supervision.

These spaces define the division between men and women in terms of spheres of activity and personal development and spheres of interest and

---

[6] For example the verse: "A woman of valor who can find?" (Proverbs 31:10). Rambam (Maimonides) states: "And our Sages commanded that a man should honor his wife more than his own body and love her like his own body. And if he has money he should benefit her according to his wealth. And he may not impose upon her excessive fear, and his speech with her should be gentle and he should not be impatient or angry" (Hilchot Ishut 15:19). See Weinroth, A., *Feminism and Judaism*, Tel Aviv: Yedioth Ahronoth/Hemed Books (2001) (Hebrew), in which he seeks to show that attitudes toward women in the Jewish sources express honour, and that many restrictions originate from an intention to safeguard and protect women.

responsibility. This division is still supported in the present day by (separate) socialization processes that begin at a very early age and continue throughout an individual's life. These processes simultaneously occur in the formal and non-formal institutions of Haredi society.[7] The separation and different status of men and women is a cornerstone of the Jewish religious worldview and way of life, which shape the culture of Haredi society.

There are various expressions of the control over women within religious cultural discourse and ideology, some overt and others latent. Until recently, women tended to accept the male hegemony without question as part of the normative, "natural" course of life. They willingly adopted definitions of reality as defined and shaped by men. The absence of equality is manifested in all aspects of life, including marital relations. Women's legal status is inferior to that of men (*ba'al*, the Hebrew for husband, also indicates property). The control over and supervision of the woman's body are expressed in the religious concepts of purity and impurity, whereby she is required to adhere to restrictive rules of conduct. Her primary function is to fulfil her motherhood potential by observing the commandment "Be ye fruitful, and multiply". The attitude toward women in terms of the sexual-sensual aspect, as engendering original sin and possessing the potential to lead men into sin, also mandates the imposition of restrictions and proscriptions whose function is to protect men. An expression of this can be found, for example, in the assertion, "The voice of a woman is nakedness" (Tractate Kiddushin 70:71), the incontestable acceptance of which in Haredi society excludes women from the male public space (e.g., the proscription against playing women singers on "Arutzei Hakodesh" [The Sacred Channels], the Haredi radio stations) to prevent them from leading men into sin. The policing of the woman's body, which is expressed in her obligation to maintain her modesty by covering it, was imposed for the same reasons. Even if many women have adopted this obligation in the present day as a normative measure of beauty and religious observance that embodies the verse, "Your beauty is measured by your modesty", it does not obscure its original reason.

---

[7] Gender segregation exists not only in educational institutions and synagogues, but also in Jewish celebrations – ritual circumcision, bar mitzvah and wedding ceremonies and even in children's amusement parks and playgrounds.

Economic Influences: The Woman as Breadwinner

Menachem Friedman describes the changes that have taken place in women's status in traditional Haredi society due to the influence of change processes in Western society. The establishment of the Beit Ya'akov network of girls' schools and its establishment under the aegis of Agudat Israel contributed to the legitimacy of the change processes. (Friedman, 1998). The expansion of the Haredi "society of scholars" to unprecedented proportions results from adopting the Haredi ideal in the form of a religious scholar frequenting a house of Torah learning, which created a new reality wherein women became the family's primary breadwinners. Friedman argues that this was a reverse process to that which took place in the nineteenth century. As the number of educated young women increased, so did the disengagement from modernity. Women willingly undertook tasks to enable men's devotion to Torah studies, while they were being rewarded by their very partnership with a man, who by means of his studies assured them of a place in the next world (Friedman, 1991; Friedman, 1995; Friedman, 2006; Heilman & Friedman, 1991:197-265; Shilhav, 2005).

In Haredi society family is a supreme value that perpetuates the perception of the woman in her traditional roles as bearing responsibility for raising children and taking care of the household (El-Or, 1995; El-Or, 1997). Whilst a high birth rate reinforces this perception, it also places the responsibility for the family's livelihood on women.[8] The outcome of this position, which is one of the main characteristics of Haredi society, is a change in the status of professional women who are the primary breadwinners.[9] The majority of Haredi men are only exposed to religious content, whereas the general and professional education of women is broader than that of most men.[10] The competition over the limited number

[8] The estimated population growth rate in Haredi society is 6% per annum, compared to 1.3% in Israel's entire Jewish population.

[9] The proportion of Haredi women in the workforce in 2004 was 48%, compared with approximately 58% of non-Haredi women. From: Gottleib, D., *Poverty and Labor Market Behavior in the Jewish Ultra-Orthodox Society in Israel*, Jerusalem: The Van Leer Institute (2006). A 2010 Israel Central Bureau of Statistics study shows that 61% of Haredi women work.

[10] A study of Haredi women's education showed that 46.6% of Haredi women hold a non-academic higher education diploma; 10.4% of Haredi women hold a BA and 3.7% hold an MA. The parallel data obtained for all other Jewish women are 18.2%, 17.2% and 10.1% respectively. From: Schwartz, E., *Employment Data in the Haredi Sector* (2008), a report submitted to the Knesset Research and Information Center's Labor, Welfare, and Health Committee.

of mandated teaching positions sought new employment options, which frequently increased women's contact with secular society. The new professions allowed women to be included in journalism, advertising, accounting, computers[11] and even engineering,[12] which are considered neutral in ideological terms (unlike science, which challenges religious thinking) (Ilan, 2000).

In his article, Friedman describes the first wave of changes. It began in Europe when women, influenced by modernity, opened up to education and going out to work, and continued in Israel during the 1950s in the process of withdrawal and disengagement from modernity (Friedman, 1988). It is our contention that Haredi society is now in the second wave of change, which began in the early 1990s. The demographic growth of Haredi society; an Israeli-born Haredi generation that did not experience life in the Diaspora; the geographic expansion into new neighbourhoods and cities (Friedman & Shilhav, 1985; Shilhav, 1991). The ongoing encounter with Israeli secular society, and the effects of using the media, are all factors influencing changes in Haredi women's status. We should, however, qualify the above and state that this process does not hold true of Haredi society in its entirety. Whereas the level of supervision over men studying in religious study frameworks is high, it seems here too that

---

[11] The increasing number of computer-related jobs raised grave concern in the spiritual leadership. See, Horowitz, N., Haredim and the Internet. *Kivunim Hadashim*, 3 (2000) 7–30 (Hebrew), and Tsarfaty, O. & Blais, D., Between Cultural Enclave and Virtual Enclave: Haredi Society and the Digital Media, *Kesher*, 32 (2002) 44–47 (Hebrew). In the Haredi city of Beitar Illit women are employed in high-tech companies. Matrix IT built the Talpiot Development Center in the city and employs some 400 women programmers. ImageStore, which provides electronic imaging services, employs some 130 Haredi women. There are currently several programs (such as the Tzofia Program run by the Ministry of Industry, Trade and Labor and the Joint Distribution Committee) engaged in training women and placing them in a variety of spheres of employment in collaboration with computer companies and even Israel Aerospace Industries.

[12] Due to growing needs and demands, the Ministry of Industry, Trade and Labor opened two engineering career paths for Haredi women: engineering studies at colleges for married women as an alternative to teacher training, at the conclusion end of which they receive an engineering diploma; the second track incorporates engineering studies into Haredi seminaries for girls (see http://www.pmo.gov.il/Files/tmt120109). The poverty rate in Haredi population is considerably higher than that in the general population. Approximately 52% of families were classified as poor in 2006. From: Shiluv Milward Brown website – market studies and strategic planning for the Haredi sector, http://www.shiluvmb.co.il.

women's exclusion from them provided women with some room to manoeuvre and led to a process of change (Kaplan, 2007).

The influence of living in a modern country is evident in various aspects of Haredi society, even if the official rhetoric still rejects modernity. Going to work exposes Haredi women to the same hardships experienced by secular working women – the virtually unattainable balance between family commitments and work demands. Similar situations produce similar conflicts, and thus Haredi and secular women find themselves facing similar problems. But whereas the official discourse in secular society presents the appearance of striving for equal rights between men and women, the dominant, official discourse in Haredi society is one of inequality by choice.

The Orthodox-feminist movement

The influence of the feminist movement on Orthodox women became evident at a later stage. The first Conference on Women and Orthodoxy was held in New York in 1996.[13] According to Ross, the ideological encounter between religious perceptions and feminist ideas can be likened to the unattainable meeting of parallel lines, for the perception of women's status in Judaism fundamentally contradicts feminist thinking. The various levels of the feminist struggle present the religious woman with objectives that clash with her religious lifestyle and religious law. Feminist critique threatens the male hegemony, the source of whose authority is Divine and challenges the religious practices being observed for generations.[14]

---

[13] In was only in the early 1980s that the book by American Orthodox-feminist Blu Greenberg was published: Greenberg, B., *On Women and Judaism: A View from Tradition*, Philadelphia: Jewish Publication Society of America (1981). See Ross, T., *Expanding the Palace of Torah: Orthodoxy and Feminism*, Tel Aviv: Alma and Am Oved (2007) (Hebrew).

[14] Tamar Ross expresses a wish, whilst recognizing the depth of the change required: "I believe that feminism need not be seen as a threat to traditional Judaism, and that Jewish tradition itself provides ways and means of dealing with the challenges. My optimism does not stem from a definitive picture of what these ways and means entail. It stems rather from a belief in belief itself, and the conviction that the true measure of belief lies in its ability to assimilate the lessons to be learned from whatever challenges it is destined to face. The challenges that feminism presents are challenges that carry the potential to enhance Judaism and make it more meaningful for all its believers, male and female alike" (Ross, 2005, xvi).

The conflict experienced by Orthodox women occurred due to the increasingly growing tension between two conflicting outlooks: maintaining a strictly religious lifestyle and accepting a religious view that deprives women in from virtually every aspect of life, and exposure to modern culture's value of equality between the sexes. As in the general feminist movement, Haredi women, too, are not in full agreement regarding how the struggle should be fought or its emphases (Shiloh, 2001). At present the struggle focuses on four main aspects: (1) some seek to bring about a change in women's literacy – whereas one approach seeks to include women in the men's world of study, an the other seeks a separate religious fulfilment for women, namely Gemara studies (El-Or, 1998; El-Or, 1992; Kahat, 2001); (2) the religious-ritual aspect, such as Torah reading and observance of the commandments like men;[15] (3) the participation of women as leaders in public life, in positions of leadership, such as rabbinical court advocates, membership to rabbinical councils, and even the ordination of women rabbis, which would allow them to make Jewish law rulings; and (4) struggle against women's legal discrimination, e.g., the struggle against women being refused a divorce by their husband. (Golinkin, 2001)

Two principal trends are becoming evident: the first seeks to bring about change within male society, and the second seeks to create an alternative alongside it. Present days constant tensions between women's status and their position in matters of religion constitute fertile soil for the adoption of a variety of feminist ideas of varying intensity among religious and Haredi society. This It is not the radical feminism of the secular West, although the effects could be radical in the long term.[16]

The establishment of the "Kolech" (Your Voice) movement (by Dr Chana Kahat) as an Orthodox-feminist movement for women who define themselves as committed to Jewish law, Jewish tradition and gender equality

---

[15] It is interesting to note that Yeshayahu Leibowitz (1999), who presented a radical view regarding the need for change in women's status in Judaism, claimed he saw no religious reasons for women to observe commandments that apply to men, for "there is nothing in it to imply service to God". In contrast, he views the exemption of women from Torah study as depriving them of a basic Jewish right, which renders their "Jewishness" inferior to that of men.

[16] Today, religious women are bound by two sets of laws: on the one hand the laws of the state that treat women and men equally, and on the other, the religious laws that discriminate against women. The origins of the influence of feminist ideas can be attributed both to American Orthodox-feminism and to the feminist discourses and activities in Israeli society. The lively feminist discourse in religious Zionist circles filters too into circles that overlap both of these communities.

is one of the manifestations of the change processes. The following appears on the movement's Internet website (!), which also applies to the feminist movement:

> One of the central characteristics of our century is the revolution of women's status in the public and personal domains alike. The religious woman, who is committed to Jewish law and at the same time aspires to develop her religious life as well, is not absent from this event. (kipa.co.il)

Echoes of the feminist demand for equality between men and women, for sharing the burden of duties defined as "women's duties", are filtering through to Haredi society, influenced by religious-Haredi women serving as a mediating group (Sheleg, 2000) and are manifested in the media discourse.

THE NEW HAREDI MEDIA MAP

There is no one single attitude in Haredi society in Israel toward the use of the media (Kaplan, 2001; Ilan, 2000; Levy, 1990; Tsarfaty & Blais, 2002). However, two principal general approaches can be discerned in the official discourse: the first is the traditional approach that rejects any use of mass media whatsoever (with the exception of newspapers) as part of its refusal of modern life in general, and since the media are identified with heretical content. Using newspapers as a means of communication is perceived as legitimate in Haredi society since it preserves the Jewish culture's special attitude toward the written word (Kouts, 1999). Later, newspapers would fill a dual function, both as an effective means of preserving intra-community religious solidarity, and as a means in the struggle against modernization and change processes. The second approach is an instrumental one which until the early 1990s was considered marginal and unique to Chabad Hasidism (Tsarfaty, 2005). After its adoption by the Shas movement and other groups in Haredi society, it became more central. It proposes that the media stay neutral and does not reject them as long as they convey religious content and worthy values.

Up to the 1990s the newspaper media discourse was typified by a primarily male discourse in terms of both content and language. The engagement of the religious newspapers in political and religious subjects, which characterize the public domain, perpetuated the exclusion of women from the media discourse. Until the early 1990s the newspapers were mainly politically ideological or associated with factions that viewed their vocation as educating, inculcating values, and constructing a reality in accordance with their worldview. Amnon Levy articulately defined this point when he asserted that "The Haredi press is characterized more than anything in that it reports on life as it ought to be, and not on life as it is" (Levy, 2002, p. 240).

The new Haredi media map began taking shape toward the end of the 1980s and the first half of the 1990s, and was influenced by the changes taking place in the institutional structure of the general media in Israel, and by the introduction of new media technology. Before long these changes were adopted by Haredi society as well. It transpired that despite the declared desire for isolation and detachment, the wall erected by Haredi society against secular society was not impregnable. From time to time the religious-spiritual leadership rallied when it found itself facing challenges posed by media technology. An important stage in the change process occurred with the publication of commercial Haredi magazines, such as *Mishpacha* (Family), *Mishpacha Tova* (Good Family) and *Sha'a Tova* (Good Time). Alongside these magazines, intergroup publications grew to unprecedented dimensions, whether in the form of synagogue newsletters or more stylish formats (Cohen, Y., 2000; Rappel, 1991). The establishment of Haredi pirate radio stations called "Arutzei Hakodesh" (The Sacred Channels) (Limor, 1998) increased exposure to worlds of new content for men and women alike. Toward the end of the 1990s, computer and Internet use spread considerably. Nowadays it seems that the adoption of new media technologies by many in Haredi society – especially the Internet and cellular telephones – challenges accepted attitudes, undermines the rabbinical leadership's ability to supervise, and directly exposes increasingly growing sections of this population to what is going on in secular society. Furthermore new behavioural patterns caused by the media are developing alongside the traditional ones.

Women's magazines

Women's magazines emerged at the end of the eighteenth and early nineteenth centuries in Europe, especially in England, reflecting the role distinction whereby men are breadwinners and women are housewives.[17] Women were perceived as a group with defined interests (Ballaster et al., 1991). The accepted premise was that women read differently to men, and moreover, that women needed guidance and protection against forbidden

[17] For a historical review on the development of women's magazines, see Byerly, C M & Ross, K., *Women and Media: A Critical Introduction*, Malden, MA: Blackwell Publishing (2006).

knowledge. Women's magazines developed advice and guidance styles, alongside Cinderella and My Fair Lady stories. From the outset these magazines were structured around the tension between women's representation, in which the magazines constitute a form of expression for their voice, and the attitudes expressed in the guidance and advice they provided. The magazines guided and instructed on how to be a "woman" and "feminine", and moral guidance constituted an inseparable part of the writing (Herzog, 2000).

Femininity in the nineteenth century was embodied in the privacy of the home and "matters of the heart". Gradually incorporated to the discourse on woman as a romantic figure was the discussion on the body, whose beauty was accentuated by a corset. In general terms, women's magazines presented femininity as a universal model, but with the passing of the years and as domestic practices changed, so did the definition of femininity. Development in women's magazines over the years is evident. Emphasis in the 1930s and 40s was on the family and motherhood, and in the 1950s and 60s the home was depicted not only as a place of work but also as one for enjoyment. Further dimensions were added to femininity, and the woman was presented as a housewife, mother, wife, consumer, beautiful and attractive (and later as enjoying sex). In the 1980s the feminine role was increasingly defined by means of shopping, i.e., the woman as a consumer. An identical number of pages devoted to editorial material and advertising could be found in women's magazines. Femininity was presented as a body constructed by commodities, clothing and accessories, and through home pictures that included numerous such commodities. Advertising and editorial writing styles became virtually indistinguishable, with each magazine employing a glossy chromo format. Content was concentrated on personal stories that focused on success and failure, and included a long series of advice on how to manoeuvre between the personal and the public (Beetham, 1996). As the meaning of "femininity" became more complex and trapped in contradictions, dependency on women's magazines as a source of information and support increased. At the end of the nineteenth century, magazines that had begun as instructional now presented an image of the magazine as a sort of friend, and served as an arena for intimate discourse between women.

Since the 1960s, with the second wave of feminism, sharp criticism has been levelled against women's magazines for representing an inferior stereotypical perception, and reading these magazines has been perceived as reproducing the oppression of women (Freidan, 1974; Tuchman, 1978). A frequently heard contention has been that women's magazines set women's agenda and perpetuated their traditional feminine contents (Ferguson, 1983).

In the wake of popular culture studies in the 1980s, which highlighted the activeness of female readership, feminist research also began displaying a more positive attitude toward the women's magazine genre. The feminist movement developed a love-hate relationship with women's magazines and their recurring promises of change, personal transformation, and reformation of women. Researchers who adopted Gramsci's hegemony concept (Gramsci, 1971) contended that magazines were not only a site for repressive ideological manipulation of women, but also an arena for political struggle and negotiation between interests of control and subordination by means of multiple contradicting representations. Janice Winship (1987) embraced Gramsci's approach in her seminal study and examined the dynamism in the content of British women's magazines between 1950 and 1980 against the backdrop of changes in women's status in British society. According to Winship, women's magazines offered survival skills in order to collaborate with the dilemmas of femininity relevant to a specific period. She contends that at the end of the 1960s the rise of the women's movement led to increased coverage of political issues in these magazines, including subjects that were previously perceived as unacceptably "feminist" (a study of American women's magazines between 1940 and 1960 even indicates multiple messages on the same subject and in the same issue) (Walker, 2000).

The research approach emphasizing the multiple voices and functions provided by a women's magazine for its readers was also supported by feminist media researcher Liesbet van Zoonen. According to her, reading women's magazines provided a sense of friendship, as well as entertainment, information and advice (Van Zoonen, 1994).

Two main points emerge from a historical review of women's magazines: the first is that according to the dominant hegemonic reading, the magazines confine women's femininity to the private-home sphere and the body; and the second is that the definition of woman and femininity is the ongoing process of a changing cultural construction (Herzog, 2000).

WOMEN'S MAGAZINES IN ISRAEL

Two types of women's magazines emerged in Israel – commercial magazines such as *LaIsha* (For Women), alongside journals published by women's organizations such as *Yarchon Na'amat* (Na'amat Monthly). Over the years the two types became increasingly similar. The magazines began imitating the commercial press with the aim of winning the hearts of women readers, while the commercial press became more serious in order to win over the educated reader (Cohen, Z., 1971).

All the editors had concurred that women's magazines were a fundamentally economic project (Fishbein, 2000). Their content matter was of interest but not world-changing; they provided a story that made people feel good and irked no one, since they were writing for a majority that was not seeking revolutions. "It should not precede reality, but only attend it" (Herzog, 2000, p. 49).

COMMERCIAL WOMEN'S MAGAZINES[18]

Israel's first commercial women's magazine, *Olam HaIsha* (Woman's World), was first published in 1940 and closed down in 1948. The La-isha (For Women) women's magazine was first published in January 1947 as a modest weekly supplement of the *Yedioth Achronoth* daily, and in July that year became an independent weekly defined as "the popular weekly for home and family". The issue's first editorial expressed the magazine's aspiration to fill a void in the press by covering "areas that fill her [the woman's] special world: homemaking, the education of her children, sewing her dresses, and so forth" (Cohen-Avigdor, 1999). By the end of the 1950s the magazine boasted thousands of readers, and it highlighted leisure and entertainment, while avoiding important social issues. In April 1958 the *Ma'ariv* daily published *Olam* Ha-isha (Woman's World), which stayed in circulation until December 1961. In April 1967, *Ma'ariv* founded the still existent *At* (You) monthly (Almog, 2007).

Both La-isha and *At* are part of Israel's main media conglomerates. La-isha is part of the one whose flagship is the *Yedioth Ahronoth* daily owned by the Mozes family, while *At* belongs to the one that includes the *Ma'ariv* daily owned by the Nimrodi family. For many years the editors of both magazines were men, which is the case in the majority of the international women's magazines.

According to Almog, up to the 1980s women's magazines were a platform for the replication of women's traditional gender roles. The home was presented in them as the woman's realm whose principal roles are to be mother and wife, and they did not encourage women to go to work. By contrast, Herzog thinks that women's magazines should not be studied in such a simplistic approach, and that even in an earlier period women's magazines contained intimations of the construction of less traditional and

[18] For more on this subject, see Herzog (2000) and Lachover (2010).

less monolithic models of femininity. In this spirit Leiden (2000) examined La-isha from a historical perspective as an arena for the emergence of a women's discourse.

Lachover recently conducted a study (2010) seeking to identify the domain of femininity offered to women in the popular women's commercial magazines in Israel – *At* (you) and La-isha – during the Six-Day War and the end of the 1960s. According to her conclusions, both magazines offer diverse versions of femininity. In normal times women's magazines are fertile in lively discourses on the values of the private space that are excluded from the public discourse, and give prominent expression to the traditional model of femininity. But in time of war there is a temporary change, and national-male rhetoric assumes pride of place but does not completely exclude personal discourse. These findings support the theoretical research premise with regard to women's magazines, to the effect that they give partial, even contradictory, definitions of femininity (Gill, 2007, pp. 199–204; Winship, 1987). "The blend of personal and public, intimate and collective, dependent and independent, conformist and critical opinions in and La-isha and *At* in wartime attests to the flexibility of women's magazines, and their ability to adapt themselves to women's dilemmas at different times" (Lachover, 2010, p. 28).

Religious women's magazines

The general Haredi press is characterized by addressing a primarily male readership, thus preserving the centrality of the male media discourse. An interesting trend is the development of supplements for women and children. As a consequence of maintaining the boundaries of modesty, there is no reporting on or pictures of women, and they are addressed in defined sections. Thus, for example, due to the Chabad movement's unique attitude toward the mass media (Tsarfaty, 2005), it was found that as early as the 1980s the *Kfar Chabad* (Chabad Village) weekly began publishing a women's magazine (defined as a supplement) called *Be-ohalei Chana* (In the Tents of Hannah). The editorial section, written by Rivka Gofein, presents a political-moral stance, with questions on Jewish law answered by a rabbi, a discussion on festivals, the connection with the Lubavitcher Rebbe, as well as messianism and redemption.

Levy contends that the women's sections explain to mother and daughter what to do and how to behave. They are devoted to clear social guidance intended to educate women in their traditional roles, and the subject matter is mainly in the form of a letter or a story. She found that in general there is scant reporting on women in the general Haredi press, which is concentrated in the women's sections and typified by a writing style of stories with a clear moral, educating for traditional roles. According to her, the existence of separate supplements facilitates a feminine writing style and, most importantly, women can, on the face of it, use the magazine as their own since they do not pose a threat to men by their participation in the same magazine (Levy, 1990).

The political party dailies also publish women's sections (as home supplements). Yated Ne'eman has published *Bayit Ne'eman* (Loyal Home) since 1985, while in 2005 Hamodia began publishing *Habayit Shelanu* (Our Home) as a separate supplement. The sections on women and the home play a role in conveying a clear educational message: to educate women for their traditional roles and strengthen the definition of their function in the home.

Similar to the feminization process that took place in the secular press (Limor & Caspi, 1994; Lavie, 2000), some feminization also took place in the Haredi press. The fact that women were entering the sphere of journalism was initially an expression of economic necessity as well. They joined the magazines as writers for women and children, editors and illustrators. The women writing in these magazines usually did so under either a pseudonym or their first name, while the men continued to be the magazine's supreme professional authority.

Unlike the political party newspapers, the commercial ones were driven by economic considerations, and were thus unable to ignore two readerships with a significant consumption potential – women and children. The early 1990s debate on "spiritual supervisory committees" (or censorship committees) reflects the commercial newspaper owners' desire for a degree of openness in content. In the 1990s attempts were made to publish commercial magazines for Haredi women, the most notable of which, *Hila* (1996–1999) and *Lilach* (1995–2004), were published in a format similar to that of the secular women's magazines, but did not last.

Economic considerations are notable in an analysis of religious-Haredi women's magazines. Advertisements – at a ratio of 40% to 60% editorial content – enables the publication of eighty monthly chromo pages at a relatively lower cost than other women's magazines, "since the advertisement purchaser has no problem selling advertising space to baby food manufacturers approved by Badatz" (rabbinic court) (Hanegbi, 2000). The premise is that it is easier to sell advertising space when there is a defined market segment, and when this market segment possesses genuine purchasing power (Ross, 1993). This premise also applies to women's magazines in general, and even more so to Haredi women's magazines.

"LET YOUR VOICE BE HEARD" – A NASCENT WOMEN'S FEMINIST DISCOURSE

Before presenting a thematic analysis of the discourse in women's magazines, we would like to note the conspicuous absence of photographs of women in Haredi women's magazines in comparison with secular women's magazines. One can find photographs of men and an abundance of photographs of children and even infant girls (which usually adorn the cover pages). The woman is devoid of face and body. Due to the strict observance of woman's modesty and the supervision imposed on magazines, the physical representation of women has been erased, and this can perhaps be viewed as a "symbolic annihilation" (Tuchman, 1978).

A thematic analysis of the *Mishpacha* and *Betoch Hamishpacha* magazines reveals interesting characteristics of the women's discourse developed in the commercial Haredi press. The central topic in all the writing genres is the domestic sphere in accordance with the traditional perception of the woman's role in the family, and talk about raising children, the household, and relationships between women in the family and the community. There are also stories about work and livelihood, study and volunteering. We seldom found references to marital relations, however.

The women's discourse will be presented in accordance with the three journalistic writing genres examined: the editorial section, personal columns and articles.

Editorial sections

The editorials in both magazines represent the religious ideological position on women's status. The sample of editorials reveals that the subject matter pertains to the roles of the woman-mother (housework, raising children, and so forth). No exceptional statements were found that represent feminist thinking or introduce voices that deviate from the prevailing rhetoric about women in Haredi society. Thus, the editorials represent a primarily conservative position. The following are two stories about parent-children relationships, from which we can learn about the sharp gender distinction between boys and girls, and the guidance toward adopting social roles around observance of the commandment of honouring one's parents, which is central in Haredi society.

The hero of the first story is Haim, a four-year-old infant who wakes up in the middle of the night to go to the bathroom without waking his parents. In the morning he explains and expands on the heroic deed: "I didn't want to wake you up, I wanted to be like Dama Ben Netina".[19] Two weeks later his mother sprains her ankle on the stairs, and the anxious Haim asks her, "Mother, are you in pain? . . . In that case I shall pray to God to take away the pain", he searches his memory for all the Psalms he knows and recites them with the seriousness reserved for children under four years of age, or the servants of God from the Stories of the Tzaddikim (the Righteous) about the early generations (*Betoch Hamishpacha*, 387, 2007).

The concern of children for their parents and their desire to please them is represented through this story. The choice of the story, at the centre of which stands a boy who observes the commandment, is not coincidental. The heroic deed is ascribed to a boy rather than a girl, and his reference model for observing the commandment is the masculine figure of a tzaddik (righteous Jew). The infant's desire to help his mother is naturally translated into his life experience, namely prayer, but it is not spontaneous prayer, as one might expect from a young child, but prayer from the Book of Psalms, which is somewhat surprising – how many Psalms does a four-year-old infant know by heart? The glorification of the boy peaks when his natural righteousness is compared to servants of God from the Tales of the Tzaddikim. Thus the story perpetuates the conservative gender model for a boy's behaviour with regard to observing the commandment of honouring one's parents, and young Haim does not deviate from the behaviour expected of him.

The heroine of the second story is a little girl.

> The Honoring One's Parents Campaign» created a problem in our home: what can a girl do who has hardly any duties in the home because her mother simply doesn't need her help? We can rack our brains: she has no

---

[19] Dama Ben Netina was a highborn gentile who is described in the Babylonian and Jerusalem Talmud as a paragon of observing the commandment to honour one's parents. The most famous story about him appears in Tractate Kiddushin (Jerusalem, 61:72; Babylonian, 31:71): The Sages went in search of a replacement for one of the precious stones that had fallen out of the High Priest's breastplate and was lost. They came to Dama Ben Netina to purchase the stone, but he refused because removing it from the chest in which it was kept would wake up his sleeping father. The Sages raised their offer, but Dama Ben Netina was adamant in his refusal. The Sages had already turned to leave when he came after them with the stone. He refused payment and even reprimanded the Sages, saying: "What? Do you think that I would sell the honour of my fathers for mere coins?"

> younger brothers and sisters to look after. There are no toys to tidy up because apart from when our nephews visit, the house is tidy. She tidies up her room in any case. . . . She folds the boys' shirts expertly on Fridays after the big pressing operation – so what should she do? All her friends do things . . . and only she . . ." (*Betoch Hamishpacha*, 389, 2007)

In this instance the editor focuses on the assortment of duties designated for a girl – all within the boundaries of housekeeping and housework. Unlike the first story, the girl does not possess special virtues other than being tidy and her desire to help, and there are no paragons to serve as role models for her. The recommended approach for a girl focuses on performing tasks around the home. Even the creative solution ultimately provided reinforces the boundaries of the gender role – in order to enable her to observe the commandment to honour one's parents it was decided to allow the girl to wash the dairy flatware and silverware(!). Beyond that, reference to the community and normative functioning is evident – "All her friends do things", as a model of comparison directed toward correct behaviour.

Both stories address the commandment to honour one's parents, but offer different gender models for boys and girls. Thus, the editorial section represents a traditional-conservative perception that directs the boy toward spiritual activity by means of prayer and proposes a tzaddik as a reference model, whereas a practical household activity is proposed for the girl.

In contrast with this traditional statement, meticulous textual examination reveals new ideas in the journalistic article and personal column genres that receive cautious expression, which is essential to avoid creating resistance.

Personal Columns

Both magazines include a wide variety of columns and articles (some under pseudonyms, as we have seen), not all of which survive over time. From a thematic aspect, stories in this genre engage extensively in family matters, with child rearing occupying a central place in the discourse. Another prevalent topic is relationships with other women in the family – the mother, the *schvigger* (mother-in-law in Yiddish), sisters, and other women in the community. Unlike the editorials, the stories in the personal columns address the husband as well, and his role in the home and the family. The detailed descriptions of day-to-day events, in a writing style that presents how to cope with dilemmas and functional recommendations for solving problems, gradually reveal the change-taking place in women's status.

One of the interesting columns that appeared in *Mishpacha Tova* throughout the studied period is entitled "Miniatures". The choice of name for the column can be interpreted as playing down its importance. It presents "little stories" related in the first person as an expression of experiences shared by and meaningful to women. The column presents women's monologues on various issues, and affords a peek into the day-to-day life of Haredi women, their difficulties and hardships, their desires and frustrations, and their ways of coping.

Liza describes herself:

> "I've always been an independent girl . . . I never really accepted various requests for help . . . I refused to take on the burden and commitment of helping on a regular basis . . . I wanted to feel that I was a free woman. I wanted to be my own mistress. I couldn't stand being taken into account without being asked first . . . I wasn't there to serve all the married grown ups and nephews. I have my own life . . . that is my freedom. I love my family and I thank God for each and every one of them, but I want to live a full life, I want my quiet, I want my own private corner and time. I don't know why I was born different in this respect from most other girls my age and of similar standing. There's something in me that doesn't like to fit in, to be a part, to go with the flow." (*Mishpacha Tova*, 84, 2006, our emphases)

The understanding that family relationships require investment – here too in appropriate measures – only matures when Liza is forced to remain in bed due to a high-risk pregnancy, alone, detached from her family. The monologue relates the story of a young woman, an individualist by nature, from a large family, who builds a wall of privacy around her and does not behave as she is expected to within her family and community. As a result, she is subjected to insulting remarks from her surroundings, and her mother is the only person who understands how she feels. The writer struggles and ruminates throughout the monologue that abounds with statements that are unacceptable with reference to girls. However, the very fact of their presentation constitutes the wish to give a different voice to that of the official rhetoric, albeit the social order is preserved by the proposed conformist solution that reinforces the importance of family relationships at the conclusion of the monologue. Concerning the overt message, the value of family stands at the centre. The daughter's enlistment to help care for the family's needs constitutes normative behaviour. At the same time, in the latent message, a certain degree of legitimacy is accorded for a girl/woman to be different, to think and behave differently, as long as it does not cause any serious damage to family relationships. The fact that Liza's mother understands how she feels indicates that the family framework has not been breached or damaged, and perhaps it is also an expression of sisterhood.

Another interesting example is the personal column entitled "Od Nedaber" (We'll Talk) by Elkana. Even in the absence of any certainty that the column is indeed written by a man, its very existence and the messages conveyed in it from a male perspective are in themselves far-reaching innovations. Assuming that some men should read the magazine as well, the stories presented in the column represent male behaviors that deviate from the traditional role distinction. And assuming that most of the readers are women, most of the stories are flattering to them.

The author writes humorously about his experiences and in the first person, and this time – about the encounter between two men doing the weekend grocery shopping. During their long wait in line at the checkout, a conversation develops between the writer and another man (who constantly consults with his wife on his cell phone about the items he is about to purchase), who complains to the writer:

> "I really don't like shopping . . . I really don't like it, not at all, I just can't stand it. . . . So you're probably surprised I'm here. . . . It's for two reasons, first, women don't think about money when they shop, and it's a waste of money. This way I alone control the shopping without one agora going to waste. . . . Look, it's Thursday today and my father-in-law, God bless him, announced at the last minute that he's coming over for the Sabbath to spend time with all his offspring, may they multiply, my wife has to wash all the floors, so I said right away, I'll be in charge of shopping and she'll have time to do all the cleaning, without problem."

Two and a half hours later he calls his wife again and the following dialogue ensues:

> "How come I'm here two and half hours and you haven't finished cleaning?" he yelled into the phone, spitting sunflower seeds. "Women nowadays are so spoilt. . . . Do you get it, I've been here two and a half hours to give her time to clean the house, and what does she tell me now . . . that she had to keep running to the phone to answer me the whole time, and that if she'd gone shopping herself she'd have finished the shopping and the cleaning and still had time to rest." (Elkana, 2007, our emphases)

On the one hand, sharing a burden that is considered feminine attests to the change-taking place, while on the other it conveys a message to the readers that for men to do the shopping constitutes normative behavior. The dialogue between the men presents a stereotypical and chauvinistic perception of women – and at the same time criticizes it and praises the woman, even if it is still within the boundaries of accepted gender roles. The narrator critically and ironically presents the image of a man shopping. The man who agrees to help his wife justifies this help with his ability to save money, unlike his spendthrift wife (a familiar feminine stereotype), but in fact it transpires that he is dependent and wasteful, for he cannot decide on the purchase of an item without frequent telephone consultations with her.

The wife stays at home to clean and thus fulfils her role, but her crushing response at the end of the story places the man in a ridiculous light. Between the lines appreciation is expressed for her ability and efficiency. The story thus presents a subversive voice criticizing the gendered functioning of men in Haredi society.

Articles

Articles and reports on a specific subject are published in every issue, including exposure to new spheres of knowledge and expertise – albeit the frame of reference would be family and children, such as psychological counseling, discussions on learning disorders and children with disabilities (a subject that was taboo until recently), counselling for couples, occupational counselling and a variety of consumer articles and sections.

The first example is an article about coping with the birth of twins and triplets, and focuses on the question of whether to separate the children or keep them together.

> Many mothers will actually prefer to continue their regular jobs outside the home for financial considerations, and even out of a desire to return to the normal course of their life as soon as possible. The little ones can be left in the care of a child minder. In many cases mothers will prefer to bring a child minder into their home to look after the children and do some light housework as well. Michal's triplets have been going to a local day nursery since they were three months old. . . . Calmly and with a smile she receives three satisfied and contented babies at four o'clock every day. (Hadar, 2005, our emphases)

In Haredi high birth rate society in which women are primarily defined according to their function as mothers, the very act of clearly placing the woman's needs and desires at the centre of the debate is an extraordinary statement. From the legitimacy of going back to work after childbirth from the need of the mother to resume the regular course of her life is an expression of a new women's discourse that places the woman at the center of her expectations and not society's. The possibility of caring for children outside the home in a day nursery is also positively presented as a legitimate option.

In this example and the following one, the maternal role of the Haredi woman, which is traditionally perceived as the essence of a woman's fulfilment, is discussed; the following article describes how Haredi women create additional content for their feminine identity. Alongside raising children, they devote time to self-fulfillment, as long as emphasis is placed on the fact that this does not intrude on their necessary tasks.

A long article deals with women taking part in a women's theatre group (!) that performs in schools and at women's evenings, and includes three photographs: an empty dressing room, a lighted but empty theatre stage and an actress in a wig getting ready in front of a mirror in the dressing room (photographed from the back, her face obscured). The writer focuses on the women – an actress, a director and drama therapist, and a producer. In their interviews she tries to answer the question: "What hides behind women who decide to perform?" Shlomit: "An ordinary woman who sends her children off to school in the morning, goes shopping on Rabbi Akiva Street, and functions like every other woman living in Bnei Brak. Once in a while there's a play and she goes out to rehearsals . . . then Shlomit goes back to being an ordinary mother in house slippers and headscarf." Also described is the experience of being in the theatre, the reactions of the enthusiastic audience and the applause, which differentiate performance arts from other arts. The "feedback" accords power, but one should beware of becoming addicted to fame, cautions the actress. It may also lead to harassment and invasion of her privacy when she happens to meet her audience in the street. The actress describes the play, which was attended by 3,000 women, and claims that due to their belief in conveying the message, actresses can be successful even without any professional training. Most of the plays are performed without remuneration for the actresses (there is even mention of women paying for the privilege of performing). Performing is also a pleasure, they all responded without embarrassment, a type of different experience. "Where would I have had the opportunity between washing floors and meatballs cooking in the pot?" (Pele, 2005, our emphases)

The article focuses on a recreational activity and a hobby that provides enjoyment to the participants, which is an innovative topic in Haredi women's discourse. The writer presents her women readers with feminine models of women who look and function like every "ordinary" woman in the Haredi street, but incorporate a new and exciting hobby into their life. Despite the warnings, reservations and problems presented in the first and second person, it can be argued that the article constructs a new Haredi women's identity. The legitimacy to engage in "performance", which is mostly alien to the traditional way of life, is justified by contribution to the community, but does not conceal the personal reward of enjoyment achieved by every amateur actress.

CONCLUSIONS

If we assume that the construction of perceptions of femininity can be better observed in women's magazines than in other popular genres (Lachover, 2010; Walker, 2000; Winship, 1987), the models of femininity presented in the commercial magazines *Mishpacha Tova* and *Mishpacha* indicate processes of change taking place among Haredi women in Israel. These processes have been taking place intensively for about two decades in Hardei society, and are a positive influence in women's status. Commercial women's magazines constitute fertile soil for expressing and sustaining these changes.

As in secular women's magazines, here too women are primarily situated in the inner sphere. Women's representation tends to perpetuate the traditional perception of distinguishing gender roles and thus preserves the existing social order. Women's discourse in Haredi magazines generally replicates the perception that positions women in the private domain. This is evident in terms of content, in the roles of the women presented, and in the messages perpetuating the gendered role system. However, the first buds of change are evident. Other voices are being heard, alongside the central, traditional, dominant voice in the editorials, which are primarily expressed in the personal column and article genres.

It can be stated that commercial magazines and supplements such as *Mishpacha Tova* and *Betoch Hamishpacha* are "sphericules" (Gitlin, 1998) that contribute to the development of a new women's discourse in Haredi media, which until recently excluded women and silenced their voices under a religious-ideological guise. These magazines constitute an important site for the emergence of a lively discourse on issues associated with the private domain, which are usually absent from Haredi public discourse, and provide a public arena for the personal-family discourse.

It is our contention that these magazines constitute a site for creating and reinforcing women's solidarity. They create and reflect a discrete women's community, as shown by previous studies on secular women's magazines (Ballaster et al., 1991; Herzog, 2000; Lachover, 2010; Winship, 1987). We also found that, as in secular women's magazines, the studied magazines excel in flexibility and adapt themselves to women's dilemmas at different times. Hence, the changes occurring in Haredi women's status, their involvement in new spheres of interest, the combination between their traditional roles in the home and self-fulfilment and diverse social interactions outside the family, are manifested in journalistic content as presented in the reviewed examples.

The commercial magazines for Haredi women in Israel today, *Mishpacha Tova* and *Betoch Hamishpacha*, focus on processes of personal change, how to be a "better" woman, and the promise of reform for the female reader possessing self-discipline and high moral values. The call for transformation is based on advice presented in the form of an intimate and familiar dialogue between the reader and someone close to her (Gill, 2007). The dialogue takes place primarily in the writing genres of personal columns and in some topical articles published in the magazines. "In this discourse we are afforded a peek into the construction of seemingly authentic feminine definitions" (Lachover, 2010, p. 3).

Our study shows that the maternal role is at the center of the discourse in Haredi women's magazines, i.e., raising and educating children as a central theme in the life of Haredi women, as stated in *Mishpacha Tova* in its mission statement: "Everything a mother needs to know from every aspect of life". Thus, the magazine in effect serves as a discussion platform on the modern practices of fulfilling traditional roles. It provides a legitimate arena for diverse women's voices to be heard and for the construction of new models of femininity, in which feminist ideas can be identified as well.

In our estimation, at least some of the new topics filtering into the discourse originate from the perception of women as consumers. As we have seen, secular women's magazines emerged concurrently with the discovery/creation of the woman consumer (Beetham, 1996; Winship, 1987). The model was replicated from secular women's magazines. Beyond the large number of advertisements in these magazines, we also found that the editorial sections discussed many topics that introduce new products and services to Haredi women (such as psychological treatments, medical products, nutrition, personal care products, vacations, and leisure activities). Since appealing to the consumer woman runs counter to the values of a life of modesty and abstemiousness, which are central values in Haredi society, a new basis has been created for the appearance of different and even contradictory feminine images (diverse models of femininity), even in the same issue (as presented by Walker, 2000).

To a great extent, commercial Haredi women's magazines represent the dramatic processes taking place in Haredi society, in which forces of change – economic, ideological, and structural – struggle with forces of preservation and tradition. Future research can investigate whether the buds of feminist discourse identified in the present study mature and assimilate into a characteristic discourse in women's magazines in the coming years.

REFERENCES

Almog, O (2007). *Farewell to "Srulik": Changing Values Among the Israeli Elite*, Haifa: University of Haifa and Zmora Bitan. (Hebrew)

Azmon, Y (1995). Judaism and the Exclusion of Women from the Public Sphere, in Y. Azmon (ed.), *A Window on Women's Lives in Jewish Societies*, Jerusalem: The Zalman Shazar Center. (Hebrew)

—. (2001). Constructing Gender Identity and Power, in Y. Azmon (ed.), *Hear My Voice: Representations of Women in Israeli Culture*, Jerusalem: Van Leer Institute and Hakibbutz Hameuchad. (Hebrew)

Ballaster, R, Frazer, E, Beetham, M & Hebron, S (1991). *Women's Worlds: Ideology, Femininity and Women's Magazines (Women in Society)*, London: Macmillan.

Beetham, M (1996). *A Magazine of Her Own?: Domesticity and Desire in the Woman's Magazine, 1800–1914*, London and New York: Routledge.

Brown, M E (1989). Soap Opera and Women's Culture: Politics and the Popular, in K Carter & C Spitzack (eds), *Doing Research on Women's Communication: Perspectives on Theory and Method*, Norwood NJ: Ablex Publishing.

Buber-Agassi, J (1982). Women's Status in Israel, in D Izraeli et al. (eds), *The Double Bind: Women in Israel*, Tel Aviv: Hakibbutz Hameuchad. (Hebrew)

Cohen, Y (2000). Politics, Alienation, and the Consolidation of Group Identity: The Case of Synagogue Pamphlets, *Rhetoric and Public Affairs*, 3(2), 247–276.

Cohen, Z, (1971). Women's Magazines in Israel: A Review, *The Annual Book of Journalists*, Tel Aviv: Journalists Association. (Hebrew)

Cohen-Avigdor, N (1998). *Women Politicians (Compared to Men) in Israeli Women's Magazines: The Way they were Portrayed During the Knesset Election Years 1959, 1977, 1996*, MA Thesis, Ramat Gan: Bar-Ilan University. (Hebrew)

—. (1999). Women's Magazines, in Z Elgat & D Paz (eds), *Woman 2000: The Stories, Dramas, Style, and Beauty in Israel (LaIsha Album, 1948–2000)*, Tel Aviv: LaIsha. (Hebrew)

Elior, R (2001). Present but Absent, Still Life, and A Pretty Maiden who has No Eyes: On the Presence and Absence of Women in the Hebrew

Language, in Jewish Culture and in Israeli Life, in Y. Azmon (ed.), *Hear My Voice: Representations of Women in Israeli Culture*.

Elkana, (2007). "Od Nedaber", *Betoch Hamishpacha*, 807.

El-Or, T (1992). *Educated and Ignorant: Ultra-Orthodox Jewish Women and Their World*, Tel Aviv: Am Oved. (Hebrew)

—. (1995). Ultra-Orthodox Jewish Women, in S. Deshen (ed.), *Israeli Judaism: The Sociology of Religion in Israel*, New Brunswick: Transaction, 149–169.

—. (1997). Visibility and Possibilities: Ultra-Orthodox Jewish Women between the Domestic and Public Spheres, *Women's Studies International Forum*, 20(5), 149–169.

—. (1998). *Next Passover: Women and Literacy among the Religious Zionists*, Tel Aviv: Am Oved. (Hebrew)

Ferguson, M (1983). *Forever Feminine: Women's Magazines and the Cult of Femininity*, London: Heinemann.

Fishbein, (2000). In Herzog, H, Women's Magazines in Israel: An Arena for Reproduction or for Challenge? *Kesher*, 28. (Hebrew)

Freidan, B (1974). *The Feminine Mystique*, New York: Dell.

Friedman, M, (1988). *The Haredi Woman*, Jerusalem: The Jerusalem Institute for Israeli Studies. (Hebrew)

—. (1991). *The Haredi Society: Sources, Trends, and Processes*, Jerusalem: The Jerusalem Institute for Israel Studies. (Hebrew)

—. (1998). "The King's Daughter is All Glorious Without": The Haredi Woman, in D Ariel, M Leibovic & Y Mazor (eds), *Blessed Be He Who Made Me a Woman?* Tel-Aviv: Yedioth Ahronoth/Hemed Books, 189–205. (Hebrew)

—. (1995). The Haredi Woman, in Y Azmon (ed.), *A Window on Women's Lives in Jewish Societies*, Jerusalem: The Zalman Shazar Center, 273–290. (Hebrew)

—. (2006). "For the Miracles": The Prosperity of the "Torah World" (Yeshivot and Kollels) in Israel, in I Etkes (ed.), *Yeshivot and Battei Midrash*, Jerusalem: The Zalman Shazar Center, 431–442. (Hebrew)

Friedman, M & Shilhav, Y (1985). *Growth and Segregation – The Ultra-Orthodox Community of Jerusalem*, Jerusalem: The Jerusalem Institute for Israel Studies. (Hebrew)

Gill, R (2007). *Gender and the Media*, Cambridge: Polity Press.

Gitlin, T (1998). Public Sphere or Public Sphericules? In T Liebes & J Curran (eds), *Media, Ritual, Identity*, London: Routledge, 168–174.

Golinkin, D (2001). *The Status of Women in Jewish Law: Responsa*. Jerusalem: The Schechter Institute of Jewish Studies' Center for Women in Jewish Law.

Gramsci, A (1971). *The Prison Notebooks* (trans. and ed. Q Hoare & G Nowell Smith), New York: International Publishers.

Hadar, Tamar (2005). "Otzrot Bitzrorot" (Bundles of Treasure), *Betoch Hamishpacha*, 285.

Hanegbi, (2000) in: Herzog, H., Women's Magazines in Israel: An Arena for Reproduction or for Challenge? 50.

Heilman, S.C. & Friedman, M., 1991. 'Religious Fundamentalism and Religious Jews: The case of the Haredim', in: M.E. Marty & R.S. Appleby (eds.), Fundamentalisms Observed, The University of Chicago Press, Chicago & London, pp. 197-265

Herzog, H., (2000). Women's Magazines in Israel: An Arena for Reproduction or for Challenge? *Kesher*, 28. (Hebrew)

Ilan, S, (2000). *Haredim Ltd.*, Jerusalem: Keter. (Hebrew)

Kahat, C (2001). Women's Status and Torah Study in Orthodox Society, in Y Azmon (ed.), *Hear My Voice: Representations of Women in Israeli Culture*, 355–364.

Kaplan, K (2001). The Media in Haredi Society in Israel, Kesher, 30, 18–31. (Hebrew)

—. (2007). Internal Popular Discourse in Israeli Haredi Society, Jerusalem: Zalman Shazar Center. (Hebrew)

Katz, J (1978). *Tradition and Crisis*, Jerusalem: The Bialik Institute. (Hebrew)

Kouts, G (1999). *Studies in the History of the Hebrew Press*, Tel Aviv: Yaron Golan. (Hebrew)

Lachover, E (2010). Models of Femininity in Israeli Women's Magazines During the Six-Day War. In M Shilo & G Katz (eds.), *Gender in Israel: New Studies on Gender in the Yishuv and the State*, Sde-Boker: Ben-Gurion Institute for the Research of Israel and Zionism. (Hebrew)

Lavie, A (2000). News Is News – It Has No Gender, *Patuach*, 4, 45–74. (Hebrew)

Levy, A (1990). *The Ultra-Orthodox*, Jerusalem: Keter. (Hebrew)

Leiden, S (2000). "LaIsha" (For Women) – An Israeli Weekly for Women That Defines Home, Self and Contemporary Reality, *Kesher*, 28, 36–42. (Hebrew)

Limor, Y (1998). *Research Report: Pirate Radio in Israel, 1998: A Situational Picture*, Jerusalem: The Hebrew University. (Hebrew)

Limor, Y & Caspi, D (1994). The Feminization of the Israeli Press, *Kesher*, 15, 37–45. (Hebrew)

Neria Ben-Shahar, R, Women in the Haredi Press, MA Thesis, Jerusalem: The Hebrew University. (Hebrew)

Peleh, M (2005). "Behind the Mask", *Betoch Hamishpacha*, 276.

Rappel, Y (1991). Synagogue Newspapers in Israel, *Kesher*, 10, 109–112. (Hebrew)

Ravitzky, A (1993). *The Revealed End and the Jewish State – Messianism, Zionism, and Religious Radicalism in Israel*, Tel-Aviv: Am Oved. (Hebrew)

—. (2006). On the Boundaries of Orthodoxy, in Y Salmon, A Ravitzky & A S Ferziger (eds), *Jewish Orthodoxy: New Perspectives*, Jerusalem: Magnes Press, 1–20. (Hebrew)

Ross, R (1993). Women's Businesses, *Tikshoret*, May Issue, 40–47. (Hebrew)

Ross, T., 2004. Expanding the Palace of Torah: Orthodoxy and Feminism, New England University Press, Boston

Rubin, S (1987). *Trends of Tradition and Change in Women's Magazines in Israel*, MA Thesis, Jerusalem: The Hebrew University of Jerusalem. (Hebrew)

Salmon, Y (2006). Jewish Orthodoxy in Eastern Europe. In Y Salmon, A Ravitzky & A S Ferziger (eds), *Jewish Orthodoxy: New Perspectives*, Jerusalem: Magnes Press, 367–380. (Hebrew)

Salmon, Y, Ravitzky, A & Ferziger, A S (2006). *Jewish Orthodoxy: New Perspectives*, Jerusalem: Magnes Press. (Hebrew)

Sheleg, Y (2000). *The New Religious Jews: Recent Developments Among Observant Jews in Israel*, Jerusalem: Keter. (Hebrew)

Shilhav, Y (1991). *A "Shtetl" (Small Town) Within a Modern City*, Jerusalem: The Jerusalem Institute for Israel Studies. (Hebrew)

—. (2005). The Ultra-Orthodox (Haredi) Women, *Mifne* 46, 53–55. (Hebrew)

Shiloh, M (ed.) (2001). *To Be a Jewish Woman*. Proceedings of the First International Conference: Woman and Her Judaism, Jerusalem: Kolech and Urim. (Hebrew)

Sivan, E (1990). The Enclave Culture, *Alpayim*, 4, 45–97. (Hebrew)

Tsarfaty, O & Blais, D (2002). Between Cultural Enclave and Virtual Enclave: Haredi Society and the Digital Media *Kesher*, 32, 44–47.

Tsarfaty, O (2005). Le mouvement hassidique haba''d et les médias: la question d'Eretz Israël et le processus de paix israélo-arabe dans les journaux de Haba''d 'Sihat ha-shavoua' et 'Kfar haba''d' (1990–1995) Lille: ANRT.

Tuchman, G (ed), (1978). *Hearth and Home: Images of Women and the Media*, New York: Oxford University Press.

Van Zoonen, L (1994). *Feminist Media Studies*, London: Sage.

Walker, N (2000). *Shaping Our Mother's World: American Women's Magazines*, Jackson: University Press of Mississippi.

Winship, J (1987). *Inside Women's Magazines*, London and New York: Pandora Press.

CRISE DE L'IDENTITE COLLECTIVISTE DES JEUNES EMPLOYES CHINOIS DANS LES ENTREPRISES A CAPITAUX ETRANGERS

XI JIANG[1]

Résumé

La culture est évolutive et dynamique. Elle n'en finit pas de changer en fonction des circonstances intérieures et extérieures qui transforment un groupe social.

Depuis longtemps, les employés chinois sont considérés comme ayant un sens du collectif et disposant d'un esprit coopératif, bien que celui-ci soit relativement moins fort que chez leurs voisins coréens et japonais. Mais la donne change. Depuis ces dernières années, on constate de plus en plus de différences sur le plan de l'esprit collectif chez les jeunes employés chinois nés après le lancement de la réforme économique, par rapport aux générations précédentes. Ces différences sont d'autant plus manifestes et perceptibles qu'ils travaillent en coopération avec leurs supérieurs ou collègues issus des pays ou régions asiatiques où la réalité de l'esprit collectif est plus présente. Cela peut entraîner parfois des conséquences néfastes. Les médias chinois, et notamment la presse, se font de plus en plus l'écho de cette situation. Comme en témoigne par exemple le reportage sur une secrétaire pékinoise qui avait refusé fermement de travailler après avoir quitté l'entreprise; ou encore celui de Foxconn, entreprise taïwanaise reconnue par son art du management très collectiviste à la japonaise, dont une dizaine d'employés se sont jetés dans le vide en moins de six mois.

Ainsi, nous nous demandons, quelle est l'identité d'adhésion au collectif actuelle des jeunes employés dans les entreprises à capitaux étrangers? Quels sont les changements par rapport aux générations précédentes et à quoi sont-ils dus? Quelles sont, au niveau du comportement et de la façon de penser, les représentations du changement de l'identité collectiviste des jeunes employés chinois dans les entreprises à capitaux étrangers.

[1] Guangdong University of Foreign Studies.

Au travers d'une double méthodologie: une enquête quantitative et des entretiens approfondis auprès de jeunes employés chinois des entreprises à capitaux étrangers en Chine, nous pouvons conclure que, les jeunes employés chinois sont coopérants et reconnaissent l'importance du travail en équipe, mais que, parallèlement, ils demandent également plus d'autonomie et font plus attention à leurs intérêts personnels. Les origines de leurs nouveaux comportements et façons de penser se situent à deux niveaux.

Un niveau interne. La politique de l'enfant unique et la compétition sociale plus dure (qui fait suite à une circulation plus libre du peuple chinois au sein de la Chine et à une disparité économique entre régions) transforment également les comportements des jeunes employés chinois.

Un niveau externe, le développement des nouvelles technologies sous le contexte de la mondialisation et de la modernité, ainsi que l'accès de plus en plus facile aux productions culturelles influencent aussi fortement les comportements des jeunes employés chinois.

Mots-clés : Identité, jeune, Chinois, entreprise

La dimension culturelle collectivisme-individualisme, depuis qu'elle est proposée par Geert Hofstede après sa une vaste étude dans les filiales IBM dans les années soixante et soixante-dix (Hofstede, 1994), est considérée par des chercheurs comme la dimension de valeur la plus importante à travers les cultures (Carroll & Gannon, 1997). Pour Hofstede, les intérêts du groupe dépassent ceux de l'individu dans les cultures collectives. Et dans ce cas-là, l'identité d'une personne se fait par son appartenance à un tel ou tel groupe donné (Hofstede, 1997). Comme le disent Stone-Romero and Stone, le « soi » dans un groupe collectif est très interdépendant et lié fortement à une famille, un groupe de travail ou une communauté et cette interdépendance est considérée comme essentielle pour le bien-être. Ainsi, les membres ont tendance à être préoccupés par le bien-être des collectifs (Stone-Romero & Stone, 2002, p 287, Gundulic, Zivnuska & Stoner, 2006). Tout ce qu'on fait l'est dans l'espoir d'un bénéfice pour l'intérêt de tout le groupe, et même

> « un comportement comme le mensonge est acceptable pour les collectivistes si elle bénéficie au groupe » (Moon & Franke, 2000, p 54, Swaidan & Hayes, 2005).

Être déloyale par rapport à son groupe est une chose très grave et on sera certainement puni et marginalisé très vite par les autres membres du groupe. En contrepartie, le groupe s'efforce de protéger ses membres durant toute leur vie en vue de garder et faire se perpétuer une indiscutable loyauté. Dans les cultures collectives, les employés sont fidèles aux entreprises où ils travaillent. Et la relation entre eux rappelle souvent celle entre le fils et son père dans une famille (Hofstede, 1997). De plus, alors que les employés des cultures individualistes font tout leur possible pour réaliser les objectifs personnels et le succès individuel, les employés des cultures collectives préfèrent établir une relation coopérative avec leurs collègues pour atteindre un but collectif et une réussite de tout le groupe. Ils apprécient beaucoup le sentiment d'appartenance à telle ou telle communauté et à un groupe. Etre membre d'un groupe est très important dans l'image de soi (Felfe, Yan & Six, 2008). C'est la raison pour laquelle on suppose souvent qu'ils établiront une relation forte avec leur entreprise et lui montreront un engagement élevé.

La société chinoise est cataloguée par beaucoup de chercheurs anthropologues et sociologues comme collectiviste (Hofstede, 1994, Trompénaars & Hampden-Turner, 2009), et les employés chinois sont considérés comme ayant un sens de la collectivité et un esprit coopératif, bien que celui-ci soit relativement moins fort que chez leurs voisins coréens et japonais. En revanche, la culture est évolutive et dynamique, et elle n'en finit pas de changer en fonction des circonstances internes et externes qui transforment un groupe social (Loth, 2006). En raison de la mondialisation, de la politique de la réforme et de l'ouverture de l'économie, la société chinoise a connu, depuis ces trente dernières années des changements considérables que ce soit au niveau économique ou culturel. Les valeurs, comportements et façons de penser des employés chinois ne sont ainsi plus les mêmes qu'avant. Par exemple, on constate récemment de plus en plus de différences sur le plan du collectivisme chez les jeunes employés chinois, nés après le lancement de la réforme économique, par rapport aux générations précédentes. Ces différences sont d'autant plus manifestes qu'ils travaillent en coopération avec leurs supérieurs ou collègues issus des pays ou régions asiatiques où la réalité de l'esprit collectif est plus forte et cela peut entraîner parfois des conséquences néfastes.

Affaire d'« E-mail Gate » et la vague de suicides chez Foxconn

Les médias chinois, et notamment la presse, se font de plus en plus l'écho de cette situation.

En 2006, un reportage sur la « guerre » entre une secrétaire pékinoise et son supérieur singapourien a attiré beaucoup l'attention des Chinois. Cette jeune fille, Rebecca Hu, qui a reçu dans la nuit du 8 au 9 avril 2006 un mail de la part de son patron lui reprochant de quitter le travail trop tôt et lui demandant de ne plus quitter le travail jusqu'à ce que tous ses supérieurs partent quelle que soit l'heure. Très fâchée, elle a répondu à ce mail sur un ton très ferme et a transféré sa réponse à tout le personnel de l'entreprise (Lin, 2008, P. 17-20). Cela a provoqué de grandes discussions dans les médias chinois et surtout sur l'Internet. La plupart des cadres d'entreprise plus âgés, qu'ils soient chinois ou pas, ont jugé cette réaction inadmissible et ont pensé qu'une secrétaire comme Mlle Hu qui n'avait pas d'esprit d'équipe et qui ne savait coopérer avec ses collègues n'était pas du tout compétente. Des personnes se sont même demandées comment les jeunes employés sont devenus si individualistes et égocentriques.

Au contraire, Mlle Hu a obtenu un soutien quasi-absolu parmi les internautes chinois, qui ont pour la plupart le même âge qu'elle, sur les forums d'Internet.

> « Pourquoi doit-elle obligatoirement rester au bureau jusqu'à ce que tous ses supérieurs le quittent, alors qu'elle a déjà terminé son travail ? »
>
> « Si jamais un jour son patron, ou ses collègues travaillent jusqu'à 3h du matin, cela signifie-t-il que Mlle Hu n'aura pas d'autre choix que de coucher au bureau ? »,
> « Il est évident que le travail, c'est seulement le travail, et il faut bien le séparer de la vie personnelle.»
>
> « Il est inadmissible que le patron nous impose de continuer à travailler après l'heure à laquelle où nous aurions dû quitter le bureau. »
>
> « Moi, je déteste travailler en dehors des heures légales, et je préfère passer plus de temps avec mes enfants».

Début 2010, un autre évènement dans le sud de la Chine a bouleversé toute la société chinoise. Depuis le début de cette année, Foxconn, entreprise transnationale taïwanaise qui fabrique l'iPhone d'Apple et d'autres icônes des appareils technologiques utilisés dans le monde entier, a connu une vague de suicides pendant 5 mois: seize personnes ont choisi de se jeter dans le vide. Ce sont tous des jeunes de moins de vingt-cinq ans qui ont à peine commencé la vie active. Cette tragédie a ouvert un fort débat dans la presse chinoise sur l'incompatibilité entre la culture d'entreprise taïwanaise, qui est très réputée pour son caractère très collectiviste, et les comportements et façons de penser des jeunes employés chinois. Selon des reportages médiatiques, ces derniers sont très disposés pour s'adapter à une vie professionnelle « hypercollectiviste » et à vivre toujours dans une « cité » où la vie professionnelle et la vie privée ne sont jamais vraiment séparées (Wang, 2010).

En effet, Foxconn n'est pas la seule entreprise taïwanaise qui se confronte à cette situation complexe. Depuis le début du siècle, on note de plus en plus de cas similaires (même s'ils ne sont pas aussi graves que la série de suicides chez Foxconn) au sein des entreprises japonaises ou coréennes, qui sont également culturellement collectivistes.

Problématique de la recherche hypothéses

Suite à la discussion et aux événements ci-dessus qui ont été tous les deux fait l'objet de discussion dans la presse et sur l'Internet, nous pouvons dire qu'il existe une vraie crise de l'identité collective parmi les jeunes employés chinois. Nous pouvons ainsi formuler nos questions de recherche comme suit :

Quelle est l'identité collectiviste actuelle des jeunes employés dans les entreprises à capitaux étrangers?

Quels sont les changements par rapport aux générations précédentes au niveau des comportements et des façons de penser ?

Et enfin et surtout, quelles sont les origines des changements de l'identité collectiviste des jeunes employés chinois dans les entreprises à capitaux étrangers?

Ce sont les questions auxquelles nous allons essayer de trouver les réponses au travers de notre recherche.

Notre problématique peut ainsi conduire à la formulation des hypothèses de notre travail comme suit :

La culture évolue au fil et à mesure du temps, mais avec un rythme progressif et lent. Il en va de même pour la culture chinoise. Malgré des changements économiques et sociaux de ces dernières trente années, la société chinoise reste encore culturellement collective. Il est vrai qu'il existe des changements de comportements et de façon de penser parmi les jeunes : ils demandent plus d'autonomie et se consacrent de plus en plus à leurs propres intérêts et à leur développement personnel. Mais en général, ils ne nient pas complètement leur identité collective. Ces jeunes chinois disposent toujours d'un esprit collectif et reconnaissent bien l'importance de la coopération, surtout dans le travail.

L'évolution de la culture d'un groupe ou une société est souvent influencée aussi bien de l'extérieur que de l'intérieur. Pour les jeunes employés chinois, leur changement d'identité culturelle collective peut se percevoir à deux niveaux : un niveau interne et un autre externe. Le premier est lié aux changements sociaux en Chine depuis le lancement de la réforme chinoise : la politique de l'enfant unique, l'assouplissement des politiques concernant la circulation des Chinois à l'intérieur de la Chine, la disparité économique inter-régionale etc. En ce qui concerne le niveau externe, la mondialisation et le développement rapide des nouveaux médias, y jouent un grand rôle.

Méthodologie

Afin de mener à bien notre recherche, nous avons choisi d'utiliser dans notre travail une double méthodologie : une enquête effectuée auprès d'employés dans les entreprises à capitaux étrangers en Chine, et des entretiens approfondis avec des personnes concernées par notre recherche.

En ce qui concerne l'enquête, elle s'est fait par la distribution des questionnaires. Le questionnaire est composé par plusieurs questions fermées. Nous y trouvons également des questions démographiques sur l'âge, le sexe, le niveau d'éducation, etc. Nous avons choisi de distribuer notre questionnaire auprès des employés qui travaillent dans trois grandes villes chinoises : Pékin, Shanghai et Canton. Ce sont les villes centrales des régions chinoises où se trouvent la plupart de l'investissement étranger et aussi des entreprises à capitaux étranger. Après avoir obtenu l'accord des sondés, les questionnaires ont été envoyés par courriel à leur adresse électronique, souvent celle personnelle mais non professionnelle en vue de protéger leur vie privée. Des questionnaires ont été également envoyés par voie postale directement aux domiciles des interrogés selon des demandes particulières.

Pour le choix des personnes interrogées, nous l'avons fait en fonction des caractéristiques de notre problématique de recherche ainsi que des objectifs de notre travail. Nous avons interviewé bien sur des jeunes employés chinois dans les entreprises à capitaux étrangers en Chine, notamment ceux qui sont nés après le lancement de la réforme économique. Ce sont des personnes dites souvent « des nouvelles générations ». En même temps, nous avons également interviewé leurs collègues plus âgés (plus de trente ans), afin de mesurer les différences des valeurs, comportements et façons de penser entre eux et leurs collègues jeunes sur la notion du collectivisme. Mais quelle que soit leur âge, ce sont principalement des ingénieurs, comptables, secrétaires, chefs de produit, attachés de presse ou conseillers juridiques qui travaillent pour la plupart dans l'importation-exportation, les services commerciaux, la fabrication, la pharmacie et l'informatique, autrement dit les domaines qui attirent la majeure partie de l'investissement international sur le territoire chinois. Des individus ayant un bon niveau d'éducation, nos interviewés parlent couramment au moins une langue internationale et ont souvent l'occasion de coopérer avec d'autres employés issus de cultures différentes. Pour ce qui est du sexe des sondés, nous avons essayé de respecter une parité hommes-femmes. Enfin, pour assurer l'exactitude de cette enquête, nous avons traité les résultats obtenus par des méthodes d'analyse statistiques à l'aide de logiciels informatiques.

Concernant les entretiens, il s'agit d'interrogatoires approfondis auprès de questionnés de notre enquête et également de leurs collègues. Les premiers entretiens ont été menés de manière semi-directive. C'est-à-dire, un plan de questions a été préparé à l'avance. Par exemple, les différences du collectivisme entre les jeunes employés chinois dans les entreprises à capitaux étrangers et les représentations de ces différences au travail. Les deuxièmes entretiens ont été tous non-directifs. Nous avons voulu, à travers ces entretiens, bien connaître leurs avis et opinions, ainsi que les raisons de leurs choix lors de l'enquête. Tous les interrogés ont eu le droit de refuser de répondre à une ou plusieurs questions ou d'y répondre plus tard par mail ou d'autres façons après les entretiens.

Il est évident que nous ne pouvons nous entretenir avec toutes les personnes enquêtées. Ici, nous exposons les critères de choix comme suivants : discuter avec les personnes qui sont susceptibles de nous fournir plus d'informations utiles qui peuvent éclairer le plus possible nos orientations de recherche. Tout d'abord des jeunes employés chinois qui ont vraiment envie d'échanger avec nous et nous montrer ce qu'ils pensent sur leur identité collective au travail. Ensuite, ce sont des employés plus âgés qui ont plus d'occasions de travailler ensemble avec les jeunes employés chinois, et qui ont également la préoccupation d'échanger avec ces derniers. Que ce soit l'enquête ou les entretiens approfondis, ils sont tous dans le cadre d'une thèse concernant les différences culturelles dans les entreprises à capitaux étranger en Chine. Comme la Chine est un pays grand et la relation interpersonnelle y est particulière, il nous a fallu plus de temps pour établir une relation de confiance avec nos questionnés et interviewés avant d'obtenir leur accord pour l'enquête et les entretiens. Ainsi, ce travail de terrain a duré au total presque une année.

Résultat du travail sur terrain

Nous avons pu faire une enquête auprès de cent huit personnes qui travaillent dans les entreprises à capitaux étrangers en Chine et effectuer vingt cinq entretiens approfondis.

Les résultats que nous avons obtenus de cette enquête répondent bien à nos deux premières questions posées comme problématiques et correspondent bien à notre première hypothèse.

Globalement, quel que soit l'âge qu'ils aient, tous les sondés chinois reconnaissent que le travail en équipe est plus efficace que l'action individuelle. En ce qui concerne le rôle important de la décision collective lors de la coopération de l'équipe, il n'existe pas non plus une grande différence entre les employés plus âgés et les jeunes employés chinois (moins de trente ans, c'est-à-dire qu'ils sont nés après le lancement de la réforme économique en 1978). En revanche, s'il existe de vrais conflits entre les employés et leurs collègues, plus de quatre-vingt pour cent de jeunes employés chinois choisissent très vite de quitter les entreprises où ils travaillent. En outre, plus de soixante pour cent des jeunes employés chinois ne pensent pas que l'aide à d'autres personnes est plus importante que le succès individuel, alors que plus de cinquante pour cent des employés chinois plus âgés ont tendance à donner « un coup de main » à leurs collègues qui sont vraiment en difficulté pour accomplir leur travail. En ce qui concerne le rapport entre la vie professionnelle et la vie privée, plus de soixante pour cent des sondés de moins de trente ans pensent que « c'est très important que mon travail me permette d'avoir suffisamment de temps libre, pour moi et pour ma famille » et estiment que « le développement personnel et l'intérêt individuel sont plus importants que ceux de toute l'équipe ». Ainsi, il n'est pas surprenant de constater que presque soixante-dix pour cent des jeunes employés chinois (ayant moins de trente ans) acceptent de changer fréquemment de job, si cela leur permet de développer leurs capacités et leurs compétences personnelles, contre un taux de moins de cinquante pour cent chez les employés plus âgés.

A partir des résultats de l'enquête, nous pouvons constater que, les jeunes employés chinois ne renoncent pas totalement à la culture collectiviste, ils sont encore coopérants et reconnaissent toujours l'importance du travail en équipe, mais en même temps, ils demandent plus d'autonomie et font de plus en plus attention à leurs propres intérêts et objectifs personnels.

Les origines des changements sur la notion du collectivisme parmi les jeunes employés chinois sont tirées plutôt des entretiens. Elles sont assez compliquées. Elles sont effectivement à lire à deux niveaux.

Un niveau interne. La politique de l'enfant unique et la compétition sociale plus dure (qui fait suite à une circulation plus libre du peuple chinois au sein de la Chine et à une disparité économique entre régions) transforment également les comportements des jeunes employés chinois.

Un niveau externe, la mondialisation et le développement des nouveaux médias permettent aux cultures occidentales, en particulier américaine, d'influencer plus fortement les comportements des jeunes employés chinois au travers principalement des productions culturelles (la musique, le film, la publicité, etc.).

ANALYSES

Origines internes

Politique de l'enfant unique. La politique de l'enfant unique en Chine en est la première raison. Cette politique, mise en vigueur en 1978 juste après le lancement de la réforme économique chinoise dans la même année, se pratique d'une manière parfois très stricte en ville, ne permet à un couple de n'avoir qu'un seul enfant. Selon le rapport du recensement de la population du Bureau National des Statistiques de Chine, jusqu'à l'année 2010, on compte déjà plus de cent millions d'enfants uniques en Chine1.

De par le rôle important de la famille dans la société chinoise (Carluer & Jiang, 2011), une famille traditionnelle chinoise a souvent envie d'avoir, à condition que la situation financière de la famille le permette, autant d'enfants que possible. Mais la donne a beaucoup changé en raison de la politique de l'enfant unique. La structure familiale est devenue beaucoup plus simple comme quatre-deux-un : Le « quatre » représente les parents d'un couple ; le « deux » implique le couple lui-même et enfin le « un » est leur enfant unique. Des chercheurs chinois expliquent cette structure familiale par un schéma de pyramide inverse. Les quatre grands-parents se trouvent au niveau le plus inférieur, ensuite les parents au milieu, et enfin l'enfant unique de la famille qui se situe au niveau le plus haut de la pyramide. Nous pouvons ainsi nous apercevoir au travers de ce schéma que l'enfant unique est le plus important pour toutes les familles chinoises contemporaines. Unique, autrement dit hors pair, ce sont des enfants qui véhiculent l'espoir de toute la famille. Ils sont par conséquent considérés comme le « trésor » de leurs parents et grands-parents, et ces derniers, font souvent leur possible pour satisfaire tous les besoins de leurs enfants, en leur fournissant les meilleures conditions de vie et d'éducation. Devenant le point central de la vie quotidienne de la famille, ces enfants se dotent inévitablement de caractère de comportements et valeurs plus individuels

[1] Selon le rapport du 6ème recensement de la population du Bureau National des Statistiques de Chine, http://www.stats.gov.cn/tjgb/rkpcgb/

par rapport à leurs générations aînées. Ils grandissent dans une situation toute différente. Sans frères ni sœurs, ils s'amusent et travaillent à la maison tout seul depuis l'enfance, ne possèdent guère l'esprit de partage mais sont souvent encouragés par leurs parents à être plus ambitieux et compétitifs en vue de parvenir à réussir, car ils sont le seul « espoir de toute la famille ».

Ainsi, au niveau de la relation interpersonnelle professionnelle, ils ne suivent ni la tradition confucianiste, ni l' « esprit collectiviste communiste ». Dans beaucoup de cas, ils sont sévères envers leurs collègues lors de coopération et les erreurs commises par ces derniers sont souvent inacceptables. Cette mentalité, jugée « extrêmement égocentrique » par des plus âgés, est déjà devenue un sujet de controverse en Chine. Des jeunes l'apprécient et la considèrent comme étant une marque de la personnalité. Mais plus nombreux sont ceux qui la critiquent beaucoup, comme dans l'article « Générations de post-80s: plus individuels? »2, publié dans le Journal de Jeunesse de Chine le 14 mars 2008, l'auteur affirme que ces jeunes des « générations post-80s », qui ne veulent ni ne savent coopérer avec d'autres collègues, doivent apprendre à bien s'insérer au sein des entreprises.

Compétition sociale plus dure. Certes, la réforme économique a activé le développement de l'économie chinoise et a amélioré le niveau de vie du peuple chinois au cours des derniers 30 ans. En revanche, les régions différentes en bénéficient de manière diverse. L'investissement direct étranger est un moteur important de l'essor économique chinois, mais sa répartition sur le territoire chinois est loin d'être équilibre. Les régions à l'est, celles côtières, grâce aux politiques avantageuses, ont reçu plus de 80% de l'investissement direct étranger pendant les derniers trente ans et ont ainsi pu se développer beaucoup plus vite que les régions à l'intérieur de la Chine. D'où une forte inégalité économique entre les régions côtières à l'est et celles au centre et à l'ouest.

Selon les chiffres du Bureau National des Statistiques de Chine, pour Shanghai, la ville la plus riche et développée en Chine, le PIB par habitant a déjà dépassé dix millions dollars soit un chiffre équivalent à celui en Slovaquie et d'environ dix fois plus que celui en Guizhou, la province la plus pauvre chinoise (qui est aussi pauvre que la Moldavie ou Le Pakistan). De plus, nous notons que, sans aucune exception, toutes les cinq régions les plus riches (les villes de Shanghai, Pékin, Tianjin, les provinces du Zhejiang et du Jiangsu) sont des régions côtières et se localisent à l'est

[2] *Générations de post-80s: plus individuels ?*, Journal de Jeunesse de Chine, 14 mars 2008

de la Chine, et que les cinq régions les plus pauvres (La région autonome du Tibet, les provinces du Guangxi, du Yunnan, du Gansu et du Guizhou), se trouvent toutes à l'ouest de la Chine3.

En outre, la Chine est un pays très décentralisé en matière de fiscalité. A cause de la disparité économique entre les régions riches et les régions pauvres, il existe ainsi un grand écart dans la fiscalité des régions. Comme les gouvernements locaux reposent principalement sur la perception des impôts locaux pour subvenir aux services publics de base, tels que l'éducation primaire et les soins de santé, les régions riches disposent de plus de moyens pour assurer un niveau de vie beaucoup plus élevé que les régions pauvres à travers les dépenses publiques. Il existait peu de différences entre les régions sur le taux de survie infantile au début des années 90 alors qu'une grande différence a été constatée en 2000 avec les chiffres étroitement liés au PIB par personne dans chaque région. Autre exemple, en ce qui concerne l'éducation, le taux d'entrée au lycée a déjà atteint presque cent pour cent dans les régions riches mais encore moins de quarante pour cent dans les régions pauvres en 2003 （Dollar, 2007）.

L'assouplissement du système de « Hukou » et l'inégalité de niveau de vie en Chine conduisent de plus en plus de Chinois à se déplacer vers les régions riches à l'est de la Chine. Selon Xie ling-li, chef de la Commission du Plan Familial et de la Population de la Municipalité de Shanghai, on compte environ six millions six cent mille de « nouveaux shanghaiens »4, autrement dit les personnes qui ne disposent pas de « Hukou » de la ville de Shanghai. Si l'on ajoute celles qui ne sont pas nées à Shanghai mais qui ont obtenu le « Hukou » shanghaïen par telle ou telle voie « régulière » ou « irrégulière », ce chiffre sera plus élevé.

Les « nouveaux habitants » des régions côtières à l'est de la Chine sont principalement composés de deux populations : Pour la première, ce sont des ouvriers-paysans qui cherchent un revenu plus élevé à grâce au travail dans les régions développées afin de subvenir aux besoins de leurs familles à la campagne. Des personnes plus jeunes qui ont fait leurs études universitaires dans les grandes villes constituent la deuxième partie des « nouveaux habitants ». En Chine, les universités prestigieuses se trouvent principalement dans des grandes villes. Selon le palmarès des universités chinoises 2008, plus de la moitié des universités du Top dix se localisent dans les villes à l'est de la Chine. Attirées par les meilleures conditions de

[3] Selon l'annuaire des statistiques 2010 du Bureau des Statistiques National de Chine, http://www.stats.gov.cn/tjgb/

[4] Chiffre publié par la Commission du Plan Familiale et de la Population de la Municipalité de Shanghai, http://www.popinfo.gov.cn/stat/ssh/

travail, les chances abondantes et le salaire plus élevé, ces jeunes élites choisissent de travailler dans ces grandes villes après leurs études. Le « Rapport du développement social de Pékin 2007», publié par l'Académie des Sciences Sociales de Pékin, montre que plus de vingt-deux pour cent des diplômés des universités pékinoises en 2007 choisissent de travailler dans les sociétés transnationales, juste dernière ceux qui sont recrutés par les unités d'Etat. En ce qui concerne les régions de travail, des grandes villes du Golfe de Bohai (où se trouvent Pékin et Tianjin), du Delta de Yangtsze (dont Shanghai est le centre économique) et celui du Fleuve de Perle (qui est la région autour de la ville de Canton) sont leurs premiers choix.

Ainsi, avec l'arrivée de ces nouveaux arrivants, la compétition dans le monde professionnel devient plus dure. Les postes ne sont pas infiniment nombreux mais le nombre de candidats compétents est énorme. Presque tous nos sondés et interviewés ont confirmé leur stress au travail, leur soif d'avoir plus de temps libre avec les amis et la famille. Et en même temps, afin de ne pas se faire marginaliser dans cette compétition dure, les jeunes employés chinois ont commencé à se préoccuper de plus en plus de leur développement personnel en vue d'atteindre leurs objectifs individuels. « J'aimerais vraiment passer plus de temps libre, et je ne peux pas toujours rester avec mes collègues, vingt-quatre heures sur vingt-quatre heures et sept jours sur sept», « Comment puis-je supporter toujours les erreurs de mes collègues ? C'est impossible. Le temps est précieux et ne nous attend pas. » « Si l'entreprise ne me permet pas de valoriser tout mon potentiel, j'envisagerai de changer de job. » « Le développement individuel est bien sûr plus important que la contribution à l'entreprise », nous racontent des jeunes employés chinois lors de nos entretiens.

Origines externes

Développement des nouvelles technologies. Selon le sociologue Anthony Giddens, la modernité est caractérisée par la dissociation et le rallongement des mesures du temps et de l'espace. Les relations sociales dans une société moderne ne sont plus forcément entre les personnes de notre entourage et ne se passent non plus dans un lieu géographiquement donné, et

> « la mondialisation peut ainsi être définie comme l'intensification des relations sociales planétaires » (Giddens, 1994, P.70).

Ainsi, ce qui se passe dans une ville asiatique peut être influencé, au travers d'un mécanisme complexe, par un évènement qui a eu lieu dans un autre coin du monde. Les gens qui partagent un même sentiment d'appartenance n'habitent pas forcément dans un même quartier ou même pays et il leur est possible d'imaginer la vie sur un autre territoire éloigné bien qu'ils ne l'aient jamais visité. On peut communiquer par Email dans les temps différés au lieu d'une communication où tous les acteurs sont présents dans un lieu géographiquement donné. Tout ce dont nous parlons ici représente la distanciation et la délocalisation spatio-temporelles proposées par Anthony Giddens. Et les nouvelles technologies, telles que l'Internet et le téléphone mobile, accélèrent le processus dynamique de distanciation et de délocalisation et nos relations sociales, qui ont été localisées dans un temps et un lieu donné, s'étirent de plus en plus loin aussi bien dans l'espace que dans le temps.

Selon les dernières statistiques du Centre de l'information du réseau Internet en Chine (CNNIC en anglais), le nombre d'internautes en Chine a déjà dépassé quatre cents cinquante sept millions, soit plus de vingt pour cent des internautes mondiaux. Parmi eux, ceux qui ont moins de trente ans représentent environ soixante pour cent. En même temps, avec le développement rapide de nouvelles générations de téléphones portables, notamment le smartphone, de plus en plus de jeunes internautes chinois commencent à naviguer davantage sur Internet au travers de leurs téléphones portables. Selon un rapport sur l'analyse des comportements de navigation d'Internet des utilisateurs chinois de smartphone, ceux qui ont moins de trente ans représentent encore une grande partie : environ soixante-dix pour cent des utilisateurs5. Chaque jour, ces jeunes chinois lisent des informations ou romans, jouent aux jeux en ligne, publient et partagent, au travers de blogues, microblogues ou de sites de réseaux sociaux, leurs photos, journaux personnels, joies et émotions avec des amis dans le monde entier.

Certes, dans une société moderne, la distanciation et la délocalisation spatio-temporelle au travers des nouvelles technologies permettent aux personnes de communiquer plus facilement et librement, mais elles engendrent également des conséquences pas toujours positives que nous ne pouvons négliger. Progressivement, on se connecte de « personne à personne » dans un espace plutôt virtuel au travers d'Internet et de

---

[5] Selon les statistiques du « 27ème rapport du développement d'Internet en Chine », publié par le Centre d'Information du Réseau d'Internet de Chine, presque 60% d'internautes chinois sont moins de 30 ans. ***27ème rapport du développement d'Internet en Chine***, publié par le Centre d'Information du Réseau d'Internet de Chine, Pékin, Janvier 2011.
http://www.cnnic.net.cn/dtygg/dtgg/201101/P020110119328960192287.pdf

téléphone mobile. On est davantage habitué à échanger et à discuter à l'aise avec des personnes lointaines que l'on ne connaît ni voit jamais, mais on a du mal à communiquer en vis-à-vis avec les collègues. En outre, la liberté extrême sur Internet provoque en simultanéité un refus des devoirs et responsabilités pour certaines personnes. Elles fuient la société réelle, acquièrent de plus en plus des caractères individualistes et en même temps, se sentent de moins en moins appartenir à son équipe et coopèrent moins avec leurs collègues.

> « Je préfère communiquer avec mes collègues par téléphone ou mail et évite de discuter avec eux en vis-à-vis, car je me sens mal à l'aise pour les affronter. Or, on ne peut toujours communiquer virtuellement. Ce qui m'angoisse beaucoup».
>
> « Je me sens très à l'aise pour échanger avec des amis sur Internet, dans un site de réseau sociaux ou un forum, mais lorsque je suis en face de mes collègues, je sens moins d'esprit commun».
>
> « Il existe moins de règles dans le cyberespace et la vie sur Internet me rend plus libéral. Mais il est impossible d'être tout à fait libéral au travail et je ne sais pas comment concilier mon esprit de libéralisme et le professionnalisme. »

Propos de jeunes employés chinois recueillis lors de nos entretiens.

Influence des productions culturelles occidentales

En même temps, la mondialisation et le développement de nouvelles technologies permettent également aux jeunes Chinois d'accéder plus facilement et librement aux productions culturelles occidentales, tels que le film, la musique et les séries télévisées.

Les productions culturelles ont pu entrer sur le marché chinois au début des années quatre-vingt du dernier siècle, mais les politiques étaient très strictes. Il a fallu quelques mois ou une année de contrôle avant que les Chinois puissent regarder un film américain qui avait déjà été diffusé aux Etats-Unis ou en Europe il y a un an. Et il a également existé un quota sur l'exportation des produits culturels étrangers. Au fur et à mesure de la réforme économique, les politiques sont devenues plus souples et les quotas ne sont plus aussi limités. En outre, le développement de nouvelles technologies permet d'accélérer la diffusion des productions culturelles en Chine. Sur les sites web d'hébergement de vidéo ou des logiciels de télévision Internet de technologie pair à pair comme ppstream ou pplive, on peut trouver très facilement des films ou sériés télévisées qui ont à peine été diffusés aux Etats-Unis, bien que la plupart de ces vidéos soient entrées en Chine par voie « irrégulière » et aient été souvent piratées. Selon les statistiques de CNNIC en 2010, environ 62% d'internautes chinois sont habitués à regarder des films et séries télévisées étrangères sur Internet6, et comme toujours, les jeunes en constituent la plus grande partie. Par exemple pour ceux qui regardent régulièrement les séries télévisées américaines, ce sont des jeunes majoritairement âgés entre dix-huit ans et trente ans, qui sont soit étudiants soit de jeunes employés des entreprises, en particulier dans les entreprises à capitaux étrangers (He & Yao, 2007). En plus, les nouveaux médias, comme les microblogues (twitter, ou d'autres sites chinois) et les sites de réseaux sociaux, qui connaissent tous les deux un développement considérable dans le marché chinois, facilitent également la circulation des informations, critiques, recommandations et le partage des productions culturelles au sein de la communauté des jeunes.

Ces productions culturelles non seulement permettent aux jeunes Chinois de mieux connaître d'autres pays et de découvrir d'autres cultures, mais aussi influencent implicitement ou explicitement les comportements et modes de penser des jeunes Chinois. Par exemple, la liberté individuelle, la chasse au succès personnel, ou l'héroïsme individuel, tout ce qui est incorporé comme valeurs dans les films ou la musique de l'Occident, en particulier des Etats-Unis, jouent un rôle assez important et transforment l'identité collectiviste traditionnelle des jeunes Chinois. Ils commencent à demander plus de liberté et d'autonomie aussi bien dans la vie quotidienne qu'au travail. Tout comme ce qu'ont choisi nos sondés de l'enquête et ce que nous ont déclaré nos interviewés :

> « Je ne peux plus coopérer sans condition avec mes collègues, si les autres ont fait des fautes, et la décision de l'équipe n'a ainsi pas toujours plus de valeur que celle de l'individu ».

> « Je reconnais que le développement personnel est plus important dans la vie professionnelle ».

> « J'ai vraiment plus de temps libre à moi et pour ma famille. »

---

[6]Selon les statistiques du « 27ème rapport du développement d'Internet en Chine », publié par le Centre d'Information du Réseau d'Internet de Chine, presque 60% d'internautes chinois sont moins de 30 ans. ***27ème rapport du développement d'Internet en Chine***, publié par le Centre d'Information du Réseau d'Internet de Chine, Pékin, janvier 2011.
http://www.cnnic.net.cn/dtygg/dtgg/201101/P020110119328960192287.pdf

« Je quitterai la société sans hésitation s'il y a plus de chances pour moi de mieux développer mes capacités et mes compétences dans une autre entreprise ».

Conclusion

La culture n'est pas figée, elle est dynamique et évolue en fonction de l'environnement et de paramètres internes au groupe social.

Depuis le lancement de la réforme économique, la société chinoise a connu des changements considérables, aussi bien dans le domaine économique que culturel. Les façons de penser, ainsi que les comportements des employés chinois, qui sont souvent catalogués comme collectivistes, ne sont également plus les mêmes qu'avant, en particulier chez les jeunes générations. Bien qu'ils soient encore coopérants et reconnaissent l'importance du travail en équipe, ces jeunes employés, selon les résultats de notre enquête et nos entretiens, sont bien différents des générations de leurs aînés et demandent plus d'autonomie et font de plus en plus attention à leurs propres intérêts et objectifs personnels.

Mettre en synergie les actions des personnes différentes afin d'arriver à un objectif collectif est un impératif universel de la gestion, comme ce que disait Philipe d'Iribarne il y a plus de vingt ans (D'Iribarne, 1989). Mais il reconnaît également,

> « et partout cet impératif est difficile à satisfaire. Car il faut coordonner, mais sans étouffer pour autant, sans casser l'enthousiasme de chacun, ses désirs d'aller de l'avant, d'innover, de créer, sans le démotiver »,

et surtout,

> « comment faire entrer chacun dans un projet commun sans décourager les fortes personnalités ? » (D'Iribarne, 1989, P.255-256).

En guise de conclusion, nous nous posons également la question suivante : comment dans le contexte de la mondialisation, faire coopérer les Chinois plus âgés, qui sont plutôt culturellement collectivistes, avec les jeunes employés chinois, qui connaissent actuellement une crise de cette identité collectiviste, demandent plus d'autonomie personnelle et se préoccupent davantage de leur développement individuel ainsi que de leur vie personnelle.

Bibliographie

Boase, J, Horrigan, J, Wellman, B, & Rainie, L (2006). *The strength of Internet ties.* Récupéré le 25 janvier, 2006, from http://www.pewinternet.org/~/media//Files/Reports/2006/PIP_Internet_ties.pdf.pdf

Carluer, C & Jiang, X (2011). *Différences culturelles asiatiques sur la notion de collectivisme : enjeux pour le management interculturel dans les entreprises à capitaux étrangers en Chine.* Article présenté au sixième séminaire interculturel sino-français de Canton, Canton.

Carroll, S J, & Gannon, M J (1997). *Ethical dimensions of international management. Thousand Oaks*, CA: Sage.

D'Iribarne, P (1989). *La logique de l'honneur : gestion des entreprises et traditions nationales.* Paris: Edition du Seuil.

Dollar, D (2007). *Poverty, inequality and social disparities during China's economic reform.* World Bank Policy Research Working Paper 4253. June.

Felfe, J, Yan, W, & Six,B (2008).*The impact of individual collectivism on commitment and its influence on organizational citizenship behaviour and turnover in three countries. International Journal of Cross Cultural Management*, 2008 8. 211–237.

Giddens, A & Meyer, O (1994). *Les conséquences de la modernité.* Paris : l'Harmattan.

Gundlach, M, Zivnuska, S & Stoner, J (2006). Understanding the relationship between individualism-collectivism and team performance through an integration of social identity theory and the social relationship model, *Human Relations,* 59, 1603–1632.

He, G & Yao, Y (2007). Analyse d'audience sous la technologie de transmission pair à pair. *Recherche de Jeunesse*, Octobre, 68–71.

Hofstede, G (1994). *Vivre dans un monde multiculturel: comprendre nos programmations mentales.* Paris : Les Ed. d'Organisation.

Lin, J (2008). Des révélations sur l'affaire de la plus courageuse secrétaire dans l'histoire. *Culture des entreprises contemporaines.* Octobre, 17–20.

Loth, D (2006). *Le management interculturel.* Paris : L'Harmattan.

Moon, Y S, & Franke, G R (2000). Cultural influences on agency practitioner's ethical perceptions: A comparison of korea and the U.S. *Journal of Advertising*, 29(1), 51–65.

Sims, R L (2009), Collective versus individualist national cultures comparing Taiwan and U.S. employee attitudes toward unethical business practices. *Business & Society,* 48(1), 39–59.

Stone-Romero, E F & Stone, D L (2002) *Cross-cultural differences in responses to feedback: Implications for individual, group, and organizational effectiveness.* In G R Ferris (ed.), *Research in personnel and human resources management* 21 (pp. 275–331). Stamford, CT: JAI Press.

Swaidan, Z, & Hayes, L A (2005). Hofstede theory and cross cultural ethics conceptualization, review, and research agenda. *Journal of American Academy of Business*, 6(2), 10–15.

Trompénaars, F & Hampden-Turner, C (2010). *L'entreprise multiculturelle.* Paris : Maxima.

Wang, J (2010). Problèmes chez Foxconn : trop de contrôles, manque de communication. *Business de Chine*, le 24 avril.

COMMUNION: AN APPROACH TOWARDS (RE)DEFINING COMMUNITY— THE ROMANIAN CASE

ADRIAN LESENCIUC, ION TEOFIL CREȚU AND VIANA POPICĂ

Abstract

Our work will discuss an issue from the field of communication in close relationship with sociology in a philosophical manner. The prolix way of the world in a reality of hyper-communication is due to the lack of objective communication and even the loss of any sense in defining communication. In order to perceive communication effectively we must go deeper than the conventional epistemological point of view of communication theory, and relate it closely to the social frameworks (community and society) in which it occurs. In Romania, communion (in Romanian, *cuminecare*) is representative and approached from a philosophical point of view (Noica, 1987). The genuine separation of concepts does not stand as a dichotomy, but as an ontological difference in the principle of Unity. Our reason is inclined to conceptualize in separate terms, avoiding dichotomous views. Behind the difference between communication and communion is the genuine meaning of being. Moving from communication theory and semiotics to metaphysics is the key to comprehending the fulfilment of the reality of interrelations. The rich sociological signification in Noica's philosophical dimension can be correlated with Tönnies' theory referring to community and society. To establish the correlation between Tönnies' concepts and our concepts, we did not look for distinctions between the sociologist's theoretical terms, but what is common to them. By defining the concepts of communion, community and society as correlative concepts, we develop an idea that defines social reality as an entity in continuous change. In a world of "hyper-consumerism", over-communication does not cancel the communion, but increases it, not in teleological but natural intentions. We feel our senses in communion and we progress by communicating within community and society. Social reality, revealed under these two aspects, does not disable communication and attenuate the communion or vice versa; even so the two dimensions of social relations, which reflect the liquidity of modernity, constantly model it. Social reality is dynamic and is animated by its components, the functions between them and more, because a whole is never the sum of its parts.

We aim at revealing the inter-determinations between community and society by comprehending the role of communion and communication that represent the essence of social reality. Furthermore, our goal is to identify how the Romanian identity, as defined in the spirit of communion, meets the European identity, and exploits its limits through communication.

Keywords: communication, communion, community, society, identity

Introduction

In our attempt to explore the fertile dichotomy intended over more than a century by Tönnies, community vs society, we tried an interpretation from the Romanian cultural point of view. As a living organism built around common inheritance, community can be associated with the Romanian communion, restful communication, implying meanings, while society – a group organized around utilitarian principles, represents the necessary frame for the development of restless communication. These dichotomous pairs correspond to others, culture-civilization, respectively actions oriented towards success – actions oriented towards understanding, expressed in monochronic or disjunctive spaces, or paradoxically, assumed and interpreted in a natural way in polychronic spaces, – including Romanian cultural space. How then is identity defined within the limits of community and society? How does it define the identity in terms of communication with and without rest? How are Europe and the European identity defined from the perspective of a monochronic and from a polychronic space? And finally, how is community (re)defined in terms of communion?

Community and Communication

Aristotle's remark about Man – *zoon politikon* – is probably the first thought that depicts an ontological link between communication and community. Moreover, the word (*logos*) binds Aristotle's hierarchical structures of community (*koinonia*) – highlighting both the dimensions regarding the constraints and the self-constraints when it comes to communicational conditioning. Only by trying to understand the relational complexity of organized social groups in communities can we comprehend the communication that is added to (and incorporates) relationships. Thus, the Palo Alto School reveals Paul Watzlavick's relational foundation (Watzlawick et al., 1967, pp. 132–133) considering that "every communication has content and relational aspects such that the latter classifies the former and is therefore a metacommunication". This implies every participant in the communicational act of defining the relation. Rules of communication are predefined within the community, while the community is built on the fundament of natural relations between the members of the social group.

The German sociologist Ferdinand Tönnies introduced two epistemologically relevant concepts in the field of sociology: Community and Society (*Gemeinschaft* and *Gesellschaft*). The distinction is ontological and reflects the world state from a social perspective. If we consider collective will as the basis of social relations, Tönnies discriminates between two forms of group organization according to their natural changing capacity to transform intentions into actions: natural/essential, respectively utilitarian/rational. The essential will (*Wesenswille*) gives birth to communities – an organic primordial construct, managing internal relations and opening to others in order to embed, seduce; the rational will (*Kürwille*), implying different aims and associated meanings, contributes to the foundation of a conscious construct, seen as the sum or the common denominator of selfish interests: society. Community is a living organism based on inheritance: a language, beliefs, and habits, ritual, which cancels the resultant of centrifugal daily actions. A community consists of individuals that perceive each other as an extension of family relations (Tönnies, 2002, pp. 37–38). This type of social group is built on interiorized norms, not on norms filtered by reason. Created by contractual relations with public or private institutions, society could be perceived, in the limits of this definition, and outside the natural as a group where individuals remain separated, distant, even alienated. The German sociologist marks in categorical terms the fracture of this form of social organization from the natural, organic community: "A *Gesellschaft* of life would be a contradiction in and of itself" (Tönnies, 2002, pp. 33–34). From this perspective, it is natural to perceive community-society relationships in terms of irreducibility:

> Tönnies' formulation sets this irreducible dichotomy: *Gemeinschaft* is "more alive", is "the lasting and genuine way of living together", while *Gessellschaft* "is transitory and superficial" (Tönnies, 2002, p. 35).

Therefore, "*Gemeinschaft* should be understood as a living organism, *Gesellschaft* as a mechanical aggregate and artifact" (idem). (See Dobrescu, 2002, p. 47.)

The community-communication relation is complex and implies reciprocal interconditioning. The explanation for this interconditioning in connection with the acceptance of community meanings as a sum of meanings from its members is insufficient. Even if the locution "Meanings are in people" offers a way to understand the community meanings, "our individual meanings can neither be added nor multiplied; the sum of our significance and the product of our meaning is nothing" (Shepherd, 2001:27). These relationships should certainly be comprehended in the spirit of community, and within community, embedding the dynamic of becoming one with the community. Aristotle reminds us that with assumed nuance of subjectivity, community comprehension from the inside makes possible the understanding of the profound senses of binds in the relationship between *logos* and *koinonia*, mediated by *koinos*.

Community or Communion? The Dichotomy that Defines the Communication Unit

In Romanian the term communication etymologically derives from "common/*comun*" (meaning: that belongs to somebody or to everybody), *comun* being a derivative of the Latin term *communis.* This term originates from the Latin verb *communicare* and in Romanian represents a doublet of *cuminecare* (translated in our text as "communion"). Most languages stick to the meaning of communication as relation and transfer between people. Communication is a fluid concept, in continuous change between the epistemic core and the symbolical form:

> Two poles, one – the epistemic core – describable and readable by definition (from which we can escape through a "Critique. . ."), the other pole – the symbolic form, shrouding in such manner our thoughts and acts, that, theoretically, we cannot describe it. (Sfez, 2002a, p. 10)

The symbolic form which Sfez refers to is not conceptual but in intuitive communion; the epistemic core is, by definition, the information and its value determined by the communication actors and/or the historical-social context. The two poles (the epistemic core and the symbolic form) will be described in our communication and communion (*comunicare* and *cuminecare*) paper.

First of all, the distinction between *comunicare* and *cuminecare* is philosophical. It was first reported in Noica (1987). The philosophical charge opened by Noica, loaded with a rich sociological signification, can be interpreted as being related to Tönnies' theory referring to community and society. Eternal community represents the living and fertile spirit of man, born of nature:

> Without moving, passing, born and dying, flickering and extinguishing, making, transformation, fulfilment, you cannot understand the term nature (in Romanian fire)" (Noica, 1987, p. 35).

Naturally, man is in communion (cuminecă). In community man is in communion, because "the communion is in the bosom of something towards something". Community is based on an agreement, on traditions and beliefs; it is spiritually evolving within and through (*întru*) trust, habits and religion – the metaphysical inheritance of community. Community is communion, the place of (nuances of) meanings and gaining. Society is, in fact, the epistemic core. The societal structure is "a mechanical one, a conglomerate, a type of agglutination. People don't live together, they coexist independently of each other" (Dobrescu, 2007, p. 47). Communication is the control and the operability function within society. Society is communication, the place of understanding and receiving, while we are in progress "through an increase of communication, but we won't really progress if we don't gain an increase of communion" (Noica, 1987, p. 188).

Society builds networks and fluxes of formal communication, key-positions as gate-keepers in organizational communication, and rules of efficiency, but it is not able to find the "seed" of informal communication. (Moreover, it is not able to find rules to subordinate and to rationally direct it for the organization's purposes, even to abolish it.) The communication increase can be recorded and can be analysed in terms of discursive production, adequate to the purposes, but this increase does not lead to relational increase.

People are in communion through a shared passion for sense (*rost*, in Romanian) – in Noica's terms, the sense is seen as a way of preparing the life (Noica, [1980] 2009, p.24) – basically, the sense that unites them. Communion could only be in sense, within the Natural. When approaching each other, men communicate the need (*dorul*, in Romanian) for communion. It is an unspoken faculty of our will, whose substance is felt in the mystic universe as spoken by Eros, Philia and Agápe. What is

Natural, in the spirit of traditions, beliefs, customs and religion, is maimed by too much communication. Our desire to communicate deviates us from communion towards spirit, and hedonistically engages us in a space overflowed by communication, incapable to communicate. In such a space, corroded by technology and oriented to purposes, society communicates without communion. The dichotomy between communication and communion is not fertile in every culture or language. In the absence of an adequate language support, by only observing the communicational fulfillment, Sfez formulates, apparently as a paradox, the deviation from communion:

> Only in a society that does not know how to communicate, whose values fall apart, and which cannot be unified by worn-out symbols, do people talk with so much pathos about communication. A centrifugal society, without any adjustment. (Sfez, 2002b, p. 16)

Unfortunately, man forgets that satiety is one form of the misery. We don't find rest by just communicating. Everything is already said. In love, culture and life, we are in communion because we are at rest.[1]

Other Dichotomous Pairs: Exceeding the Logics of Disjunction through Communication

The Occident, reasoning against the natural and not in its spirit, interestingly contributes to the appearance of a false lead in the teleological oriented linear construct. This perspective, when associated to monochronic peoples, which implies planning, programming, fragmentation, selection, priorities and purposes, is the base of the utilitarian social structure (society), which alienates:

> In the Occident, we are alienated, apart from nature. We are victims of a certain number of false ideas: for example, we think that life has a sense, so we are not predisposed. We wallow in this belief despite the multiple proof to the contrary. We lead our fragmented, compartmentalized lives. We have learned to think in a linear manner and not in a synthetic one, not unscientifically or due to the lack of intelligence or capacities, but because profound cultural currents structure our lives through complex ways,

---

[1] In Romanian, the term "rest" means both *rest* and *change*. "Rest" is a term with a special semantic load, suggested to Noica, unwilled, by his son. His boy thought that when you don't have enough money, the store would give you the change, in order to cover the bill. So is it in culture, but you have to come with your own *money*, the Romanian philosopher tells us.

> whose ensemble forms an organized system which is not consciously formulated. (Hall, [1976] 1979, p. 17).

This monochronic organization limits the perception of events, maintains it within the limits of an imagined causality, alienates and creates distances between individuals within the same social group and makes impossible the perception of the context. This form of organization, in which connections are artificially built and not naturally maintained, fuelled by communications (communicating reasons), allowed the artificial suspension of the individual in the significations network devised by himself (Geertz, 1973, p. 5).

The construct of the society as a triumph of reason does not prevent the crossing of the linearity, but the formulations are poor in "natural content" and in cultural signification. For example when Habermas reevaluates the autonomous subject (taken from the social connections' frame), he observes that he cannot build in the limits of subjectivity and tries a restoration of the authority of reason in a space of inter-subjectivity (but not of the "inter-subjectivity" in Fichtean terms, reduced to mutual objective relationships, or in Hegelian terms, contributing to the beginning and development of the modern culture through science, releasing the subject). For of this reason, Habermas suggests the replacing of the individual "I" with the "I" built on the structure of the community, also realizes a repositioning of the notion of reason and contributes to the replacement of rationality in the limits of universal-individual mediation through an "inter-subjective" form of the social subject expression: "Within a communicational community, that works in cooperation constraint" (Habermas, 2000a, p. 71).

This community is not a utilitarian structure and communication is not oriented to achieve its goals. Moreover, in such a communicating structure, the social subject does not only refer to Mead's dichotomy between I and Me, that is between the answer of the organism to the attitude of others and the organized set of attitudes assumed by someone (Mead, 1934, p. 175). Habermas broadens the analysis and proposes the terms of theoretical or cognitive conscience (Met) and practical conscience (Mep), while Mead's "I" cannot be translated as "Ich" or "Ego", but by native conscience, by the socialized I. The re-interpretation of the social interaction theory represents the premise of Mead's assignments, according to Habermas, of the "rudiments" of a theory of communication according to which the linguistic communication is possible only from the perspective of the social integration of the actors oriented to achieve this goal. In Habermas' terms, Mead's communication theory does not only imply intelligibility, does not review only the semantic and syntactic fields, but also the pragmatic one, studying the communicative action. The distinction made by Habermas at the level of the social "I" is continued by the sketching of a frame of social reasonable understanding through the perspective of communicative action theory. We find in the German philosopher another suggestive dichotomy regarding our field of interest: actions oriented towards success vs actions oriented towards understanding. The first, the instrumental actions, aim to achieve the goals, based on the same capacity type of transforming the intentions into action: the rational will, like in Tönnies' society. The others, when analyzed using dialogical logics and reported to the predominant context of communication (being the cultural context), action oriented towards understanding or communicative actions as named by Habermas, imply the consensus, understanding, and natural, based on the same type of will: essential will, like in the case of community. In the same vision, to identify the "increase of communion" as Noica says, the German philosopher does not associate the action oriented towards success with the reconstructed rationality. The communicative actions (a poor formulation considering the Romanian communion), associated with the actualization of cultural and group values, the strengthening of the sense of belonging, the social integration and the delineation of individuality, are seen as being rational: a ration of communion increase in order to support and fulfill the communication increase.

In addition to the classical dichotomy between society and community, duplicated within the Romanian spiritual space by the distinction between communication and communion, we can identify another conceptual pair reducible to rational will vs natural will: civilization vs culture. The two terms, built in the light of disjunctive logic, are perceived differently in different cultural spaces, even in the heart of Western Europe (in German, *Kultur* has a wider semantic field, in French *civilisation* covers a larger area) and are easy to differentiate from each other by relating to own goods or products: if, in the first case, the products, of an organic community/culture are symbolic goods, in the other case, a society/the civilization can produce goods. Tönnies also marked the distinction and identified the areas of reference as such: "There exists a *Gemeinschaft* of language, of folkways or mores, or of beliefs; but, by way of contrast, *Gesellschaft* exists in the realm of business, travel or sciences" (2002, p. 34).

Fortunately, the last derived pairs exceed the disjunctive logic, building the foundation of an indivisible whole, in which each part presumes the other. Let's try, for analytical purposes, to represent the studied pairs:

$$\frac{\text{Essential will (\textit{Wessenswille})}}{\text{Rational will (\textit{Küwille})}} = \frac{\text{Community (\textit{Gemeinschaft})}}{\text{Society (\textit{Gesselschaft})}} = \frac{\text{Culture}}{\text{Civilization}} = \frac{\text{Actions oriented towards understanding}}{\text{Actions oriented towards success}} = \frac{\text{Communion}}{\text{Communication}}$$

The relation presented above, being under disjunctive pressure in Western space, is essentially built over antagonisms and exclusions and can be read in two different registers. The first register undoubtedly is the one of separation from the analysed terms. This perspective leads to two parallel discourses: one about efficiency/success and the other about inwardness. Both discourses are auto-reflexive; they understand the communication as a whole and either establish recipes for efficiency, or confront their own limits of production, about the logic that governs them – the logic of goods, of merchandise. Both discourses can be registered in the corpus of "political economy of sign".

Let's see if and how this communication remains a model or restructures the antagonisms, not only in the Romanian space, liable to completion and shaping, but even in the interior of monochronic spaces, eroding the very reason of the causal reasoning chains. Fortunately, the contrastive forms of communication assigned to communication and communion by Noica could also be found in the American cultural space. John Dewey, the father of the Chicago School, distinguished (by overlapping the dichotomy between society and community) the communicational perspective between communication as transmission and communication as ritual. The prefiguration of the ritual communication was also doubled by the prefiguration of the distinction between representative and expressive communication in Sfez' vision: "Society not only continues to exist by transmission, by communication, but it may fairly be said to exist in transmission, in communication" (Dewey, 2001, p.8).

The transmission view of communication, that could be defined by terms like "sending", "transmitting", "giving information to others", doubled by the possibilities of hoarding according to Cooley's vision (1909, pp. 68–69), contrasts with the ritual view of communication, that could be defined in the following terms: "sharing", "participation", "association", "fellowship", James Carey "the possession of a common faith". Carey identifies in this ritual perspective the common structure of values, which is atypical for American scholarship,[2] but still actual and enhanced:

[2] "The ritual view of communication has not been a dominant motif in American scholarship. Our thought and work have been glued to a transmission view of communication because this view is congenial with the underlying wellsprings of American culture, sources that feed into our scientific life as well as our common,

> This definition exploits the ancient identity and common roots of the terms "commonness," "communion," "community," and "communication." A ritual view of communication is not directed toward the extension of messages in space but toward the maintenance of society in time; not the act of imparting information but the representation of shared beliefs. (Carey, [1989], 2009, p. 18).

By defining this dichotomy, it becomes simple to understand why, by exposing the meaning without rest, the sense loses itself and society substitutes other different meanings for the revealed world through the projections of ideals created by the community. American communication as a ritual, impoverished and removed from the academic sphere, resonates with the Romanian "communion".

About the Limits of Active Communication or a Way to Return to Community

When everything flows as a whole, without rest, laws of the social group superiorly regulate the circulation. These laws ensure the transparency of fluxes (in pictures, the transparency of contents), without having to sustain the relations, as someone could commute anytime, anywhere, on every resonant fluctuation, on every reverberation with sense (apparently), on every explanation that is searched in the visible, transparent network, of a society emptied of any relations and saturated with fluxes. A real relation continues virtually, man being a simple "terminal of multiple networks" (Baudrillard, [1987], p. 12).

In such a space, over-saturated with senseless communication, being loses its identity, because the communication is being and being happens in communication. Norbert Wiener (in 1957) said that the law within things can be seen as of communication, confirming the first axiom of the school of Palo Alto: "One cannot not communicate" (Watzlavick et al., 1967, pp.48-49), and on the other hand, being together is *logos*, we cannot let the happening or the being to be in the organized horizon of communication fluxes without rest/sense (*rest/rost*). This would represent a tautological loss of our being in the web of technology. The return to language is necessary but impossible to understand when the language, like blood vessels, does not ensure the internal flux of its own being in the spirit of interior communication, but it requires transfusion through a set of

---

public understandings. There is an irony in this. We have not explored the ritual view of communication because the concept of culture is such a weak and evanescent notion in American social thought." (Carey, [1989] 2009, p. 15)

transparent canals. “The language is the house of Being”, Heidegger tells us. Unity in communication is the mystical confession of Being. People bound to each other through words are in communion and become one.

> Each dialogue, each meeting is being:
> Let me remind you of a thought of the ancient philosopher who asked: when you gather together,
> Which one gathers with the other?
> Which one becomes two?
> . . . But when a friend meets a friend
> . . . Who will gather with whom, which friend will become two? (Noica, 2007, p. 146)

Within the limits of active communication, identity is lost. From the perspective of community, Bauman (2001, p. 11) warned,

> The identity evaporates from the moment its condition starts to disintegrate, meaning when the balance between the communication from “the inside” and the one from “the outside”, once inclined strictly inwards, becomes more balanced, blurring the distinction between “us” and “them”. The identity evaporates from the moment the communication between the insiders and the outsider become more intense and has more weight than the reciprocal changes between the insiders.

However, Young (2001, p. 13) observed the paradox that “when community collapses, it invents identity”. This is the paradox that marks the reports of society and community today: as society erodes community more intensely, so does the community strengthen. The identity of communities becomes, in this profound way, one of culture living with the civilization, of cohabitation of organizing around the fundament of report between Gemeinschaft-Gesellschaft, engine of organization in the existential plan.

CHALLENGES OF IDENTITY: THE ROMANIAN CASE

Identity – a real or projected characteristic of persons (or objects, phenomena, events, statements), substituting for each other, a manner of self-definition in relation to others, or self-identification in relation to absolute self-consciousness – varies depending on the size of reference group and predominant dimension: biological, psychological, or socio-cultural. But we think that identity varies depending on the type of reference social group – community or society – and thus, depends on the dominant type of communication: with or without rest. Therefore, not only the biological and psychological dimensions are problematic in our approach, but the socio-cultural one, as it is not important to analyse socio-cultural identity markers: language, nationality, religion, a certain social class, some communicational patterns, different habits, and norms governing daily life. Rather, the awareness of reporting to others is important, especially the type of causal relationship with other and the dominant type of will. In terms of multiple relationships (usually, in terms of additivity, and not in terms of interconnection), the identity of the individual does not imply a clear boundary or location in a framework separated from the others, or reference to a single group, but a series of successive and relative stages between individual identity and the anthropological identity of the species (Georgiu, 1997, p. 77). In a similar manner, we can identify from an identity perspective a set of concentric closings: from the planetary level (the identity of species) to the individual level (the identity of the ego, that constitutes the core for the proximity of the birthplace, of the region, of the country). At a conference held Leigh University, Pennsylvania, in 1991 Vaclav Havel asserted that:

> I believe that every circle, every aspect of the house must be given what it deserves. It is senseless to deny or, worse, to exclude one aspect for another; neither should it be regarded as less important or inferior. They are part of our natural world and a correctly organized organic society must respect all and give them the chance of fulfilment. (Brumaru, 2001, pp. 194–195)

Let's consider, for the purposes of this presentation, the paradoxical structure of formulations concerning successive dichotomous pairs. We could first of all ascertain the paradox of uncommunicative communication provided by Sfez (2002a, 2002b), secondly the paradox of the vacuous, defaced, insoluble, arbitrary, fortuitous sign (Baudrillard, 1997), and thirdly the paradox of vulgarizing culture and communication (Ramonet, 2000). Moreover, we could encounter a paradoxical rationality allocation to action oriented towards reaching understanding (communicative actions) (Habermas, [1980] 2000b), that aligns with Rorty's opinion regarding philosophy's role as "guardian of rationality". Last but not least, we could report a paradoxical relationship between identity and communication (Young, 1999; Bauman, 2001). Without the rest in communication, the "complete" assertion needs to slide on the other side of Möbius strip, not realizing that this side is not a different one. Communicating "with rest", the paradox enter the logics of normality, of nature. Community and society can coexist, can feed and promote each other. Nature can "flood" the rational realm, making sense and fertilizing it. Culture is built with civilizations' values, assimilated in the innovative effort, but still fights for its identity. Actions oriented towards success are supported by those oriented towards understanding, and not vice versa, through the insertion of validity claims. Not only must the "interaction leads by norms" prevail, but also the game of perspectives, understood in relations to "decentralizing of understanding the world" (Habermas, [1980] 2000b, p.128), could be exploited, while decentralizing is based not on complex and additive structures.[3] Communication without rest is, in fact, communication with rest – but with an abandoned rest. For understanding and utilizing these conceptual pairs over the limits of the paradoxical expressions, sometimes insufficient in the monochronic fragmentation (made by fragments causally brought together), the openness towards paradoxical logics is necessary. This openness is a characteristic of the Romanians, Blaga ([1936] 1985, p. 260) assures us: "Our people assimilate the precepts in a more organic way, and somehow less aware". Consequently, how could Europe be seen without strangling the national identity?

Two fundamental works, which were published almost simultaneously, realize the challenges of the European identity: Edgar Morin's *Penser l'Europe* (1990) and Constantin Noica's *Modelul cultural European* (1993), both emphasize the principle of multiple unity, hence identity. The first of these work came from the core of Western Europe, carrying the values of this space, and speaks of a Judeo-Christian-Greek-Latin European culture. The second work, born in the polychronic reflux of the

---

[3] In this respect, Habermas finds useful a stopover on the structure of the actions oriented towards understanding (focusing on the differentiation between this type of action and actions oriented towards success) in order to understand the mechanisms of action coordination, to emphasize the relationships between action and linguistic act, to identify the background of *Lebenswelt*, the process of reciprocal understanding of world and *Lebenswelt*, to establish the validity claims and the world perspective for defining the decentralizing of understanding the world through the game of perspectives. Convinced that the ontogenesis of the speaker and of world perspectives leads to decentralized understanding, the German philosopher tries to complete the world system of perspectives. The approach is not easy, and concerns the consideration of some divergent directions, such as speaker, participant and observer perspectives. According to the forms of reciprocity, to the orientation towards action (cooperation, conflict, etc.), to the form of reciprocity (authority-based complementarity, interest-based symmetry) and not to the action systems, Habermas distinguishes four pre-conventional types of action Depending on the type of action and on the social-cognitive structure of interaction, they underlie a more complex definition of the issue, ensuring the translation from the pre-conventional behaviour to the strategic action and then the translation to the conventional stage of the interaction.

Romanian space, speaks about the Byzantine foundations of Europe. It expresses the rational paradox within the natural, communicating with rest about the birth date and birthplace of Europe:

> Everything began in 325, at the Council of Nicaea, convened by the king and continued with other six meetings [of bishops] till 787. . . . In 325, in a decisive manner, a new culture started. . . . Against any Gnosticism, unable to understand how three [persons, hypostases of the Trinity: Father, Son and Holy Spirit] could be one [one single substance, one single being, God's being], it was decreed that three are actually one. (Noica, 1993, pp. 69–71)

The other work, born outside the area where naturally 3=1, strives by appealing to the dialogic approach – different logics complexly (complementary, competing and antagonistic, as Morin noted) connected in a unit – to design the multiple:

> The difficulty of conceiving Europe is, primarily, the difficulty of thinking the one in multiple, the multiple in one: *unitas multiplex.* It is, at the same time, the difficulty of conceiving the identity in non-identity. Thus, to conceive how European unity lies in dissension and heterogeneity, we must appeal to two principles of intelligibility, able to clarify the complex phenomena of this order: the dialogic principle and the recursion principle. (Morin, [1990] 2002, p. 28)

In the natural order, a multiple Europe could be perceived through communion (*cuminecare*). Through and within communion, one and multiple are mutually implied. Despite the fact that through communion, communication and identity are not excluded, but enriched, in the spirit of communication, one and multiple are mutually exclusive.

Conclusions

Space of paradoxes naturally interpreted, Romanian culture coagulates around community values and through communication with rest. The identity (required where the dialogic principle is difficult to conceive) is not a mark of inclusion. In essence, inclusion is not additive, but embedding. If inclusion is rather a result of practice than a result of reflection on the other, a profound sense of inward orientation could be discovered. But, the apparent inward orientation is due to the indissoluble relationship with space, not with time. In this respect, the Romanian being discovers a framework of successive closures in order to strengthen the value systems, understood as "closures towards opening" (Noica). This process implies being's enrichment, defined through the agency of the all-comprehensive adverb "home". In fact, communion (*cuminecare*) means both opening of being towards being and closure of beings in the Cultural Being (being "in the bosom of something towards something"). Noted that Cultural Being is multiple, nonlinear, natural and organic.

We identified three attempts to reconfigure the contemporary community: first, essentially European, through unitas multiplex; second, from American cultural space, through cultural creativity, aiming to return to community as a solution to social problems (a transcultural new community built by blending cultures and values); and third, as a result of the current crisis seen as a result of failure of a social form of organization (now that the seed of a "new" state capitalism is sprouting), implying the reconfiguration of community within the limits of society and the natural extension of community while the bankruptcy of organization in the spirit of rational will. Each of these three attempts is, in fact, a projection, a germinating seed. First of these, the seed of European multiple unities, sprouts in the fallow soil of southeastern Europe, and dries under the sun of Western rationality. Maybe the rest from the communicational circuit could irrigate and lead to the harvest of a mature plant, with fruit raised from the seed of a Byzantine idea.

References

Baudrillard, J [1987] (1997). Celălalt prin sine însuşi, Cluj-Napoca: Casa Cărţii de Ştiinţă.

Bauman, Z (2001). Comunitatea. Căutarea siguranţei într-o lume nesigură, Bucharest: Antet.

Blaga, L (1936) [1985]. "Spaţiul mioritic. În L. Blaga, *Opere 9", Trilogia culturii.* Bucharest: Minerva.

Brumaru, A I (2001). Despre fiinţa românească. Bucharest: Viitorul românesc.

Carey, J W [1989] (2009). *Communication as culture*, revised edition. New foreword by G Stuart Adam. New York: Routledge.

Cooley, C H [1909] (1963). *Social Organization: A Study of the Larger Mind,* New York: Charles Scribner's Sons.

Dewey, John. (2001). *Democracy and Education* [electronic series], Hazleton, PA: Pennsylvania State University.

Dobrescu, P (2007). Gabriel Tarde şi Ferdinand Tönnies: epoca mulţimilor devine epoca publicurilor. In P Dobrescu, A Bârgăoanu & N Corbu, Istoria comunicării. Bucharest: comunicare.ro.

Geertz, C (1973). *The Interpretation of Cultures,* New York: Basic Books.

Georgiu, G (1997). Naţiune, cultură, identitate, Bucureşti: Diogene.

Habermas, J [1980] (2000a). Discursul filosofic al modernităţii. 12 prelegeri. Bucureşti: AllEducaţional.

—. [1980] (2000b). Conştiinţă morală şi acţiune comunicativă, Bucureşti: AllEducaţional.

—. (1997). *The Theory of Communicative Action,* Vols 1 & 2. Cambridge: Polity Press.

Hall, E T [1976] (1979). *Au-delà de la culture,* Paris: Éditions du Seuil.

Lesenciuc, A, Nagy, D Susan, A M & Cincan, M (2009). *The identity of communities, as a foundation of the European construct*, Paper presented at The 6th International Conference: New Challenges in the Field of Military Sciences. Budapest: Zrínyi Miklós National Defence University.

Mead, G H (1934). *Mind, Self, and Society from the Standpoint of a Social Behaviorist.* Chicago: University of Chicago Press.

Morin, E [1990] (2002). *Gândind Europa,* Bucharest: Trei Publishing House.

Noica, C [1980] (2009). Povestiri despre om: după o carte a lui Hegel, Bucharest: Humanitas.

—. (1987). Cuvânt împreună despre rostirea românească, Bucharest: Editura Eminescu.

—. (1993). *Modelul cultural European,* Bucharest: Humanitas.

—. (2007). *Jurnal de idei*, Bucharest: Humanitas.

Ramonet, I (2000). Tirania comunicării, Bucharest: Doina.

Sfez, L (2002a). O critică a comunicării, Bucharest: comunicare.ro.

—. (2002b). *Comunicarea,* Iaşi: Institutul European.

Shepherd, G J (2001). Community as the interpersonal accomplishment of communication. In Gregory J Shepherd & Eric W Rothenbuhler (eds). *Communication and Community*. Mahwah, NJ: Lawrence Erlbaum Associates.

Tönnies, F (2002). *Community and Society,* Mineola, NY: Dover Publications.

Watzlawick, P, Beavin Bavelas, J & Jackson, D D (1967). *Pragmatics of Human Communication: A Study of Interactional Patterns, Pathologies, and Paradoxes,* New York: Norton.

Young, J (1999). *The Exclusive Society,* London: Sage.

COMMUNICATION INTERCULTURELLE PROVOQUEE: ENTRE IDENTITE ET RECADRAGE PRESENTIEL

CHRISTIAN AGBOBLI AND OUMAR KANE

Résumé

Depuis que la communication interculturelle a acquis une dignité scientifique à travers les écrits d'Edward T. Hall, les spécialistes de ce domaine n'ont eu de cesse d'essayer de la cerner, de la circonscrire et de l'analyser à travers 1) des concepts-clés tels que ceux d'identité, d'intégration, de représentations médiatiques, etc. et 2) des pratiques concrètes dans lesquelles l'interaction avec l'autre occupe une place centrale. Comme le soutiennent Halualani, Mendoza et Drzewiecka (2009), la communication interculturelle mettait traditionnellement l'accent sur une perspective fonctionnaliste et interprétative pour se situer ensuite sur le versant critique en analysant les rapports de pouvoir et de domination.

Notre contribution porte sur l'étude du cas d'une table-ronde organisée en 2010 à travers l'articulation de la théorie et de la pratique. Cette table-ronde dont le thème était la question de l'intégration et de l'usage des technologies de l'information et de la communication (TIC) s'est déroulée dans un contexte universitaire et a été marquée par la présence (sur le panel et dans le public) de personnes issues de diverses communautés culturelles. En nous inspirant de plusieurs recherches et théories en communication interculturelle, notamment aux rites d'interaction (Goffman, 1974), à la double-contrainte (Bateson, 1980) et aux dimensions cachées de la culture (Hall, 1971), nous analyserons, d'une part la rencontre culturelle générée par l'altérité et, d'autre part, le processus de recadrage culturel induit par la communication interculturelle. Les résultats de l'analyse révèlent des catégories clés qui mettent en lumière les relations entre identité et altérité dans un contexte provoqué de communication interculturelle : l'identité des acteurs en présence, le rôle de la langue, la fonction du dispositif technique, les contextes culturels et l'importance du temps.

Mots-clés : communication - identité – acteurs - langue – temps

Les relations que les individus entretiennent les uns avec les autres se déroulent par le biais de la communication. La communication est souvent présentée comme une solution aux maux dont souffre l'humanité. Cependant, il faut se garder d'analyser naïvement la communication sociale :

> « on ne parle jamais autant de communication que dans une société qui ne sait plus communiquer avec elle-même, dont la cohésion est contestée, dont les valeurs se délitent, que des symboles trop usées ne parviennent plus à unifier » (Sfez, 2001,).

L'auteur dresse néanmoins le parcours de la communication, présentée comme une forme de « tautisme » qui rend la communication problématique. La communication est une sorte d'autisme dans le sens où elle reflète un contexte fermé où elle se parle à elle-même. Pour Wolton (2005 p.13) :

> « La communication, c'est toujours la recherche de la relation et du partage avec autrui. Elle traverse toutes les activités : loisirs, travail, éducation, politique, concerne tous les milieux sociaux, les classes sociales, tous les âges, les continents, les riches comme les pauvres. »

Pourtant, il spécifie que la communication ne saurait exister sans son pendant, l'incommunication. Si la communication avec les gens de notre propre groupe culturel n'est pas toujours évidente, elle l'est encore moins lorsqu'on aborde la communication entre gens de cultures différentes.

L'objectif de la présente réflexion est d'analyser les phénomènes à l'œuvre lors d'une communication interculturelle « provoquée » ainsi que le processus de recadrage culturel qui en résulte. Cette réflexion portera sur l'étude du cas d'une table-ronde organisée en 2010 et dont le thème tournait autour de la diversité, des dispositifs techniques, de l'identité et de l'intégration. Nous commencerons par cerner le contexte de l'événement à travers une mise en contexte puis nous présenterons la méthodologie de recherche employée. La deuxième partie explicite sur les enjeux théoriques et pratiques qui sous-tendent la communication interculturelle. La troisième partie repose sur une analyse interprétative du cas et identifiera un certain nombre catégories pertinentes (acteurs, contexte, langue, ...).

Contexte: de la genèse de l'événement à la méthodologie de la recherche

Riggins (1997, p. 3) soutient que le terme « autre » comme catégorie de la pensée spéculative peut être retracé chez Platon « qui l'utilisait pour représenter la relation entre l'observateur (soi) et l'observé (l'autre) ». Lévinas (cité par Kapuscinski, 2006) considère que la rencontre avec l'autre est un « événement fondamental ». En effet, la rencontre avec l'autre demeure un mystère et un événement qui modifie « soi » et « autrui » tout en établissant un lien relationnel. Faisant une analyse de la recherche interculturelle en France, Rafoni (2003) dresse différentes caractéristiques de cette tradition de recherche. Premièrement, elle soutient que le caractère dynamique de ses objets est une constance malgré la diversité des perspectives choisies. Selon cette auteure (2003, 17-18), « Ils [les objets] procèdent d'échanges, de liens mais aussi de tensions entre des cultures distinctes, quoiqu'il s'agit moins de se pencher sur le passé que sur des relations interculturelles en train de se faire ». Ensuite, les recherches interculturelles sont un prolongement et une actualisation de l'anthropologie des contacts culturels et de la théorie de l'acculturation en privilégiant « un contact direct interpersonnel ou intergroupal de représentants de différentes cultures ». La présente réflexion s'insère dans le sillage des traditions de recherche francophone sur la communication interculturelle en y développant une perspective interprétative, compréhensive et critique. Avant d'aborder notre angle méthodologique, précisons le contexte de l'événement.

La table-ronde: organisation et description

La table-ronde qui fait l'objet de la présente analyse a été organisée en 2010 et portait sur l'utilisation d'un dispositif technique par des immigrants et les enjeux de leur insertion dans la société québécoise[1]. Cette table-ronde a connu la participation de différents acteurs : les panélistes (au nombre de cinq dont une qui était à Cuba et intervenait à travers le dispositif technique), l'animateur, le public présent sur place et

[1] Nous ne pouvons donner plus de détails sur la nature et les objets de la table-ronde en raison de notre engagement à respecter la confidentialité des participants et des organisateurs.

le public de blogueurs présent par le biais de la communication technologique. La rencontre, qui a débuté à17 heures, était prévue pour durer deux heures et devait se terminer par un cocktail. Le temps de parole prévu pour les panélistes était de sept minutes chacun et des échanges avec le public étaient prévus à la fin de chaque intervention. L'événement devait être trilingue : français, anglais et espagnol. La particularité de cette table-ronde était qu'elle était accessible par Internet.

Cette rencontre a été rendue possible par des contacts établis entre les organisateurs d'une activité destinée à l'art et à la culture au Québec et les auteurs de cet article. Ces organisateurs ont accepté que la table-ronde soit utilisée comme objet de recherche sous condition d'une garantie d'anonymat. Par le biais d'échanges réguliers, le déroulement de la table-ronde a été établi d'un commun accord. Les principales balises étaient d'une part le respect des règles universitaires ou de l'idée que s'en faisaient les auteurs du présent article, et d'autre part un certain degré de liberté pour les organisateurs, notamment la possibilité de remercier certains de leurs partenaires. D'ailleurs, il était convenu qu'un de leurs partenaires, conseiller en immigration, puisse intervenir pendant deux minutes.

Dans les faits, la rencontre ne s'est pas exactement déroulée comme planifiée. D'abord, la logique temporelle fut modifiée : les panélistes ont parlé plus longtemps que prévu, les échanges ont été plus longs et la table-ronde dans son ensemble a duré plus de trois heures de temps. Le discours de tous les panélistes n'a pas été traduit. La table-ronde a fait apparaître deux animateurs plutôt que celui nommément désigné selon l'accord initialement conclu. De plus, des moments de tension ont pu être décelés.

Le décalage entre la planification de la table-ronde et le résultat final, le constat de la place prise par l'identité d'origine, les échanges avec plusieurs des participants (panélistes et membres du public) ont suscité en nous des interrogations qui se sont muées en motivations de recherche.

ORIENTATIONS MÉTHODOLOGIQUES

Selon Gohard-Radenkovic (2010, p.59),

> « les anthropologues et sociologues s'intéressent désormais à l'identification des stratégies et logiques des individus en interrelation avec les enjeux et logiques des institutions et de leurs discours, dans ces expériences de cohabitation et de mobilité, qui sont d'abord et avant tout, une expérience de l'altérité dans la diversité ».

Pour les communicologues, l'interculturel est avant tout un enjeu d'interactions et d'échanges qui nécessite l'étude des conditions qui rendent la communication possible dans un contexte particulier. C'est le sens de l'affirmation de Rafoni (2003, p. 20) :

> « Les recherches sur la communication interculturelle doivent s'aligner sur celles des sciences de l'information et de la communication, soit s'intéresser aux médias, à la littérature ou plus généralement à l'art, non pas seulement en tant qu'objet esthétique, mais en tant que phénomène socioculturel et objet communiquant. Mais elles doivent aussi s'interroger sur la quotidienneté, dans des situations de communications non verbales, sources de hiatus entre les cultures ».

Notre démarche méthodologique, de type qualitatif, s'inspire de l'ethnométhodologie telle que développée par Garfinkel (1967). Considérée comme une rupture avec la recherche sociologique traditionnelle, l'ethnométhodologie est

> « la recherche empirique des méthodes que les individus utilisent pour donner sens et en même temps accomplir leurs actions de tous les jours : communiquer, prendre des décisions, raisonner (Coulon, 1987, p. 23–24) ».

L'ethnométhodologie est donc une étude des activités quotidiennes, elle analyse les activités de sens commun par opposition à la pensée savante. De plus,

> « l'observation attentive et l'analyse des processus mis en œuvre dans les actions permettraient de mettre au jour les procédures par lesquels les acteurs interprètent constamment la réalité sociale, inventent la vie dans un bricolage permanent (Coulon, 2003, p. 25–26) ».

Pour rendre compte et interpréter cette réalité construite par les acteurs, l'ethnométhodologie a recours à quelques concepts clés : « la pratique » qui reflète les activités banales de la vie quotidienne, « l'indexicalité » qui désigne l'incomplétude des mots qui ne prennent sens que dans leur contexte d'occurrence, l'« accountability », c'est-à-dire les descriptions ou comptes-rendus des activités pratiques. Le « membership » réfère à la maîtrise du langage naturel qui donne un sens au monde qui l'entoure.

Tout comme l'ethnométhodologie, nous nous inspirons de la phénoménologie sociale de Schutz (1987), notamment lorsqu'il aborde le caractère construit des cultures et les aptitudes interprétatives de l'étranger lorsqu'il arrive dans un nouveau pays. L'interactionnisme symbolique constitue un de nos référents théoriques, notamment à travers l'importance des aspects symboliques dans les interactions humaines formelles ou informelles.

Pour rendre compte à la fois de l'altérité et de l'identité, une situation de communication interculturelle provoquée nous a semblé être un bon terrain de recherche. Dans ce sens, l'étude de cas est la méthode de recherche idoine. Pour Gagnon (2005) reprenant Woodside et Wilson,

> « l'étude de cas comme méthode est appropriée pour la description, l'explication, la prédiction et le contrôle de processus inhérents à divers phénomènes, que ces derniers soient individuels, de groupe ou d'une organisation » (p. 2).

Certes, il ne s'agit pas d'une recherche dans le sens classique du terme puisque le design de la recherche s'est fait après la table-ronde. Une fois l'activité terminée, les échanges avec les participants et une analyse post-événementielle nous ont amenés à construire un canevas de recherche *a posteriori* afin d'analyser les événements qui se sont déroulés pendant la table-ronde. Nos techniques de cueillette de données reposent principalement sur l'observation participante, c'est-à-dire que nous avons joué un rôle dans la situation observée et avons participé directement aux événements. Cette technique nous a permis d'être considérés comme des participants comme les autres et a su prévenir le développement d'un biais quelconque de la part des autres participants. Parallèlement à l'observation, nous avons utilisé la documentation disponible : sites web, communiqués, courriels et photos.

Enjeux théoriques et pratiques de la communication interculturelle

L'interculturalité, bien qu'étant née dans les études anthropologiques a su rapidement s'émanciper de son carcan disciplinaire pour s'interdisciplinariser. En effet, plusieurs disciplines telles que l'anthropologie, la sociologie, les sciences de l'éducation, la communication, l'histoire traitent de la recherche interculturelle (Stoiciu et Hsab, 2011 ; Gohard-Radenkovic, 2010).

Avec cette tradition de recherche sont développés plusieurs concepts-clés dont le binôme identité-altérité. La notion d'identité est fortement reliée à celle de culture. Les premières conceptions de la culture démontraient une quasi-osmose entre l'identité et la culture. Edward Tylor (cité par Cuche, 1997, p. 24) par exemple définissait la culture comme « l'ensemble des habitudes acquises par l'homme en société» alors qu'Alfred Kroeber (cité par Cuche, 1997, p. 22) définit la culture comme

une sorte de « super-organisme », indépendant des personnes et des rapports sociaux qui les unissent ou les opposent, sorte de réalité supérieure qui détermine la conduite des individus (repris par Cuche, 1997). A partir de la rupture radicale effectuée par Malinowski qui s'est rapproché des peuples qu'il observait et analysait, on a commencé à concevoir la culture comme une construction sociale. Ainsi, l'identité n'était plus perçue comme figée mais comme étant évolutive. Néanmoins, la construction de la relation à l'autre et sa nature restent complexes.
L'autre a souvent été nié ou encensé mais rarement reconnu comme semblable à soi. Or l'autre est un élément constitutif de notre identité. C'est ce qui fait que l'identité suppose l'altérité.

Jacques Demorgon et Marie-Nelly Carpentier (2010) ambitionnent de poser les jalons de la recherche interculturelle fondamentale. Posant les obstacles liés à la recherche interculturelle fondamentale, ils relèvent les confusions générées par la culture contemporaine, l'absence d'unanimité autour du terme « interculturel », l'absence de discipline clairement consacrée à l'ensemble des questions interculturelles et la multiplicité des acteurs. Pour ces auteurs, la recherche interculturelle devrait se pencher sur l'intérité qui est une dimension inséparable de la diversité des personnes, des groupes et des sociétés.

> « L'intérité, comme notion générale, se réfère à la temporalité entière : elle est après, mais elle est aussi pendant et avant. Au plan biopsychologique, l'intérité n'est pas seulement interaction post individuelle, elle précède notre individuation à travers la lignée des ancêtres. Elle est peut-être ce à quoi nous aurons toujours du mal à nous référer, une sorte de « fond de la vie » selon le mot de Kimura. Au plan psychosocial, l'intérité est constituée par l'ensemble des stratégies et des cultures humaines en interférence. Notre identité, individuelle et collective, s'oriente de façon constructive en s'y référant et de façon destructive en la déniant. L'intérité stratégique du monde vivant est créatrice de la biosphère dans laquelle l'humain apparaît avec une liberté de se programmer de façon changeante (Carpentier & Demorgon, 2010, pp. 34–35) ».

Afin d'étudier l'intérité cachée de l'humanité, Carpentier et Demorgon proposent d'analyser quatre grands visages de l'humain : le processuel, le problématique, le sectoriel et le sociétal. L'humain processuel nous intrigue particulièrement dans notre réflexion en raison de ses liens avec la communication. En effet, il correspond à l'analyse des processus utilisés dans la rencontre de l'humain avec lui-même. Cette intérité repose sur les transformations effectuées par le biais d'échanges pacifiques ou non.

Le cœur de la communication interculturelle se retrouve dans des interrogations théoriques et des pratiques qui mettent l'accent sur les interactions comme constitutives du processus de communication entre porteurs de cultures différentes. Etymologiquement, le mot « communication » vient du latin comunicare qui signifie mettre en commun, être en relation. Ce mot a eu différentes définitions qui gravitent autour de deux pôles : l'échange et la transmission. Ces deux caractéristiques reflètent deux tendances importantes. Dans le premier cas, celui de l'échange, la communication est étroitement associée à la démocratie, à la volonté de partager, de maintenir la société cohérente entre ses différents membres. On y décèle une vision optimiste de la communication. Myron W. Lustig et Jolene Koester (1996, p. 29) ont défini la communication comme « a symbolic process in which people create shared meanings ». Dans le deuxième cas, celui de la transmission, la communication est davantage reliée au contrôle, à la volonté d'induire un changement, à la propagande. Ces deux visions de la communication ont été bien imagées par Yves Winkin (1981, p. 26), lorsqu'il fait la distinction entre le modèle orchestral de la communication et le modèle télégraphique :

> « le modèle orchestrale revient en fait à voir dans la communication le phénomène social que le tout premier sens du mot rendait très bien, tant en français qu'en anglais : la mise en commun, la participation, la communion. »

La communication interculturelle en tant que sous-champ de la communication vit les mêmes tensions que sa discipline-mère. Toutefois, elle a ses propres particularités. En effet, la communication interculturelle réfère à la communication entre individus provenant de cultures différentes. Pour Samovar and Porter (1991, p. 10), la communication interculturelle a lieu lorsqu'un message est produit par un membre d'une culture afin d'être consommé par un membre d'une autre culture. Quant à Spitzberg, il définit la communication interculturelle comme :

> «an impression that message behavior is appropriate and effective in a given context.» (Spitzberg, 1994, p. 354).

Cette définition, très large, vise principalement la mise en place de critères d'évaluation : «appropriateness» (respect des normes, règles et valeurs) et «effectiveness» (atteinte des buts ou objectifs communicationnels). Pour Gudykunst et Kim, la communication interculturelle «is a transactional, symbolic process involving the attribution of meaning between people from different cultures.» (1992, pp. 13–14). Au-delà des différentes définitions de la communication interculturelle qui renvoient soit à des perspectives plutôt généralistes sur la rencontre de culture, soit à son caractère orchestral ou télégraphique, la communication interculturelle reflète une volonté affichée de succès : comment rendre cette communication interculturelle possible ?

Edward T. Hall, l'un des principaux théoriciens de la communication interculturelle, a développé une réflexion où il articule communication et culture. La culture est vue comme un « système de communication » (Winkin, 1981, p. 88). Afin de bien cerner la communication entre gens de cultures différentes, Hall propose de définir les caractéristiques de la culture. Il identifiera entre autre les cultures polychroniques et monochroniques et précisera différents rapports au temps et à l'espace. Si les réflexions de Hall sur la communication interculturelle relèvent de l'interpersonnel, il les introduit aussi dans une logique de communication organisationnelle notamment dans les relations entre gens d'affaires allemands, américains, français ou japonais.

D'autres auteurs mettent l'accent sur la communication entre les groupes. Ainsi, Gudykunst Ting-Toomey, Hall et Schmidt (1989) qui s'inspirent de la psychologie sociale analysent la communication interculturelle sous l'angle des rapports identitaires, des groupes et de la langue. Ils affirment que

> «language is a critical aspect of the study of intergroup communication in general and intercultural communication in particular» (Gudykunst, Ting-Toomey, Hall & Schmidt, 1989, p. 157).

Mais ils constatent aussi que les recherches ayant été menées sur les incidences du langage sur les facteurs psychosociaux (identité ethnolinguistique, stéréotypes, etc.) et sociologiques (vie groupale, normes de langage, etc.) ont été trop peu intégrées à la recherche en communication interculturelle. Parallèlement à leur réflexion sur l'importance du langage et sa trop faible présence dans la recherche en communication, Gudykunst et al. soutiennent que la langue n'est pas un simple moyen de communication mais représente le facteur d'unification et le préréquis de survie d'une culture particulière.

L'interactionnisme symbolique bien qu'étant initialement développée en sociologie, a été largement intégré dans la recherche en communication interculturelle. En effet, le syntagme *interactionnisme symbolique*, forgé en 1938, reflète une multiplicité de points de vue développés par des auteurs tels que George Herbert Mead ou Herbert Blumer issus de l'école de Chicago. Selon Baszanger (1992), trois idées primordiales permettent de comprendre l'interactionnisme : une vision de la société comme production collective ; les ressources de l'activité humaine s'élaborent essentiellement dans des relations intersubjectives qui évoluent dans le temps ; les êtres humaines sont perçus comme réflexifs, créatifs et actifs. Les interactionnistes mettent en évidence le caractère symbolique de l'action sociale et l'importance du langage. La notion d'interaction et les processus dynamiques renvoient à une conception orchestrale de la communication interculturelle. L'importance que les auteurs de ce domaine accordent à la langue laisse apparaître celle-ci comme dimension constitutive du rapport à l'autre tout comme les dimensions cachées de la culture que sont les valeurs, le temps, l'espace.

Erving Goffman (1974) s'interroge sur les rites d'interactions (les comportements rituels, verbaux et non-verbaux) qui se manifestent en milieu social organisé. Goffman recherche le schéma d'interaction, les

> «relations syntaxiques qui unissent les actions de diverses personnes mutuellement en présence (Goffman, 1974, p. 8) ».

Pour cet auteur, nous vivons dans un monde social où existe un canevas d'actes verbaux et non-verbaux accepté, reconnu et utilisé. Il emploie la notion de « face » qui se définit comme

> «la valeur sociale positive qu'une personne revendique effectivement à travers la ligne d'action que les autres supposent qu'elle a adoptée au cours d'un contact particulier (Goffman, 1974, p. 9) ».

La communication interculturelle est fortement ancrée dans la pratique, dans le processus d'interaction entre gens de culture différentes. Si les chercheurs essaient de l'analyser en la catégorisant, en faisant ressortir des récurrences, la communication interculturelle ne se dévoile que lorsqu'elle est en train de se dérouler. La section qui suit nous permet d'articuler les pratiques de communication interculturelle telles qu'elles se sont données à notre observation et les théories qui y réfèrent.

La communication interculturelle en train de se faire

La plupart des chercheurs en communication interculturelle ont développé leur approche sur une base pragmatique en observant ou en interviewant leurs interlocuteurs. Pour Jandt (2010), la communication interculturelle renvoie aux interactions en face-à-face entre gens de cultures différentes et implique des difficultés lorsque peu de symboles sont partagés entre la source et le récepteur. Laray M. Barna (1997) a dressé une liste de six obstacles à la communication interculturelle parmi lesquels l'anxiété, les stéréotypes et les préjugés, et le langage. La rencontre qui fait l'objet de la présente réflexion reflète le caractère dynamique de la communication interculturelle en train de se faire. Si l'on fait exception de projets mûrement réfléchis tels que le management interculturel par exemple, la communication interculturelle est toujours non déterminée, dans le sens où on ne peut prédire son issue. La communication entre individus de cultures différentes dans un cadre déterminé par avance modifie la spontanéité reliée à la communication interculturelle perçue comme possibilité de rencontre et d'échanges. Lorsqu'on quitte chez soi pour aller à la rencontre d'autrui, on doit laisser place à l'imprévu, d'autant plus que notre interlocuteur peut provenir de n'importe quelle culture. La table-ronde que nous avons organisée illustre bien cette part d'imprévu qui peut surgir dans le déroulement planifié d'une activité de communication. De plus, cette rencontre a permis, à l'instar de Marc et Picard (2008) de prendre en compte la complexité des situations réelles en se basant sur cinq éléments : les acteurs, le partage du sens, le contexte, le système de régulation et la dynamique interactionnelle. Les acteurs, qui ont une identité, une personnalité, une histoire, etc., s'influencent mutuellement. Ces acteurs vont échanger du sens en interprétant les messages perçus. Le contexte influence le comportement des interactants par la situation et le « co-texte[2] ». Le système de régulation renvoie aux contraintes, aux normes et aux règles qui président à la communication. La dynamique interactionnelle met de l'avant les enjeux opératoires ou symboliques.

Aux fins d'analyser notre cas en lien avec la communication interculturelle et son rapport à l'identité, nous avons subdivisé la situation de communication en trois catégories : les acteurs, la langue, et l'espace-temps.

LES ACTEURS

Les acteurs de la situation que nous avons étudiée sont : le cadre universitaire comme espace structurant l'interaction, les blogueurs, les techniciens, le public et les traducteurs. Le cadre universitaire reflète l'environnement physique de l'université, le lieu dans lequel s'est déroulée la rencontre. De plus, l'animateur de la table-ronde était un professeur d'université qui avait un programme bien établi selon l'agenda de l'événement convenu préalablement entre les parties.

---

[2] Pour Marc et Picard (2008, p.74), le co-texte « appartient au domaine langagier et correspond à ce que les linguistes appellent « l'environnement discursif d'une séquence », c'est-à-dire l'ensemble des mots et propositions qui, placés autour d'une expression lui donnent un sens ».

Les blogueurs constituent les acteurs centraux de la rencontre puisqu'ils étaient invités à prendre la parole lors de cette rencontre qui leur était dédiée. Dans cette catégorie figurait une blogueuse qui participait aux échanges à distance par le biais du dispositif technologique mis en place. Il s'agit d'une blogueuse dissidente cubaine dont la présence a restructuré les interactions. En effet, en présentant cette blogueuse, une intervenante a évoqué ses faits d'armes ainsi que les difficultés qu'elle a eu à subir de la part du régime cubain. Au début, suite à des problèmes techniques, la communication ne fut pas possible avec Cuba. Cette difficulté a eu une incidence imprévue puisqu'elle a favorisé un discours militant très fort. En effet, une autre blogueuse présente dans la salle soutenait que le problème communicationnel était du à la censure du régime castriste qu'elle soupçonnait d'avoir coupé la connexion Internet de la dissidente. Une fois, la connexion rétablie, la blogueuse voulait faire dire à la dissidente cubaine que la police se trouvait en bas de chez elle et était la cause du problème de connexion. Mais ce n'était manifestement pas le propos de la blogueuse dissidente.

Les techniciens/consultants constituent d'autres acteurs majeurs de la rencontre qui ont eu une influence notable sur le déroulement des interactions. Pour permettre au public virtuel de blogueurs de se connecter, des consultants en immigration ont proposé d'offrir leur infrastructure technologique afin de permettre aux internautes hispanophones de contribuer aux débats. Comme ces consultants comprenaient le français et l'espagnol, ils ont rapidement débordé l'animateur pour prendre sa place afin d'animer la rencontre et de lire les commentaires des internautes. D'une certaine manière, ils ont utilisé leur avantage technologique et leur bilinguisme français/espagnol pour modeler la rencontre selon leurs propres attentes. Ce faisant, le statut d'animateur de la rencontre a progressivement migré vers les techniciens/consultants au détriment du schéma initialement prévu par les organisateurs.

Le public était constitué par des individus intéressés par la thématique de manière large, pas des étudiants et par les internautes blogeurs essentielement latino américains. Ces deux types de public (en présentiel et à distance) ont beaucoup participé aux échanges en posant des questions et souvent en monopolisant la parole.

Les traducteurs étaient les membres de l'organisation qui ont préparé la table-ronde avec nous. Une des membres du panel a même par moments joué le rôle de traductrice. On pouvait donc noter trois traducteurs[3] en incluant le consultant en immigration.

La dynamique engagée par les différents acteurs reflètent leur identité (personnelle et sociale), la prise en compte de leur culture et la spécificité du contexte dans lequel ils oeuvrent. Si on se fie à Paul Ricoeur (1992), l'idée d'un *Soi* ancré dans l'histoire conjugue permanence et changement. Ainsi, certains traits sont stables : le caractère, c'est-à-dire,

> « l'ensemble des marques distinctives qui permettent de réidentifier un individu humain comme étant le même » (p. 144).

D'autres peuvent être modifiés au cours de l'existence du sujet ; la permanence de certains projets prend la forme d'une fidélité à des engagements. Dans un sens, l'identité personnelle est le maintien de soi dans la parole donnée. Quant à l'identité sociale, elle peut être définie comme étant « that part of an individual's self-concept which derives from his [or her] knowledge of his [of her] membership in social group (or groups) together with the value and emotional significance attached to that membership» (Asante & Gudykunst, 1989, p. 147). On y retrouve donc le concept de membre développé par l'ethnométhodologie qui y voit une appartenance permettant de donner sens au monde.

L'analyse de la séquence d'interaction permet de voir la culture en action. Clifford Geertz propose cette définition de la culture

> «... the man is an animal suspended in webs of significance he himself has spun, I take culture to be those webs, and the analysis of it to be therefore not an experimental science in search of law but an interpretative one in search of meaning.» (Geertz, 1973, p. 5).

Pour cet auteur, la culture est ce qui donne sens, ce qui structure et oriente le passage de la pensée à l'action :

> «As interworked system of construable signs […], culture is not a power, something to which social events, behavior, institutions, or processes can be causally attributed; it is a context, something within which they can be intelligibly [...] described.» (Geertz, 1973, p. 14).

Dans cette perspective, l'individu est acteur de la culture qu'il crée. Les interactions constatées pendant la table-ronde permettent de corroborer cette thèse. Ainsi, pendant les échanges avec le public, un

[3] Les trois traducteurs sont le consultant, la directrice de l'organisation avec laquelle nous collaborions ainsi qu'une panéliste.

moment de recadrage culturel est apparu puisque le consensus[4] québécois a volé en éclat. En effet, face au discours sur le régime cubain, un des membres du public a remis en question la vision acceptée d'un régime cubain dictatorial. Cette remise en question a causé un long moment de tension et de gêne. A partir de cet instant, la dynamique des échanges a été différente et a reflété la construction d'une sous-culture différente de celle envisagée par les organisateurs. La mise en relation des interactants et de leur identité personnelle et la modification de la situation de communication par le biais de la confrontation ont permis l'émergence d'une identité de groupe.

LA LANGUE

Les anthropologues, les philosophes et certains spécialistes de l'interculturalité l'avaient déjà soulevé. La connaissance ou l'apprentissage de la langue constitue un élément central de la communication interculturelle. Toutefois, elle n'en constitue pas la caractéristique unique. Gudykunst et al. (1989) démontrent, études à l'appui que le langage influe directement sur l'identité sociale. Ces études démontrent de plus que la relation langage/identité est particulièrement présente dans le processus identitaire des groupes ethniques. L'identité sociale et ses composantes liées au langage correspondent à l'identité
ethnolinguistique. Par exemple, les membres de groupes ethniques utilisent différentes stratégies de distinction par le langage afin de se définir comme membre d'un groupe ou comme «non-membre» d'un groupe extérieur. Inversement, si l'identité sociale d'un groupe se transforme, son langage évoluera aussi (Gudikunst & al., 1989, reprenant Giles & al. et McNamara).

Comme nous l'avions mentionné, trois langues ont été utilisées pendant la table-ronde : le français, l'anglais et l'espagnol. Le français est la langue officielle de l'Université du Québec à Montréal (UQÀM) où se tenait la rencontre. Il y avait donc une obligation officielle de tenir la table-ronde dans cette langue. Toutefois, comme plusieurs des panélistes et des membres du public, notamment les internautes, sont hispanophones, une traduction devait être réalisée. Dans le même temps, un des panélistes provenait de l'Ontario, province unilingue anglophone et il fallait donc

---

[4] Par consensus québécois, nous entendons un élément de trait culturel des Québécois qui n'aiment pas comme on dit « la chicane ». Dans ce sens, le consensus repose sur le fait de ne pas faire de critiques intempestives ou d'accepter les propos de l'interlocuteur sans nécessairement le remettre en question.

intégrer cette troisième langue dans la rencontre. En séance, il a été convenu de traduire les propos de tous les panélistes en français ou en espagnol selon la langue de départ. Toutefois, les propos de l'une des panélistes n'ont pas été traduits. Paradoxalement, il s'agissait de la seule panéliste qui était « québécoise de souche », c'est-à-dire une Québécoise blanche catholique. De plus, la table-ronde a davantage été hispanophone. L'espagnol est devenu la langue véhiculaire entre les participants, transformant ainsi l'identité sociale du groupe et illustrant toute la force de « l'indexicalité » (Garkinkel, 1967).

De plus, la question de la langue est associée au fait qu'il n'y avait qu'un seul micro. Comme l'animateur universitaire ne parlait pas espagnol, il a dû souvent céder son micro aux traducteurs. Une redistribution du « pouvoir » a pu être de ce fait constatée. La table-ronde a pu illustrer la fameuse « hypothèse Sapir-Whorf » qui affirme que la langue détermine notre culture puisque la langue n'est pas un simple élément de transmission mais façonne nos pensées, nos croyances et nos attitudes.

L'ESPACE ET LE TEMPS

Parmi ses différents objets de réflexion, centres d'intérêt, Michel Foucault (1967) s'est intéressé à l'espace : « il n'est pas possible de méconnaître cet entrecroisement fatal du temps avec l'espace ». Dans sa réflexion, il évoque une science, l'hétérotopologie, qui étudierait les hétérotopies, ces espaces absolument autres. Présentant les utopies qui sont des lieux précis et réels et qu'on peut déterminer, il propose des contre-espaces qui sont localisés. Pour lui, les hétérotopies sont

> « des lieux réels, des lieux effectifs, des lieux qui ont dessinés dans l'institution même de la société, et qui sont des sortes de contre-emplacements, sortes d'utopies effectivement réalisées dans lesquelles les emplacements réels, tous les autres emplacements réels que l'on peut trouver à l'intérieur de la culture sont à la fois représentés, contestés et inversés, des sortes de lieux qui sont hors de tous les lieux, bien que pourtant ils soient effectivement localisables. Ces lieux, parce qu'ils sont absolument autres que tous les emplacements qu'ils reflètent et dont ils parlent. »

En prenant l'exemple du cimetière, du théâtre, du jardin, etc., il avance que l'hétérotopie a pour règle de juxtaposer en un lieu réel, plusieurs espaces qui seraient incompatibles. La table-ronde comme prétexte de rencontre interculturelle reflète l'hétérotopie dont parle Foucault puisqu'elle peut être conçue comme un lieu de superposition d'identités, de référents, de langues et de cultures différents.

Comme nous l'avons mentionné, la rencontre a lieu à l'université. Toutefois, l'espace était aussi virtuel par le biais d'Internet. Le temps était réglé au quart de tour. La table-ronde devait durer deux heures de temps a duré finalement plus de 3 heures. Censée commencer à 17h, elle a finalement débuté à 17h30. De même, le cocktail a dépassé la durée prévue. En fait, les différences relatives au temps et à l'espace ont construit un lieu où la rencontre ne va pas de soi. Dans le même temps, les réflexions d'Edward T. Hall sur la proxémique ou le territoire ont pu être détectées lors de la rencontre. Plus spécifiquement, la rencontre illustre la distinction que Edward T. Hall et Mildred Reed Hall (1990) effectuent entre temps polychronique et temps monochronique. Pour ces auteurs, avec le temps monochronique, on ne prend en considération et on ne fait qu'une seule chose à la fois. Ce temps est important et on le traite comme une chose tangible qu'on peut dépenser, perdre ou gaspiller. Quant au temps polychronique, il est caractérisé par la diversité et la simultanéité des activités. Il place davantage l'accent sur l'activité, la tâche, l'interaction que sur le respect scrupuleux des programmes. Ainsi, certains chocs peuvent apparaître lorsque des gens de culture de temps polychronique rencontrent des gens de culture de temps monochronique comme ce fut le cas lors de la table-ronde.

Conclusion

A travers l'analyse, trop succincte, de ce cas pratique d'interaction interculturelle provoquée dans l'espace académique, un certain nombre d'éléments émergent relativement clairement. D'abord il apparaît que la communication interculturelle reflète le processus par lequel l'identité et l'altérité se déploient pour mettre en scène la rencontre en gens de cultures différentes. L'aboutissement de cette communication dépend de la logique des acteurs et du sens qu'ils accordent à la rencontre. En l'occurrence, un problème technique banal a été investi d'une signification politique et a complètement changé la dynamique prévue des échanges qui prennent place non seulement dans l'espace feutré d'une institution universitaire, mais aussi dans un espace social marqué historiquement par une certaine tendance à ne pas heurter autrui en public. Le surgissement d'échanges très durs sur fond de contentieux herméneutique de la politique cubaine semble montrer qu'il suffit de peu pour changer la dynamique prévue et faire surgir le dissensus. Par ailleurs, le partage d'une langue commune, en l'occurrence l'espagnol, par la majorité des intervenants, a été saisi comme prétexte par certains acteurs qui ont modifié l'ordonnancement de l'événement dans le but de promouvoir leur image corporative. La technologie, c'est-à-dire la plateforme technologique destinée à faciliter les échanges entre le public présent sur place et les blogueurs connectés à distance a également joué un rôle de premier plan dans la structuration des échanges puisque le technicien de service s'est vu investir d'un pouvoir de médiation qui lui a permis d'imposer son rôle au détriment de celui de l'animateur initialement prévu. Ces quelques exemples, analysés ici à la lueur des acquis théoriques de la recherche en communication interculturelle, montrent qu'il s'agit d'un phénomène d'échange complexe dans lequel des éléments culturels, politiques, économiques et symboliques sont impliqués sans qu'il soit toujours facile de les distinguer.

BIBLIOGRAPHIE

Asante, M K, Gudykunst W B & Newmark E (eds) (1989). *Handbook of International and Intercultural Communication*, Newbury Park, CA: Sage Publications.

Barna, L M (1997). Stumbling blocks in intercultural communication. In L A Samovar & R E Porter (eds), *Intercultural Communication: A Reader*, pp. 337–346, 8th edition. Belmont, CA: Wadsworth.

Bateson, G (1980). *Vers une écologie de l'esprit, t II*. Paris : Éditions du seuil.

Bszanger, I (1992). Introduction. In A Strauss. *La trame de la négociation : sociologie qualitative et interactionnisme*, Paris : L'Harmattan.

Carpentier, M-N & J Demorgon (2010). La recherche interculturelle : l'intérité humaine cachée. In G Thésée, N Carignan & P R Carr (eds). *Les faces cachées de l'interculturel : De la rencontre des porteurs de cultures*, pp. 33–53. Paris : L'Harmattan.

Coulon, A (1987). *L'ethnomédogologie*. Paris : Presses Universitaires de France.

Cuche, D (1997). Nouveaux regards sur la culture: L'évolution d'une notion en anthropologie. Sciences Humaines. 77.

Gagnon, Y (2005). *L'étude de cas comme méthode de recherche : guide de réalisation*. Sainte-Foy : Presses de l'Université du Québec.

Garfinkel, H (1967). *Studies in Ethnomethodology*. Englewood Cliffs, NJ: Prentice-Hall.

Geertz, C (1973). *The Interpretation of Culture*. New York: Basic Books.

Goffman, E, (1974). *Les rites d'interaction.* Paris : Éditions de minuit.

Gohard-Radenkovic, A (2010). De la diversité à la différence, de la différence à la différenciation. In G Thésée, N Carignan & Paul R Carr (eds). *Les faces cachées de l'interculturel : De la rencontre des porteurs de cultures*. Paris : L'Harmattan.

Gudykunst, W B, Ting-Toomey, S, Hall B J & Schmidt K L (1989). Language and Intergroup Communication. In M K Asante & W B Gudykunst (eds). *Handbook of International and Intercultural Communication* (pp. 145–162). Newbury Park, CA: Sage Publications.

Gudykunst, W B & Kim, Y Y (1992). *Communicating With Strangers: An Approach to Intercultural Communication*. New York/Montréal : McGraw-Hill.

Hall, Ed. T. (1971). La dimension cachée. Paris : Éditions du seuil

Halualani, R T, Mendoza, S L & Drzewiecka, J A (2009). "Critical" Junctures in Intercultural Communication Studies: A Review. *Review of Communication*, 9(1), 17–35.

Jandt, F E (2010). *An Introduction to Intercultural Communication: Identities in a Global Community*. Los Angeles/London/New Delhi/Singapore/Washington DC: Sage.

Kapuscinski, R (2006) « Rencontrer l'Étranger, cet événement fondamental ». In *Le Monde Diplomatique,* (Janvier), 14–15.

Lustig, M W & Koester, J (1996). *Intercultural Competence: Interpersonal Communication Across Cultures.* New York, Harper Collins College Publishers.

Marc, E & Picard D (2008). *Relations et communications interpersonnelles.* Paris : Dunod, 2è édition.

Rafoni, B (2003). La recherche interculturelle. État des lieux en France. *Questions de communication,* 4, 13–26.

Ricoeur, P ([1990] 1992). *Soi-même comme un autre*. Paris : Seuil.

Riggins, S H (1997). The Rhetoric of Othering. In S H Riggins (ed.), *The Language and Politics of Exclusion: Others in Discourse* (pp. 1–30). Thousand Oaks, CA: Sage.

Samovar, L A & Porter R E (1991). *Intercultural Communication : A Reader*. Belmont, CA: Wadsworth.

Schutz, A (1987). *Le chercheur et le quotidien : Phénoménologie des sciences sociales.* Paris : Méridiens Klincksieck.

Spitzberg, B (1994). Intercultural communication competence. In L A Samovar & R E Porter (eds). *Intercultural Communication: A Reader* (pp. 353–365). Belmont, CA: Wadsworth.

Stoiciu, G & Hsab, G (2011). Communication internationale et communication interculturelle : des champs croisés, des frontières ambulantes. In C Agbobli & G Hsab (eds). *Comunication internationale et*

communication interculturelle : regards épistémologiques et espaces de pratiques. Sainte-Foy : Presses de l'Université du Québec.
Winkin, Y (1981). *La nouvelle communication*. Paris, Éditions du Seuil.
Wolton, D (2005). *Il faut sauver la communication*. Paris : Flammarion.

L'IMAGE DES ACTEURS HUMANITAIRES AUPRES DES HAÏTIENS: SAUVEURS OU COLONISATEURS ?

COLETTE NGUEMEDYAM DJADEU

Résumé

Depuis les années 80, Haïti connaît une affluence d'acteurs humanitaire qui justifient leur présence par le taux de pauvreté très important dans ce pays. Haïti serait le pays le plus pauvres des Caraïbes.

Le tremblement de terre du 12 janvier 2010, par son caractère très destructeur, aurait été pour Haïti une occasion de révéler avec plus d'écho au monde entier, la situation de précarité dans laquelle vivent ses populations depuis plusieurs années. Il a attiré davantage d'acteurs humanitaires : on estime à 900 ONG venu du monde entier, recensées au lendemain de cette catastrophe humanitaire, sans compter les organisations de l'ONU déjà présentes sur le terrain.

Du côté des Haïtiens, cette invasion de charité « occidentale » ne fait pas toujours l'unanimité. Pour certains, l'activité humanitaire en Haïti est salutaire car elle répond effectivement aux besoins des populations que le gouvernement Haïtien n'arrive pas à gérer. Pour d'autres, derrière l'apparence de sauveur pour les plus pauvres, il y a surtout une volonté politique de recolonisation d'Haïti.

Ainsi, les organisations humanitaires étant pour la plupart étrangères avec souvent beaucoup de personnels expatriés, la perception des étrangers par les Haïtiens vivant en Haïti varie selon la classe sociale et le milieu de vie, entre le « riche sauveur » et l' »envahisseur concurrent » voir le complice des colons.

A partir des éléments du contexte politique et social haïtien, je me propose de faire dans ma communication une description analytique des différentes conceptions de l'identité Haïtienne par rapport aux étrangers en Haïti.

Mon corpus de travail sera constitué d'articles de la presse Haïtienne et internationale, puis de quelques extraits d'entretiens effectués avec des

Haïtiens bénéficiaires d'ONG, fonctionnaires d'organisation humanitaire ou du gouvernement haïtien. Je m'appuierai par ailleurs sur des articles élaborés par des analystes de l'actions humanitaire en Haïti ou ailleurs.

Mots-clés: acteurs humanitaires – identité – haïtiens- images

L'histoire d'Haïti est marquée par une longue crise socio politique. Au cours des 30 dernières année (1983-2011), le pays a connu plus de quatorze (14) gouvernements et cinq (5) coups d'état accompagnés à chaque fois d'actes d'assassinats et de pillage et trois (3) interventions de forces étrangères sur le territoire national. Les forces militaires et de police des Nations Unies (www.minustah.org) arrivées en Haïti depuis 2004 y sont encore aujourd'hui et la durée de leur mandat reste jusqu'ici indéterminée. Ainsi, les éléments historiques ci-dessous sont essentiels pour comprendre les différences perceptions de l'étranger en Haïti. Nous commencerons donc par des éléments d'histoire et des réalités sociales et économiques haïtienne avant de voir comment en sont influencées les représentations des « autres », alors mêmes qu'ils viennent dans un contexte d'aide humanitaire, comme après le tremblement de terre de 2010.

Quelques éléments de l'histoire politique d'Haïti et son contexte socio économique (Ardouin, 1847; Madiou Fils, 1843)

Depuis sa découverte par Christophe Colomb, Haïti a connu à plusieurs reprises des occupations étrangères. Certaines de ces occupations sont souvent justifiées par les crises politiques et la situation sociale marquée par un taux élevé de pauvreté.

De la découverte espagnole à la Révolution française

L'île sur laquelle est établie la république d'Haïti était peuplée par les indiens Arawaks (ou Taïnos) et les Caraïbes. Ils avaient nommé leur île, Ayiti, la « Terre des hautes montagnes », Quisqueya et Bohio.

L'espagnol Christophe Colomb explore l'île d'Ayiti pour la première fois en 1492. Frappé par la richesse de ses sols, il entreprend de la conquérir ainsi que ses habitants.

Les indiens d'Haïti sont contraints à la servitude alors qu'ils ont l'habitude d'une vie calme et oisive. Ils organisent pour se défendre une révolte armée contre les espagnols envahisseurs. Beaucoup d'indiens ont péris dans les mines profondes où ils étaient forcés de travailler. C'est ainsi que fut progressivement exterminé le peuple des premiers habitants d'Haïti.

Vers 1517, Pour repeupler l'île d'Haïti par des hommes et femmes forts capables de résister au travail rudes, le royaume d'Espagne fit venir des esclaves noirs de Séville puis de l'Afrique.

Au XVIIe siècle, la France impose sa présence dans l'île en reprenant peu à peu aux Espagnols le contrôle de sa partie occidentale. L'économie reposait à l'époque sur l'esclavage. Ce système engendra des troubles qui aboutirent, en 1791, à la révolte des Noirs, conduite par le général haïtien Toussaint-Louverture. À la faveur de la Révolution française, les insurgés obtinrent satisfaction. Un décret de la Convention abolit l'esclavage en 1794. Toussaint-Louverture se rallia alors au gouvernement français, avant d'afficher, en 1801, son intention d'établir en Haïti une république noire.

De la lute des Noirs contre les mulâtres à l'intervention américaine

Entre 1804 qui est l'année de l'indépendance de l'île d'Hispaniola par Jean-Jacques Dessalines et 1865 qui correspond à la restauration de la république d'Haïti telle qu'on la connait aujourd'hui par le mulâtre Nicolas Geffrard, ce pays a connu une succession de crise politique interne marquée par des luttes de pouvoirs entre noirs et mulâtre.

En 1915, les Etats unis, déjà présents en République dominicaine, s'intéresse à Haïti et l'occupe militairement. Un gouvernement soumis aux volontés du colonisateur est mis en place. Ce dernier s'engage en contre partie à fournir au pays une assistance politique et économique.

En 1918, les Américains réprimèrent dans le sang une révolte paysanne (plus de 15 000 morts). L'hostilité de la population à l'égard de l'occupant grandit, et conduit finalement, en août 1934, au départ des Américains.

De Papa Doc à la surveillance de l'ONU

Après le départ des américains, des luttes de pouvoir internes continuent en Haïti jusqu'à l'élection de François Duvalier - dit "Papa Doc" (perspective.usherbrooke.ca), ancien membre du gouvernement, élu président de la république d'Haïti en 1957. Il impose pendant ses années de présidence une politique extrêmement répressive (interdiction des partis d'opposition, instauration de l'état de siège, le 2 mai 1958). Le régime Duvalier s'appuyait sur une milice paramilitaire, les Volontaires de la

Sécurité nationale, surnommés les « tontons macoutes », qui semait la terreur dans les rangs de l'opposition et parvint à étouffer toute résistance.

À la mort de François Duvalier le 21 avril 1971, Jean-Claude Duvalier son fils, accède à la présidence de la République. Il commence par appliquer la politique de son père, avant d'amorcer une timide libéralisation du régime.

En 1986, un soulèvement populaire renverse Jean-Claude Duvalier, qui va se réfugier dans le sud de la France. Après le régime Duvalier, Haïti connait une nouvelle série de crise politique.

La première intervention des Nations Unies en Haïti remonte à 1993. En septembre 1993, le Conseil de sécurité a établi la première opération de maintien de la paix dans le pays, la Mission des Nations Unies en Haïti (MINUHA).Toutefois, en raison du refus de coopérer des autorités militaires haïtiennes, la MINUHA n'a pas pu être complètement déployée à l'époque et s'acquitter de son mandat.

En juillet 1994, le Conseil de sécurité a autorisé, par sa résolution 940 (1994), le déploiement d'une force multinationale de 20 000 membres pour faciliter le retour rapide des autorités haïtiennes légitimes, maintenir la sécurité et la stabilité dans le pays et promouvoir l'état de droit. La force multinationale a été suivie par une série de missions successives des Nations Unies de 1994 à 2001.

Souscrivant aux recommandations du Secrétaire général, le Conseil de sécurité a adopté la résolution 1542 du 30 avril 2004, établissant la MINUSTAH (Mission des Nations Unies pour la stabilisation en Haïti) pour une durée initiale de 6 mois et a demandé que la passation de pouvoirs de la force multinationale intérimaire s'effectue le 1er juin 2004.

En 2011, la MINUSTAH, perçue comme une puissance militaire étrangère, est encore présente en Haïti.

Ces différents moments d'occupation du territoire haïtien par des puissances étrangères constituent l'un des éléments central de la mémoire collective haïtienne. Elles se transmettent de génération en génération à travers les programmes scolaire sur l'histoire d'Haïti et contribue à créer une identité haïtienne qui est plus ou moins revendiquée par les Haïtiens en fonction de leur catégorie sociale : « Haïti, la première république noire indépendante »

La réalité sociale et économique en Haïti de l'indépendance à nos jours

La nouvelle société qui émerge de la lutte pour l'indépendance se construit en tant que telle tout au long du 19e siècle. Elle prend appui sur le morcellement des anciennes grandes habitations sucrières coloniales, l'occupation par les anciens esclaves des terres montagneuses et la poursuite du commerce d'exportation des denrées agricoles et des produits forestiers. Sur les ruines du morcellement extrême de l'espace colonial va se construire une vie régionale dense et forte autour d'un port d'exportation et d'un arrière-pays producteur de denrées.

Il s'observe en Haïti une pauvreté massive entretenue par des inégalités importantes. Toutes les mesures de la pauvreté corroborent cette situation que l'on se réfère à l'approche monétaire, à celle de la pauvreté humaine ou encore à l'approche subjective (DSNCRP, 2008-2010). Un rapport préparé pour le Programme des Nations Unies pour le Développement (PNUD) sur le profil de la pauvreté en Haïti à partir de l'ECVH-2001 indique qu'au total, 55% de la population haïtienne – 4,4 millions de personnes – vivent dans des ménages qui se situent en dessous de la ligne de pauvreté extrême de 1 US$ (PPA) par personne par jour. D'autre part, 71% – ou près de 6,2 millions sur une population haïtienne de 8,1 millions – vivent dans des ménages qui se trouvent en dessous la ligne de pauvreté de 2 US$ (PPA) par personne par jour. (Carte de la pauvreté d'Haïti, 2004) 40% des plus pauvres de la population n'ont accès qu'à seulement 5,9% du revenu total, tandis que les 20% des plus nantis captent 68%. Les indicateurs sociaux indiquent que le pays fait face à un accès très précaire en services sociaux de base tels que l'éducation, la santé, l'eau courante et l'assainissement. Par ailleurs, la malnutrition affecte environ 50% des enfants de moins de 5 ans, et environ la moitié des Haïtiens adultes est analphabète (55%). (ECVH, 2003) Le système éducatif en Haïti est fortement marqué par l'exclusion. Il contribue à perpétuer et à renforcer les inégalités à travers une offre scolaire limitée, surtout en milieu rural ; une différenciation de l'offre scolaire impliquant que les plus pauvres n'ont généralement accès qu'à une éducation de faible qualité. (GTEF, Août 2010)

C'est alors dans ce contexte historique, social et économique qu'interviennent des acteurs de l'aide humanitaire et de développement.

Les représentations des acteurs de l'humanitaire et du développement

Les acteurs de l'aide humanitaire et de développement se donnent pour mission de travailler dans le sens de rétablir l'équilibre social en apportant des réponses aux besoins latents des populations défavorisées et exclues.

Ainsi, les principaux secteurs d'intervention des organisations humanitaires en Haïti sont : l'Agriculture, la santé, la sécurité alimentaire, la santé, l'eau et l'assainissement, la sécurité sociale, la micro finance. Dans le secteur de l'éducation précisément, les organisations humanitaires favorisent par leurs actions, l'accès aux écoles à des enfants issus des communautés les plus défavorisées. Ceci à travers le parrainage d'enfants et des partenariats avec des écoles communautaires.

Notons que ces organisations humanitaires sont pour la plupart des organisations étrangères, financées et dirigées par des étrangers (non Haïtien). De plus en plus nombreuses depuis 1954 (900 ONG recensés après le séisme du 12 janvier), ces organisations remplacent souvent l'Etat en matière d'intervention sociale. L'OCHA (office of coordination of humanitarian affairs) en a recensé 512[1] au lendemain de tremblement de terre (mars 2010) dont 469 organisations internationale et seulement 26 nationales. Par ailleurs, le ministère de la planification via son Unité de Coordination des Activités des Organisations Non-Gouvernementale (UCAONG) a enregistré et reconnue Entre 1982 à septembre 2011, 500 ONG[2] dont 317 sont étrangères.

Par conséquent, de manière générale l'idée qu'on se fait de l'aide humanitaire et du développement en Haïti c'est bien une intervention étrangère. L'image qu'en ont les Haïtiens varie selon qu'ils en sont bénéficiaires ou non d'une part et d'autre part, en fonction de leur capacité d'objectivité.

Les ONG et organisations internationale/étrangers comme sauveurs

Par leurs activités visant à apporter des réponses aux besoins latents des populations défavorisées et exclues de la société haïtienne, les acteurs de l'aide humanitaire et du développement sont perçues comme sauveurs par les bénéficiaires directs de leur programme d'aide. Ces derniers sont souvent assimilés aux étrangers, ce sont des bienfaiteurs pour le peuple exclu et misérable d'Haïti. Dans ce sens, Des victimes du séisme du 12 janvier 2010 vivant dans des camps, interrogés sur leur perception de l'aide humanitaire en Haïti, adhèrent totalement à l'idée selon laquelle «

[1] Données édité su site de l'OCHA par Jessie Altagrace Vital, chargée de la gestion de l'information et du système d'information géographique à l'unité de gestion de l'information de l'OCHA en Haïti.
[2] Liste des ONG reconnues de 1982 à nos jours, http://www.mpce.gouv.ht/ongreconnue.pdf

Haïti est le pays des ONG », « ce sont les ONG qui font tout pour nous [3]», affirment-ils. Dans cette même logique, Maxime Laguerre (2008), ancien bénéficiaire du programme de parrainage de World vision en Haïti, s'exprime en ces termes dans un poème dédié à l'ONG World Vision :

> « Vous faites de moi le doux soleil qui se lève, et dont les rayons éclairent pour toujours.
>
> O Dieu que ce mot soit à jamais l'objet de mes lèvres, qu'il ne cesse d'être ma vie, mon avenir et mon amour ! Grâce à vous, je revois tous mes rêves envolés, je vis en moi tout mon désir intérieur,
>
> Je ne suis pas et ne serai non plus un être dévoyé, car vous êtes l'ombre qui m'épargne des foudres du malheur. Grâce à vous je respire l'air de l'espoir, et ne revient plus en moi le désespoir.
>
> Je suis sauvé de la dame aux yeux méchants qui est misère.
>
> Que Dieu vous accorde ses faveurs en tout temps, vous qui êtes le symbole de mon existence, l'atmosphère qui m'entoure et dans laquelle je vis longtemps »

Ainsi, comme sauveurs, les ONG participent à la réintégration sociale des populations exclues. On retrouve dans cette perception des acteurs humanitaires une vision puriste et idéaliste qui voudrait que ces derniers, par leurs actions, contribuent à améliorer les conditions de vies des hommes tout en luttant pour le respect de leurs dignités humaines.[4] En Haïti, Cette vision s'oppose à la celle qui conçoit l'humanitaire comme mode d'impérialisme ou de recolonisation occidentale.

Les ONG et organisations internationales/étrangères comme acteurs de colonisation

Du côté de certains intellectuels et homme politiciens haïtiens, la présence des organisations humanitaires est souvent perçue comme une stratégie de recolonisation, dans la même logique que Ricardo Setenfur, représentant spécial en Haïti de l'OEA (organisation des Etats Américain) qui affirme que

> « la présence des troupes de l'ONU en Haïti après le tremblement de terre, alors que ce dernier ne connaissait pas de guerre civile et n'était pas une menace internationale, apparaît comme une manière de geler le pouvoir Haïtien et de transformer les Haïtien en prisonnier sur leur propre îles. Il

[3] Extrait d'entretien avec des victimes du 12 janvier 2010 vivant dans des camps

[4] Définition de l'humanitaire du Portail d'information et d'initiation à l'action humanitaire http://www.humanitaire.ci

> existe selon lui une relation perverse entre la fragilité du pouvoir haïtien et la puissance des ONG (le bien est privée grâce aux médecins, hôpitaux, écoles et nourritures qui arrivent du monde entier, alors que le mal est public puisque l'Etat Haïtien n'est présent que par la police) ; ce qu'il appelle « éogénisation ». En Haïti, la coopération internationale a fait place à la charité, ce qui bafoue un peu la souveraineté du pays. L'implication excessive des coopérants empêche la consolidation des structures de société civile. Sous couvert d'action humanitaire et avec l'argument massue bien qu'usé de « d'état en faillite », la communauté internationale a privé du droit du peuple haïtien à la possibilité d'auto-organisation et de d'avoir sa propre prise en charge ». (Cunill, 2011)

Dans le même sens, pour le Comité d'Action Contre l'Occupation pour la Libération d'Ayiti (CACOLA):

> « Sous prétexte de répondre à l'urgence humanitaire, la dite 'communauté internationale' menée par l'impérialisme états-unien a mis en place une tutelle qui masque à peine la réalité d'une occupation. »
> (www.npa2009.org, 2011)

Il perçoit aussi la Commission Intérimaire pour la Reconstruction d'Haïti (CIRH) comme un « gouvernement parallèle codirigé par Bill Clinton », et surtout, comme une « stratégie impérialiste du gouvernement Américain sur le territoire Haïtien ».

Dans la même logique des fonctionnaires haïtien pendant des entretiens, pour répondre à la question des difficultés du gouvernement haïtien dans la coordination humanitaire déclare: « C'est la main qui donne qui dirige… les bailleurs de fonds financent les projets des ONG sur le terrain sans tenir compte des relations que ces dernières entretiennent avec l'Etat… les budgets de certaines ONG dépassent celui de l'Etat, ce qui leur donne une superpuissance.», de leur point de vue, « les ONG ramassent des fonds au nom d'Haïti et les gèrent sans tenir compte de l'Etat d'Haïti ».

Pour Charles VORBE, Professeur à l'université d'Etat d'Haïti et directeur de recherche du centre d'étude en population et développement

> « l'humanitaire est aujourd'hui une des formes principales que prends l'idéologie dominante. Sa fonction sociale n'a rien à voir avec les discours grandiloquents sur les valeurs humanistes. Il en est ainsi en Haïti où depuis le séisme de 12 janvier dernier et l'effet d'amplification de ses conséquences sur la société haïtienne dû en grande partie au caractère néocolonial de cette dernière, l'on assiste, sous couvert d'aide humanitaire, à une véritable intervention militaire américaine qui vise au renforcement de la domination étrangère sur le pays » (Vorbe, 2011)

Cette perception est partagée par beaucoup de Haïtien, hommes politiques, de fonctionnaires du gouvernement et entrepreneurs privés, etc. elle peut être analysée comme un élan nationaliste, protecteur et défenseur de l'indépendance haïtienne. C'est une vision géopolitique de l'aide humanitaire. Les haïtiens qui adhèrent à cette vision sont très souvent « anti-ONG » ce qui pourrait susciter des sentiments et attitudes d'hostilité vis-à-vis des acteurs humanitaires.

A côté de cette perception « refoulante » des acteurs humanitaires, il peut arriver que des haïtiens préalablement « anti ONG » se retrouvant dans certains contextes, reconsidèrent leur point de vue en reconnaissant l'intérêt social de ces derniers.

Les ONG et organisations internationales/ étrangères comme partenaires du gouvernement

Parce qu'ils ont participé en tant que acteurs de l'humanitaire ou du développement à la mise en œuvre des activités sur le terrain en faveur des populations vulnérables ou alors parce qu'ayant collaboré avec des acteurs humanitaires dans des planifications stratégiques d'activités, certains haïtiens adoptent la perception des ONG comme partenaires du gouvernement dans l'action social.

C'est ainsi qu'un fonctionnaire de l'UCAONG[5] (unité de coordination des actions des ONG) fait l'observation suivante :

> « les ONG sont acteurs de développement en Haïti, elles fournissent une aide importante à la population. On ne peut pas se passer de leurs interventions. L'UCAONG essaye d'intégrer les actions des ONG dans le programme d'investissement public d'où l'obligation qu'ont les ONG de nous soumettre régulièrement leurs programmes d'actions et rapports d'activités ».

Dans la même logique, un salarié haïtien de la MINUSTAH (Mission des nations unies pour la stabilisation en Haïti), organisation fortement perçue comme outil impérialiste de l'occident en Haïti de part les forces militaire qu'elle y déploie, déclare :

> « la présence de la MINUSTAH en Haïti s'est fait en accord avec l'Etat Haïtien, c'est une mission d'accompagnement des institutions publiques et non une force d'occupation ».

---

[5] Unité relevant du ministère de la planification et de la coopération/gouvernement d'Haïti

Cette vision des ONG et organisations internationales donc des acteurs humanitaires qui apparait comme intermédiaire entre les deux premières est souvent exprimée par quelques haïtiens parmi lesquels ont retrouve des salariés d'organisations humanitaires ou des bénéficiaires de programmes humanitaires. D'après cette logique, la présence des humanitaires en Haïti résulte effectivement d'un état de déséquilibre social constaté, où les plus faibles ne peuvent pas toujours compter sur les structures publiques étatiques pour satisfaire leur besoins de base à savoir (santé, éducation et nutrition). L'invasion des ONG et acteurs humanitaires serait une manifestation flagrante du manque de leadership du gouvernement dans la régulation de leurs activités en faveur des populations. Les adeptes de cette vision encouragent fortement le renforcement des capacités du gouvernement par les organisations internationales et les bailleurs de fonds, dans le contrôle et le suivi des activités des acteurs humanitaires.

Conclusion

De tout ceci, il ressort ce qui suit : la connaissance de l'histoire d'Haïti contribue à créer chez les haïtiens une certaine méfiance vis-à-vis des étrangers et plus particulièrement ceux venant des « pays occidentaux ».

Entre les représentations des acteurs humanitaires en Haïti comme sauveurs d'une part, perception très présentes chez les bénéficiaires directs de l'aide humanitaire et colonisateurs d'autre part, conception très nationaliste de l'humanitaire étranger et envahisseurs, se développe progressivement une représentation des acteurs humanitaires comme partenaires de l'Etat. Elle est issu des haïtiens ayant vécu l'aide humanitaire en tant que acteurs ou bénéficiaires qui, souvent partagées par leurs sentiments, essayent de trouver de manière plus objective, une nouvelle perception des acteurs humanitaires dans leurs pays.

C'est dans cette même logique que le Groupe URD écrit dans le cadre d'une étude de la gestion de crise en Haïti

> « Il est en effet à craindre que cette coordination sans les Haïtiens devienne soit une source de tension forte entre le système de l'aide et le gouvernement, soit un processus qui entraîne à terme la délégitimisation d'un Etat haïtien déjà bien affaibli ses difficultés à porter une parole publique forte pour rassurer les populations »[6].

---

[6] Etude en temps réel de la gestion de la crise en Haïti après le séisme du 12 janvier 2010 Mission du 9 au 23 février, Groupe URD (urgence- réhabilitation-développement), 4 avril 2010. www.reliefweb.in

Beaucoup d'analyste et d'acteur de l'aide humanitaire s'accordent pour soutenir l'idée selon laquelle, malgré ses faiblesses, il revient au gouvernement haïtien de s'imposer en tant que Etat souverain, en assurant la coordination et la régulation de tous les acteurs humanitaires sur le territoire nationale.

Au regard de ce qui précède, le véritable challenge du gouvernement haïtien et des acteurs humanitaire semble être : Comment construire un partenariat en préservant l'autorité de l'Etat Haïtien ?

BIBLIOGRAPHIE

(2008) *Sonnet à World Vision*, par Maxime Laguerre, enfants parrainé par la World Vision, dans rapport de l'année du 30ème de World Vision en Haïti.

Ardouin, Beaubrun (1847) *Etudes sur l'histoire d'Haïti*, Desobry et E Magdeleine, LIB. Editeurs, Paris

Charles VORBE (mai 2011) *Séisme, humanitarisme et interventionnisme en Haïti*, dans Cahiers du CEPODE/ FSH/UEH.

Madiou Fils, Thomas (1843) *Histoire d'Haïti*, imprimerie de JH Ourtois, Port au Prince.

Documents

République d'Haïti/Ministère de l'économie et des finances/Institut Haïtien de statistique et d'informatique (2003) *Enquête sur les conditions de vie en Haïti* (ECVH).

Républiqye d'Haïti, Ministère de la planification (2004) *Carte de la pauvreté d'Haïti.*

République d'Haïti, Ministère de la planification (2008-2010) *Document de stratégie nationale pour la croissance et la réduction de la pauvreté* (DSNCRP).

Rapport du groupe de travail sur l'éducation en Haïti (GTEF) (Août 2010) *Pour un pacte national sur l'éducation en Haïti.*

Site Internet

www.minustah.org

http://perspective.usherbrooke.ca/bilan/pays/HTI/fr.html site de l'université de Sherbrooke

Martinez Cunill, Daniel - *Haïti. Le côté obscur de la coopération internationale*, article publié le 29 janvier 2011 sur www.Rebelion.org

Anxiety and Uncertainty in Expatriate Everyday Life: Identity Boundary Regulation within Estonian Online Communities

Kristel Kaljund and Anne-Liis Peterson

Abstract

In postmodern Europe the Internet increasingly substitutes for the modern expatriate community, providing an arena for expatriates to represent the sense of cultural distinctiveness they feel, and allowing them to pass on and multiply the representations created and sustained in their daily interpersonal communications in a novel cultural environment. In this context, our paper looks into the nature and characteristics of psychological reactions to the intercultural everyday, which are often reactions to anxiety and uncertainty. Our qualitative textual analysis focuses on the representation of feelings experienced offline and represented online – crucial indicators of a lack of security – by people of Estonian origin (PEO) who live in Western Europe (specifically Luxembourg). We analyse the elements of PEO expatriate self-identity construction, as maintained by identification with others and other groups. Taking the existential security-vulnerability of one's identity as the primary motivation dialectic for human interaction, the analysis reveals expatriates' latent goal: to reinforce existential security and diffuse identity vulnerability via identity boundary regulation. Inclusion and differentiation are performed and represented in PEO weblogs to enhance or verify positive self-conceptions with supportive others. Expressions of "being themselves" include maintaining the perceived dominant position and symbolic capital PEO expatriates held in their home culture; their self-representations within and towards a culturally hostile environment are politically loaded. We have selected the identity–cognitive security model to discuss how PEO expatriates in Western Europe fulfil their need for positive regard and symbolic capital confirmation.

Key words: Expatriates, everyday life, anxiety and uncertainty, boundaries of identity

INTRODUCTION

In postmodern Europe, the Internet increasingly substitutes for the modern expatriate community, providing (among its many other functions) an arena for expatriates in Europe to represent the sense of cultural distinctiveness they feel in daily intercultural situations. Furthermore, the internet serves as a means of passing on and multiplying these representations, created and sustained in expatriates' daily interpersonal communication, in a novel cultural environment.

Recent research shows that "newer technologies, such as email and the Internet, [are] used most frequently and [have] among the highest satisfaction scores. … [C]ommunication via some types of information and communication technology can be just as satisfying to individuals on overseas assignments as personal visits" (Cox 2004, p. 215). Besides multiplying the expatriate experience, this is one of the reasons why expatriates nowadays do not necessarily need closer contacts to locals for their psychological well-being, while their connection to their original neighbourhood (whether online or offline) remains stronger than ever.

In this context, our research into expatriates' online representations looks into the nature and characteristics of psychological reactions to intercultural everyday life, which are often reactions of anxiety and uncertainty that potentially threaten both the cultural adaption and social competence of expatriates. Our qualitative textual analysis takes a close look at the online representation of feelings experienced offline, by people of Estonian origin (PEO) living and experiencing their daily lives in Western Europe (specifically Luxembourg). Inclusion and differentiation are performed and represented in PEO weblogs to enhance or verify positive self-conceptions with supportive others. We have selected the identity–cognitive security model, to discuss how PEO expatriates in Western Europe fulfil their need for positive regard and symbolic capital confirmation, and to examine some consequences of this set of intercultural conditions.

EXPATRIATES

For our purposes, expatriates can be defined as temporary cultural sojourners, voluntarily staying in an unfamiliar cultural environment for employment reasons. They are specialists, a highly qualified workforce. Nevertheless, further examination of this group reveals an interesting contradiction: expatriates are primarily seen as international business people; yet, although work-related cross-cultural travel covers all occupational levels, many of the so-called *arbeiter* group are often, in reality, immigrants or intending immigrants (Ward, Bochner & Furnham, 2001). However, the present research concentrates on those who perceive themselves to be abroad on only a temporary basis, i.e. who do not wish to immigrate.

There is a large and growing literature on the expatriate experience, most studies being conducted with workers in managerial and professional roles (Ward et al., 2001). Moreover, the number of Estonian expatriates is constantly growing; for instance, Estonia's EU membership saw the emergence of a new community in Belgium and Luxembourg. However, since World War II (when 70,000 Estonians fled the expected Soviet terror), the number of Estonian expatriates has not been comparable to, for example, Poles or Lithuanians. There are no significant Estonian economic refugee communities or diaspora groups in Europe. Last but not least, these are people who are virtually present, doing white-collar jobs using computers; and since they are educated, they can be expected to reflect upon their expatriate/cultural experiences in written form.

THE EFFECTS OF ANXIETY AND UNCERTAINTY UPON EXPATRIATE EXPERIENCE

William B. Gudykunst has noted the importance of the mindful management of anxiety and uncertainty for effective communication. Anxiety and uncertainty management theory is complex, and its validity is not universally recognized; nonetheless, it warrants further qualitative research. For the present study it served as a starting-point and inspiration, which led to further theoretical considerations.

Anxiety "…stems from feeling uneasy, tense, worried, or apprehensive about what might happen. /-/ The anxiety we experience when we communicate with others is usually based on negative expectations. /---/ One of the behavioral consequences of anxiety is avoidance" (Stephan & Stephan, in Gudykunst & Nishida, 2001, p. 59). To be motivated to communicate with others, our anxiety has to be below our maximum thresholds and above our minimum thresholds (Gudykunst & Nishida, 2001). If our anxiety level is high, we rely on simplistic information processing to reduce tension: we see the world in stereotypical terms, making inadequate evaluations of the behaviour of those we communicate with. If our anxiety level is low, we are not motivated to communicate with locals; we keep to ourselves, and do not integrate or learn about our cultural environment. If our anxiety level is neither too high nor too low, we feel comfortable while interacting with others (*ibid.*). Anxiety can paralyze us because we fear the consequences of inappropriate behaviour, which may make others perceive us negatively; on the other hand, it is anxiety that makes us mindful, and therefore effective in communication (Stephan, Stephan & Gudykunst, 1999).

Uncertainty is the inability to predict and explain our own and others' behaviour (Gudykunst, 1993). "Uncertainty is a cognitive phenomenon. Predictive uncertainty is the uncertainty we have about predicting the other's attitudes, feelings, beliefs, values, and behaviours" (Berger & Calabrese, in Gudykunst & Nishida, 2001, p. 56). As with anxiety, effective communication requires that our level of uncertainty is between our minimum and maximum thresholds (Gudykunst 1993). If our uncertainty level is high, we lack the confidence necessary to draw conclusions about the behaviour of others, about the reasons behind their behaviour, about their attitudes and feelings; in a word, we are unable to predict the behaviour of others. If our uncertainty level is low, we will be overconfident in interpreting the behaviour of our communication partners, i.e. we will not be aware of reality (Gudykunst & Nishida, 2001).

> [U]ncertainty and anxiety consistently decrease over time, as positive expectations, perceived quality of communication, and perceived effectiveness of communication consistently increase over time. … [I]t is not just the quality of contact between members of different groups, but also the quantity of the contact that is important (Hubbert, Gudykunst & Guerrero, 1998, p. 41).

RESEARCHING VIRTUAL COMMUNITIES

This study was initiated based upon the intuition that, in a Europe characterized by the free movement of employees and electronic mediation, the internet increasingly substitutes the modern expatriate community as an arena for the maintenance of cultural distinctiveness and reflection in Anthony Giddens's sense (Giddens, 1993). In the same context, this study inquires about some of the crucial characteristics of collective identity in online expatriate communities; since our approach was based upon Gudykunst and related authors, we needed to know how wide the range of expatriate representations of anxiety and uncertainty is. Starting from these considerations, we worked out an identity–cognitive security model, incorporating Erik Erikson's identity–health model as well as the identity–interaction model most commonly associated with the work of Erving Goffmann. Central to the identity–health model is the proposition that individuals have a need for positive regard or identity confirmation. The identity–interaction model stresses that an individual's identity is formed and maintained through social interaction (Blacking, 1983, p. 49). Using Gudykunst's conceptualization of the mindful management of anxiety and uncertainty, we found cognitive security to be one of the key dimensions and motivational factors of expatriate everyday life, as represented in online texts (weblogs) produced by PEO expatriates living and working in Western Europe.

The sample group used is PEO expatriates residing in Luxembourg and working for the European Union. From February – May 2011 their representations were observed through qualitative textual analysis of an expatriate web portal, les.lu. The internet gives offline expatriate communities the ability to connect online and inhabit a virtual space, thus strengthening the offline community and multiplying representations of their own culture. Furthermore, a group such as PEO expatriates can experience their cultural identity and reflexively design its borders in the same sphere.

Besides forming and joining online networks that consist of both static and dynamic arenas, the online presence of a community includes the representation of oneself in web portals and weblogs. In the case of online expatriate communities, like the one formed by PEO, a textual network contains reflexive discourse derived from various aspects of everyday life in a strange cultural environment, such as news, work, and entertainment. In our case, the network formed in a portal or weblog strengthens ties between members of the offline expatriate community. The ability to set up such networks is a useful community-forming resource provided by the internet, as are the activities of browsing and blogging, and the ability to virtually participate in community life. The nature of these phenomena means that both the decisions taken in relation to the identity of expatriate community members, and the tools used to maintain the necessary elements and boundaries, can be mutually encouraged; they thus provide the community with psychological well-being and identity security.

The act of decoding online representations often requires the researcher to invoke offline contexts and reflexivity in the interpretive process. In the present study, these contexts refer to the offline PEO community, which is represented online through the texts in the chosen portal. Scholars have described this as providing a "window on something that exists outside language" (Ryan, 2001, p. 91). When a group of PEO browse and create les.lu, they look through the same windows; consequently, familiarity and agreement with the signs contained in those texts develops. According to some theorists, when such identification is shared by a group of people, they increasingly develop as a virtual or abstract community (Holmes, 1997; Willson, 1997). Community habitation in a weblog occurs through the process of interacting with other participants, whose identities and discourse reflexively construct a more desirable reality both within the virtual space and in participants' minds. The more engaged a community member is in the processes of blogging and commenting, the greater is their immersion in this virtual arena – although this does not mean that their offline experience is any less important as a source of online reflection and reality construction. Taking all of the above into account, our conclusions about the nature of identity in the online PEO expatriate community derive from the qualitative textual analysis of their portal and linked weblogs.

THE INFLUENCE OF EXPATRIATE EXPERIENCE UPON IDENTITY

"[T]he matter of cultural experience is an issue of personal identity development and reformulation" (Weinreich, 2009, p. 135). The development of intercultural identity has been conceptualized differently by various researchers, who have worked out categories of different kinds of adaption. From an interculturalist perspective, John W. Berry has addressed the topic of social identity, stating that cross-cultural interactions challenge one's sociocultural identity and even one's self-conception (Berry, 2003; Maertz, Hassan & Magnusson, 2009, p. 68).

Identity questions are crucial to the process of cultural adaption: "...acculturative stress comes not only from uncertainty [regarding] how to behave appropriately, but also from internal conflicts ... As Project GLOBE scholars recently stated, 'The dexterity to adjust one's behavior is a critical requirement. Not everyone can do this' (Javidan, Dorfman, Sulley de Luque, & House, 2006, p. 85)" (Maertz et al., 2009, p. 67). This point is evident in interactions on les.lu: for example, a PEO described a situation in which different bodily borders and different ways of creating politeness collided:

> I did not know what to think /…/ when one well-dressed lady attacked me physically at a classical music open-air concert. /…/ [Later, as an answer to comments] She attacked me because I passed her, wanting to go somewhere else. I was simply changing my position.
> —2007

But, as Henri Tajfel and other scholars have taught us, social identity forms "that part of an individual's self-concept which derives from his [or her] knowledge of his [or her] membership of a social group (or groups) together with the value and emotional significance attached to the membership" (Tajfel, 1978, p. 63 in Ting-Toomey, 1993, p. 83; Tajfel, 1982, p. 70). Stella Ting-Toomey offers a similar definition: "Identity is defined as the mosaic sense of self-identification that incorporates the interplay of human, cultural, social and personal image as consciously or unconsciously experienced and enacted by the individual" (Ting-Toomey, 1993, p. 74).

According to Tajfel's social identity theory, it is important for each individual to feel they acquire a positive social identity from the group(s) he/she belongs to (Tajfel & Turner, in Stroebe & Insko, 1989). Group membership, according to Tajfel, means that we are aware of belonging to a group, and we perceive that group in either a positive or negative way (Tajfel, 1982). Most people have positive self-conceptions and wish to enhance or verify these self-conceptions with supportive others: thus, an individual tends to associate with people who provide affirmative feedback on positive self-views, while avoiding people who engage in negative appraisals of one's self-identification (Ting-Toomey, 1993). On les.lu one finds frequent expressions of a desire to avoid local people, and descriptions of voluntary exclusion. For example, according to one of the expatriates:

> We tried to watch the game on the big screen at Knuedler square as well, but we soon realized it wasn't a good idea. It was because of the crowd hanging around there that we left and ended up in an empty pub …
> —2008

"[I]dentity can be defined as a continuous process, aiming at the development and maintenance of positive psychological distinctiveness, as well as a sense of continuity and social belongingness" (Tajfel 1974, Lange & Westin, in Liebkind, 1983, p. 187); consequently, each individual is always in a continuous process of identity work. "Individual identity orientations derive from previous experience, as well as from intentional, future aspirations, and the psychological processes of self-categorization, self-evaluation and identification act as crucial transmitters between the personal and the social levels of identity" (Liebkind, 1983, p. 187).

In the age of nation-states in the European sense, one of the most useful approaches to social identity is provided by the concept of ethnic identity, "that part of the totality of one's self-construal made up of those dimensions that express the continuity between one's construal of past ancestry and one's future aspirations in relation to ethnicity" (Weinreich, 2009, p. 128, see also DeVos, 1983, p. 135). European researchers agree that ethnic identities seem to be relatively stable phenomena (Liebkind, 1983), despite the changeable nature of individuals' cultural environments in contemporary Europe. Ethnicity provides us with a coding system to translate new information and divide it into "natural" or "unnatural" categories, based upon our ethnic "bank of knowledge". Ethnicity is the meaning system that we live in: it helps us to manage our everyday experience, and to feel that we understand ourselves and the rest of the world.

Boundary Maintenance

Frederik Barth's *Ethnic Groups and Boundaries* (1969) investigates the boundary-maintaining mechanisms which keep groups distinct (DeVos 1983, p. 140). It argues that "…ethnic 'identity' is one that cannot be measured easily by consistently applicable, objective, behavioral criteria. … Ethnic identity cannot be studied by giving specific attention to objective features of physical differences, territory, language, religion, occupational and economic features or other cultural traits." For Barth, "the problem is … one of 'boundary maintenance', whatever the contrastive features employed to define a group" (DeVos 1983, p. 135). These contrastive features, used to maintain boundaries, can be found in any aspect of everyday life – such as the celebration of annual festivals:

> Yesterday we walked around the town briefly and discovered that Christmas!!!! had arrived in town and the Christmas market was crowded. /…/ they had nothing to offer that I could relate to Christmas, apart from mulled wine. And that mulled wine was rather well-hidden among the usual hamburgers, sauerkraut, waffles and oriental stuff. Thus the whole circus had a rather contrary effect on me.
> —2007

Although Christmas is a pan-European event, local traditions and food (like sauerkraut) are here rejected as unfamiliar; borders between "our" Christmas and "their" Christmas are recreated and represented on les.lu.

Barth's thoughts link to those of Stella Ting-Toomey, according to whom the primary motivation dialectic for human interaction is the existential security-vulnerability of one's identity: our goal is to reinforce existential security and diffuse identity vulnerability via identity boundary regulation. A secondary motivation is inclusion/differentiation (evident in auto/hetero-stereotypes and prejudices) (Ting-Toomey, 1993, p. 82). The importance of preserving group boundaries while developing a superordinate identity must also be acknowledged (see Hewstone and Brown, 1986), and this is frequently evident in representations of the expatriate everyday:

> Obviously the two and half years I have spent in Luxembourg have made me much more patient towards the world around me and have raised my tolerance as a client. Well, is that good or bad?! :) In the end, I did get the bagel I had ordered, accompanied by several excusez-moi's, and so I did not find it necessary to discuss the matter in detail. /…/ besides, as I plan to go back there to drink coffee, I don't want to risk the service personnel adulterating my coffee with something unnatural the next time.
> —2006

Anxiety and uncertainty can be addressed in very different ways. In the context of cultural adjustment, psychologists also employ the cognitive dissonance perspective introduced by Leon Festinger (1957). This has generally been defined as "a negative state of uncomfortable arousal resulting from an inconsistency between two cognitions, or between behavior and some cognition. … [D]issonance is aroused when a discrepancy is detected between a behavior/cognition and a personal standard or self-expectancy for competence and morality (e.g., Aronson & Carlsmith, 1962; Thibodeau & Aronson, 1992). In this approach, the aim of dissonance reduction is to maintain one's individual self-images of competence and morality against threats from inconsistency. This approach emphasizes rescuing the individual image in the self-concept that is threatened" (Maertz et al., 2009, p. 68). Threatened self-images of competence, in particular, link directly to our research. One of the best examples is a statement that is typical of the weblogs studied:

> [Places of entertainment] are full of European officials and bankers and most of the time they talk about how long they have lived in Luxembourg, about specific details of this or that job and about nobody liking living in Luxembourg.
> —2008

STATUS OF THE SOCIAL GROUP

The status of the social group one belongs to is an important determinant of social identity. "Various group memberships … affect the valence of our self-conception via social comparison. To the extent that our salient ingroup compares favorably with other relevant social and cultural groups, we achieve a positive social identity. Conversely, to the extent that our salient ingroup compares unfavorably, we would attempt different options such as changing the identity group if possible, changing the comparative criteria dimensions, or downgrading the comparative group via ingroup aggression" (Ting-Toomey, 1993, pp. 83–84). Different options can be pursued when we attempt to resolve cognitive dissonance and find more balance and integrity for ourselves. A tangible example of a PEO downgrading a comparative group is evident in this representation of the nut market in Vianden:

> In order to get anywhere at all, you had to fight your way through a crowd of drunken guys on the narrow main street. On top of that, it was certain that some sausage, ketchup, mustard or a bit of liqueur would stick to your shoes. People drank liquor straight from the bottle, showing no manners at all. /…/ German schlagers echoed in the valley, one after another or at the same time, horrible party music mixed with some Metallica songs. On top of that you heard people yelling and it sounded as if there were animals screaming for help as well. /…/ After experiencing that madness and having escaped as fast as we could, it was difficult to persuade Sergo that Vianden is actually one of the loveliest spots in Luxembourg that is really worth visiting and we could come back here one day.
> —2007

As such examples suggest, "…a person's overall sense of self-worth is heavily dependent on the effective regulation of identity/boundary issues and the satisfaction derived out of the appropriate management of the security-vulnerability dialectic and the inclusion-differentiation dialectic" (Ting-Toomey, 1993, p. 89; see also Stroebe & Insko, 1989; Paalamo, Uljas & Sagara, 1998).

Reality and Selfhood when Living Abroad

Even a temporary stay in a strange cultural environment calls for an adjustment in the way we see ourselves, and for new decisions concerning where we now belong. "Expatriate work … launches a secondary experience of how fragile our taken-for-granted reality and selfhood are, and potentially opens up the possibility of new forms of subjectivity without the fear of losing one's core self" (Peltonen 2007, p. 889). Yet this is only a possibility, one which cannot be accomplished by sheer will alone, and in many cases identity is endangered (see Weinreich, 2009, p. 125).

As "a discrepancy between individual construals and reality – especially if it concerns one's self-construal – is psychologically uncomfortable and normally leads to a process of reconstruction"

(Liebkind, 1983, p. 190), the self-categorization will have to be corrected according to the novel situation. "There are … two ways of diminishing an experienced threat to one's core identity: to loosen the structure to avoid invalidation or to tighten up increasingly, in order to define current identity content more clearly than before" (McCoy, Liebkind, 1983, p. 191). "The battle for the achievement and preservation of social recognition may use structurally tight identities as instruments" (Liebkind, 1983, p. 191), as is the case with PEO in Luxembourg wanting dignity and a positive self-conception.

Most research relates cultural identity to long-term immigrant adjustment (Berry, 1997; Boekestijn, 1989; Moyerman & Forman, in Sussman, 2002, p. 392). "As sojourners recognize the temporary nature of their cultural experience, one might reasonably argue that their motivations and expectations regarding cultural adjustment and adaptation differ substantially from those of immigrants" (*ibid.*). This is one of the reasons why expatriates maintain their identity boundaries so firmly, i.e. why they tend to create and keep a cultural identity "bubble". Literature on intercultural adjustment and competence clearly states that positive contact and a less biased attitude, which invariably lead to identity adjustment, both promote the well-being of expatriates and their professional performance; however, the threat of losing one's self, alongside the meaning system with which one makes sense of the novel outside world, counterbalances these incentives. It is therefore unsurprising that expatriates and immigrants seek to maintain identity boundaries.

At the same time, we could say that identity maintenance in favour of selected elements of expatriates' home culture can be seen as rational, since several studies show that strong home culture identification is linked to the psychological well-being of sojourners, whereas the loss of that connection causes mood disturbance (Ward et al., 1994, 1999, 2000; Luo, in Sussman, 2002, p. 404). Taking into consideration the diversity of factors considered here, Eastern European expatriates living in Western Europe arguably support their psychological well-being by preserving strong group boundaries (see Valk, Karu-Kletter & Drozdova, 2011). Some evidence for this claim was found when researching les.lu. As one expatriate explains:

> You can spend years in Luxembourg without the somewhat painful pokes the local culture gives you having a serious influence on you. For instance, 95% of my life takes place in Estonian and the other 5% I spend buying bread or vegetables in a shop or once a week drinking coffee with someone I know. /…/ it seems to me that my vocabulary, which consists of twenty-some words in the local language, is bigger than that of many who have

> lived decades in Luxembourg. /…/ life just goes on, already four years and a month, or 49 months, or soon that'll be 1,500 days.
> —2008

Similarly, Stephen P. Banks's research into identity among U.S. expatriate retirees in Mexico found that this group construct an identity through othering the hosts; moreover, apparently positive statements regarding Mexicans actually hid implicit criticism and claims of superiority. "That adjustment narrative reveals a struggle to conserve cultural identities" (Banks, 2004, p. 376); "…expatriate retirees … strive to preserve their home cultural values, and in so doing they strive to preserve those values that earmark a desirable self-identity" (Banks, 2004, p. 377). While the relationship to the host culture in this case is very different to the position of PEO in Luxembourg, the desired identity position is the same. One of the expatriates summarizes this concisely:

> Although we are tourists, we do live here :)
> 2006

CULTURAL ADJUSTMENT STRATEGIES AND IDENTITY

Any culture contact is accompanied by changes in people's ethnic identities. Interculturalists have often articulated the dilemma in simplistic terms: "individuals exposed to heterogeneous cultural influences … can either become or resist becoming multicultural" (Ward, Bochner and Furnham, 2001, p. 31). Based upon that consideration, Colleen Ward et al. divide the identities of individuals who have been exposed to culture contact into four categories: passing, chauvinist, marginal and multicultural. The first are those who adopt the new culture (especially if it has a higher status than the original culture); the second group rejects cultural influence altogether, strengthening their original national feelings; the third feels at home in neither culture; while the last acquires the much-debated multicultural personality, becoming mediating persons (Ward et al., 2001; Bochner, 1981).

The classic categorization of acculturation patterns stems from John W. Berry, who describes four patterns of adjustment (separation, assimilation, integration, and marginalization), based upon whether individuals or groups identified with one, both, or neither cultural group in an intercultural situation (Berry, 2003). The assimilating individual loses his or her own cultural identity and adopts the host culture; the integrating individual adapts to the host culture while also maintaining their original ethnic identity; the separating individual does everything to hold on to his or her culture, avoiding contact with members of other cultures (including the host culture); and marginalization strategy applies, according to Berry, to individuals who lose touch with their own culture but do not respond by adopting the host culture: they supposedly alienate from ethnic identity as such (Berry 2003, p. 24). J. Ben Cox, re-evaluating Berry's conceptualization, assigns new designations to the concepts while focusing specifically on expatriate experience, renaming the aforementioned identity groups as home-favoured, host-favoured, integrated, and disintegrated (Cox 2004, p. 205).

The key problem with Berry's model is that it assumes individuals always have a choice in the adjustment strategy they employ, not taking into account the demands of the host society or the specific situation of each individual. These factors mean that, in reality, expatriates are presented with only a few options, setting boundaries to identity formation. There are often expectations placed on the individual by his or her ethnic group and background.

Other ways of classifying intercultural identity are put forward by Milton J. Bennett and Nan M. Sussman. Bennett conceptualizes intercultural identity in two patterns of cultural marginality: constructive marginal and encapsulated marginal. Constructive marginals are able to integrate their cultural identities, while encapsulated marginals experience conflict between the cultural perspectives they have learned (Bennet, 1993b). Sussman (2000) classifies cultural identity in four patterns: subtractive, additive, affirmative, and intercultural. The subtractive pattern results in expatriates feeling less comfortable with the norms and values of their home culture, while the additive pattern results in individuals feeling closer to the host culture's norms and values. The affirmative acculturation strategy reflects strong identification with home, while the intercultural strategy is characterized by identification with both cultures in the expatriate's self-conception.

Berry's cultural adaption strategies also inspired Jan Pieter van Oudenhoven, Karen van der Zee and Mariska van Kooten (2001), who worked out four categories which reflect the identity work done by expatriates; these categories take two significant characteristics of this group into consideration, namely the importance of their job, and the perceived temporary character of their stay. The four categories are: free agents, going native, hearts-at-home and dual citizens (*ibid.*), which correspond respectively to Berry's marginalization, assimilation, separation and integration strategies.

Although controversial, the concept of an ideal type of multicultural personality should at least be introduced here, since today it is in general undeservedly dismissed. The concept was initially popularized by Peter S. Adler, who defines the genuinely multicultural person as "a human being whose identifications and loyalties transcend the boundaries of nationalism and whose commitments are pinned to a larger vision of the global community", "a person whose essential identity is inclusive of different life patterns and who has psychologically and socially come to grips with a multiplicity of realities". Adler claims that "the multicultural person is intellectually and emotionally committed to the basic unity of all human beings while at the same time recognizing, legitimizing, accepting and appreciating the differences that exist between people of different cultures" (Adler, 1998, pp. 225, 227).

The concept of this kind of mediating individual has fascinated mostly male scientists, especially white, Western men, belonging to cultures with high status, who clearly believe that we have choices in the ways we define ourselves: "…a new self-consciousness emerges from the awareness that all values are relative and at the same time from the awareness that the culture is universal" (von Barloewen, 1993, p. 309). Bennett has even insisted that "[t]here is no natural cultural identity for a marginal person" (Bennett, 1993a, p. 63).

No evidence of this personality type was found by our research. However, in the context of this study it should be pointed out that "identity development … is interactive, highly dependent on context, and ultimately rooted in gender, race, ethnicity and religion" (Sparrow, 2000, p. 173); it is surrounded by boundaries. Lise M. Sparrow explains that "I think of myself not as a unified cultural being but as a communion of different cultural beings. Due to the fact that I have spent time in different cultural environments I have developed several cultural identities that diverge and converge according to the need of the moment. … I don't think people change who they are /…/ but I'm aware. I can never change who I am but I can change my awareness" (Sparrow, 2000, p. 190).

Discussion

Having looked at how the representational dimensions of virtual cultural communities act as carriers and multipliers of personal intercultural experience, we agree with Hermann Bausinger that "people have discovered their own way out of the dilemma of wanting identity. Their way is a clear departure from ideological identity. People, in general, no longer trust vague and distant entities, like nations, to take care of their being themselves. They have, on the contrary, made efforts to settle their identity in their own neighbourhood, as a part and an outcome of the inconspicuous structures of everyday life" (Bausinger 1983, p. 340). This trend is clear in our sample, which illustrates the desired and constructed identities of people who have retreated from the environment of Estonian national ideology. For these expatriates, it is primarily a political, rather than an ideological matter: they seek an identity and, in their everyday life within the host culture, others will either reward them with that identity; grant it only partially; or deny it altogether. The decisions made by these expatriates concerning emancipatory politics, and particularly those concerning life politics in Giddens's sense (Giddens, 1993), have always to do with the question of how to acquire (and maintain) recognition within their own cultural community. Self-actualization and the drawing of identity boundaries mostly serve this exact purpose, being means of avoiding the anxiety and uncertainty that continuously threaten expatriates' everyday life and psychological well-being. Nowadays, self-identity is a reflexive accomplishment that is maintained, controlled and shaped in the circumstances of a rapidly changing and increasingly globalized social life. As Giddens has noted, "the individual must integrate information deriving from a diversity of mediated experiences with local involvements in such a way as to connect future projects with past experiences in a reasonably coherent fashion. Only if the person is able to develop an inner authenticity – a framework of basic trust by means of which the lifespan can be understood as a unity against the backdrop of shifting events – can this be attained" (Giddens 1993, p. 215).

Everything that PEO expatriates do in Luxembourg is culturally coded, linked to and integrated within cultural memory. However, their perception of this environment as one which is threatening to their identity clearly shows that PEO live in Western Europe with above-average anxiety levels (compared to expatriates in general), deriving from identity insecurity, which exhausts the self-system (see Ting-Toomey, 1993, p. 80). Every individual needs a safe, healthy and coherent narrative of self-identity, and continually strives towards that goal. This takes us back to culture and politics. The PEO expatriate culture is collective; it includes and differentiates; but, most importantly, it provides cultural sojourners with an exclusive, coherent identity. Yet that coherence, being conservative by nature, has boundaries which provide a defensive function: they reflexively filter out and modify new ideas, reproduce identity, and reconstruct memory and symbols. These defensive processes collectively serve an important purpose: to maintain (at least subjectively) the PEO community's dignity and social position, as well as its various capitals, according to Pierre Bourdieu's theory (Bourdieu 2003, p. 36; Lauristin 2004, pp. 252–253). In threatening situations, the will to protect the self grows (Bloom 1990, p. 153), and consequently the community's sense of internal inclusion and external differentiation also increase.

It is therefore crucial to admit that there is a certain rationality in intercultural communication, as well as in identity construction and the maintenance of identity boundaries, which supports the psychological well-being of PEO expatriates. If we simply dismiss as irrational the decisions that expatriates in Western Europe take concerning their identity, or the ways in which they resist cultural adaption, we will underestimate collective identities as a whole. Such identities give life a meaning that goes beyond the everyday experience of individuals. Moreover, as the British-Hungarian social scientist George Schöpflin has cautioned, if we disrupt or fragment a collective's system of constructing past and future, it can fall into a devastating crisis (Schöpflin 2005, p. 105). PEO expatriates in Luxembourg stand at a crossroads of political and power-centred tensions in contemporary multicultural Europe, and in this context they make rational, conservative and sustainable identity choices. By acknowledging both their individual and collective choices and applying existing social, psychological and intercultural knowledge in practice, we can facilitate the development of intercultural communication competence in today's multicultural Europe.

REFERENCES

Adler, P S (1998). Beyond Cultural Identity: Reflections on Multiculturalism. In M J Bennett [ed.] *Basic Concepts of Intercultural Communication: A Reader*, Main, pp. 225-245.

Banks, S P (2004). Identity Narratives by American and Canadian Retirees in Mexico. *Journal of Cross-Cultural Gerontology*. 19(4), 361-381.

Bausinger, H (1983). Senseless Identity. In A Jacobson-Widding (Ed.). *Identity: Personal and Socio-Cultural: A Symposium. Acta Universitatis Upsaliensis* (pp. 337-345.). Uppsala: Humanities Press.

Bennett, M J (1993a). Towards Ethnorelativism: A Developmental Model of Intercultural Sensitivity. In R M Paige [Ed.] *Education for the Intercultural Experience* (pp. 21-71). Yarmouth, ME: Intercultural Press.

Bennett, M J (1993b). Cultural Marginality: Identity Issues in Intercultural Training. In R M Paige (Ed.). *Education for the Intercultural Experience* (pp. 109–136). Yarmouth, ME: Intercultural Press.

Berry, J W (2003). Conceptual Approaches to Acculturation. In K M Chun, P B Organista & G Marín (Eds.). *Acculturation: Advances in*

Theory, Measurement and Applied Research (pp. 17-37). Washington, D.C.: American Psychological Association.

Blacking, J (1983). The Concept of Identity and Folk Concepts of Self. In A Jacobson-Widding (Ed.). *Identity: Personal and Socio-Cultural: A Symposium* (pp. 47-65). Uppsala: Humanities Press.

Bloom, W (1990). *Personal Identity, National Identity and International Relations.* Cambridge: University Press.

Bochner, S (1981). *The Mediating Person: Bridges between Cultures.* Boston: G K Hall & Co.

Bourdieu, P (2003). *Praktilised Põhjused. Teoteooriast.* Tallinn: Tänapäev.

Cox, J B (2004). The Role of Communication, Technology, and Cultural Identity in Repatriation Adjustment. *International Journal of Intercultural Relations.* 28(3-4), 201–219.

DeVos, G (1983). Ethnic Identity and Minority Status: Some Psycho-Cultural Considerations. In A Jacobson-Widding (Ed.). *Identity: Personal and Socio-Cultural: A Symposium* (pp. 90-113). Uppsala: Humanities Press.

Giddens, A (1993). *Modernity and Self-Identity: Self and Society in the Late Modern Age.* Cambridge: Polity Press.

Gudykunst, W B & Nishida, T (2001). Anxiety, Uncertainty, and Perceived Effectiveness of Communication Across Relationships and Cultures. *International Journal of Intercultural Relations.* 25(1), 55-71.

Gudykunst, W B (1993). Towards a Theory of Effective Interpersonal and Intergroup Communication: An Anxiety/Uncertainty Management (AUM) Perspective. In R. L. Wiseman & J Koester [Eds.] *Intercultural Communication Competence* (pp. 33-71). Newbury Park, London, New Delhi: Sage.

Festinger, L A (1957). *A Theory of Cognitive Dissonance*. New York: Row Peterson.

Hewstone, M and Brown, R (Eds.) (1986). *Contact and Conflict in Intergroup Encounters: Social Psychology and Society.* Cambridge, MA: Basil Blackwell.

Holmes, D (1997). Virtual Identity: Communities of Broadcast, Communities of Interactivity. In D. Holmes (Ed.) *Virtual Politics: Identity and Community in Cyberspace* (pp. 26-45). Thousand Oaks, CA: Sage.

Hubbert, K N, Gudykunst, W B & Guerrero, S L (1998). Intergroup Communication Over Time. *International Journal of Intercultural Relations.* 23(1), 13-46.

Lauristin, M (2004). Eesti Ühiskonna Kihistumine. In M Lauristin (Ed.) *Eesti Elavik 21. Sajandi Algul: Ülevaade Uurimuse Mina. Maailm. Meedia Tulemustest* (pp. 251-285). Tartu: Tartu Ülikooli Kirjastus.

Liebkind, K (1983). Dimensions of ***Identity*** in Multiple Group Allegiance. In A Jacobson-Widding (Ed.). *Identity: Personal and Socio-Cultural: A Symposium* (pp. 187-203). Uppsala: Humanities Press.

Maertz, C P Jr, Hassan, A & Magnusson, P (2009). When Learning is Not Enough: A Process Model of Expatriate Adjustment as Cultural Cognitive Dissonance Reduction. *Organizational Behavior and Human Decision Processes*. 108(1), 66-78.

Oudenhoven, J P, Zee, K I & Kooten, M (2001). Successful Adaptation Strategies According to Expatriates. *International Journal of Intercultural Relations*. 25(5), 467-482.

Paalamo, H, Uljas, J & Sagara, K (1998). Helsingin Ja Tallinnan Nuoret: Kontaktit Ja Asenteet Kulttuurien Kohdaessa. In Tutkimuskatsauksia. Helsinkin Kaupunkin Tietokeskus. No. 4. Helsinki.

Peltonen, T (1998). Narrative Construction of Expatriate Experience and Career Cycle: Discursive Patterns in Finnish Stories of International Career. The International Journal of Human Resource Management. 9(5), 875-892.

Ryan, M L (2001). *Narrative as Virtual Reality: Immersion and Interactivity in Literature and Electronic Media*. Baltimore, MD: The John Hopkins University Press.

Schöpflin, G (2005). Rahvusriik, Moodsus, Demokraatia. In *Vikerkaar*, 10-11, 97-108.

Sparrow, L M (2000). Beyond Multicultural Man: Complexities of Identity. In *International Journal of Intercultural Relations*, 24(2), 173-201.

Stephan W G, Stephan, C W & Gudykunst, W B (1999). Anxiety in Intergroup Relations: A Comparison of Anxiety/Uncertainty Management Theory and Integrated Threat Theory. *International Journal of Intercultural Relations*. 23(4), 613-628.

Stroebe, W & Insko, C A (1989). Stereotype, Prejudice, and Discrimination: Changing Conceptions in Theory and Research. In D Bar-Tal, C F Graumann, A W Kruglanski & W Stroebe (Eds.). *Stereotyping and Prejudice: Changing Conceptions* (pp. 3-34). New York, Berlin, Heidelberg: Springer-Verlag.

Sussman, N M (2000). The Dynamic Nature of Cultural Identity Throughout Cultural Transitions: Why Home is Not So Sweet? *Personality and Social Psychology Review*, 4, 355–373.

Sussman, N M (2002). Testing the Cultural Identity Model of the Cultural Transition Cycle: Sojourners Return Home. *International Journal of Intercultural Relations.* 26(4), 391-408.

Tajfel, H (1982). *Gruppenkonflikt und Vorurteil: Entstehung und Fiktion Sozialer Stereotypen.* Bern, Stuttgart, Wien: Huber.

Ting-Toomey, S (1993). Communication Resourcefulness: An Identity Negotiation Perspective. In R L Wiseman & J Koester [Eds.] *Intercultural Communication Competence* (pp. 72-111). Newbury Park, London, New Delhi: Sage.

Valk, A, Karu-Kletter, K & Drozdova, M (2011). Estonian Open Identity: Reality and Ideals. In *Trames*, 15(65/60), 1, 33-59.

Von Barloewen, C (1993). Fremdheit und Interkulturelle Identität: Überlegungen aus der Sicht der Vergleichenden Kulturforschung. In Wierlacher, A. [Ed.] *Kulturthema Fremdheit* (pp. 297-318), München: Ludicium.

Ward, C., Bochner, S. & Furnham, A (2001). *The Psychology of Culture Shock.* London: Routledge.

Weinreich, P (2009). 'Enculturation', not 'Acculturation': Conceptualising and Assessing Identity Processes in Migrant Communities. *International Journal of Intercultural Relations.* 33(2), 124–139.

Willson, M (1997). Community in the Abstract: A Political and Ethical Dilemma? In D Holmes (Ed.) *Virtual Politics: Identity and Community in Cyberspace* (pp. 145-162). Thousand Oaks, CA: Sage.

Raising Public Issues in Romanian Media: Visibility Patterns and Deliberative Practices in Debating Professional Migration Impact

Mălina Ciocea

Abstract

This paper will tackle the question of the strategic use of the theme of professional migration in Romanian media. While our media's consideration of the identity of the Romanian Diaspora is by now firmly established, the professional mobility of specialists prompted policy discourses analysing collective responsibility and appropriate institutional choices, as well as expert dialogues implying the professionalization of media speech when addressing the effects of professional migration, and identity discourses developing settings for transnational migration which involves permanent negotiation with the other.

Introducing the theme of new migration to a public issue implies not only a certain moral distance of the media towards diasporic identity (which varies with the strategic interests of the actors involved in the debate), but also an increased use of visibility patterns and deliberative practices, which can lead to a certain dynamic and intensity in the public debate.

We take these recent developments to be relevant for the broader issue of building a civil sphere. The Romanian media landscape is rich with campaigns aimed at involving the audiences in various participative formats. In the age of increasing reflexivity, the media appropriate the reflective instruments needed to turn spectators into an active, conscientious public. If one goes a step further towards the ideal of an ethical public space, then the media must be acknowledged as a moral force enabling and creating such representations. The permanent negotiation of meaning and opinion (the contrapuntal seen by Silverstone (2007) as the mediating logic governing the Mediapolis) allows the creation of a moral public life. Since citizenship has been increasingly perceived as a negotiation tool rather than a fixed, homogeneous state of public allegiance, the question of media influence has been asked along with the more problematic question of media as a relevant environment for civic life (Sassi, 2001; Coleman, 2001). The ethical role of the media derives not only from responsibility to educate the public, but from the infinitely more difficult task of inviting public action. Against this background we will discuss to what degree the employment of certain practices and discourses are serving the public interest and, more broadly, helping to develop media's conscience of civic duties and the moral implications of their choices.

Key words: Romanian media, deliberative practices, diasporic identity, public issues, and professional migration

INTRODUCTION

This paper will discuss the question of the strategic use of the theme of professional migration in Romanian media. The theme of migration constantly features on the Romanian media agenda, albeit somewhat in the background of the main discourse. It is usually brought forward by changes in host countries' policies regarding migrants or by incidents in the migrants' communities. The politicians seem to reactivate the Diaspora as a voting body during elections or use it as a living proof of misguided policies when they take a stand against foreign governments' decisions that affect the Diaspora. The surge of profound social turmoil brought about by the economic crisis has triggered increased interest in the Diaspora as a provider of money for families left behind and as a nurturing home for those who chose to emigrate in search of more felicitous living standards. While the early '90s witnessed political migration (with migrants seeking a way out of the instability of social and political life in a former Communist country) and the early 2000s, economically motivated migration, the latest wave of immigrants seems to be driven away from the country by very diverse factors, including hope for professional improvement, disappointment in public policies and political life in general, and the failure of the state to provide appropriate working environments for specialists. Following the liberalization of labour force movement in the EU, highly professionalized immigrants, among them doctors and nurses, have joined the usual construction workers; domestic helpers and nurses cut a particularly striking figure.

It is upon these recent developments that we set our analysis of deliberative practices in the media and their subsequent influence over the civil sphere, part of a larger research project about media's discourse on diasporic identity.[1] While meditation on the identity of the Romanian Diaspora is by now firmly established in our media landscape, the professional mobility of specialists has caused some changes: policy discourses which discuss collective responsibility and appropriate institutional choices, expert discourses implying the professionalization of media talk on the effects of professional migration, and identity discourses developing the transnational setting of migration, thus involving permanent negotiation with the other. The approach to the question of professional migration by the media, politicians and institutions has generated various interpretations, representations and policies relating to the Diaspora.

It is highly relevant, then, to be studying the visibility patterns and the deliberative mechanisms employed by the media with reference to migrants. Which are the types of discourse and discursive strategies preferred by journalists in building the image of migrants? What mediatization patterns are being used in reference to migrant identity and what imagery of transnational communities is being built in the media? Raising the theme of new migration to a public issue implies not only a certain moral distance of the media towards diasporic identity (which varies with the strategic interests of the actors involved in the debate), but also an increased use of deliberative practices, which lead to a certain dynamic and intensity in the public debate. Their inventory will give us an insight into the power of the social body, here represented by the press, to give an alternative to the present community of citizens. It will provide the body of evidence needed to appraise the media's role in political deliberation and construction of a civil sphere.

We will discuss to what degree the use of certain practices and discourses serves public interest and, more broadly, helps develop the media's consciousness of civic duties and the moral implications of their choices. We will draw on recent developments in cultural theory regarding the role of the media in constructing and promoting a civil sphere and will

---

[1] Research project "Diaspora în sfera politico-mediatică din România. De la eveniment la construcţia socială a problemelor publice." [*Diaspora in the Romanian Media and Political Sphere. From Event to the Social Construction of Public Issues*] (project coordinator: Professor Camelia Beciu), financed by the National University Research Council. The project is developed by the Laboratory Communication, Discourse, Public Issues (CODIPO) of the Centre for Research in Communication, Faculty of Communication and Public Relations, NUPSPA.

place our emphasis on the complex relations of power between the media and their public, on the media's role in political deliberation, and on media morality when mediating between the local community and the Diaspora.

THE ROLE OF THE MEDIA IN CREATING A CIVIL SPHERE

The changing nature of the public sphere, as announced by Habermas, invites some hopes since its appropriateness is a locus for the emerging civil society. Back in the eighteenth century, "the public sphere as a functional element in the political realm was given the normative status of an organ for the self-articulation of civil society with a state authority corresponding to its needs" (Habermas, 1989, p. 74). Now the political public sphere is subject to the influence of two competing processes: "the communicative generation of legitimate power" (whose communication processes, while interlinked and inclusive, are legitimated by weak institutions) and "the manipulative deployment of media power to procure mass loyalty, consumer demand, and <compliance> with systemic imperatives" (which is more of an interference in the public sphere, based on alternative referential frames) (Habermas, 1992, p. 452). If power is now exercised by multiple actors following competing agendas, it is to be expected that they will attempt to identify and create their own publics, consequently multiplying perspectives and encouraging eccentric (if not individual) choices. In these circumstances, the principle of rationality makes room for impulsive/emotional reaction – "rational-critical debate gave way to the consumption of culture" (Calhoun, 1992, p. 21). The pessimistic view of a degraded public sphere can be counteracted by the optimistic stance where the multiplication of publics and public spaces would allow various identities to express themselves. It is not insignificant that Habermas himself acknowledges the critical potential of the public, becoming pluralistic (Habermas, 1992, p. 438). The mutual dependency between political ideology and cultural standing introduces the topic of the reconfiguration of civil society and the public sphere. That the term "public sphere" should be allowed to signify public spheres in which a variety of self-reflexive publics are at work is quite self-understood ever since Habermas refined the idea of the public sphere as a network permitting the exchange of viewpoints. The reflexivity of publics is further emphasized by Appadurai's understanding of "mediascapes" and "ideoscapes" as constructs moulded by actors' various backgrounds. While mediascapes are rather centred on images and based on reality narratives, and ideoscapes belong to the political realm of ideologies, both are enabling for actors, since they offer pooled resources for building new contexts (be they semiotic or political).

It is now time to develop the argument that the media can offer the scene needed for the construction of a civil sphere. Two propositions derive from here: (i) that, by inviting debate, the media help highlight mutual interests by mediating between publics and (ii) in doing so, they create the possibility of public action.

The media have long been pinpointed as instrumental when negotiating and reflecting on the meanings and ideological allegiances of individuals and communities – so long that the complex relations of power between the media and their public have become a cliché (Curran, 2006, p. 139). The exchanges between media and the publics, the configuration of the knowledge circulated among the media and the public, the fields of action opening up to the empowered publics and the ethical implications of this interchange undoubtedly are the most fertile grounds to explore in future years (in the words of Couldry, "a new map of media studies" should include "two crucial landmarks (knowledge, agency) that, assuming media research still wants a critical edge, imply a third (ethics)" (Couldry, 2006, p. 187). A brief look at the evolution of the idea of media influence over civil society and political activism might prove effective. From viewing the media as reflecting and serving society to its more radical counterpart of media managing society, social theory moved towards acknowledging the relevance of the interpretive schema of the public. A version of liberal functionalism still allows the media to play a leading role in society, but sees them rather as agencies of social integration than agencies of influence. While traditional liberal analysis emphasizes media democratic functions (watchdog role, information and debate role, people's representation to authority), the radical functionalist approach uses this argument to manifest the idea that media can actively produce consensus (which involves the notion of ideological agency).

In the age of increasing reflexivity, the media appropriate the reflective instruments needed to turn spectators into an active, conscientious public. If, along this reality, one goes a step further towards the ideal of an ethical public space, then the media should be seen as a moral force enabling and creating such representations. The permanent negotiation of meaning and opinion (the contrapuntal seen by Silverstone as the mediating logic governing the Mediapolis) allows the creation of a moral public life:

> "our media provide the most pervasive and persuasive perceptual frameworks, in an increasingly global society, for the way in which meanings, representations and relationships to the other are offered and defined" (Silverstone, 2007, p. 101).

If we employ Jeffrey Alexander's definition of civil society as containing not only symbolic categories but also structures of feeling, including the idea of the public "as it has inserted itself into social subjectivity" (Alexander, 2006, p. 72), we must allow for the media (as a communicative institution) to provide interpretations and define representations of the public.

Since citizenship has been increasingly viewed as a negotiation tool rather than a fixed, homogeneous state of public allegiance, two questions are being asked along that of media influence and the more problematic relevance of media as an environment for civic life:

> Current social and organizational ties seem to be weak in their form and stability [an evidence in the fragmentation of the civil sphere], whereas the sphere of mediated communication, especially through the Net, appears to be widening and strengthening. (Sassi, 2001, p. 100; insertion mine)

The question is answered in Alexander's proposal to understand civil society as "a solidarity sphere . . . displayed and sustained by public opinion, deep cultural codes, distinctive organizations – legal, journalistic and associational – and such historically specific interactional practices as civility, criticism and mutual respect" (Alexander, 2006, p. 31), defined both in moral and cultural terms (while Habermas, as we remember, tends to include cultural commitments in ethics, rather than morals).

Citizenship is being built on these possibilities of direct engagement. Habermas' long established connection between discourse and democracy is confirmed by participatory journalism and the participatory culture at large. The citizen is increasingly more than a socially involved agent; he is a "communicative agent" (Coleman, 2001, p. 111) taking a step further from representative journalism claiming to reflect public interest into finding his own voice. Already relatively difficult to assess in terms of relevance and impact due to "the overload of information and the complexity of communication" (Singer et al., 2011, p. 167) (problems it shares with institutionalized media), participatory journalism adds a further difficulty, that of deciphering the frames of reference it uses, since "[u]ser-generated communication is situational and contextual" (ibid, p. 164). In a sceptical account of the dynamics of media power, Curran and Seaton blame the optimists for hailing the rejuvenation of civil society and new forms of political activism a little too soon: their stand extrapolates, "from the technological potential of the net, the view that a powerful engine of changes is at work, and then fastens on to a few hopeful straws of evidence to confirm the advent of a brave new world" (Curran & Seaton, [1981] 2003, p. 264).

One such "straw of evidence" encouraging future media influence is the "many-to-many" communication model that is well adapted to multiple audiences. Another is the growing representativeness of the users. In Curran's view, two more objectives should be featured in the analysis of media-democracy relationship: "To facilitate the expression of conflict and difference" and "to assist social conciliation" (Curran, 2002, p. 239). The role of the media as facilitators of civil society endeavours – as an alternative, rather than prescriptive, direction – might prove meaningful.

The media offer a battlefield for much political struggle for domination and a propitious stage for building identities and allowing them to manifest themselves.

> [C]ontemporary media culture provides forms of ideological domination that help to reproduce the current relations of power, while also providing resources for the construction of identities and for empowerment, resistance, and struggle. (Kellner, 1995, p. 2)

In building hegemony (by producing and selecting representations), media discourses are not unlike political discourses. If we allow for a broader definition of ideology beyond the obvious statements in a text, to include "[d]iscourses and figures, concepts and images, theoretical positions and symbolic forms" (ibid, p. 59), we are justified in attempting a critique of meanings and means in journalistic discourse.

It is within this frame that public issues are constructed. Announcing the theme to a public, allowing definitions and interpretations of the theme by various social actors, including the theme on the media and political agenda, initiating debates on the various meanings and implications of the theme, are stages in building the larger dimensions of the theme. Raising a theme to a public issue is a matter of policy; for instance, "[t]he way in which the press builds public issues around the European theme signals a certain positioning on the European agenda" (Beciu & Perpelea, 2011, p. 7, our translation). What kind of public space do journalists who apprehend their role as defining and responding to the public interest construct? The interpretive dimension of the journalist's work is certainly visible in discursive practices allowing for a variety of viewpoints; what if the journalist's discourse is mainly informative? "In what conditions could we admit of a distinction between interpretive journalism and informative journalism?" (Beciu, 2007).

This is largely the question directing our research into media practices as regards the theme of professional migration. The answer may be taken on looking at the instruments offered to the reader: can they form an opinion and subsequently act on it? In deciding upon the viability of such instruments, we need to look beyond the informative dimension of the text towards the ideological construct allowing generalization of meaning and towards the position assumed by the journalist in relation to the object of his discourse and public opinion at large. Leaving aside the ideal of deliberative communication, the relevant questions to ask regarding the efficacy of the journalistic discourse are: Does it reveal a general dimension? Does it mediate between actors and uses various viewpoints on the issue under discussion? (See Beciu, 2007).

Media Responsibility towards Their Public

Who are the public that the media address in discussing professional migration? As a mediator between different cultural spaces and social actors, the journalist should give voices to each of them. The idea of a pluralistic, "fractured" public, a "patchwork of co-existing and overlapping communities" (Coleman & Ross, 2010, p. 123), implies the idea of media diversifying their perspectives and banned from using moral universalism as a frame of reference and explanation for events. The Diaspora itself, a fragmented community negotiating meanings between various cultures, is hard to capture as a uniform, constant, static public.

This difficulty adds to the more problematic definition of public interest. If social solidarity is produced in the public space through symbolic negotiation (see Calhoun, 2002), then journalists are expected to create this common space for public debate, which in the long run will help create a civic culture. While the social responsibility of the journalist might be apprehended as deterministic and illiberal, it cannot be ignored that the interpretive dimension of journalistic discourse results from a certain understanding of public space and the role of the journalist. In addressing public interest, the media cannot rule out the moral stance in favour of neutrality, since the journalists themselves are citizens needing to protect a democratic society. Standards like

> "[t]he political and economic establishments, the morals of the nation and the state, the citizens' basic rights, and the conceptions of good that guide society" (Cohen-Almagor, 2005, p. 91)

inform ethical codes and performance standards and make the case for normative and ethical reporting when covering issues of vital concern for a community.

From the point of view of the public as a plurality, the question of public interest is problematic itself, since it should be allowed to accommodate this plurality.

The rise of fragmented publics and the accompanying question of media accountability pose problems as regards media policies: media should then present a "story" that is true to every public and allow various publics to understand each other and should still facilitate agreement and public action (Coleman & Ross, 2010, pp. 128–129). If such conditions are not met, then the public may fail to feel responsible for the "other" (and the Diaspora can be seen as the other, not only because of geographical distance, but mainly because of its tendency to have a plural cultural allegiance). Once the self-reflexive public is given such empowering tools, the media cannot just stage deliberation, but reflect deliberation that is taking place among various publics. One solution to the issue of media morality (as discussed by Chouliaraki, 2006, and Silverstone, 2007) would be to allow imagination to play its part in designing new patterns of collective life (Appadurai, 1996) that would help communities not only to imagine better worlds, but also construct them (Appadurai, 2000).

By encouraging reflexivity, media take a stand on inducing social change. One of its instruments is mediation, defined by Silverstone as the "dialectical process in which institutionalized media of communication are involved in the general circulation of symbols in social life" (Silverstone, 2007, p. 109). It is shaped into the ideal foundation of the Mediapolis by proper distance (which might be seen as the kinder approach to difference), trust (in the view the media take), complicity and collusion (in accepting the mediation of the media) and responsibility (for such shaping). A further step is to see mediation as a political process in respect of its potential to define public response and cosmopolitan traits in spectators (Chouliaraki, 2006, p. 18).

The dilemma lies in how to negotiate between the consequence of such mediation and public action. The ethical role of the media derives not only from the responsibility to educate the public, but also from the infinitely more difficult task of inviting public action in the name of the civic sensibility it has thus created. The moral issues involved by mediation derive from two transformations it brings about: immediacy and deterritorialization, both of which raise the issue of "rendering various moral horizons adequate" (Tomlinson, 2002, p. 252). In line with Tomlinson (who suggests the taming of moral issues from distant spaces, rather than require people to cover the "moral distance"), Chouliaraki deals with "the problematic of governmentality" associated with mediation, given its potential to influence the conduct of the public (Chouliaraki, 2006, p. 71). The long-standing issue of media power is thus confronted to by the trickier problem of media responsibility.

DISCUSSION

To what degree do the Romanian media employ reflexive discourses to meditate on the impact of professional migration on societal development? And to what degree does the employment of certain practices and discourses serve public interest and, more broadly, help develop media consciousness of civic duties and the moral implications of their choices?

To answer these questions we have followed the coverage of the theme of professional migration in one leading quality paper, Adevărul, immediately before and after a controversial declaration by President Băsescu. On 4 August 2010, President Băsescu took up a theme lately cherished by the media, the migration of doctors and its consequences for the already crippled medical system. His declarations managed to inflame spirits:

> Let us not make a drama out of the fact that we are going abroad. Romania's grand objective was the liberalization of work force. Our right to live where we are better off. Where our work is correctly paid. At this moment, the Romanian state cannot pay its doctors, teachers, their worth, it cannot, and that is reality.

Since the interview took place in the context of an IMF visit, many opinion articles made reference to the whole declaration, which stole some of the limelight from the topic under discussion here.

Such discussions on the national, government-funded TV station, TVR, are an opportunity for the president to pinpoint some issues circulating in the media on a public scene, free from the constraints of official declarations. In the days to follow, the press would usually take over the most important points and discuss them in detail. The press structure their discourse to highlight the legitimate effect of the president's speeches (the clear-cut position of the president confirms the type of reactions the public expect from him), the reinforcing effect (the president's declaration resonates with the politicians' lack of interest in the individuals' fate) and the cumulative effect (this is just one of the many offences from politicians a citizen must take).

Because of the format and context of the interview, the general feeling is that the president is presenting a definite, absolute version of the facts; the press constantly positions them in a different perspective and builds arguments to undermine the declarations made from this position of authority. On the one hand, we have a summative landmark of the state of affairs, and on the other, a detailed, well grounded, expert-based analysis of the ideas contained in the discourse as such and of the implications of the president's assertions.

Since the president's declaration touched upon individual destinies and perspectives but equally referred to the systemic problems of the economy, one could expect the press discourse to be twofold: first to present cases of doctors and their life-stories as migrants and second to invite reflection on the consequences of professional migration on Romania's development prospects. Articles in the written press generally follow this approach and, while presenting individual cases, constantly discuss implications for the common good.

How is the identity of migrants built in journalists' discourses? By the accumulation of details, journalists hope to present "the robot portrait" of the professional migrant: either young (a graduate or a resident with high expectations), or middle-aged and firmly established in his profession. Knowledge of the language, proper qualifications, professional competences ensure success abroad. When migrants are quoted, they present typical, exemplary life-stories. Images of success are obviously preferred to images of dislocation (few, if any, doctors are worse off abroad). Doctors gain a lot of money abroad, they find work easily and their choices are supported by family and former teachers. The migrants declare they want to leave for good, and will not look back. Such success stories encourage migration and a positive image of migration as a moral act, serving the individual's interest, and not the common good. In the words of one interviewee, pushing a young professional to leave the country is unpatriotic, but the articles tie in this implication with the overt encouragement from the president: since the president's discourse was cynical and depressing and discouragingly honest about the state's inability to pay its specialists, loyalty cannot be expected from ordinary citizens. We are a far cry from Obama's mobilizing discourses encouraging Americans to fight the economic crisis (Adevărul, 8 August 2010).

While individuals' stories confirm the private morals of individuals serving their own interest, the dual positioning of journalists is quite evident, since they build a catastrophic image of consequences on the Romanian medical system. The reasons presented by migrants for leaving gather in strong criticism against this very system: hospitals have poor equipment and funding and lack resources. Doctors are forced to make do with poor work conditions, which leads to low self-esteem, undermined dignity, poor living standards and depression. Salaries are at an all-time low, the spectre of massive lay-offs and the impossibility of supporting families and covering debts looms large. The collapsing system is a danger to patients who cannot be treated properly, which makes doctors very doubtful of their ability to help them. The widespread disillusion over the poor governmental and political system adds to the list of discontents. Compared with other medical systems, ours is 500 years behind. While migration is presented as a good personal option, the effects of this phenomenon are bordering disaster. Migration is referred to as "the great migration" (Adevărul, 12 August), "the exodus of white robes" (Adevărul, 20 August), an "unprecedented" phenomenon leading to catastrophe (Adevărul, 23 August). The systemic effect of definitive "temporary" migration of doctors is evident in the quote from BBC News: the system sits "at the edge of a precipice" (Adevărul, 12 August), there will be no doctors left in eleven years if the numbers of migrants stay the same. Romania loses doctors in favour of richer countries (Adevărul, 13 July) and feeds other medical systems (Adevărul, 22 July).

It is quite evident that the double standard used by the journalists in approaching the issue (the private, legitimate interest of the individual and the general interest of citizens and the country) comes partly from a faulty use of resources, on the one hand, and from choice of formats, on the other. The figures are taken from studies of professional organizations, studies of European organizations, the Ministry of Health, while the migrants' life-stories are obtained through interviews. The gathering of facts, statistics and data might suggest a wish to improve the professionalization of talks on the issue. However, the texts are largely informative and no journalists' involvement is evident, apart from the selection of themes and actors. The little interpretation we have of data or the phenomenon at large comes from sources: BBC News, Newsweek, sociologists, even interviewees. The image given of the medical system, for instance, is quite vivid, yet it is so by the accumulation of details, and not by discussion or analysis. Defects are always brought forward, but moral responsibility for shortcomings is attributed to no one.

While visibility patterns of the migrants and of the theme as such are pervasive, deliberative mechanisms are very thin on the ground. Deliberative practices in themselves can lead to the creation of a civil sphere: through the practice itself, which encourages people to form opinions, discover their voice and express opinions; through the recognition, by the media, that there is something to gain from involving the public in the debate; because the theme of the debate itself forces the construction of certain imagery about society in general (what is the ideal type of society, of social actors, of politicians?) and about debates as discursive genres in particular (what is the ideal construction of the debate, with which rules and instruments, on which appropriate themes?) The media become a moral force because of their alliance with the public, which is the result of a mutual understanding of meaning, following a negotiation. Media responsibility does not only mean facilitating the public's participation in the debate, but also channelling their forces towards public action. While reflexive instruments are among the media's appurtenances, they are transferred to the public, who are offered a debate arena, a theme and a rhetorical genre. The involvement of a self-reflexive public (where reflexivity regards not only the instruments of the debate, but also the implications of the meanings resulting from the debate on the scene of civic action) amounts to an age of maturity in the media. In the case of a mainly informative discourse on a highly sensitive issue, can we speak about the strategic use of the theme of professional migration in the media? Does the theme of professional migration become a public issue? Obviously not, although all the ingredients are present: the coexistence of private and general interests, an agreement on the centrality of the theme (if only by opposition to the intended demeaning effects of the president's intervention, who declared it a non-theme), guaranteed emotional response in the public, rippling effects in real government policies.

The theme could have allowed several discourses coming from the media: identity discourses, expert discourses, policy discourses. While the identity of the intending migrants is clearly outlined, the journalists' reflection on the identity of the changing community of migrants and especially the reflection on media identity as the locus of debate are very pale. There are slight attempts at expert discourses through data gathering; yet the refinements of research instruments or the quality of the argumentative discourse, or the approval for a certain type of engagement for that matter (preserving objectivity throughout or emotional approach for rhetoric effects, generalization – integrating resulting ideas in a larger image of society and its development) are practically non-existent. Consequently, although we might allow for the efficacy of informative discourses as long as they endow the public with instruments for civic action, it is too early to discuss the capacity of journalists in this particular media setting to raise issues. This also sheds some light on the importance of clearly defining public interest, of the media's positioning themselves in respect of this public interest and, more broadly, on the current state of affairs as regards to media consciousness of civic duties and the moral implications of their choices.

References

Alexander, J (2006). *The Civil Sphere*, Oxford: Oxford University Press.

Appadurai, A (1996). *Modernity at Large: Cultural Dimensions of Globalization*, Minneapolis: University of Minnesota Press.

Appadurai, A (2000). Grassroots Globalization and the Research Imagination. *Public Culture*, 12(1), 1–19.

Beciu, C (2007). Forme mediatice de dezbatere a normelor europene. Redefinirea "misiunii" jurnalistului – elemente analitice (I). [Media Forms of Debating European Norms. Redefining the Journalist's "Mission" – Analytic Elements (I)], *R*evista Română de Sociologie [Romanian Review of Sociology], XVIII(3–4).

Beciu, C & Perpelea, N (2011). Despre pasiunea de a defini Uniunea Europeană. Studiu introductiv [About the Passion of Defining the European Union. Introductory Study]. In C Beciu & N Perpelea (coord.), Europa în context. Identităţi şi practici discursive. [*Europe in Context. Identities and Discursive Practices*], Bucureşti: Ars Docendi, pp. 7–20.

Calhoun, C (1992). Introduction: Habermas and the Public Sphere. In C Calhoun (ed.), *Habermas and the Public Sphere*. Cambridge, MA: MIT Press.

—. (2002). Imagining Solidarity: Cosmopolitanism, Constitutional Patriotism and the Public Sphere. *Public Culture*, 14(1), 147–171.

Chouliaraki, L (2006). *The Spectatorship of Suffering*. London: Sage.

Cohen-Almagor, R (2005). *Speech, Media and Ethics: The Limits of Free Expression.* Palgrave Macmillan.

Coleman, S (2001). The Transformation of Citizenship? In B Axford & R Huggins (eds), *New Media and Politics.* London: Sage.

Coleman, S & Ross, K (2010). *The Media and the Public: "Them" and "Us" in Media Discourse.* Wiley-Blackwell.

Couldry, N (2006). Transvaluing Media Studies: or, beyond the Myth of the Mediated Centre. In J Curran & D Morley (eds), *Media and Cultural Theory.* London: Routledge.

Curran, J (2002). *Media and Power.* London: Routledge.

—. (2006). Media and Cultural Theory in the Age of Market Liberalism. In J Curran & D Morley (eds). *Media and Cultural Theory.* London: Routledge.

Curran, J & Seaton, J ([1981] 2003). *Power without Responsibility.* London: Routledge.

Habermas, J (1989). *The Structural Transformation of the Public Sphere: An Inquiry into a Category of Bourgeois Society.* Translation by Thomas Burger. Cambridge, MA: MIT Press.

—. (1992). Further Reflections on the Public Sphere. In C Calhoun (ed.), *Habermas and the Public Sphere.* Cambridge, MA: MIT Press.

Kellner, D (1995). *Media Culture: Cultural Studies, Identity and Politics between the Modern and the Postmodern.* London and New York: Routledge.

Sassi, S (2001). The Transformation of the Public Sphere? In B Axford & R Huggins (eds), *New Media and Politics.* London: Sage.

Silverstone, R (2007). *Media and Morality: On the Rise of the Mediapolis.* London: Polity.

Singer, Jane B, Hermida, A, Domingo, D, Heinonen, A, Paulussen. S, Quandt, T, Reich, Z & Vujnovic, M (2011). *Participatory Journalism: Guarding Open Gates at Online Newspapers.* Wiley-Blackwell.

Tomlinson, J (2002). Globalizare şi cultură [Globalization and culture]. Translation by Cristina Gyurcsik. Timişoara: Amarcord.

STEREOTYPES CROISES ET IDENTITES : UNE ETUDE EMPIRIQUE MENEE EN CONTEXTE UNIVERSITAIRE MULTICULTUREL

ANNE-MARIE CODRESCU

Résumé

Le questionnement initial de la présente étude visait si et comment les représentations culturelles figées sur l'Autre se modifient par le contact direct et l'interaction dans un cadre européen qui favorise l'action commune et l'apprentissage.

L'assise conceptuelle et théorique est la communication interculturelle conçue comme un processus herméneutique. L'interprétation intra- et interculturelle est soujacente dans une analyse centrée sur les stéréotypes nationaux qui prend en compte la nature ambivalente de la notion : source d'apprentissage social, le stéréotype est-il fondé sur un noyau culturel commun, ce qui expliquerait le fort attachement identitaire et les sources de dévalorisation de l'autre, ou bien se prête-t-il, par l'interaction et le contact direct, à une connaissance approfondie des racines culturelles, à l'acceptation du noyau ontologique originaire, des différences implicites entre les communautés, à la déconstruction des généralisations hâtives par la réflexion intra culturelle et la connaissance de la culture de l'Autre ?

Une enquête menée auprès d'étudiants étrangers et roumains, par des interviews en profondeur semi dirigées me permet d'entreprendre une analyse qualitative sur les stéréotypes nationaux dans un contexte universitaire européen afin de vérifier l'évolution des représentations sur soi et sur l'autre. La thèse du renforcement des stéréotypes se vérifie-elle ou, au contraire, le contact direct dans un contexte éducatif favorise-t-il une meilleure communication interculturelle dans un esprit d'ouverture et de tolérance réciproque?

Mots-clés: communication intra- et interculturelle, stéréotype, identité européenne, noyau ontologique originaire

INTRODUCTION

A l'ère de l'ouverture des frontières entre les pays de l'Europe se pose de manière prégnante la question de la communication entre des cultures différentes. Or, si appartenir à une culture signifie communiquer d'une manière spécifique, la culture d'origine et la culture cible devront prendre en considération le phénomène de l'altérité, le problème identitaire et la construction des savoirs (Chaudeau, 2007 : 6). Lorsque des individus appartenant à des cultures différentes entrent en contact il est possible que des évidences non partagées, des normes et des valeurs variables surgissent : c'est bien le moment de la confrontation entre deux visions du monde, de la rencontre avec l'étranger, avec l'étrange.

Or, les stéréotypes constituent un premier pas dans l'appréhension de la réalité et de l'autre, dont ils façonnent la représentation. Le concept a gagné en complexité grâce aux clarifications complémentaires et croisées apportées par les sciences sociales et humaines : sociologie, psychologie sociale, sciences du langage, sociolinguistique. On constate en effet une évolution intra et interdisciplinaire des études sur les stéréotypes qui contribue à l'apparition de notions de plus en plus nuancées et complexes : „reproduction quasi photographique d'un cliché cérébral" (Tarde, 1890), le „stéréotype" (Lippman, 1922) en tant que structure sociocognitive fixe, est un mécanisme simplificateur de connaissance de la réalité par le biais des similitudes. Il est fait de jugements fixes qui, développés à partir d'une base émotionnelle, fonctionnent en tant que repères sécurisants pour l'individu. Hormis cette fonction cognitive, le stéréotype a également une fonction idéologique car il reflète un ensemble d'idées, de croyances et de doctrines propres à une société.

Les interactions interculturelles ont fait l'objet d'études sur l'image qu'un peuple se fait sur un autre et sur le poids des stéréotypes dans les rapports à l'Autre, sur la „fonction identitaire du stereotype" (Camillieri et Vinsonneau, 1996, *apud* Amossy, 2005:45). Marques spécifiques des identités culturelles les stéréotypes « nourrissent » l'interculturel et justifient la diversité culturelle (Paul Ricœur, 1986). D'autres études constatent un renforcement des stéréotypes en contact interculturel qui ne saurait être surmonté que par l'action et des intérêts communs (Ladmiral et Lipianski, 1989, Demorgon, 1989).

En effet on reconnaît au stéréotype deux fonctions positives, la construction de l'identité et la fonction cognitive, d'élément structurant et organisationnel, mais aussi son revers, celui d'élément fige, caricatural de jugement de l'Autre.

Cette ambivalence du stéréotype (Amossy, 2005 :28), perçu comme repère cognitif sécurisant, par certains et barrière mentale ou entrave à la connaissance par d'autres (Pierre Mauroy, Francine Fournier, 2000), rend plus complexe l'analyse des interactions entre des cultures différentes.

Représentations et stereotypes, precisions conceptuelles

Si toute représentation relève d'une démarche identitaire, les représentations de l'étranger constituent paradoxalement l'une des voies les plus accessibles pour amorcer une réflexion sur le fonctionnement de son identité, qu'il s'agisse de l'identité nationale, de l'identité sociale ou bien des pratiques socioculturelles. Comme structure figée, simplificatrice, les stéréotypes concernent tous les modes de connaissance intra- et interculturelle et d'appartenance identitaire. Pourtant, ils ne laissent pas de place à la réflexion, alors les individus, les communautés, les pays et les langues sont caractérisés de manière intrinsèque.

Mais il est tout aussi vrai que les stéréotypes peuvent évoluer, notamment à la suite du contact direct avec l'autre. Il est avéré que l'expérience directe diminue à la fois les stéréotypes négatifs et la survalorisation du groupe ethnique d'origine (McGrady & Mc Grady, 1987, Bjerstedt, 1959).

En psychologie sociale, on distingue entre représentations et stéréotypes (Moscovici, 1988; Jodelet, 1989). Les représentations sont inhérentes à l'activité humaine. A la différence des stéréotypes, qui sont fixes, immuables, elles prennent appui sur une action dynamique, qui suppose une évolution. Ainsi la représentation sociale serait „un univers d'opinions" (J. Maisonneuve, 1988:146) tandis que le stereotype n'est que la cristallisation d'un élément, il sert d'indicateur. (Amossy & Herschberg Pierrot, 2005:50–51)

Les représentations sociales sur un groupe culturellement homogène, qui font l'objet de notre intérêt, participent d'un processus de définition de l'identité sociale. En outre, partager des représentations signifie manifester son adhésion à un groupe, affirmer un lien social et contribuer à son renforcement.

La recherche exploratoire, menée dans un groupe multiculturel d'étudiants, se concentre sur les représentations et la présence ou non des stéréotypes nationaux, afin de vérifier si et en quelle mesure ceux-ci sont une source de dévalorisation de l'autre à cause de généralisations hâtives et de leur enracinement dans le mental collectif. Stéréotypes raciaux, ethniques, nationaux, régionaux, de genre, d'âge, professionnels se construisent selon la double logique de la différence et de l'appartenance. „ L'identité suppose en effet la différence: la conscience d'appartenir à une même collectivité n'émerge que face à d'autres collectivités ressenties comme „étrangères” [1].

L'un des volets de notre démarche vise justement à identifier comment, dans une situation interculturelle, les représentations initiales et / ou les stéréotypes de l'autre ont évolué à la suite de la rencontre directe. L'autre volet se propose d'appréhender chez les sujets interviewés l'effort d'interprétation et d'adaptation qu'ils ont dû fournir en situation interculturelle. Cet effort suppose à la fois une prise de distance par rapport à soi et une ouverture vers l'autre („hors de soi en l'Autre”). (Gadamer, in belcikowski.org) En effet, la compréhension herméneutique prend appui sur la reconnaissance réciproque du noyau culturel qui définit l'identité de tout individu et de l'être en général. C'est précisément en cela que la communication interculturelle est une herméneutique.

Le sentiment d'appartenance à un groupe culturel – un pays et ses natifs – a des racines ontologiques fondées sur la manière de concevoir l'existence, les rapports à l'espace, au temps, à l'Autre. (Asante et al. , 2008 :40–41)

On reconnaît effectivement des facteurs objectifs comme soubassement de l'identité culturelle collective (histoire commune, traditions, langue, religion) doublés des éléments subjectifs inscrits dans chaque conscience individuelle.

L'identité culturelle

> « existe d'abord sous forme de représentation sociale qui permet à une collectivité de se définir et de se faire reconnaître par les autres ; cette représentation est faite d'images, de symboles, de stéréotypes, de mythes originaires, de récits historiques qui offrent à la conscience collective une figuration de sa « personnalité » et de son unité. » (Ladmiral & Lipiansky, 1989:10)

---

[1] Ladmiral et Lipianski avertissent sur le risque de reduire le sentiment d'apartenance à la seule composante nationale, car la différenciation est ressentie à d'autres niveaux de l'ensemble des représentations sur l'identité, dont l'appartenance ethnique, régionale, socio-professionnelle, religieuse ou idéologique. Leurs recherches les ont conduit à affirmer la dialectique de l'identité et de l'alterité à l'oeuvre dans les rencontres interculturelles, construites sur un jeu d' ”oppositions et liaisons”: „L'identité se trouve au point de rencontre de deux mouvements qui tendent à maintenir à la fois différence et lien, *paradigmes* et *syntagme*, dimensions constitutives de l'ordre symbolique qui fonde la culture.” Ladmiral, Jean –Rene, Lipiansky, Edmond Marc, *La communication interculturelle*, Armand Colin, Paris, 1989, p. 130

Le noyau culturel constitué par l'ensemble des caractéristiques que tous les membres de l'ensemble culturel partagent (Linton, 1936) serait l'une des « dimensions oubliées » qui président à l'organisation des relations sociales (Joly in Chaulat, 1990 :473) et ne saurait être ignoré.

Ce noyau ontologique originaire, profondément enfoui dans la conscience collective forme l'assise des valeurs, normes, représentations communes (« représentations partagées », Boyer, 2001 : 333) et se manifestent par les comportements individuels. Il explique en quelque sorte l'attitude auto-défensive des individus confrontés aux hétéro représentations ou aux hétéro stéréotypes véhiculés sur leur identité collective.

Par exemple, Mircea Vulcanescu essaie de mettre en évidence que les sources des stéréotypes sur l'identité nationale peuvent être profondément enfouies dans le mental collectif, ce qui leur confère souvent un caractère véridique et explique leur résistance. Pour le philosophe roumain, ces repères incontestables de jugement marquent et parfois empiètent sur la communication interculturelle.

Selon lui, tandis que pour les Français « la clarté et la logique sont [...] des dimensions privilégiées de l'existence, des perspectives absolues, des normes, au nom desquelles sont éthiquement jugées les accomplissements dans les autres perspectives. » (Vulcănescu, 2005:1012), ce qui domine la conception roumaine de l'existence est le sentiment d'une vaste solidarité universelle, son « caractère protéiforme incontestable » (Vulcănescu, 2005 :1034), l'inconstance et le scepticisme.

Toute auto représentation sur l'identité collective d'un groupe culturel pourrait prendre comme repère fondamental l'analyse des rapports à l'existence. Par ailleurs, le questionnement herméneutique sur les différences culturelles aboutit souvent au noyau dur identitaire, qu'il faut assumer et accepter.

Les représentations sur l'Autre sont ainsi marquées non seulement par les acquis d'expériences personnelles, par les repères culturels différents, mais également par une conception particulière de l'existence.

ETUDE DE CAS. PRECISIONS NOTIONNELLES ET METHODOLOGIQUES

Cette intervention s'inscrit dans le cadre d'une recherche plus ample[2].

---

[2] Une étude partielle a été présentée dans le cadre du Colloque franco-roumain, juin 2010, de Bucarest. Le projet d'ensemble propose une étude empirique sur les stéréotypes nationaux dans le contexte de l'identité européenne, par une analyse qualitative basée sur des interviews en profondeur semi-structurés. Un public cible est représenté par des sujets internationaux qui étudient en France (à Lyon) et proviennent d'un pays européen ou d'un pas non-européen. Une attention

Les hétéro représentations, sous leur modalité la plus névralgique, le stéréotype, font l'objet de nombreuses études interculturelles[3] menées principalement en contexte biculturel. Les notions sont encore controversées, différents auteurs proposant des alternatives notionnelles afin d'éviter l'ambiguïté sémantique du stéréotype[4].

L'auto stéréotype (Boyer, 2001/3-4, No.123 : 333–340) est appliqué par l'individu à sa propre culture. L'hétéro stéréotype est appliqué à une autre culture. Nous utilisons principalement, dans l'interprétation des réponses de cette étude, la notion d'hétéro représentations, le cas échéant celle d'hétéro stéréotype. Les notions d'auto représentation et hétéro représentation interviendront uniquement dans l'analyse des éléments de l'identité européenne.

Notre contribution voudrait dépasser l'observation biculturelle et identifier, à travers les témoignages des jeunes, étudiant en contexte universitaire multiculturel[5], et de leurs exemples d'interaction avec plusieurs cultures différentes les hétéro représentations sur leur culture d'appartenance, le poids des stéréotypes, ainsi que la présence des paramètres d'une identité commune européenne. Ce qui nous a semblé intéressant à étudier dans un tel groupe c'est précisément la pluralité des perspectives sur un sujet sensible de l'actualité. D'une part, l'aspect pédagogique : entraînés quotidiennement dans des activités d'étude, ils se confrontent à présent aux différences culturelles d'une micro société, mais ce contact de l'Autre constitue l'essence de leur future activité professionnelle. D'autre part, ils seront les membres actifs d'une société multiculturelle, et le dialogue permet une prise de conscience des problématiques sensible dans la société européenne.

Le dialogue a visé: les processus de la rencontre de l'Autre; l'importance du contact direct sur les modifications des représentations

---

particulière est accordée aux stéréotypes auxquels les étudiants roumains se confrontent dans une autre culture.

[3] En témoigne les 5 tomes de communications parues en novembre 2009, *Stereotypage, stereotypes : fonctionnements ordinaires et mises en scene,* ENS Editions, revues.org. sous la direction d'Henri Boyer.

[4] Ainsi, pour Ladmiral et Lipiansky, dans leur étude sur l'imagerie franco-allemande, l'objet de l'imagologie est l'analyse du « contenu des représentations qu'un peuple se fait d'un autre (*hétéro-images*) et de lui-même (d'*auto-images*) », Ladmiral, Jean –Rene, Lipiansky, Edmond Marc, *La communication interculturelle*, Armand Colin, Paris, 1989, p. 228

[5] Etudiants en Master 2 Communication, humanitaire et solidarite, ICOM, Universite Lyon 2 Lumiere, 2010-2011. Les entretiens se sont deroules le 9 decembre 2010.

initiales; le rôle et les fonctions des stéréotypes dans la dynamiques des rencontres; l'identité européenne: Plus précisément, les questions clés de la présente recherche ont été:

1. Sur quels fondements peut-on définir l'altérité par rapport à une culture d'accueil?
2. Quels sont les stéréotypes dominants sur le pays d'origine des répondants dans les pays de référence ?
3. Peut-on parler d'une identité européenne et quels en seraient les paramètres?

Puisqu'il s'agit d'une recherche qualitative exploratoire, au cours des entretiens des questions supplémentaires ont été nécessaires afin de clarifier certains aspects liés aux stéréotypes nationaux et/ou à l'identité européenne ou pour éliminer tout soupçon de parti pris.

L'étude de cas a été menée sur un groupe pluri-national de 16 étudiants, agés de 22 à 26 ans, d'une université française, par des interviews semi-dirigées. L'intérêt du groupe consiste essentiellement, d'une part, dans la diversité des identités d'origine (3 étrangers /13 Français, dont 2 de parents etrangers) et, d'autre part, dans les nombreux contacts avec des cultures étrangères (15 repères géographiques distincts)[6]. A la diversité géographique s'ajoutent les contextes différents qui ont permis leur immersion dans la culture de référence (personnel, éducationnel, professionnel, social, touristique).

La transcription des interviews individuelles, semi-dirigées, d'une durée totale de 241 :08 minutes nous a fourni le corpus d'analyse. L'ensemble du corpus a été divisé en 3 grands segments thématiques (altérité, hétéro représentations sur la France et sur la Roumanie et éléments d'identité européenne). Les réponses à chaque groupe de questions (structure du guide d'entretien en annexe) ont été traitées comme un discours à part, ce qui m' a permis d'identifier et d'analyser les constantes et les variables dans chaque séquence thématique. Ainsi, l'analyse textuelle a mis en évidence : les critères de définition de l'altérité; les repères de différenciation pris en compte dans les hétéro représentations évoquées; un inventaire des éléments de l'identité européenne et les arguments des sujets.

---

[6] Dans le groupe, la plupart ont eu au moins une experience culturelle dans les pays europeens (9 / 16), 6/16 dans des pays africains, 3/16 aux Etats-Unis, 3/16 en Asie et 1/16 en Amerique du Sud.

Nous avons ensuite dépouillé, structuré et organisé les résultats en prenant comme unité de référence les mots et les syntagmes utilisés par les sujets dans leurs discours.

Dans ce qui suit nous présentons une synthèse structurée de leurs réponses. Nous précisons entre parenthèses le nombre de personnes ayant donné la même réponse, par rapport à l'ensemble des 16 sujets.

DÉFINIR L'ALTÉRITÉ, CRITÈRES CULTURELS DISTINCTIFS

Le but du dialogue face-à-face a été de recueillir des témoignages sur le vécu des rencontres interculturelles des sujets, visant d'abord à leur permettre de se définir en tant qu'étrangers dans une culture différente de la leur. La plupart des étudiants définissent différemment l'altérité selon le vécu personnel de l'interaction entre les „étrangers„ et les „locaux". Pour eux; le champ sémantique du rapport à l'altérité est analysé:

- en termes de réactions de l'Autre: „être étranger"c'est un rejet / une confrontation / une comparaison / une curiosité /;
- et / ou en termes de réaction du Moi: „être étranger" c'est se remettre en question / prendre conscience de sa culture / une intégration / comprendre l'Autre;
- un sentiment d'appartenance (2): „être etranger" c'est „être européen" / „être en Erasmus".

Comme critères de différenciation entre Moi et l'Autre, le discours des participants a mis en évidence: les pratiques sociales (6), la race et les barrières linguistiques (5), l'identité nationale, le caractère, l'histoire et les relations bilatérales (5) la religion (4), les parcours de vie et de formation (1), la barrière administrative (1) et le statut de la femme (1), certains d'entre eux énumerant plusieurs. En fait, le nombre assez grand de repères s'explique par des critères de jugement de l'Autre qui leur sont familiers. L'expérience fournit des repères individuels particuliers ou des repères de vie commune, selon lesquels ils ont jugé l'intéraction avec les étrangers. Dans la culture italienne, par exemple, c'est par rapport aux pratiques culturelles locales, „le foot, les voitures", qu'on est jugé: „ben, tu es Francais, tu manges les escargots mais tu ne sais pas faire les pates" (Gaetan). On constate l'émergence spontanée d'un stéréotype courant sur les „Français, mangeurs d'escargots ou de grenouilles" dans le jugement de l'Italien.

Un autre exemple indique le fait que les repères culturels familiers, quand ils ne sont pas partagés par l'Autre, peuvent devenir aussi source d'étonnement et de dépaysement : „ ... des dessins animés pour les enfants, quand je leur parlais de trucs de base, là-bas, en Espagne, ils n'étaient pas capables de comprendre." (Elisa).

„... on est éternellement étrangers ..."

Pour la plupart des participants le contact direct reste essentiel dans les rapports interculturels car il permet de vraiment vivre la différence. C'est le cas de l'étudiant français d'origine algérienne, lors de sa première visite au pays de ses parents, pour qui „quand on y va c'est très différent", „même si je vis dans un quartier avec des gens qui viennent de là-bas, du Maghreb, de l'Afrique" (Akim).

En effet, les opinions sont très partagées sur la nécessite de se renseigner sur le pays de destination: pour la plupart le contact direct reste le plus important, il modifie ou relativise les représentations initiales. Trois d'entre eux seulement considèrent les informations préliminaires importantes pour des raisons d'insertion professionnelle ou culturelle (codes particuliers) ou pour des raisons pratiques (climat, informations touristiques).

L'altérité peut être doublement ressentie par un même sujet. Le regard et surtout le jugement de l'autre équivaut à un rejet qui place le sujet en porte-à-faux à cause de la double appartenance (identité originaire et identité acquise). C'est, par exemple, le cas de Sarah, d'origine marocaine, qui „se sent balancée entre deux cultures: au Maroc on l'appelle „personne de l'extérieur", et en France elle est vue comme étrangère aussi, „puisqu'elle est née au Maroc" (Akim, Français d'origine algérienne).

L'altérité a ete évoquée comme une expérience dramatique par quelqu'un qui fait partie une minorité « contrastante": à Haiti, où „au collège, sur 1200 élèves, on était 20 „blancs". „Donc c'était moi qui était la minorité, c'etait moi qui était vue comme différente, c'est là que je me suis remise en question, j'ai connu ce que c'est le racisme". Elle évoque l'apparence physique, cause de rejet, en contraste avec „les critères de beauté" locaux. Pourtant, de retour en France, „ qui était cense être (son) pays", elle n'était pas à sa place et s'est confrontée au désintérêt de ses semblables, puisqu'elle ne partageait pas les mêmes codes ou repères culturels (Aude). Dans les déclarations de deux interviewés, intervient un certain conflit entre l'identite personnelle[7] et l'identite sociale[8] déterminé par l'appartenance à une minorité raciale.

---

[7] L'identité personnelle est „un processus psychologique de représentation de soi qui se traduit par le sentiment d'exister dans une continuité en tant qu'être singulier et d'être reconnu comme tel par autrui", in Amossy R., Herschberg Pierrot A., oeuvr. citée, p. 44.

Toutefois, l'altérité peut aussi devenir une source d'enrichissement et de remise en question de l'identité personnelle: „on commence a se remettre en cause, a s'améliorer par rapport à ses origines, ... ce n'est pas qu'on la dénigre, mais on l'enrichit" (Rama).

Confronté aux idées reçues au sein du même groupe culturel, aux auto stéréotypes sur la place et le rôle „assignés" d'avance dans la société, se distinguer des autres, choisir un autre „parcours", c'est ce qui „renforce ou diminue le fait qu'on est étranger" (Christella). Dans ce cas, être etranger est vécu comme un paradoxe puisque, à l'intérieur d'une même culture, l'altérité est vécue en terme de différenciation sociale et éthnique. Appartenir à des éthnies différentes par ses origines familiales risque, en situation de conflit, à exposer au rejet et même à conduire à des massacres fratricides. C'est l'une des conséquences de „limiter les gens à leur seule identité" (Christella).

Selon les témoignages reccueillis, le rapport identité / altérité reste assez paradoxal, car il est fondé sur des expériences personnelles, en fonction de l'origine, du statut social à l'interieur de la culture d'accueil ou de sa propre culture. Il est à remarquer surtout dans les représentations collectives la fonction identitaire des stéréotypes et leur rôle dans la remise en question de l'identité individuelle.

„... reconnaître'altérité en nous, c'est prendre conscience que nous sommes tous des „métis" culturels" (Ladmiral et Lipianski, 1989:143)

Hétéro représentations: La France et la Roumanie

Sur les 9 questions de l'entretien, 5 étaient centrées sur les hétéro représentations de la France et de la Roumanie et de leurs habitants. Les sujets étaient encouragés à présenter comment, lors du contact direct avec les habitants des pays visités, ceux-ci se représentaient la France et ses habitants. Lorsqu'il a été question de la Roumanie, les hétéro-représentations étaient formées presqu'exclusivement à partir d'expériences vécues en France et des informations médiatisées. Même si cela reflète une situation de fait, cette assymétrie entre les représentations des deux pays a exigé une analyse et un traitement différents des données recueillies.

---

[8] L'identité sociale est „un processus psychosocial de construction et de représentation de soi résultant des interactions et des cognitions des individus concernant leur appartenance sociale" (Fischer 1996: 202), apud Amossy Amossy R., Herschberg Pierrot A., oeuvr. citée, p. 44.

Les questions sur l'image médiatique des pays et sur les sources d'information ont visé à fournir une référence complémentaire sur les thèmes qui intéressent la presse étrangère.

La schématisation, le recours à des paradigmes d'oppositions auraient simplifié l'analyse des représentations du groupe interviewé, pourtant cette approche a été considérée inadéquate vu que la complexité et la diversité des discours, l'analyse critique des participants, le dialogue sur les situations de contact ou sur l'image médiatisée des deux pays permettaient une approche plus nuancée. Un autre argument a été la capacité des étudiants à éviter les clichés, les idées reçues et d'en parler avec une certaine objectivité. C'est pourquoi j'utilise la notion d'hétéro représentations et j'essaie de découvrir, dans l'analyse du discours, les stéréotypes sous-jacents qui informent certaines représentations.

La France. Hétéro-représentations et effets d'images: une expérience directe

Les participants ont évoque d'abord les „on dit" sur la France et les Français dans les pays visités. Les critères géopolitiques, l'histoire des relations avec la France, les critéres générationnel et social ont été évoqués pour distinguer les représentations différentes sur la France. Les facteurs qui entrainent des modifications sur les hétéro images et même sur les stéréotypes sont les conjonctures socio-politiques qui modifient les comportements et les jugements: Les situations citées en exemple: la crise des banlieues en novembre 2005, le boicote économique de la France par les Etats-Unis en 2002-2003, les mouvements sociaux récents en France.

Rarement la différence par rapport aux cultures étrangères est ressentie sur une base nationale: „être française c'est reconnaître les stéréotypes, avoir une histoire partagée ou pas" (Camille).

La différence varie selon les pays et l'histoire des relations avec la France

Ainsi, pour les Européens, l'image de la France est plus favorable dans les pays nordiques et au Sud où on apprécie le dynamisme politique de Sarkozy, car „là-bas les choses bougent", en contraste avec l'immobilisme politique local (l'Espagne, en l'occurence). En fait l'image qui revient souvent est celle de „pays des grèves", ce qui confirme le stéréotype sur les Français „râleurs". Conscient d'un autre stéréotype généralisé, „xénophobe, toujours sur soi", l'étudiant apprend des mots de base dans les langues des pays visités car „ces stéréotypes, il faut les casser" (Gaetan).

En Afrique, au sein de la population, l'image est contrastée en fonction de l'histoire coloniale. Dans les anciennes colonies, se maintient encore l'image de la France comme „papa colonisateur", même si on remarque qu'elle s'estompe actuellement car elle „perd pied" par rapport aux Etats-Unis (Christella). Par contraste, les stéréotypes positifs dominent chez les catégories moins éduquées et plus agées. Pour elles, la France reste une référence cognitive, même au niveau des stéréotypes: elle continue de représenter un „idéal", le pays de la culture, „des Lumières" (4).

Hétéro stéréotypes „partis en fumée"

Aux Etats-Unis, se maintiennent des stéréotypes tres anciens, qui font référence soit à la gastronomie ou au Français, „un bonhomme au beret et à la baguette" soit au rôle de „sauveurs" des Americains (Akim). Les hétéro-images sur la France continue d'être celle d'"une mère-patrie" qui „accueille tous les étrangers", leur donne „la sécurité sociale, l'accès à l'éducation", ce qui démontre l'amalgame historique avec la période post-coloniale et justifie les idées reçues sur les Français „socialistes ou communistes" (Camille). Ceux-ci sont plutot „mal vus", ils seraient „libertins .. ayant des idées frivoles", „bêtes" „sales" (Rama, Yoann). Une remarque sur ce dernier stéréotype qui circule dans les pays anglo-saxons et en Amérique du Sud: sa source provient d'un amalgame que l'on fait avec un autre stéréotype, tout aussi faux, les Français, „inventeurs du parfum".

Les médias perpétuent l'image stéréotypée

Les images dans les médias étrangers européens sont centrées sur les grèves et les politiques restrictives contre l'immigration, la France étant perçue comme „très en recul" par rapport aux droits de l'homme (3).

Les médias africains perpétuent souvent l'image d'une nation responsable des problèmes de l'Afrique, la France étant dénigrée surtout en Algerie et au Maroc (3)

Aux Etats –Unis, malgré la fausseté de certains jugements, les médias continuent de les propager, car „ les Americains, ils se moquent un peu de la France" et „ils traitent les Français un peu de haut" (Rama).

D'autre part, le boicote des produits français aux Etats Unis, en 2002-2003 a ébranlé l'identité française dans les seuls éléments qui, dans le mental collectif, lui servaient de fondement, et des stéréotypes sont partis „

en fumée, le vin français, le fromage, la baguette, tout était enquêté" (Camille). Ce qui démontre l'effet des événements socio-politiques médiatises sur le comportement de la population, concretisé par le rejet des produits-symbôles qui avaient construit l'image stéréotypée du pays.

On pourrait dire que l'image de la France est autant marquée par le passé („pays colonisateur") que par le présent (les mouvements sociaux, „ la grogne, les grèves"), en particulier par les politiques contre les immigrés. Dans les médias étrangers elle reste plutot négative, partielle, centrée sur le sensationnel (en Espagne et en Australie on privilégie les informations „people"), „ un pays dont on apprécie la culture mais on deprécie la France" (Laetitia).

La Roumanie. L'amalgame identitaire: une expérience médiée

Les réponses portant sur la Roumanie et les Roumains sont restées vagues, prouvant la méconnaissance due principalement à l'absence d'un contact direct avec le pays et au manque d'informations. Un seul sujet y avait fait une courte incursion au delà de la frontière hongroise en 1991. Les sources principales restent le contact involontaire avec les Roumains d'éthnie rrome qui vivent en France, l'opinion des gens - les „on dit"-, les discours des médias, rarement l'entourage personnel.

C'est pourquoi dans les propos recueillis sont visibles les marques d'hésitation, les silences, la volonté déclarée de ne pas reprendre des idées reçues, un certain embarras. En fait, la Roumanie reste „un pays mystérieux" (Audrey) de l'Europe de l'Est, „méconnu" (5), visiblement absent des promotions touristiques et, implicitement, „on n'a pas l'image du peuple roumain" (Gaetan).

Le discours des participants reste assez inégal, car il contient d'une part des associations spontanées de mots isolés, qui activent des clichés ou des stéréotypes, et, d'autre part, des analyses ou explications de leurs représentations sur la Roumanie et les Roumains.

En effet, dans la premiére catégorie, les participants ont mentionné plusieurs associations spontanées (12) que je synthétise. Selon des critères geographiques, la Roumanie est un pays „froid", de l'Europe de l'Est, „l'ex-URSS", où dominent de „vastes plaines". Quatre des participants ont évoqué des critères historiques récents, „dictature, Ceausescu", „orphelinats". Les critères d'ordre économique sont plus nombreux (7) : on considère que le clivage entre l'Europe de l'Est et celle de l'Ouest place la Roumanie parmi les „pays en voie de développement", un „pays pauvre, où la main d'oeuvre n'est pas chère", ce qui justifie les délocalisations. Un sujet évoque l'image du travailleur de l'Est, qui „vient piquer le boulot des autres", promue par les partis de l'extrême droite (Sebastien). On constate la présence dominante des stéréotypes sur le pays et sur la région de l'Europe de l'Est, en général.

Les hétéro-images sur les Roumains sont plutot positives et nuancées: Le portrait robot synthèse contient des impressions formées après un contact direct avec des Roumains connus dans l'entourage personnel ou professionnel. Dans l'ensemble, pour 6 participants, il n'y a pas de différences culturelles, les Roumains seraient „tres cultivés", „d'esprit ouvert", gentils, chaleureux, humbles mais malins, spirituels et bons vivants, une participante trouvaient que „les femmes sont belles". Parmi les hétéro-images négatives sur les Roumains on a mentionné „stigmatisés" et une seule participante a évoqué les stéréotypes négatifs „voleurs", „Rroms" et „voyage".

La partie plus critique de leur discours a signalé l'amalgame „halucinant" qui existe „dans la tête des gens" entre Rroms et Roumains (11) , ce qui fait que l'on ne dit jamais des choses positives et que les „Roumains sont mal vus". Les participants ont fait état des préjugés qui existent sur les „Roumains mendiants", mais il y a aussi des jugements critiques sur la stigmatisation éthnique d'origine politique qui visait auparavant les Arabes et qui, depuis août 2010, concernent les mesures d'expulsion contre les Rroms. Une participante analyse et explique la source et le fonctionnement de ces stéréotypes négatifs dans le mental collectif: " les opinions sont fondées sur le comportement des populations migrantes, pour le Français moyen c'est une simplification" (Sarah).

Ces jugements négatifs, l'amalgame „généralisé", les stéréotypes négatifs qui existent dans l'opinion française se sont deja incrustés dans le langage: des expressions toutes faites circulent pour faire des remarques négatives sur le comportement ou l'aspects des gens. Par exemple, pour critiquer le „désordre, dans une pièce, dans une voiture", on va dire „mais, quoi on est en Roumanie?", ou bien à quelqu'un qui est mal habillé, „mis n'importe comment" on lui jette avec arrogance: „Oh, t'es rromano..." ou bien „ ah, t'es habillée comme une Roumaine". Même si l'étudiante reconnait que c'est irespectueux, elle se justifie „mais c'est des expressions qu'on dit en France" (Camille), ce qui renforce l'idée de la pérennisation du stygmate par le langage.

Pour conclure, l'image que les gens vont généraliser sur les Roumains c'est „la partie visible de l'iceberg", car c'est „ce qui leur est donné à voir tous les jours" et qui „est perçu comme un dérangement" (Yoann).

Les remarques spontanées des participants se confirment dans les réponses concernant l'image médiatisée de la Roumanie et des Roumains. La confusion persiste dans la presse, engendrée par une méconnaissance des distinctions éthniques quand „on parle des Roumains comme des Rroms", lorsqu'on fait des jugements sur les actions „des Roumains" et on passe „des informations politiques sur les Rroms" (Ramona, Benedicte, Aude).

D'autres informations diffusées sur ce pays concerne les délocalisations et la situation des étudiants français en médecine expatriés pour continuer leurs études en Roumanie ainsi que le flux inverse des jeunes médecins roumains qui travaillent dans les villages français.

Les stéréotypes négatifs du mental collectif sont consolidés par les médias et renforcés par la reprise en boucle dans les reportages ou les films inspirés par les événements. La conjoncture socio-politique (les mesures d'expulsion des Rroms en aout 2010), représente un facteur important sur la modification de l'image du pays et explique en partie cette dominante négative dans les hétéro représentations du corpus analysé, ainsi que l'image figée dans les médias français. Celle-ci persiste et „grossit" avec le temps: la preuve, les cartes des stéréotypes nationaux dans les pays européнens (adevarul.ro) , ou les émissions de télévision qui transforment l'image d'un pays dans une caricature méconnaissable.

L'IDENTITÉ EUROPÉENNE ET SES PARAMÈTRES: HÉTÉRO REPRÉSENTATIONS ET AUTO REPRÉSENTATIONS

L'Europe vue d'ailleurs

Etats-Unis: Vue de l'autre coté de l'Atlantique, „la vieille Europe c'est tout petit" avec des pays minuscules dans l'imaginaire des enfants americains (Akim).

En ce qui concerne les traits de caractère, si la modestie est considérée une qualité en Europe, elle est interprétée comme de la lacheté par les Americains „qui sont arrogants" (Akim).

En Asie. l'image de l'Europe est assimilée aux valeurs du siècle des Lumières, l'esprit, cartésien, le doute, l'esprit critique qui contrastent avec les mentalités et les croyances locales (Camille).

Les médias américains prouvent une connaissance très approximative de la géographie européenne: la carte de la France présentée sur CNN était toute déformée, Paris se trouvant à Strasbourg et les frontières de la France en Allemagne, „un amalgame" (Beatrice).

L'Europe vue par ses habitants

Selon les auto représentations des participants, elle serait marquée en son sein par le clivage entre l'Est et l'Ouest, ce qui fait que les Européens de l'Est sont encore vus comme des „sous-européens", et l'UE est encore perçue comme „une communauté occidentale" (Akim, Sebastien)

Les signes de l'appartenance identitaire européenne

Si les sujets reconnaissent à l'Europe une auto-image neutre, positive même: „on est sur une base commune" (Audrey), on partage une aire géographique commune, on n'est pas différents (Noemie), ce qui se justifie selon quelques uns par la gastronomie, les droits de l'homme, la culture, la toute-puissance passée (3), et par le programme Erasmus (2), la grande majorité (12) des jeunes interviewés n'ont pas de sentiment d'appartenance identitaire européenne. Pourtant ce dernier reste marqué surtout „chez les jeunes avangardistes" (Christella).

Les interviewés mentionnent comme arguments: les différences nationales ou ethniques („l'on est trop differents pour partager une identite commune"), déplorent le manque de valeurs européennes ou de textes fondateurs communs (Camille), soulignent l'empreinte nationale plus forte que le sentiment européen et la barrière linguistique (3).

Les déclarations contradictoires interdisent toute généralisation.

Questionnés sur les éléments communs de l'identité européenne, visibles en France, les jeunes ont cité: l'aspect financier, la monnaie commune, même si elle reste dans le contexte actuel plutot „une image", les projets transfrontaliers finances par l'UE (5); les facilités de déplacement (7); les facilités administratives (2); les tentatives de créer une langue commune (2), le sytème Erasmus (2), l'aspect juridique, le Parlement (3). L'un conclut pourtant que l'identité européenne est pour le moment „une autorité technocratique" (Benedicte).

Seule une étudiante bouroundaise exprime des sentiments positifs: l'appartenance européenne serait concretisée par le mode de vie des pays développés, l'esprit critique, les chances professionnelles et „l'ouverture vers l'ailleurs" (Christella).

Le cas particulier des deux étudiantes „en Erasmus" semble paradoxal et mérite d'être rappelé. Elles ont ressenti l'appartenance commune à une même culture, une solidarité avec les jeunes des autres pays européens, un sentiment de proximité, de solidarité spécifique à l'endogroupe (Henri Tajfel, 1969 *apud* Amosy, 2005:45), par opposition aux autochtones, aux Espagnols, représentant l'outgroupe.

CONCLUSIONS

Selon les résultats de cette étude, on peut constater que le contact direct favorise la remise en question des représentations figées sur l'Autre, permet une meilleure communication interculturelle, dans le cadre universitaire multiculturel il renforce la solidarité de groupe mais accentue la fronde envers les autochtones.

Le vécu de l'altérité dans le groupe de sujets démontre un effort d'interprétation de la culture de l'autre, une interrogation sur l'autre et le désir de confronter les représentations a priori à la réalité. Les sujets manifestent une prise de distance par rapport aux idées reçues, s'intéressent au contact direct avec les habitants, ce qui permet de reconnaître un noyau culturel individuel /collectif spécifique à enrichir et/ou à relativiser par un double apport cognitif. Le questionnement sur la culture de l'autre les amèene à reconnaitre dans certaines circonstances les effets perturbateurs des stéréotypes raciaux et nationaux.

Les efforts assumés et déclarés pour combattre, transgresser (ou déconstruire) les stéréotypes liés aux nationalités et pour assurer une plus rapide intégration dans la culture d'accueil ont été d'ordre cognitif (l'apprentissange de la langue, des codes culturels), participatif (actions de formation ou lucratives), comportemental (partager des pratiques culturelles).

Les caractéristiques du groupe, étudiants M2 - leur parcours antérieur de formation: licences en droit, sociologie, psychologie, communication, philologie –, lui confère certaines particularités: ouverture d'esprit, jugement et intelligence critiques, authenticité. Si les sujets reconnaissent la présence des stéréotypes au niveau de l'opinion et des médias, ils se défendent de „tomber dans le piège des idées reçues", préfèrent reconnaître leur ignorance du sujet que reprendre à leur compte les „on-dit" et réagissent par l'attitude ou le comportement contre les stéréotypes incrustés dans le mental collectif.

Malgré les limites d'analyse et d'interprétation imposées par le corpus, je me permets d'affirmer pour l'instant que les stéréotypes nationaux ou éthniques évoqués dans le discours perdurent surtout au sein des populations moins éduquées, construisant une identité nationale décalée ou amalgamée. Leurs effets pervers sont multiples. Cette construction figée, très partielle, est propagée par les médias, ce qui contribue à un renforcement de l'image stéréotypée d'un pays et d'un peuple. Une deuxième conséquence, plus grave, à mon avis: les stéréotypes circulent dans le langage et s'inscrivent avec le temps dans les représentations et la doxa.

Leur déconstruction peut être faite au niveau individuel, par la connaissance, le contact et une attitude d'ouverture et de tolérance.

La séquence consacrée aux signes visibles de l'identité européenne et aux sentiments d'appartenance à l'Europe permet d'avancer que, dans ce groupe, le concept reste encore flou, contradictoire, car il lui manque des éléments fondamentaux (valeurs, langue, base identitaire communes).

Bibliographie

Amossy, R, & Herschberg Pierrot, A (2005). *Stereotypes et cliches*, Paris: Armand Colin.

Asante et al. (2008). The Centrality of Culture. In *The Global Intercultural Communication Reader*, London: Routledge.

Boyer, Henry (2001). L'incontournable paradigme des représentations partagées, le traitement de la compétence culturelle en français langue étrangère, *Revue de didactologie des langues-cultures*, 3-4 (123), 333–340.

Charaudeau, Patrick (2007). Analyse du discours et communication. L'un dans l'autre ou l'autre dans l'un ? *Semen* - Sémiotique et communication. Etat des lieux et perspectives d'un dialogue, in http://semen.revues.org/document5081.html

CoE (2007). Dialogue interculturel, in http://www.coe.int/t/dg4/highereducation/InterculturalDialogue/Edo_Poglia_Rapport_1902_R.pdf

Coianiz, Alain (2005). Du culturel à l'interculturel en didactique du FLE, Travaux de didactique du FLE, 53, Montpellier: I.E.F.E. Universitatea Paul Valery.

Demorgon, Jacques (1989). *L'exploration interculturelle. Pour une pédagogie internationale,* Paris: Armand Colin.

ERICarts (2008), Sharing Diversity National Approaches to Intercultural Dialogue in Europe. Study for the European Commission, in http://ec.europa.eu/culture/archives/sources_info/studies/pdf/final_report_en.pdf [consultat le 15 februarie 2010].

Gadamer, Hans-Georg (1960). *Verite et Methode,* Paris: Seuil.

Gadamer, Hans-Georg, La méthode de l'herméneutique, in http://belcikowski.org/la_dormeuse/methode_hermeneutique.php consulte le 27.09.2010

Geertz, Clifford (1986) Diapositives anthropologiques, Le croisement des cultures, *Communications*, 43, 71–90.

Ladmiral, Jean-Rene, Lipiansky, & Edmond Marc (1989). *La Communication interculturelle*, Paris : Armand Colin.

Levesque-Mausbacher, Pascale (2001). *Pedagogie interculturelle: le discours de l'Autre*, LFDM, 318.

Lippman, Walter (1922). *Public Opinion*. New York: Free Press.

Mauroy, Pierre, & Fournier, Francine (2000). Colloque *Les stereotypes nationaux et la construction europeenne*, Vingtième siecle. Revue d'histoire, Année 2000, vol. 66, No.1.

Ricoeur, Paul (1986). *Du texte a l'action. Essais d'hermeneutique II*, Paris: Seuil.

Urban, Ewa, & Orbe, Mark P (2007). „The Syndrome of the Boiled Frog'': Exploring International Students on US Campuses as Co-Cultural Group Members, *Journal of Intercultural Communication Research,* 36(2), 117–138.

*** Livre blanc sur le dialogue interculturel. Vivre ensemble dans la dignite, lansat de Ministerele Afacerilor Externe in cadrul Consiliului Europei, Strasbourg (2008), http://www.coe.int/t/dg4/intercultural/Source/White%20Paper_final_revised_FR.pdf

http://www.adevarul.ro/actualitate/Harta_stereotipurilor_Europei-_Romanii_sunt_hoti-iar_ungurii_sunt_staruri_porno-cred_italienii_0_548345452.html /consultat 06.09.2011, ora 14.50

Annexe

Structure du guide d'entretien

Thème 1 : Altérité (Q. 1,2)

1. Que signifie pour vous être étranger dans une autre culture ? Avez-vous déjà eu de telles expériences ? Où ? Quand ? Combien de temps ?
2. Avant de visiter un pays vous renseignez-vous sur ce pays ? Quels aspects vous semblent prioritaires et pourquoi ?

Thème 2 (Q 3, 4, 5): Représentations

- représentations sur la France et ses habitants
- représentations sur la Roumanie et ses habitants

3. Que dit-on dans votre pays sur la Roumanie / France et leurs habitants respectifs ? Croyez-vous que ces opinions soient fondées ? Pourquoi ?
4. Indiquez 3 mots que vous associez spontanément à la Roumanie / France.
5. Indiquez 3 mots que vous associez spontanément à leurs habitants respectifs ?

Thème 3 (Q 6, 7) : Image des médias étrangers sur les pays concernés

6. D'après vous, quelle image les médias étrangers donnent-ils de votre pays et de ses ressortissants ? Pensez-vous qu'elle soit fidèle, neutre, négative, positive ? Pourquoi ?
7. Quelles sont vos sources d'information ?

Thème 4 (Q 8, 9) : Eléments d'identité européenne

8. Selon vous, quels sont les éléments d'appartenance identitaire européenne reconnus dans votre pays ?
9. Vous sentez-vous un citoyen européen ? Si oui, précisez les éléments qui fondent cet attachement identitaire. Si non, comment l'expliquez-vous ?

DEFINING ROMANIAN CULTURAL IDENTITY: GUIDELINES FOR AN INTERCULTURAL HISTORY OF A THEORETICAL QUEST

GRIGORE GEORGIU AND ALEXANDRU CARLAN

Abstract

Histories of knowledge, of scientific or philosophical thinking, can be easily conceived as intercultural endeavours, aiming at tracing how ideas from various cultural spaces bring their own influences to a specific field of knowledge. Intercultural perspectives are fertile in this regard, helping to overcome ethnocentrisms and limited visions, so that it wouldn't be hasty to predict that intercultural approaches will replace the dominant ethno-histories of today. Ideas, throughout history, spread into and influence various cultural spaces: beyond the evident example of particular artistic currents, one could consider, for instance, the trans-cultural spread of religions, or the diffusion of the world-image that modern science has elaborated.

Our project is inspired by recent approaches in contemporary paradigms in the social sciences. The globalized world also is an intercultural one, but one which, surprisingly, has re-ignited the problem of cultural identities, in the wider framework of the debates on ethnocentrism and cultural relativism, and with significant consequences on the policies of non-conflictual management of cultural differences. Romanian modern culture was born at the crossroad of various cultural differences, the Western ones being preeminent. Being a culture of interferences, theoretical elaborations on its identity also produced a significant reflection on interculturality. In our study, we present and analyse the relevant cases of two Romanian theorists who opted for intercultural approaches in defining Romanian cultural identity, illustrating thus how this theoretical quest is dependent on a reflexive consciousness of interculturality. Based on this analysis, we aim at providing the guidelines for a project of an intercultural history of Romanian identity theory.

Key words: intercultural communication, cultural identity, ethnocentrism, Eugen Lovinescu, Lucian Blaga.

INTRODUCTION

Under the pressure of structural changes Romania has gone through in the post-communist period, but especially due to the cultural and communicational contacts encouraged by the European integration, the Romanian culture has experienced a significant process of redefining of its identity. This process took place, simultaneously, on several levels. A first significant change regarded the redesigning of cultural institutions, emancipating them from the ideological imperatives of the communist regime and redefining their managerial statute according to the new context. A second, more important, level is that of changes of the inner structures of Romanian culture, through the gradual assimilation of new attitudes, languages and expression forms, dominant in the context of globalization. Liberated from the restrictions imposed by the communist regime, the creative agents benefited from the resumption of contacts and fertile interactions with the West, thus facilitating the integration of the Romanian culture in the intercultural communicational flows of contemporary world. The effects of these influences can be attested in social and political theory, in various areas of the artistic field, but also in the expansion of media culture, of manifestations pertaining to a new popular culture, a type of (sub)culture mimetically adopted from the repertoire of Western cultural industries.

A third aspect is related to the critical reinterpretation and rewriting of national cultural history, aiming mainly to review and revise the value judgements imposed on certain events, personalities and cultural currents during the years of the communist regime. This beneficial operation has brought along a critical and comprehensive dialogue with the past, a reinterpretation of the cultural tradition and a significant revision of our panoply of values. Various forms of opposition have had to be confronted, coming from cultural and media groups, and heated debates have been triggered because the new grid of reading and interpretation implied the rehabilitation of new personalities and demythicization of others, rearranging authors and their works on a new scale of national values – and these debates still continue.

As a consequence, these debates have contributed to the reshaping of the self-consciousness of Romanian culture, first in the narrow space of academia and later, through media reverberation, have significantly modified Romanians' perspective on their cultural patrimony as well.

Without any doubt, one result of this critical examination has been the integration of Romanian culture in the European context of interactions and interdependencies of the modern period, i.e. its repositioning in an intercultural system of multiple references. Thus, the new situation has brought back into discussion the topic of our cultural identity, which dominated the debates of the interwar period. As in the present, the relation between Europe and Romania has been the central theme. Many Romanian authors of the period before World War II emphasized and theorized the necessity of defining our cultural identity from a comparative and intercultural perspective.

Nowadays, this perspective is considered to be a fundamental methodological imperative in the approaches aiming at a critical analysis of the cultural history and the redefinition of Romanian identity in relation to the evolution of ideas and European cultural paradigms. Being in Europe, we are naturally interested to emphasize "our sources and resources of Europeanism, to examine and bring up to date our European tradition" (Martin, 2008, p. 7). For this objective we need an intercultural history of Romanian society and culture, able to explain the conditions of the process of modernization in Romania. An appropriate understanding of these influences requires an interpretative framework which appeals both to the "inner eye" and the "outer eye" (Dungaciu, 2003, p. 8), in order to re-evaluate the significance, value and originality of some works of the Romanian culture. Combining a national and European perspective, such a history would be an intercultural and geopolitical one at the same time. Our aim in this study is to prove that this type of comparative examination, dominant in some recent works dedicated to our cultural history (Boia, 1997; Alexandrescu, 2000; Manolescu, 2009; Malița, 2010), is not new to Romanian culture and can be traced back in some projects and theoretical models elaborated by Romanian authors of the interwar period, with significant contemporary echoes.

Conceptual Clarifications and Levels of Analysis

The concept of "intercultural" is a recent addition to the vocabulary of social sciences. Starting from intercultural communication, a phenomenon ever expanding in the process of globalization and generating subject matter with this very name, theorists have elaborated on the concept of "intercultural" in the contiguity of the "multicultural", sometimes even in opposition to the latter, but explicitly in opposition to monocultural and ethnocentric approaches. The network of globalization and the spaces of intercultural communication bring together actors and structures with different statuses, organized on multiple levels: individuals, groups, minorities, local and regional communities, organizations, societies, states, nations and cultures, up to forms of supranational integration (such as the EU) or those of a civilizational range. The theorists in this field have proposed a semantic specialization of the terms, establishing distinctions between: 1) intercultural communication (at a microsocial level, between persons and groups); 2) cross-cultural communication or communication between cultures, which presupposes a comparative, transversal analysis of manners in which themes and ideas are approached and interpreted in various cultures and 3) international communication between states, countries, governments, public institutions, political structures or international organizations (Gudykunst & Mody, 2002, pp. 1–5).

It is clear that these three levels overlap and rest on a common theoretical background, even though each of them is used for relatively different purposes. In many of the contemporary theories (mainly those generated in the American cultural space) there is a growing consensus on the idea that through "intercultural communication" we should have in mind a situation of direct, face to face communication, between individuals and groups with different cultural structures. This perspective can be extended, granting the term "intercultural" a general meaning, covering all three referential levels and targeting all the forms of interaction and communication between the actors and the entities that constitute the fabric of contemporary world.

A further argument for unifying these approaches under a single concept of interculturalism can be advanced if we scrutinize the methodological assumptions of these approaches, most of them emphasizing the role of the agents in intercultural communication. But, if one adopts different starting points and investigates communications looking, for instance, at genres as forms of social action through which communication is accomplished (Bawarshi & Reiff, 2010, pp. 57–73), the proposed distinction becomes less operable.

Yet, the question of the relation between agents interacting and the forms of interactions is inevitable. Individuals and groups interacting in various communication situations are the bearers of different cultural equipments, which direct their attitudes and behaviours. Consequently, it is through these agents that the communication between cultures and societies occurs. These are supra-individual, macro-sociological structures formed during history, with identities of ethnic, regional or national level. Thus, theories of intercultural communication inevitably have to approach this level, elaborating, for instance, indicators to define cultural identities and the differences between cultures (Jandt, 2010; Hofstede, 1996).

Intercultural Histories: A New Mental Map

What would be the meaning of an "intercultural history" of national cultures? According to the French author Jacques Demorgon, who created a massive work on the subject, such an approach aims at analysing the multiple interactions between societies in their historical development and the various "strategies of reply" through which societies have "singled themselves out", finding and applying particular solutions for solving general problems of humanity. "These answers, elaborated during a historical genesis, led to the formation of national cultures" in the modern epoch (Demorgon, 2002, pp. 6–7). Thus, the central concept is that of cultural identity, a necessary one when approaching cultures as integrated and coexistent symbolic entities, acting at the scale of the history.

In any culture we can discover interferences and unique combinations of general and specific traits. The interactions and contacts among societies and cultures are phenomena that have occurred, with various intensities, all along human history. But intercultural histories have become mandatory today, when the locus of most important processes is no longer "the national", but "the global" (Demorgon, 2002, p. 323). Such histories can offer us a new mental map for dealing with the present, but they can also be projected retrospectively, to provide further insight into the thesis already consecrated by anthropology that the diversity of cultures "is less a function of the isolation of groups, but a consequence of the relations uniting them" (Levi-Strauss, 1982, p. 8).

However, using a transnational framework is a necessary, yet not sufficient, condition for understanding the process of formation of modern nations and cultures, as well as the relations between them in the contemporary context. In Demorgon's view, in order to avoid unilateral interpretations, cultural analyses have to follow the epistemic track general–particular–singular, both ways, emphasizing the conceptual polarities employed in understanding human existence: unity/diversity, convergence/divergence, continuity/change, global/local, specific/universal. In other words, cultural identities can be seen as "nodes" (intersection points) of a vast network, as cumulative result of interactions, influences, acculturations, interferences, exchanges of ideas, values and symbolic practices from various societies. These identities can be understood through a complex operation which requires permanent combinations between diachronic and synchronic, genetic and structural analyses, between an internal analysis referring to specific sources and contents (local contexts, attitudes, values, traditions, adaptive strategies) and an external analysis, having as an object the cultural and geopolitical system of interactions in which it was formed. From the level of integrative frameworks (epochs, historical types of societies, forms of universalization) the analysis has to descend to the deep structure of societies) to shed a stronger light to their specific temporalities ("heterochronies") and differences between cultural identities, which are concrete, singular and unrepeatable embodiments of the human condition (Demorgon, 2002, pp. 60–61).

Identity Crisis: Discourses and Contexts

Globalization has created both a vast field of interactions among cultures and a pluralistic and competitive environment where products, ideas, values, beliefs, representations and different images of the world meet and compete. The new relations among cultures generate changes to their inner structure and value systems, but also changes concerning the strategies used to promote their image in the current communicational space. Cultures are forced to redefine their identity through openness, dialogue and confrontation on the market of symbolic and non-material goods. In this context, the studies on intercultural communication have step by step been recognized as a priority research trend for social and humanistic disciplines.

Thus, intercultural studies have to confront the fundamental problem of explaining the diversity and the identity of cultures. A programmatic UNESCO document resumes the themes of the contemporary world in these terms, appreciating that intercultural dialogue overcome ethnocentric attitudes, redrawing of the relation between "us" and "them" and non-conflictual management of cultural diversity (UNESCO, 2010). Some theorists argue that the most important challenge for the contemporary world is finding ways through which "a relational cultural identity can be built and an often aggressive, refuge-identity can be avoided", or, in other words, to find of formula for "cohabitation" and coexistence of cultural differences and identities in a common framework (Wolton, 2003, p. 69).

The impact of globalization on cultures has been interpreted through various paradigms and with different conclusions. Some of them are worth mentioning: a) a tendency toward uniformization of cultures, toward diminishing or vanishing the differences between national cultural identities; b) an expression of cultural neo-imperialism (of an American formation, mainly), a new form of hegemony (together with the economic one) of the centre over the peripheries, through media culture; c) the birth of a global culture, with no identity mark; d) a process of hybridization of cultures, as a consequence of multiple interactions between them; e) a redefinition of cultural identities under the pressure of the new contexts, in versions combining in unprecedented manners both global and local traits (see Tomlinson, 2002, pp. 104–106). The last two interpretations are central to theoretical reflection nowadays, for their explanatory power of the generalized crises of identities that globalization triggered, a crisis on which there is increasing agreement. For instance, Huntington claimed, invoking a wide range of references and examples, that in the contemporary world "a generalized crises of identities has become a global phenomenon" (2004, p. 16). But here as well, the cultural identities are understood through "pluralist analyses" and their interpretations can be seen as a "perspective effect", depending on the angle of the approach (Alexandrescu, 2000, pp. 8–10). Zygmunt Bauman claims that we witness today a disappearance of previous forms of identity and a transition towards other forms of their manifestation and expression. In the past, national identity had a statute of preeminence in relation to the "small" identities, be them individual or of a group. Today, the hierarchies are reversed. Individual identities (multiple, constructed, invented, negotiated, liquid, temporary) overcome the national identity. This is a reliable indicator of the shift towards an identity which is no longer a predetermined attribute, but a cultural construction with variable geometry. Bauman's conclusion is relevant: "identity is revealed to us only as something to be invented rather than discovered;" (Bauman, 2004, p. 15).

Discourses on identity tend to polarize between this perspective, according to which the collective identities "melt" in the "multicultural bazaar" of globalization (Bauman, 2004, p. 96), losing their former consistency, and the opposed perspective, according to which it is the apparently very generous medium of globalization that triggers a tumultuous comeback of identities, identity conflicts and tensions dominating in contemporary scene. The recent claims by some European leaders, according to whom "the project of an intercultural society has failed," can be interpreted as a confirmation of a return of the identity discourse even in the European space. There are many theorists that regard such a return as a boomerang effect produced by certain apologetic representations of globalization, according to which the humankind would move towards a "global culture", with no identity mark, a representation ignoring the importance that the issue of identity has regained. In these representations, "the progress means moving from a national to a global identity, from particular to universal, through communication, dialogue, and opportune melting (Taguieff, 2002, p. 117). The quoted author and other analysts consider this vision as having "successfully deconstructed" the issue of national identity, but also having promoted only a "vague Europeanism", an abstract universalism and the utopia of post-national space (either European or global), in which identities would melt into an "undifferentiated humankind". The promoters of these interpretations would be responsible, in a certain sense, for the recrudescence of the nationalist positions and radical political discourses.

From a scientific and explanatory point of view, histories of an intercultural persuasion are better fitted to explain the current situation, when the interactions and hybridizations between cultures gather dimensions and implications much more relevant in comparison to the past. It is important for these histories to maintain the balance between unity and diversity, between convergence and divergence, because the risk of simply replacing nationalist mythologies with globalist ones, similarly deficient, is always present. Our representation of the past is recomposed through the standpoint of the actual trends, being frequently translated in mythical narrations, "according to a logic of imagery" (Boia, 1997, p. 7). For the relativist mindset of the contemporary world, the past is permanently reinterpreted through the codes of the present, and, consequently, there is no objective history, claims Boia, since "the time of the absolute truth has long gone" – a way of speaking reminding of the theorists of post-modernity. Historical discourses differentiate according to the factors shaping them: "the civilizational space, the cultural heritage, the mindset, the historical circumstances, the formation of the historian, and, decisively, the ideological spectrum. The ideological and political pluralism translates inevitably into historiographic pluralism" (Boia, 1997, pp. 5–6). This type of cultural and historical relativism projects a very different image of the social universe in comparison with the evolutionist, positivist or determinist images dominating the intellectual scene of the nineteenth century. In post-modern paradigms, the present is projected in the past, the history of yesterday's causes is rewritten from the new perspective offered by the history of today's effects, so that what we finally get is a sum of alternative, competing versions of the events and facts of the past.

The Pressure of the Context: Influences, Imitations and Synchronizations

The debates that re-opened the file of Romanian identity can be better understood if they are systematically connected with themes that regained preeminence in the agenda of social theory. As we have already discussed, the history of a culture is, implicitly, an intercultural history. Romanian historians have naturally adopted this perspective, since the evolution of modern Romania has been determined by the variable geo-political relations among European countries and the Romanian culture (Alexandrescu, 2000, p. 12). In this paper we will refer to two complementary perspectives from the interwar period, both of them focusing on the relation between the Romanian identity and the multiple cultural influences affecting it: the theory of synchronism, elaborated by Eugen Lovinescu, and the theory of the stylistic matrix of cultures elaborated by Lucian Blaga.

Eugen Lovinescu elaborated, for the first time in the Romanian culture, an intercultural history of the process of modernization of Romania. Due to its theoretical premises, it has a wider scope, constituting an allegedly valid explanatory account to any belated, peripheral or post-colonial society. He placed the history of Romanian culture and the Romanian identity in a constellation of regional and continental influences, the western ones being preeminent in the modern epoch. As a theoretical support, Lovinescu relied on cultural evolutionism and diffusionism, mainstream approaches for such fields of inquiry at the beginning of the twentieth century. He also introduced new concepts, which maintain their relevance even for contemporary debates: spheres of influence, the mechanism of social and cultural imitation, saeculum (spirit of the Age), synchronism, autonomy of values or the mutation of aesthetic values. The most important is synchronism, through which Lovinescu anticipates the phenomenon of today's globalization, and one could draw multiple links with today's theories on the topic.

Briefly, he starts from the observation that in modernity we witness an increase in the interdependencies between societies as a consequence of the development of communication technologies and of the contagious spread of ideas and civilizational elements. In order to provide a theoretical model for these influences and interdependencies, he adopted the concept of "imitation" from the French sociologist Gabriel Tarde and tried to understand through it the process of the formation of the modern Romanian civilization. According to him, the Romanian political and cultural space gradually exited the influence sphere of the Eastern Europe, entering the Western sphere. This change of geo-political significance occurred in the first decades of the nineteenth century, when the intellectual and political elites managed to change "the historical orientation axis of the Romanian people from East to West" (Lovinescu, 1997, p. 13). Thus, Romanians have built their nation state and their modern culture under the salutary and massive influence of the Western model.

As other Romanian authors before him, Lovinescu operated with the opposition between East and West, the first one being associated with the past and with stagnation in traditional frameworks, the second one with the future, progress and modernity. His strong belief was that other peoples would adopt the model of Western civilization as well, so that the slogan *Ex occidente lux* would be valid globally. With regard to the Romanian cultural space, Lovinescu's main reference is the so-called "theory of forms without content", elaborated by Titu Maiorescu more than half a century before. This theory stated that the Western influence had as an effect only the adoption of forms (ideas and modern institutions), but their implementation of social and cultural practices (the content) generated an acute contradiction between the two components and many dysfunctions in Romanian society. This theory gained an exceptional following in Romanian thinking, because it conceptualized a fundamental problem confronting the modernization of Romania (Schifirneț, 2007). But, although a useful instrument of historical and sociological analysis, this theory has been confiscated by conservative groups. The "critique" of forms without content became thus the ideological support of the traditionalist and anti-European attitudes in the interwar period.

Lovinescu's theory was directed against those ideological trends and his demonstration was meant to refute of their arguments. His central thesis was that belated societies, such as the Romanian one, could no more evolve "organically" (from contents to forms, simultaneously), but only "revolutionary", i.e. from forms to contents. Relying on a series of ideas previously developed in the Romanian culture, he considers that these societies, once entered the "orbit" of the Western civilizational system – on its global expansion – cannot escape from this gravitational field that constrains them fatally (i.e. "objectively") to adopt, in a first stage, modern political and institutional forms from the developed societies; in the second stage, these forms would stimulate and develop their local content (economic and cultural practices).

Lovinescu explained in an interesting manner the imitative mechanism through which the external influences bring about effects in this type of society ("acculturation" would not be an inaccurate contemporary equivalent for this process). The imitation is a top-down process: from centre to periphery (from the developed societies to those developing more recently) and, within a society, from cultural and political elites towards lower classes, and from external aspects of the civilizational system (public behaviours, institutions, laws) towards the internal ones (values, attitudes, mindsets). In Lovinescu's opponents' words: from forms to content. According to Lovinescu, there is a functional solidarity, a reversible relation between the two main variables of the modernization process. Yet, in the belated countries, the imitation proceeds from civilization to culture. It starts, usually, with the adoption of political elements and public behaviour (fashion and protocol are a main subject of analysis for Lovinescu) that are to be transmuted, gradually, into practices and mentalities. The modern forms, adopted initially as external elements, "simulate" a content, but once assimilated, internalized and integrated in the social experience, they come to stimulate the creation of an appropriate content and to modify the previous cultural background (values, ways of thinking and forms of symbolic production).

Starting from the Romanian case, Lovinescu formulates "the law of synchronism", according to which, in modern history (first in the European space, but then on a global span), we can witness an increase of interdependencies between societies and a gradual solidarity among them on behalf of certain principles, values and institutions. This converging evolution occurs in all societies under the pressure of a saeculum (the spirit of the age – a concept borrowed by Lovinescu from the historian Tacitus), defined as "the totality of material and moral conditions configuring the lives of European peoples at a certain time" (Lovinescu, 1997, p. 407). This integrative concept is used by Lovinescu to synthetically refer to a multitude of factors defining and differentiating historical periods. The new saeculum of Lovinescu's times determined an increasing synchronization between modern societies, a fact leading to a progressive homogenization of the political and economic structures, and of the culture.

Lovinescu's approach leads to fertile applications, confirmations and analogies in the contemporary period, since the processes described by him have gained significant amplitude compared to the interwar period. He operated with a centre–periphery model, granting a decisive role to external factors (influences, interactions, connections) as opposed to the internal ones, to the present as opposed to the past, to innovation as opposed to tradition. At the core of his conception was the view that the context of the modernity creates an intense pressure on societies, a complex form of determinism with consequences ranging from social to aesthetic theory.

The paradigm of a single-line evolutionism, informing his theory behind his many nuances and complexities, is visible mainly in his equation of modernity and Westernization, which considers that the Western model is the only viable manner of evolution. The progressive synchronization of societies under the pressure of the new "saeculum" leads, as a consequence, to a homogenization of cultures, a thesis still central in many of today's theories of globalization. It is, perhaps, the most contended issue in Lovinescu's theory, the one most often amended by critiques, both at the moment of the publication of his book (1924–1925) and afterwards. Yet he pointed out rightly that the cultural identity is not a metaphysical reality, a substratum, but a factor permanently restructuring itself according to the saeculum. Lovinescu was interested in the historical diversity, rather than in the structural diversity of cultures. He emphasized the formative role of external influences, overlooking internal sources. In his view, the identity of the Romanian culture was just a differentiating trait within a unifying superstructure. Ignoring local traditions and contributions to the European patrimony was one of the key objections of those who elaborated alternative versions of the Romanian identities, starting with various conservative replies of the interwar period up to the discussions on protochronism in the '70s (see Papu, 1977).

The Internal Generating Structure of a Cultural Identity: The Stylistic Matrix

Systematically relating the Romanian culture to the European one is a necessary task to be undertaken by those aiming at identifying an identity profile of the Romanian culture. Yet this relation can be made from various perspectives and paradigms. Lucian Blaga elaborated an alternative model for analysing the Romanian identity, sharing yet with Lovinescu the non-traditionalistic, non anti-European perspective. His analytic approach was also an intercultural one, but his theoretical sources were completely different from those of Lovinescu. Educated in the German intellectual climate, he adopted and redefined a series of concepts and approaches developed by neo-Kantian philosophy, by the school of morphology of culture (relying on authors such as Leo Frobenius and Oswald Spengler) and by C G Jung's psychoanalysis. At the crossroads of these intellectual influences he elaborated the concept of "stylistic matrix" to define the identity of cultures and their differences.

Blaga argued that cultures should be analysed according to their constitutive dimensions: the symbolic one – since a culture is the creative instrument through which the man tries to understand the "mystery of the world"), and the stylistic one – the particularizing dimension which endows it with a specific physiognomy. The symbolic dimension is a universal one, but it is always made manifest in particular stylistic forms, within a "stylistic field" shaped by factors belonging to the collective unconsciousness of an epoch, society and national community. Blaga grouped the factors generating the differentiation of cultures under the concept of "stylistic matrix", a concept similar in function and articulation with Ruth Benedict's concept of "cultural pattern." The main factors constituting the stylistic matrix of a culture are the spatial and temporal horizons, the dominant axiological accents, the values and meanings attributed to time, movement, history and human destiny, the preference for certain values in the order of creation. (Blaga, 1985, pp. 179–180). These factors generate a "cosmotic structure" (as opposed to the Freudian, chaotic unconscious) that allows us to analyze the identity of a culture from a different perspective. Rooted in the strata of the collective unconscious, the stylistic matrix provides an orientation for any cultural creation of a people and for its historical manifestations. It can be conceived as a "prism" through which human communities and individuals perceive and interpret the world. Relying on this theoretical support, Blaga undertook an in-depth analysis of the Romanian culture, integrating it in an assembly of influences, in order to reveal its specificity. Of particular interest are his analyses on the catholic, orthodox and protestant stylistic traits within the European civilization. Blaga can be included in a tradition that stems from Max Weber and goes up to contemporary theories rehabilitating the key role of the religious factors in configuring collective identities.

In relation to Lovinescu, Blaga can be described as belonging to a paradigm of cultural relativism, in opposition to the approach of the single-line evolutionism. Yet he has not rejected cultural influences, considering that "we cannot develop without integrating in Europe" (Blaga, 1985, p. 312), but these influences are always filtered through one's cultural stylistic matrix, which has, in this regard, a function similar to that of the a priori categories of Kant. Integrated in a "network of European determinants," the Romanian modern culture was inevitably subject to various influences, some of them being considered by Blaga as "modelling influences", mostly coming from the French cultural space, other being "catalytic influences" – most of them coming from the German space. The two cultures have different internal structures, stylistic matrixes and spiritual orientations, which are reflected in a different manner in the cultures they are influencing. The French culture, of a classical and rationalist type, is presenting itself as a "model" urging other cultures to follow it. As opposed to it, the German culture, of a romantic structure, is not proposing itself as a model, but as a particular structure urging you to find "your own being". "The French culture is like a magister who demands to be imitated. The German culture is like a mentor who leads you toward yourself" (Blaga, 1985, p. 315). The Romanian culture was formed under the combined influence of the two models, but nevertheless employing the resources of its own historical and cultural roots.

It is not the point of this paper to undertake a critical examination of Blaga's philosophy, which, according to contemporary standards, would be of an over speculative metaphysical orientation. This is because our main goal is to reveal how Romanian theorists of different persuasion tried to integrate in the very description of the Romanian cultural identity topics that today would be described as pertaining to intercultural communication, not to evaluate the theoretical success of their endeavour. Yet, one possible inconsistency of Blaga's philosophy with its own terms is very relevant to our purpose and deserves pointing out: these influences, of either "catalytic" or "modelling" nature, are expected to be perceived and integrated through the categories of the stylistic matrix, since they belong, in the Kantian parlance underlying Blaga's philosophy, to the noumen, not to the phenomenon. So they are expected to be inputs for the stylistic matrix, not factors altering at a further stage the output of the stylistic matrix, as would result from their description. It is not clear, in Blaga's account, at what moment in the artistic elaboration this "modelling" occurs and how it is filtered through the stylistic matrix.

Conclusions

The globalized world is an intercultural one. The studies on intercultural communication have acquired unquestionable theoretical relevance and increasing applicative poignancy. These studies have had major consequences also for the historic discourse, producing a shift from national to transnational approaches and frameworks. Through its meanings, the concept of "intercultural" can provide a better understanding of the profound consequences of globalization. Thus, we consider that an intercultural history of cultures can provide an appropriate theoretical model regarding new modalities to define and interpret collective cultural identities, as well as the relations among them, in the context of globalization and European integration.

Romanian culture is situated in a space of interferences and multiple influences, between the West and the East, and, as a consequence, it has an intercultural vocation. This vocation can be historically accounted and it has been a subject of theoretical elaboration for Romanian authors. They have been interested in the problem of cultural differences and have proposed theoretical models within the mainstream paradigms of the Western Europe. Under the pressure of cascading changes triggered by modernization and synchronization processes, Romanian thinkers have veered towards a "relational" reading of identity and a conjunctive paradigm, which requires critical self-evaluation and permanent comparisons between complementary national and European aspects. We analysed Lovinescu and Blaga as two illustrative examples that adopted a comparative and intercultural approach for interpreting the identity of Romanian culture in its European context. Models proposed by other Romanian authors, such as Mircea Vulcanescu, should be reconsidered and re-actualized as well. The urge of systematic reevaluation of cultural identities should be doubled by a critical dialogue with the national tradition, with ideas and theoretical models of the past, for a better assessment of Romania's place in European culture.

REFERENCES

Alexandrescu, S (2000). Identitate în ruptură. Mentalităţi româneşti postbelice [Torn Identities: Postwar Romanian Mentalities]. Bucharest: Univers.

Bauman, Z (2004). *Identity: Conversations with Benedetto Vecchi.* Cambridge: Polity Press.

Bawarshyi, A, & Reiff, M J (2010). *Genre: an introduction to history, theory, research, and pedagogy*, West Lafayette: Parlour Press.

Blaga, L (1985). *Trilogia culturii* [The Trilogy of Culture]. In *Opere*, vol. 9, Bucharest: Minerva.

Boia, L (1997). Istorie şi mit în conştiinţa românească [History and Myth in the Romanian Consciousness], Bucharest: Humanitas.

Demorgon, J (2002). *L'histoire interculturelle des sociétés*, Paris: Economica.

Dungaciu, D (2003). Elita interbelică. Sociologia românească în context european [Interwar Elites. Romanian Sociology in European Contexts], Bucharest: Mica Valahie.

Gudykunst, W B, & Mody, B (eds) (2002). *Handbook of International and Intercultural Communication* 2nd ed. Thousand Oaks, CA: Sage Publications, Inc.

Jandt, E F (2010). *An introduction to Intercultural Communication: Identities in a Global Community* 6th ed. Thousand Oaks, CA: Sage Publications.

Hofstede, G (1996). *Managementul structurilor multiculturale, Software-ul gândirii* [Cultures and Organizations. Software of the Mind] Bucharest: Economică.

Lovinescu, E (1997). Istoria civilizaţiei române moderne [History of Modern Romanian Civilization]. Bucharest: Minerva.
Manolescu, N (2009). Istoria critică a literaturii române [A Critical History of Romanian Literature]. Piteşti: Paralela 45.
Maliţa, M (2010). Cuminţenia pământului: Strategii de supravieţuire în istoria poporului român [Modesty: Strategies for Survival in the History of Romanian People] Bucharest: Corint.
Martin, M (2008). *Identit*ate românească – identitate europeană [Romanian Identity – European Identity] vol. I. Bucharest: Cuvântul.
Papu, E (1977). Din clasicii noştri [From Our Classics]. Bucharest: Eminescu.
Schifirneţ, C (2007). Formele fără fond, un brand românesc? [Forms Without Content – a Romanian Brand?]. Bucureşti: Editura Comunicare.ro.
Levi-Strauss, C (1982). Rasă şi istorie [Race and History]. In Rasismul în faţa ştiinţei, Bucharest: Politică.
Taguieff, P-A (2002). Naţionalism şi antinaţionalism: Dezbaterea pe marginea identităţii franceze [Nationalisme et antinationalisme. Le débat sur l'identité française]. In Cordellier, S & Poisson E (eds). Naţiuni şi naţionalisme. Bucharest: Corint.
Tomlinson, J (2002). Globalizare şi cultură [Globalization and Culture]. Timişoara: Amarcord.
Wolton, D (2003). *L'autre mondialisation.* Paris: Flammarion.
UNESCO World Report (2010). *Investing in Cultural Diversity and Intercultural Dialogue*. Unesco.

PERCEVOIR L'ALTÉRITÉ, SE SENTIR AUTRE L'ALTERITE A TRAVERS TROIS PHILOSOPHES FRANÇAIS: MICHEL FOUCAULT, EMMANUEL LEVINAS, PAUL RICOEUR

ODILE RIONDET

Résumé

L'appel à communication met en avant une thématique médiatique : quel jeu jouent les médias dans la construction de la figure de l'autre, de l'étranger, de la différence ? Cette thématique est déclinée selon le types de discours, l'organisation qui le prend en charge, l'usage des technologies de l'information et de la communication pour rendre les groupes et les identités affirmées, visibles. Sans nier les enjeux de ce point de départ, il nous semble important, dans ce colloque, de nous interroger sur le sentiment même de l'altérité : qu'est-ce qu'un autre ? Et qui est le moi qui a le sentiment qu'il y a, face à lui, un autre ?

La philosophie a une large antériorité dans le traitement de ces questions. J'ai donc souhaité me tourner vers les philosophes. De nombreux auteurs étaient possibles. J'en ai retenu trois selon des critères précis : des auteurs contemporains, travaillés fréquemment dans ma discipline (Communication), correspondant à des problématiques qui sont les nôtres. Enfin, et c'est ce qui m'a sans doute le plus retenue, ces auteurs nous offrent la possibilité d'envisager la question de l'altérité non comme une opposition, identité contre identité, mais comme une part de nous-mêmes, comme une partie prenante de notre travail sur nous-mêmes, lorsque nous cherchons à savoir qui nous sommes.

Cela correspond, je le sais, à une hypothèse anthropologique : un être humain travaille sur lui-même, c'est bénéfique, les relations aux autres ne menacent en rien la découverte de lui-même, mais y aident. Ces philosophes sont tous trois dans cette perspective. J'assume l'hypothèse que représente ce choix d'auteurs. J'ai pris le parti de les traiter simplement par ordre alphabétique, d'une part parce qu'il fallait trouver un principe simple, mais cette règle formelle n'est pas sans intérêt sur le fond, car Michel Foucault part de la question de soi avant d'interroger la relation à l'autre, Emmanuel Levinas est beaucoup plus centré sur la rencontre interindividuelle et Paul Ricoeur a beaucoup à nous dire sur les identités collectives. Dans un second temps, nous verrons comment, à partir de ces auteurs, se pose les questions du rapport entre altérité et identité du point de vue personnel, du point de vue de la connaissance, du point de vue éthique et politique.

Mots-clés : altérité, identité, autre

Cet article a donc pour objectif de reprendre la question de l'identité en profondeur, en évitant de nous en tenir à l'allusion ou à l'accumulation de références, qui ne sont trop souvent que construction rapide autour de textes que l'on a à peine pris le temps de comprendre. Ce qui implique un réel travail sur les auteurs, la nécessité d'entrer dans le détail de leur pensée. Seul un travail de fond des penseurs de l'identité permet d'éviter de tomber dans des idées toutes faites, dans la répétition des arguments d'autrui, qui ne sont qu'une manière de renoncer à penser.

Cette manière de travailler est en elle-même une vision de l'identité et une perspective de recherche. Car elle signifie, dans sa pratique même, qu'il est ridicule d'opposer l'entrée dans la pensée d'autrui avec un renoncement à une pensée propre. Bien au contraire : plus je fais l'effort de compréhension, plus je confronte ce que je lis à ma propre manière de voir. Plus je cherche à articuler mes acquiescements et mes objections, plus la synthèse, qui décadre mes lectures pour les recadrer dans ma cohérence propre, sera complexe. Ainsi, s'il y a ici quelque pédagogie, ce qui pourrait être justifié dans un colloque rassemblant enseignants et doctorants, nous pouvons la lire dans l'explicitation de la pensée des auteurs comme dans la démarche méthodologique consistant à entrer dans le détail d'une pensée pour permettre la pleine expression de la sienne. N'est-ce pas déjà, dès cet instant, une manière de débattre de la notion d'identité ?

Trois philosophes contemporains: Michel Foucault et l'herméneutique du sujet

Michel Foucault est l'un des auteurs les plus cités dans notre discipline. J'ai choisi ici les cours au Collège de France en 1982, qui portaient sur L'herméneutique du sujet. Ces cours se situent à la fin de sa vie professionnelle, et il les présente à plusieurs reprises comme une synthèse de ses écrits antérieurs, un instant récapitulatif de sa pensée.

En quoi la question du « souci de soi » est-elle quelque chose de la question de l'altérité ? Elle l'est à un double titre : dans le travail sur soi, tout au long de l'Antiquité, l'autre est médiateur, bien que d'une manière différente selon les Écoles philosophique. Et parce que le travail sur soi met au jour un autre « soi », parfois inattendu : il y a en chacun un soi qui s'ignore, qui a besoin d'apparaître, un soi qui est autre que ce que l'on pense d'abord de soi-même ou de celui qui s'est manifesté aux autres pendant un certain temps. Il y a en soi-même une altérité fondamentale que l'autre (le maître) aide à révéler. Nous voyons que cette approche de Michel Foucault permet dès le départ une interprétation particulière du titre même de ce colloque, qui accole identité et communication interculturelle, laissant aux intervenant le choix du mode de relation à établir entre les deux. L'identité ne saurait être, dans cette perspective, le contraire de la communication avec l'autre, car l'autre est le vecteur de la structuration de l'identité. Et ceci même si, de l'aveu même de Michel Foucault, il y a une dimension qui a manqué à toute l'Antiquité : une véritable « herméneutique du sujet », c'est-à-dire le fait de se considérer soi-même comme une sorte de mystère dont il faudrait découvrir la vérité.

Un autre en soi-même

On peut considérer le souci de soi comme caractéristique de toute l'Antiquité grecque. « C'est une attitude : à l'égard de soi, à l'égard des autres, à l'égard du monde.» (Foucault, 2001:12) C'est une forme d'ascèse ou de spiritualité qui parie sur la capacité du sujet à se modifier, se déplacer, changer. La question émerge avec Platon et concerne alors les jeunes aristocrates appelés à participer à la décision de la cité, à gouverner. Il faut donc mettre en place des pratiques de transformations du sujet pour garantir la qualité de sagesse des dirigeants : des techniques de concentration, de retraite, d'endurance, apprendre à résister aux tentations. Le soi dont il faut s'occuper, c'est l'âme. L'âme en tant que sujet de l'action.

On retrouvera cette préoccupation dans des Écoles philosophiques plus tardives et chez les Romains, mais avec des modifications. Le souci de soi ne concerne pas que la jeunesse, c'est un art de toute la vie, jusque dans la vieillesse. Car le vieillard connaît le prix de chaque instant de la vie, bénéficier de la tranquillité, peut donc atteindre la plénitude, jouir de lui-même, vivre chaque jour comme s'il était le dernier. Vivre chaque matin comme s'il était l'enfance et chaque soir comme s'il était la fin. Il. Le souci de soi s'élargit à d'autres populations, pas seulement celle des gouvernants, mais ne constitue pas pour autant une loi éthique universelle : « Jamais dans la culture antique, dans la culture grecque et romaine, le souci de soi n'a été effectivement perçu, posé, affirmé comme une loi universelle valant pour tous les individus, quel que soit le mode de vie qu'il adopte. » (Foucault, 2001:109) Ce qui lui semble être la même matrice que celle du christianisme : « C'est cette forme que l'on va retrouver au cœur même du christianisme, réarticulée dans le christianisme autour du problème de la Révélation, de la foi, du Texte, de la grâce, etc. [...] Disons en d'autres termes que le rapport à soi, le travail de soi sur soi, ont été en Occident conçus et déployés comme la voie, la seule voie possible qui mène de l'universalité d'un appel qui ne peut être, de fait, entendu que par quelques-uns à la rareté d'un salut dont nul pourtant n'était originairement exclu.» (Foucault, 2001:116)

Qu'est-ce qui permet de garder la maîtrise de soi ? Les discours de la raison compris comme vrais. Il faut aussi que ces discours soient en nous comme une voix intérieure. Il faut donc que nous nous les soyons appropriés, par des techniques de mémorisation comme par notre effort intellectuel. Cependant « il ne s'agit pas de découvrir une vérité dans le sujet ni de faire de l'âme le lieu où elle réside par une parenté d'essence ou un droit d'origine ; il ne s'agit pas non plus de faire de l'âme l'objet d'un discours vrai. Nous sommes encore très loin de ce que serait une herméneutique du sujet.» (Foucault, 2001:481)

La préoccupation d'un affinement de soi qui dure toute la vie est, là encore, une manière de préciser notre interprétation du titre du colloque : l'idée même que l'identité n'est pas fixée à un moment précis de notre histoire personnelle est donc largement ancrée dans la culture gréco-romaine et peut constituer un héritage que nous désirons assumer.

L'autre comme médiateur

La pratique de soi porte sur les soins de son corps, la santé, les devoirs familiaux et religieux, les activités agricoles, l'amour. La pratique de soi est diététique, économique et érotique. On peut y ajouter une sorte d'examen de conscience du soir, une revue de la journée destinée au maître. Le rapport verbal avec l'autre est donc une vérification des pratiques du soi. C'est ici que se pose la question de l'Autre comme médiateur indispensable dans la pratique de soi, le maître, l'exemple, un modèle de comportement. L'autre est celui qui a la compétence, connaît les principes, a les aptitudes et les savoir-faire. L'autre est décisif dans la constitution du sujet comme sujet. Il l'aidera à surmonter l'irrésolution, à se constituer comme individu stable, qui est lui-même et sait qui il est dans sa constance. Cet Autre est philosophe, le seul médiateur qui peut aider à se trouver soi-même. Les Écoles de philosophie reçoivent ainsi le public régulier de ceux qui viennent pour s'exercer à une fonction, et le public ponctuel, de ceux qui viennent à l'occasion d'un problème particulier. Parfois, dans les plus grandes familles, un philosophe est attaché comme conseiller au maître de maison. Il y a donc une sorte de direction de conscience comme type de relation sociale exercé par le philosophe.

Ce personnage du philosophe, qui détient les techniques de soi, devient cependant ambigu et est discuté. En effet, le souci de soi est un temps de détachement. Alors, le Prince a-t-il besoin d'une vie de loisirs cultivés, le philosophe est-il utile ou pas aux politiques dans leur action, ne devient-il pas à un moment une sorte de trouble-fête agressif qui ne sait que critiquer l'action sans avoir jamais été capable de la mener ? Progressivement, la fonction cathartique et la fonction politique du souci de soi vont se distinguer. Il y a des valeurs qui polarisent la vie et qui peuvent se trouver en décalage avec l'action politique. « Et il me semble qu'il n'est guère possible de faire l'histoire de la subjectivité, l'histoire des rapports entre le sujet et la vérité, sans l'inscrire dans le cadre de cette culture de soi, qui connaîtra ensuite dans le christianisme – le christianisme primitif, puis médiéval – et puis ensuite à la Renaissance puis au XVIIème siècle, toute une série d'avatars et de transformations. » (Foucault, 2001:173)

Qu'est-ce que ces réflexions apportent à notre sujet ? Que nous ne pouvons réfléchir identité et altérité comme deux fixités qui se font face, et parfois s'affrontent. Michel Foucault nous rappelle que l'Europe, dès sa naissance, s'est fondée sur une pensée qui désigne l'humain comme mouvement, comme transformation, une transformation qui affecte progressivement toute la vie et des cercles d'individus de plus en plus larges. L'altérité est en chacun, parce que la marge de progression est en chacun. Et un Autre choisi, aimé, un lien affectif, n'est pas une étrangeté à affronter, mais une aide à la révélation de soi.

Cette perspective n'est évidemment qu'un seul des aspects de la question de l'identité et de l'altérité. Le fait d'avoir une identité de groupe notamment, une identité nationale, politique, n'est pas réellement posée. Michel Foucault met en avant la préoccupation de soi et du mouvement en soi comme un élément commun à toute la culture occidentale. En ce sens, il aborde un peu la question de l'identité de groupe. Mais en quelque sorte en creux, laissant à d'autres le soin de décrire cette particularité héritée par notre civilisation.

Et ceci notamment parce que son interprétation omet trois points centraux : le premier est que le salut chrétien, dont il marque bien ce qu'il doit à l'Antiquité, va opérer une série de ruptures fondamentales : il est appuyé sur la collectivité croyante, mais à destination de tous, croyants et non-croyants. Ensuite, leur foi est connue de Dieu seul et en aucun cas évaluée par des maîtres. Enfin, le «salut » dont il s'agit n'est pas l'accès à la sérénité individuelle, mais un état de justice dans l'humanité qui peut passer par des drames individuels, des échecs, des deuils et des morts injustes, assumés pour garder la cohérence de la parole et de l'action. Or, nous affirme Michel Foucault, sur le plan philosophique, le salut est une « activité permanente du sujet sur lui-même, qui trouve sa récompense dans un certain rapport du sujet à lui-même.». (Foucault, 2001:178) Autrement dit, on se sauve soi-même pour aboutir à soi-même. La justice comme la place de la justice sont donc d'autres dimensions que nous verrons chez Emmanuel Levinas et chez Paul Ricoeur.

Emmanuel Levinas face au visage de l'Autre

Toute la philosophie d'Emmanuel Levinas est celle du mystère de la relation à l'autre. La question de cette relation, potentiellement cruelle, alors qu'elle devrait être celle d'une rencontre évidente de visage humain à visage humain, renvoie à l'invraisemblable inhumanité de l'Holocauste. Pour lui, il n'est pas d'humanité sans sens d'autrui. Et l'identité la plus juste est celle qui se donne précisément pour identité l'attention à autrui. « Vie des vivants dans la lutte pour la vie ; histoire naturelle des humains dans le sang et les larmes des guerres entre personnes, nations et classes ; matière des choses, dure matière. […] Et voici que surgit, dans la vie vécue par l'humain – et c'est là que, à proprement parler, l'humain commence, pure éventualité, mais d'emblée éventualité pure et sainte – du se vouer-à-l'autre. […] C'est cette rupture de l'indifférence – de l'indifférence fût-elle statistiquement dominante -, la possibilité de l'un-pour-l'autre, qui est l'événement éthique |…], la vocation d'un exister-pour-autrui plus fort que la menace de la mort. » (Levinas, 1993 :10) Avec Emmanuel Levinas, nous allons donc aborder un autre aspect de notre interprétation du titre du colloque : s'il y a un lien entre identité et communication interculturelle, ce n'est pas seulement parce que l'autre m'aide tout au long de ma vie à découvrir ma propre identité, mais parce que, si je veux être moi-même au maximum de ma personne, je dois construire mon humanité. Or, cette humanité nous est commune : chacun, à développe sa propre personnalité à partir d'un modèle partagé de l'humanité.

Identité juive

Ce qui nous intéressera particulièrement chez Emmanuel Levinas est sa capacité à penser à la fois une identité juive forte et l'universalité. Il se sent d'une part profondément juif, car: « on est dans le judaïsme, comme on est en soi-même [...], car l'appartenance s'incurve en destin. » (Levinas, 1987 :85) Mais il ne s'agit en aucun cas d'une forme de nationalisme. Il s'agit de partir de son identité, de sa particularité, pour se demander à quoi sa particularité peut servir, en quoi ce que l'on est manifeste quelque chose d'important de l'humanité. Israël est une pièce de l'histoire universelle et a servi à quelque chose dans l'histoire universelle. C'est vrai de tout individu singulier et de tout peuple particulier.

Cette vision assumée d'un « messianisme » de tout peuple (pour ce qui le concerne celui d'Israël) pourrait être dangereuse : un peuple qui se sent investi d'une mission n'est-il pas profondément dangereux pour ceux qui s'opposeront à sa mission autoproclamée ? Cela ne peut fonctionner que si, dans le même temps, nous avons le sentiment aigu, la certitude, l'expérience constante, de notre fragilité et de nos approximations, si nous sommes individuellement et collectivement capables de nous éprouver, si les décisions prises sont longuement évaluées Ce qui signifie; sur un plan personnel, que le regard que nous jetons sur nous est un regard pour nous éprouver (et nous retrouvons ici la culture de l'épreuve de soi) : nous ne nous connaissons pas réellement nous-mêmes. « Personne n'est identique à soi [sociologues, nous rechercherons les lois sociales comme des influences intersidérales, [...] philologues et historiens, nous contesterons à chacun jusqu'au pouvoir même d'être auteur de son discours. » (Levinas, 1993 :36) Par notre entourage, nous sommes les héritiers d'une mentalité que nous nous approprions et qui, en même temps, nous échappe dans beaucoup de ses dimensions. « La notion de mentalité consiste à affirmer que l'esprit humain ne dépend pas seulement d'une situation extérieure – climat, race, institutions, et même habitudes mentales contractées qui viendraient fausser la lumière naturelle – mais qu'en lui-même il est dépendance [...] qu'antérieurement à la représentation il est engagé d'une façon saisissante dans l'être.» (Levinas, 1993 :65-66) Le moi est ambigu et énigmatique, il n'est pas isolé et il y a donc toujours une dimension de responsabilité dans le simple fait d'exister en un lieu : ma place au soleil, sur quoi ou sur qui a-t-elle été conquise pour que je puisse l'occuper ? L'identité juive, comme interrogation sur soi et comme engagement envers l'autre, est précisément cette mentalité interrogative sur soi, un soi qui intègre l'autre et la responsabilité que nous avons envers lui. Comme le peuple d'Israël, par sa particularité-même, apporte quelque chose d'unique à l'histoire du monde, ainsi chacun, de par sa particularité-même, apporte quelque chose d'unique au milieu dans lequel il vit.

La rencontre

Emmanuel Levinas est un phénoménologue. Comme Merleau-Ponty, il focalise son attention sur le senti, la perception, et notamment la perception de l'autre. Nous faisons l'expérience de l'altérité dans le simple fait de vivre dans le monde, d'être au monde, dans un monde qui ne nous appartient pas, car la nature elle-même est autre, elle nous est étrangère. Et cette expérience est aussi celle de la rencontre humaine. Que se passe-t-il entre deux individus ? Toute rencontre provoque la certitude immédiate que l'on a affaire à de l'humain. Que l'humain a quelque chose de sacré et d'absolu, qu'il n'est pas seulement un humain particulier mais aussi que toute l'humanité est manifestée en lui. Et qu'il est profondément étranger, irréductible à ce que je vois ou pense de lui. Il est à la fois don (celui de son visage pour la relation) et résistance. Toute rencontre est indissociablement accompagnée d'une double certitude : que l'on a en face de soi quelqu'un qui vous ressemble et quelqu'un qui vous échappe, aussi mystérieux que la nature. Mais ce sentiment d'être en face de l'inconnaissable, de ce que l'on ne peut jamais maîtriser entièrement, est le début de toute curiosité, de toute connaissance, de toute pensée même : « La pensée commence avec la possibilité de concevoir une liberté extérieure à la mienne. » (Levinas, 1993:29)

Dans la rencontre, les subjectivités se touchent sur le modèle des mains qui se touchent. La relation de l'autre à moi est construction progressive de ce qui peut être un univers commun. En ce sens, aucun humain ne peut se réaliser en étant seul, en voulant échapper à l'échange, qui implique dans sa définition même des emprunts de l'un à l'autre. L'humain isolé est déficient, incomplet, impossible même. « Un être particulier ne peut se prendre pour une totalité que s'il manque de pensée » et s'il existe entre deux être humains de la violence, elle ne fait que révéler « des individus qui confondent leur particularité avec la totalité ». (Levinas, 1993:25) Alors, si toute pensée est le résultat d'une rencontre des subjectivités, confrontation des manières toujours différentes – de par la différence des personnalités – de voir le monde et de le comprendre, alors l'humanisation et la culture sont les fruits de la rencontre et de la capacité à prendre l'autre en compte et « le savoir est, par lui-même, relation à un autre de la conscience. » (Levinas, 1993:161)

La relation qui s'instaure entre deux individus va certes immédiatement leur assigner des places, elle ne sera pas exemptes des différences de statut ou de pouvoir. C'est pourquoi il faudra se demander à quel moment une relation est juste, à quel moment les situations de direction sont acceptables, non humiliantes, ne relèvent pas de l'abus de pouvoir ou de la violence, à quel moment le commandement reçu peut et doit être respecté. C'est cette dimension qui porte une interrogation éthique.

Il y a ici un élément que nous n'avions pas encore perçu dans nos textes, mais qui est fortement organisateur de la relation à l'autre. Car la relation entre deux individus, deux groupes, deux peuples, intègre toujours un troisième terme : un objectif, une idée de la justice, une représentation de l'humanité…C'est ce troisième terme qui servira de référence et d'arbitre en cas d'opposition. Ainsi, si l'on parle d'identité et de communication interculturelle, il faudra se demander, dans les cas vécus comme des chocs, s'il peut exister un troisième terme ordonnateur de la relation.

L'autre comme injonction éthique

Nous l'avons vu, l'humanité commence avec la prise en compte de l'autre, de l'immensité de sa différence. Il n'est pas là pour me regarder vivre, pour être le simple témoin de mes actions, pour être un acteur obligé dans une pièce conçue par moi. L'humanité commence avec la sortie de soi. L'autre est pour moi une transcendance, c'est-à-dire un extérieur que je ne pourrai jamais maîtriser, qui me provoque à m'adapter, à me reprendre, à me transformer, à inventer. C'est dans ce mécanisme de l'obligation de la sortie de soi et dans la prise en compte de l'inattendu de l'autre que naît la question de l'éthique. Selon les termes d'Emmanuel Levinas, c'est « la transcendance du pour l'autre qui instaure le sujet éthique qui instaurent l'entre-nous. » (Levinas, 1993:9)

Si nous prenons au sérieux l'altérité de l'autre, si nous nous mettons dans cette disposition où nous acceptons que l'autre nous fasse bouger en nous-même pour lire et comprendre l'humanité qu'il manifeste et nous en nourrir, alors nous assumons notre responsabilité vis-à-vis de lui. « La rencontre d'Autrui est d'emblée responsabilité pour lui. La responsabilité pour le prochain qui est, sans doute, le nom sévère de ce qu'on appelle amour du prochain [...] Je n'aime pas le mot amour qui est usé et frelaté. Parlons d'une prise sur soi du destin d'autrui.» (Levinas, 1993:121) Il y a ainsi une sorte d'asymétrie : autrui est celui dont je me sens responsable, quel qu'il soit.

Mais pourquoi cela a-t-il un sens de se sentir responsable d'autrui ? Comment justifier que ce sentiment soit juste, soit meilleur ou plus humain que la volonté de puissance, pourquoi ne pas trouver plus normal que les compétences inégales des forts et des faibles, les appétits de pouvoir inégaux, engendrent des situations normales d'inégalités des richesses et de la pauvreté, des situations sociales ? Et même, les situations d'oppression n'ont-elles pas été voulues en quelque sorte par ceux qui n'ont pas jugé bon de se défendre ou de se révolter ? La réponse à cette question est dans la foi juive. Si le comportement d'attention aux faibles, l'attention à la justice, la sensibilité extrême au détail de toutes les formes, même les plus minimes, de pouvoir ou de violence, est un comportement le plus humain, c'est parce qu'il correspond au point où l'humain se rapproche le plus de Dieu, cela correspond à sa spiritualité fondamentale. Une spiritualité particulière du judaïsme. Lorsque le prophète Élie part dans la montagne et attend son Seigneur, il entend le fracas du vent, celui de tremblement de terre. Mais le Seigneur n'est ni dans l'un ni dans l'autre. Mais lorsque Élie entend « le bruissement d'un murmure ténu », alors il sait que le Seigneur est là. Ainsi, la vérité de l'homme est dans cette attention au ténu, au presque rien, au presque imperceptible, à ce qui fait le moins de bruit, ce qui a le moins de puissance, le moins de pouvoir, pour en comprendre la force vitale. C'est cette façon d'être qui est le plus fort de l'humanité, contre les cohérences de violence de l'univers.

Que tirer d'Emmanuel Levinas alors pour notre propos ? Que le « travail sur soi » peut correspondre non seulement à une tentative pour atteindre un bien-être et une sérénité, mais aussi et sans doute surtout à échapper à la tentation de la violence. Que le « travail sur soi » est fondamentalement lié à la rencontre de l'autre humain. Et que l'attention exercée, portée vers l'extériorité de ce que nous sommes n'est pas une perturbation de notre identité, mais bien le propre d'une humanité dont la vocation d'ouverture correspond au plus profond de ce qu'elle est, de ce à quoi elle aspire. Par rapport à Michel Foucault, il s'intéresse de plus à la dimension de l'identité collective et aux relations entra pays, entre institutions, entre civilisations. Là encore, il n'envisage pas d'opposition entre identité et altérité. Car si l'identité se définit comme capacité d'un groupe à manifester son ouverture à l'inconnu, alors l'identité porte en elle-même la relation à l'altérité et l'intégration en soi de l'altérité.

Paul Ricoeur et la construction de soi par l'autre

Paul Ricoeur a deux manières de décrire l'autre comme faisant partie de soi : dans la relation et dans le récit, par l'intermédiaire du texte. N'est-ce pas notre expérience quotidienne, de lire et de nous retrouver transformés par ce que nous avons lu ? Et ce travail incessant nous inscrit dans des traditions, des civilisations, des nationalités, que nous assumons et critiquons à la fois inévitablement. Il y a donc trois points de sa pensée qui nous intéresseront ici : le soi face à l'autre, le soi face à l'altérité d'un texte, la relation à une tradition ou une identité qui nous précède. Pour Ricoeur, si nous effectuons ce travail constant de construction, c'est parce que nous sommes inconnus à nous-mêmes, pleins de nos ombres inconscientes. Et parce que notre identité est toujours structurée entre notre personnalité propre et la multiplicité des influences héritées et dont il nous faut apprendre à évaluer l'importance pour nous – ou y renoncer. La communication interculturelle dont il est question ici est celle d'une distance historique avec ce qui nous constitue.

Le soi face à l'autre

Réfléchir sur soi-même et l'autre, c'est d'abord se poser cette question : comment pouvons-nous être sûrs de nous-mêmes ? Et cette question est une partie d'une autre, plus générale : de quoi pouvons-nous être certains, qu'est-ce qu'être certain de quelque chose ? Comme Emmanuel Levinas, Paul Ricoeur a hérité cette question de la phénoménologie : il y a une similitude entre l'approche de l'autre et l'approche du monde, dans les deux cas, face à ce qui n'est pas nous, nous avons des réactions d'accueil ou de rejet. Parfois une hésitation surmontée. Pour répondre à cette question de la certitude, il prendra ses distances aussi bien avec Descartes qu'avec Kant ou Nietzsche. Pour Descartes, il y a une possibilité d'être certain tant de nous-mêmes que de ce qui nous entoure parce que, au fond de nous, il y a une puissance ultime de jugement qui nous permet, à un certain moment, de tenir les choses pour vraies. Kant distingue entre la sensibilité qui nous donne les objets et l'entendement qui nous les fait penser. Nietzsche, en « maître du soupçon », désigne nos incohérences, nos incapacités, notre instabilité. Mais Husserl montre que notre vie est faite de changements, que nous sommes à la fois nous-mêmes et non identiques du début à la fin de notre existence. Et ceci parce que ce que notre perception est comme celle d'un dé dont nous ne voyons pas simultanément toutes les faces. Et c'est cette relation changeante à notre environnement, à l'autre et à nous-mêmes aussi, qui fait notre dynamique dans la vie et construit malgré toutes nos mouvances notre persévérance dans une manière de répondre au changement.

Pouvons-nous alors penser une « herméneutique de soi » qui ne soit « ni éclatante ni déchue », autrement dit avons-nous une vérité de nous-mêmes, une vérité qui ne soit ni défensive ni introuvable, quelque chose comme « une créance sans garantie, mais aussi en tant que confiance plus forte que tout soupçon.» (Ricoeur, 1990:35) Nous avons des intentions, des désirs, des raisons d'agir. Cela pourrait sembler être notre permanence. Mais la psychanalyse nous a appris à les accueillir et les soupçonner en même temps. La psychanalyse a montré notre force de désir comme l'ambiguïté de ce désir. Autrement dit « il faut perdre le moi pour trouver le je.» (Ricoeur, Essais d'herméneutique, :24) Cette perspective soupçonneuse était absente dans l'Antiquité que nous présente Michel Foucault. « Entre l'imagination qui dit "je peux tout essayer", et la voix qui dit "Tout est possible, mais tout n'est pas bénéfique (entendons : à autrui et à toi-même)", une sourde discorde s'installe». (Ricoeur, Essais d'herméneutique, :198)

Cette discorde ne pouvait être perçue comme inconscience de nous-mêmes par les Grecs. Et pourtant c'est dans cette discorde que le phénoménologue identifiera la force dynamique pour l'individu quand il est en relation à un autre. C'est cette discorde que l'acte de la promesse transfigure en concorde fragile : « je peux tout essayer", certes, mais : "ici je me tiens".» (Ricoeur, Essais d'herméneutique,)Il y a donc en nous une relative incertitude de ce que nous sommes. Et en même temps, le regard de l'autre nous apprend à nous tenir droit, car il manifeste une attente à laquelle nous désirons répondre. « La question devient : qui suis-je, moi, si versatile, pour que, néanmoins, tu comptes sur moi ? » Ce n'est pas un orgueil stoïcien, car nous savons parfaitement quelle est notre fragilité. Mais c'est un engagement vis-à-vis de l'autre. C'est par lui et pour lui que nous nous affirmons nous-mêmes comme des individus fiables et constants.

L'expérience de l'autre est toujours une expérience de passivité dans une certaine mesure: car l'autre agit sur nous, pour nous, avec nous, et cela transforme ce qui aurait été notre trajectoire, notre volonté, notre action. Est-ce un déni de ce que nous devrions être, de ce que nous sommes au fond de nous-mêmes ? La question, posée en termes philosophiques, devient « Comment rendre compte du travail de l'altérité au cœur de l'ipséité? » (Ricoeur, 1990:368) Autrement dit : que se passe-t-il quand un individu compose avec un autre, quand il veut à la fois rester lui-même et intégrer une nouveauté qui vient de l'autre, et qui peut être une forme d'obligation, ou après tout lui sembler bénéfique, intelligente, nécessaire ou même exaltante ? Peut-être peut-on répondre en considérant que la diversité des expériences de passivité est le répondant existentiel de la notion théorique d'altérité. Il y a donc inévitablement, de par le simple fait que nous ne sommes pas seuls, « une altérité constitutive du soi » (Ricoeur, 1990:378), ce qui justifie le titre d'un de ses ouvrages Soi-même comme un autre. L'autre est pour nous comme une injonction, que nous intériorisons, comme une responsabilité vis-à-vis de nous-mêmes et de lui, par sa seule présence. En ce sens, l'autre peut-être aussi bien un individu particulier que nos parents (réels ou fantasmés), ou une représentation de nos ancêtres, de nos obligations nationales, ou une représentation de Dieu.

Nous retrouvons ici, plus développée, l'idée que nous avions pointée chez Emmanuel Levinas. Il n'y a jamais deux entités fermées, précises et closes, qui négocient et comptent les points de ce que l'une gagne et l'autre perd dans une confrontation de leurs différences. Il y a, dans toute relation que nous vivons, une marge naturelle d'hésitation et d'ouverture à l'imprévu, car cet imprévu est toujours susceptible de devenir un facteur de plus grande cohérence de ce que nous sommes. Et entre nous, il y a toujours une possible référence à un troisième terme au nom duquel nous raisonnons. Ainsi, nous n'avons pas à obéir à l'autre ou le faire obéir, lui ressembler ou l'obliger à nous ressembler, mais nous nous accordons parfois tous deux pour reconnaître l'importance d'une valeur, d'un objectif, d'une référence, d'une aspiration, pour effectuer chacun le mouvement qui nous rapprochera tous deux de notre désir.

Le soi face à l'altérité du texte

Que vient faire ici la problématique du texte ? Le texte est pour nous une des formes de l'altérité. Une altérité qui peut être de personne (l'auteur), d'univers (l'univers d'un récit), de distance dans le temps qui nous le rend étranger (le récit historique ou le texte ancien). Pour un phénoménologue, la question sera là encore d'analyser ce qui se passe en celui qui cherche à comprendre un texte. Ainsi, dans une perspective d'herméneutique du sujet, c'est-à-dire si l'on s'intéresse à la manière dont un individu découvre ce qu'est en lui sa vérité, la question de savoir ce que l'individu peut comprendre renvoie à une anthropologie, une certaine vision de l'humain. « A la question : à quelle condition un sujet connaissant peut-il comprendre un texte, ou l'histoire, on substitue la question : qu'est-ce qu'un être dont l'être consiste à comprendre ? » (Ricoeur, Essais d'herméneutique, :10) Autrement dit :comprendre est un mode d'être et c'est ce mode d'être de la compréhension qui intéresse le philosophe.

Il faut apprendre à prêter attention, à recevoir un texte comme on apprend à recevoir quelqu'un. C'est beaucoup plus difficile que d'être certain a priori. Un texte est comme une proposition de relation, une proposition qu'il nous faut interpréter. Or, interpréter est toujours un effort d'ouverture et d'attention : « Toute interprétation se propose de vaincre un éloignement, une distance, entre l'époque culturelle révolue à laquelle appartient le texte et l'interprète lui-même. En surmontant cette distance, en se rendant contemporain du texte, l'exégète peut s'approprier le sens : d'étranger, il veut le rendre propre, c'est-à-dire le faire sien ; c'est donc l'agrandissement de la propre compréhension de soi-même qu'il poursuit à travers la compréhension de l'autre. Toute herméneutique est ainsi, explicitement ou implicitement, compréhension de soi-même par le détour de la compréhension de l'autre. » (Ricoeur, Essais d'herméneutique, :20)

Cette dernière phrase introduit alors un point essentiel tant pour Paul Ricoeur que pour notre questionnement : notre relation à l'autre, au texte, au récit, à ceux qui nous ont précédés et dont nous écoutons l'histoire n'a de sens que pour la conduite de notre vie, pour l'orientation de notre action. Et, en sens inverse, les autres nous regardent vivre et « lisent » en quelque sorte nos actes comme ils liraient une histoire, notre histoire. On peut faire ainsi un double parallèle entre l'action et le texte : les textes lus nourrissent nos actions et nos actions sont décryptées par les autres comme ils interpréteraient un texte. Comme le texte, une action s'adresse à quelqu'un, elle est fixée, elle est sous-tendue par des actes mentaux, elle est autonome, elle a une pertinence et une importance, des conséquences attendues ou inattendues. Ainsi, parler de communication interculturelle n'est pas faire référence à une situation statique et intellectuelle dans laquelle chacun évaluerait la « culture » de l'autre, mais se demander dans quelle mesure une action commune est possible malgré des différences d'appréciation. Et souvent, le passage à l'action est une entrée en communication plus forte que toute parole, et qui contourne les fixités stéréotypées dans lesquelles nous pouvons nous exprimer et dont nous ne pouvons ou savons pas sortir.

La relation à ce qui nous précède

Cette perspective d'une relation au texte et à l'histoire comme vecteur d'action inscrit l'individu dans une identité collective : il appartient à un peuple, une nation, un État, une civilisation, dont il existe éventuellement des fondements scripturaires. Notre identité est à la fois personnelle et nationale, collective, historique. Nous héritons aussi des représentations de ce qu'il faut espérer, des enjeux à poursuivre. Nous avons des ancêtres, des solidarités requises. Nous nous sentons inscrits dans des lignées auxquelles nous devons d'être ce que nous sommes, et auxquelles nous devons des comportements, des attitudes, des faits, des paroles. Et nous construisons individuellement et collectivement notre « identité narrative », c'est-à-dire ce que nous disons de nous-mêmes comme groupe.

C'est vrai de notre vie personnelle, sociale et politique. C'est vrai aussi de notre vie de chercheur. Tout individu, tout chercheur, est précédé par quelqu'un. Il se sent appartenir à une lignée, à une école. Tout savoir « est précédé par une relation d'appartenance que nous ne pourrons jamais entièrement réfléchir ». (Ricoeur, Essais d'herméneutique, :363) Le savoir objectivant est un travail de distanciation temporelle, positive. La recherche est un effort constant de détachement, car ce savoir sera toujours partiel et que nul n'est sans amarres. En ceci, il se distingue des premières positions d'Habermas, lorsque ce dernier définit la réflexion éthique comme un rejet de tout ce qui est traditionnel et une épuration de tout ce qui peut être de l'ordre de la convention. Pour Paul Ricoeur, l'argumentation n'est pas opposition à une tradition, mais « instance critique opérant au cœur de convictions ». (Ricoeur, Essais d'herméneutique, :334) Il existe une vérité du sujet, et « la vérité est procès de reprise des significations disponibles dans des significations neuves. » (Ricoeur, Essais d'herméneutique, :245) La vérité d'un individu est qu'il porte toujours un héritage, même s'il en renie volontairement certaines parties. Et la vérité épistémologique d'un chercheur est qu'il n'est jamais débarrassé de toute idéologie ou de toute représentation héritée.

La question est de savoir comment nous nous situons entre notre vie aujourd'hui et notre héritage, un héritage que nous pouvons raisonner, contester, mais que nous ne pouvons pas ne pas avoir ni avoir vécu. Nous vivons ainsi deux sortes d'herméneutiques de nous-mêmes : l'une qui part d'aujourd'hui pour nous interroger sur hier, l'autre qui part d'hier pour nous interroger sur notre avenir. Les autres font partie de nos espoirs, de nos projections, de nos idéologies (héritées) et de nos utopies (orientées vers l'avenir que nous rêvons). Tout groupe a une idéologie, car tout groupe a besoin de se donner une image de lui-même pour prendre conscience de ce qui le constitue comme groupe. L'idéologie vise à en perpétrer la mémoire, ré-insuffler l'énergie dont le groupe initial était porteur. L'idéologie relève en ce sens d'une « théorie de la motivation sociale ». Nos identités politiques et sociales renvoient donc toujours à une idéologie, car une nation a une identité narrative, une rationalisation de ses pratiques collectives, qu'elle construit aussi en définissant ce qui la distingue des autres. Et tout groupe porte ses utopies, c'est-à-dire un avenir souhaité, un état idéal qui motive l'action. Nous avons donc à faire, face à nos identités nationales, le même travail de distance et de critique que celui qui nous faisons comme chercheurs.

La dimension de la relation à l'altérité ici évoquée est la dimension collective : quels récits répétons-nous de notre pays, de notre groupe social, du parti politique auquel nous appartenons ? Ces récits sont porteurs de l'image positive et particulière que nous revendiquons, de l'histoire qui nous a amenés à ce que nous sommes, de l'avenir auquel nous aspirons. Nos imaginaires historiques se travaillent d'abord à l'intérieur de nos groupes d'appartenance et nous ne cessons de fait, à travers nos expériences et nos actions, d'interroger cet imaginaire. La rencontre interculturelle peut être aussi définie comme une vérification de la justesse de ces imaginaires.

Altérité et identité

Au bout du compte, qu'avons-nous appris sur notre sujet « Percevoir l'altérité, se sentir autre » ? Il est bien évident que le titre lui-même induisait une position précise, que nous avons précisée et assumée : le choix des philosophes eux-mêmes visait à travailler la part d'altérité qui est en chacun de nous, la part de l'autre dans notre construction identitaire, et présenter l'identité non comme un état stable, mais en mouvement. Ce sont ces points que nous allons reprendre ici sous forme de synthèse.

Altérité et identité du point de vue personnel

Le premier point est qu'il y a un autre en soi. C'est ce que nous dit Michel Foucault : il y a en chacun de nous un soi qui s'ignore, qui est sans doute mieux que ce que nous sommes à un instant donné, et qu'un maître aide à révéler. Il ne s'agit pas ici de n'importe quel autre, mais bien d'un maître. Et ce qui se révèle est ce qui est encore inaccompli, non pas un mystère. C'est en ce sens qu'il dit que, dans l'Antiquité, il n'y a pas d'herméneutique du sujet. Par contre, il met bien en évidence le fait que cette préoccupation de soi, réservée au début à un instant de la vie, devient progressivement une préoccupation constante : l'autre qui est en soi a besoin de se développer jusqu'aux derniers instants. L'objectif est d'abord l'acquisition de compétences sociales. Puis il devient d'acquérir le bien-être intérieur, le sentiment de la plénitude de la vie. Il s'agit donc là d'un art non pas utilisable par tous, mais seulement pour ceux qui disposent de temps. Ce qui amène une forme de tension : le philosophe-maître exige un temps que l'acteur politique ou social n'a pas.

Pour Levinas, la question centrale est celle de la relation à l'autre, de sa construction, pas de la construction de soi. Il ne s'agit pas de savoir comment se construire, comment être au maximum de ses compétences ou de son bien-être, mais de savoir comment dépasser la violence spontanée qui peut nous saisir face à l'autre dont la différence est en elle-même une forme d'agression, de question, d'interrogation, parfois de reproche. Il y a aussi chez Levinas un point que l'on retrouvera développé chez Ricoeur :

le doute sur soi-même, sur son identité, comme acquis incontournable de la modernité. Il y a donc à l'égard de soi, à l'inverse de l'Antiquité, une forme de soupçon que Foucault n'évoque pas. Car l'autre qui est en moi peut-être inconscient, immaîtrisable, violent. Il peut être pour moi-même un mystère, une préoccupation. La psychanalyse est passée par là. Le moi qui sent une altérité en soi est profondément soupçonnable. Et il a besoin de l'autre humain (tout autre humain, pas seulement d'un maître) pour se construire. Et s'il a besoin d'une image de maître, cette image est multiple : cela peut être notamment sa nation, sa culture. Et quand le maître devient intérieur, alors l'humanisation de l'individu a avancé, surtout si le maître intérieur a permis de mettre en évidence la nécessaire relation de dons entre humains.

Ricoeur pose quant à lui explicitement la question de « l'herméneutique du sujet » dont Foucault remarquait qu'elle n'existait pas comme telle dans l'Antiquité. Et cette herméneutique, il estime que, pour être humanisante, elle ne doit être « ni éclatante ni déchue ». Autrement dit : l'autre qui est en chacun de nous et qu'il nous faut découvrir tout au long de notre vie ne doit provoquer en nous ni honte ni volonté de puissance et d'imposition. Certes, la psychanalyse nous a appris à nous suspecter. Mais nous parvenons malgré tout à nous tenir quelque part, par nos choix répétés, par nos décisions constantes, même minuscules, de ce que nous acceptons et refusons. Nous parvenons à garder face aux autres un visage à peu près constant, et ils savent en quoi ils peuvent compter sur nous. Et les autres, de la même manière, ne nous menacent nullement en étant autres, car ils nous montrent des manières de faire, de vivre, que nous pouvons recevoir, reprendre, comprendre, imiter ou non. Si nous savons accueillir l'altérité en nous, nous saurons identifier ce que nous pouvons nous approprier de l'autre.

Si nous nous référons au thème général de notre colloque, cela signifie que l'identité humaine est fondamentalement constituée d'une ouverture à l'autre qui est la condition même de l'humanisation. Le « et » qui relie les deux termes indique donc une conjonction des deux notions.

Altérité et identité du point de vue éthique et politique

Chez Foucault, la dimension sociale et politique est présente, mais en quelque sorte marginale par rapport à la question : le souci de soi émerge d'abord comme un problème de formation de l'homme public, mais s'étend ensuite au groupe des patriciens. Et le fait de travailler sur soi pour être capable de gérer la cité est l'un des paramètres d'une société où le pouvoir est exercé par une élite. La question de l'altérité n'est donc pas celle de nos démocraties. Le « salut » que chacun doit atteindre est individuel. L'enjeu de la transformation de soi est l'amélioration de l'individu qui veut aboutir à lui-même.

Emmanuel Levinas pose la question de l'identité collective à travers la judéité. Mais cette identité collective des juifs n'est pas opposée à l'universel. Pour Emmanuel Levinas, il n'y a pas d'opposition entre être profondément soi, profondément juif et être universel. Car le judaïsme, l'identité juive, consiste en un effort particulier d'humanisation : celui de se demander à quoi un individu, un groupe, un peuple peut servir à l'humanité, ce que son originalité lui apporte. Il y a donc une recherche de coordination de la différence dans la culture juive. Si l'on apprend à être un bon juif, on apprend l'ouverture à l'autre. L'identité acquise, l'identité qui marque l'idéal d'humanité est dont une identité qui cherche la différence nécessaire à toute complémentarité. Chacun est responsable des autres, il y a une solidarité humaine fondamentale de tous les humains qui est requise par une véritable humanisation. Et une solidarité qui s'adresse d'abord aux plus faibles. Ce qui est une différence fondamentale avec les débats du souci de soi de l'Antiquité, où le travail sur soi est destiné aux individus actifs politiquement ou à ceux qui disposent de loisirs.

Chez Paul Ricoeur, chaque individu particulier se construit à travers les autres, mais des autres qui sont aussi des visages d'autorité : des parents réels ou fantasmés, une représentation de nos ancêtres, de notre nation, une représentation de Dieu. L'autre qui est en nous est aussi cette image de ce que nous nous devons à nous-mêmes et de ce que nous devons aux autres. Il y a une dimension inévitablement collective de l'altérité en soi. Et un autre exigeant, qui en même temps s'adresse à tous. C'est l'image de cet autre qui est importante, car elle est pour nous comme un centre auquel nous nous référons dans nos choix. Or, cette image centrale peut être profondément différente, solliciter ou pas la coopération entre les individus et les groupes. Car, contrairement à l'Antiquité, Levinas comme Ricoeur estiment que la réflexion n'a de sens que pour l'action et qu'une réflexion n'isole pas de l'action.

Il y a cependant, suivant les individus et les groupes, une représentation différente de l'humanisation. Il y a notamment chez Levinas et Ricoeur non seulement une référence à l'autre personne humaine, mais une référence à l'Autre (avec une majuscule), image centrale de référence. Et cette image ordonnatrice des comportements est clairement une image d'ouverture. Cette manière de voir n'est pas forcément partagée. Sans doute les débats sur l'identité et la communication interculturelle se comprennent-ils comme une opposition des deux termes lorsque la référence centrale n'est pas la même.

ALTÉRITÉ ET IDENTITÉ DU POINT DE VUE DE LA CONNAISSANCE

Nous retiendrons enfin les aspects épistémologiques de la question de l'altérité en soi, c'est-à-dire la dimension de connaissance impliquée par l'attention à ce qui n'est pas soi. L'Antiquité fait appel au maître pour que le jeune patricien acquière une compétence pour remplir une fonction sociale. Pour Levinas, les liens étroits entre les individus aboutissent à la construction d'un « accord intersubjectif » sur les situations rencontrées, qu'elles soient observation du monde ou situations sociales. L'autre est donc essentiel pour que je puisse expliciter le monde où je vis. Pour Paul Ricoeur enfin, il y a une similitude complètement explicitée entre les modes de compréhension du monde et les raisonnements que nous mettons en oeuvre pour comprendre l'autre : comprendre est un mode d'être qui nécessite toujours ouverture et attention.

Au bout du compte, nous avons affaire à des auteurs pour lesquels il n'y a pas d'identité sans altérité, parce que l'autre est toujours d'une manière ou d'une autre constitutif de moi. Mais le reconnaître ne suffit pas. L'identité est une représentation de soi-même et de son projet. Or, certaines identités intègrent l'altérité dans leur projet-même. Et l'on peut alors se demander, pour revenir aux questionnements de ce colloque, quel rôle joue les médias. N'ont-ils pas fréquemment une définition stéréotypée de l'identité comme opposition à l'altérité ? Dans la mesure où les philosophies ici évoquées ont à la fois une perspective proche (la part d'altérité en chacun) et d'importantes différences dans leurs description des objectifs de la vie, on peut alors suggérer qu'il serait tout à fait passionnant d'analyser les anthropologies sous-jacentes des journalistes et des acteurs médiatiques, anthropologies porteuses d'une palette de relations entre identité et altérité.

BIBLIOGRAPHIE

Foucault, M (2001). *Herméneutique du sujet*. Gallimard-Seuil.
Levians, E (1963 et 1976). *Difficile liberté*. Albin Michel.
—. (1982). *L'au-delà du verset*. Éditions de Minuit.
—. (1987). *Hors sujet*. Livre de poche.
—. (1971). *Totalité et infini*. Livre de poche.
—. (1991). *Entre nous, Essais sur le penser-à-l'autre*. Grasset.
Ricoeur, P (1990). *Soi-même comme un autre*. Seuil.
—. (1969). *Essais d'herméneutique*. Seuil.
—. (2005). *Parcours de la reconnaissance*. Gallimard.
Riondet, O Paul Ricoeur, le texte, le récit et l'histoire », BBF.
Riondet, O « Emmanuel Levinas, le Livre et l'Autre », BBF.

ENCOUNTER BETWEEN THE WESTERN GAZE AND THE PICTURESQUE OTHER IN THE TOURIST CULTURE

SIMONA BUCŞA

Abstract

The contact and intercultural encounters between tourists and natives may be regarded as a unique form of intercultural relationships and communications, built in a distinctive space within tourism culture. The present research, which is part of a larger project on tourist discourses produced in dynamic tourist cultures, aims to track encounters between the powerful Western gaze and the weak but picturesque Other. In addition, it seeks to unveil the representations of this encounter in tourist discourses, also answering how the relationship between Western gaze and picturesque Other is nurtured for cultural consumption purposes. The research method is the semiotic analysis of both guidebooks and travelogues, taking into account the visual and textual representations of the romantic, picturesque, and nostalgic tourist gaze. The analysis addresses two aspects of the tourist discourse, i.e. the promotional tourist discourse that makes up the tourist guidebooks, and, on the other hand, the Western traveller/tourist discourse from travelogues. A parallel analysis of these two types of tourist discourses within the boundaries of the tourist culture attempts to further delineate the space where the Western gaze meets the Other, including where they negotiate the consumption of signs and representations of romanticism, picturesque and nostalgia.

Key words: Western gaze, the Other, tourist culture, romantic space, semiotics

INTRODUCTION

The nature of interactions between tourists and natives has been overlooked by researchers in various fields of study and research, from sociology, psychology and anthropology to communication studies, discourse analysis or semiotics. This is because these encounters are set up not only on economic but also on increasing social and cultural relations. This shows that the contact between tourists and natives may be regarded as a unique form of intercultural interaction, taking place in a particular and clearly delineated space within the boundaries of a distinctively constructed culture, i.e. the tourist culture. In this paper I attempt to glean insight into tourist culture and space, as constructed in the tourist discourse of both guides and tourists. The tourist I pursue is the new tourist, the "untourist" (Huie, in Corrigan, 1997), the "New Moral Tourist" (Butcher, 2003). This Western "untourist" and the Other native meet in a romantic space which is part of a "context model that organizes the ways our discourses are strategically structured and adapted to the whole communicative situation" (Van Dijk, 2008, p. 71). These context models envisage the intentions and goals of the nature-oriented "romantic gaze" (Urry, 2002), so I based the qualitative research on the following hypothesis: Tourist discourse, both promotional and traveller discourse, (re)constructs the signs of romanticism and the picturesque in a new space where the Western gaze and the Other meet. The research question I aim to answer is: How are signs of romanticism negotiated in the relationship between the Western gaze and the picturesque Other?

CORPUS AND METHODOLOGY

Corpus

The small-scale study included two promotional sites of two travel companies, both members of the Romanian Association of Ecotourism, each one with a distinct profile. These sites were chosen based on quality and professionalism of design, compliance with the principles of ecotourism and the guestbook available on both sites. The information used for this study is strictly what was available on both websites.

One site belongs to DiscoveRomania, owned by a Romanian tour guide, self-described as "a small travel company specialising in rural and ecological tourism". Its slogan, "Step into the Gateways to Real Romania," guides the traveller's gaze to a romantic space where "real" "typically turns out to mean 'rural' – what is real or authentic for the New Moral Tourist is not to be found in cities or towns, which remind him of home, but in rural, 'sustainable lifestyles'"(Butcher, 2003, p. 78). Furthermore, Butcher associates the adjective "real" with Urry's "romantic tourist gaze, well away from the masses" (ibid.).

From the very beginning, the tourist discourse appeals to the traveller's imaginative experience of romanticism and what it connects with, i.e., authenticity, genuineness, and nostalgia. "Real Romania" is the first sign of romanticism occurring in the tourist discourse.

The other site belongs to Equus Silvania, owned by Western professionals in wildlife biology and horse trail guiding. It's described as a guesthouse lying "in the foothills of the Transylvanian Carpathians" and includes a horse riding facility that "combines western standards and animal treatment with Romanian tradition, cuisine and lifestyle." Its slogan, "Horseriding and Nature at its Best", guides the traveller gaze to a romantic space where "nature" is associated with the remote realms of untouched and virgin nature. The nature or

"landscape preferences and values for wilderness to which they appeal reflect cultural influences originating in European Romanticism" (Squire, 2003, p. 80).

This site is interesting because the owners are not Romanians but care for traditional Romanian things. The results of the analysis for this site are very interesting because the travellers do not come into contact with natives but with Western people and thus the only romantic sign they share is nature and what it connects with: adventure, exploration, experience. On the other hand, it is the owners' Western gaze itself that is reflected in the so-called discourse of the Picturesque Other.

Both companies have guestbooks available on their website. As a consequence, this was the source for the travellers' discourse I analysed in this paper, as a parallel to the promotional discourse of the tourist sites.

Methodology

The method chosen for analysis is the semiotic analysis of discourse undertaken by Barthes (1997), namely analysis of signs of romanticism, represented in the tourist discourse of both promotional sites and related guestbooks as part of a mythological system on two levels of significance. The two signs of romanticism considered myths and analysed as a semiological system are "nature" and "noble savage". The term "noble savage" is borrowed, within the context of tourist studies, from Hennig (2002) who carries out research in an attempt to understand the relationship between tourism and modern myths. The modern myths he considers to have special significance for tourism are "nature, the noble savage, art, individual freedom and self-realization, equality and paradise" (Hennig, 2002, p. 174).

The reasoning at the base of a mythological system-oriented analysis is that all texts of tourist discourses are reproductions of previous texts that evolve in "a chain of associated concepts" (Fiske, 1989, p. 169) and these texts may be regarded as a "mythological system." Analysing texts within the mythological system is based on the idea that signs of romanticism represented in tourist discourses are actually a chain of previous significances concerning the Other. Referring to texts and romanticism, Thompson advances a similar idea of "a vast matrix of prior texts, anecdotes, and images that thus underpins and informs Romantic ideas, practices and representations of travel" (Thompson, 2007:11).

Chaining significances on levels of significances is accurately illustrated by Barthes (1997, p. 241): "myth is a special system, in that it is constructed from a semiological chain which existed before it: it is a second-order semiological system. That which is a sign (namely the associative total of a concept and an image) in the first system, becomes a mere signifier in the second."

Other methods that offer great support in analysing the tourist discourse of both promotional sites and travellers as a chain of tourist experiences taking place in the tourist culture are the experience and context models developed by Van Dijk (2008). The two genres of tourist discourse that are analysed in this paper are in fact representations of a chain of experience models and mental models of travellers and the tourist experience is regarded as a whole, from the promotional discourse on DiscoveRomania or Equus Silvania sites to the traveller discourse on their related guestbooks. Without considering the basic categories of context models that enable the production of discourses, i.e. setting (time, period, space, place, environment), participants, their roles, relations, intentions and communicative actions (Van Dijk, 2008, p. 76), it is impossible to construct a discourse to be understood and continued. Although this method is not fully applied in this research, it is going to be essential for further research in the field of tourist discourse.

TOURIST CULTURE AND ROMANTIC SPACE

Tourist Culture – Intercultural Encounter

Many contemporary researchers have approached the concept of tourist culture, but all of them have based their studies, to a greater or less extent, on Goffman's dramaturgical sociology and theatrical frame (1991, 2007). That frame looks at social interactions as performances on a stage where individuals play a role assigned to them according to the performance type and manage their stage impressions. Goffman's theories and concepts of "back region", "front region" and "backstage" refer to acting on an actual stage; in other words, the use of practices and strategies specific to dramaturgy are used to describe the contextual boundaries of the meeting between the tourist and the host. These conceptual frames have been approached in cultural studies in tourism and have led to the creation of a new frame for tourism, i.e. tourist culture and new concepts used to delineate this frame, such as "staged authenticity" (MacCannell, 1999), "staged experience" (Rojek, in Paterson, 2006, p. 137) and "masqued ball" (Trottier, in Laplante, 2000, p. 96).

MacCannell interprets Goffman's concepts thus: "the front is the meeting place of hosts and guests or customers and service persons, and the back is the place where members of the home team retire between performances to relax and to prepare" (MacCannell, 1999, p. 92). This space is considered authentic and, as a consequence, it is sought out by tourists; however, as MacCannell states (1999, p. 101), his position is reiterated by Paterson (2006, p. 137): "it is always possible that what is taken to be entry into a back region is really entry into a front region that has been totally set up in advance for tourist visitation."

MacCannell calls this concept "staged authenticity". Rojek's concept of "staged experience" (cited by Paterson, 2006) has nothing to do with the romantic traveller but with the post-tourist who accepts the idea of play and inauthenticity. Paterson traces a border between MacCannell's tourist who "desires to consume only authentic experiences" and Rojek's post-tourist who "is attracted by experience as an end in itself and not by what the experience teaches about one's inner resources, or whether the attraction is authentic" (Paterson, 2006, p. 137). Paterson maintains the name of tourists for travellers "still motivated by a romantic impulse, to encounter nature as a form of self-improvement or moral instruction." I shall use the name given by Corrigan (1997), namely the "untourist" who, together with the post-tourist, as the author further argues, is likely "to be the elite tourist categories of the future, the former representing the postmodern strand of culture discussed in Urry (1990) and the latter growing out of the environmental strand" (Corrigan, 1997, p. 145).

L. Trottier's idea about tourist culture is taken by LaPlante (2000). Thus, tourist culture is seen as "an intersection of individuals' real life who disguise themselves as tourists and hosts to simulate the intercultural encounter on an ephemeral stage. Their masks do not deceive anyone but make the meetings more lively like a masked ball" (Trottier in LaPlante, 2000, p. 96).

The tourist image built up by "the original culture of the tourist" comes into contact with the "original culture of the visited society," leading to intercultural contact. It is this intercultural meeting that gives rise to tourist culture as defined and illustrated below by Trottier (in LaPlante, 2000, p. 96). Trottier maintains that this culture is a product of the postmodern culture due to its artificiality: "tourist culture is a product of postmodern culture due to its artificiality. The acted life of tourism is without consequences because it is a paranthesis in both individual's life and postmodern society" (Laplante, 2000, p. 97).

Wearing, Stevenson and Young (2010) argue that "tourist cultures are a complex of relationships that occur with, through, and in space – both real and imagined" (2010, p. 2) and understand "tourist cultures through the conceptual lenses of experience and space" (2010, p. 6).

The authors introduce the concept of space as its traditional meaning changes, but I shall return to this issue in more detail later in the paper. Beyond space, another essential element of the tourist culture introduced by Wearing, Stevenson and Young (2010) is the self and the construction of the traveller self within the boundaries of the tourist culture. Indeed, the idea of moving "beyond traditional activity-based analyses of tourism to an approach that is space and subject-centered" (2010, p. 12) is to be found, as the authors themselves underscore, in works by Edensor (1998), or Rojek and Urry (1997). All the above-mentioned researchers, including those cited by Wearing, Stevenson, and Young, originate their analyses in Goffman's theories and agree that the traveller self is constructed following the "interactions of the tourist in, and with, the spaces of tourism, and the relationships which tourists form with people and places as part of these interactions" (2010, p. 12).

I find very interesting the reference to Grosz's work (cited in Wearing, Stevenson, and Young, 2010, p. 9) which "provides a useful starting point for developing a way of thinking about tourist cultures in terms of interaction and experience, rather than as objectified activities or sights".

I support and attempt to conduct my research starting from the same premises, that tourist culture is defined by interaction and experience. In addition, I add the prodigious and influential work of Wang (2002) who, without specifically talking about tourist culture, actually makes us think in terms of a tourist culture and tourist space when dealing with the experiential and symbolic consumption through "three consecutive stages: pre-travel, on-trip experiences and post-travel" (Wang, 2002, p. 200).

All the stages, i.e. pre-travel (which "involves the consumption of images and representations"), on-trip experience (which "involves consumption of experiences") and post-travel stage which "involves the symbolic effect of the consumption of tourism" (2002, p. 200) are interlinked and can only exist or be analysed within the framework of the tourist culture.

The encounter between the Western traveller and the picturesque Other which I analyse in this paper does not occur at a particular moment, space or place. Moreover, it is not solely a social interaction. It is an encounter nurtured by the tourist experience – either the imaginative experience, or the experience during the travel, or the experience after the travel. In these encounters, by pursuing specific signs attached to a specific space, in my case the romantic space, goes beyond the social interaction, namely the construction of self-identity that "has the potential for enlargement and growth through the engagement of the tourist with other environments, peoples, societies and cultures" (Wearing, Stevenson & Young, 2010, p. 36).

To emphasize this idea, I appeal to the same authors who, also inspired by the work of Lefebvre (1991), reiterate the idea of "culture which locates the ways of life of a group of people as being intrinsically related to the spaces and places within which they conduct their lived (travel) experiences"; thus "Tourist cultures, and thus the traveler self, are multiple and contradictory, constructed and reconstructed through the negotiation of experience that occurs in the context of tourist space" (Wearing, Stevenson & Young, 2010, p. 12).

A concept that must be clarified is that of space and tourist space. As with contemporary researchers and their works, I consider space from the perspective of symbolism. Although it is beyond the scope of this paper to theorize the tourist space, as such a theorization is a topic for independent research, for my research it is important to define space from the current perspective on cultural studies, as space reflects on the tourist discourse I analyse in this paper.

Tourist Space – Romantic Space

Redefining space

In contemporary cultural studies, space and place are redefined. According to Barker (2004), unlike the modern social theory that considered the space fixed, after the seventies cultural theory, inspired in particular by the work of Foucault, refocused its interest towards the construction of spaces and places by discourse, power, and discipline. Thus "space can be understood as a social construct with the social itself being spatially organized" and "is constituted by a dynamic set of processes that are implicated in questions of power and symbolism" (Barker, 2004, p. 186). Place, on the other hand, is "a site or location in space constituted and made meaningful by social relations of power and marked by identifications or emotional investments. As such, a place can be understood to be a bounded manifestation of the production of meaning in space" (2004:144). Barker further distinguished space and place "in terms of absence-presence. That is, place is marked by face-to-face encounters and space by relations between absent others."

In other words, Romania's rural landscape may be considered a place where the romantic Western traveller meets the picturesque Other and is "the product of physical presence and social rituals" and, at the same time, may be regarded as a text reproduced in tourist sites, letters, narratives, or blogs, a space with "symbolic and power-saturated character" (Barker, 2004, p. 187). It may be regarded as the domain of "romanticism" and "nostalgia" in the light of a "romantic" and "egocentric" gaze or, on the contrary, the domain of human expansion and development in the light of an "anthropocentric" gaze. Newsome, Moore and Dowling (2003) look at the environmental from the ecocentric and anthropocentric perspective, whereas Urry (2002) looks at the environment from a romantic perspective.

Gregory (1994), citing Duncan, emphasizes the idea of regarding landscape as both a text and space where both the sender and the receiver produce and reproduce meanings. "Landscapes anywhere can be viewed as texts which are constitutive of discursive fields, and thus can be interpreted socio-semiotically in terms of their narrative structure, their synecdoches and recurrence. This applies as much to late twentieth century" (Duncan, in Gregory, 1994, p. 145). These texts, continues the author, "encourage the reader to carve it up, to rework it, to produce it. Although it cannot mean anything at all [i.e. there are limits to interpretative possibility], it is a space in which the reader as writer can wander, in which signifiers play, signifieds becoming signifiers in an endless process of deferment" (Duncan, in Gregory, 1994, p. 145).

In this paper we see how landscape and its meanings are represented in two different genres of discourse: tourist sites and travelogues, part of the same type of discourse, and tourist discourse, how the symbolic meanings of space are negotiated in the tourist culture in the perspective of the "romantic gaze" (Urry, 2002). The following section introduces the signs of romanticism as perceived by contemporary travellers. Who the contemporary travellers are is another issue to be addressed in this paper so as to reach the actual analysis of the discourse produced for and by this new type of traveller.

Romantic space – sign and significance

Urry, J (2002) introduces the concept of "romantic" gaze as opposed to that of "collective gaze," "in which the emphasis is upon solitude, privacy and a personal, semi-spiritual relationship with the object of gaze" rather than "the presence of large numbers of other people" (Urry, 2001, p. 43). The romantic perspective is represented in the idyllic discourse on landscape and aims at the new environment-oriented tourist who is seeking to evade "the natural world in all its undisturbed, pristine glory" in an "an undisturbed vista of natural beauty, without ugly man-made buildings, and often unpolluted even by fellow human beings" (Paterson, 2006, p. 119). Paterson also adds that the romantic gaze is a "product of the Western European romantic tradition" and that it is "such a historically pervasive tradition that current tourist practices are inevitably shaped by it, in the propensity for walking or cycling holidays, for hill-walking and mountaineering." The romantic perspective is represented in both genres of tourism discourse analyzed in this paper: "you will be part of that lost paradise," "unique beauty of nature's area," "fantastic landscape" (extracts from tourist discourses). Therefore, the way in the "Romantic movement" (Urry, 2002) back in the late eighteenth and early nineteenth centuries "emphasis was placed on the intensity of emotion and sensation, on poetic mystery rather than intellectual clarity, and on hedonistic expression" (Urry, 2002:20) led, as Urry continues, not only "to the development of scenic tourism" (Urry, 2002:20) but also to the "emergence of mass tourism" (Urry, 2002:44). Nowadays the "Romantic movement" tracks down the lost paradise of Romanticism, serving "to suggest that one could feel emotional about the natural world and scenery" (Urry, 2002:20).

Thus, the romantic gaze moves away from the collective gaze towards solitude and the sublime nature, in a space of romantic symbolism. The romantic space is all about feelings and sensations to which particular signs give rise. For instance, the beautiful forests of Transylvania give rise to the sensation of a "fairy-tale", while the villages bring about a feeling of nostalgia and sentimentalism, making travellers feel "as though you've gone back with a time-machine" (Equus Silvania guestbook).

Thinking romantically means thinking in terms of authenticity, exploration, adventure, experience, nostalgia, sentimentalism, sensation, or emotions. This is the reason why we may talk about a romantic space within the boundaries of modern tourist culture in terms of symbolism. Here all travellers, Culler says, are semioticians. "Tourists are the agents of semiotics: all over the world they are engaged in reading cities, landscapes and cultures as sign systems" (Culler, 1988). They interpret the signs of romanticism in light of their romantic associations. On the one hand, promotional discourses on websites with focus on the new "untourists" introduce signs of romanticism in order to appeal to the Western gaze in search for authentic experiences, unspoiled nature, and real adventures in the picturesque Other. On the other hand, travellers' discourse reproduces the signs of romanticism in the light of their own experience. To further develop the idea, we can say that whereas promotional discourses produce signs in the romantic space of a context model that is based on the experience model of the Western romantic tourist, i.e. imaginative experience regarding the picturesque Other, travellers' discourse produces signs in the romantic space of a context model that is based on a new experience model of the Western romantic tourist, i.e post-travel, experience regarding the picturesque Other. These context models, consecutive and interrelated, enable the romantic space and implicitly, through signs and representations, the romantic discourse to be produced. It is rather reproduced and negotiated in a close relationship between the Western gaze and the picturesque Other, viewing the intentions and goals of the nature-oriented "romantic gaze."

Before analysing the two romantic signs, namely nature and noble savage, I am going to briefly place these signs and their significances within the boundaries of the romantic space. Nature is definitely a romantic sign with meanings that have evolved through the centuries. The occurrence of nature as a romantic symbol connected with "emotion and sensation" (Urry, 2002, p. 20), "imagination and feelings" (Wang, 2000, p. 82), the "sublime and heroic seeking" (Thompson, 2007, p. 29), and as a "redeeming and renewing force" (Hennig, 2002, p. 175) was marked by all the above-cited authors in the late eighteenth century, especially in the English society, where nature "gained a positive meaning" (Wang, 2000, p. 82). The Romantic Movement has turned the meanings of nature from medieval and early modern periods when mountains for instance "were perceived as hideous, hostile places best avoided by all sane, God-fearing men" into "objects of aesthetic pleasure" (Thompson, 2007, p. 29). In other words, "a taste and passion for landscapes and nature was one of the original characteristics of the Romantic Movement and romanticism" (Wang, 2000, p. 82). As Thompson puts it,

> beside the influence of romance, sentimentalism, and Gothic in the Romantic interest in travel as misadventure . . . the growing taste for sublime landscapes was another factor in the perilous predicaments Romantic travellers sometimes found themselves in. (Thompson, 2007, p. 12)

The "aesthetic relationship with nature" (Hennig, 2002, p. 174) has been continuously nurtured up to present day. The only differences are the places where the romantic space is manifested. The romantic gaze is oriented towards unknown, unexplored places where nature can still be found in its untroubled splendour. Romania, still rural and known, similar to other developing societies, is seen as "pre-modern, natural and more authentic than modern societies" (Selwyn, in Dorsey et al., 2004, p. 757) and seems to embody a "refuge from modernity", "a rural utopia where tourists may evade from the present into an authentic and nostalgic past" (Short, in Sharpley, 2004, p. 377). There's an idea that "by contact with nature", in its whole beauty, "its purifying powers will somehow be transferred" to travellers (Hennig, 2002, p. 175).

The same meanings may be applied to the "noble savage." He or she is part of the nature that untourists look for, the embodiment of the authentic style of life unlike the inauthentic Western societies. Experiencing the authenticity of a different culture and a lack of authenticity in one's personal culture is stressed by MacCannell who says "Sightseers are motivated by a desire to see life as it is really lived, even to get in with the natives" (MacCannell, 1999, p. 94).

According to Hennig (2002), the imagery of the noble savage developed, along with nature, "in the late 18th century accounts of the South Sea Islands" and "became one of the main counter-images to the developing industrial civilization" (Hennig, 2002, p. 176). The noble savage, adds Hennig, "lives in harmony with the forces of nature, in contrast to modern man, who has become alienated from his origin." This image of the picturesque native from remote, untroubled destinations, either textual or pictorial, appears in all genres of tourist discourse, from guidebooks and travel sites to travelogues and travel blogs. They show "villagers who still plough by hand and wear traditional costumes" (site

DiscoveRomania); "people still live a very simple life without electricity and running water" (Equus Silvania site).

To conclude, I return to J. Urry's romantic gaze and "its role in constructing nature as an absolutely central positional good" (Urry, 2002, p. 137). This good is not important economically, but rather culturally. Thinking of Fiske's concept of cultural economy (2009), that it is meanings and pleasure that circulate not money, or of Baudriallard's theory of consumption cited by Urry (2002), that we increasingly consume signs or representations, the same idea is emphasized by Paterson (2006), who underscores that in tourist culture, consumption is turned into the "consumption of particular signs, markers or representations, the tourist's attention being directed to them through an anticipative engagement with discourses of travel and nature through brochures and advertisements for example" (Paterson, 2006, p. 118).

All the above statements considered, we can interpret nature and the noble savage in terms of signs and representations of a romantic gaze that develops within the contextual models of the romantic discourse. Who the participants are in these context models makes the subject of the following section.

New Types of Tourists and the Western Gaze

The evolution and changes in Western societies have had a considerable impact on tourism as well. G. Hughes (2004), citing Krippendorf and Poon, explains the development of new types of tourism as part of economic, social, and cultural changes from Western societies as part of the "de-industrialization" of many territories of Western Europe and North America.

> The demise of semi-skilled or unskilled occupational categories under the twin pressures of automation and global relocation of production, and the contemporaneous expansion in service employment, coincided with, and contributed to, transformations in institutional structures including those of class, family, gender, and nation. (Hughes, 2004, p. 499)

Hughes also shows the difference between economic and cultural changes. From an economic perspective, Western societies have moved from industrial (Fordist) to post-industrial (post-Fordist) production. From a sociocultural perspective, Western structures moved from modern to postmodern. Consequently, continuing Hughes's idea, the development of new types of tourism may be explained through a change in consumers who belong to the new and emerging middle class employed in the economy of post-industrial services. This new class is defined by Urry (2002) as the "service class," which

> consists of that set of places within the social division of labour whose occupants do not own capital or land to any substantial degree; are located within a set of interlocking social institutions which collectively 'service' capital; enjoy superior work and market situations generally resulting from the existence of well-defined careers, either within or between organisations; and have their entry regulated by the differential possession of educational credentials. These serve to demarcate the service class from more general white-collar workers and generate distinctions of cultural capital and taste. (Urry, 2002, p. 80)

The new types of tourists, as Poon (cited in Hughes, 2005, p. 499) describes them, are interested in travel that involves enjoying the natural environment while respecting the integrity of local communities. Fewer in number, the new tourists are highly sought after because they are alleged to be more discerning. They look for authenticity, novelty, spontaneity and adventure and are keen to learn about the natural environment and new cultures.

This new, more discerning tourist has various names. Corrigan names him or her the "untourist," but other names include "ecotourists, green tourists, cultural tourists, alternative tourists, educational tourists" (Huie, quoted in Corrigan, 1997, p. 145). The untourist "is out to track down authenticity . . . cares for people, maintains unspoiled environments, authenticity, and value-for-money". In addition, "Their main categories are the traditional ones of romantic reactions to industrial societies" (Corrigan, 1997, p. 144).

Butcher (2003, p. 78) calls these travellers "New Moral Tourists" who "really want to experience the country and its people" and for whom "a rough-and-ready experience is a virtue". The New Moral Tourist discourse is less of a "hegemonic discourse" (concept introduced by Bruner, 1991) because the romantic discourse also means equality, placing the picturesque Other in a privileged place from which he has a lot of things to learn:

> for New Moral Tourists, not only is otherness sought after, but there is a sense in which it can be elevated above one's own culture. . . . The tourist gaze fixes upon sites that appear to offer an unmodern existence; an existence from which the tourist feels they have much to learn. The New Moral Tourist gaze is a gaze in awe. (Butcher 2003, p. 78)

Thus the Western romantic tourist does not look at the Other with superiority, but with admiration. Yet, adds the author, the admiration remains only so long as the Other remains regarded as undeveloped and primitive. Thus, promotional discourses have the tendency to describe natives as even less developed than they actually are for the sake of money. This leads the discourse to the verge of a hegemonic discourse that according to Bruner (1991, citing Pratt, 1985, p. 120) "fixes the Other in a timeless present" in which only powerful ones who have power and money decide what stories to be told: "The tourists come to Africa to see the spectacular landscape, the wild animals, and the primitive tribes, and as this is what they are prepared to pay for, it is what will be served to them" (Bruner, 1991, p. 241).

This is the other side of the story, not explored in my research because the co-participants in the context model of the tourist discourse analysed here are also romantics who wish to remain in nature and to return to tradition: "we want to show you the best of Romania – because we are fascinated by it as well!" (site DiscoveRomania); "they organize two large nature and landscape conservation programmes in the Carpathians and the Transylvanian Hills" (site Equus Silvania).

All things considered, both the untourist and the tour guide, whose discourses are analyzed here as part of the same "epistemic community" (concept used by van Dijk, 2008), share the same sociocultural knowledge and values, including respect and love for nature and natural things. They share the same "romantic gaze".

Discussions and Conclusions

Interpreting the results

In order to analyse the two signs of romanticism, namely nature and the noble savage, with the precise aim of proving that these signs are negotiated within the framework of the relationship between Western gaze and picturesque Other that is formed and maintained in the romantic space of a chain of context models, the first step was to outline four categories of romantic image. These categories were pervasive throughout the two sites, DiscoveRomania and Equus Silvania, and their related guestbooks: nature-gaze, noble savage, adventure-exploration, nostalgia-sentimentalism. The categories were designed to take into account the romantic gaze of all the participants in discourse production. When looking for their textual representations, I considered four types of action: for nature, depicting; for adventure, acting; for nostalgia, dreaming; and for the noble savage, meeting.

Table 24-1 illustrates the category hierarchy in the promotional discourse of the DiscoveRomania site. Due to the main activities and focus of the travel company, organizing trips for tourists in "the most picturesque and perhaps the most genuine realm of Romanian life" (extract from the site) in rural Romania, the classification is almost predictable: nature-gaze, adventure-exploration and on the same position, nostalgia-sentimentalism and noble savage. A few representations of the four categories of romantic images are as follows:

> crossing its threshold, you will enter the world of the grass blade, of the deep woods, fields and wild flowers, mountains teeming with wildlife [nature-gaze]

> walk and climb in the mountains, or explore dense pine and beech forests still inhabited by the Carpathian bear [adventure-exploration]

> you will be part of that lost paradise, where time has a different meaning [nostalgia-sentimentalism]

> villagers who still plough by hand and wear traditional costumes [noble savage].

On the other hand, the guestbook on DiscoveRomania (Table 24-2) portrays a different hierarchy, i.e. noble savage, adventure-exploration and nature-gaze and nostalgia-sentimentalism. The explanation may reside in the arguments of Butcher (2003) when pondering the cultural sensibilities of the New Moral Tourist. Thus, Butcher argues that for the New Moral Tourist

> the host society is often subject to a romantic gaze by the tourist in search of a sense of authenticity – its culture is seen as unsullied by consumerism and embodying spiritual values and a sense of community sought after in more wealthy tourism-generating regions. "Culture" coheres nirvana, protecting it from the modern assault. (Butcher, 2003, p. 82).

Moreover, adds the author, the New Moral Tourist is like an anthropologist who is "interested in learning about the culture of the host" (ibid.).

The noble savage is, therefore, a sign of romanticism, a modern myth whose levels of significances will be analysed in the following subchapter.

Table 24-1. Comparison Picturesque Other – Western Gaze (DiscoveRomania)

Picturesque Other (website)		Western Gaze (guestbook)	
Nature-gaze	33%	Noble Savage	35%
Adventure-Exploration	31%	Nature-gaze Adventure-Exploration	25%
Nostalgia-Sentimentalism Noble Savage	18%; 18%	Nostalgia-Sentimentalism	15%

The hierarchy in the Equus Silvania site is different, mainly due to the fact that the owners are themselves the Western gaze. They "discovered" and love the noble savage who is "still deeply rooted in their traditions". This explains why the noble savage ranks second after nature-gaze (predictable since the slogan of the site is mainly oriented towards nature) but before adventure-exploration and nostalgia-sentimentalism.

Likewise, the guestbook hierarchy is also the result of the guesthouse's Western ownership. Because guests come into contact only with their Western horse trail guide, they miss meeting with the natives, the noble savage. Consequently, the noble savage ranks fourth, after nature-gaze, adventure-exploration and nostalgia-sentimentalism. However, we notice that nature is closely linked with countryside, and rural areas that have a strong impact upon travellers, the sites of "beautiful landscapes, fairytale forests and villages that made you feel as though you've gone back with a time-machine". As Butcher says, "they seek timelessness, not change, in a rapidly changing world" (Butcher, 2003, p. 82).

The following table shows a parallel analysis between the discourse of the picturesque Other and that of the Western gaze, as categorized according to the categories of the romantic signs.

Table 24-2. Comparison Picturesque Other – Western Gaze (Equus Silvania)

Picturesque Other		Western Gaze	
Nature-gaze	39%	Nature-gaze	36%
Noble Savage	25%	Adventure-Exploration	30%
Adventure-Exploration	20%	Nostalgia-Sentimentalism	22%
Nostalgia-Sentimentalism	16%	Noble Savage	12%

Mythological System

Nature and the noble savage become independent texts in a modern mythical system, constructed and consumed by the romantic gaze within the romantic space of a clearly delineated contextual model. The myth constantly shifts and so does its significances. The origin of the myths is not important anymore because, as Barthes says, "text unity does not reside in its origin but its destination" (Barthes, 1997, p. 148).

Nature and the noble savage are not simple signs to be understood at a denotative level as a linguistic system made up of the acoustic expression and concept. The two signs become myths, "meta-language" in which reading does not take account of the linguistic system anymore. Rather, "the image loses some knowledge to better receive the knowledge in the concept" (Barthes, 1997, p. 247).

I shall trace the two signs within the two context models of the two genres of tourist discourse, the promotional discourse and the travelers discourse, making use of the mythological system.

At the first level of signification, that of connotation, nature refers to plant and animal life as distinct from man. At the second level of signification, that of myth, the concept of nature is associated with emotion, sensation, nostalgia. The sign, the signification that correlates the signifier and the signified, is discursively represented through the following texts:

> a fiery land with a striking natural beauty that stirs your heart (DiscoveRomania site),

or, less strongly,

> endless forests and spectacular views are the characteristics of this journey (Equus Silvania site).

The next concept model asserts that where the main participant is the Western gaze, a new genre of discourse is produced that still preserves the boundaries of the romantic space. Thus, the concept of nature is still associated with emotion, sensation and nostalgia, but they are much stronger, especially in case of those who traveled with Equus Silvania. The sign is discursively represented through the following texts: "Thanks to Transylvania for being so wild and free and for letting us canter over your velvet pastures" (Equus Silvania guestbook), and

> "it really was beyond my wildest dreams" (DiscoveRomania guestbook).

As for the noble savage, at the first level of signification, that of connotation, noble savage refers to a picturesque primitive creature. At the second level of signification, that of myth, the concept of noble savage is associated with authentic, genuine, timeless. The sign, i.e. the signification that correlates the signifier and the signified, is discursively represented through the following texts: "simple way of life" or "warmly hospitable people" (DiscoveRomania site).

The sign representation in Equus Silvania is stronger and makes appeal to traveler desires, like their own, to step into the noble savage space: "meeting people with us is something authentic, off the beaten track, and will give you a true insight into how people live in the small villages at the foot of the Carpathian Mountain" (Equus Silvania site).

The post-travel context model offers a different approach to the noble savage as a sign in the mythological system. In the DiscoveRomania guestbook, at the second level of significance, the concept of noble savage is associated with sacred, religious feelings. The sign is represented as follows:

> "the highlight had to be our weekend in Botiza and the service on Easter Monday."

The sacred relation with the noble savage is very strong and has a significant impact upon the Western gaze. The travellers were received in the sacred space of the Romanians and to them this meant "real Romania".

The choice of mythological system enables us to see that the participants involved in discourse production or understanding are given the freedom to read the meaning of texts in light of their own romantic view.

Conclusions

The choice of two methods of research allowed me to trace and keep a better account of the romantic signs in the two genres of tourist discourse submitted to analysis. Van Dijk's contextual models helped me to pursue the tourist experiences that occurred within the boundaries of the tourist culture and the tourist space where the encounter between the Western gaze and the Picturesque Other took place.

An important conclusion is that experiences, both imaginative and post-travel, are transferred from one discourse to another by means of context models. This results in discourses based on common experiences lived in the tourist culture.

All the participants in tourist discourse, the tour guides and the travelers, reconstruct signs of romanticism in this new, romantic space where the Western gaze and the Other meet. Barthes' mythological system helped me interpret these signs.

The hypothesis is tested and the research question is answered. The signs of romanticism are negotiated in light of all participants' travel or romantic experience. An example is the interchangeability of the Western gaze that is either reflected in the traveller discourse or in the promotional discourse. From this point of view, the study is very interesting and opens new paths toward new research.

In conclusion, Romania, along with other isolated, remote, and yet unexplored tourist destinations, has attached meanings and representations associated with "the Other" in relation to "the Western," which leads to "a significant influence on their choice of destination and their motives and behaviour as tourists" (Saarinen, 2004, p. 442).

The promotional tourist discourse reflects the Western imagination and is generally created to represent the Western myth of nature, the picturesque native, exploration, and sensation. In this study, we saw that traveller discourse also reflects the Western imagination, but this imagination is negotiated in the context of personal experiences. The myths of nature and noble savage are transferred from one context model to another, but their significance is negotiated as well, dependent on the goals and intentions of participants. This means that the tourist culture and the romantic space gives the freedom to construct and reconstruct the signs of authenticity and romanticism, emphasizing again the idea that it is the significance we attach to objects that matters, not the object itself.

References

Barker, C (2004). *The Sage Dictionary of Cultural Studies*, London: SAGE Publications.

Barthes, R (1997). *Mitologii*, Iaşi: Editura Institutul European.

Bruner, E M (1991). Transformation of Self in Tourism. *Annals of Tourism Research*, 18, 238–250.

Butcher, J (2003). *The Moralisation of Tourism: Sun, Sand . . . and Saving the World?* London: Routledge.

Corrigan, P (1997). *The Sociology of Consumption*, London: Sage Publications.

Culler, J (1988). *Framing the Sign: Criticism and Its Institutions*, Norman: University of Oklahoma Press.

Dorsey, E R, Steeves, H L, & Porras, L, E (2004). Advertising Ecotourism on the Internet: Commodifying Environment and Culture. *New Media Society* 6, 753–779.

Edensor, T (1998). *Tourists at the Taj*, London: Routledge.

Edensor, T (2001), Performing Tourism, Staging Tourism: (Re)producing Tourist Space and Practice. *Tourist Studies,* 1(1), 59–81.

Fiske, J (1989). *Understanding Popular Culture*, London, New York: Unwin Hyman.

Goffman, E (1991). *Les cadres de l'experience*, Paris: Les Editions de Minuit.

—. (2007).Viaţa cotidiană ca un spectacol, Bucureşti: Comunicare.ro.

Gregory, D (1994). *Geographical Imaginations*, Oxford: Blackwell Publishers.

Hennig, C (2002). Tourism: Enacting Modern Myths. In Dann, G M S (ed.).*The Tourist as a Metaphor of the Social World,* Wallingford: CABI Publishing;

Hughes, G (2004). Tourism, Sustainability, and Social Theory. In Lew, A A, Hall, C M & Williams, A M (eds). *A Companion to Tourism* (pp. 498–509), Oxford: Blackwell Publishing.

Jaworski, A & Pritchard, A (eds) (2005). *Discourse, Communication and Tourism,* Clevedon: Channel View Publications.

LaPlante, M (2000). *L'expérience touristique contemporaine*, Québec: Presses Universitaires du Québec.

Lefebvre, H (1991). *The Production of Space*, Oxford: Blackwell Publishing.

Lew, A A, Hall, C M & Williams, A M (eds) (2004). *A Companion to Tourism*, Oxford: Blackwell Publishing.

MacCannell, D (1999). *The Tourist, a New Theory of the Leisure Class*, Berkeley, CA: University of California Press.

Newsome, D, Moore, S, Dowling, R K (2002). *Natural Area Tourism: Ecology, Impacts and Management*, Clevedon: Channel View Publications.

Paterson, M (2006). *Consumption and Everyday Life*, London: Routledge.

Pratt, M L (1985). Scrathes of the Face of the Country; or, What Mr. Barrow Saw in the Hand of the Bushmen. *Critical Inquiry*, 12, 119–143.

Rojek, C, Urry, J (1997). *Touring Cultures: Transformations of Travel and Theory*, London: Routledge.

Saarinen, J (2004). The Social Construction of Tourist Destinations. In Lew, A A, Hall, C M & Williams, A M (eds). *A Companion to Tourism* (pp. 154–173), Oxford: Blackwell Publishing.

Sharpley, R (2004). Tourism and the Countryside. In Lew, A A, Hall, C M & Williams, A M (eds). *A Companion to Tourism* (pp. 374–386), Oxford: Blackwell Publishing.

Squire, S J (2003). Rewriting Languages of Geography and Tourism. In Ringer, G (ed.). *Destinations: Cultural Landscapes of Tourism* (pp. 80–100), London: Routledge.

Thompson, C (2007). *The Suffering Traveller and the Romantic Imagination,* Oxford: Oxford University Press.

Urry, J (2002). *The Tourist Gaze*, London: Sage Publications.

Van Dijk, T (2008). *Discourse and Context: A Sociocognitive Approach*, Cambridge: Cambridge University Press.

Wang, N (2000). *Tourism and Modernity: A Sociological Analysis*, Amsterdam: Pergamon.

Wearing, S, Stevenson, D & Young, T (2010). *Tourist Cultures: Identity, Place and the Traveller*. London: Sage Publications.

*** www.discoveromania.ro

*** www.equus-silvania.com

Patterns of Communication in Public Space in Romania

Corina Daba Buzoianu
and Cristina Cîrtiţă-Buzoianu

Abstract

The study focuses on communication in the media public space in Romania and argues that strong and open societies are based on solid communication in the public space. We start from Levi-Strauss' idea that a society is a group of people who communicate. We try to analyse how communication in the public space is being shaped in Romania and what messages it comprises.

Our analysis shows that in Romania, currently, communication in the public space is connected to political matters, although it is not assimilated into the political discourse. The messages regard subjects that involve political actors and create a debate that is pointed towards the decision-makers of the state. In order to study the phenomena of communication in the Romanian public space, we analysed the messages regarding this type of communication and the discourses of the representatives of the civil society. This analysis includes media monitoring of the most circulated newspapers in Romania and the interpretation of the messages that reached their target audience. Therefore, we focused on the content of communication in public space messages in order to see the subject matters that exist in the Romanian public space.

Our study points out not only that these messages are somehow connected to political matters, but also that they involve a certain image of the Romanians that is being shaped and spread through the media. Therefore, by communicating negative messages and by orienting the communication in the public space to political matters, media shapes the communication process by promoting only one part of the communication, leaving the matters regarding the society in the background. We conclude that, as long as communication in the public space focuses only on matters that are connected to politics, society will not be able to strengthen itself and will not be able to adapt to changes.

Key words: communication in public space, media analysis

This paper presents the results of an ample study aimed at analysing communication mechanisms in the public space in Romania. The study investigated if its actors generate social debates on fundamental themes and to what extent the messages in this type of communication space are linked to the political and institutional zone. We started from Levi-Straus's idea that "a society is a group of people who communicate" (Levi-Strauss, 1963, p. 296) and we tried to analyse how communication in the public space is being shaped in Romania and what are the messages that it comprises. This paper uses the concept of public space as it was defined by Eric Dacheux as a space of mediation between civil society and the state, a space that favours contradictory debates and the emergence of public opinion (Dacheux, 2008, p. 11). In that sense we are speaking of a symbolic space that represents one of the fundamental requirements of a functioning democracy. Our analysis considered only the public space messages that are transmitted through mass communication. According to this analysis, the public space is identified with the public sphere, as it was defined by Jürgen Habermas: a space specific to democratic societies where citizens debate common interest issues:

> By public sphere, we mean first of all a realm of our social life in which something approaching public opinion can be formed . . . Newspapers, magazines, radio and television are the media of public sphere. (Habermas, 1997, p. 105)

This research analyses the public space messages broadcast by the mass media in the first half of 2011 and aims to investigate the content of these messages in order to discover their structure and functionality. Our research takes into consideration public space actors such as non-governmental organizations, unions, writers and other cultural personalities, and also psychologists and other citizens with a public persona. In addition, we monitored well known journalists who, due to their frequent television appearances and their many mass media articles, have become opinion leaders. In order to analyse the structure of communication in the public space, we also surveyed political and institutional communication messages in terms of the themes they generate, in order to identify possible correlations and connections between these types of communication.

The method used was the public relations content analysis model designed by Michelson & Griffin (2005), where the message content is interpreted according to the communication lifecycle. In addition, we used quantitative and qualitative analysis to interpret the recorded and monitored messages. The hypothesis to be validated was: the more public space communications are interconnected with the political and institutional spheres, the less civil society they create and the less open society will be. Therefore we departed from the premise that post-communist societies are confronted with an underdeveloped civil society, and public space communications are limited to responding to themes imposed by the political class and rarely generates new themes. The investigation of the lack of real autonomy of public space messages from the political and institutional areas takes into account Romania's post-revolutionary history as well as the political, economic and social context of the year 2011.

The raw research data were obtained by monitoring three daily publications with national coverage in Romania (Jurnalul Naţional, Adevărul and *Evenimentul zilei*) through the months of January to July 2011. They were chosen because, according to market studies,[1] during the period taken into consideration they held the greatest share of the market.

Analytic Methodology

The research for the current paper was based on the method developed by Michaelson and Griffin, who proposed a new public relations content analysis model through which we can investigate the content of messages while keeping in mind the purposes of the communication, which they call the communication lifecycle (Michaelson & Griffin, 2005, p. 7). Essentially, while monitoring we recorded those articles where there were messages from the actors of the public space. These messages were then introduced in categories depending on the themes and actors communicating. Afterwards, the content of the message was analysed, its form and the transmitter's attitude, and also those elements aimed at evaluating the efficiency of communication in the public space:

> awareness of the issue; the capacity to build sufficient knowledge and understanding about the issue, and the capacity to create a level of interest in the preference of the issue or at least a recognition of its relevance to the message recipient. (Michaelson & Griffin, 2005, p. 8)

---

[1] According to data reported by BRAT (www.brat.ro).

For a complete picture of what the Romanian media public space communication means, we monitored all political and institutional messages related to the themes debated by the actors of communication in the public space. The monitoring results were processed in order to investigate the connection between the Romanian public space communication with the political and institutional spheres, and the efficiency of these types of communications.

CONTEXT

The analysis that took place during the first months of 2011 gave us the opportunity to study and interpret the Romanian media public space. The context in which the analysis was performed is extremely important in the interpretation of the data both because Romanian because of the events occurring since the beginning of 2011. The way in which the Romanian media public space is structured is substantially linked to the lack of a consolidated civil society or of a developed civic spirit. Under the leadership of the Romanian Communist party, the state suppressed civic initiatives, while the public space was controlled by the state. Since 1989, the relationship between the state and the governmental sector, as well as the one between the public administration and the public, went through structural changes. Therefore the Romanian public space is not fully developed due to the lack of a tradition of public debate specific to democracies, as well as the lack of civic initiatives. In the first two years after the revolution, the non-governmental sector, although quite fragile, militated in street protests and was excluded from governmental programmes, acting as a spectator to the political games (Lamburu & Vameşu, 2010, p. 96). Between 1992 and 1996, due to the founding of the non-governmental organizations such as the Civic Alliance, the Group for Social Dialogue, the Student Union, the Human Rights League, Pro-Democracy and the Timisoara Society, the public space went through the first functional and discourse change. At that time, the non-governmental sector started to consolidate and a partnership was shaped with the governmental sector. The state's efforts to ensure the entry of Romania into the European Union were doubled by programmes and debates organized by non-governmental organizations between 2002 and 2008. After 2008, the relationship between state and civil society was marked by a crisis in which communication and cooperation were reduced to a minimum (Lamburu & Vameşu, 2010, p. 99).

During the period when the monitoring took place, the media agenda included such themes as the state reform, national education, the health system, the economic crisis, the political class, Romanian society, the price of gas, job loss, the changes to the constitution and regionalization.

Some of these themes were present for no longer than three months while others kept the media's interest for the entire monitored period. This was the case of the education reform theme that emerged in January with the national education law and ended in June with the Baccalaureate exam. If the changes in education generated heated debate and street protests, the restructuring of the health sector did not bring out extensive protesting social movements but rather small localized protests that received little attention in the media public space. An interesting case is that of the Romanian society theme and the political class, both remaining highly visible throughout the entire period. The amount of visibility, however, was structured differently for those actors who communicated via mass media. The communicators were well known journalists, writers and cultural personalities, whereas in the case of the political class the messages were presented by representatives of state institutions, politicians and the mass media.

The theme of state reform was initiated by the president and afterwards taken up by the media during the first two months of the year. The economic crisis kept the interest of journalists particularly in March, while the increase in gas prices was a visible theme in January and February. The economic crisis and job losses in April and June, the increase in gas price and the border corruption produced messages in the public space, which were followed by organized or spontaneous protests.

The increase in gas price, though an important subject, was barely debated in the media public space. The protests of drivers were ridiculed and did not succeed to create a significant message. The job losses were regarded by the authorities as a continuation of the state reform process. The public space reactions were limited to sporadic protests of those directly affected and there was no solidarity from other social categories. As for border corruption, the subject was abundantly covered by the media. The coverage generated an attitude of condemnation within public opinion, although the suspicions did not extend to the political class. Therefore, this theme became more of a method of turning the publics' attention away from the more significant problems. The other two themes debated during this period, administrative regionalization and the constitutional reform, were covered by reporting the diverging statements coming from the political class rather than presenting the point of view of the civil society. While in June the issue of regionalization caused friction within the governing coalition, the constitutional reform, in the same month, led to a conflict between state institutions, the presidency and the Constitutional Court, as well as to strong reactions from the opposition.

In France and Greece we saw ample protests and violence from the civil society, which expressed the public's attitudes towards the authorities. In Romania, the protests were mostly limited to marches. The media interviewed union leaders; many of them lacked legitimacy, due to the large personal wealth or to the number of corruption allegations they have amassed.

Data Analysis

Monitoring the three sources from January to June 2011, we found 3347 articles containing messages transmitted by political actors and representatives of state institutions. The raw data shows that, in the period surveyed by this analysis, in the three newspapers there were 4171 articles from all categories, including mass-media, political actors, representatives of state institutions and public space actors. Of the total number of articles, 2725 included messages from the institutional sphere, 622 messages from the political class (political actors who are not part of the structures of power or any other form of public administration), 709 articles contained information, opinions and commentary from journalists on various themes, and 115 articles including messages from actors in the media public space. The communication of actors from the media public space represented only 2.75% of the communication taking place through the mass-media, political communication reached 14.91%, and the greatest percentage was that of institutional communications at 65.33%. Of the total number of articles, 17% were written by journalists that did not match any of the above mentioned communication spaces (Figure 25-1).

The actors in the media public space who communicated through the mass media were non-governmental organizations, unions, writers, well-known journalists, psychologists, cultural personalities and also citizens who enjoyed media attention without being a part of the aforementioned categories. Among all of these media public space actors, the most communicative were the non-governmental organizations reaching 24.34%, followed by the well-known journalists at 21.73% (Figure 2). In our monitoring, we differentiated between well-known journalists and publicists, the latter having less name recognition. Although during the monitored period the government decided to restructure and fire employees in a number of areas, the union communications amassed to only 18.26%. Several individuals managed through their actions to attract media attention and to enter the media public space (11.30%), as in the case of Adrian Sobaru and Alice Rotta who were unknown to the public before the events that they initiated. Writers (7.82%), publicists (3.48%) and cultural figures (2.61%) had limited visibility in the media public space. Among the professional categories, the rectors, reacting to the national education law proposed by the Ministry of Education, Research and Innovation, were the most prominent. Because their protests and the one of the drivers were not organized by unions, these two categories were considered separately from teachers, employees of the health system or the Postal services.

The themes were categorized in order to allow for analysis of the way the actors' interest was structured, as well as for measuring the visibility of messages in the media public space (Figure 3). The monitoring showed that the messages centred on the education reform (15.65%) including the National Education Law and the changes to the Baccalaureate, measures addressing the economy (12.17%), job losses (7.83%), the labour code (6.96%), territorial reorganization (5.22%), social welfare (5.22%) and public health (5.22%).

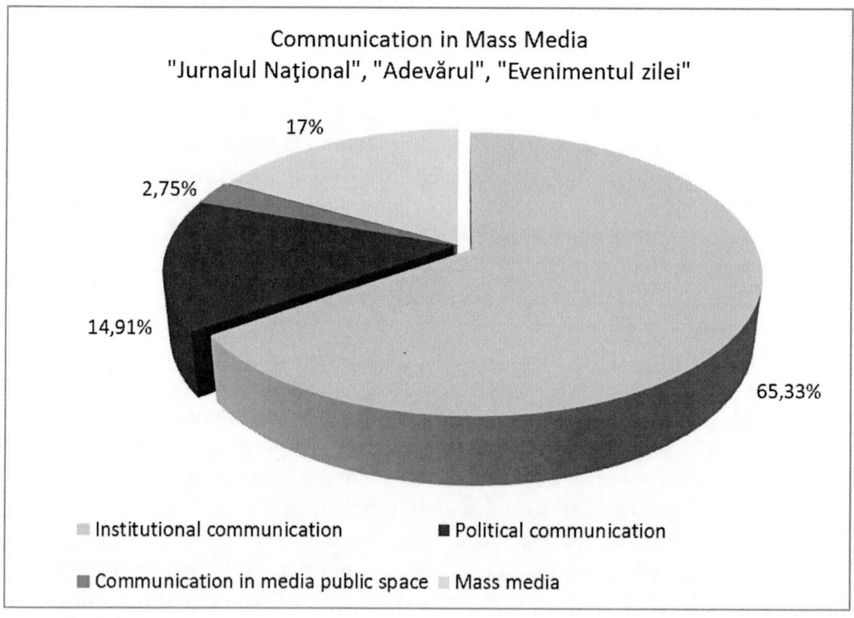

Figure 25-1

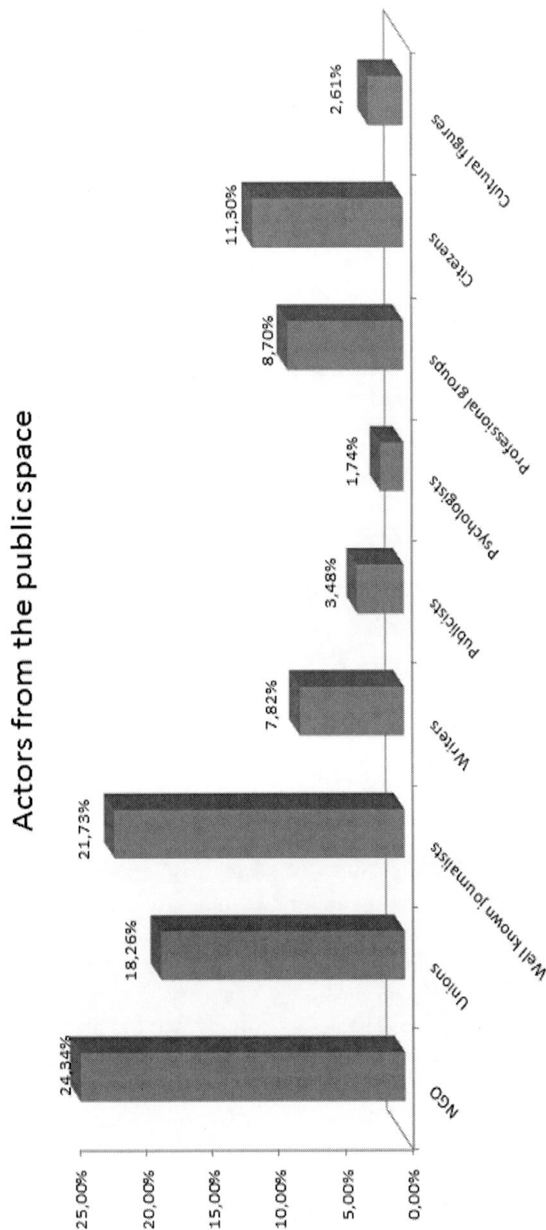
Actors from the public space
25,00%
20,00%
15,00%
10,00%
5,00%
0,00%
24,34%
18,26%
21,73%
7,82%
3,48%
1,74%
8,70%
11,30%
2,61%
NGO
Unions
Well known journalists
Writers
Publicists
Psychologists
Professional groups
Citezens
Cultural figures

Figure 25-2

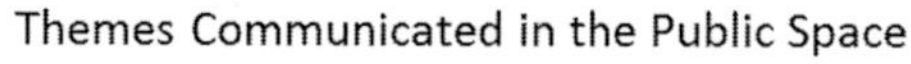

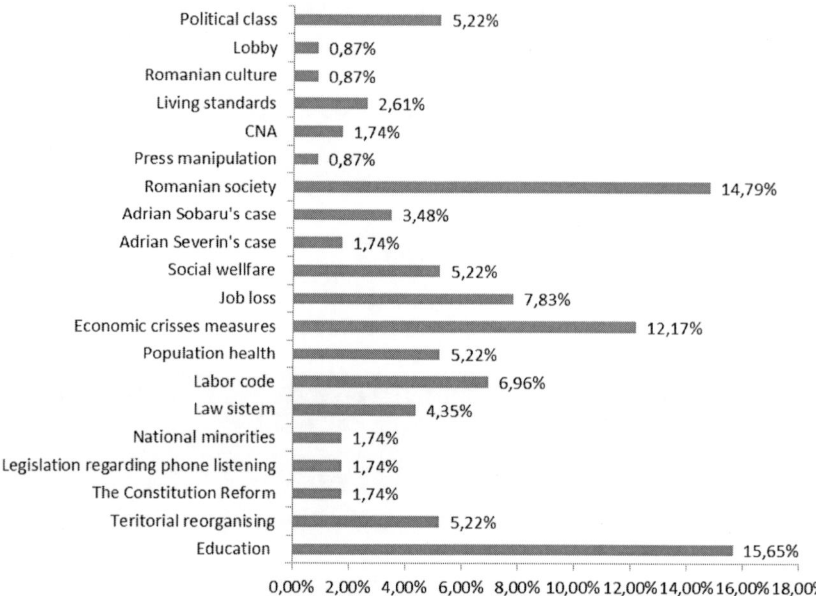

Figure 25-3

The theme with the most visibility was education. Non-governmental organizations were the most communicative on the topic of education – they occupied 40% of the coverage – but unions were also quite active at 29.41%. The well-known journalists spoke of education in 7% of the articles. For them, the more important topics were the economic crisis (48.28%), the territorial reorganization (13.79%), and the Romanian society (10.34%). This last theme proved to be particularly interesting and held one of the highest positions in the visibility hierarchy of the messages in the media public space. The actors communicating about the Romanian society were well-known journalists (10.34%), psychologists, cultural personalities and publicists, writers (75%) and citizens (33.33%). Of the messages on this theme, 85% had a negative connotation, suggesting deep dissatisfaction with the way Romanian society functions and is organized.

These messages paint a picture of the Romanian citizen, constructing a negative ethno-image. The proliferation of these messages and the use of negative notes, together with the defamation of an entire political class due to mistakes of individuals, has lead to the framing and spreading of a negative ethno-image in the media public space.

In order to investigate how messages were structured depending on the actors, we qualitatively analysed their communications. The result indicated that non-governmental organizations (see figure 25-4) intervened in the public space mainly with messages related to education – 40% of the time. In this area, the most visible was the Parents' Association and various student groups from all over the country. The legislative initiatives related to tapping and lobbying were exclusively communicated by non-governmental organizations, particularly the Pro-Democracy Association and Transparency International. The territorial reorganization and social protection (particularly maternity aid) themes had a smaller preponderance in the content of the messages communicated by non-governmental organizations in the media public space (each at 6.66%).

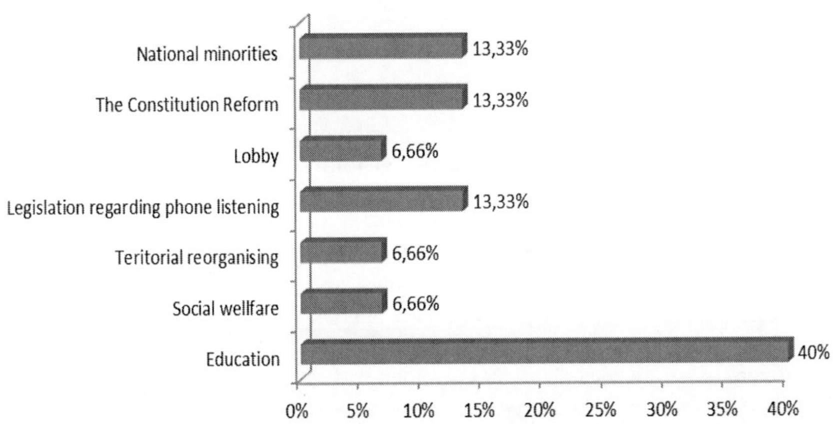

Figure 25-4

Unions (as shown in Figure 25-5) gave more importance to education (29.41%), job loss (26.47%), labour laws (23.53%) and social protection (11.76%). These percentages are not surprising if we take into consideration the context of our analysis.

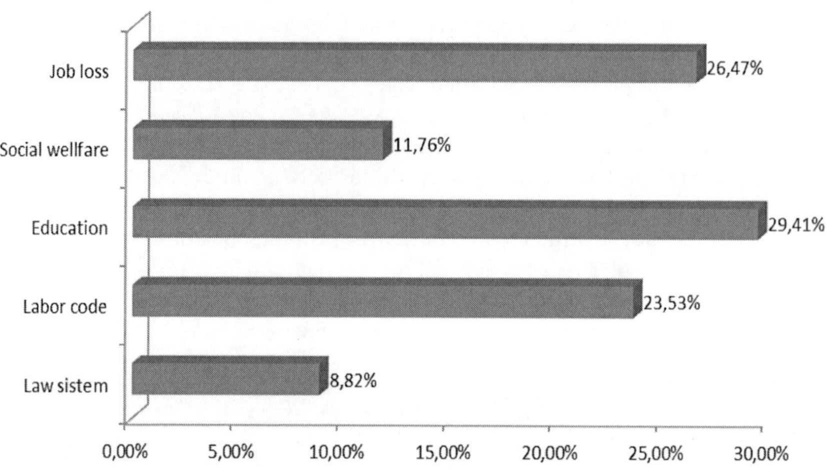

Figure 25-5

Another interesting aspect of how communication was structured in the Romanian media public space is the visibility garnered by individuals' messages when they took an initiative in response to an issue (Figure 25-6). Although in the hierarchy of communicating actors these cases took the fourth place at 11.30%, the way in which they communicated and the fact that they were covered by the media was an overall gain for the media public space. Without the advantage of having a famous name and the resources of non-governmental organizations and unions behind them, the citizens who succeeded in making themselves heard mainly transmitted messages related to the status of the Romanian society (33.33%) and to the political class (33.33%). In both cases the attitude is negative. Similarly to other actors in the public space, the messages created a negative image of Romanian society.

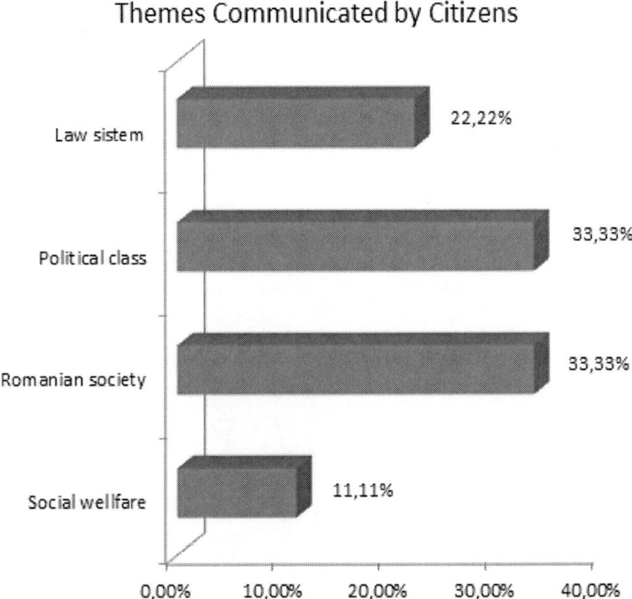

Figure 25-6

In order to validate the hypothesis and evaluate communicative efficiency in the media public space through the communication lifecycle methodology, we included an analytic comparison of the themes transmitted by actors of the media public space, and of those transmitted by the political class, institutional sphere and mass media. It is an important distinction, as the themes did not coincide each month, meaning that not all of the themes transmitted by the political class and institutional representatives were taken up by actors in the public space. The analysis highlights a dependence of the public space communications of the themes propelled by the political and institutional sectors. The public space communication dealt with a lack of the resources to generate and impose its own themes.

The data obtained while monitoring the media pointed out that the political actors, state institutions' representatives and the mass media mostly communicated on themes such as education, the health system, the economic crisis, job losses, pay cuts and the rise in gas price. While in the case of actors in the public space the communicative attitude was primarily negative, in the case of these actors the attitude was often neutral (Figure 25-7).

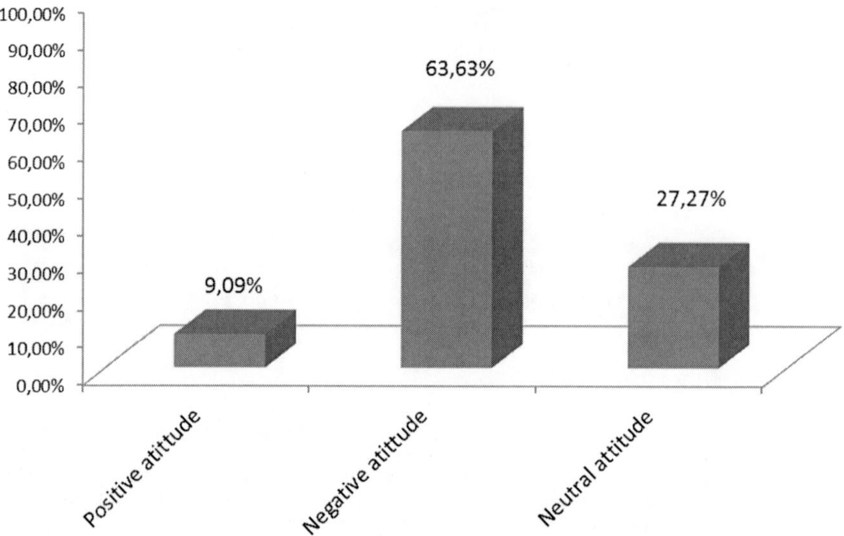

Figure 25-7

A surprising aspect is that the theme of education, which was so important and publicized by the actors in the public space, was far less important to the political and state institutional actors. They communicated less on the topic, 18.82% and 12.94% respectively (Figure 25-8). One possible explanation is the level of inefficiency exhibited by members of the political class and the representatives of state institutions in the way communication themes were chosen. They preferred to rely instead on the health system reform and job losses, although these two topics were not as visible in the media public space, as was stated above.

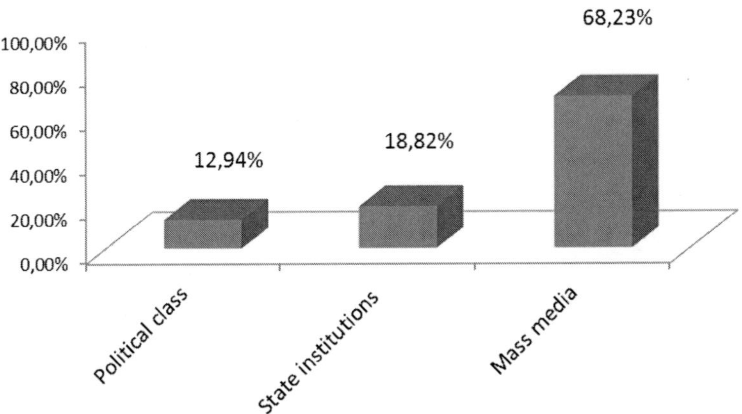

Figure 25-8

A comparison of the messages sent by actors in the media public space to those coming from the political and institutional sphere and those coming from the mass-media shows that communication in the Romanian public space is dependent upon the themes generated by the political and institutional representatives. Messages sent by actors in the media public space were picked up and multiplied by all three of the monitored newspapers. This can be explained by the fact that the themes are of general interest, like education, job losses, the labour code and the health system. However their retransmission is amplified by other actors who have access to the media machine. The theme of Romanian society was not generated by the political or institutional representatives, but rather it was a consequence of the way in which the political class is depicted. From this perspective, the theme of Romanian society is an extension of the theme of the political class and promotes, as mentioned, a negative ethno-image.

The messages transmitted by the actors in the media public space were less numerous than those that used other communication spaces, which in turn influenced the efficiency of this form of communication. The significantly lower number of messages in the media public space implies a discourse lacking visibility and notoriety.

The effectiveness of the communication in public spaces to create a level of interest in the issue was partially confirmed by the fact that the actors did not generate or impose themes in the media public space to be debated by the public. Nevertheless, communication in the public space can attract public interest to some extent. The limited efficiency of this type of communication comes from the reduced amount of messages transmitted through the media space and the fact that it is based on negative messages in regard to Romanian society.

Conclusions

Currently, communication in the Romanian media public space is reactive and makes limited attempts to inform and direct public opinion and to determine how those in the government act. The actors in the media public space do not succeed in imposing debate themes or to generate discussions within the public. Our analysis revealed that only those themes transmitted by those in power are picked up, although authorities are usually seen negatively by the civil society and the public. This phenomenon is not surprising because there is no tradition of public debate or communication in the public space in Romania.

The lack of civil actions within the contemporary Romanian civil society, despite a few extreme or insignificant attempts, is compounded by the ideological incoherence of intellectuals, who either limit themselves to being polemic journalists or are involved in politics.

Our working hypothesis is confirmed. The more public space communication is linked to the political and institutional sphere, the less civil society it develops and the less influence it has, leading to a society that is overall less open to change.

Although there is a negative image of the political class and a negative ethno-image is promoted, the actors in the media public space do not pick up the theme of state reform. The explanation may be the lack of any trust in the statements of political leaders in regards to the positive and profound changes to take place in Romania.

The media expansion is ample and gathers at the social level the debated agenda and creates inhibitions in terms of civil initiatives. Levi-Strauss' vision, which involves the communication component in the social, is confirmed. In the case of the Romanian media public space, the communications do not come from the civil society but somewhat from the exterior, since it is limited to reactions to the political class. Politics currently dominate the entire social agenda, either as a result of a strategy that inhibits public communication, or due to the lack of experience of Romanian society, which is still going through a transition and is incapable of undertaking essential changes.

References

Arendt, H (2006). *Originile totalitarismului,* Bucureşti : Humanitas.

Dacheux, É (ed.) (2008). *L'espace public*, Paris: CNRS Éditions.

Habermas, J (1997). The Public Sphere. In R E Goodin & P Pettit (eds), *Contemporary Political Philosophy: An Anthology,* Oxford: Blackwell Publishers.

Lamburu, M & Vameşu, A (eds) (2010). *Rom*ânia 2010. Sectorul guvernamental: profil, tendinţe, provocări, material realizat în cadrul proiectului "Catalogul Societăţii Civile" implementat de Fundaţia pentru Dezvoltarea Societăţii Civile şi finanţat de Trust for Civil Society in Central and Eastern Europe. Available online at www.stiriong.ro.

Levi-Strauss, C (1963). *Structural Anthropology,* New York: Harper Torchbooks.

Michaelson, D & Griffin, T L (2005). *A New Model for Media Content Analysis,* USA: Institute for Public Relations. Available online at www.instituteforpr.com.

Wolton, D (2009). *Informer n'est pas communiquer*, Paris: CNRS Éditions.

Daily newspapers

Adevărul, 1 January – 30 June 2011 collection.
Evenimentul Zilei, 1 January – 30 June 2011 collection.
Jurnalul Naţional, 1 January – 30 June 2011 collection.

Web resources

www.brat.ro
www.instituteforpr.com
www.stiriong.ro

PART THREE:

PROFESSIONAL IDENTITIES AND NETWORKS

DEPROFESSIONNALISATION DU JOURNALISME OU RETOUR AUX SOURCES ?

ARNAUD NOBLET

Résumé

Constater la déprofessionnalisation du journalisme, c'est partir, explicitement ou implicitement, du postulat de l'existence d'un modèle jusqu'ici prédominant : celui d'une pratique journalistique essentiellement professionnelle. C'est en effet ce mètre-étalon qui semble aujourd'hui fortement et de plus en plus écorné, notamment avec l'apparition et le développement d'Internet.

Toutefois, on peut s'interroger sur les caractéristiques et l'origine même d'un tel modèle référentiel : d'où vient-il ? représente-t-il l'essence de ce que nous nommons « journalisme » ? comment et depuis quand s'est-il imposé ? En fait, en l'absence de définition consensuelle, ce que nous entendons par « journalisme » apparaît comme un objet historiquement construit, comme le résultat d'un processus d'écriture de l'histoire (ce que le discours historique a désigné comme tel) ou, pour le dire autrement, comme une construction historiographique.

Nous partons ici de l'hypothèse que la vision articulée autour de l'exercice professionnel du journalisme (dont nous constatons la remise en cause à l'ère d'Internet) n'est pas immuable et absolue. Elle se serait en fait développée et imposée en France au sein de l'historiographie et de la vision savante du journalisme à partir du début des années 1980. Dès lors, on aurait assisté à l'affirmation d'une tendance historiographique nouvelle qui, sans faire totalement disparaître les modèles référentiels initiaux marqués par l'imprimé périodique et l'arrimage démocratique, prendrait désormais et majoritaitement en compte le journalisme comme profession et les journalistes comme groupe professionnel. De fait, depuis une trentaine d'année, ce prisme « professionnaliste » du journalisme semble imprégner une grande partie des travaux de recherche et en constituer un arrière-plan déterminant.

Afin d'examiner la validité de notre hypothèse, nous avons choisi de faire porter notre étude sur un corpus relatif à l'historiographie française de la presse et du journalisme (Noblet, 2010). Précisons d'emblée qu'il ne s'agit pas de faire l'histoire de l'objet lui-même mais bien d'examiner la façon dont a été élaborée et écrite son histoire à travers le temps, opération dont nous sommes les héritiers plus ou moins conscients quand nous parlons aujourd'hui de journalisme. Car tous ces travaux, ces lectures multiples participent, comme le remarque Loraux (1993) d'une tradition sédimentée qui nous travaille sans même que nous nous en avisions.

Mots-clés : journalisme, deprofessionnalisation, historicité, historiographie, internet

Régimes d'historicité et régimes d'historiographie

Dans le cadre de notre questionnement, il nous a semblé pertinent de mobiliser, en l'adaptant à nos besoins, la notion de « régime d'historicité », développée en France principalement par l'historien spécialiste de l'Antiquité François Hartog et dont les principales étapes d'émergence et les influences « nourricières » (notamment les travaux de Reinhart Koselleck et de Paul Ricoeur) ont fait l'objet d'une synthèse récente (Delacroix, 2010). La polysémie et la plasticité d'une telle notion donnent incontestablement beaucoup de liberté au chercheur. Liberté dont nous avons usé voire abusé pour adapter l'instrument, pour le « configuer » en quelque sorte, selon nos besoins et les particularités de l'objet étudié. Nous avons notamment développé notre travail à partir de l'idée selon laquelle un régime d'historicité renverrait « à une sorte de logique d'arrière-plan, une logique d' « ombre » dirait Michel Foucault, articulant ensemble les dimensions temporelles du passé, du futur et du présent, organisant leur conditionnement réciproque » (Lenclud, 2006, p. 1071). C'est sur la mise à jour de cette logique d'arrière-plan qu'il nous a semblé pertinent de nous arrêter, tout en étant conscient de ce que cette dernière peut avoir d'insaisissable et de protéiforme.

Le choix de mener nos travaux sur la base d'un corpus historiographique s'inspire directement des réflexions de Hartog et Lenclud (1993). Selon eux, « le régime d'historicité définirait une forme culturellement délimitée, donc conventionnelle, de relation au passé : l'historiographie serait l'une de ces formes et, en tant que genre, un élément symptomatique d'un régime d'historicité englobant » (p. 26). Ainsi, les modèles historiographiques mis en œuvre pourraient-ils être les produits de régimes d'historicité spécifiques. A chaque régime d'historicité correspondrait en quelque sorte une historiographie qui l'accompagne et le manifeste. Mais également qui contribue à lui donner forme.

En ce sens, en aboutissant à définir le récit comme "gardien du temps", les travaux de Paul Ricoeur apportent une contribution décisive permettant d'appréhender ce qu'est et peut être un régime d'historicité et d'historiographie (Hartog et Lenclud, 1993). Paul Ricoeur emploie le terme de récit pour désigner toute opération narrative de « mise en intrigue » (intrigue devant être entendue comme une figuration du monde vécu). Ce processus s'avère nécessaire pour rendre intelligible le déroulement de l'action historique. Sans cela, les événements n'apparaissent que comme une succession où dominent la variété et la discordance. Selon Ricoeur (1983),

> « composer l'intrigue, c'est déjà faire surgir l'intelligible de l'accidentel, l'universel du singulier, le nécessaire ou le vraisemblable de l'épisodique » (p. 70).

Hartog et Lenclud (1993) avancent qu'une hypothèse forte émerge de l'ouvrage de Ricoeur : celle qui voudrait que c'est en recevant des récits qu'individus et communautés se constituent dans leur identité propre, soulignant ainsi le

> « lien fondamental entre les formes de fabrication/réception des récits et la conscience de soi d'une société (son régime d'historicité) » (p. 32).

Dans cette perspective, ceux qui participent à la production historique ne sont pas seulement de simples reflets d'un ordre du temps ou les marqueurs de l'émergence d'un nouveau régime d'historicité, ils en sont aussi les acteurs et les producteurs (Garcia, 2002). L'historiographie apparaît alors comme un élément qui, à la fois manifeste et constitue un régime d'historicité donné, ce dernier l'influençant et l'irrigant en retour. Les procédures propres au « faire de l'histoire » renvoient à une manière de « faire l'histoire » (Certeau, 1975).

Ainsi, l'historiographie révèle des schémas et des motifs pré-établis. Selon Lenclud (2006), ce sont de tels motifs qui participent à la mise en ordre du temps et « confèrent une unité d'arrière-plan aux discours historiques, ou régimes d'historiographie (…). Ils charrient une série d'évidences ; ils constituent de la sorte comme un a priori » (p. 1077). Des arrières-plans qu'il peut sembler pertinent de déconstruire, à l'image du travail entamé depuis plusieurs décennies par exemple au sein de l'historiographie anglo-saxonne, que cela soit aux Etats-Unis (McChesney et Salomon (éds.), 1993) ou outre-Manche (Curran et Seaton, 1981).

UN RÉGIME HISTORIOGRAPHIQUE PROFESSIONNALISTE DOMINANT

Quelles sont alors ces toiles de fond, les arrière-plans de notre perception actuelle du journalisme ? Au sein du corpus étudié, et en écho notamment aux découpages proposés par divers spécialistes des médias (Kalifa et Vaillant, 2004), on peut distinguer trois axes essentiels, s'ajoutant et coexistant, qui nous paraissent marquer fortement l'historiographie du journalisme et de la presse depuis 150 ans et créer les grandes constantes des régimes historiographiques dont nous sommes les héritiers : tout d'abord, une référence fondatrice à la presse écrite imprimée périodique (pas de journalisme sans journal) ainsi qu'un arrimage démocratique et républicain (pas de journalisme sans liberté et, à l'inverse, pas de liberté sans journalisme). Ces deux grandes tendances dominent schématiquement le paysage historiographique jusqu'aux années 1980. A partir de là, s'impose une vision que nous qualifierons de « professionnaliste », plus centrée sur les pratiques journalistiques et le groupe social des journalistes (pas de journalisme préalablement à sa structuration professionnelle) (Noblet, 2010).

Dominique Kalifa et Alain Vaillant (2004) évoquent à ce propos une séquence historiographique qui s'inscrirait dans une logique plus sociale, passant d'une histoire des journaux à une histoire des journalistes et du journalisme. Alors que les décennies passées n'avaient prêté attention

> « qu'aux grandes plumes, aux polémistes célèbres ou aux patrons de presse, on porte alors le regard vers les acteurs plus obscurs, et notamment les journalistes qui font irruption dans le paysage historiographique » (p. 200).

Ce tournant historiographique, dont les premières manifestations remontent essentiellement à une trentaine d'années nonobstant quelques précurseurs isolés (Voyenne, 1959), se caractérise notamment par une évolution terminologique et un déplacement des répères et des découpes chronologiques.

Un des signes perceptibles de l'évolution du prisme historiographique est tout d'abord la multiplication des termes « journalisme » et « journalistes » dans les titres et les sous-titres d'ouvrages. Ces deux termes y apparaissent plus fréquemment en trente ans (9 fois entre 1976 et 2007) qu'en cent trente ans (5 fois entre 1846 et 1976). Dans le détail, on citera pour la période commençant à la fin des années 1970/début des années 1980 et allant jusqu'en 2007 plusieurs travaux universitaires : Des petits journaux aux grandes agences. Naissance du journalisme moderne

(Palmer, 1983) ; Histoire du journalisme et des journalistes français (Delporte, 1995) ; Les journalistes en France. 1880-1950 (Delporte, 1999) ou encore Les journalistes (Mathien, 1995) et Les journalistes. Histoire, pratiques et enjeux (Mathien, 2007). Cette tendance est également perceptible chez les auteurs issus du monde professionnel, notamment chez les deux journalistes-historiens, auteurs pour l'un de l'ouvrage Les journalistes français (Voyenne, 1985), et pour l'autre de L'invention du journalisme (Ferenczi, 1993).

On assiste également à une modification des découpages chronologiques : les anciennes bornes classiques de l'historiographie de la presse (1631, 1789, et dans une moindre mesure 1881) ont tendance à s'estomper, au profit de l'apparition de nouvelles dates liées à l'histoire culturelle et à l'histoire du journalisme proprement dit. C'est le cas notamment pour la détermination des origines du journalisme avec l'apparition de césures spécifiques à l'objet. A cet égard, Des petits journaux aux grandes agences. Naissance du journalisme moderne (Palmer, 1983) marque un tournant important. Dès le début de l'ouvrage, Palmer, dépassant le repère classique de la loi de 1881, inscrit en effet son étude au sein de la période 1863-1914. Si 1914 est une borne chronologique jusque là couramment utilisée par l'historiographie de la presse dans le cadre de découpages qui reprennent les grandes scansions de l'histoire politique française, il n'en est pas de même pour l'année 1863. Cette dernière détrône en quelque sorte la césure habituelle de 1870-71 (fin du Second Empire/Commune/débuts de la Troisième République). Elle impose la date de création du premier grand quotidien populaire français, Le Petit Journal de Moïse Millaud, comme nouveau repère historiographique de la seconde moitié du XIXe siècle.

Par la suite, la date de 1863 et plus largement les années 1860 en tant période symbole de la naissance de la presse industrielle seront utilisées par de nombreux travaux comme une référence chronologique pivot, un « palier » dans l'histoire du journalisme : c'est par exemple le point de départ donné dans l'ouvrage Médias et journalistes de la République (Martin, 1997) ou encore celui proposé par Ruellan (1997) pour le découpage qu'il propose de l'histoire du journalisme. On peut également trouver une expression de cette tendance dans la contribution de Kalifa (2000) dont le titre affiche clairement le parti-pris de découpage : « L'entrée de la France en régime médiatique : l'étape des années 1860 ».

A côté des années 1860, d'autres nouveaux repères, bousculant ceux qui étaient jusque là communément admis, vont également s'imposer au sein de l'historiographie de la presse et du journalisme au cours de ces trois dernières décennies. C'est le cas des années 1830. Un historien comme Charle (2004) fait ainsi commencer son « siècle de la presse » à cette date (pour l'achever en 1939), justifiant ce choix de 1830 comme point de départ (plutôt que celui de la Révolution française) dans la mesure où

la révolution de Juillet a eu pour origine les ordonnances de Charles X, dont la plus importante suspendait la liberté de la presse périodique. La mobilisation et la protestation des journaux et des journalistes et des milieux politiques libéraux ont été l'étincelle de la révolte populaire victorieuse. (…) C'est donc la première fois qu'on peut parler d'un pouvoir médiatique sur les masses, socialement mesurable et politiquement décisif (p. 10-11).

Le positionnement chronologique de Charle est confirmé (voire nourri) par d'autres travaux, issus pour certains des études littéraires (Therenty, 2001), qui insistent par exemple sur le caractère novateur de la création de La Presse par Emile de Girardin, parfois présenté comme l'inventeur de la presse périodique industrielle (Barbier et Bertho Lavenir, 1996) et qui mettent en exergue l'année 1836 comme « an I de l'ère médiatique » (Therenty et Vaillant, 2001).

Les deux périodes de 1830 et de 1860 ne sont pas à opposer radicalement aux yeux de la nouvelle tendance historiographique. Considérer les bornes chronologiques de façon trop hermétique, en oublier la porosité et d'une certaine manière l'étalement, reviendrait à figer l'analyse dans des attitudes peu productives. Comme le remarquent Kalifa et Vaillant (2004), il est ainsi possible d'envisager l'idée d'

> « un séisme majeur, dont l'épicentre est situé quelque part vers le mitan du siècle (la décennie 1860), mais dont les premières secousses sont largement antérieures (la décennies 1830) et les rejeux, récurrences ou refus largement postérieurs » (p. 204).

L'INTÉGRATION DU MODÈLE HISTORIOGRAPHIQUE PROFESSIONNALISTE AU SEIN DES SIC

A partir des années 1980-1990, plusieurs représentants des Sciences de l'information et de la communication comme Michael Palmer, Michel Mathien ou Denis Ruellan prennent place aux côtés des journalistes professionnels et des historiens de métier au sein du corpus étudié, reflet de l'importance croissante de cette discipline dans le domaine des études sur le journalisme.

C'est en effet au sein des SIC que vont désormais s'inscrire une grande partie des études dans ce domaine (notamment celles mobilisant l'histoire) même si, comme le remarque Pélissier (2005), ces travaux sont initialement marquées par une relative dispersion, et qu'il faille attendre

> « la première moitié des années 1990, pour qu'un nombre significatif de chercheurs de cette discipline, dans la lignée des travaux pionniers d'Yves de La Haye, Rémy Rieffel ou Jean-François Tétu produits au cours de la décennie précédente, s'engagent dans de véritables dynamiques de recherche sur le journalisme et les journalistes » (p. 34).

Ainsi, le modèle historiographique professionnaliste, incarné notamment par la focalisation sur la loi de 1935 et sur le processus qui a amené à sa rédaction et à son vote, est rapidement intégré au sein des Sciences de l'Information et de la Communication dans les années 1990. Ceci est notamment visible à travers la multiplication des travaux, colloques et autres journées d'études, ayant pour thème l'identité professionnelle des journalistes. Au sein de notre corpus (et nonobstant bien sûr leurs autres travaux), les ouvrages, parus, dans la décennies 1990, de Mathien (1995) et Ruellan (1997) représentent bien cette installation du modèle historiographique centré sur la construction de l'espace professionnel et du groupe social des journalistes. Le premier coordonne avec Rieffel un ouvrage collectif issu d'un colloque, intitulé L'identité professionnelle des journalistes (Mathien et Rieffel, 1995); le second fait quant à lui paraître une étude sur la structuration du groupe ayant pour titre Le professionnalisme du flou (Ruellan, 1993) Les travaux de ces deux chercheurs (parmi d'autres) se focalisent ainsi sur la constitution du groupe social des journalistes professionnels, sur son histoire, ses repères, ses pratiques, bref sur les différents aspects de son processus de professionnalisation.

D'autres chercheurs (dont un nombre important en Sciences de l'information et de la communication) vont également aborder dans les années 1990 et 2000 les questions liées au professionnalisme, à la professionnalisation et à la profession de journaliste. Quelques exemples des travaux publiés sur ces thèmes sont listés par exemple par Le Cam et Ruellan (2004) ; on trouve déjà quelques années plus tôt une liste des chercheurs

> « qui ont signalé ce fait "professionnel" et l'intelligence de son organisation » dans Ruellan (1997).

Des journées d'études sont organisées : par exemple, en mai 2003, celle du CRAPE (Centre de recherche sur l'action politique en Europe) de l'université de Rennes, en collaboration avec l'Institut Français de Presse de l'université Paris 2, sur le thème « le journalisme comme profession. Regard international comparé ».

Notre objectif n'est pas ici de résumer et encore moins de discuter les positions de ces différents travaux, dont une vue d'ensemble peut être notamment trouvée dans Pélissier (2005), mais bien de voir en quoi leurs analyses sont marquées, au moins en partie, par le présupposé historique que « le » journalisme, c'est le journalisme de type professionnel né quelque part entre la deuxième moitié du XIXe siècle et les années 1930 (voire les années 1940). Pour prendre une image, on pourrait évoquer l'existence d' « attendus » comme il en existe dans le domaine judiciaire. Ces attendus seraient présents de manière plus ou moins implicite, souvent en arrière-plan. L'attendu principal se traduirait ici de la façon suivante : attendu que le terme « journalisme » est utilisé ici selon sa figure référentielle professionnelle, etc.

La force de cet attendu professionnaliste, ou de ce nouveau régime d'historicité, dépend bien évidemment de la prégnance du modèle historiographique correspondant. Cette prégnance repose notamment sur le charisme scientifique des auteurs qui portent les travaux majeurs sur ce thème, voire sur les capacités de structuration de la recherche autour de ces axes professionnalistes, permettant de les rendre attractifs. Cette structuration scientifique volontariste est particulièrement visible à partir de la fin des années 1990, notamment dans le cadre du REJ (Réseau d'études sur le journalisme). Cette structure, initiée principalement par Denis Ruellan dont les travaux constituent en partie le socle initial de travail, va contribuer à la diffusion du prisme « professionnaliste » qui va alors imprégner (à travers la production scientifique des membres du réseau) une grande partie des travaux de recherche sur le journalisme et en constituer l'arrière-plan déterminant, canalisant de fait les bases de la rélfexion (Noblet 2010). Un arrière-plan valant comme nous l'avons vu pour définition, prisme à travers lequel sera jaugé et jugé, souvent implicitement, le journalisme (et ce même si le propos se veut une remise en question voire une déconstruction de ce modèle référent).

Il y aurait là en quelque sorte, au cœur même de l'étude du journalisme, un positionnement amphibie : en l'absence d'une définition, ce sont les caractéristiques mouvantes du groupe socio-professionnel des journalistes qui l'auraient remplacée et auraient fini par l'aspirer, la vampiriser en tant que base de réflexion.

Un processus de déprofessionnalisation du journalisme… ou de l'histoire du journalisme?

Dans ce cadre scientifique et historiographique, la prise en compte de l'essor d'Internet peut donner lieu selon nous à un double niveau lecture :

celui du constat et de l'étude d'un processus d'affaiblissement voire d'effacement des caractéristiques professionnelles qui seraient consubstantielles au journalisme ; mais également celui d'une remise en cause du prisme historiographique à travers lequel ces évolutions sont analysées.

Une première lecture consiste à souligner qu'avec l'apparition et le rapide développement d'Internet, il n'est plus nécessaire d'avoir le statut de « journaliste professionnel » pour « faire » du journalisme (Gillmor, 2004). Cette question, qui suscite la polémique, s'est incarnée en de nombreuses expressions qui tendent à désubstantialiser, voire à déprofessionnaliser la notion même de journalisme en lui accolant des qualificatifs ; on parle alors de journalisme « amateur » ou encore de journalisme « citoyen » (Ruellan, 2007) pour exprimer cette

> « possibilité offerte à tout individu de collecter, hiérarchiser, analyser l'information, de "faire du journalisme" pour son propre compte et celui de la communauté à laquelle il appartient » (Deslandes, Fonnet et Godbert, 2009).

Le lien peut être fait ici avec le public journalism, mouvement développé par des journalistes dans les années 1980 et 1990 aux Etats-Unis (Watine, 2003 ; Tétu, 2008). Ainsi, les diverses catégories (journaliste, amateur, public) se chevauchent, perdent progressivement de leur pertinence, et le magistère des journalistes de métier se voit ébranlé par un phénomène, qui semble sur Internet primordial : l'indifférenciation croissante entre journalisme professionnel et journalisme non-professionnel (Estienne, 2007).

Un exemple récurrent et emblématique de ce brouillage des frontières est l'accréditation croissante de blogueurs pour la couverture d'événements, notamment politiques. Ce phénomène, fréquent en Amérique du Nord, tend à se développer en France. Le journal canadien Le Devoir s'inquiétait déjà de cette pratique il y a quelques années, dénonçant une

> « nouvelle confusion des genres dans une profession qui, déjà, pratique le croisement des styles » (Chouinard, 2008).

En France, cette évolution est également fortement critiquée par les « garants de la profession », notamment la Commission de la carte d'identité des journalistes, dont le vice-président affirme :

> « à force de dire que tout le monde peut être journaliste, on dévalorise ce métier et on occulte le fait que la bonne information a un coût. Après tout,

on ne parle pas de "chirurgien citoyen". Le terme de "citoyen" ne sert qu'à habiller une dévalorisation de l'information et une précarisation de la profession » (cité dans Ternisien, 2009).

Ce mouvement de « déprofessionnalisation » des journalistes s'exprime également, en creux, dans une tendance à la « professionnalisation » des non-journalistes dont l'indicateur le plus marquant est la rémunération croissante des « amateurs de l'information ». Rappelons que ce qui permet de qualifier un « journaliste », c'est notamment sa rétribution principale pour l'exercice de sa profession. Or aujourd'hui, il n'est pas rare que des « non journalistes » (blogueurs notamment) soient rémunérés voire embauchés par des sites web de presse. Nous n'en concluons pas que les amateurs, par la seule présence de cette rémunération (qui reste le plus souvent faible, irrégulière et secondaire), accèdent à un statut professionnel, mais, indéniablement, les frontières qui avaient été érigées de manière hermétiques lors de la constitution du groupe professionnel tendent à s'effriter (Ruellan, 1997).

Le dernier aspect à souligner est que les journalistes et les médias concourent eux-mêmes à renforcer le flou entre les frontières et à banaliser leurs pratiques en favorisant l'émergence en leur sein de contenus amateurs (commentaires, blogs, photos, vidéos, etc.) qu'ils intègrent, de manière plus ou moins poussée, dans leurs propres productions journalistiques (Noblet et Pignard-Cheynel, 2010), créant progressivement une « économie de la participation » (Deslandes, Fonnet et Godbert, 2009). Certains vont même plus loin en jouant des modèles journalistiques pour valoriser – et canaliser – la participation amateur. Une étude menée en 2009 montre que l'une des figures les plus nobles – ou en tout cas les plus « mythiques » – du journalisme, le reporter, est ainsi fréquemment mobilisée par les sites d'information en ligne dans leurs dispositifs de captation des contenus non journalistiques (Noblet et Pignard-Cheynel, 2009). De la sorte, ces mécanismes, qui relèvent en fait davantage de stratégies d'audience et de logiques marketing, n'en contribuent pas moins à brouiller les contours mêmes de la profession.

Résonances, résurgences, hypothèses

Un deuxième niveau de lecture lié aux effets de l'essor d'Internet relève quant à lui d'une remise en cause du prisme historiographique à travers lequel la déprofessionalisation du journalisme est aujourd'hui analysée Dans cette optique, l'onde de choc provoquée par Internet bouscule le régime d'historicité professionnaliste du journalisme, c'est-à-dire la tendance historiographique appréhendant ce même journalisme à travers, à partir et en référence à un statut et à des pratiques professionnelles. En déconnectant le couple « journalisme » et « professionnel », Internet remet en même temps en cause ce mètre-étalon historiographique professionnaliste. Effet indirect, une fois cette digue rompue, apparaissent alors de multiples possibles, des points de départ différents, autres en tout cas que la figure captatrice d'un journalisme « moderne » né entre la deuxième partie du XIXe siècle et la Deuxième Guerre mondiale et dont le statut et les pratiques « professionnels » entreraient seuls dans le champ du pensable (à analyser, critiquer, déconstruire,…).

L'historiographie foisonne de ces autres possibles. Des figures jusqu'ici mises en veille, considérées comme des formes « primitives » du journalisme (par exemple orales ou manuscrites), formes reléguées aux marges du discours voire écartées par nombre d'auteurs, et rejetées souvent avec ironie et condescendance dans les catégories/chapitres « préhistoire », « proto-histoire » de la presse voire « proto-journalisme » comme le constate Noblet (2010). La déconstruction du prisme professionnaliste sous l'effet notamment d'Internet brouille de tels contours. Surgissent alors diverses pratiques comme autant de résonances, de figures alternatives qui questionnent aussi bien les statuts, les fonctions que les supports. Citons ici quelques exemples à titre d'illustration : pratiques journalistiques assumées par des esclaves à Rome et rapportées par Hatin (1859-1861) ou

> « existence de professionnels ou de semi-professionnels de l'information dès l'Antiquité » (Voyenne, 1985) ;

journalisme manuscrit clandestin assuré par les nouvellistes ou recherche quotidienne de nouvelles effectuée par des domestiques appointés sous l'Ancien régime (Ginisty, 1917) ; images encore d'un journalisme occasionnel et mobile pratiqué par des catégories sociales itinérantes (comme les colporteurs) pour lesquelles l'information collectée et restituée constitue une plus-value dans l'exercice de leur métier principal (Tavernier, 1902) ; etc.

Évidemment, la raison du lecteur d'aujourd'hui se rebiffe : tout ceci n'est pas du journalisme dira-t-on. Mais si le regard se porte sur la page blanche des définitions et sur le brouillage des statuts et des pratiques, décuplé à l'ère d'Internet, le doute surgit. Et ce journalisme que nous connaissons ou croyons connaître apparaît alors pour ce qu'il est, c'est-à-dire un pensable historiquement construit par le discours historiographique. Le processus de cette construction résulte d'un « tri entre ce qui peut être compris et ce qui doit être oublié pour obtenir la représentation d'une intelligibilité présente » (Certeau, 1975). Ce tri n'a toutefois pas entièrement effacé les traces des options écartées et ces dernières ressurgissent parfois, tels des refoulés.

Les questionnements qui en résultent peuvent concerner les marges historiographiques, en demeurant toutefois dans une logique professionnaliste : par exemple, comme se le demande Feyel (2007), les « journalistes » et gazetiers de l'Ancien régime voire du début du XIXe siècle doivent-ils être intégrés au sein d'un journalisme envisagé en tant que pratique professionnelle et doit-on refuser au journalisme né de Renaudot puis de la Révolution, tout caractère professionnel ? Et de souligner qu'avant 1880-1890, il y eut des journalistes qui firent carrière et une éthique fondant les pratiques habituelles du métier, dans lesquelles se reconnaissaient les journalistes et leurs publics.

Mais il est possible faire un pas de côté plus important vis-à-vis de cette focalisation professionnaliste de l'historiographie dont une des conséquences est un relatif assèchement des perspectives. Comme nous l'avons vu, l'onde de choc perturbatrice que constitue le développement du web ces dernières années active (voire réactive) de nouvelles zones d'attraction potentielles, à travers notamment la résurgence d'anciennes figures historiographiques qui bousculent les régimes d'historicité traditionnels. Réintégrer ces pratiques dans le périmètre référentiel de ce que le chercheur considère comme « le » journalisme peut alors permettre de déplacer l'angle d'attaque, de revisiter les frontières de l'analyse et de poser certaines hypothèses.

A cette aune, et au regard des multiples figures « journalistiques » de semi-professionnels, d'intermittents et d'itinérants qui se nichent dans les marges de l'historiographie, on peut même se demander si la figure du journaliste professionnel telle que nous l'entendons aujourd'hui (c'est-à-dire ayant émergée entre la deuxième moitié du XIXe siècle et la première moitié du XXe) ne serait pas qu'une parenthèse de quelque 150 ans au sein d'une histoire de pratiques bien plus anciennes, des pratiques dont certaines caractéristiques profondes resurgiraient aujourd'hui, par exemple en écho au développement des réalités dites « amateurs ».

CONCLUSION

En guise de conclusion, notons que les interrogations provoquées par l'onde de choc d'Internet quant au statut professionnel du journaliste et à l'éventualité d'un journalisme « amateur » ou « citoyen » ne semblent pas spécifiques à la situation présente et qu'elles rencontrent sur leur chemin rétrospectif d'autres questionnements plus anciens :

Faut-il que le journalisme soit un métier ? Est-ce qu'il n'est pas permis de se représenter dans un avenir quelconque des journaux qui ne soient plus rédigés seulement par des plumes de profession, mais par des gens de diverses classes qui subsisteraient d'autre chose que de la publicité [entendue au sens de publier] même ? (…) Si on voulait faire le recensement des gens capables présentement d'exprimer leurs idées sur le papier de façon correcte, sensée et même éloquente, on arriverait sans doute à un chiffre considérable. Pourquoi donc le journalisme n'utiliserait-il pas toutes ces forces vives ? (Frémy, 1866)

De tels propos s'avèrent d'une étonnante actualité au regard des évolutions actuelles alors qu'ils datent du Second empire. Selon leur auteur, lui-même homme de presse, il s'agit de

> « tailler le journaliste, non plus comme autrefois, dans l'étoffe du bel esprit et du fantaisiste mais dans celle du citoyen » (p. 379).

Le jour viendra ainsi où,

> « la presse, n'étant plus ni exploitation ni coterie, ne sera plus que l'expression de l'opinion publique elle-même, transcrite par un choix de citoyens-rédacteurs » (p. 382).

BIBLIOGRAPHIE

Barbier, F & Bertho Lavenir, C (1996). *Histoire des médias, de Diderot à Internet,* Paris : A. Colin.

Certeau, M de (1975). *L'écriture de l'histoire,* Paris : Gallimard.

Charle, C (2004). *Le siècle de la presse (1830-1939),* Paris : Seuil.

Chouinard, M-A (2008, 30/10). « Médias - Le poids du blogue », *Le Devoir.* http://www.ledevoir.com/politique/canada/213187/medias-le-poids-du-blogue, page consultée le 7 mars 2010.

Curran, J & Seaton J (1998). *Power Without Responsibility : the press and broadcasting in Britain (1ère édition 1981),* Londres-New York : Routledge.

Delacroix, C (2009). « Généalogie d'une notion ». Dans C Delacroix, F Dosse & P Garcia, (dir.), *Historicités* (pp. 29–45), Paris : La Découverte.

Delporte, C (1995). *Histoire du journalisme et des journalistes en France, du XVIIe siècle à nos jours,* Paris : Presses universitaires de France.

—. (1999). *Les journalistes en France (1880–1950). Naissance et construction d'une profession,* Paris : Seuil.

Deslandes, G, Fonnet, L & Godbert, A (2009). « Éthique des médias sociaux et économie de la participation: Vers une nouvelle approche éditoriale ? Une étude comparative », *Global Media Journal - Canadian Edition*, 2(1), pp. 41–61.

Estienne, Y (2007). *Le journalisme après Internet*, Paris : L'Harmattan.

Ferenczi, T (1993). *L'invention du journalisme en France. Naissance de la presse moderne à la fin du XIXe siècle,* Paris : Plon.

Feyel, G (1999). *La presse en France des origines à 1944. Histoire politique et matérielle,* Paris : Ellipses.

—. (2008). « Histoire de l'invention d'une profession », *Médiamophoses*, 24, pp. 145–151.

Frémy, A (1866). *La révolution du journalisme.* Paris : Librairie centrale.

Garcia, P (2002). « Les régimes d'historicité : un outil pour les historiens ? Une étude de cas : la "guerre des races" ». *Revue d'histoire du XIXe siècle*, 25. Mis en ligne le 07 mars 2008 : http://rg19.revues.org/index418.html, page consultée le 05 mars 2009.

Gillmor, D (2004). *We the Media. Grassroots Journalism by the People, for the People,* Beijing : O'Reilly.

Ginisty, P (1917). *Anthologie du journalisme, du XVIIe siècle à nos jours*, 2 vol, Paris : Delgrave.

Hartog, F & Lenclud, G (1993). « Régimes d'historicité », In *L'Etat des lieux en sciences sociales*, Textes réunis par A. Dutu et N. Dodille. Paris: L'Harmattan.

Hatin, E (1859–1861). *Histoire politique et littéraire de la presse en France avec une introduction historique sur les origines du journal et la bibliographie générale des journaux depuis leur origine*, 8 vol, Paris : Poulet-Malassis et de Broise.

Kalifa, D (2000). « L'entrée de la France en régime médiatique : l'étape des années 1860 ». In J Migozzi (dir.), *De l'écrit à l'écran. Littérature populaire : mutations génériques, mutations médiatiques*. Limoges : Pulim.

Kalifa, D & Vaillant, A (2004). « Pour une histoire culturelle et littéraire de la presse française au XIXe siècle ». *Le Temps des Médias*, 2004(1,2), pp. 197–214.

Le Cam, F & Ruellan, D (2004). « Professionnalisme, professionnalisation et profession de journaliste au Brésil, en France et au Québec : un essai de comparaison », In Legavre, J.-B. (dir.), *La presse écrite : objets délaissés*. Paris : L'Harmattan.

Lenclud, G (2006). « Traversées dans le temps », *Annales. Histoire, Sciences Sociales* (5), pp. 1053–1084.

Loraux, N (1993). « Eloge de l'anachronisme », *Le genre humain* (27), pp. 23–39.

Martin, M (1997). *Médias et journalistes de la République*, Paris : O.Jacob.

Mathien, M (1995). *Les journalistes*, Paris : Presses universitaires de France.

—. (2007). *Les journalistes. Histoire, pratiques et enjeux*, Paris : Ellipses.

Mathien, M & Rieffel, R. (dir.) (1995). *L'identité professionnelle des journalistes,* Strasbourg : CUEJ/Alphacom.

McChesney, W R & Salomon W S (éds) (1993). *Ruthless Criticism. New perspectives in U.S. Communication History*, Minneapolis, London : University of Minnesota Press.

Noblet, A (2010). *Les régimes d'historicité du journalisme. Héritages et transformations à l'ère d'Internet* (thèse de doctorat non publiée), Université Lyon 2, Lyon.

Noblet, A & Pignard-Cheynel, N (2009). « La mobilisation du mythe du journaliste-reporter sur le web, nouvel Eldorado participatif ? », *Communication présentée au congrès Nouveaux médias et information - convergences et divergences (actes sur CD-ROM).* Athènes, Grèce.

Noblet, A & Pignard-Cheynel, N (2010). « L'encadrement des contributions "amateurs" au sein des sites d'information : entre impératifs participatifs et exigences journalistiques ». In F. Millerand, S. Proulx & J. RUEFF (dir.), *Web social. Mutation de la communication* (pp. 265–282). Québec : Presses Universitaires de Québec.

Palmer, M (1983). *Des petits journaux aux grandes agences. Naissance du journalisme moderne (1863–1914)*, Paris : Aubier.

Pelissier, N (2005). *Ecrire sur le journalisme. Etude de la dispersion d'un savoir scientifique. Le cas de la France (1937–2005)*, Document présenté en vue de l'Habilitation à diriger des Recherches.

Ricoeur, P (1983). *Temps et récit*, Paris : Seuil.

Ruellan, D (1993). *Le professionnalisme du flou. Identité et savoir-faire des journalistes français*, Grenoble : PUG.

—. (1997). *Les pros du journalisme. De l'état au statut, la construction d'un espace professionnel*, Rennes : Presse Universitaires de Rennes.

—. (2007). « Penser le "journalisme citoyen" » *M@rsouin.* http://www.marsouin.org/IMG/pdf/Ruellan_13-2007.pdf, page consultée le 11 mars 2010.

Tavernier, E (1902). *Du journalisme, son histoire, son rôle politique et religieux*, Paris : H. Oudin.

Tétu, J-F (2008). « Du "public journalism" au "journalisme citoyen" », *Questions de communication*, (13), p. 71-89.

Thérenty, M-E (2001). « Physiologie du chercheur sur la presse », In M-E Thérenty & A Vaillant, *1836 : l'an I de l'ère médiatique*, Paris :

Editions Nouveau Monde.

Thérenty, M-E et Viallant, A (2001). *1836 : l'an I de l'ère médiatique*, Paris : Editions Nouveau Monde.

Ternisien, X (2009). « Les blogs : info ou influence ? », *Le Monde*, 6/3.

Voyenne, B (1959). « Les journalistes », *Revue française de sciences politiques*, 9(4), pp. 901–934.

—. (1985). *Les journalistes français. D'où viennent-ils ? qui sont-ils ? que font-ils ?,* Paris : Centre de formation et de perfectionnement des journalistes/Retz.

Watine, T (2003). « Le modèle du journalisme public », *Hermès* (35), pp. 231–239.

FACTUALITY AS A CRISIS COMMUNICATION TOOL—CASE STUDY: ROŞIA MONTANĂ GOLD CORPORATION

GEORGE DAVID AND ION CHICIUDEAN

Abstract

In most cases of crisis-prone situations, the stakeholder perceptions are substantially affected by emotions, particularly negative ones. This emotional approach, hardly based on evidence and facts, often turns in an aggravating feature able to worsen the events into a crisis.

The easiest position organizations are tempted to adopt in such cases, as far as crisis communication is concerned, is to respond emotionally: denial, diminution of responsibility, diminution of the danger perceived, blaming the accidental factors, promises and good intentions etc.; however, such an approach often doesn't produce beneficial outcomes, actually escalating the spiral of anger instead of calming it down.

If the organizational response had been based on neutral information, facts and solid evidence, the stakeholder resentment would have been better managed to the advantage of the organization.

The Roşia Montană Gold Corporation, a Canadian-Romanian joint venture specializing in gold extraction, has recently initiated such a communication strategy based on factuality in its attempt to extract gold in Romania: after they had initially been confronted with a great many negative public emotions and activist positions blaming the project, the company in a first phase renounced any kind of public communication, in hope that the project presented to the Government would speak for itself through its professional approach; as governmental agencies appeared to be influenced in their decisions by the public antagonism, the company decided to try to change public perceptions based on subjective erroneous interpretations.

Based on this case, we will analyse in our study how factual approaches could benefit organizations confronting crisis situations.

Key words: factuality, crisis management, factual communication, crisis prevention, stakeholder perceptions.

Introductory Remarks

Communication during the development of a crisis cannot be managed only by engaging more human and material resources. The structure, content and philosophy of communication need to be changed, because the pre-established directions of interpretation and understanding can disappear during crises. This requires communication to operate as a vital component of the support provided to the people in order to understand and interpret correctly the situation they find themselves in (Reynolds, Hunter-Galdo & Sokler, 2002). Communication must also assume a prophylactic role by making possible the avoidance of potentially dangerous negative attitudes, behaviours and actions of individuals, groups and communities.

Avoiding the stakeholders' negative behaviours is essential to achieve an efficient two-way communication, designed to foster an interested, involved, rational, concerned, solution-oriented public. Otherwise, certain elements that are hard to control may hinder crisis management and disturb organizational communication: contradictory, desperate, hostile manifestations; irreconcilable positions; argumentative and justifying discourses to explain the manifestations and the positions adopted; media involvement with consequences at the level of representation (when media become the spokesperson of the discontented, the organization/institution is in a delicate situation), and at the discourse level (the discourse of the involved publics, processed and filtered by the press, becomes more elaborate, more radical and harder for the organization to influence).

Things can worsen if unprofessional communication practices are added to the crisis situation: mixed messages coming from various specialists; delayed information which becomes obsolete because of the rapid development of events; excessively reassuring messages; recommendations made to stakeholders without having been tested or analysed by experts; leaving myths, rumours and intentionally exaggerated predictions uncorrected (Reynolds, Hunter-Galdo & Sokler, 2002); late involvement of the public relations resources (Leinemann & Baikalţeva, 2004).

When an organization is in a crisis situation, its internal and external communication tends to be more reactive, unplanned, incoherent, ambiguous and emotional. A faulty internal communication of the organization's changes and perspectives often leads to the occurrence of conflicts and the weakening of the organization's internal cohesion. Although, at least theoretically, the importance of internal communication during crises is well recognized and accepted, in real life it tends to be neglected as a consequence of the "media actions being privileged" (Libaert, 2008, p. 102). Internal communication should be treated at least as equally important as the communication with media, because, if the internal publics do not feel as being part of the "inside", they will then behave as the external publics do. This requirement is more important today, as organizations can operate on wide geographical areas, with indefinite borders, with its members spread in different locations and in diverse social and cultural environments.

Incoherent and contradictory external communication regarding the goals and the ways of achieving them can bring the organization in a conflicting situation with one or more organizations/institutions in the environment/area/country where it runs its business. The consequences of a conflicting situation can turn into radical measures or decisions with negative outcomes for the functioning of the organization and for the public promotion of its own interests, thus creating the conditions for the organization to enter a crisis. Examples can come from organizations that do not make public their degree of risk in operation, the technological processes used by them being likely to affect the environment, the people's health and safety.

In such situations, the competent authorities decide, under the pressure of public opinion and of the activists, to stop the projects intended or under way, restrict or stop the functioning of those companies, and therefore cause them to enter a crisis. Such a situation will be further analysed in our case study. These organizations' communication in the public space is usually limited to defensive reactions, justification and answering questions asked by journalists and by stakeholders (local communities, environmental organizations and state authorities).

The lack of coherence and transparency in communication may cause the organization to break its relations, at local, national, and international level, with other organizations and categories of stakeholders that might be an important support in overcoming the crisis. Moreover, when the managers' effort during a crisis is focused especially on solving the material, financial and technological aspects and less on communication and the involvement of the human factor, the stakeholders' attitudes, behaviors and actions, generated most often by frustration and other negative feelings, can be unpredictable and counterproductive for the organization (Chiciudean & Ţoneş, 2010).

In order to avoid stakeholders' negative emotions and reactions, the organizations must substantiate communication by facts and actions that illustrate both the interests of the organization and those of the stakeholders. The organizational communicators must be aware of the importance of an interactive communication process: the organization is not supposed just to speak, it is also supposed to listen to what its publics have to say. They must keep in mind that it is crucial to avoid any speculations at all costs, by releasing only factual information based on certainty, not on projections or predictions which are based on uncertain results of possible future events. This imperative requirement implies both maximum transparency and visibility in the public space of all decisions made and actions taken by the organization, and building a relationship based on trust with its publics. In other words, factuality must be used as a crisis communication tool in the context of a relationship based on mutual trust.

Literature Review

Communication Context Based on Factuality

Cabin and Dortier (2010) have elaborated an interesting vision on organizational communication, mentioning that the organization members consider it both the source of all unclear, debatable aspects and the instrument that can provide solutions to all problems that might arise. The privileged status of organizational communication is favoured by the emergence of certain illusions, which are responsible for all the distortions occurring in this area: the illusion of an easily achievable communication; the illusion that the message will be understood by the receiver just as the sender understands it; the illusion that there is only one single valid form of communication, the one in which the message has been sent.

Such illusions appear in all types of communication, including crisis communication. Their consequences are driven by how changes take place in the actual organizations that are transforming permanently, not only due to technological progress, but also to the development of new concepts such as autonomy, transversal organization, team projects, participation, responsibility etc. (Cabin & Dortier, 2010). Without clarity, consistency and continuity in communication, without compatibility between messages, procedures and behaviours, between words and facts, the organization should not expect recognition and legitimacy (Christensen, Firat & Torp, 2008). The key to solving the problem is transparency through factual, candid communication.

When the activities carried on by organizations have consequences on certain groups of people or on other organizations/institutions, the hazard of risks arises. The affected groups' awareness of the risks and of their interest gives rise to activism and to taking sides, thus generating the conditions for a conflict to break out. With the purpose of magnifying the negative perception of risk, most often, the involved groups try to get media attention due to the fact that journalists tend to give events a higher profile (Regester & Larkin, 2003).

The public's increased interest in the risk caused by the organization's activity puts pressure on those who manage the risks, forcing them to take action on the spur of the moment. In such a situation, adopting an inadequate communication policy, such as silence, may bring about insurmountable difficulties for the organization. Poor communication is harmful for leaders, for personnel and for organization as a whole. Stakeholders evaluate communication and lay the entire blame on the organization for all the negative aspects during the crisis. This blame is invoked constantly; it is uttered at an early stage, being voiced throughout the crisis and even after the crisis is over (Ramirez, 2010).

Factuality as a Crisis Communication Tool

Libaert views factuality in the wider context of crisis management, drawing attention to the fact that "the reality of an event is blurred by perception and by different representations of the involved parties" (Libaert, 2008, p. 1).

Therefore, without a global, well-articulated communication strategy, it is unlikely that the organization may conduct an effective crisis communication process (Libaert, 2008).

In order to control communication and its credibility, the perception that crisis communication manipulates people's understanding must be erased. In this respect, the essential message to be issued must be prepared with deepest thinking and utmost caution. To this end, it is extremely important to have the answers to the following questions: What do we want to say about this type of event? Do we take a positive or a defensive attitude? How could it happen? Has it happened before? Can it happen again? What are the consequences? (Libaert, 2008).

The organization must build and maintain its stakeholders' trust. That is why, both at the level of discourse and at the level of facts, it is very important that the organization's attitude meets the public's expectations. This can become feasible if the discourse is endorsed constantly by facts which prove its accuracy. In order to meet the public's expectations with regard to facts, the organization must ascertain the significance of the activities that prove the clear control over the crisis: withdrawal of products, cessation of trading or manufacturing those products, firing the accountable employees, etc. Communication that is not based on demonstrable facts runs the risk of being inefficient (Libaert, 2008).

People's safety is important during a crisis. Many organizations have this reaction deriving from their firm belief. They try to reassure people with regard to their safety and to build a better cooperation with them. However, "in order to be efficient, reassurance must be accompanied by communication based on evidence, namely on real, concrete and verifiable actions which prove that the organization faces up to the problem, and which show the organization's determination to solve the crisis" (Libaert, 2008, p. 81).

In many cases visualization is necessary. To strengthen the power of the word, images that can be understood instantly due to their symbolic value are useful (Libaert, 2008).

Regester and Larkin (2003) also emphasize the role of revealing the facts in shaping people's attitude and behaviour when faced with a crisis. Companies often label a problem wrongly, because they concentrate on technical aspects and ignore those aspects related to perception; therefore negative consequences will appear soon. The solution is to "take the right actions to fix the situation, to be seen while taking action and heard while saying the right words" (Regester & Larkin, 2003, p. 143).

During a crisis, people need to be reassured quickly about certain things, mainly to know that all measures had been taken to prevent the occurrence of the event.

The organization going through such an experience must be able to produce the image of a group of competent and benevolent people who immediately took action to solve the situation. The leader of the organization must take responsibility for the consequences of the crisis by sending three simple messages: this is what happened; this is what we are doing about it; this is our attitude regarding what happened. This kind of communication, based on facts, will make people's anger disappear and will reassure people that the organization is making all possible efforts under a most difficult situation (Regester & Larkin, 2003).

An important principle of contingency planning, as shown by the authors, is that facts create reputation in a much more effective way than words in an advertisement or in a glossy brochure. In the current climate of corporate responsibility, promises are received with scepticism or disbelief. This type of approach can turn the company into a target, should a mistake occur in its operations. The evidence of relevant facts is an essential element to create a positive image.

The essence of good reputation consists in determining the management to enhance performance so that facts may speak for themselves. The underlying principles of crisis management, which can make the desired performance feasible, are: developing a positive attitude towards crisis management; bringing the performance of the entire organization to the level of the public's expectations; building the organization's credibility through a number of responsible facts; seeking and capitalizing on opportunities during a crisis (Regester & Larkin, 2003). "Everything finally breaks down to facts versus statements. Evidence of responsible facts is the organization's insurance policy when and if something bad happens" (Regester & Larkin, 2003, p. 187).

Other authors (Reynolds et al., 2002) identify important methodological aspects of communication factuality. The definition of crisis communication establishes differences between the types of factors involved in the communication process and refers firstly to the factual communication of an organization in its relation with its stakeholders and publics. Factuality must be based on solid empirical information so that an individual can judge its accuracy without the help of an expert.

The core of crisis communication is the reality that the organization is going through a crisis and it has to react, and its reaction must be based on facts. The speed with which facts are spread out can be an indicator of the organization's readiness to manage the crisis. If the public cannot find out that the organization solves the problem, if the public does not know the efforts made, then they are made in vain. The public will be interested in factual information, and some people will expect to be given instructions for action. In order to take action according to the desired factual communication, certain guidelines are necessary: prioritize information about facts and consistently repeat it; avoid offering details shortly after the event happens; communicate with one single voice; offer only consistent messages based on facts (Reynolds et al., 2002).

Lukaszewski (2000a, 2000b) also deals widely with the analysis of using facts in crisis communication. The aspects he highlights are of a thorough methodological nature. He points out the imperative of using the power of facts in order to organize the top management of the organization into an operational, concentrated, motivated, productive, thinking, deciding team when a crisis happens.

Facts are important, especially in situations with a strong emotional impact, which is why the use of fact-sheets is recommended to quickly give the public the accurate and vital information. This technique helps the organization to buy time, by providing answers to the frequent questions reporters ask about company and its operations, and to manage the reputation created due to reporters' and victims' stories (Lukaszewski, 2000c, 1.3). The power of facts will make the management's and the legal advisors' strategic decisions be more focused on the existing situation, will reduce mistakes, will open the way to a better management of crisis communication.

Fearn-Banks (2011) proposes an extremely interesting idea with regard to the public perception of the true events occurring during a crisis. In limit situations, the public perceives the truth about events as being provided by the public opinion. An organization in crisis must prove to its stakeholders, and quite often to the general public, that the prevailing negative opinion is not factual. Unlike in a court of justice, where a person is innocent until proven guilty, in the tribunal of the public opinion, a person or organization is guilty until proven to be innocent.

Under such conditions, Holladay (2010) suggests that factual information coming from primary respondents (the first who answer the questions arising in a crisis situation) might be used to outline the crisis framework in ways that are unfavorable to the organization. If the first respondents are predominantly present in the media reports, and the organization's spokespersons are absent, the organization may be perceived as not having control over the crisis.

The problem is that media need to fill up the gap of information, and the lack of organizational spokespersons does not prevent journalists from reporting the crisis. However, factual reports can also create confusion and wrong perceptions in certain conditions. Cohn (2000) speaks about the danger that such confusions may occur: sometimes, insignificant facts may be perceived as generating certain situations, although the reality is quite different. In January 1982, an airplane of the Air Florida company crashed, and in July 1984 the company went bankrupt; the statement of a spokeswoman hired by company from a consultancy said that Air Florida went bankrupt because of that air crash, although, in reality, bankruptcy was provoked by the company's rapid growth and the resulting incapacity to control the debts properly.

Other authors (Heath & O'Hair, 2009) point out the relation between factual communication and the organization's behaviour towards those affected. To improve trust and credibility, according to the authors, a fundamental role is played by information and expertise, alongside the organizations' care and attention for the affected publics. They become more credible the more they are perceived as working to support the interests of those at risk. This is the reason why, in risk and crisis situations, facts count, and, at the same time, the source-organization's concern and attention give life to facts, not conversely.

The relation between facts and the organization's attitude towards those affected also embraces ethical and moral aspects. Bowen (2009) pleads for the need to include and communicate facts in an ethical context, by establishing the major facts, based on a strong ethical sense, as well as the relevant themes and topics and the way of solving them. Part of this process implies engaging in dialogue with the public, which should rely on the organization's honesty and total transparency toward its publics.

> Actually, this is about a universal imperative requirement saying that between organizations and the public there should be a relation based on transparent communication of facts, honest interpretation of these, and on complete release of information. (Bowen, 2009, p. 358)

Case Study

In order to illustrate the theoretical approaches already mentioned, we have chosen to present a case study about an organization which has opted for this type of factual communication after several years of searching for effective corporate communication in a very complex and sensitive project. We believe that this method is able to offer pertinent answers to questions such as:

- How does factual communication influence the communication potential of an organization in crisis?
- Which is the correlation between factual communication and persuasion in a crisis?
- What are the potential dangers of factual communication in a crisis?

Our research has been mainly based on the analysis of various kinds of documents produced and made public by the parties involved, such as administrative and official papers, public statements, media reports, expert opinions, and statistics. We also interviewed Roşia Montană Gold Corporation (RMGC) representatives on the company's communication strategy and its outcomes.

Chronology

A mining joint-venture was established in 1997, in the Romanian county of Alba – a well known area for gold extraction (this kind of activity has been documented through indubitable archeological evidence since the second century AD). The main shareholders are the Canada-based company Gabriel Resources (80.46%) and the Romanian state-owned mining company Minvest Deva (19.31%). Since 1999, the company has been named Roşia Montană Gold Corporation (RMGC). Its main goal consists of gold and silver mining.

The estimated quantities of metals to be extracted from the 23.8 sq km area Roşia Montană – the most promising site in Alba County from this perspective – go up to 314 tons of gold and 1480 tons of silver (RMGC – Mining Project: Geology). According to its own statements (RMGC – Quick Facts), the company Gabriel Resources has invested in this venture in Romania more than US$400 million so far, and plans to allocate more than US$2.5 billion for the further development of the Roşia Montană mining project.

On 14 December 2004, RMGC submitted to the Romanian Ministry of Waters and Environmental Protection its application for the Environmental Agreement for the development of the Roşia Montană Gold and Silver Mining Project. Following this submission, approximately 120 NGOs and individuals both from Romania and abroad (according to the figures released by one of the most vocal opponents – the Alburnus Maior Association) began to show their opposition to the project. Their disagreement contributed to a public opinion characterized by resistance to such a plan.

This high level of negative emotions has also been encouraged by the resistance to the project of several organizations with great public visibility, such as the Romanian Academy, the Romanian Orthodox Church, the Romanian Catholic Church, the Romanian Unitarian Church, the Romanian Royal House, Greenpeace and the European Federation of Green Parties. The media involvement should also be noted: from a primary emotional approach following the stereotypes already settled in the public opinion, media reports have gained more balance today; however, media opposition is still significant and, in our opinion, it remains one of the major risk factors when it comes to this project.

Confronted with such an emotional perception both over the RMGC's mining project and over the company itself, the Romanian authorities (local and national) have expressed their worries about the impact of the project, and consequently avoided endorsing it, even when RMGC called them to adjudicate. A number of 16 public presentations (two of them in Hungary) took place in 2006, in order to explain the project and to answer their questions. Following this phase, in January 2007 the Romanian Ministry of Environment (ME) submitted to RMGC some 5600 questions asked both by organizations and individuals. RMGC presented its answers in May 2007, in a 12,600-page document.

From September 2007 to September 2010, the ME did not examine the project, believing that the urbanism certificate was suspended *de jure* and therefore it was "in impossibility of continuing the procedure of environment impact assessment and issuance of the environment agreement" (Ministry of Environment – Note regarding the suspension [...]).

With the submission of a new urbanism certificate in May 2010, the endorsement procedures have been resumed in the same climate of reluctance. However, on 12 July 2011 the National Commission for Archeology, reporting to the Ministry of Culture, approved the issuance of an archeological discharge certificate for a part of the perimeter, thus seeming to open the way to a more rapid approval of the whole project.

Within the larger communication context, marked by the economic and political conditions, by the specifics of Romanian media environment, by cultural patterns and stereotypes, there have been – in our opinion – several elements particularly favoring this kind of negative perceptions, elements which RMGC should have been aware of from the very beginning:

1. The word "cyanide". Indeed, this chemical product is supposed to be used while extracting gold from rocks. Although experts claim that "the fear of cyanide arises from several historical sources. It is this fear that is sometimes exploited to generate negative public sentiment against mining" (Mudder, 2007, p. 7), the fear still remains. It is the same public opinion perceptional mechanism as in the case of other "dangerous" words such as "dioxine" or "nuclear".
2. The word "patrimony". The Roşia Montană perimeter hosts a consistent archeological and cultural heritage, particularly coming from the Roman times, all of it related to or created by mining activities. By a very common association based on the cause-effect thinking mechanism, whoever tries to mine in the respective area will damage this patrimony.
3. The public reluctance over business companies, which, according to the attribution theory, are perceived as presumably "guilty".
4. The same public stereotype consisting of a lack of enthusiasm when it comes to foreign companies trying to exploit national valuable resources such as oil or gold.

These points were considered when the new communication strategy was drafted back in 2009. The strategy resulted in a massive integrated communication campaign, with components such as advertising, public relations and public affairs, advocacy, publicity.

Actors Involved

Roşia Montană Gold Corporation – actor directly involved: since the very beginning of the gold-mining project, in the stage of real estate acquisitions, RMGC paid special attention to communication with the local community and its components, aiming to obtain their acceptance and to avoid oppositions and disagreements. General publics, as well as national media, did not represent one of the top communication priorities until the project was submitted to the ME in December 2004.

Since that moment to September 2007, when ME declined its capacity of examining the project due to the suspension of the urbanism certificate, communication efforts were made in a reactive manner, trying to counterbalance the wave of hostile opinions made public by various actors.

Since September 2007, organizational efforts have been directed essentially to fine-tuning the project so that it could speak for itself and thus be rapidly approved by authorities; this way, communication efforts were reduced – or at least they appeared to be – in the hope that the project, based on solid argumentation, would gain credibility and trust, this way being eventually endorsed by authorities.

As this strategy of silence proved to be ineffective, a new stage of communication efforts began by 2009, with a massive campaign designed to change attitudes on a large scale.

The Romanian State (through its institutions and agencies) – actor directly involved: According to RMGC evaluations, the Romanian State would get a direct benefit of US$1.8 billion coming from taxes, duties, royalties and other taxes specific to mining activities; the overall estimated benefits for the Romanian economy, coming from jobs created, logistic facilities and infrastructure required for this project, rehabilitations, would be about to US$4 billion (RMGC – Benefits for the Romanian State); according to the details provided by RMGC officials, this estimation was based on the gold price in force at that time, US$900 per ounce, but it later almost doubled (price listed on http://goldprice.org/gold-price.html on 12 August 2011: US$1760.12 per ounce). In contrast, one of the major adversaries, academician Ionel Haiduc, the President in function of the Romanian Academy, claimed that

> the Romanian State (governmental or national budget) will benefit from a legal exploitation royalty of 2% of the profit (estimated by some sources at 4.4 million USD per year), which is very little compared to the company's turnover. The State income, affected by the tax and customs fee exemptions made to the firm, thus eventually consists in a profit which is deplorable (insignificant). The only taxes collected by the State budget would be those on the employees' salaries. In conclusion, if the benefits of RMGC are beyond any doubt, the benefits of the Romanian State (budget) and of the community in the area are minimal, uncertain and disputable. (Haiduc, 2003, p. 77)

However, the public pressure (including media scrutiny) over political and governmental institutions still remains high, thus delaying the endorsement of the mining project.

The Chamber of Deputies, one of the two bodies of the Romanian Parliament, has been involved in the evaluation of the RMGC project since 2002. Since 2006, through its Committee for Public Administration, Territorial Planning and Ecological Balance, the Chamber of Deputies has been involved more substantially. Committee members, together with the President of the Chamber, made a site visit, ministries and governmental agencies were asked to affirm their positions and the committee made public its concerns on economic and social aspects (with a particular view on social consequences of resettlement and relocation). However, in spite of these concerns, a remark has been made since the very beginning of the social aspect analysis:

> Socially and culturally, the area is on a decline, so that people leave for other regions able to offer them better life conditions. In spite of its touristic potential, Roşia Montană still remains an isolated spot, with no potential investments able to reinvigorate the village other than in mining. (Chamber of Deputies – Roşia Montană Project).

The government ministries and agencies, as well as the political parties involved, have also adopted a reticent attitude as a result of the public pressure. Therefore, they have taken this project as a "hot potato", trying to pass it to anybody else whenever a decision had to be made. As a recent example, the above-mentioned issuance of the archeological discharge certificate, which seemed to unfreeze somehow the endorsing process, has quite rapidly been followed by a stepping back statement of the Minister of Culture.

Local community – actor directly involved. Since the very beginning of the project, the local community has been split in two major factions, one of them agreeing to the project and its consequences, the other one opposing it. The first faction, including the mayor of Roşia Montană, seems to be larger and more vocal: in an open letter addressed to the Minister of Culture and posted on Facebook on 18 July 2011, the mayor, Eugen Furdui, claimed that "in an overwhelming majority, we, the Rosians, believe in the RMGC's investment in mining and support it. Only this way we would have a modern infrastructure, jobs, cleaner waters, a rehabilitated environment and a settlement where tourists may come joyfully" (Roşia Montană City Hall, 2011). RMGC backs this group and supports part of its projects. As a result, all the mayors and other officials from Roşia Montană, no matter their political orientation, have consented to the project, because it has substantially contributed to the local budgets.

The other group is structured mainly around the Alburnus Maior NGO. They also benefit from a certain public recognition, but their resources appear to be short. As to its dimensions, even RMGC opponents talk about the "minority of locals who do not want to move from village" (Dohotaru, 2011). The essential reason for this division is given by the long tradition of mining (particularly gold mining) in the area. Indeed, mining still represents the most convenient choice when it comes to local sustainable development; other projects, such as tourism, agriculture, cattle, timber, dairy/cheese production, did not gain much credibility and acceptance, because they have not been supported by appropriate resources able to back them in the long run.

Alburnus Maior Association – actor directly involved. In 2000, when RMGC had already started the real estate acquisition process, some of the locals and owners from Roşia Montană gathered in an association called Alburnus Maior (the old Roman name of the settlement); based in Roşia Montană, this NGO has declared itself as the representative entity of about 400 families in the area that have chosen to oppose the RMGC project for social, cultural, environmental and economic reasons. Since then, they have been fighting against the relocation and resettlement initiatives of RMGC, the use of cyanide, the presumed damage of archeological and cultural patrimony, and the extended surface mining projects in the area (Alburnus Maior – About Us).

With declared activist purposes, Alburnus Maior initiated in 2002 the campaign "Save Roşia Montană", which has become quite visible to the public and is still developing; however, at least some of its components, such as the FânFest music festival, have lost some of their credibility and local acceptance.

The public/media perception (both nationally and internationally) of this NGO is mainly positive, which, combined with the visibility of Alburnus Maior, stands for one of the major threats to the RMGC project. At the same time, the NGO has a vast reputation among environmental activists; as a matter of fact, Stephanie Roth – a former environmental journalist who turned to environmental activism and won the Goldman Environmental Prize in 2005 – has been one of the key supporters of this NGO since the beginning. Alburnus Maior is not the only organization/association opposing the project.

Gabriel Resources Ltd. – actor indirectly involved – the majority owner of RMGC. The company was founded in Canada and was initially chaired by Vasile Frank Timis, a businessman of Romanian origin whose involvement in the extracting industries worldwide is significant. According to a press release, he resigned in May 2003, but "will continue to assist Gabriel, as an independent consultant, in connection with the development of the Roşia Montană project" (Gabriel Resources Ltd, 2003). The company is listed on the Toronto Stock Exchange.

Minvest Deva S.A. – actor indirectly involved – is a Romanian state-owned company sharing 19.31% of RMGC. The company's website makes no mention at all of RMGC and the mining project from Roşia Montană.

Greenpeace – actor indirectly involved. The Romanian branch of the well known environmental international organization has placed the campaign against the RMGC project among its top seven priorities, along with nuclear energy, climate change, energetic (r)evolution, energetic efficiency, selective waste collection and ocean protection. "Greenpeace has involved itself in this campaign since the very beginning of the project, resolutely expressing its opposition against the mining operation in Roşia Montană" (Greenpeace Romania Activity Report 2010, p. 9). Five activist protests were developed in 2010, with the purpose of stopping the project or at least making it more ecologically friendly.

On February, 2011, Greenpeace Romania released the results of an opinion poll conducted by the end of 2010 by the Sociological Research and Branding Company. According to this survey, only 9% of Romanians totally agreed and 15% partially agreed. The DK/NA percentage was 38%; on the other hand, no mention was made of the size and structure of the sample population. Although 71% of respondents claimed that they had heard about the project, 48% of them declared themselves uninformed and another 10% avoided answering (DK/NA).

The Romanian Academy – indirect actor, belonging to the interpretation area, particularly to the scientific interpretation. According to its tasks, the Romanian Academy issued several points of view based on analysis of various aspects, such as: environmental consequences; potential threats on archeological patrimony; geological aspects; local influences on the labour market; predictable benefits for RMGC, for local population, and for the Romanian State; economic, social, legal, ecological and technological risks; political aspects. The general conclusion of such research has been negative to the project:

> Taking into account the consequences, both damaging to the environment and threatening to human communities in the area, considering also the archeological and historical aspects, the Romanian Academy, which gives expression to the positions of the most prominent scientists and humanists of the country, solicits to those responsible to prevent the achievement of this project. (Romanian Academy, 2003)

This position was reaffirmed on 1 March 2011, when three of the academicians agreed to take part in the Independent Group for the Study of Roşia Montană Patrimony – a faction more favourable to the RMGC project. A new confirmation came out on 27 July 2011, when a press release issued by the Presidium of the Romanian Academy stated that it

> has decided to maintain the before-mentioned position and concerns on the potential consequences and risks, especially on medium- and long-term. The Presidium calls for the authorities to responsibly analyze the effects of the execution of gold and silver mining projects in the Apuseni Mountains, so that national interest not be negatively affected. (Romanian Academy, 2011)

The position adopted by the Romanian Academy in 2003 – before the submission of the project to administrative endorsement – is thus still unchanged, although major changes and corrections have been made to the project since then, and in spite of RMGC's repeated public demands for its re-evaluation (see, for instance, RMGC – Open Letter Addressed to the Romanian Academy).

The scientific authority of the Romanian Academy and its public visibility and reputation enhance the significance of this opinion, often used as a solid argument by opponents.

The media – indirect actor. Because of insufficient information provided by RMGC, journalists initially interpreted facts in response to the general public opinion. Later, as the ongoing information campaign was developing, they were provided with enough genuine data for interpretion and consequently the manner of reports has become less and less hostile towards the project, and, at the same time, more and more informative. This evolution will be discussed later on, when we will interpret the results of the campaign.

Most of media have accurately approached the components of the integrated campaign. However, supposedly invoking professional deontology codes (Romanian Media Club – Journalist's Deontological Code, art. 8), media belonging to the Adevărul Holding refused to publish RMGC advertisements; in fact, Peter Imre, CEO of the holding, publicly declared that "Roşia Montană is a controversial project, and we do not want us to be connected with it. It is a project that I consider deeply immoral".

Opinion leaders and influencers – indirect actors: supporters, mediators, sceptics and opponents. Among supporters, one can find politicians, scientists, artists. Adriean Videanu, for instance, former Minister of Economy, declared from the very beginning of his mandate that "we want to include in the Program of Governance the start of the RMGC project as fast as possible, because the gold market is favoring such projects" (HotNews.ro, 2009).

Another political statement, which is significant in our opinion due to the specific position of the speaker, came from Laszlo Borbely, then Minister of Environment:

> I have recently visited a gold mine in Sweden, to see exactly how cyanide mining works. I have to mention that the technological process used there is identical to what would be used at Roşia Montană. I saw how gold can be mined safely for environment and nature, and Sweden is not a country to take environmental risks. The European Directive has established maximum limits for cyanide concentration. For new investments, the maximum limit must be below 10 ppm. The investor from Roşia Montană sets a maximum level of 5 ppm. (Ministry of Environment – Roşia Montană – Press Release).

However, his support was moderate and based on solid facts, according to his own declaration:

> Laszlo Borbely underscored that, in his capacity as Environment minister, he will fully comply with the European and the Romanian legislation with respect to the gold and silver exploitation project in Roşia Montană. "I am

neither in favor nor against the Roşia Montană project," the minister said. (Financiarul – Minister Laszlo Borbely: All Procedures Relating to Roşia Montană will be resumed)

Among politicians, the Romanian president Traian Băsescu has a spectacular evolution: from a moderate position, as we will show a little further on, Băsescu has become one of the most vocal supporters, insistently urging a solution favourable to the RMGC project. He expressed his new opinion on 18 August 2011, when he requested the Government "to have courage" to tell the Romanians that this project must be done (Mediafax, 2011). Since then, he has used any opportunity to speak of his support and to recommend the Government to take appropriate action.

In the same group of supporters, relevant names can also be found in the scientific world, such as Dennis G. Rodwell, an architect specializing in cultural heritage and sustainable development, who rejected in a report the utility of placing Roşia Montană on the UNESCO Tentative List for Romania; or Terry I. Mudder, said to be "the world's No. 1 expert in the use of cyanide", who also released a technical statement deconstructing the emotional allegations on the use of cyanide:

> It is sincerely hoped the information provided herein will provide the People of Romania a balanced and renewed perspective about the benefits of cyanide when used prudently and properly. The banning of cyanide and curtailing of its use will not eliminate the many risks people are exposed to and must cope with every day. Clearly, the benefits of cyanide outweigh its detriments, and our society and lives would be adversely affected without it and its useful products we rely upon every day. (Mudder, 2007, p. 12).

The opinions of both of them have adequately been made public on the company's website (RMGC – Experts' Opinion).

Among journalists, we would mention the name of Corina Drăgotescu, TV moderator, who declares herself in favour of the project.

Some of the supporters (among them NGOs, trade unions, entrepreneur associations, the head of the National Council of Small and Medium Enterprises Association) have lately (June, 2011) gathered in a Support Group for the project.

RMGC has been making substantial efforts to gain approval from opinion leaders. As an example, the company arranged two tours to the gold mines in New Zealand for 30 people, most of them prominent media editors, in September 2009 and September 2010. Since the beginning of 2011, an Independent Group for Monitoring Roşia Montană Cultural Patrimony has been formed, among its members being three academicians as well as experts in history, archeology and culture. Though affirming its members' independence, the group has confirmed the logistic support offered by RMGC.

Mediators seem to recognize that there is a matter of option and negotiation. Traian Băsescu, the Romanian president, positioned himself in this category, declaring that "solutions must be found on Roşia Montană" and "things must be approached in a very realistic way" (Adevărul, 2009). However, since 18 August 2011, the President has declared himself an explicit supporter, often advocating for the project. Unfortunately, mediators have had little success, because of the high political risks generated by any type of decision, either favouring or banning the project.

Sceptics have little expectation that the project will eventually succeed somehow due to bureaucracy, unclear legislation, various pressures exerted and political dangers implied. Emil Boc, the then Prime Minister, as well as Adrian Năstase, former Prime Minister, are two of them.

Among the opponents, one can find politicians and political organizations led by political/electoral reasons, religious entities (as already mentioned) led by emotional approaches, business competitors and other kinds of opinion leaders. Among them is the Presidential adviser Peter Eckstein-Kovacs, who resigned on 1 September 2011, citing the incompatibility of his opinion about the project with the new attitude of the Romanian president (HotNews.ro – Traian Băsescu has signed the decree [...]).

Mihai Goţiu, journalist, has also long been very vocal based on his insights as an active supporter of the "Save Roşia Montană" project. Sânziana Pop, editor of the weekly *Formula As* with a large circulation, is also one of the fervent opponents. Organizations can also be found in this category, such as the Soros Romania Foundation, a well-known entity in the sphere of Romanian NGOs.

Talking about indirect actors, we have to point out that there is also a category of organizations and individuals that have interfered, trying to gain capital from a positive public image as a result of their intervention in a situation with great public visibility. As an example, the Romanian Union of Architects (RUA) has recently (end of July 2011) addressed a letter both to the National Council of Audiovisual and the Romanian public television, blaming the RMGC's TV spots running on screens: in a very emotional style (phrases such as "harsh exploitation", "catastrophes", "questionable project", "debatable cases"; rhetorical questions), the letter urged the recipients to stop the release of the incriminated TV spots, but without bringing any new, unbiased motivation in the support of this request, which leads to the idea that the real purpose was to use an opportunity of achieving a positive image.

Threats Perceived

In our opinion, there are two main categories of threats to be identified in this situation: those perceived by stakeholders (general public included) and those perceived by RMGC.

For the state, one of the RMGC's stakeholders directly involved, the essential threats refer to:

1. major environmental damage;
2. unfavourable political consequences, both internally and internationally;
3. little economic profit;
4. devastation of historical, archeological, cultural patrimony.

The local population (quite enthusiastic about jobs and new housing conditions) also perceives a number of economic, social, cultural, and environmental threats:

1. potential labour accidents caused by the use of cyanide;
2. resettlement and relocation (including building demolition and graveyard relocations): the skills and qualifications of the relocated people are no longer able to produce income in the new life and work environment;
3. danger of contamination due to the existence of the tailings management facility storing toxic waste;
4. devastation of the local landscape, as well as of the local cultural heritage;
5. keeping down the development of economic alternatives such as tourism or agriculture;
6. failure of the existing local production systems;
7. loss of goods and income sources;
8. annihilation of local social networks.

The general public, whose opinions have been influenced by the emotional statements made by various primary respondents (Holladay, 2010) since the very beginning of the project and playing a contextual role, has identified indirect threats such as:

1. environmental damage;
2. devastation of patrimony;
3. poor economic advantage for the State;
4. harm to the local community.

For RMGC, the delay of the project, combined with the probability it will be definitely banned, represents the essential threat, which actually makes this case a crisis situation. The company cannot start running its business and might never launch it. In fact, the postponement of a decision, either positive or negative, *sine die* is the main threat perceived by the company, according to its representatives.

Connected to it, there are threats generated by subjective public perceptions both of the company and of the presumed outcomes of its operations: work accidents, environmental damage, enforced resettlement and relocation, fraud to state revenue.

Communication Plan

Confronted with public disregard, RMGC had to re-evaluate its communication strategy, which had proved to be ineffective to date. At that moment, the company was finding itself a victim of an attack, in the circumstances described by Benoit in his approach to the image restoration theory:

> The key to understanding image repair strategies is to consider the nature of attacks or complaints that prompt such responses or instigate a corporate crisis. An attack has two components:
> 1. The accused is held responsible for an action.
> 2. That act is considered offensive. (Benoit, 1997, p. 178)

Indeed, both components were carried out: RMGC was accused for its project of gold mining and, at the same time, the project itself was blamed for its presumed threats.

The RMGC team recognized this state of facts in 2008, when the failure of the "strategy of silence" was obvious: the hope that stakeholders – especially government institutions – would be given the "real picture" only through functional messages (organizational doings speaking for themselves) had proved to have little success.

Aware of the importance of not only doing things, but also speaking about them, the team first conducted quantitative and qualitative sociological research on the perceptions of the RMGC project. The research revealed a sharp polarization of opinions, which were not based on solid arguments. The predominance of negative perceptions had been favoured by the non-communicative attitude adopted by RMGC since September 2007.

The research also revealed three important myths already rooted in public opinion: the environmental disaster ("they dig out our mountains and poison our waters"); the social disaster ("they forcibly resettle people and destroy villages"); the economic failure ("strangers come to steal our gold"). The problem of patrimony was almost non-existent then, both among ordinary people and decision makers or opinion leaders.

Using the results of this research, a new communication strategy has been set up, based on the concept of "de-mythicization of myths": communication based on the recognition of the need of a binomial "myth vs truth", trying to deconstruct myths by genuine facts, figures and data communicated appropriately.

Among the objectives of the new strategy, one can discern some dealing with factual communication and the new approach: to inform and educate public opinion, based on rational evidence, as to the project benefits and details, in order to transform the public perception of the project from negative to neutral. Consequently, to generate an informed attitude of the stakeholders and the general public, to make them able to evaluate the project without prejudice, without influences of public opinion, myths or urban legends.

This need of factuality has been directed then in two directions: on one hand, through the projection of communicated facts, the intended strategy was going to enlarge the topic of RMGC project from the local level aimed so far to a national one, so that national authorities and publics are informed of benefits brought by the project nationally. On the other hand, a large communication campaign was planned, based on four pillars: economy, environment, patrimony and community. The economic pillar, of strategic importance, was designed to communicate factually the major impact of this project in Romania, whilst the other three were given the role of "de-mythicization of myths".

Following these four pillars, several facts were listed:

1. Economy: the amount of US$4 billion representing the benefit of the Romanian State and details about how this amount would be generated; jobs to be created – 2300 direct jobs during the construction phase, 800 direct jobs in the operation phase, up to 3000 indirect jobs in the same phase; additional investments to be encouraged, such as in maintenance, spare parts, transportation, civil and industrial construction, insurance etc.; excerpts from the

business plan posted on company's website; optimistic signals for other entrepreneurs waiting for investing in gold extraction (18 other exploitation licenses have already been issued, but investors remain cautious, evaluating the attitude of the Romanian administration towards RMGC).

2. Environment: NGOs and opinion influencers had already constantly used the word "cyanide" in order to generate public fear; additionally, another myth has been spread out about an alleged EU interdiction of using cyanide in gold mining, Romania thus violating the European legal framework. The company's decision has been to approach this topic through an informative campaign meant to say "truths about the RMGC project as to cyanide and environment", consisting of do-you-know-type questions. This campaign has aimed to release and reinforce details like: RMGC will clean up waters with no expense to Romanian taxpayers; at the end of the extraction, the whole perimeter will be replanted with vegetation; RMGC will provide a financial pledge to guarantee the environmental rehabilitation, which will be updated annually, according to the legal provisions in force; EU allows the use of cyanide in gold mining; RMGC observes all the European environmental standards, more than that, in the waste detoxification process, the final concentration of cyanide will not go over 5-7 mg/l, although European legislation allows a maximum concentration of 10 mg/l; many states, among them the USA, New Zealand, Spain, Finland and Sweden, allow the use of cyanide in gold extraction; webcam live images from a river confluence show how un-rehabilitated old mining works are still polluting local waters; another webcam from the total of five shows the existing state of the area Cetate, where the old mining ceased and no environmental recovery has been done so far.
3. Patrimony: as we have already pointed out, the archeological patrimony in the Roşia Montană area did not represent a major concern before 2008. On the other hand, public investments in maintenance had been poor; this is why the patrimony has been constantly damaged. RMGC released details about: the financial support given to archeological research and conservation; the support given to the government's Alburnus Maior National Archeological Research Program; its own contributions made in the conservation and restoration of patrimony in protected areas such as the historical center of Roşia Montană, the Roman vestiges in Carpeni, the funerary monument and industrial techniques in Tău

Găuri, and the natural monuments in Piatra Corbului; studies on how to encourage tourism through opportunities offered by the local archeological, historical, cultural and natural patrimony, which are not viable in a "tourism without industrial development" option; when the first building in the Roşia Montană historical centre was restored and transformed into the museum "Gold of Apuseni Mountains", media events and opportunities were arranged, then news releases on the number of visitors have been periodically released; two webcams offer live images from the Roşia Montană historical centre.

4. Community: a brand new housing area (Recea) was built in the neighbourhood of the city of Alba Iulia for relocated people; assistance has been given in a unique relocation program in Romania; the project would re-launch the local declining economy; apart of jobs, the project would also offer new housing conditions, education, infrastructure, economic and social opportunities; release of authentic, indisputable testimonials of locals telling about community wishes and expectations; webcam live images from the residential area Recea, where about 125 families have already moved, are available round-the-clock.

A page of "Experts' opinion" is also available on the company's website, where diverse opinions coming from experts (both individuals and organizations) are cited. Another section deals with frequently asked questions (the most sensitive ones), and a news feed is accessible as well. All the information in the company's website can be obtained through RSS feeds or shared through mail and messaging, as well as through the most accessed social networks (Facebook, Twitter, LinkedIn). The accessibility of key information and messages is easy, so that users get them with little effort.

Not only facts have been used to enhance credibility, but communicators also have been carefully selected, so that they give reliability to the messages spoken out: the RMGC General Manager, Dragoş Tănase, reputed experts, such as the academician Răzvan Theodorescu, the financial consultant and former banker Bogdan Baltazar, and the cyanide expert Terry I. Mudder.

Results of Factual Communication

Adapted to various target publics, this communication campaign, which is still developing, has used a large scale of both BTL and ATL techniques.

Periodical evaluations of RMGC's communicational efforts show that the campaign results at this stage correspond to the initial objectives. According to data provided by the company, at this stage there have been measurable partial outcomes:

1. Since 2008 to 2010 the total number of media reports on the Roşia Montană project has grown up to 4 times, thus showing the media awareness on this topic; the media awareness has grown up primarily as a results of publicity campaigns (with an informational component instead of advertising), which acted as a "trigger" for editorial columns.
2. The percentage of positive media reports has doubled, that of negative ones has halved, and the percentage of neutral reports has grown by 40%.
3. According to monthly and annual studies by IMAS (a Romanian opinion polling institute) between 2008 and 2011, approximately one third of the public opinion is in favour of the project, another third is against, and the remaining others still do not have a clear attitude. That means there is no dominant opinion at the level of the general public.
4. More than 100,000 "RMGC friends" on Twitter (August 2011).

As to the correlation between factual communication and persuasion in a crisis, we must remember here the ethical and moral implications already mentioned (Bowen, 2009). Ethical sense, honesty and transparency must shape a communication strategy, because the attempt to persuade somebody generates the risk of crossing over the boundary between persuasive information (releasing relevant facts able to convince) and manipulation (suggestions with little support in real life). Such a danger was suspected by the National Council of Audiovisual (NCA) in 2009, when a decision was released urging RMGC to observe the legal frame of correct information in some of its TV spots ("observing the legal frame of correct information" meant "explaining the amount of 4 billion USD said to represent the benefit of the Romanian State"). Consequently, RMGC adapted the spots, adding factual information on benefits. A new intimation has recently been submitted to NCA by the Committee of Ethics of the Romanian Advertising Council (RAC), which has suspected deceptive practices in some of the RMGC's spots currently running on TV screens.

However, NCA rejected the charge for two reasons: first, the alleged spots had ceased to be released on TV before the complaint was made; secondly, RAC itself had previously endorsed the release of the incriminated spots, affirming that they did not violate the RAC code!

Conclusions, Lessons Learned

The case of RMGC gold mining project in Romania is exceptionally complex, with numerous actors and events involved and consequently with evolutions and consequences difficult to predict. This is why the evaluation of such a case is not easy and there is a danger of reaching wrong conclusions unless they are drawn with prudence.

Getting back to the initial questions, we can conclude that factual communication is an indispensable tool in crisis situations. The RMGC case clearly shows that, particularly in such circumstances, organizations cannot communicate successfully only by doing the right things. Those things must be communicated to the right publics in the right manner in order to produce the right perceptions, attitudes and behaviours.

In our opinion, this case study gives pertinent answers to the first question: how factual communication influences the communication potential of an organization in crisis. Indeed, functional messages resulted from organizational operations are not enough, especially in crises, they must be accompanied by the corresponding deliberate messages: i.e., facts communicated appropriately. Therefore, crisis management plans must include consistent communication planning, not only dealing with threats in an appropriate manner.

RMGC lost the opportunity of being proactive in the first phases, which led to the consolidation of a consistently negative public opinion. Nowadays, no matter how proactive the company is, a long-term plan of image repair is needed. Results will not appear instantly, because correction of public perceptions and attitudes takes longer than their creation.

As to the second question, concerning the correlation between factual communication and persuasion in a crisis, we must mention the difficulties of image restoration/repair after losing communication control. Ethical and moral risks can also come up if attention given to persuasion prevails over factual information. In this case, persuasion may cross often the border to manipulation and this has been one of the reasons for which RMGC opponents have constantly contested the company's communication efforts.

As for the question referring to potential dangers of factual communication in a crisis, losing credibility is another major threat.

As a final conclusion, the RMGC case illustrates how facts can be used to give more success to an image restoration/repair strategy. At the same time, by showing how costly restoration/repair efforts are, this case calls for taking into consideration proactive policies in crisis management, which can provide better value for the resources engaged.

References

Adevărul. (2009). Băsescu: "Solutions Must Be Found on Roşia Montană" (July 18, 2009), Retrieved 9 August 2011 from http://www.adevarul.ro/actualitate/politica/Trebuie-Montana-Rosia-solutii-gasite_0_81592174.html

Alburnus Maior. *About Us*. Retrieved 9 August 2011 from https://www.facebook.com/alburnusmaior/info

Atkins, Joanne (2011). Roşia Montană, a community at war with itself. *Cotidianul.ro* (26 July), retrieved 9 August 2011 from http://www.cotidianul.ro/Rosia-Montana-a-community-at-war-with-itself-152968/

Benoit, William L (1997). Image Repair Discourse and Crisis Communication. *Public Relations Review,* 23(2), 177–186.

Bowen, Shannon A (2009). Ethical Responsibility and Guidelines for Managing Issues of Risk and Risk Communication. In Heath, R L & O'Hair, H D (eds), *Handbook of Risk and Crisis Communication* (pp. 343–363). New York: Routledge.

Cabin, P & Dortier, J-F (2010). *Comunicarea: perspective actuale* (*Communication: current perspectives*), Iaşi: Polirom.

Chamber of Deputies. Roşia Montană Project. Retrieved 5 August 2001 from http://www.cdep.ro/pls/dic/site.page?id=591

Chiciudean, I & Ţoneş, V (2010). *Gestionarea crizelor de imagine* (*Image Crisis Management,* Bucharest: Comunicare.ro.

Christensen, L T, Firat, F A & Torp, S (2008). The Organization of Integrated Communications: Toward Flexible Integration. *European Journal of Marketing*, 42(3/4), 423–452.

Cohn, R (2000). *The PR Crisis Bible,* New York: Truman Talley Books, St. Martin's Press.

Coombs, W T (2007). *Ongoing Crisis Communication. Planning, Managing, and Responding* (second edition), Thousand Oaks, California: Sage Publications.

Dohotaru, A (2011). FânFest, alternate deliberative frameworks and a day of fight for Roşia Montană", *CriticAtac* (9 August). Retrieved 12 August 2011 from http://www.criticatac.ro/9237/fanfest-cadre-deliberative-alternative-si-o-zi-de-lupta-pentru-rosia-montana/

Fearn-Banks, K (2011). *Crisis Communications: A Casebook Approach*, fourth edition, New York: Routledge.

Financiarul (2010). Minister Laszlo Borbely: All Procedures Relating to Roşia Montană will be resumed. (22 June). Retrieved 15 August 2010 from http://www.financiarul.ro/2010/06/22/minister-laszlo-borbely-all-procedures-relating-to-rosia-montana-will-be-resumed/

Gabriel Resources Ltd. (2003). *Resignation Of Frank Timis As A Director* (press release, 20 May). Retrieved 8 July 2011 from http://www.gabrielresources.com/ro/PressReleases.asp?ReportID=156029&_Type=Press-Releases&_Title=Resignation-Of-Frank-Timis-As-A-Director

Greenpeace Romania. (2011). *Activity Report 2010*.

—. (2011). Only 9% of Romanians Agree to the Roşia Montană Project (press release, 25 February). Retrieved 8 August 2011 from http://www.greenpeace.org/romania/news/sondaj-independent-rom-nii-p

Haiduc, Ionel. (2003). The Roşia Montană Mining Project: Between Risks And Benefits. *Academica* (13-14), 77–80.

Heath, Robert L & O'Hair, H D (2009). The Significance of Crisis and Risk Communication. In Heath, R L & O'Hair, H D (eds). *Handbook of Risk and Crisis Communication* (pp. 5–30). New York: Routledge.

Holladay, Sherry. (2010). Are They Practicing What We Are Preaching? An Investigation of Crisis Communication Strategies in the Media Coverage of Chemical Accidents. In Coombs, W T & Holladay, S (eds). *The Handbook of Crisis Communication* (pp. 159–180). Oxford: Wiley-Blackwell.

HotNews.ro. (2009). *Adriean Videanu: the RMGC Project Will Be Included in the Program of Governance* (18 December). Retrieved 9 August 2001 from http://economie.hotnews.ro/stiri-companii-6742272-adriean-videanu-proiectul-rosia-montana-inclus-programul-guvernare.htm

—. (2011). Traian Băsescu a semnat decretul de eliberare din funcţia de consilier prezidenţial a lui Peter Eckstein-Kovacs (Traian Băsescu has signed the decree releasing Peter Eckstein-Kovacs from his duties as Presidential adviser). (12 September). Retrieved 12 September 2011 from http://www.hotnews.ro/stiri-politic-10103812-traian-basescu-semnat-decretul-eliberare-din-functia-consilier-prezidential-lui-peter-eckstein-kovacs.htm

Leinemann, Ralf & Baikalţeva, Elena. (2004). Eficienţa în relaţiile publice (Effectiveness in Public Relations). Bucharest: Comunicare.ro.

Libaert, T (2008). Comunicarea de criză (Crisis Communication). Bucharest: C.H. Beck.

Lukaszewski, J (2000a). *War Stories and Crisis Communication Strategies. A Crisis Communication Management Anthology*, vol. I, New York: The Lukaszewski Group.

—. (2000b). *Crisis Communication Planning Strategies. A Crisis Communication Management Workbook*, vol. II, New York: The Lukaszewski Group.

—. (2000c). *Media Relations Strategies During Emergencies. A Crisis Communication Management Guide*, vol. IV. New York: The Lukaszewski Group.

Lukaszewski, J E (2005). *Crisis Communication Plan Components and Models. Crisis Communication Management Readiness*, vol. III, New York: The Lukaszewski Group.

Mediafax (August 18, 2011). Băsescu: Proiectul Roşia Montană trebuie făcut, dar cu renegocierea partajării beneficiilor (Băsescu: The Roşia Montană Project must be done, but with a re-negotiation of benefits). Retrieved 18 August 2011 from http://www.mediafax.ro/politic/basescu-proiectul-rosia-montana-trebuie-facut-dar-cu-renegocierea-partajarii-beneficiilor-8630726

Ministry of Environment. *Note regarding the suspension* de iure *of the Urbanism Certificate no. 105/27.07.2007 for the Project Rosia Montana*. Retrieved 24 July 2011 from http://www.mmediu.ro/protectia_mediului/rosia_montana/pdf/NOTE_Suspension.pdf

—. (21 June 2010). Roşia Montană – Press Release. Retrieved 15 August 2011 from http://www.mmediu.ro/media/comunicate/06_Iunie_2010/21.06.2010a.htm

Mudder, Terry I. (2007). *Technical Statement Regarding Cyanide (submitted to the Government, Parliament, and People of Romania on August 13, 2007)*. Retrieved 23 July 2011 from http://en.rmgc.ro/sites/default/files/experts_opinion/Terry-Mudder-Technical-Statement.pdf

Obae, Petrişor (July 30, 2010). "Adevărul" No More Wants Advertisement from Roşia Montană. Retrieved 14 August 2011 from http://www.paginademedia.ro/2010/07/adevarul-nu-mai-vrea-publicitate-pentru-ro%C8%99ia-montana/

Ramirez, Duane E. (2010). ERP Crisis Management Through Leadership Communication. *International Journal of Management and Information Systems,* 14(1), 15–18).

Regester, Michael & Larkin, Jude. (2003). Managementul crizelor şi al situaţiilor de risc (*Crisis and Risk Management).* Bucharest: Comunicare.ro.

Reynolds, B, Hunter-Galdo, J & Sokler, L (eds). (2002). *Crisis and Emergency Risk Communication.* Atlanta: Centers for Disease Control and Prevention.

RMGC. *Benefits for the Romanian State*. Retrieved 31 July 2011 from http://en.rmgc.ro/rosia-montana-project/economy/benefits-for-the-romanian-state.html

—. *Experts' Opinion*. Retrieved 9 August 2011 from http://en.rmgc.ro/about-us/points-of-view/experts-opinion.html

—. *Mining Project: Geology*. Retrieved 20 June 2011 from http://en.rmgc.ro/rosia-montana-project/mining-project/geology.html

—. *Open Letter Addressed to the Romanian Academy* (5 November 2009). Retrieved 12 August 2011 from http://www.rmgc.ro/media/comunicate-de-presa/rmgc/scrisoare-deschisa-adresata-academiei-romane.html

—. *Quick Facts*. Retrieved 20 June 2011 from http://en.rmgc.ro/media/quick-facts.html

Romanian Academy. (2003). *Point of View of the Romanian Academy on the Mining Projec*t Roşia Montană (presented in a scientific conference on 4 March 2003). Retrieved 6 August 2011 from http://www.acad.ro/com2003/pag_com03_0304.htm

—. (2011). *Press Release on the Gold Mining Project in the Apuseni Mountains* (27 July 2011). Retrieved 7 August 2011 from http://www.acad.ro/com2011/doc/ComunicatRosiaMontana-27iulie2011.doc

Romanian Media Club. *Journalist's Deontological Code.* Retrieved 11 August 2011 from http://clubulromandepresa.ro/?page_id=322

Roşia Montană City Hall. (2011). *Open Letter Addressed to the Minister of Culture, Mr. Kelemen Hunor*. Posted on Facebook on 18 July and retrieved 9 August 2011 from http://ro-ro.facebook.com/notes/primaria-rosia-montana/scrisoare-deschis%C4%83-c%C4%83tre-domnul-ministru-kelemen-hunor/250491034966242

Websites accessed

Alburnus Maior, http://rosiamontana.org/
The Chamber of Deputies,
http://www.cdep.ro/pls/dic/site.page?den=rosiam-istoric
Gabriel Resources Ltd., http://www.gabrielresources.com/
Greenpeace Romania, http://www.greenpeace.org/romania/
Ministry of Culture, http://www.cultura.ro/
Ministry of Environment,
http://www.mmediu.ro/protectia_mediului/rosia_montana/rosia_montana.htm
Minvest Deva S.A., http://www.minvest.hd.ro/
No Dirty Gold (international campaign led by Earthworks),
http://www.nodirtygold.org/
Roşia Montană Gold Corporation, http://en.rmgc.ro/

THE IMPACT OF THE NEW TECHNOLOGIES ON THE JOURNALIST'S STATUS AND ON MASS COMMUNICATION EDUCATION

TUDOR VLAD AND LEE B. BECKER

Abstract

The broad field of journalism and mass communication has been affected in recent years by two powerful forces: the economic crisis and the new technologies. For almost two centuries, the legitimacy of the occupation of journalist had been a result of the printing and distribution of the journalists' products via mass media. The occupation of journalist had been legitimized through the media organization that the individual worked for or contributed to. Now, the new technologies have changed this situation and are challenging the status of professional journalists. This paper discusses how the emergence of new communicators, such as citizen journalists, bloggers and community journalists, has the potential to impact professionalization in the field of journalism.

In the same way that changes in the media landscape have created uncertainty for those who work in various communication occupations, those changes and their effects on the labour market have created uncertainties for journalism and mass communication education. In recent years, many US schools of journalism and mass communication have operated changes in their curricula and in the recruitment of new faculty to address the evolving needs of their graduates. The efforts of those schools, as assessed in the most recent Survey of Journalism and Mass Communication Enrollments, are presented in this paper.

INTRODUCTION

For a long time, the occupation of journalist was directly related to established media organizations. The journalists were people who worked in or contributed to newspapers, magazines, radio stations or television. The status of their occupation was legitimized by the final product, which was the result of the collaboration between newsroom, business departments and channels of distribution.

The new communication technologies and the turmoil in the traditional media industry have raised questions about the future of the occupation of journalism. Graduates of journalism and mass communication programs in the United States were confronted with a tough job market at the end of the last decade. The drop in 2008 in the level of full-time employment six to eight months after graduation – from 70.2% of graduates in 2007 to 60.4% in 2008 – was the largest change recorded in the 23 years that the same methodology had been used to track these statistics (Becker et al., 2009). The turmoil was not limited to the entry-level segment of the job market. An estimated 5900 full-time jobs were cut in US newspaper newsrooms in both 2008 and 2009 (Project for Excellence in Journalism, 2009, 2010). Television, radio and news magazines also trimmed their staffs, often by eliminating positions at the top.

New Technology's Impact on Mass Communication Education

Many of those journalists and of more recent journalism graduates tried to use their communication skills by setting up their own web operations or joining others in doing the same. If successful, these activities mean that the occupation of journalism has a different meaning and does not necessarily suggest or imply a relationship with established media companies.

In addition, the journalists employed by established media and those who have gone out on their own have found themselves in competition with other groups of individuals, often labelled "citizen" journalists (Keen, 2007); Project for Excellence in Journalism, 2009, 2010), "community journalists" or "bloggers". Based on the model of journalists' professional associations, new organizations such as Media Bloggers Association and the National Association of Citizen Journalists were created in the United States to protect the rights of their members and to provide them with training materials.

All this process suggests a transformation and deprofessionalization of the journalistic occupation itself (Nossek, 2009). Given the collapse of the economic model of the old journalistic organizations and the emergence of other types of mass communication outlets that are managed by people with no formal journalism education, it is even possible to question whether journalism will remain an occupation. Chris Anderson, editor in chief of *Wired* magazine, speculated that journalism may simply become a hobby (Hornig, 2009).

The turmoil has affected other communication occupations as well. The easy access of amateurs to the tools of graphic design, databases needed for sales, and the distribution capabilities of the web also mean that everyone can become an advertising or public relations professional.

In the same way that changes in the media landscape have created uncertainty for those who work in various communication occupations, those changes and their effects on the labour market have created uncertainties for journalism and mass communication education. For a long time, the curriculum in journalism and mass communication programmes in the United States – which are heavily oriented toward undergraduate education – followed the industry. The research conducted in most of these programmes was based on assessments and evaluations of various segments or operations within the media industry. The expectations of the industry managers from these programmes were that they produce graduates who would become parts of the system, and not to lead the industry toward its future, by innovation or revolution. As a result, journalism and mass communication education reflects the crisis and the uncertainty of the industry: some schools are trying to adjust their curricula, others are trying to change them dramatically, while others do nothing. Although most of the observations in this paper are about communication occupations and educational institutions in one country, namely the United States, the issues are likely to generalize to other settings. While all media systems have their unique characteristics, as the work of Hallin and Mancini (2004) shows, they also have common characteristics. The same is probably true about educational institutions (Froehlich & Holtz-Bacha, 2003).

In the sociology of work literature, an occupation is defined as a social role played by adult members of society that directly and indirectly yields social and financial consequences (Hall, 1994). Occupations frequently have been compared and sometimes confused with an ideal type, a profession. In Wilensky's (1964) classic characterization, occupations go through four key, defining steps in the process of becoming a profession. First, the occupation establishes training schools for admission. Second, the occupation forms professional associations. Next, it attempts to regulate the practice of the profession through legal protection. Finally, it adopts a formal code of ethics. In addition, professions have been viewed as occupations with a special service orientation toward society. The occupation of journalist has never reached the status of profession, either for economic reasons (lack of need of extended education to produce people who can report, write or edit) or for ideological reasons (freedom of speech). Some media experts have argued that this current phase in the evolution of mass media might be favourable for this transition from journalism as an occupation toward journalism as profession, but the reality seems to contradict this view.

Freidson's (1994) concept of a market shelter has been very important in the discussion of professions. Professions gain and then maintain control in the economic marketplace by creating such a shelter, which keeps out competitors and controls who qualifies for the profession. Once a market shelter is in place, professionals control both the supply and the demand of workers and the work they do. The control over qualification is based on presumed skills needed for practice in the profession, which include objectivity or neutrality. This is one reason why professional journalists disregard the work of citizen journalists: because they are engaged, that is, have a point of view. Citizen journalists are often drawn from the ranks of citizen activists, and it is these more activist journalists that the journalists being thrown out of traditional media organizations confront. It should not be so surprising that the traditional journalist, clinging to traditional notions of professionalism, is not enamoured with the competition.

One of the problems with market shelters, as Timmermans (2008) argued, is that they can stifle innovation. The professionals thus find it difficult to adapt to a changing technological or economic landscape while being protected but also restricted by the shelter. Implicit in this notion is the recognition that occupations can deprofessionalize over time as well as professionalize.

Deuze (2007), in his study of media work in the era of the Internet, argued that responsibility has increasingly shifted from the organization to the individual. Cultural production employers and managers stress the importance of enterprise as an individual outcome, rather than as an organizational one. Work is much more flexible than in the past, he argues.

What seems clear is that occupations have confronted the current technological changes in work at different stages of professional development and are likely to respond to those changes in different ways. Journalism and the communication occupations have struggled to make the case that their practices were based on unique skills sets acquired through their education and training. Journalists have argued that they know news when they see it because of their skills. Advertising and other promotional practitioners have argued that they could create messages based on artistic skills they possessed and honed. The creative producer could say she or he knew good art. But this also suggests that communication experts doubt the abilities of their sources and audiences. Many journalists, according to McQuail (1997) feel that the audience members lack the skills and qualifications needed to judge their work. The market shelter, with its emphasis on the characteristics and consequences of news, has isolated the professionals from their sources and the audience.

The members of the traditional occupation of journalists claim that they possess a set of skills that require specific training and are recognized through credentials. Education thus becomes an essential prerequisite for entry into occupations that are labelled as professions, and occupations that are seeking to become professions give prominence to educational training. The routines that produce news are what journalists learn in their university studies, where classrooms are often designed to mimic the real world environment of broadcast and print organizations. The students are taught how to work a beat, how to identify sources, and how to define what is news. This latter is what comes closest to the "esoteric" knowledge required of a profession, and it helps explain why journalists treat citizens with less respect than official sources, who are expected to have a better sense of what news is. University programmes in journalism and mass communication play an important role in discussions about the communications occupations and their efforts at professionalization (Becker, Fruit & Caudill, 1987; Froehlich & Holtz-Bacha, 2003).

In recent years, US schools of journalism and mass communication have shown signs of experimentation in their courses, spurred by turbulence and change in the media industries and professions, but still many programmes are based on traditional structures and practices. A 2005 study showed that changes in the news industry such as "convergence" of media platforms were much on the minds of school administrators and faculty, but movement toward adapting knowledge areas and curricular tracks was slow and cautious. Change tended to derive from individual faculty initiative rather than from formal institutional shift (Lowrey, Daniels & Becker, 2005). According to a 2009 survey of US programmes, most maintain traditional "silo" structures, separating print journalism from telecom from advertising/public relations (Becker, Vlad & Desnoes, 2010).

Reluctance to change curricula is due to a variety of factors across different levels of analysis. Preferences of unit administrators may play a role, as may faculty's focus on research rather than on fit between undergraduate curricula and changing media. Organizational factors such as unit size and level of unit resources likely have an impact. A survey of journalism and mass communication programs showed that academic departments' operating budgets had dipped (Becker, Vlad & Desnoes, 2010). And influential alumni tied to specialized industries may encourage persistence of differentiated tracks.

The most recent survey of journalism and mass communication enrolments (Vlad et al., 2011) showed that a vast majority of the programme reported engaging in a number of strategies to update the digital media skills of their faculties, from sending them on training programmes to hiring permanent and adjunct professors with those skills. Only 3.6% reporting doing nothing in this regard (Chart 1).

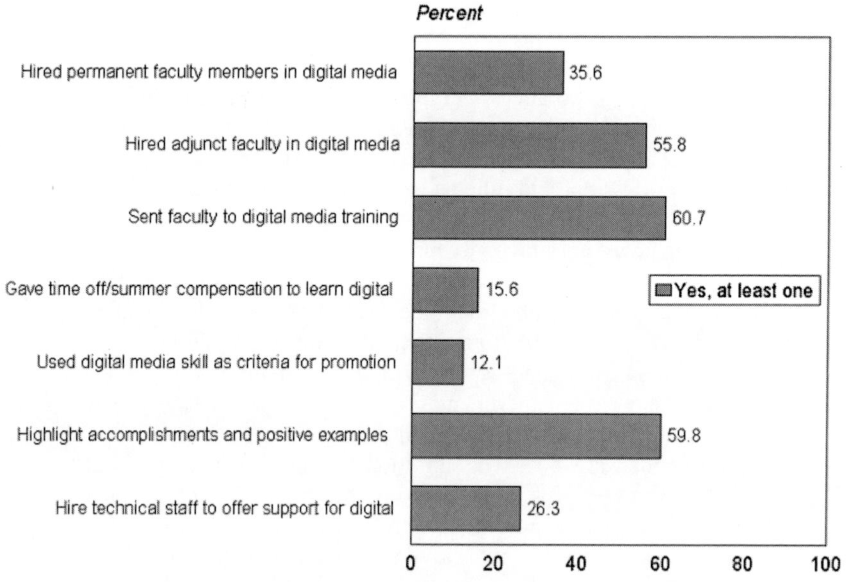

Fig 27-1. Personnel strategies for digital media

More than eight in 10 of the administrators said that they made changes in their curricula (Chart 2). One in 10 had added a digital course or even emphasize, and the same ratio had added multimedia courses (Chart 3).

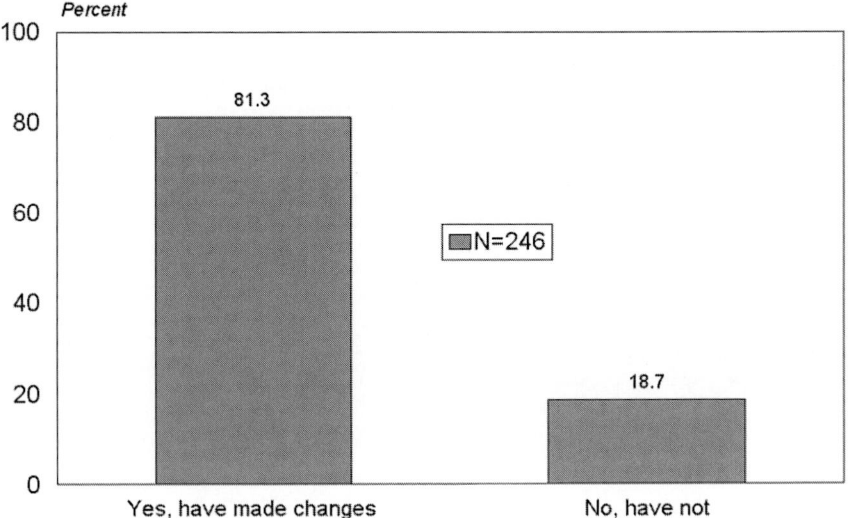

Fig 27-2. Made changes in the curriculum

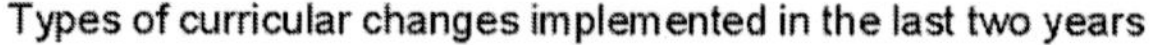

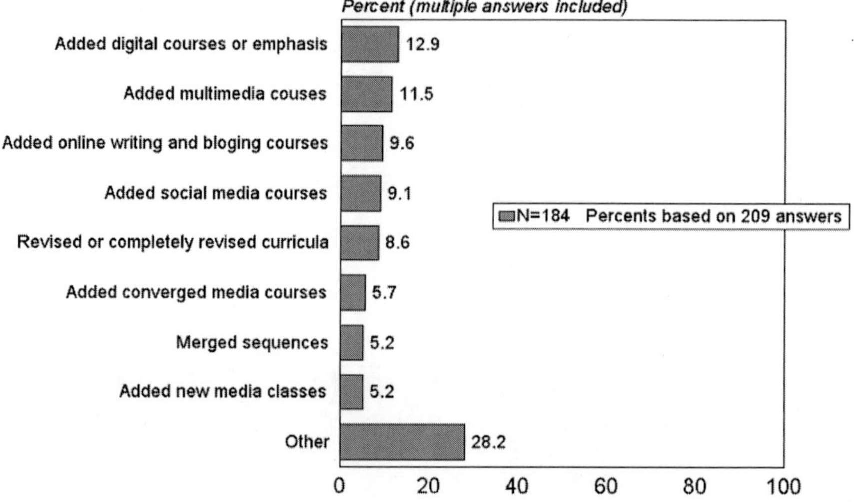

Fig 27-3. Changes made in the curriculum

Many programmes, but not all, have incorporated web layout and design, writing, reporting and editing for the web and using audio and video for the web in their curricula (Charts 4 & 5).

Becker (2008) has suggested a number of possible activities that journalism and mass communication programs should consider undertaking in this new occupational environment. One important avenue is credentialing. Journalism and mass communication programs might put more emphasis on degrees and titles, and create easy verification of these degrees via Internet link and in easily accessible data bases.

In their report of the Carnegie-Knight Initiative of the future of journalism education, Donsbach and Fiedler (2008) suggested that stronger distinctions should be made between the American first degree, the bachelor's degree, and the second, the master's degree.

Research in the journalism and mass communication academic environment might focus more on anticipating how the industry will evolve and thus contributing more to the non-academic occupational world.

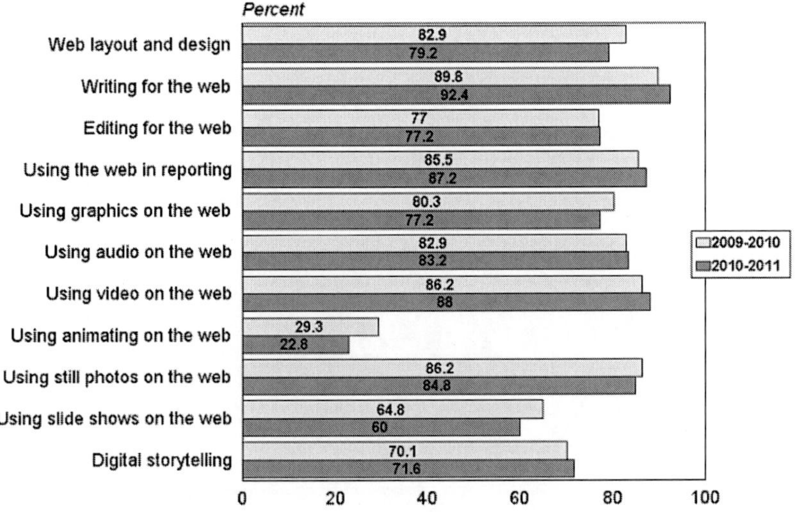

Fig 27-4. Skills taught in curricula I

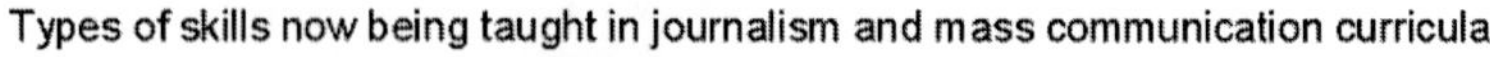

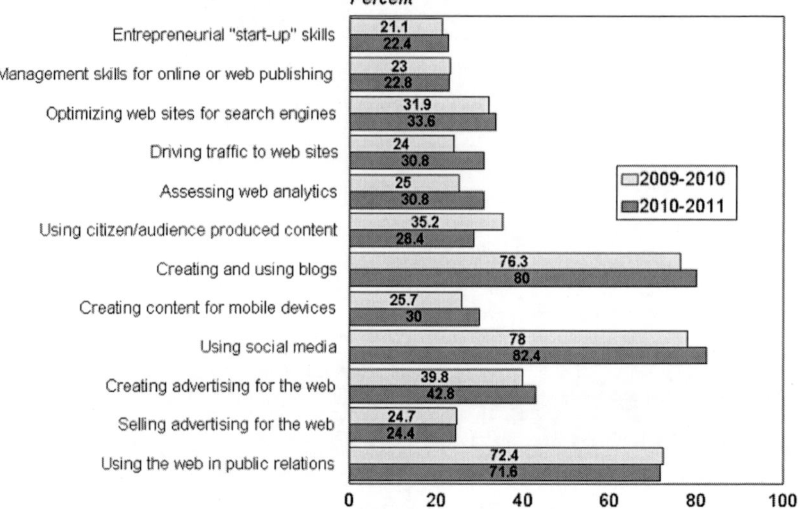

Fig 27-5. Skills taught in curricula II

The communication curricula will need to include more courses on the skills of entrepreneurial operation. All communicators are going to need to know how to survive as small businesses. They are going to need to know the skills to manoeuvre in a very competitive environment in which their own skill sets will be challenged and mimicked by others. Here the public relations and advertising market experience is likely to be particularly informative.

In the past, journalists have not worried much about the audience for their products. They have relied on the organization where they did their work to assemble the audience. Without the organization, the journalists are going to need to understand how to create and manage an audience. Here, too, public relations and advertising have an advantage. They have not had ready access to an audience for their messages in the past. They already have a heightened sensitivity to audiences and the techniques for gaining access to them.

Conclusion

Journalism and mass communication programmes in the United States have considered journalism to be their core, since it is from that journalism heart that the curricula in public relations and, to a lesser extent, advertising have grown. It might well be the case that the academic enterprise needs to examine more fully the experiences of those who have been working in other communication areas and make some of those experiences the centrepiece of curricular reform and certification.

If all communication occupations are becoming more individualized, in at least some sense more deprofessionalized, and more open to amateurs, those parts of the field, specifically public relations, with more experience in such an environment could provide guidance for the future. The nature of communication work is changing dramatically, raising serious questions about the nature of the communication occupations themselves. The work in the future will be less likely to be carried out in large organizational settings. It will be more likely to be carried out in competition with amateurs, that is, individuals without any specialized training in the occupations.

In the current environment, where everyone can easily acquire and use the technical skills, communication education either helps to provide the knowledge skills for differentiation of the professional from the amateur, or it will contribute to the demise of the communication occupations as they exist today.

References

Becker, L B (2008). The Most Pressing Challenge for Journalism and Mass Communication Education. In A C Osborne (ed.), *The Future of Journalism and Mass Communication Education* (pp. 78–79), Baton Rouge, LA: LSU Manship School of Journalism.

Becker, L B, Fruit, J W & Caudill, S L (1987). *The Training and Hiring of Journalists*, Norwood, NJ: ABLEX.

Becker, L B, Vlad, T, Olin, D, Hanisak, S & Wilcox, D (2009). *2008 Annual Survey of Journalism & Mass Communication Graduates.* Retrieved 12 July 2009 from http://www.grady.uga.edu/annualsurveys/Graduate_Survey/Graduate_2008/Grad2008Fullcolor.pdf

Becker, L B, Vlad, T & Desnoes, P (2010). Enrollments Decline Slightly and the Student Body Becomes More Diverse. *Journalism and Mass Communication Educator,* 65, 224–249.

Deuze, M (2007). *Mediawork,* Cambridge: Polity Press.

Donsbach, W, & Fiedler, T (2008). *Journalism School Curriculum Enrichment*, Harvard University.

Freidson, E (1994). *Professionalism Reborn*, Chicago: University of Chicago Press.

Froehlich, R, & Holtz-Bacha, C (eds) (2003). *Journalism Education in Europe and North America.* Cresskill, NJ: Hampton Press.

Hall, R H (1994). *Sociology of work*, Thousand Oaks, CA: Pine Forge Press.

Hallin, D C, & Mancini, P (2004). *Comparing Media Systems*, Cambridge: Cambridge University Press.

Hornig, F (2009). Who Needs Newspapers when you have Twitter?" *Wired* (28 July). Retrieved 29 July 2009, from www.salon.con/new/feature/2009/07/28/wired/print.html

Keen, A (2007). *The Cult of the Amateur*. New York: Random House.

Lowrey, W, Daniels, G & Becker, L B (2005). Predictors of Convergence Curricula in Journalism and Mass Communication Programs. *Journalism and Mass Communication Educator* 60, 32–46.

McQuail, D (1997). *Audience Analysis*, Thousand Oaks, CA: Sage Publications.

Nossek, H (2009). On the Future of Journalism as a Professional Practice and the Case of Journalism in Israel. *Journalism*, 10(3), 358–361.

Project for Excellence in Journalism (2009). *The State of the News Media 2009.* Pew Project for Excellence in Journalism. Retrieved 12 August 2009 from http://www.stateofthemedia.org/2009/index.htm

—. (2010). *The State of the News Media 2010.* Pew Project for Excellence in Journalism. Retrieved 15 June 2010 from http://www.stateofthemedia.org/2010/

Timmermans, S (2008). Professions and their Work: Do Market Shelters Protect Professional Interests? *Work and Occupations,* 35(2), 164–188.

Vlad, T, Becker, L B, Kazragis, W, Toledo, C, & Desnoes, P (2011) 2010 annual survey of journalism & mass communication enrollments. Retrieved 24 August 2011 from http://www.grady.uga.edu/annualsurveys/Enrollment_Survey/Enrollment_2010/Enrollment_Report_2010_color.pdf

Wilensky, H (1964). The Professionalization of Everyone? *American Journal of Sociology*, 70(2), 137–158.

LES CONTOURS D'UNE COMMUNAUTE IMAGINEE : LE THEME-EVENEMENT EUROPE A L'INTERIEUR DES JOURNAUX TELEVISES FRANÇAIS (1951–2009)

JEAN-CLAUDE SOULAGES

Résumé

L'hypothèse qui sous-tend notre démarche postule que l'examen sur une longue période d'un genre informatif dans son régime de croisière, c'est-à-dire celui que présentent quotidiennement les journaux télévisés de différentes chaînes nationales traitant d'un même thème-événement, est à même de constituer un révélateur productif quant aux variations concernant les pratiques discursives informatives des acteurs médiatiques mais aussi, à travers les modalités de hiérarchisation et de traitement éditorial de ce dernier, d'offrir le reflet tangible des imaginaires qui les sous-tendent. Cette démarche prend appui sur deux postulats théoriques, le premier relatif au processus d'*agenda setting* tel que l'ont défini Mc Comb et Shaw (1972) et le second relatif aux modes de production de la réalité sociale décrits par Eliseo Veron (1981). Ces deux approches confirment le statut de l'actualité événementielle telle qu'elle s'impose dans nos sociétés médiatisées performée par l'action et les interactions continues de la sphère médiatique. Elles corroborent le constat que dressait déjà Pierre Nora (1972), selon lequel les sources de l'Histoire sont désormais essentiellement issues de ce type de constructions. Dès lors, cette médiation qui a toujours existé à travers l'archive, nous pousse à interroger la nature de celle que les médias télévisés nous proposent aujourd'hui. Car, en pratiquant un travail de médiatisation, les acteurs du champ journalistique conduisent des opérations plus ou moins conscientes de consolidation ou bien d'imposition d'un certain nombre de valeurs, croyances, points de vue qui visent à encadrer les appartenances identitaires ou symboliques des communautés de public.

Dès lors, les médias ne doivent plus être considérés seulement comme des médiateurs ou de simples messagers. Ils assurent d'autres fonctions et entre autres, celle d'élaborer les archives du temps présent et donc du regard porté par les hommes sur l'univers qui les entoure. Si les interfaces médiatiques nous transmettent continûment des informations sur l'actualité événementielle du monde, ce monde qu'elles exhibent devient par leur intermédiaire imaginairement le nôtre. Comme nous le rappelle Bernard Stiegler (1994) à la suite de Leroy Gourhan, les objets techniques, sont toujours à considérer comme des « monuments » au moyen desquels quelque chose de la mémoire de l'humanité a été déposé et enregistré.

Mots-clés : journaux télévisés, champ journalistique, thématique Europe

La thématique Europe à l'intérieur des journaux télévisés français (1951–2009)

Il en va ainsi des archives de la télévision. L'accès à ces matériaux mémoriels constitue donc une opportunité et une aide précieuse dans le champ de la recherche. Surtout lorsque cette recherche porte sur la télévision française. Car, avec la création de l'Inathèque de France, une institution unique au monde, les bases documentaires professionnelles de l'Institut National de l'Audiovisuel, constituées à partir du travail d'indexation systématique des documents audiovisuels depuis 1949 sont enfin accessibles aux chercheurs. Pour ce faire, elles ont été reformatées au cœur de la Bibliothèque de France en vue de recherches de type scientifique. Il nous est ainsi possible d'y explorer la mémoire télévisuelle de notre collectivité sur plus de soixante années et d'en tirer un certain nombre de constats. Il va de soi qu'il ne s'agit en aucun cas d'un accès immédiat et transparent à l'actualité mais de l'accès à un document archivé et indexé par les services de documentation de l'Ina, document qui lui-même renvoie au regard journalistique porté sur un événement à un moment t de l'histoire nationale. Attentif à ce cadre de recherche, le chercheur doit donc toujours resté vigilant tant dans son approche méthodologique que quant à ses hypothèses interprétatives.

Un thème événement comme la question de la construction européenne, aujourd'hui plus que jamais sous les feux de l'actualité, se prête d'évidence à ce type d'examen. En effet, on peut faire l'hypothèse qu'il a connu différents types de déclinaisons ainsi que des traitements médiatiques spécifiques au cours des dernières décennies. Cette approche, qui prend appui sur les bases documentaires de l'Inathèque à travers différentes démarches méthodologiques éprouvées, innove toutefois par un nouveau mode d'instrumentation. En effet, l'évolution des outils statistiques mis à la disposition des chercheurs et entre autres de Mediacorpus [1], permet désormais d'importer et de traiter de façon statistique l'ensemble des descripteurs affectés aux différents reportages par les documentalistes de l'INA dans leurs fiches documentaires. L'interrogation a donc porté sur la recension des sujets traitant cette question depuis 1951 à travers le croisement de descripteurs précis renvoyant à la notion de communauté européenne (Europe, politique étrangère, CEE, UE, etc…). A l'issue de cette opération, la base de données crée rassemble 28 024 sujets toutes chaînes confondues indexés à travers 130 000 descripteurs portant sur le thème-événement Europe (voir exemples de fiches en annexe 1, 2, 3).

Cette démarche se décompose en deux moments d'analyse :

— un premier purement quantitatif basé sur la recension du volume de sujets traitant de la question européenne dans les différentes éditions des journaux français, c'est-à-dire le relevé de la fréquence et de la distribution de ces occurrences sur une période très étendue (1951–2009).

— la seconde démarche vise à prendre en compte les données relatives aux contenus événementiels de ces programmes d'information en les regroupant autour de différentes thématiques repérées et suivies dans le flux des quelques 28 024 sujets recensés durant cette période à travers des descripteurs secondaires rémanents (agriculture, économie, sidérurgie, etc.). Au moyen d'un traitement automatisé des fiches documentaires et du visionnement d'échantillons de sujets, il devient alors possible de percevoir l'évolution sémantique de la couverture de la thématique par les différentes chaines françaises.

L'ÉTUDE QUANTITATIVE

Au vu des résultats obtenus, la couverture de la thématique Europe obéit à une montée en charge progressive. Cette couverture devient réellement significative (d'un point de vue statistique et thématique) à partir de l'année 1972. Le tableau ci-dessus synthétise la distribution des différents sujets de 1972 à 2009.

---

[1] Ces outils ont été développés lors de différentes études conduites par le Centre d'Analyse du Discours (CAD) dès 1990 sur le conflit en ex-Yougoslavie et celle menée dans le cadre des projets ALFA de la CEE, portant sur la médiatisation de la pandémie de SIDA regroupant différents pays latins (Argentine, Brésil, Portugal, Espagne, France).

Années	Nombre de sujets	Actualité européenne
1972	58	
1973	45	
1974	51	
1975	44	
1976	60	
1977	112	
1978	199	
1979	**322**	**Élections européennes**
1980	286	
1981	265	
1982	207	
1983	251	
1984	**578**	**Élections européennes**
1985	261	
1986	292	
1987	408	
1988	487	
1989	**1097**	**Élections européennes**
1990	603	
1991	762	
1992	1661	Référendum sur le traité de Maastricht.
1993	1320	
1994	**1142**	**Élections européennes.**
1995	531	
1996	884	
1997	902	
1998	928	
1999	**1473**	**Élections européennes.**
2000	926	
2001	1174	
2002	1400	
2003	1514	
2004	**1502**	**Élections européennes.**
2005	1966	**Référendum sur le traité constitutionnel**
2006	840	
2007	889	

2008	1148	
2009	**1436**	**Élections européennes.**
Total.	28024	

Fig 28-1: La couverture du thème-événement toutes chaînes confondues en nombre de sujets

La genèse du thème-événement ; une Europe sans visage

La période précédente 1951/1971 (qui n'apparaît pas ici dans le tableau) est marquée par la mise en place progressive du réseau d'information télévisée national tel que nous le connaissons aujourd'hui. Si l'on exclut la permanence des compétitions sportives entre les pays du vieux continent, l'intrusion d'une thématique liée à la question européenne demeure encore tout à fait marginale dans l'agenda des premiers journaux télévisés français. Du reste lorsqu'elle y apparaît, cette dernière demeure systématiquement rattachée aux péripéties de l'actualité politique nationale[2]. De façon symptomatique, dans de nombreux sujets cohabitent les descripteurs France et Europe ou bien apparaît lors du travail d'indexation des documentaristes le descripteur très englobant « politique étrangère ». Cet effet de relégation caractéristique de ces deux décennies est renforcé par la couverture télévisuelle de ce que l'on pourrait appeler des " cérémonies du pouvoir " qui donnent lieu à de brèves relations académiques purement factuelles qui interviennent lors de conférences de presse des chefs d'état français, De Gaulle, Pompidou ou lors de rencontres avec leurs homologues européens en France (voir annexe 1). Dans ces premières éditions des journaux télévisés, l'Europe apparaît comme un territoire extérieur et une instance éloignée voire séparée de la collectivité nationale, cantonnée à la seule incarnation des représentants institutionnels des Etats nations ; une Europe sans peuple, sans économie, sans visage, en marge de l'actualité nationale.

Une montée en charge discontinue

A cette entrée en matière succède une montée en puissance continue de la thématique à partir de 1972 ; de 58 sujets on passe à plus de 1000 en 2001. L'examen attentif de cette lente progression met en évidence le

[2] Tout au long de cette période les descripteurs Europe (Europe, CEE, marché commun, etc.) sont systématiquement associés à ceux relatifs à l'actualité franco-française.

caractère tout à fait discontinu de cette tendance. Caractère discontinu mais non aléatoire. En effet, si les années correspondant aux élections européennes attestent d'une focalisation significative sur la question européenne, on peut souligner que chacun de ses pics (1979, 1984, 1989, 1994, 1999, 2004, 2009) est suivi d'une montée en charge qui se maintient à un nouveau régime de croisière nettement plus élevé que dans les années qui précèdent. À l'année 1979 succède un régime de plus de 200 sujets, l'année 1984 de 400 sujets, l'année 1989 de plus de 600 sujets, l'année 1994 de 800 sujets, 1999 de 1000 sujets. Le maximum étant atteint en 1992 (1661 sujets) lors de la ratification du traité de Maastricht et en 2005 du référendum sur le traité constitutionnel (1966 sujets).

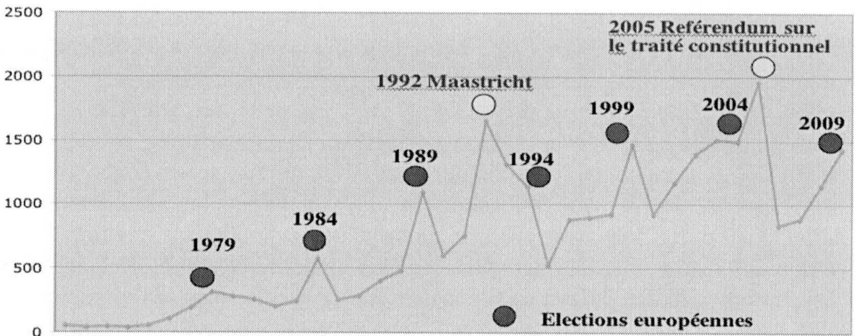

Fig 28-2 : La montée en charge du thème-événement 1972–2009.

Ainsi l'agenda institutionnel des élections européennes, loin de refléter une simple couverture conventionnelle et factuelle de l'actualité européenne, semble avoir été directement à l'origine, à travers la constitution de ces différents paliers dans la couverture médiatique, d'une dynamique décisive pour le regard médiatique porté sur la question. Contrairement au pensum qui veut que ce type d'élections ait très peu d'impact sur la communauté nationale, son caractère itératif dans l'actualité télévisée semble avoir servi, pour les instances informatives, d'accélérateur et de déclencheur déterminants débouchant sur un élargissement du spectre informatif et une mobilisation accrue concernant ce nouveau domaine événementiel.

UNE COUVERTURE INÉGALEMENT RÉPARTIE

La distribution de la couverture télévisuelle peut être observée de façon relativement fine et fiable depuis 1995 (grâce à la recension exhaustive des documents télévisuels de l'ensemble des chaînes françaises depuis la création de l'Inathèque). Si cette montée en charge progressive apparaît comme un dénominateur commun à toutes les chaines, un examen attentif met en évidence un traitement tout à fait inégal suivant les différentes rédactions nationales. On constate immédiatement la spécificité du traitement informatif de la chaîne franco-allemande Arte dont le point de vue, loin de se cantonner à un simple procédé de regard croisé sur deux communautés nationales, affiche une sensibilisation explicite et continue à cette question. On peut remarquer le moindre intérêt manifesté par TF1 (chaîne commerciale) à l'égard de cette thématique alors que les chaînes de service public la devancent, France 2 systématiquement, France 3 de façon épisodique.

Années.	**ARTE**	**Canal +**	**France 2**	**France 3**	**M6**	**TF1**
1995	128	17	103	80	26	86
1996	247	41	232	179	96	156
1997	284	45	184	154	63	176
1998	239	44	214	77	65	209
1999	**200**	**64**	**309**	**248**	**99**	**291**
2000	308	57	220	163	47	212
2001	408	51	226	190	41	303
2002	350	60	265	193	47	334
2003	417	82	325	272	56	301
2004	**330**	**70**	**298**	**172**	**63**	**249**
2005	369	128	507	301	119	523
2006	258	43	167	123	34	189
2007	251	71	190	142	36	184
2008	315	107	270	170	67	216
2009	**282**	**136**	**212**	**172**	**49**	**167**
Total	4386	1016	3722	2636	908	3596

Fig 28-3 : La couverture du thème-événement par les chaines françaises en nombre de sujets

ÉLÉMENTS D'UNE CARTOGRAPHIE SÉMANTIQUE DE LA QUESTION EUROPÉENNE À L'INTÉRIEUR DU FLUX INFORMATIF TÉLÉVISUEL NATIONAL

Cette approche tout à fait expérimentale repose comme cela a été évoqué plus haut sur le traitement statistique des descripteurs affectés aux différents sujets par les services de l'INA. Ce traitement statistique nous a permis d'isoler des sous-thématiques ou « domaines scéniques » ainsi que les procédés récurrents dans le traitement informatif des chaînes françaises. Ce recours à des bases documentaires déjà constituées ne peut en aucun tenir lieu du travail de visionnement et d'indexation original (irréalisable techniquement) de plus de 600 heures de programmes. Mais, les données recueillies par l'INA, issues d'un même genre (le journal télévisé), présentent, pour ce qui concerne ces sujets essentiellement factuels liés à l'actualité, une homogénéité et une stabilité certaine. Chacune des fiches documentaires associées à un reportage contient des données techniques (durée, réseau, producteurs, nom des locuteurs, etc.), un bref résumé en texte libre et de 5 à 10 descripteurs renvoyant à un vaste thésaurus remis à jour tous les 6 mois (voir annexes).

Nous avons retenu pour la présentation synthétique de ces résultats, la périodisation qui s'est dégagée de la première étape purement quantitative de ce travail, c'est-à-dire l'existence des différents paliers observés consécutifs aux différentes échéances électorales européennes.

Les années 1972–1979 ; l'autonomisation du thème-évènement

L'année 1972 est marquée par une autonomisation manifeste du domaine européen qui n'est plus traité désormais comme un simple enjeu politicien purement franco-français ou une rubrique rattachée à la politique étrangère mais est doté d'une indépendance par rapport à l'actualité nationale ou internationale et apparaît ainsi dans une dimension transnationale et tout à fait autonome. Contrairement à la période précédente, purement cérémonielle et formelle, la relation de la scène télévisuelle européenne est caractérisée par une forte personnalisation de ses différents protagonistes. À travers leur nomination réitérée, de véritables " personnages " de l'actualité européenne entrent en scène, chefs d'état, ministre des affaires étrangères ou européennes[3], ballet

[3] Parmi les personnalités les plus citées : Harold Wilson, Edward Heath, Léo Tindemans, Gaston Thorn, Roy Jenkins, Helmut Schmidt, Simone Veil, Olivier Stirn, etc.

diplomatique qui va de pair avec une sorte de ratification de la communauté de destin des états nationaux fondateurs. On peut souligner, du point de vue du traitement médiatique, l'institutionnalisation progressive de rubriques spécialisées consacrées exclusivement aux questions européennes, assurées désormais par des journalistes spécialistes du domaine. Le regard médiatique se porte sur la constitution d'un « marché commun », appréhendé essentiellement dans sa dimension économique et législative ; les sous thématiques récurrentes sont liées aux problèmes de l'agriculture et de l'industrie lourde. Parallèlement, la question de l'adhésion de nouveaux membres entraîne une focalisation sur certains pays s'accompagnant de multiples débats agitant l'actualité nationale ; parmi ces états, les plus cités sont la Grande Bretagne, l'Espagne, le Portugal, la Grèce.

Les années 1980–1984 ; l'intégration dans une économie supranationale

Aux sous-thématiques de la période précédente viennent se greffer progressivement, celle de la pêche, de la viticulture mais aussi celle de la sécurité, du terrorisme. Contrairement à la période précédente qui proposait un simple inventaire prospectif et factuel des échéances de l'union, cette période est marquée par la couverture récurrente de conflits sociaux dont la nature apparaît nettement franco-européenne (la viticulture, la pêche, la sidérurgie, les chantiers navals, etc.). Ces sujets opposent régulièrement la dynamique législative et formelle des instances européennes aux réactions virulentes de groupes sociaux dont les conditions économiques et sociales se trouvent mises en cause. Cet antagonisme atteint même les sommets de l'État lors de la remise en question de la politique socialiste du second gouvernement Mitterrand (l'évocation d'une sortie possible du serpent monétaire). Cette silhouette d'un pouvoir morcelé, lointain et sans visage, responsable et acteur dans certaines évolutions subies par certains secteurs de l'économie nationale, est renforcée par un nouveau type de traitement médiatique tout à fait symptomatique, celui entourant les « conférences aux sommets » qui deviennent des cérémonies rituelles donnant lieu à de multiples compte rendus conséquents étalés sur plusieurs jours ; Maastricht 1981, Bruxelles 1982, Athènes 1983. Innervant de multiples sujets socio-économiques, les discours sur l'économie française intègrent quasi systématiquement désormais cet horizon européen.

Les années 1985–1989 ; l'Europe de la régulation

La période est marquée essentiellement par la mise en avant de l'élargissement des relations économiques tout azimut, de l'Europe avec les USA, le Japon, etc. L'apparition de grands programmes de coopération scientifique et technique marque également la période. La dénomination " marché commun " est délaissée au profit de celle " d'union monétaire, économique ou douanière ". L'actualité européenne se confond de plus en plus avec des séries de réunions techniques interministérielles, bi ou multilatérales. Progressivement l'Europe est de plus en plus assimilée à l'image de centres de décision extranationaux, Bruxelles ou plus rarement le Parlement Européen, organes périphériques traversés par des alliances ou des oppositions supranationales (le couple franco-allemand, l'Europe du Sud, du Nord, etc.). Parallèlement, dans les discours, la dominante économique a pris le pas sur la dimension historico-symbolique entourant le projet d'édification européenne. La production régulière de textes législatifs et de directives multiples rejaillit sur des domaines événementiels de plus en plus diversifiés. De nouvelles thématiques apparaissent, l'environnement, les transports, l'énergie dont les échéances et les enjeux s'inscrivent d'emblée dans une dimension supranationale.

Les années 1990–1994 ; vers une identité supranationale

L'orientation thématique jusque là cantonnée aux domaines économique et social s'élargit à la politique monétaire ainsi qu'aux affaires diplomatiques consécutives aux conflits dans le Golfe et dans les Balkans. Confrontée à la chute du bloc soviétique et à la montée en puissance d'un " nouvel ordre mondial ", la question européenne est agitée durant cette période par des préoccupations géopolitiques et stratégiques qui lui confèrent une authentique dimension planétaire qu'elle ne présentait pas jusqu'alors. Mais cette nouvelle identité prospective est fragilisée par les atermoiements et les nombreuses tergiversations des pouvoirs décisionnaires que les acteurs médiatiques ne se privent pas de mettre en exergue. Les discussions autour de la ratification du traité de Maastricht constituent un seuil dans la médiatisation des échéances européennes et une sorte de point de rupture susceptible de conduire à une impasse et à un arrêt du processus de construction. C'est sans aucun doute, cette période conflictuelle qui représente, dans les nombreuses relations des instances médiatiques, un pas décisif vers le processus d'édification de l'union européenne. De toute évidence, que cela soit de façon velléitaire le plus souvent ou sous le mode de la déploration, l'entité européenne a acquis son autonomie symbolique et une consistance supranationale, en se détachant laborieusement des particularismes nationaux.

Les années 1995–2001 ; vers une identité européenne

Cette période se caractérise par de nombreuses interrogations d'ordre économique et monétaire. Une nouvelle thématique transversale s'immisce dans le débat franco-européen et participe le plus souvent à en brouiller les cartes ; celle liée à la mondialisation de l'économie. De nouvelles thématiques voient le jour, celle de la monnaie unique, de l'euro, des droits de l'homme, de l'exception culturelle, de l'immigration, de l'élargissement aux pays de l'ex-bloc de l'Est, etc.

Toutefois, durant cette période, un nouveau type de traitement s'affirme dans les pratiques journalistiques, déjà en germe dans la période précédente. De nombreux sujets, intégrant la dimension européenne sont diffusés, déconnectés de tout agenda politique ou institutionnel référables aux instances européennes ou nationales. Ce sont essentiellement des sujets de société ou bien traitant de la vie quotidienne, des modes de vie, des habitus sociaux, de l'organisation du travail ou des transports, etc. qui donnent lieu à une présentation systématiquement contrastive. Dans cette nouvelle forme de reportage, les pratiques sociales ou économiques ou bien les tranches de vie des acteurs sociaux nationaux sont documentées de façon délibérée à la lumière d'un point de vue synoptique qui les confrontent à celles de leurs homologues européens (voir annexe 2 et 3). Désormais, le regard porté sur l'actualité nationale par les rédactions nationales s'inscrit délibérément dans un horizon européen.

Les années 2001–2005 ; interrogations et débats

Ces années se caractérisent par une prédominance d'une vision géopolitique et l'esquisse d'un nouvel ordre mondial, toutefois le 11 septembre, la guerre en Afghanistan et en Irak, sont des événements dans lesquels l'Europe affiche ses divisions et le plus souvent son absence de gouvernance commune. La monnaie commune par contre apparaît comme une étape incontournable dans un processus inéluctable d'approfondissement de l'intégration européenne. Le débat autour de la ratification du traité constitutionnel européen innerve l'espace médiatique franco-français et déborde le cadre des journaux télévisés quotidiens pour alimenter toute une série d'émissions de paroles dans lesquelles la thématique est discutée. L'ensemble des acteurs mais aussi la majorité des locuteurs sollicités plaident pour la ratification du traité en y percevant un seuil qualitatif dans le processus de construction européenne.

Les années 2005–2009 ; le backlash

Le « Non » français à la ratification du traité européen intervient comme un hiatus dans la couverture du thème-événement. D'évidence, les médias n'avaient pas anticipé la possibilité du rejet du texte législatif par les électeurs. Les journalistes (mais aussi les politiques) abandonnent les postures volontaristes précédentes au profit pour certains d'une remise en question voire d'une critique explicite des modalités de la gouvernance supranationale. Symptomatiquement, les rubriques spécialisées ainsi que certaines magazines consacrés à la question européenne disparaissent. L'irruption de la crise financière à la fin de cette période conditionne le traitement de l'actualité européenne ; l'économie, la gestion par à coup de ces crises. Les seuils de couverture de la thématique stagnent et sont systématiquement centrés sur les crises successives. Délaissant les projets ou les réalisations communes, ce sont la complexité mais le plus souvent les impasses de la gouvernance européenne qui font désormais l'essentiel de la couverture de l'actualité européenne.

Vers une "naturalisation" de la question européenne dans les pratiques des instances informatives

Certes, il serait souhaitable d'approfondir ce type d'études en analysant certaines périodes-charnières ou bien des formes ritualisées de la couverture télévisuelle (les sommets européens), toutefois, l'observation de ce vaste corpus de documents télévisuels permet de discerner certaines des logiques médiatiques à l'œuvre à l'intérieur de ce domaine événementiel. Dans un premier temps, d'évidence, ce ne sont pas tant des orientations politiques gouvernementales ou éditoriales mais la simple répercussion de mécaniques purement institutionnelles qui ont prédominé dans l'orientation du regard médiatique. L'unique activité participative et implicative à une identité européenne en gestation, représentée par l'agenda cyclique des élections européennes a pu concourir, à travers la mobilisation des instances informatives, à une forme d'incarnation effective de cette entité dans les discours médiatiques. Cette itération durant plusieurs décennies a débouché de façon patente sur une sensibilisation accrue à la question de la naissance de cette nouvelle Europe. Au terme de la période examinée, ce nouveau " cadre de description " semble avoir été intégré de façon organique dans les routines des acteurs de l'information. Le traitement de ce thème n'obéit plus, comme on a pu l'observer dans les premières décennies, aux contraintes de l'agenda programmatique de l'actualité institutionnelle ou des agissements des acteurs du monde politique. Elle a été insensiblement, en quelque sorte, naturalisée et intériorisée par les acteurs de l'information pour venir constituer une sorte d'arrière-plan structurel dans de nombreuses questions d'actualité purement nationale. Comme le constate Louis Quéré, « d'une information reflet, on est passé à une information générative et opérationnelle ». On perçoit bien ici toute la dimension constructiviste et prospective de la pratique informative impliquée dans ce processus " d'individuation " des événements qui « passe, comme le fait remarquer ce même chercheur, par la schématisation d'un divers hétérogène sous une totalité intelligible et par son affiliation à un contexte de description ». (Quéré, 1999:274)

En dépit de l'apparente régression qui succède au choc du non de 2005 et aux soubresauts des crises financières à partir de 2007, on peut discerner les contours et l'esquisse d'une authentique communauté d'identité qui prend forme progressivement dans les modes de configuration de la réalité événementielle et dont les journalistes incarnent les porte-voix. A travers ce jeu performatif de construction de la réalité sociale, les médias véhiculent et assurent ainsi la consolidation de nouvelles identités d'appartenance. La question qui se pose alors est bien celle de savoir si l'identité européenne obéit aux mêmes schémas de construction que ceux qui ont œuvré à la naissance des identités nationales. Ici, ce sont moins les hypothétiques racines culturelles communes, la langue ou la culture commune, ni un corps de fonctionnaires étatiques qui encadrent ce nouvel imaginaire (trans)national, mais en partie l'ombre portée d'un pouvoir institutionnel vertical transnational en voie de constitution et sans doute, corrélativement, si l'on retient les postulats avancés par Benedict Anderson (1996), le lent travail de sédimentation et de symbolisation se constituant par paliers, assuré par l'actualité événementielle telle que les médias de masse et entre autres l'information télévisée la produisent. Et c'est manifestement dans l'entrelacs de leurs discours que nous assistons à la naissance d'une nouvelle « communauté imaginée » (imagined communitie) (Anderson, 1996) ou de ce qu'Étienne Balibar (2001) perçoit désormais comme une « identité secondaire » rémanente, indissociable de nos univers de croyance et de nos cartographies du « proche et du lointain ». Il est évident que ce processus entraîne en partie une déconstruction effective du paradigme de l'Etat-Nation avec tous ses risques, ce qui explique les effets récents de balancier et de backlash. A la lumière de ces observations, on peut s'interroger sur la naissance de ce « patriotisme supranational » pour lequel militent Jürgen Habermas et certains théoriciens qui reposerait sur un système démocratique de lois et une "démocratie procédurale" et non "communautariste et identitaire" comme d'autres chercheurs tel Charles Taylor l'avancent. En effet, comme l'attestent certain éléments de cette cartographie sémantique, l'Europe n'a toujours pas de visage, pas de centre, pas d'incarnation, en un mot, tout ce que s'efforcent de distiller les médias dans la discursivité sociale, d'où sans doute cette aporie paradoxale observable en fin de période, un discours incertain sans véritable objet et dénué de responsabilité énonciative. Une des rares certitudes étant que ce sont bien les discours médiatiques qui sont d'évidence aujourd'hui les lieux où circulent les imaginaires d'appartenance et surtout où surgissent les conflits de définitions qu'ils engendrent.

FICHES DE L'INATHÈQUE DE FRANCE

Annexe 1
Titre propre : Arrivée Wilson Orly
Titre collection : JT 20 heures
Canal de diffusion : 1
Canal : Réseau 1
Date de diffusion : 18 06 1967
Durée : 00 01 12
Genre : Journal télévisé.
Générique : Jou, La Taille, Emmanuel de
Descripteurs : France, Paris, visite, Wilson Harold, Premier ministre, politique extérieure.
Résumé : le premier ministre britannique en visite en France après le rejet de la demande d'entrée de l'Angleterre dans le marché commun européen. M Wilson arrive à Orly avec sa femme ; accueil par les personnalités : garde d'honneur ; il passe les troupes en revue.
Société de programme ORTF
Producteurs Paris ORTF : 1967

Annexe 2
Titre propre : Les médecins généralistes en Europe
Titre collection : TF1 20 heures
Titre programmes : TF1 20 heures [émission du 22 janvier 1996]
Chaîne de diffusion : TF1
Canal : Réseau 1
Date de diffusion : 22 01 1996
Jour : Lundi

Heure de diffusion : 20 06 12
Heure de fin de diffusion : 20 07 34
Durée : 00 01 22
Genre : Journal télévisé.
Type de description : Sujet
Générique : Jou, Jungfer Viviane
Descripteurs : Union européenne, politique sociale, santé, médecin généraliste, consultation.
Chapeau reportage : Présentation des systèmes de santé dans différents pays de l'union européenne, Allemagne, Espagne, Italie et Grande Bretagne. Explication de leur fonctionnement, des tarifs et de la durée moyenne d'une consultation.
Commentaire sur images d'illustration et infographies.
Société de programme TF1
Producteurs Producteur, Boulogne: TF1 2002

Annexe 3
Titre propre : L'homoparentalité en Europe
Titre collection : Arte information
Titre programmes : Arte info [émission du 26 février 2001]
Chaîne de diffusion : ARTE
Canal : Réseau 5
Date de diffusion : 26 02 2001
Jour : Lundi
Heure de diffusion : 19 59 15
Heure de fin de diffusion : 20 00 45
Durée : 00 01 30
Genre : Journal télévisé.
Type de description : Sujet
Générique : Jou, Julien, Lionel
Descripteurs : Europe, homosexuel, adoption, enfant.
Chapeau reportage : tour d'horizon de l'homoparentalité à travers l'Europe, avec l'adoption d'enfants par des couples homosexuels, une situation qui bouge mais est loin d'être uniforme en matière de droit selon les pays. Commentaire sur images d'illustration et cartes géographiques.
Société de programme ARTE
Producteurs Producteur, Strasbourg : Arte GEIE, Association relative aux télévisions européennes 2002

BIBLIOGRAPHIE

Anderson, B (1996). *L'imaginaire national, réflexions sur l'origine et l'essor du nationalisme*, Paris : La Découverte.

Balibar É (2001). *Nous citoyens d'Europe ? Les frontières, l'État, le peuple*, Paris : La Découverte.

McCombs M E & Shaw E (1972). The Agenda-setting Function of the Press. *Public Opinion Quarterly*

Nora P (1972). « L'événement monstre », Communications n° 18, Paris : Le Seuil.

Quéré, L, (1999) "Evénement et temps de l'histoire" in *L'événement en perspective*, (sous la direction de Jean-Louis Petit), *Raisons pratiques*, N° 2, Editions de l'Ecole des hautes Etudes en Sciences sociales, Paris, p. 274.

Stiegler B (1994). *La technique et le temps I, La faute d'Epiméthée,* Paris : Galilée.

Veron E (1981). *Construire l'événement, les médias et l'accident de Three Mile Island*, Paris : éditions de Minuit.

THE USE OF SOCIAL NETWORKS FOR BUILDING POLITICAL BRANDS: A COMPARATIVE PERSPECTIVE

DIANA MARIA CISMARU

Abstract

Social networks represent a new development in political communication. The rapid changes in the new media space have brought social networks in the first line of public communication, while blogs are in the second line. Presence and activity in social networks have become an obligation for political actors who intend to build a solid brand in the public space. The involvement in social networks produced a change in the communication strategy: the online relationship with publics became the focus of communication. This paper aims to compare the use of social networks in political communication in two very different societies, American and Romanian. Important political leaders in Romania have had a recent entry in social networks. The comparison with American political leaders and their presence in social networks intends to emphasize the different stages in the evolution of political communication in the two countries. The analysis starts with a few outlines of the use of social media, including communication strategies used in political branding, and ends with features of profiles in social networks. The social networks chosen for analysis are Facebook and Twitter, the most powerful and the most specific in the social media landscape.

Key words: social networs, political brands, communication strategies

INTRODUCTION

Nowadays, the "magic of communication" seems to be everywhere in the public space. Often, practice seems to constitute the entire field of political communication (Nimmo, 1977). However, political marketing is only the instrumental part: the collection of strategies, techniques and processes by which the political actors/organizations influence and persuade the public opinion, in order to be elected (adaptation of the definition of Gerstle, 2002, p.14). While the practice of political marketing evolved it specialized in narrower areas (and political communication in social media is one of the areas of specialization) (Strother, 1999). But the behavioural perspective ignores the "human side", the interaction of political communication, and eliminates many important variables. From a theoretical perspective in the field of political communication, the digital approach focuses both on the strategic perspective of political actions and on human interaction (Gerstle, 2002, p.: 14). The focus on human interaction, having its origin in the paradigm of symbolic interactionism (Blumer, 1969), is revived today, through the development of social media in the public space. "Politics in web 2.0" has interaction as its main feature. Social media have created a new actor in the public (virtual) stage: the ordinary citizen (Dominick, 2009). This is the main revolution that has been accomplished by social media: ordinary citizens have been brought into the political debate as powerful actors, similar to traditional journalists. The online space has special rules, and social influence and status are an effect of complementary factors. Though it is apparently only a mirror of the events of the real space, the virtual space can also have the function of generator for the real space.

In the political communication field, there is a clear tendency to construct political brands in the online space. The hypothesis of this chapter is that Romanian politicians and their communication advisers underestimate the power of communication in social networks, as they underestimated the importance of social media in the pre-electoral years.

RECENT CHANGES IN THE SOCIAL MEDIA SPACE

Social networks are online communication platforms which function similarly to the natural social networks, and they are based on direct interpersonal contacts. They offer, through their mission statements, the promise of an open and connected world, in which users have the possibility to share their experiences and interests: "*Giving people the power to share and make the world more open and connected*" (as defined in the "information" section of Facebook). Other social networks bring the promise of efficient communication, in real time, transcending the limits of space and time: "*Twitter is a real-time information network that connects you to the latest information about what you find interesting. Simply find the public streams you find most compelling and follow the conversations*" (as defined in the "about" section of Twitter).

The presence of a public actor in social networks is evaluated by the public by the quality of interaction and of "added value" he or she brings in conversation with publics. The public has an egocentric attitude: the online reaction is produced by the immediate benefits to the audiences (Tapscott, 2011). Only if the public actor has a proposal that is interesting, useful and attractive for the user, is the message treated as relevant and will it receive the attention of the public.

In Romania, in 2007–2009 social media had a rapid growth, through the use of the blogosphere (Cismaru, 2012). The blogosphere doubled its volume between 2008 (30,000 blogs) and 2010 (over 70,000). At the end of 2011, 4,1 million users of Facebook existed in Romania, 400,000 LinkedIn accounts and 51,065 Twitter accounts were registered (according to the monitoring sites Facebrands and Zelist, respectively).

The Effects of Political Communication in Social Networks

The attractiveness of Facebook for users comes from the variety of instruments for selection and interpretation of content. The "news feed" is a powerful news channel that allows users to select the news from „trusted sources" in a single flow of information. Giving feed-back also is easy (it can be a simple "like," without expressing any other ideas). The additional tools for receiving information (for example, by accessing personal account with a mobile phone) have increased the potential audiences. For political communication, the opportunity comes when the account has thousands of fans: the advantage of disseminating messages directly to public, without the intermediate interpretation of traditional media (TV and radio), is impressive. Another opportunity is the transformation of the Facebook account in a channel to release messages to the press (Cismaru, 2012, p. 108).

The second network examined in this paper, Twitter, is centered more on information than on communication. The main feature in this network is the length of the messages (limit of 140 characters, including spaces, in a tweet) and the limitation of the tools. Twitter communication is focused on two aspects: the information (novelty value - the messages are news in the personal and public space) and the audience. The Twitter account is a "personal news channel" and the user delivers what he considers to be news to the other users in his personal network (followers). Comparing Twitter with Facebook, even if the "news feed" from Facebook is also a news channel, Facebook has a stronger social significance (messages are longer and rich in interpretation and interaction, through comments). On Twitter, the usefulness of the information is the only variable which manages the user's behaviour inside the network. For political actors, this is of particular interest, because they have the opportunity to build and express their status as opinion leader. Also, they usually have public positions and have new information to share; they can build their political capital of public trust by delivering useful information to users. Both Facebook and Twitter users potentially are opinion leaders (local or specialized) and they can be very effective agents when releasing the messages and issues promoted by a political actor.

For the practitioners of strategic communication, social media in general (and social networks especially) offer advantages that shouldn't be neglected. One of the advantages is that the strategy can be redesigne, according to public reaction, and constructed gradually until a satisfactory formula is reached. The mainstream media channels, used in traditional communication strategies, did not offer this possibility (Iacob, Cismaru & Pricopie, 2001, pp. 200- 201). Still, Romanian political communication is paying little attention to the effective practices of image building and to the use of communication channels as effective promotional means of political attitudes. Many political actors do not have profiles in social media, or they have only a formal presence in the virtual space.

At the level of political parties, the situation is similar. The political parties' pages are mainly instruments of information for journalists, analysts or supporters, but they are not built for a relationship with key publics. Even when these sites have an interactive section, the section is rarely managed (no one answers questions or comments).

Obama's 2008 campaign had great success because it attracted new categories of voters, especially among younger people. The Net Generation asks for government politics which allow the participation of citizens with balanced ideas in the decisional process (Browning, 2002). Also, the "Net Generation" asks for a move from politics to policies, and for responsible decisions made in a truly democratic way.

In the Romanian space, the politicians and the communication teams have understood the importance of the virtual space, but they acted only during the limited time of the campaign. In recent Romanian history, the 2009 electoral campaign is the best example of the importance of the online space in political communication. Social networks were not priority channels for political communication; the main instruments were the sites (for example, sites "opposing" a candidate, promotional sites for an idea or for opinion leaders). The winner in the online space was Crin Antonescu, with 50–60% of the votes from Internet users. The second candidate in the online campaign was president Traian Băsescu, with a dynamic strategy focused on his combative voters (short texts, contrasting design and interactivity). The online space was a generous source for votes. In the case of Crin Antonescu, the notoriety he needed to reach the third position was built in the online space. For the winner, Traian Băsescu, the sites brought the voters he needed to win the second tour. Large budgets invested in the online space were not a guarantee for success in the virtual space: as an example, Mircea Geoană had a fine strategy but weak results (only 12% adherents in the online space). The factors of success for all candidates were the interactivity, the freshness of perspective and the originality in constructing messages.

Methodology

As a method, a comparative analysis of several politicians' profiles on Facebook and Twitter was chosen. The criteria of selection of the cases were: (a) the public visibility and notoriety of political actors; (b) their activity in social networks (presence and continuous activity); (c) the importance of political actors and their institutional positions.

The Romanian politicians were then compared with two American politicians, Sarah Palin and Barack Obama. The comparison took into account the difference of volume between the network publics (the American is 20 times bigger in terms of social network users). Also, the difference in lifestyle was considered (Americans spend more time online). The analysis focused on the quality of profiles in social networks, not on the quantity of messages.

The criteria of analysis for Facebook were: the originality of the content (the text is conceived for Facebook in terms of length, style and subjects), the number of friends/fans (depending on the page character, individual or organizational page), the frequency of posts (the actualization of the content), the richness of information (combining writing and visual, the use of all tools), and interactivity (feed-back and moderation politics).

For Twitter, some basic elements were considered in the analysis: the frequency of posts (number of posts) and the current activity (some accounts have an unbalanced rhythm of posting, with long pauses), the type and the inner consistency of messages, the relationship between followers and following.

Another important element for the analysis on Twitter was the type of tweets. Thus, five categories of tweets were identified: information tweets (that transmit news of general or specific public interest), professional tweets (about the current professional activity), tweets of attitude (that intend to build a certain image profile), tweets of relationship (that aim to build and maintain a relationship with publics), and personal tweets.

The Results of Analysis

Facebook Results

The accounts of five Romanian politicians were selected (the most visible and important political actors and also the most active in social networks). The preliminary research showed that the majority of the other Romanian politicians had no online accounts in social networks.

The sample cases which resulted from selection were:

Crin Antonescu, third favorite in the 2009 electoral presidential campaign and the most persistent in the online space in that campaign. Currently he is the president of the third most powerful party in Romania, the National Liberal Party.

Victor Ponta, current president of the Social Democrat Party, the most powerful opposition party at that time. He is one of the new political personalities, who became notorious after the electoral campaign in 2009. His presence in social networks was modest in terms of audience, but constant.

Sorin Oprescu, the Mayor of Bucharest, former independent candidate in the 2009 presidential elections 2009 (the fourth in the contest). He has often been visible in the real public space and is very popular in Bucharest. His presence in the online space also was low, but constant.

Elena Udrea, Minister of Development and the president of the Bucharest local organization of the Democrat Liberal Party until 2012. She has been a notorious and controversial personality in Romanian politics. She was, beginning with 2008, the most active politician on her own online communication channels (being the first politician who had a personal site, blog, Facebook and Twitter accounts.)

Remus Cernea, president of the Green Party, a small and non-parliamentary Party, but notorious as a candidate in the 2009 electoral campaign, when he managed to become visible by personal means – using social media as main channels for building his notoriety. In September 2011, he was the political actor with the greatest audience on Facebook (31,000 fans).

Table 29-1

Crin Antonescu	
Content	30 % original (repostings from blog, announces about presence in media, with a short introduction).
Friends/fans	19,518
Frequency of posts	2- 5 messages per month, started to write after a long pause in May 2011
Quality of information	Only wall messages and news (reposted by syndication)
Interactivity	There is no feed-back, only moderation rules.
Victor Ponta	
Content	30% original
Friends	3209
Frequency	Daily
Quality of information	Fine structure of static information (about the political programme of the party) but the messages are mixed with users' messages, who are allowed to post on the wall.
Interactivity	Weak
Sorin Oprescu	
Content	10% (repostings and photos)
Friends/fans	4998
Frequency of posts	Daily
Quality of information	Users are allowed to write on the wall, messages of the politician are lost from public attention.
Interactivity	None
Elena Udrea	
Content	80% original (reposting from blog to notes but posting original short messages with a great interest from fans).
Friends/fans	18,500
Frequency of posts	1- 2 daily messages
Quality of information	Great variety of subjects, combined with photos and videos
Interactivity	Likes for constructive comments and direct answers.

Remus Cernea	
Content	70% original (reposting with consistent introduction); there are subjects opposed to Romanian orthodox values (sexual alternate orientation);
Friends/fans	30,779
Frequency of posts	3- 5 daily posts
Quality of information	Fine organization, written and visual are combined
Interactivity	Personal answers to comments
Barack Obama	
Content	80% original: Texts for Facebook or texts reposted from other sources
Friends/fans	22,134,574
Frequency of posts	2- 4 daily posts
Quality of information	Very high, combines written and visual information, reposted articles from other sources have a consistent introduction
Interactivity	Huge number of comments (thousands of comments to a posts) moderated by administrators.
Sarah Palin	
Content	30% original (only notes are original, wall is allowed for others)
Friends/fans	3,203,234
Frequency of posts	3 posts per week
Quality of information	Fine organization but lacks variation. The classic articles are posted as Notes. Their target is a traditional and stable public, a little older than the average age of Facebook users. The information is uniform (photos are not used).
Interactivity	There is feed-back from moderators.

As the analysis shows, Romanian politicians lack understanding of the networks' main features (focus on public's interests, accessibility and interaction). Romanian politicians did not have a consistent activity on their accounts (for example, the lack of original content, on Crin Antonescu's profile) or the communication is one-way and non-targeted, as for Victor Ponta and Sorin Oprescu. Elena Udrea (member of Government) and Remus Cernea (ex-presidential candidate) were the only ones with a correct perspective on Facebook.

The American politicians' strategy included high interactivity, constant actualization, a consistent line in the content (Sarah Palin), and a complexity of messages addressed to targeted audiences (Barack Obama).

Twitter results

The politicians who are present in the virtual space are usually present on more than one network. Almost the same group of Romanian politicians was selected for Twitter. The only case that was changed was Remus Cernea, who had no profile on Twitter. Remus Cernea was replaced by Mircea Geoana, with a more visible activity on Twitter. Mircea Geoana was the former president of the then most important opposition party (the Social- Democratic Party) and also the former President of the Romanian Senate. In the 2009 presidential elections, he almost won the second-round contest with president Basescu, when several exit polls designated him as winner. Those exit polls did not count the votes from abroad, which were given mainly to president Basescu (and thus, Mircea Geoana is now called "the one-night president" by Romanian journalists). On Twitter, Mircea Geoana is a relevant case because he met all the criteria of political visibility, constant online activity, and importance of position in the public space. While comparing the Romanian accounts of politicians with the two selected cases from United States, the age of account in case of Obama and Sarah Palin could not be found out, because the accounts are old and rich in content.

Table 29-2

Crin Antonescu	
Age of account	@CrinAntonescu09 – 2 July 2009 There are two alternate accounts with a small number of followers and only few tweets.
Number of followers	1397
Number followed	79
Number of tweets	79
Frequency of tweets	Unequal rhythm of posting, 1- 2 tweets weekly until November 2010, when the activity stopped.
Content of messages	Self promotion, attacks on those exercising power; links to discourses and own interventions, comments of the political party's programme.
Current activity	There is no current activity.
Victor Ponta	
Age of accounts	@Victor_Ponta – 16 June 2010 There are three alternate accounts which are only intentions (small number of followers and no tweets)
Number of followers	313
Number followed	182
Number of tweets	118
Frequency of tweets	4 – 5 posts weekly Variable, breaks of 10- 14 days with no tweets.
Content of messages	Declaration about the administrators of accounts. Content includes self- promotion messages, critiques of competitors, presence in media announcements, public statements and interviews; expression of position in public issues.
Current activity	Normal activity. The account is a vehicle for the opposition's ideas.
Mircea GEOANĂ	
Age of account	27 October 2008
Number of followers	1318
Number followed	787

Number of tweets	379
Frequency of tweets	Varied; sometimes 1- 4 daily, other times 1–2 weekly. Pauses are shorter than two days.
Content of messages	Constant information about public activities. Attitudes of interest for the electorate. Official messages of the president of the Senate with several occasions. Reference to political and military studies. Media presence and interviews. Lack of tweets of relationship.
Current activity	Communication is intense and consistent. Expression of attitudes towards internal events.
Sorin Oprescu	
Age of account	9 July 2009
Number of followers	1085
Number followed	1280
Number of tweets	125
Frequency of tweets	1 tweet per week, sometimes 1 message to ten days. Unequal frequency, with long pauses (20 January - 15 May)
Content of messages	Information about activities as mayor (events, projects). Announcements about the presence in mass -media (interviews). No tweets of relationship. Some tweets are very short and alternate with the informal ones.
Current activity	Frequency is lower in the last period. Only activities with high public impact are underlined.
Elena UDREA	
Age of account	19 October 2009
Number of followers	1195
Number followed	1
Number of tweets	134
Frequency of tweets	2 – 3 daily

Content of messages	Professional (activity inside the Ministry of Development and Tourism); attitudes towards political events; information in public agenda problems; announcements about the agenda and media presence Tweets of relationship – 25%.
Current activity	Alternate subjects, with the dominant note of the ministry but also on attitude problems. Big volume of information concentrated in tweets. Constant frequency of posts.
Barack OBAMA	
Number of followers	9,210,800
Number followed	692,540
Number of tweets	1494
Frequency of tweets	4- 7/daily
Content of messages	There are two accounts; the personal one is from the perspective of electoral competition (role of a politician in competition), and @ObamaNews which wires institutional information (role of a president).On both accounts, a variety of subjects and messages wired.
Current activity	Regular posting, the president's personal tweets signed BO.
Sarah PALIN	
Number of followers	603,599
Number followed	116
Number of tweets	985
Frequency of tweets	1- 5/daily
Content of messages	Great number of tweets of attitude. Participation in human tragedies. Participation of politician's family in the construction of the personal brand.
Current activity	Not constant, there are pauses in vacations, which create the perception of sincerity.

There were notable differences between the Romanian accounts and the two American examples. Romanian politicians (with the exception of Mircea Geoană and Elena Udrea) were more superficial in their communication on Twitter accounts. The Romanian politicians were present on this social network, but they did not consider it as a priority or as an opportunity; they did not adapt their communication instruments to their political targets. The variety of tweets was weak, and they posted only professional tweets (but they were not expressed in a useful and friendly way). In most cases, the interaction with the audience (by tweets of relationship) was weak or did not exist (Sorin Oprescu, Victor Ponta, Crin Antonescu). For Mircea Geoana, the perspective was complex (the content was rich and specialized) but too formal for the publics' features on Twitter and on social networks in general.

Conclusions

Several Romanian politicians started using Facebook and Twitter during the 2009 electoral campaign, but they had a limited use of these networks, mostly as a tool of transmission for messages conceived for other channels. Their attitude was unidirectional (towards the public, but not back). The availability to listen and answer to the feed-back of publics was very limited. They did not adapt their messages to the characteristics of Facebook and Twitter. Political communication should pay attention in the future to public reactions and also to bidirectional communication.

References

Blumer, H (1969), *Symbolic Interactionism*, Englewood Cliffs, New Jersey: Prentice Hall.

Browning, G (2002), *Electronic Democracy: Using the Internet to Transform American Politics*, Medford, New Jersey: Information Today.

Cismaru, D-M (2012). *Social media și managementul reputației [Social media and reputation management*], Bucharest: Tritonic.

Dominick, J R (2009). Ipostazele comunicarii de masă. Media în era digitală, *[Mass media communication in the digital age],* Bucharest: Comunicare.ro.

Gerstle, J (2002). *Comunicarea Pol*itică [Political Communication], Jassy: Institutul European.

Iacob, D, Cismaru, D-M & Pricopie, R (2011). Relaţiile publice-eficienţă prin comunicare, [*Public Relations – cohesion and efficiency through communication*] Bucharest: Comunicare.ro.

Nimmo, D (1977). Political Communication Theory and Research: An Overview. , In B D Ruben, *Communication Yearbook*, I, New Brunswick: Transaction Books.

Strother, R (1999). Foreword., in D D Perlmutter (ed.), *The Manship School Guide for Political Communication*, Louisiana: Louisiana State University Press.

Tapscott, D (2011). Crescuţi digital. Generaţia Net îţi schimbă lumea *[Educated digitally. Net Generation changes the world],* Bucharest: Publica.

http://www.facebook.com/facebook#!/facebook?sk=info, accessed 13 May 2011.

http://twitter.com/about, accessed 13 May 2011.

www.facebrands.ro, accessed 5 January 2012.

www.zelist.ro/zetweety, accessed 5 January 2012.

OS DE LA, LA TRANSCENDANCE DES ENVIRONNEMENTS INFORMATIQUES

VINCENT MABILLOT

Résumé

Cet essai s'inspirant d'un article d'Umberto Eco analysant les différences entre Windows et Mac sous l'angle d'une guerre de religions sémiotique, s'intéresse aux différentes apparences du système d'exploitation GNU/Linux. L'objectif est d'évoquer des hypothèses sur les relations entre l'esthétique des interfaces, leurs usages et les idéologies qui pourraient être sous-jacentes. Derrière se pose la question de l'ouverture ou de la clôture des dispositifs communicationnels qu'autorisent certains choix en apparence esthétiques. Il ressort que les interfaces numériques sont le lieu d'expressions idéologiques. Une interface, un système ne sont pas intuitifs ou naturels, ils sont une construction héritée de modèle idéologique se reflétant dans la considération de la place de l'autre (l'utilisateur) et des usages qu'on lui reconnaît, qu'on lui autorise. Par leur élaboration multi-communautaire dégagée de rationalisation marketing, la diversité des logiciels libres et de leurs environnements en font un terrain d'observation de la diversité potentielle de l'informatique permettant de repérer différents modèles « idéologisés ».

Mots-clés : Logiciel libre, religion, sémiotique, informatique, médiologie, identité, diversité, idéologie, altérité, alternative

DOS LE PROTESTANT, MAC LE CATHOLIQUE, WINDOWS L'ANGLICAN ET GNU/LINUX ALORS ?

En 1993 dans l'Expresso, Umberto Eco s'amusait d'une analyse sémiotique de la guerre de religions opposant Windows et MacIntosh. Pour mettre face à face les deux chapelles, il observait le fonctionnement des différents systèmes informatiques de l'époque en osant une analogie avec les signes extérieurs du religieux. Il comparait ainsi le système DOS, utilisé jusque là sur la plus grande partie des PC (en particulier ceux des entreprises) à la religion protestante. L'interface relevait selon lui du calvinisme le plus austère. Marqué par un système fonctionnant en ligne de commande et où le moniteur n'offrait au démarrage qu'une triste invite clignotante dans l'attente d'une saisie rigoureuse qui lancerait une application. Ainsi, si l'on respectait à la lettre les écritures, le programme s'exécutait et nous gagnions ainsi notre droit au paradis numérique.

À DOS, il opposait le catholicisme du MacIntosh[1]. Ce dernier au travers de son interface graphique, était alors tout à la gloire du culte de l'icône. Opposition radicale où l'image se substituait au commandement. Il faut adorer l'image sans aller voir la réalité qu'elle recouvre, mais se fier à sa transcendance transmise par les concepteurs de cet environnement. Ce qu'il y a derrière l'icône, son fonctionnement, échappe à la rationalité. Pour preuve ? L'icône de la poubelle dont la signification serait une action de suppression permet aussi d'éjecter une disquette de l'appareil. Parallèlement si les fichiers qui sont sur la disquette sont copiés sur le bureau de l'ordinateur puis mis dans la poubelle, ils sont en fait supprimés de la disquette... Donc ils n'étaient que symboliquement sur le bureau...

Microsoft, propriétaire de DOS, commence à déployer massivement, à l'époque de l'article d'Umberto Eco, son propre environnement graphique, Windows 3.1[2]. Selon Umberto Eco, il est associable à l'anglicanisme, ce subtile mélange de catholicisme et de protestantisme. Il offre les fastes somptueux de l'église romaine même si derrière l'icône se trouve la ligne de commande DOS. Mais il se targue de rappeler que sous ces environnements, il y a le langage machine, le fondement, la relation directe qui convertit la quête humaine en des traitements d'informations binaires. Cette couche mère, il la compare au Talmud rappelant que toute une vie d'étude et de sagesse ne permettront jamais d'en maîtriser toutes les vérités.

Le texte d'Umberto Eco est brillant de perspicacité et d'humour. Il met à l'œuvre avec justesse une interprétation de l'univers des signes informatiques avec des idéologies sous-jacentes qui fonctionne. Même s'il faut bien se garder d'aller au-delà d'une relation symbolique entre religion et operating system, il serait certainement tentant d'aller fouiller d'un peu plus près les modèles organisationnels, décisionnels et communicationnels

[1] 1984 passage à un environnement graphique chez Apple reprenant...

[2] Les versions 1.0 (1985) et 2.0 (1987) de Windows, très proche de l'environnement graphique d'origine GEM n'était qu'un coup d'essai, il faut attendre Windows 3.1(1990) pour que cet environnement devienne l'environnement par défaut des ordinateurs PC qui seront désormais pré-installés avec un système windows et non DOS (Wikipédia, 2011a).

des équipes de développement de ces systèmes pour voir si on les retrouve dans la représentation et la préconisation d'usage visibles.

Sur cette base, nous avons donc eu envie de poursuivre et creuser la petite réflexion du sémioticien en essayant d'intégrer à sa réflexion la place de GNU/Linux qui se présenterait comme une alternative libre à Mac et Windows.

La genèse de GNU/Linux

En 1993, Umberto Eco n'a pas forcément connaissance de l'existence de ce nouvel OS[3] qui est devenu opérationnel en 1991, depuis qu'un jeune étudiant finlandais, Linus Torvalds a proposé à la communauté GNU, un noyau (un kernel) qu'il a placé sous licence libre GPL et qui va prendre le nom de Linux.

Si pour le libriste[4] averti, ce paragraphe introductif est limpide, il mérite certainement quelques éclaircissements pour le profane.

Au commencement, il y avait le projet GNU, dont l'acronyme récursif « GNU is Not Unix » est à la fois une blague potache d'informaticien et bien l'idée d'un système qui se redéfinit lui-même en permanence en référence à un système qu'il n'est pas , UNIX. L'initiateur du projet GNU, Richard Matthew Stallman[5], est considéré comme un des inventeurs du concept de logiciel libre.

L'histoire raconte que RMS n'ayant plus la possibilité d'améliorer les logiciels qu'il utilisait au MIT pour piloter l'imprimante (ceux-ci étant devenus propriétaires du fabricant de l'imprimante qui interdisait leur modification), décida d'initier un mouvement redonnant des libertés aux utilisateurs de logiciels. Pour que l'on soit libre dans l'utilisation de l'informatique, il faut que dès l'allumage de l'ordinateur l'environnement système soit libre. Le projet GNU consiste donc, dès 1984, à proposer un environnement complet et des logiciels pouvant fonctionner sur ordinateur classique et que cet ensemble pourraient être accessible à tous et modifiable par chacun. Ce projet GNU se développe sous l'impulsion de RMS et d'une communauté de hackers[6].

---

[3] OS : Acronyme d'Operating System (Système opérationnel, environnement du système)

[4] Libriste : utilisateur d'environnement et de logiciels libres

[5] Richard Matthew Stallman est aussi connu par son pseudo de hacker, RMS que nous utiliserons par la suite pour faire référence au personnage.

[6] Par hackers, il faut entendre des « codeurs capables de tailler, modifier, bricoler, améliorer un programme existant ». Le hacker pourrait se traduire en français par « bidouilleur » (Williams, Stallman, et Masutti, 2010). Il n'est pas par définition un

Il naît en 1985, sous l'impulsion de RMS, la FSF (Free Software Foundation) dont l'objectif va être de promouvoir le logiciel libre. Pour protéger cette liberté, RMS et l'avocat Eben Moglen créent en 1989 la première version de la GPL (General Public License) qui protège juridiquement les libertés d'utilisation, d'observation, de modification et d'utilisation. La licence protège le droit de l'auteur mais aussi celui de l'utilisateur.

Par libre, il faut entendre donc que les logiciels répondent à quatre libertés fondamentales :

- Liberté 0 : liberté d'utiliser, sur son ordinateur ou sur d'autres machines, capables d'interpréter le programme
- Liberté 1 : liberté d'étudier, de savoir comment est fait le logiciel, comment il est organisé. Le code source[7] doit être accessible. C'est aussi un gain de transparence sur le fonctionnement du programme pour éviter qu'il fasse des actions à notre insu.
- Liberté 2 : liberté de modifier, si on a les compétences ou qu'on trouve quelqu'un les ayant. On doit pouvoir améliorer, corriger ou faire évoluer le programme.
- Liberté 3 : liberté de diffuser, à qui on le souhaite y compris en se faisant rémunérer, sous réserve bien sûr de distribuer le programme avec les trois autres libertés. Cela implique de maintenir l'accès au code source du logiciel et donne le droit au nouvel utilisateur de redistribuer à son tour le logiciel (y compris gratuitement... même s'il l'a payé initialement).

Mais voilà jusqu'en 1991, le projet GNU reste expérimental et même si de nombreuses parties de l'environnement et de ses outils d'élaboration sont fonctionnels, le système dans son ensemble n'est pas opérationnel. C'est à ce moment de l'histoire que Linus Torvalds propose sur une liste de discussions un noyau qui va permettre de rendre l'ensemble opérationnel. Entre 1992 et 1993, les discussions et les échanges vont finir

---

« hors la loi » ou un « pirate ». Cette association est abusive. Cette activité (presque ce sport cérébral) n'est pas illégale par définition. Elle ne le devient que lorsqu'elle est pratiquée sur des logiciels ou des systèmes dont les conditions d'utilisation interdisent de les modifier.

[7] Lorsqu'un logiciel est créé, il est d'abord écrit dans un langage de programmation (qui ressemble à un texte avec une structure et une syntaxe spécifique). C'est le code source. Puis ce « fichier source» est « compilé », c'est à dire convertit en fichier binaire exécutable par la machine mais incompréhensible pour l'humain.

par consacrer « Linux » comme noyau opérationnel du projet GNU[8] donnant naissance à ce que l'on devrait généralement appeler le système « GNU/Linux [9]».

Cette union est aussi symptomatique de l'activité collaborative planétaire qui s'organise autour des réseaux télématiques et du réseau internet car l'annonce de Linus Torvalds, à l'époque jeune étudiant finlandais, et la discussion de celle-ci vont se faire par l'intermédiaire de liste de discussion et le partage de ressources FTP. Elle marque la capacité d'individualité de différents niveaux de reconnaissance institutionnelle en situation d'éclatement géographique à constituer des communautés contributives efficaces.

Mais c'est aussi bien là que l'on peut à nouveau retrouver toute la dimension « religieuse », disons plus généralement « idéologique » des operating system. Le projet d'un OS libre est le fruit de discussion de controverses et d'échanges houleux marqués sur la manière de faire, la différence entre être intègre ou intégriste, les modalités de décisions... Plusieurs courants apparaissent et c'est à partir de là que nous allons réinterroger les modèles communicationnels des OS libre au travers d'une analyse sémiotico-religieuse dans le prolongement de celle d'Umberto Eco.

LES MÉDIATEURS CHARISMATIQUES DU MOVEMENT DU LOGICIEL LIBRE

Si on a vu préalablement par quels signes extérieurs d'interface les environnements propriétaires classiques pouvaient être rapprochés de certaines religions, peut-on se risquer au même exercice avec GNU/Linux ?

L'histoire du logiciel libre s'inscrit dans un ensemble de cohésions et de controverses idéologiques qui prennent souvent l'apparence de querelles de personnes s'incarnant lors des « conciles » que sont les grandes rencontres qui ponctuent la vie événementielle des communautés du logiciel libre. Mais derrière ces prises de paroles, il y a des conceptions, des visions idéologiques qui dépassent les personnalités.

---

[8] GNU se prononce g-nou avec un g presque muet. En anglais le mot sonne ainsi pratiquement comme « new » mais aussi comme le gnou qui est l'animal emblématique du projet.

[9] RMS rappelle depuis les 1993 systématiquement à chacun de ses interlocuteurs que Linux seule est une appellation erroné du système car elle ne concerne que le noyau du projet et qu'en oubliant de préciser GNU/Linux on ne consacre que le travail de Linus Torvalds au détriment de celui du reste de la communauté (Williams, Stallman, et Masutti, 2010).

Par exemple, si le choix de Linus Torvalds de mettre son noyau sous la licence GPL est un choix initialement opportuniste pour protéger son code tout en laissant à d'autres la possibilité d'y contribuer (Torvalds et Guignot, 2011), pour d'autres comme RMS, le choix de la licence est d'abord éthique (Williams, Stallman, et Masutti, 2010). Une position idéologique qui sera au centre de controverses notamment portées par une autre personnalité emblématique du logiciel libre, Eric S. Raymond[10] qui sera à l'origine de l'OSI (Open Source Initiative) considérant que ce qui importe ici est une approche qu'il considère comme pragmatique et efficace. Selon lui, le modèle de l'Open Source et donc de l'ouverture du code (la recette de cuisine du logiciel) et la possibilité de chacun de l'améliorer, permet un développement plus créatif, plus adapté au besoin. Même s'il qualifie son modèle de « bazar », il défend que celui-ci s'impose au monde de l'informatique, non pour des raisons morales, mais parce qu'il obtient plus vite de meilleur résultat que le modèle des « bâtisseurs de cathédrales » auquel il associe les tenants d'une ingénierie de développement fermée (Raymond, 1997).

Au fil du temps différentes chapelles vont s'établir proposant leurs versions du système et la façon de l'utiliser.

Dans l'univers du logiciel libre, lorsqu'une nouvelle branche d'un logiciel s'écarte du projet principal, on parle de fork. Il arrive que les divergences soient durables et deviennent antagonistes. Mais au fil des années on a pu voir des projets se réunifier et surtout les groupes de développeurs travaillent en intégrant cette idée du fork y compris au sein des projets. Ils ont développer des outils permettant de tester différentes variantes et de faire des regroupements. L'important étant pour ces communautés, de maintenir le contact et le dialogue entre elles pour s'accorder sur des « formats » interopérables.

C'est notamment le cas avec l'environnement GNU/Linux qui a vu se démultiplier sous formes de distributions[11].

---

[10] Eric S. Raymond (connu aussi sous le pseudonyme ESR), se revendique comme « Libertarian » poussant la logique du refus de contrôle de gouvernemental en revendiquant la liberté d'être armé pour ne pas dépendre d'une autorité pour sa propre sécurité. Hacker et promoteur de technologies de défense de la vie privée, il a contribué à mettre en place des outils d'anonymisation accessibles pour des pays victimes de répressions policières (notamment dans le cadre des révolutions arabes de 2010-2011).

[11] Une distribution est à la fois le système d'exploitation plus une sélection de logiciels installés ou installables ainsi que des technologies de maintenance de l'ensemble. La variété des déclinaisons est visible sur la page web suivante : http://upload.wikimedia.org/wikipedia/commons/8/8c/Gldt.svg ainsi que sur le site

Les variations sont là encore des divergences de concepts, de personnalités, de constitution[12] mais aussi de disponibilités personnelles des contributeurs.

Il en découle une grande variété des « mises en scène » de GNU/Linux et des logiciels libres.

SOBRIÉTÉ ET ÉVANGÉLISATION

Si l'on s'en réfère à l'étude de David Lancashire (Lancashire, 2005), le logiciel libre est plutôt développé (proportionnellement au nombre de connectés à internet) dans les pays du nord de l'Europe et en Amérique du Nord (d'un point de vue absolu). Si la dimension culturelle est relativisable selon cet auteur (notamment en prenant en compte l'impact des investissements et le taux de recrutement), ce sont tout de même des cultures initialement héritières du protestantisme. Ceci permettait d'imaginer qu'il y ait un « fond » protestant dans l'univers des signes linuxiens.

À l'écran, on retrouverait ainsi le culte de la ligne de commande, le retour à l'écriture à une époque où l'informatique est portée par des interfaces graphiques. On y retrouve l'austérité de DOS telle qu'évoquée dans la première partie de cet article.

La ligne de commande est encore plus exigeante que sous DOS : pas question de faire l'impasse sur la différence entre majuscules et minuscules, les options doivent être invoquées dans l'ordre, l'utilisateur doit savoir où il se situe dans l'organisation de ses répertoires et dans les noms de fichiers. Il existe bien des commandes « ls » (pour lister répertoires et fichiers), « man » (pour manuel) ou « help » (aide) pour s'y retrouver ou pour accéder aux « livres » expliquant les commandes.

Sam Williams (Williams, Stallman, et Masutti, 2010) y retrouve même une dimension talmudique de l 'écriture lorsqu'il décide de placer son livre sous licence GPL FDL, une licence créée sur la base de la GPL mais pour s'appliquer plus particulièrement aux spécificités de la documentation.

Il y a donc avec le projet GNU/Linux un mouvement de retour aux fondamentaux de l'informatique, aux temps originels et une recherche des pratiques antérieures associée à une forme de vulgarisation qui aurait été

---

http://distrowatch.com/

[12] Les communautés se dotent souvent de règles de fonctionnement pouvant prendre la forme de constitution définissant les modalités de prise de décisions collectives (voir le travaux de Vanessa David présenter en parallèle de cet article). Par exemple la communauté Debian utilise dans différentes situations le vote Condorcet pour consensualiser certaines décisions (O'Mahony et Ferraro, 2007).

introduite par les interfaces graphiques.

Au-delà ensuite des atours de l'usage, il y a aussi la pratique des utilisateurs. La quasi-totalité de la population utilisant un ordinateur n'a pas débuté ou grandie dans un univers d'operating system libre. L'initiation, la transmission traditionnelle du savoir numérique est passée par un premier contact avec des environnements propriétaires (renforcé par les pratiques commerciales illégales mais tolérées des ventes liées[13]). Pour presque tous les utilisateurs de systèmes libres, il s'agit d'un choix passant par un parcours de conversion volontaire, un cheminement personnel.

Ce parcours de *conversion* n'est pas sans rappeler l'approche protestante où l'adhésion à la foi est un choix, une confession, une affirmation individuelle (Samuel, 1996). S'y ajoute une dimension d'engagement dans la communauté visant à faire connaître, à permettre aux autres d'accéder à la connaissance. Dans la quasi absence d'un circuit de commercialisation d'ordinateur sous GNU/Linux, la transmission de la pratique, l'accompagnement à l'installation[14] et l'aide se construit de proche en proche et au sein de communauté d'utilisateurs. L'utilisateur de logiciel libre est encore bien souvent un militant qui prêche, explique et cherche à convaincre. Un rôle qu'incarne à la perfection RMS.

Au-delà, c'est l'organisation même des communautés de libristes qui nous rappelle le protestantisme. Les groupes d'utilisateurs sont constitués en LUG (Linux Users Group) qui sont autonomes les uns des autres mais auxquels il n'est pas obligatoire d'adhérer ou de participer pour se revendiquer libriste. Les LUG, notamment en France, ne recherchent pas l'accompagnement des institutions au travers des subventions par exemple. Sauf pour des événements exceptionnels, ils fonctionnent en fonds propres. Les LUG s'honorent généralement de trouver des solutions économiques, humbles et raisonnables : Les signes extérieurs de modernité

---

[13] La vente liée consiste à vendre un ordinateur avec un operating system pré-installé sans donner le choix à l'utilisateur d'acquérir l'ordinateur où il pourrait choisir le système de son choix. C'est le cas pour la plus grande partie des ordinateurs actuellement commercialisés avec les systèmes Windows ou MacOSX. Bien que cette pratique soit condamnable et condamnée, elle reste très largement tolérée notamment en France. Pour plus d'information:
http://non.aux.racketiciels.info/

[14] Les groupes d'utilisateurs organisent par le biais d'association ou entre eux des « install parties ». Séances au cours desquelles les utilisateurs expérimentés assistent celles et ceux qui veulent « convertir » leur machine. Toutefois cette opération s'est simplifiée et est très documentée sur internet rendant tout à fait possible pour de nombreux « partisans » de tester voir d'installer en toute autonomie.

peuvent facilement être « disqualifiés» s'ils sont considérés comme ostentatoires (y compris concernant l'attractivité visuelle des sites)[15]. Être « design et tendance » est probablement suspect de vouloir séduire par la forme plutôt que par le fond (la très grande majorité des LUG n'ont pas de charte graphique, leur site ne sont illustrés bien souvent que par une bannière de présentation...).

Cette affirmation de simplicité et cet attachement à être indépendant des pouvoirs politiques [16] sont encore une fois des caractéristiques que manifestent les églises protestantes.

L'EMPREINTE DE L'ISLAM, ANICONISME ET PLACE DE LA FEMME ?

Toutefois il est une autre grande religion monothéiste iconoclaste et sans clergé directif centralisé, l'Islam. Là encore, les adeptes de la ligne de commande ramènent l'écriture au centre de l'expression. L'icône y est suspecte. Si GNU/Linux utilise le serveur X Windows pour gérer des applications graphiques, le déploiement d'environnements graphiques va se développer à partir de 1997-1998 avec les environnements KDE et Gnome (ce dernier voyant le jour au Mexique, le plus catholique des états nord-américain !).

Si l'écriture reste la référence, la pratique voudrait que l'utilisateur connaisse de mémoire les commandes de base. Ce qui implique un travail d'apprentissage, de récitation régulière qui est une manière aussi d'entretenir la confession de foi.

L'utilisation de la ligne de commande implique une certaine rigueur que nous avons déjà évoquée. Mais les commandes de bases sont communes à toutes les distributions. L'écriture originelle est une langue commune à chacun. Mais dès que l'on ajoute des couches supplémentaires (notamment lorsqu'il va s'agir de gérer l'organisation et la maintenance du système, les schismes apparaîssent. L'interprétation de la gestion des

[15] On pourrait presque dire qu'en opposition à l'esthétisme épuré et minimaliste d'Apple, l'univers GNU/Linux érige le moche, le naïf et le surchargé comme marque d'authenticité et de probité.

[16] Les libertariens du libre pourraient d'ailleurs être sur la même longueur d'onde à ce sujet. Bien que farouchement athée, taquinant des idées ultra-libérales et proche des thèses de Ayn Rand, de nombreux libristes (nord américains) à l'image de ESR ou encore de Jimmy Wales (fondateur de wikipédia) se revendiquent ou s'inspirent de ce courant, notamment pour justifier rejeter l'interventionnisme « normatif » de l'état, notamment dans la vie culturelle et associative. En synthétisant fortement leur réflexion, pour être une organisation « non-gouvernementale », il ne faut pas toucher d'argent du gouvernement (c'est à dire des impôts). (Mangu-Ward, 2007)

commandes (à défaut des commandements) et la promotion du système, se caractérisent par différents courants. De même l'Islam connaît une séparation majeure entre deux courants (sunnite et chiite). On peut s'essayer à superposer ce schisme au sein de l'Islam avec les ruptures entre les libristes « pragmatiques » comme Linus Torvalds ou Eric S. Raymond et les « idéologues » comme RMS. Mais la superposition serait complexe.. Si les deux premiers peuvent être apparentés au sunnisme par leur adaptabilité au contexte de l'époque, leur rapport désengagé avec les modèles électifs et la place de l'auteur, les positionne certainement plus du côté du chiisme [17]. L'école de la « FSF » serait plutôt sunnite par l'électivité des représentants, mais son conservatisme dogmatique et son attachement au martyr plutôt qu'à la compromission est potentiellement rapprochable du chiisme.

Profitons aussi de cette partie pour évoquer la place ambiguë des femmes.

Dans la représentation occidentale courante, les femmes sont déconsidérées par l'Islam par rapport aux hommes. Pourtant une grande partie des spécialistes de cette religion rapporte que cette vision est abusive, et que la vie du prophète Mahomet[18] lui-même montre que la place de la femme dans la société musulmane est beaucoup plus émancipée qu'on ne veut bien le dire. De même l'univers du logiciel libre n'affiche aucun ségrégationnisme de genre formel, mais force est de constater que la présence des femmes est réduite à environ 2% du corps des développeurs[19] (Hancock, 2008b).

GNU/LINUX EST BOUDDHISTE

L'archétype de l'accoutrement du libriste, en short et en tongues, cheveux longs et barbu (bedonnant au fil du temps), lui vaut aussi d'être « reconnu » comme un hippie de retour de Katmandou, porteur de signes extérieurs de bouddhisme. Cette « zen attitude » serait l'expression du

---

[17] Tony Mobily explique ainsi que Linus Torvalds fait partie des « Dictateur Bienveillant à Vie » et que son rôle est indispensable à la conduite d'un projet open source. Il rappelle que malgré tout personne n'est contraint de le suivre et que c'est la confiance des autres membres de la communauté qui accepte ce rôle (Mobily, 2008).

[18] La femme de Mahomet fût d'abord sa patronne Khadija de 15 ans son aînée (Gaudin, Bressolette, Crombe, Delahoutre, et Collectif, 2009).

[19] On trouvera aussi une traduction de l'article de Terry Hancock sur le site Framablog avec en prime une discussion passionnée entre les lectrices et les les lecteurs (Hancock, 2008a).

détachement de la quête des apparences et l'expression de l'humilité. La machine n'est pas un jouet, mais un objet de quête de la connaissance, une recherche quasi-intérieure et individuelle qui dans la libération du code conduirait à un renoncement de soi. Le modèle « économique » devient alors celui du don, de la charité servant à nourrir l'enveloppe matérielle dans le renoncement du profit personnel.

D'emblée, nous véhiculons un archétype et une réduction occidentalisée de la complexité du bouddhisme qui peut être considéré comme philosophie, doctrine ou religion[20]. Pour simplifier notre propos, nous montrerons rapidement comment s'expriment dans l'univers linuxien trois caractéristiques de l'existence (l'impersonnalité, l'impermanence, l'insatisfaction) et trois poisons du bouddhisme (avidité, colère et ignorance) (Wikipédia, 2011b).

L'impersonnalité est certainement une vertu revendiquée mais en même temps elle entre en conflit avec la place de l'auteur. Si le logiciel libre revendique que l'auteur n'est pas propriétaire, il défend l'existence de son statut qui, du coup, entretient une forme de personnalisation. Mais les voies de l'impersonnalité se manifestent au travers de plusieurs « relativisations » de l'auteur-personne. Chaque application est accompagnée de sa licence ou de fichiers de « crédits » permettant de lister les auteurs et contributeurs. L'utilisation de pseudonymes (comme RMS, ESR...) produisent un détachement de l'individu physique et social pour en faire un membre d'une communauté le reconnaissant (Danet, 1997). La dépersonnalisation s'effectue ensuite dans la liste des crédits par l'accumulation du nombre de contributeurs.

Du côté de l'utilisateur, l'impersonnalité pourrait se trouver dans l'absence d'élément affichant, manifestant son unicité. Mais résolument le système est personnel car au démarrage de chaque session, qu'on soit en mode graphique ou en mode « terminal » (la ligne de commande), il faudra commencer par s'identifier.

Bien sûr ce propos est de plus en plus à nuancer avec l'institutionnalisation, la normalisation de l'environnement lors de son déploiement dans le secteur professionnel.

En revanche l'insatisfaction et l'impermanence sont des caractéristiques très présentes. Dans la mesure où le code source est par essence ouvert à toute modification, la correction et l'amélioration sont parties intégrantes de l'univers du libriste. Chaque logiciel propose dans ses menus et ses fichiers des informations pour faire des « retours de

---

[20] Albert Samuel indique même qu'on pourrait considérer le bouddhisme comme une religion agnostique , athée (Samuel, 1996).

bugs[21] ».

L'impermanence se lit aussi dans l'importance accordée aux numéros de version. Chaque projet définit une politique de numérotation des versions et des qualifications [22] pour spécifier chaque évolution du programme. Le numéro de version est presque systématiquement affiché pendant le lancement de l'application. On le trouve aussi dans le menu « À propos » des applications graphiques. Même si une version est appelée stable, elle reste l'objet de mise à jour (souvent automatisée) chaque fois que l'on constate une « imperfection » du monde au travers de la découverte a posteriori d'un bug.

L'avidité, qui pourrait consister à utiliser un logiciel libre pour s'installer sur des ordinateurs en proposant ensuite des extensions payantes, est une stratégie peu développée car elle est contraire à une logique d'indépendance des utilisateurs. Elle est donc peu visible ou se manifeste exceptionnellement par des fonctionnalités qui sont grisées[23].

Ignorance et colère sont d'un point de vue éthique des poisons pour le libriste. GNU/Linux pour des raisons généralement économiques n'est pas installé sur les ordinateurs. L'acte d'installation amène donc l'utilisateur à devoir apprendre quelques pré-requis sur ce qu'il va faire. De même l'installation d'une nouvelle application ou l'enclenchement des mises à jours nécessitent une validation de sa part qui vaut pour un avertissement à être conscient et connaissant de l'acte qu'il va engager. Un exemple typique est celui de l'ajout d'extensions au navigateur web Firefox. Lorsque l'utilisateur choisit d'installer l'un d'elles, la boîte de dialogue permettant de démarrer l'opération est inactivée pendant quelques secondes avec un compte à rebours visible. Cette temporisation est un choix de développement visant à ce que l'utilisateur réfléchisse à deux fois avant de cliquer. On voit ici comment la patience est complice de la connaissance.

---

[21] Retourner un bug consiste à informer la communauté des développeurs des problèmes et dysfonctionnements rencontrés.

[22] Alpha pour les premiers tests, Béta pour stabiliser les fonctionnalités et évolutions retenues, Realease candidate (RC) pour les versions en cours de validation, avant de qualifier de « Stable » lorsqu'il n'y a plus de bugs de fonctionnement.

[23] C'est le cas pour des applications existants sous une version « communautaire libre » et une version « incluant des fonctionnalités propriétaires ». Il s'agit généralement de produits développés à l'origine par une entreprise qui à libéré le « noyau » de l'application pour l'ouvrir à d'autres développeurs et bénéficier d'une visibilité dans les annuaires de logiciels gratuits et/ou libre. L'application de mindmapping Xmind ou le système de base de données MySql pourraient rentrer dans cette catégorie.

LE BESTIAIRE ANIMISTE DU GNU

Ce qui amuse et rend souvent sympathique au premier abord celui qui découvre l'univers du logiciel libre, c'est son côté Arche de Noé.

Un grand nombre de logiciels libres sont associés à des animaux qui illustrent les icônes de lancement, les splashscreens[24], qui servent à illustrer les démonstrations ou des produits dérivés[25] servant à financer les projets.

Un panda roux enroulé autour d'un globe permet de lancer le navigateur Firefox. L'association fonctionne parfois sur l'analogie d'une caractéristique de l'animal qui illustre l'utilisation de l'application : les oiseaux sont associés à des programmes de messageries ou de communication (comme par exemple Pidgin ou Adium[26]), un mulet représentre eMule qui sert à transporter des fichiers échanger de pair à pair sur le réseau eDonkey. Toutefois l'association peut sortir de cette caractéristique analogique. Ceci renforce la dimension « animiste » qui rend alors le choix de la bête comme appartenant à des relations entre un monde visible et les forces mystiques ou ancestrales d'un monde naturel aux lois invisibles. L'animal est souvent le jumeau de l'homme et en fouillant on trouve des choix de mascotte qui relèvent plus d'une histoire personnelle que d'une symbolique reliant l'animal et le programme.

Le plus célèbre d'entre tous est certainement le manchot Tux, mais il apparaît surtout comme illustration dans les applications ou personnage dans des jeux, car il n'est pas utilisé comme icône de lancement (car pour le lancer il faudrait avoir démarré l'ordinateur sous... GNU/Linux[27]. Toutefois il est symptomatique des voies animistes qui s'insinuent dans la communauté linuxienne. En effet, c'est après avoir été mordu par un manchot dans un zoo australien que Linus Torvalds a proposé que cet animal deviennent la mascotte de Linux. Il raconte différentes versions de l'anecdote. Dans l'une d'entre elle, la morsure aurait été suivie d'une fièvre délirante le plongeant dans une sorte d'extase envers les manchots. Mais il conclut généralement par une version plus simple : il adore les

[24] Écran s'affichant au lancement du programme.

[25] De nombreux sites de projets proposent une boutique de « goodies » vendant des tee-shirts, des peluches, des mugs...

[26] Programmes de messageries instantanées multi-protocoles (Jabber, Gtalk, MSN, AIM...)

[27] Certains puristes taquins pourraient s'amuser à commenter cette évidence en indiquant qu'on pourrait bien lancer GNU/Linux dans une machine virtuelle depuis un autre OS. La redondance trollesque de cette note de bas de page n'a donc d'intérêt que pour les lecteurs qui s'en amuseraient.

manchots et trouve que c'est un animal «goofy and fun[28] » (Baker, 2007).

Au-delà de l'aspect amusant que certains trouveront probablement infantile, on peut émettre l'hypothèse que cette attachement à des animaux, que cet espèce d'animisme potache exprime une relation particulière à la machine. L'utilisateur de système GNU/Linux est imaginé (et se vit) comme un geek, c'est à dire une personne ayant une relation particulière avec l'ordinateur. Un héritage d'une culture cybernétique qui n'en fait pas une machine, mais un être. A cette hypothèse culturelle, s'ajoute une hypothèse socio-politique. La société animiste est une société sans Etat (Gaudin, Bressolette, Crombe, Delahoutre, et Collectif, 2009), et on retrouve là le crédo des libertariens tel Eric S. Raymond.

GNI[29]/DIEU GNI/MAÎTRE

Et finalement si la production de signes sous GNU/Linux était plutôt du côté d'idéologies ou de réflexions matérialistes.

L'éthique communautaire pourrait produire des objets ayant par exemple une connotation marxiste pour reprendre la terminologie de Roland Barthes. L'investissement des pays sud-américain marxistes ou anti-capitalistes dans le mouvement du logiciel libre est croissant notamment sous l'impulsion du Vénézuela, de Cuba, du Brésil, du Pérou, de l'Uruguay... (Criado, 2008) Mais il paraît difficile d'identifier des symboles marxisants au niveau des interfaces ou des applications. Tout au plus peut-on repérer sur les principaux gestionnaires de bureau une icône permettant de changer d'utilisateur sur même ordinateur. Cette possibilité donne ainsi une dimension « collectiviste » à une machine qui n'est plus celle d'un utilisateur unique. Notons toutefois que cette fonctionnalité n'est pas spécifique à l'environnement GNU/Linux.

On peut interroger alors une sémiotique qui pencherait vers une expression libertaire voire libérale et qui se traduirait notamment par la personnalisation à outrance de l'environnement en commençant par le bureau mais aussi dans les nombreuses applications qui offrent la possibilité de « skiner » l'apparence et la présentation des interfaces. C'est le cas par exemple de Firefox qui peut porter des « tenues » différentes. C'est aussi le cas controversé de Gimp. L'application d'infographie nativement propose une interface mutlti-fenêtrée où les palettes d'outils comme les images possèdent leurs propres fenêtres. L'utilisateur peut à loisir, en fonction de ses besoins et de sa pratique, les positionner de

[28] Qu'on traduira par «taré et amusant ».

[29] GNI ne veut rien dire, il sert juste l'esthétique du titre et se prononce « ni ».

manière très personnelle. Mais la conséquence est une accumulation de fenêtres sur le bureau. Certains utilisateurs (notamment les « nouveaux arrivants ») souhaiteraient regrouper toutes ces fenêtres en une seule. Cette demande a longtemps fait l'objet de discussions entre utilisateurs et développeurs. Si à partir de la version 2.8, les utilisateurs auront le choix, à ce jour les tenants du multi-fenêtrage argumentent que sous GNU/Linux, l'utilisateur dispose de plusieurs bureaux entre lesquels il peut naviguer facilement. Il peut donc ouvrir son GIMP sur un bureau dédié évitant ainsi un éparpillement au milieu des fenêtres de d'autres applications. Cette méthode et forme d'organisation ne saute pas aux yeux du « nouvel arrivant ». Il n'a pas le réflexe de cette pratique qui nécessite au départ d'avoir une représentation de son environnement comme allant au-delà du visible.

Si jusqu'à maintenant nous avions principalement évoqué un système austère, généralement basé sur la ligne de commande, il nous apparaît, avec cette personnalisation poussée à l'extrême,nécessaire d' évoquer un glissement vers une approche plus ludique et plus hédoniste de l'interface devenue graphique.

Sous l'impulsion notamment des Mexicain Miguel De Icaza et Federico Meno Quinter, GNU/Linux va s'habiller à partir de 1997 d'un environnement graphique, Gnome[30]. Ce qui se joue avec cette interface, c'est une approche plus manipulable, plus esthétique. Pour séduire le « geek », elle offre des fonctionnalités (notamment des appliquettes) parfaitement inutiles si ce n'est pour le plaisir des yeux ou de la bidouille. L'un des exemples typique est Wanda, un petit poisson que l'on peut installer dans la barre de menu et qui bouge ses nageoires. Une combinaison de clics et de touches spécifiques permet de libérer le poisson qui va alors nager sur l'ensemble de l'écran.

Complété par le système d'affichage « compiz fusion », la gestion des fenêtres devient un moment d'auto-satisfaction pour l'utilisateur qui va pouvoir gérer des effets d'apparition et de disparition sur les fenêtres, créer de la 3D en trompe l'œil et des transparences pour gérer des superpositions d'applications.

L'univers informatique devient alors un terrain de jeu, un espace que l'on décore, que l'on aménage, un prétexte à des réglages sans fin qui justifient un sur-investissement du temps passer avec la machine (en argumentant du contraire... il faut que ce soit convivial compte tenu du temps où l'on va l'utiliser).

---

[30] Si à la même époque le gestionnaire de fenêtres KDE est un peu en avance sur Gnome, ce dernier semble être le plus utilisé.

Conclusion

Cette exploration rudimentaire des interfaces GNU/Linux ne prétend pas rendre compte de résultats d'observations. Nous avons plutôt esquissé une série de portraits de la diversité des mises en formes et de leurs relations avec des usages.

Nous souhaitons bien sûr à partir de ce premier jet, mettre en œuvre des observations plus systématiques pour vérifier les hypothèses que nous soulevons. Ils serait pertinent d'aller à la rencontre des équipes de développement et des utilisateurs. Nous pourrions alors envisager rendre compte plus précisément de la relation entre l'usage et le fonctionnement de l'interface pour repérer des impacts « idéologiques » et des arrangements ou subversions qui se dégageraient de ces dispositifs.

Nous retiendrons cependant que l'univers du logiciel libre et de l'open source est traversé par la diversité. Que l'engagement idéologique s'inscrit dans les interfaces et les usages qu'ils sous-tendent. Certes on peut les considérer parfois comme des paradoxes à première vue. Par exemple, le fait que pour installer une nouvelle application ou effectuer certaines opérations sur le système nécessite de devoir avoir des droits d'administrateur impliquerait un lien de dépendance, et donc une altération de la liberté de l'utilisateur. Mais généralement l'utilisateur est l'administrateur ou en a les droits[31].

Cette extrême diversité des possibles donne probablement à GNU/Linux une image de complexité produisant de l'inquiétude et du doute quant à l'appropriation du système pour les utilisateurs d'informatique peu confiants dans leurs compétences. Pourtant, le système se décline en « distributions » qui sont des assemblages « clés en main » en fonction des utilisations et des compétences[32].

Cet œcuménisme des usages et de leur mise en scène permet aussi de faire de cet environnement un terrain d'exploration et c'est probablement pour cette raison que même si GNU/Linux n'est présent que sur 2% d'ordinateurs personnels (source : NetmarketShare – Aout 2011), il a une notoriété qui dépasse de loin le cercle de ses usagers.

Cette variété des usages est une des raisons qui motive actuellement

---

[31] En général l'utilisateur principal de la machine dispose des droits d'administration. Mais pour des raisons de sécurisation et de temporisation des réflexes, on lui demande son mot de passe en guise d'accord chaque fois qu'une opération pourrait compromettre le système.

[32] Il existe des « distributions » pour les enfants non-lecteurs, pour les utilisateurs chevronnés, pour tenter de récupérer le contenu d'un disque dur, pour installer sur un téléphone portable (Wikipédia, 2011c)...

notre engagement dans l'observation des pratiques communicationnelles au sein de la communauté du logiciel libre. Pratiques qui ont le mérite de rendre visible la mise en œuvre de dispositifs de communication et de décisions en explorant de nombreux modèles organisationnels.

Bibliographie

Baker, S (2007). « The History of Tux the Linux Penguin ». In : *wikiid!* [En ligne]. [s.l.] : [s.n.]. Disponible sur : http://www.sjbaker.org/wiki/index.php?title=The_History_of_Tux_the_Linux_Penguin (consulté le 1 novembre 2011)

Criado, M A (2008). « Linux conquista América Latina ». In : *Framablog* [En ligne]. [s.l.] : [s.n.]. Disponible sur : http://www.framablog.org/index.php/post/2008/11/12/linux-conquista-america-latina (consulté le 2 novembre 2011)

Danet, B (1997). « Playful Expressivity and Artfulness in Computer-mediated Communication - General Introduction ». *Journal of Computer-Mediated Communication* [En ligne]. Vol. 1, n°2,. Disponible sur : < http://jcmc.indiana.edu/vol1/issue2/genintro.html > (consulté le 1 novembre 2011)

Gaudin, P, Bressolette, C, Crombe, V, Delahoutre, M (2009). *Les grandes religions*. [s.l.] : Ellipses Marketing. ISBN : 2729841709.

Hancock, T (2008a). « Les femmes et le logiciel libre », In : *Framablog* [En ligne]. [s.l.] : [s.n.]. Disponible sur : http://www.framablog.org/index.php/post/2008/10/21/femmes-et-logiciels-libres (consulté le 31 octobre 2011)

—. (2008b). « Ten easy ways to attract women to your free software project » In : *Free Software Magazine* [En ligne]. [s.l.] : [s.n.]. Disponible sur : http://www.freesoftwaremagazine.com/columns/ten_easy_ways_attract_women_your_free_software_project > (consulté le 31 octobre 2011)

Lancashire, D (2005). « Code, Culture and Cash : The Fading Altruism of Open Source Development », *First Monday* [En ligne]. Special issue #2 : Open Source. Disponible sur : http://firstmonday.org/htbin/cgiwrap/bin/ojs/index.php/fm/rt/printerFriendly/1488/1403 > (consulté le 30 octobre 2011)

Mangu-Ward, K (2007). « Wikipedia and Beyond », In : *Reason Magazine* [En ligne]. [s.l.] : [s.n.]. Disponible sur : http://reason.com/archives/2007/05/30/wikipedia-and-beyond (consulté le 2 novembre 2011)

Mobily, T (2008). « Dictators in free and open source software ». *Free*

Software Magazine [En ligne]. [s.l.] : [s.n.]. Disponible sur : http://www.freesoftwaremagazine.com/columns/dictators_free_and_open_source_software (consulté le 31 octobre 2011)

O'Mahony, S & Ferraro, F (2007). « The emergence of governance in an open source community », *Academy of Management Journal,* 50(5), pp. 1079–1106.

Raymond, E (1997). « La cathédrale et le bazar », [s.l.] : [s.n.]. Disponible sur : http://www.linux-france.org/article/these/cathedrale-bazar/cathedrale-bazar.html (consulté le 30 octobre 2011)

Samuel, A (1996). *Les religions aujourd'hui.* 4e éd.[s.l.] : Editions de l'Atelier. ISBN : 2708232096.

Torvalds, L & Guignot, P (2011). « Linus Torvalds : l'interview anniversaire des 20 ans du noyau - LinuxFr.org ». In *LinuxFr* [En ligne]. [s.l.] : [s.n.]. Disponible sur : http://linuxfr.org/news/linus-torvalds-l%E2%80%99interview-anniversaire-des-20%C2%A0ans-du-noyau (consulté le 30 octobre 2011)

Wikipedia (2011a). *Microsoft Windows* [En ligne]. *Wikipédia.* 2011a. Disponible sur : < http://fr.wikipedia.org/wiki/Microsoft_Windows > (consulté le 2 novembre 2011)

—. (2011b). « Bouddhisme ». In : *Wikipédia* [En ligne]. [s.l.] : [s.n.]. Disponible sur : http://fr.wikipedia.org/wiki/Bouddhisme#Les_trois_caract.C3.A9ristiques_de_l.27existence. (consulté le 1 novembre 2011)

—. (2011c). *Liste des distributions Linux* [En ligne]. *Wikipédia.* Disponible sur : http://fr.wikipedia.org/wiki/Liste_des_distributions_Linux (consulté le 2 novembre 2011)

Williams, S, Stallman, R & Masutti, C (2010). *Richard Stallman et la révolution du logiciel libre. Une biographie autorisée,* [En ligne]. 1er éd. [s.l.] : Eyrolles. Disponible sur : http://www.eyrolles.com/Informatique/Livre/richard-stallman-et-la-revolution-du-logiciel-libre-9782212126099. ISBN : 2212126093.

NONVERBAL SENSITIVITY AND NETWORK CENTRALITY: USING OUR ABILITIES TO INTERPRET EMOTIONS AND BECOME POPULAR

LOREDANA IVAN

Abstract

Predicting a positive relationship between nonverbal competence and centrality in their class network, we used DANVA-2 (Nowicki, 2004) to assess 54 adolescents' abilities to decode others' emotions. Unlike previous studies (Custrini & Feldman, 1989; Konold et al., 2010) that measured popularity based on the evaluations of significant others (parents, teachers), we suggested a structural approach, based on Social Network Analysis. We referred to the network centrality as an indicator of the participants' relational capital. We also discussed the possible influences of gender and sex role identity (Bem, 1981), both on the nonverbal sensitivity and on the group centrality. The results prove the importance of using high stake situations when testing an individual's abilities to decode emotions.

Key words: nonverbal sensitivity, decoding emotions, network centrality, sex role identity

INTRODUCTION

In the modern workplace, the ability to interact with others – colleagues, subordinates, clients, and so on – establish and maintain social contacts and to predict and influence the behaviour of others is considered both a part of an individual's personal success and a dimension of professional success. The relevance of social skills in predicting outputs of human interactions has been widely debated in social psychological literature for the past 20 years (Goleman, 1995; Bandura, 1997; Capella,

1997; Saarni, 1999; Hess & Philippot, 2007; Greene & Burelson, 2008; Spitzberg, 2008). This concept is generally described as a constant behavioural adjustment to others, a process of mutual adaptation and accommodation with certain assertive value by which individuals define flexible goals relative to groups, gaining rewards and achieving social status. However, the insulated influence of social competence over the specific analysed outputs could be difficult to prove mostly because the concept itself is broad and context-related (see Ivan, 2008; 2009).

Nonverbal sensitivity is one dimension of the broader concept of social skills, referring to one's ability to code and decode nonverbal messages and use nonverbal elements to estimate or predict others' emotions, attitudes and behavioural intentions (Ivan, 2009, p. 135). There are similar concepts in social psychological literature, including "emotional competence", "self-efficacy", "emotional intelligence" and "communication skills", denoting different aspects of the individual's social skills. "Nonverbal sensitivity" is commonly used when particularly describing people's ability to code and decode nonverbal elements (see Hall & Bernieri, 2001).

Certainly when coding and decoding nonverbal messages one can notice individual differences based on personal characteristics or abilities to access different channels of communication, but there are also group differences and occupational or cultural differences (Slama-Cazacu, 2007; Ivan, 2008; Hall, 2009; Barrier, 2010). Standardized instruments are needed in order to emphasize these differences in nonverbal competences. Although there are researches focused mainly on the encoding of emotion (e.g. Wagner, Buck & Winterbothsam, 1993), it is methodologically problematic to elaborate standardized instruments to measure an individual's ability to encode nonverbal elements because it is difficult to establish a standard or a proper expression of an emotion associated with a peculiar situation (see Hall, 2009). This is why the current international research focuses on nonverbal or interpersonal sensitivity as the ability to decode the emotions of others and to make inferences about that stimulus (a person's emotional state or personality traits) or other aspects related to the context of interaction.

Several research instruments and alternative methodologies have been used to assess interpersonal sensitivity (Hall & Bernieri, 2001). Among them, standardized tests have been considered valid methodological approaches. The pioneering work of Rosenthal and his colleagues (1979) produced one of first standardized instruments to assess nonverbal sensitivity: the Profile of Nonverbal Sensitivity (PONS). It consists of 220 two-second paralinguistic or visual slides representing 20 interpersonal situations enacted by the same female encoder. Other similar measurements, the Interpersonal Perception Task (IPT; Archer & Contanzo, 1988) or the Diagnostic Analysis of Nonverbal Accuracy (Nowicki & Duke, 1994) are also widely quoted in the literature.

People's nonverbal sensitivity, briefly defined as the ability to decode nonverbal cues, has already been related to: 1) An individual's performance on particular tasks, such as accuracy in detecting lies or deception (Ekman & O'Sulivan, 1991; Ekman, 2009) – those who recognized basic emotions when stimulus was presented for a quarter of a second have better performance in distinguishing stimulus persons who lied or told the truth; 2) Leadership styles (Riggio, 2001; Knapp & Hall, 2005) – task-oriented leaders proved to be more nonverbal sensitive than goal-oriented leaders; 3) Value orientation – those who strongly embraced social values and were less dogmatic also proved to be nonverbal competent (Hall, Andrzejewski &Yopchick, 2009); 4) Job type or professional interests – subjects professionally trained to pay attention and decode subtle nonverbal elements, including criminalists or artists, scored higher on the nonverbal sensitivity tests, indicating that nonverbal competence could be trained (Ekman & O'Sulivan, 1991; Ekman & Friesen, 2003; De Paulo et al., 2003).

NONVERBAL SENSITIVITY AND GENDER DIFFERENCES

The idea that women are more nonverbal sensitive than men is widely debated (see Saarni, 1999), and the empirical evidence seems to support such hypothesis. A meta-analysis conducted by Judith Hall (1978) using 75 studies of nonverbal accuracy found that women scored significantly better than men regardless of sample size, age of the judges and sex or age of the stimuli person. Using the PONS test to assess nonverbal sensitivity, Rosenthal and his collaborators (1979) reported a consistent gender effect in 80% of the tested samples (N = 2615). Previous research conducted in Romania (Ivan, 2009; Ivan & Duduciuc, 2011) also found that female students were more accurate than male students, especially on body-only items, on the PONS test. However, several studies using other nonverbal sensitivity measures, including DANVA, failed to produce any gender differences (e.g. Rosip & Hall, 2004; Mullins-Nelson, Salekin & Leistico, 2006).

When discussing gender differences in nonverbal sensitivity, some scholars (Hall, 1990; Saarni, 1999) claim that women perform better in measures because in European cultures – where most of the studies have been conducted – females are encouraged to express and read emotions as part of their social role. With that contention, researchers are using gender role identity to explain differences in social competences. It is also plausible that we are not dealing with real gender differences but rather with sex role differences, meaning a correlation between sex role identity (Eagly, 1987, 1997) and nonverbal decoding skills may be more consistent than a correlation contingent on biological sex differences. One's sex role identity, also described as one's psychological sex, describes the degree to which one self-identifies with stereotypical masculine or feminine characteristics. Following the socialization explanation, we could expect that individuals who define themselves by including feminine characteristics, regardless of biological sex, would perform differently in nonverbal decoding tasks from those who define themselves by masculine characteristics. In fact, one study (Schneider & Schneider-Düker, 1984) conducted on 40 students (20 males and 20 females) using the Bem-Sex Role Inventory (BSRI; Bem, 1981) to assess feminine or masculine self-identification concluded that "masculine" female students and "feminine" male students tended to have higher nonverbal decoding accuracy. This study also failed to produce evidence for simple biological sex differences. The current research analysis of the importance of sex role identity in regard to nonverbal accuracy argues that, although biological sex might not influence participant performance in decoding nonverbal cues, sex role identity could be used as a relevant predictor.

Nonverbal Sensitivity and Group Centrality

The relation between nonverbal sensitivity and an individual's centrality in groups has been assessed mainly on children. Using subjects between the ages of five and twelve, two similar studies (Hubbard & Coie, 1994; Boyatzis & Satyaprasd, 1994) argued that children with high abilities to decode emotions enjoy more appreciation among their peers, are more actively involved in playing with others in groups and are better in negotiating frustrating situations. Previously gathered data (Walden & Field, 1990; Cassidy & Berlin, 1994) also showed that individuals with high nonverbal sensitivity are preferred as interaction partners and easily accepted in groups. Moreover, research conducted on students (Saarni, 1999; Carton, Kessler & Pape, 1999) confirm the results obtained in children's groups – students with better performances in emotional decoding tasks have been evaluated by their teachers as better adjusted to their classmates. Recently, studies conducted on adults in formal networks (Byron, Terranova & Nowicki, 2007; Elfenbein et al, 2007) have connected social competences, particularly nonverbal ones, with an individual's appreciation of others, defined as working partners. Essentially, individuals who are highly nonverbal sensitive received more gratification from their work colleagues. One methodological problem with the studies mentioned above is the way centrality in groups has been measured, using the unspecific evaluation of others – parents, teachers, colleagues – without a structural approach on the real position of the individual relative to the other group members. Research conducted on children and adolescents assessed centrality in groups according to teacher, parent and self evaluations, while studies conducted on teamwork took into account cumulative evaluations of collegues, subordinates and managers. A study run by Nowicki and Duke (1994) tried to overcome these limitations by testing the relation between nonverbal sensitivity and the structural position of subjects in their social networks using a different methodology. Participants (primary school children) were provided with a list of all the names of their classmates and asked to circle the names of the three children they liked the most and draw a line through the names of the three children they liked the least. Such an approach allows us to calculate one sociometric score of "Like" and "Dislike" for each of the participants in the experiment. Nowicki and Duke (1994) proved that children who were better at decoding nonverbal cues were also more popular among their classmates.

One possible approach to connecting nonverbal sensitivity and an individual's centrality in groups is the Social Network Analysis (SNA). SNA, reviving the relational resources in explaining behavior, has been an important topic in sociological and anthropological research for more than thirty years (Lévi-Strauss, 1968; Coleman, 1990) and has recently become an expansive research domain. For the past ten years, SNA has also been used in economics and political science on issues related to trust and interdependence (see Flap, 1999; Scott, 2000; Knoke & Yang, 2008), major topics in current social and political agenda. Specialists in the area have evaluated the way the structural positions of individuals in their networks could be a factor in finding personal or professional opportunities, such as a better job or a life partner (Moerbeek, Ultee & Flap, 1995; Bellotti, 2008). Alternatively, this sometimes keeps individuals in places they do not find any gratifications, despite the availability of alternatives (Rusbult & Martz, 1995; Lewis et al., 2008). Another research line linked social networks with social stratification, where networks are treated as forms of social capital and relational resources (Downey, 1995; Sandu, 2005).

The present research uses micro social network analysis to find whether highly nonverbal sensitive individuals are also central in their formal networks. The concept of centrality denotes a social actor's popularity and visibility (Wasserman & Faust, 1994, pp. 169–219) in addition to indicating the level of the actor's involvement in direct or mediated ties within the network.

The relation between network centrality and nonverbal sensitivity works in two ways. On the one side, highly nonverbal sensitive social actors could easily anticipate the reactions of others and pay more attention to their subtle cues. Thus, they have proper reactions in interactional situations and, as a result, gain visibility and multiple connections. On the other side, having a central position in the network offers a social actor the possibility of access and control to the informational flow, experience that could enrich one's social competence.

When discussing centrality in adolescent groups, several studies (e.g. Butovskaya, Timentschik & Burkova, 2007) conclude that boys and girls have different means to achieve popularity: girls prefer to interact with fewer classmates, spending more time with them, while boys prefer larger groups. Moreover, boys who like school are more popular in peer groups than girls who like school. Those studies also concluded that some stereotypical "masculine" characteristics, such as aggression, could increase a female's chances of becoming popular in peer networks. This means we should also test the moderator effect of sex and sex role identity on group centrality when evaluating adolescent networks. The sex role identities of participants could influence the process of status attainment in adolescent groups. Both popularity and nonverbal competence could be linked with self-role identity.

Nonverbal Sensitivity Testing in High Stake Situations

Most studies testing individuals on their ability to decode nonverbal cues have been conducted in neutral or low-stake situations, without subjects' expectations of reward or repercussion for high or poor performance that one would experience in real life. In a recent publication (Ivan 2009, pp. 219–220), I presented the dispute between social psychologists and economists about using financial incentives to reward performances in experiments – psychologists believe subjects should be intrinsically motivated to perform the experimental tasks while economists agree financial incentives would increase subjects' performance.

When discussing those two alternatives – high-stake versus low-stake experimental situations – only for the nonverbal sensitivity topic, Ekman and Frank (1997) concluded that high stake situations allow more reliable results and could be generalized beyond the particular context created for the experiment. They proved that an individual's ability to decode lies and deception could be generalized beyond the specific lie or deceptive situations they are asking to judged, but only in high-stake situations, when the subjects are rewarded or punished for their performance. The authors mostly refer to social rewards, not necessarily financial incentives.

There are also researchers (Phillips, Tunstall & Channon, 2007; Tracy & Robins, 2008) who addressed the question of inhibitory and stimulatory factors in nonverbal behaviour decoding tasks, showing cognitive load could act as an inhibitory factor. The researchers examined cognitive load as associated to complex tasks or tasks that require considerable memory effort. High-stake situations also require intense cognitive effort. For the present research, we compare individuals' nonverbal decoding performance in two adolescent groups, including one in which we increased the stake of the experimental situation through financial incentives. We wanted to test what happens with an individual's nonverbal sensitivity when the stake associated with nonverbal accuracy is high, a context often replicated in real life.

We previously experienced difficulties including financial incentives in experiments on Romanian student samples (Ivan, 2009) because participants in our initial experimental group did not actually believe they would receive any money. This happened mainly because Romanian students rarely take part in experiments, so the situation was uncommon and the idea of being rewarded for their performance in such a situation was even more far-fetched. Cumulatively, the financial incentives were difficult to take seriously. When research is conducted in places with low experiment culture, ad hoc rewards, rather than promised rewards, could be used as a procedure in order to be sure subjects interpret the situation as a high-stake one.

Method

Participants

A group of 54 adolescents (36 girls and 18 boys), aged 16 to 17, from a high school outside Bucharest took part in the experiment. Formally, the 54 students were distributed in two classes, one with 30 pupils (28 girls and 2 boys) and one with 24 pupils and we conducted the experiment separately on the two groups as a part of their extracurricular activities.

Individual Measures

Nonverbal sensitivity testing

The Diagnostic Analysis of Nonverbal Accuracy

DANVA 2 Adult (Nowicki, 2004) has been used to measure nonverbal sensitivity both on visual and audio channel. The Adult Faces are composed of 24 items (static) with different encoders expressing one of four emotions – happy, sad, angry or fearful – with high or low intensity. Participants fill in an answer-sheet after seeing each stimulus person, choosing the emotion (from the four possible options) they think the stimulus person might feel. The Adult Postures component of the test also consists of 24 body-only items where subjects perform a similar task, choosing the proper emotion, when they cannot see stimulus person's face. In the case of Adult Voices, the 24 items are presented only on an audio channel, with different encoders saying the same sentence, "I am going out of the room now, and I will be back later," with different voice inflexions associated to the emotion the stimulus feels. Subjects then perform the same task, choosing one of the four emotions after hearing each item.

Participants' centrality

First, we obtain relational data in both groups using a sociometric questionnaire with a roster of names. We opted for a free-choice design, with no restrictions for the number of chosen actors, which was recommended in the literature (Wasserman & Faust, 1994) when assessing centrality in ego-centred networks. Four relational ties were analysed, two related to school issues and two to extracurricular issues: "cooperation in a school project", "asking help to do a homework for a course you have missed", "follow someone's advice to go on a funny trip", and "borrow money". Separate rosters containing only classmate names were given to the two experimental groups. To assess the "cooperation in a project" network, we asked participants, "With whom would you like to work on school project?" The answers were dichotomous for each individual from the list. The data was analysed using the Social Network Analysis software tool UCINET (Borgatti, Everett, & Freeman, 2002). We calculated every individual's centrality in each of the networks using degree centrality for the non-directional relational ties, for example "cooperate with somebody in a project", and we added in-degree centrality as an indicator of centrality in directional examples, such as "asking help for a homework".

Popular actors are most often the "object" and not the "source" of the relation and in-degree and out-degree centrality are used in SNA to make such distinction. Note that in the case of directional ties, those who have no contribution to the analysed network are deleted. We have also used normalized centrality in order to control for the networks' size.

Second, we tested the centrality of the adolescents using the Nowicki and Duke (1994) indicators mentioned above. Participants were asked to circle, from the roster of names, people they liked the most and draw a line through people they liked the least, using a free choice design (no specific number of answers was required). We computed scores from the "Like" and "Dislike" indicators for each participant, and the normalized scores were used when analyzing the data, in order to control for the network size.

Sex role identification

The Bem Sex Role Inventory (BSRI; Bem, 1981) has been used to assess participant self-description in "masculine" or "feminine" terms. A Romanian back-translated version of the BSRI was initially pre-tested on a group of 30 adolescents before being integrated in current research. The instrument consists of 60 scales of bipolar attributes stereotypically associated with masculinity and femininity. After calculating "femininity" and "masculinity" scores for each individual, the instrument separates participants into four possible categories of sex role identity: F (individuals with high femininity scores), M (individuals with high masculine scores), MF (psychological androgyny, both feminine and high masculine scores above the mean), and N (non-differentiated – individuals with both masculine and feminine scores below the mean).

Procedure

The first adolescent group (30 participants; we refer to this as non-incentive group) was tested with DANVA-2 Adult, the test presented as a measure of their ability to decode nonverbal cues on face, posture and voice. They then completed the sociometric questionnaire, using a code to preserve the anonymity of their answers. Students marked codes in the questionnaire that corresponded to the names from the list, advised to choose only people from their class. Participants were also tested using BEM and additional information about participant age and gender was requested. Each student also filled out a personal code identical to the one from the roster of names. In the end, they were required to circle the colleagues they liked the most and the colleagues they like the least from the list of their classmate's names.

In the second adolescent group (24 participants, we refer to this as incentive group) the procedure was similar, but participants were told a financial incentive would be offered after their completion of the DANVA, pending their performance. The incentives were shown before starting the research, and participants were assured they could receive 1 RON (Romanian currency) for each DANVA item correctly identified, just after finishing the test. A research assistant conducted the evaluation and offered the incentive for their performance before we continued the experiment using the other measures. The research was conducted during the daily school programme of the students and was followed by a discussion as a part of debriefing.

Results

Participants' Nonverbal Decoding Accuracy

The nonverbal decoding abilities of our sample are close to the normative adolescent group (15-18 years of age): $M = 4.2$, $SD = 2.3$ for DANVA adult faces ($N = 333$); $M = 6.5$, $SD = 3.4$ for DANVA adult voices ($N = 333$); and $M = 10.9$, $SD = 3.4$ ($N = 136$) for DANVA adult postures (Nowicki, 2004, p. 36).

There were significant gender differences only in the case of posture items, with female participants being significantly better at decoding nonverbal cues specific to the four basic emotions when posture items were presented, as compared to male adolescents, $t(52) = -2.657$, $p = .01$. Although the mean number of errors for DANVA voice items was less for males than for female participants, the differences are modest and not statistically significant.

We tested the nonverbal decoding accuracy for the two groups – incentive and non-incentive – trying to prove that when we raised the stakes for the nonverbal decoding tasks, participants improved their performances. We obtained significant mean differences for DANVA posture items, $t(52) = 2.029$, $p < .05$), and modest mean differences for DANVA face items, $t(52) = -1.867$, $p < .06$). However, the number of female students from the non-incentive group was significantly higher than the number of male students, and the differences obtained for DANVA posture items are actually caused by the fact that females proved to be more accurate in decoding posture items. When we controlled for gender, we did not find any significant differences in DANVA postures scores between the incentive and the non-incentive group. Although modest, the presence of the incentive increased participant accuracy in decoding basic emotions on face items, probably because people pay more attention to subtle cues in high-stake situations. One possible explanation for the increased accuracy of the financial incentive group, only in case of DANVA face items, could be that decoding emotions on face is a common task for most people and accuracy is very much dependent on the importance of the situation.

Fig 31-1 Means and standard deviation for nonverbal decoding accuracy scores (DANVA)*

Level of nonverbal sensitivity	**DANVA faces**	**DANVA postures**	**DANVA voices**			
	M	SD	M	SD	M	SD
Females (N = 36)	4.8	2.4	6.6	2.4	6.6	3.0
Males (N = 18)	4.5	2.9	8.5	2.0	5.6	1.8
Incentive group (N = 24)	4.0	2.4	8.0	1.8	6.0	2.9
Non-incentive group (N = 30)	5.3	2.6	6.7	2.7	6.6	2.5
Total (N =54)	5.0	2.6	7.0	2.4	6.0	2.6

* DANVA scores are calculated by counting the number of errors of nonverbal sensitivity (The lower means fewer errors in emotion decoding).

Sex Role Identity and Nonverbal Accuracy

The scores for he Bem Sex Role Inventory (BSRI) reveal that most of the adolescents could be integrated in the androgyny type (N = 24) or in the non-differentiated type (N = 20). Only 6 participants could be defined as "masculine type" and 4 participants as "feminine type", according to their "femininity" and "masculinity" scores (M = 4.9, SD = .74, for the femininity scores; M = 4.3, SD = .62, for the masculinity scores). It could be that typical feminine self-descriptions are developing when individuals reach maturity while adolescents, who are in a process of identity formation, incorporate both masculine and feminine characteristics. The scores on "masculinity" and "femininity" were not significantly different in regard to gender. Scores on "masculine" dimension modestly correlated with scores on "feminine" dimension, although the relation is negative as we might have expected (r = —.02, p > .05), proving that adolescents tend to include both masculine and feminine characteristics in their gender self-identity. When we analysed the correlation between the feminine or masculine sex role identity in participants and their abilities to decode basic emotions, we found support for a possible negative relation between feminine sex role identity and emotion decoding accuracy. Although there were no differences between boys and girls in the accuracies on DANVA adult faces, we found significant sex role differences in the accuracies on the DANVA adult faces (except for the happy faces items). As we can see in Table 31-2, participants with high femininity scores had significantly more errors in decoding sad face items (r = .37, p < .01) and fear face items (r = .26, p < .05) when controlling for the incentives. It seems that the more participants described themselves in stereotypical feminine terms, the less they managed to decode basic emotions on face items (especially the negative ones: sad and fear).

Fig 1-2. Correlation[a] matrix: emotion decoding (DANVA adult [b]) and sex role identity (BSRI)

	BSRI Femininity	BSRI Masculinity	DANVA sad faces	DANVA fear face	DANVA total face	DANVA fear voices
BSRI Femininity	—					
BSRI Masculinity	—.024	—				
DANVA sad faces	.379**	—.017	—			
DANVA fear face	.265*	—.095	.375**	—		
DANVA total face	.340**	—.085	.644**	.796**	—	
DANVA fear voices	—.277*	—.171	—.054	.171	.057	—

*p < .05 two-tailed, **p < .01 two-tailed

[a] Partial correlation, with controlling for the incentives

[b] DANVA scores are calculated based or emotion decoding errors

We also compared the mean nonverbal decoding errors between the non-differentiated group (N = 20) and the androgyny group (N = 24) and we found that non-differentiated group had more errors in decoding fear voices, t (42) = —2.609, p = .01, and they were also less popular among their classmates: the "Dislike" scores are significant higher compare to the androgyny group, t(42) = —1.961, p < .05.

Centrality Measures and Nonverbal Sensitivity

The four centrality measures- the standardized scores for "Like" and "Dislike" indicators, using Nowicki and Duke (1994) procedure and the degree centrality measurements for the four types of relational ties ("cooperate in a school project", "asking help to do a homework", "following someone advise to go on a funny trip", "borrow money"'), and Social Network Analysis have been correlated to the nonverbal accuracy of the participants. We found that the "Liked" scores significantly correlated with the ability to decode sad faces (r = .29, p < .05, when we controlled for the incentives), as well as with the ability to decode happy posture items (r = —.42, p < .01, when we controlled for the incentives). The "Dislike" scores significantly correlated with the ability to decode DANVA posture in general (r = .30, p < .05) and especially angry posture (r =.292, p<.05) and fear posture (r =.250, p <.07), when controlling for the gender effect. In other words, students who were popular in their groups made more errors in decoding sad faces but were significantly better at decoding happy postures, while students who were less popular had difficulties in interpreting angry postures and fear postures.

When correlations were calculated for the centrality in all four relational ties, we obtained similar results: subjects who were central in the "funny trip" network were also better at decoding happy facial expressions (r = —.29, p < .05) and scored lower when decoding angry faces (r = .30, p< .05). We also obtained a significant relationship between centrality in the "asking help to do homework" network and student ability to decode happy postures (r = .36, p < .01), as well as between the centrality in the "borrow money" network and student ability to interpret angry posture items (r = .31, p < .05), although it is difficult to interpret that. It could be that those central in "borrow" networks express anger less often and have also difficulties in decoding subtle cues of this basic emotion.

One interesting analysis comes in a comparison of the six centrality measures, formulating possible predictors for being liked or disliked in an adolescent network. First of all we found gender differences both on "Like" and "Dislike" indicators, t(52) = 5.300, p < .001; t (52) = 3.819, p

< .001), with girls being more "liked' and "disliked" than boys. It could be that girls are usually more active in adolescent groups, making them more visible for peers evaluation. We also found differences between mean "Like" and "Dislike" indicators between the two tested classes: the one with 28 girls and 2 boys, and the one with 8 girls and 16 boys, t(52) = 19.240, p < .001; t (52) = 5.140, p < .001. It looks like in female dominated classes, popularity is structured differently that in mixed adolescent classes. We also found a higher level of degree centrality for the "cooperation in a project" network in female dominated classes as compared to the mixed one, t (52) = 2.884, p < .01.

Table 31-3 shows how centrality in the adolescent network is defined: individuals who are central in one specific network– "cooperate in a project" for example– tended to be central in other networks as well, such "asking help with a homework." The level of centrality in school related networks correlated with one other (r = .34, p < .05), but the degree centralities in non school-related networks were even more related (r= .42, p< .01).

Fig 31-3. Correlation[a] matrix between emotion decoding (DANVA adult [b]) and centrality measures

	Like score	Dislike score	Cooperate in a project	Asking help with a homework	Go for a funny trip	Borrow money
Like score	—					
Dislike scores	–.819**	—				
Cooperate in a project	.279*	–.094	—			
Asking help with a homework	.141	–.054	.340*	—		
Go for a funny trip	.004	.134	.299*	.463**	—	
Borrow money	–.107	.213	.231	.230	.442**	—

*p < .05 two-tailed, **p < .01 two-tailed
[a] Partial correlation was reported, controlling for the class membership
[b] DANVA scores are calculated based on emotion decoding errors

The results show that using the "Like" and "Dislike" procedure, as Nowicki and Duke (1994) suggested, is not necessary useful in assessing centrality, at least for the adolescent networks. The "like" index correlates only with the "cooperate in a project" centrality index and not necessary with popularity in other networks ties. People tended to declare they would cooperate in the project with peers they liked, but the "Liked" indicator could not predict whether someone was popular in other types of networks, such as "go for a funny trip".

Discussion

We found gender differences in nonverbal sensitivity using DANVA, but only in the case of posture items. These results are consistent with previous research conducted on Romanian students (Ivan & Duduciuc, 2011) using the PONS test. Decoding facial expressions of emotions is a common and easier task than decoding emotions using only body posture, which is why posture items could better discriminate between higher and lower nonverbal accuracy. Generally speaking, a significant number of studies have shown gender effect in the case of nonverbal accuracy tests. The studies using DANVA, however, have failed to produce consistent gender effects, probably because the test itself uses four basic emotions and it has already been proven that such universal emotions are recognizable, regardless of the socialization context (see Ekman & Friesen, 2003; Ekman, 2007).

When comparing nonverbal accuracy scores between the two groups – financial incentive group and non-financial incentive group – we found that incentives have influenced DANVA performance, especially on the face items, which were easy to decode. If high-stake situations do indeed allow more reliable data on nonverbal sensitivity measures, in a sense they discriminate better between higher and lower sensitive individuals, and the experimental procedure described here could be a solution to increase the validity of nonverbal sensitivity measurements. I could not agree more with Ekman and Frank (1997) and their idea that the impact of high-stake situations in experiments that use the evaluation of others, based on nonverbal elements, is insufficiently explored in the current literature and could be one of the sources of the contradictory results on some topics. The current research results allow us to speculate that raising the stakes could increase individual performances only for familiar tasks, while being focused on the payoff could have modest effects in unusual tasks.

Using high-stake situations, either by financially rewarding subjects for performance or by creating situations in which subjects will estimate rewards or constraints for performance, would bring nonverbal sensitivity tasks in artificial experimental situations closer with those from real life in addition to greatly contributing to reliable measures of nonverbal competences that allow researchers to generalize their results across different decoding situations.

We also found support for a possible relationship between sex role identity and emotion decoding accuracy. The results are surprising because they indicate that feminine sex role identity negatively correlated with abilities to decode the DANVA face items. A possible explanation could be that participants who describe themselves in stereotypically feminine terms (with high feminine scores) are becoming overconfident in their abilities to decode emotions, with negative impact on their final performance. Because we lack data about participant involvement and focus on the task requirements, it is difficult to interpret the negative relation between "femininity scores" and nonverbal sensitivity accuracy. Moreover, most of our participants could not be integrated as "feminine type" or "masculine type" using the Bem Sex Role Inventory because we used an adolescent group as our subject pool (an age group just beginning the process of self-identity formation). Most of the students from our sample were either "psychological androgynous" or "non-differentiated." Of participants with both high masculine and feminine self-identity (called androgyny group) and those with no clear sex role identity (called non-differentiated) are the following, the latter group made more DANVA mistakes and were also less popular.

The results regarding the relationship between network centrality and nonverbal accuracy illustrate that participants who were particularly liked in their class made more errors in decoding sad faces but were significantly better in decoding happy postures. Those who were less liked had difficulties in interpreting angry postures and fear postures. Such results also suggest that group popularity could be related with an individual's nonverbal abilities, and we proved that such a relationship exists in non-school- related ties, such as "going for a funny trip."

Regarding participant network centrality, girls proved to be significantly more liked and disliked by their peers and also seemed to be more actively involved in their class networks than boys. We hypothesize that in female-dominated classes, popularity is structured differently than that in mixed-adolescent classes. It could be interesting to research the role of nonverbal sensitivity and sex role identity in adolescent groups dominated by males, by females, or gender equal.

The size of our adolescent group is a major limitation for the results to be generalized. However, Social Network Analysis is difficult to conduct on larger groups and requires that group members would know each other.

ACKNOWLEDGEMENTS

This work was supported by the strategic grant POSDRU/89/ 1.5/S/62259, Project 'Applied social, human and political sciences. Post-doctoral training and post-doctoral fellowships in social, human and political sciences,' co-financed by the European Social Fund within the Sectorial Operational Program Human Resources Development 2007–2013.

REFERENCES

Archer, D & Costanzo, M (1987). *Interpersonal Perception Task*, Berkeley: University of California.

Bandura, A (1997). Cultivate self-efficacy for personal and organizational effectiveness. In E A Locke (ed.), *The Blackwell Handbook of Principles of Organizational Behaviour* (pp. 120–137), Oxford: Blackwell Reference Online.

Barrier, G (2010). *La communication non verbale: Comprendre les gestes: perception et signification* (5th ed.), Paris: ESF.

Bellotti, E (2008). What are friends for? Effective communities of single people. *Social Networks,* 30(4), 318-329.

Bem, S L (1981). *Bem Sex Role Inventory Professional Manual*, Palo Alto, CA: Consulting Psychologists Press.

Borgatti, S P Everett, M G & Freeman, L C (2002). *UCINET for Windows: Software for Social Network Analysis*, Harvard University: Analytic Technologies.

Boyatzis, J C & Satyaprasd, C (1994). Children's Facial and Gestural Decoding and Encoding: Relations between Skills and Popularity. *Journal of Nonverbal Behavior*, 18(1), 35–55.

Butovskaya, M L, Timentschik, V M & Burcova, V N (2007). Aggression, Conflict Resolution, Popularity, and Attitude to School in Russian Adolescents. *Aggressive Behavior*, 33, 170–183.

Byron, K, Terranova, S & Nowicki, S (2007). Nonverbal Emotion Recognition and Sales Persons: Linking Ability to Perceived and Actual Success. *Journal of Applied and Social Psychology*, 37, 2600–2619.

Capella, J (1997.) Behavioral and Judgment Coordination in Adult Informal Social Interactions: Vocal and Kinesics Indicators. *Journal of Personality and Social Psychology*, 72(1), 119–131.

Cassidy, J & Berlin, J L (1994). The Insecure/Ambivalent Pattern of Attachment: Theory and Research. *Child Development*, 65(4), 971–991.

Carton, S J, Kessler, A E & Pape, L C (1999). Nonverbal Decoding and Relationship Well-being in Adults. *Journal of Nonverbal Behavior*, 23(1), 93–100.

Coleman, J (1990). *The Foundation of Social Theory*, Cambridge: Cambridge University Press.

Custrini, R J & Feldman, R S (1989). Children's Social Competence and Nonverbal Encoding and Decoding of Emotions. *Journal of Clinical Child Psychology*, 18(4), 336–342.

De Paulo, M B et al. (2003). Cues to Deception. *Psychological Bulletin*, 129(1), 74–118.

Downey, D (1995). When Bigger is not Better: Family Size, Parental Resources, and Children's Educational Performance. *American Sociological Review*, 60, 746–761.

Eagly, A H (1987). *Sex Differences in Social Behavior: A Social Role Interpretation*, Hillsdale, NJ: Erlbaum.

—. (1997). Sex Differences in Social Behavior: Comparing Social Role Theory and Evolutionary Psychology. *American Psychologist*, 50, 1380–1383.

Ekman, P (2007). *Emotion Revealed: Recognizing Face and Feeling to Improve Communication* (2nd ed.), New York: Henry Holt.

—. (2009). *Telling Lies: Clues to Deceit in Marketplace, Politics, and Marriage* (3rd ed.), London and New York: W W Norton.

Ekman, P & Frank, G M (1997). The Ability to Detect Deceit Generalizes across Different Types of High-stake Lies. *Journal of Personality and Social Psychology,* 76(6), 1429–1439.

Ekman, P & Friesen, V W (2003). *Unmasking the Face: A Guide to Recognizing Emotions from Facial Expressions*, New York: Malor Books.

Ekman, P & O'Sulivan, M (1991). Who can Catch a Liar? *American Psychologist*, 46(9), 913–920.

Elfenbein, H, Foo, M D, White, J, Tan, H H & Aik, C (2007). Reading your Counterpart: The Benefit of Emotion Recognition Accuracy for Effectiveness in Negotiation. *Journal of Nonverbal Behavior*, 31, 205–223.

Flap, H (1999). Creation and Returns of Social Capital: A New Research Program. *La Revue de Tocqueville/ The Tocqueville Review*, 20(1), 10–21.

Goleman, D (1995). *Emotional Intelligence,* New York: Bantam.

Greene, O J & Burelson, R B (eds) (2008). *Handbook of Communication and Social Interaction Skills* (3rd ed.), Mahwah, NJ: Lawrence Erlbaum Associates.

Hall, J (1978). Gender Effects in Decoding Nonverbal Cues. *Psychological Bulletin*, 85(4), 845–857.

—. (1990). *Nonverbal Sex Differences: Accuracy of Communication and Expressive Style*, Baltimore MD: Johns Hopkins University Press.

—. (2009). Nonverbal Behavior in Social Psychology Research: The Good, the Bad and the Ugly. In C Agnew, D Carlston, W Graziano & J Kelley (eds), *Then a Miracle Occurs: Focusing on Behavior in Social Psychological Theory and Research* (pp. 412–438). New York: Oxford University Press.

Hall, J, Andrzejewski, A S & Yopchick, E J (2009). Psychosocial Correlates of Interpersonal Sensitivity: A Meta-analysis. *Journal of Nonverbal Behavior*, 33(3), 149–180.

Hall, J & Bernieri, F J (eds.) (2001). *Interpersonal Sensitivity: Theory and Measurement*, Mahwah, NJ: Lawrence Erlbaum Associates.

Hess, U & Philippot, P (eds.) (2007). *Group Dynamics and Emotional Expression*, New York: Cambridge University Press.

Hubbard, A J & Coie, D J (1994). Emotional Determinants of Social Competence in Children's Peer Relationships. *Merrill-Palmer Quarterly*, 40, 1–20.

Ivan, L (2008). Antrenarea competenţei de comunicare nonverbală (*The Nonverbal Sensitivity Training*). In S. Chelcea, L. Ivan & A. Chelcea. *Comunicarea non*verbală: gesturile şi postura [*Nonverbal communication*], 2nd ed. (pp. 213–235). Bucharest: Comunicare.ro.

—. (2009). Cele mai importante 20 de secunde. Competenţa în comunicarea nonverbală. [*The most important 20 seconds. Nonverbal competence],* Bucharest: Tritonic.

Ivan, L & Duduciuc, A (2011). Social Skills, Nonverbal Sensitivity and Academic Success: The Key Role of Centrality in Student Networks for Higher Grades Achievement. *Review of Research and Social Intervention*, 33, 151–167.

Knapp, L M & Hall, J (2005). *Nonverbal Communication in Human Interaction* (4th ed.), Belmond, CA: Wadsworth.

Knoke, D. & Yang, S. (2008). *Social Network Analysis* (2nd ed.), London: Sage Publications.

Konold, T R, Jamison, K R, Stanton-Chapman, T L & Rimm-Kaufman, S E (2010). Relationships among Informant Based Measures of Social Skills and Student Achievement: A Longitudinal Examination of Differential Effects by Sex. *Applied Developmental Science*, 14(1), 18–34.

Lévi-Strauss, C (1968). *Structural Anthropology*, New York: Basic Books.

Lewis, K *et al.* (2008). Tastes, Ties and Time: Social Network Dataset Using Facebook.com. *Social Network*, 30(4), 330–342.

Moerbeek, H, Ultee, W & Flap, H (1995). "That's what Friends are for": Ascribed and Achieved Social Capital in the Occupational Career. Fourth European Social Network Conference, London.

Mullins-Nelson, J L, Salekin, R T & Leistico, A-M (2006). Psychopathy, Empathy and Perspective: Talking Ability in a Community Sample: Implication for the Successful Psychopathy Concept. *International Journal of Forensic Mental Health*, 5(2), 133–149.

Nowicki, S & Duke, M (1994). Individual Differences in the Nonverbal Communication of Affect: The Diagnostic Analysis of Nonverbal Accuracy Scale. *Journal of Nonverbal Behavior*, 19, 9–35.

Nowicki, S (2004). *Manual for the Receptive Tests of Diagnosis Analysis of Nonverbal Accuracy 2*, Department of Psychology, Emory University.

Phillips, H L Tunstall, M & Channon, S (2007). Exploring the Role of Working Memory in Dynamic Social Cue Decoding Using Dual Task Methodology. *Journal of Nonverbal Behaviour*, 31, 137–152.

Riggio, E R (2001). Interpersonal Sensitivity Research and Organizational Psychology. In J Hall & F J Bernieri, *Interpersonal Sensitivity: Theory and Measurement* (pp. 127–143). Mahwah, NJ: Lawrence Erlbaum Associates.

Rosenthal, R, Hall, J A, DiMateo, M R, Rogers, L P & Archer, D (1979). *Sensitivity to Nonverbal Communication. The PONS Test*, Baltimore, Maryland: John Hopkins University Press.

Rosip, J C, & Hall, J A (2004). Knowledge of Nonverbal Cues, Gender, and Nonverbal Decoding Accuracy. *Journal of Nonverbal Behavior*, 28, 268–286.

Rusbult, E C & Martz, M J (1995). Remaining in an Abusive Relationship: An Investment Model Analysis of Non Voluntary Dependence. *Personality and Social Psychology, 21(6), 558–571.*

Saarni, C (1999). *The Development of Emotional Competence*, New York: Guilford.

Sandu, D (2005). Dezvoltare comunitară. Cercetare, practică, ideologie [Community Development: Research, Practice and Ideology], Iaşi: Polirom.

Schneider, J & Schneider-Düker, M (1984). Sex Roles and Nonverbal Sensitivity. *Journal of Social Psychology,* 182, 281–282.

Scott, P J (2000). *Social Network Analysis* (2nd ed.), London: Sage Publications.

Slama-Cazacu, T (2007). Viaţă, personalitate, limbaj – analize context*ual-dinamice [Life, Personality and Language – Contextual Dynamic Analysis]*, Bucharest: Minerva.

Spitzberg, H B (2008). "Perspectives on nonverbal communication skills. In L K Guerrero & M L Hecht, *The Nonverbal Communication Reader* 3rd ed. (pp. 21–27). Long Grove, IL: Waveland Press.

Tracy, L J & Robins, W R (2008). The Automaticity of Emotion Recognition. *Emotion*, 8, 81–95.

Wagner, H L, Buck, R & Winterbothsam, M (1993). Communication of Specific Emotions: Gender Differences in Sending Accuracy and Communication Measures. *Journal of Nonverbal Behavior*, 17, 29–53.

Walden, T A & Field, M T (1990). Preschool Children's Social Competence and the Production and Discrimination of Affective Expressions. *British Journal of Developmental Psychology,* 8, 65–76.

Wasserman, S & Faust, K (1994). *Social Network Analysis: Methods and Applications: Structural Analysis in Social Sciences*, Cambridge: Cambridge University Press.

LE DISCOURS DE SOLIDARITE INTERNATIONALE: L'IDENTITE DE L'AUTRE A TRAVERS LES PRATIQUES DES ONG

DANA POPESCU JOURDY
AND ELISABETH VERCHER

Résumé

Dans le cadre d'une théorie de la rationalité et de la communication solidaires, l'article analyse la construction de l'identité de l'Autre dans le discours des organisations de solidarité internationale partant de l'exemple des interventions en Haïti après le tremblement de terre de 2010.

Il s'agit de mettre en évidence l'articulation entre mise en scène de l'action et construction de l'identité de l'Autre lointain dans une double logique : éthique et institutionnelle. Notre hypothèse est que la manière d'agir des ONG de solidarité internationale définit la représentation de la figure de l'Autre à travers les discours d'accompagnement des projets conçus et mis en place par les organisations.

L'analyse sémiotique des discours et des dispositifs des sites Internet est déclinée en fonction des étapes du parcours génératif des pratiques de communication, notamment le témoignage, le plaidoyer et la communication visant la collecte de fonds. Ces variables constituent pour nous des éléments qui fondent la construction de l'identité de l'Autre dans le discours des ONG. Ainsi, l'image de l'Autre apparaît comme fragmentée, tributaire principalement à la manière dans laquelle les structures définissent et organisent leurs missions. Trois niveaux discursifs – factuel, émotionnel et performatif – participent successivement à la construction de la figure de l'Autre. De la même façon, dans cette construction discursive la logique de l'engagement et celle de l'efficience institutionnelle sont déclinés par les ONG en rationalités communicationnelles cohérentes. En fin de compte, à travers ces articulations, la construction de la figure de l'Autre se réalise par un rapprochement symbolique entre la victime, l'action des ONG et le nous-mêmes, relation absolument nécessaire à la légitimation et la réalisation de l'action de solidarité.

Mots-clés : identité, ONG, solidarité, l'Autre

Introduction

Cet article s'inscrit dans d'une recherche plus ample que nous menons sur la figure de la solidarité, sur la construction du paradigme de la solidarité, élément central de ce que nous appelons « communication solidaire », définie comme la mise en scène institutionnelle des projets et des valeurs à vocation explicitement solidaire et/ou humanitaire.

En regardant son étymologie, le mot « solidarité » renvoie à un principe juridique. Dans le Code de Justinien, le mot latin solidus se rapporte à l'interdépendance des débiteurs entre eux. Chacun est engagé, en termes de dette et de responsabilité, pour le tout (in solidum). Le concept – qui rejoint sans doute l'idée pythagoricienne du nombre – insiste sur une totalité, une unité dont la sollicitude s'exerce sur chaque être qui la constitue. In solidum reconnaît donc la responsabilité solidaire entre plusieurs acteurs pour une dette reconnue et considérée comme étant commune.

C'est ainsi que le paradigme de la solidarité devient le point de départ de nos travaux. Car il nous amène à nous interroger notamment sur la manière particulière dans laquelle l'attitude solidaire participe au fondement de l'identité des acteurs.

Rationalité et communication solidaires

L'articulation entre communication et solidarité institutionnalisée est ici envisagée comme une articulation entre éthique et identité, comme une rationalisation éthique des rapports sociaux. Tandis que la sociabilité se fonde sur l'indistinction en termes d'identité, la solidarité est une forme d'expression de la différence perçue et vécue collectivement. Elle passe obligatoirement par des logiques d'engagement et de stratégies de motivation qui contribuent à la définition de sa propre identité à travers l'identité de l'Autre.

De plus, la solidarité comporte une importante dimension imaginaire qui exprime l'idéal politique d'une société dans laquelle, grâce à l'action des acteurs, le manque et la souffrance n'existerait plus. Les projets déroulés dans le cadre des organisations solidaires réunissent une diversité d'acteurs autour de cet imaginaire.

Ainsi, la solidarité inscrit l'identité des acteurs impliqués dans une logique particulière d'articulation entre le singulier et le collectif, logique définie par trois dimensions : l'imaginaire de l'égalité citoyenne, le niveau symbolique de la différence complémentaire à l'Autre et le réel de l'action solidaire.

Partant de ces constats, il s'agit notamment d'analyser le paradigme de la solidarité dans les pratiques et les discours des organisations. La solidarité est pensée ici comme forme spécifique de rationalité, constituant un cadre qui va définir des formes spécifiques de communication.

Tout d'abord, la question qui se pose ici est de savoir dans quelle mesure l'organisation qui met en pratique une action institutionnelle particulière autour d'un projet à vocation explicitement solidaire génère une forme de rationalisation – dans le sens wébérien du terme – de l'action solidaire et humanitaire et dans quelle mesure cette rationalité constitue un cadre qui va définir des discours et des pratiques spécifiques de communication.

Pour répondre à cette question, nous définissons la rationalité solidaire - une « rationalité de valeurs » plutôt qu'une « rationalité de finalité » - qui passe obligatoirement par des logiques d'engagement et de stratégies de motivation et contribue à la définition de sa propre identité à travers l'identité de l'Autre. Ainsi, cette forme spécifique de rationalité implique pour l'organisation une (re)définition identitaire comme acteur social, à savoir le choix des actions avec une finalité collective, l'affirmation d'une conscience politique, ainsi que la construction des médiations autour d'un projet et des valeurs portées par ce projet.

Dans un deuxième temps, nous avons identifié, dans le domaine de la communication des organisations, ce que nous appelons un « modèle de communication solidaire », modèle qui comporterait quatre niveaux discursifs :

- La définition de la « dette » (cause, manque, etc.) commune autour de laquelle les organisations construisent leurs rapports de solidarité.
- L'affirmation de la responsabilité commune des différents acteurs institutionnels, qui devient ainsi des membres d'une communauté solidaire
- L'expression de l'engagement des parties solidaires, élément essentiel pour le « contrat » solidaire et pour l'accomplissement d'une missions, mais aussi modalité d'assumer les valeurs choisies donnant un sens à l'action
- Les médiations entre les acteurs pour assurer le principe d'unité qui déterminera également l'unité de l'action.

Ainsi, la rationalité solidaire impliquerait des formes spécifiques de communication et des rhétoriques spécifiques. L'analyse de la construction du paradigme de la solidarité dans le discours des organisations nous montre dans un premier temps que cette construction se réalise principalement sur deux niveaux : la redéfinition de l'identité de l'organisation et la construction de sens autour des valeurs et de projets.

La question qui se pose ici est donc de savoir dans quelle mesure cette forme spécifique de rationalité, la rationalité solidaire, constitue un cadre/modèle qui va définir des pratiques spécifiques de communication et la construction d'une rhétorique de la solidarité. Dans quelle mesure le paradigme [VANDERDORPE, 1990] de la solidarité devient un modèle de reparamétrage des pratiques et génère des nouvelles formes de participation et de visibilité dans l'espace public. Et comment cette « rationalité solidaire » articulera des formes spécifiques de communication à des formes rhétoriques spécifiques.

LE PARADIGME DE LA SOLIDARITÉ INTERNATIONALE

Dans le cas des organisations qui définissent leurs missions autour de la solidarité internationale, nous assistons à une transformation des éléments de notre paradigme de la solidarité selon la dimension internationale de l'action. Dans un même temps, le modèle de la communication solidaire prend en compte les aspects interculturelles de la représentation de l'Autre. Ainsi, la prise en compte de la souffrance de l'Autre lointain implique une dimension imaginaire renforcée présente aussi bien dans la définition de la dette morale que dans l'éthique de l'action. Les principes qui guident le projets et les pratiques, les valeurs qui fondent les discours de solidarité internationale se basent désormais sur les concepts d'universalisme et d'humanisme.

Plus fortes encore que le désir d'action, les motivations des actions institutionnalisées de solidarité internationale sont inscrites dans des logiques idéologiques marquées. Nous connaissons, par exemple, les débats autour des rapports Nord-Sud qui ont définit pendant des siècles l'action de solidarité internationale comme une action de soutien des « pays développées » envers de « pays pauvres » ou « en développement », rapports qui se trouvent actuellement remis en question par la mondialisation et l'apparition des « pays émergents ». Depuis peu, l'Europe et les États-Unis ne sont plus les principaux fournisseurs de financement de l'aide internationale. Les « nouveaux acteurs » de solidarité internationale se trouvent actuellement plutôt en Amérique Latine (Brésil) ou au Moyen Orient (Arabie Saoudite). Un autre exemple significatif constitue le positionnement spécifique des organisations en termes d'engagement. Entre les doctrines urgentistes ou celles de développement les différences et même les tensions se font de plus en plus ressentir.

Notre hypothèse porte ici sur l'idée que la manière de « faire de la solidarité internationale » a un impact direct sur la représentation de la figure de l'Autre à travers les discours d'accompagnement de l'action et des projets construits par les ONG.

UNE MISE EN SCÈNE INSTITUTIONNELLE DE LA FIGURE DE L'AUTRE

Pour notre analyse, nous avons choisi l'intervention de plusieurs ONG françaises dans contexte de la crise survenue en Haïti suite au tremblement de terre de 2010. Nous mettons en évidence le fait que des dispositifs communicationnels spécifiques s'articulent à chaque niveau de l'action pour créer des entités discursives unitaires. De l'autre côté, nous regarderons comment ces unités discursives sont-elles intégrées dans les stratégies de communication des organisations [BERTIN, 2007]. L'analyse sémiotique des discours et des dispositifs mis en place s'articule à une analyse des parcours génératifs des pratiques de communication.

Ainsi, nous analysons l'articulation entre trois éléments :

- le type de projets proposés par chaque ONG et la mise en scène de l'action
- la construction de la figure de l'Autre
- les stratégies de collecte de don

Les variables choisies pour notre analyse correspondent aux éléments récurrents présents dans les discours d'accompagnement existants sur les sites Internet des organisations faisant partie de notre corpus[1].

Notre analyse concerne notamment la mises en scène des missions que les ONG se sont fixés pour intervenir en Haïti, la manière dans laquelle la population locale est définie en termes de « bénéficiaire » des ces actions, ainsi que les aspects financiers (mode de collecte de fonds et la visibilité financière des résultats). Nous pensons que ces variables observés dans notre corpus participent à la construction de ce que nous appelons la figure de l'Autre dans le discours des organisations de solidarité internationale.

Nous présenterons ici les détails des résultats pour 5 organisations : Action contre la Faim, Architectes de l'Urgence, la Croix Rouge française,

[1] Il s'agit de 30 organisations francophones

Médecins du Monde et Solidarités International.

1. L'IMAGE DE L'AUTRE INTÉGRÉE À LA MISE EN SCÈNE DE L'ACTION DE SECOURS

Le choix des types d'actions d'une ONG se fait en fonction des compétences de chaque organisation, mais également en fonction de ce que celle-ci détermine comme étant les « besoins » d'une population confrontée à une crise. Ainsi, l'identité de cette population est mise en scène par une triple articulation : l'identité de l'ONG en termes de missions et compétences, la nature de la crise et la « vulnérabilité » qu'elle provoque. L'Autre devient ainsi le bénéficiaire « logique » de l'action de secours mise en place par l'ONG.

Pour Action contre la Faim, les interventions menées en Haïti sont : la santé mentale, la sécurité alimentaire et l'accès à l'eau et au conditions d'hygiène. L'accès à cette page dédié à Haïti se fait en passant par les rubriques : « Nos combats », puis « Nos missions ». Les autres pays présents sur le site sont situés notamment en Afrique, mais également en Amérique Latine et le Moyen Orient.

L'organisation Architectes de l'Urgence, fondation française reconnue d'utilité publique, intervient également en Haïti dans ses domaines spécifiques de compétence : l'évaluation et la mise en sécurité des bâtiments affectés par le tremblement de terre, relogement des sinistrés, réhabilitation et la construction de maisons, écoles, dispensaires et hôpitaux. La représentation de la population haïtienne est réduite ici à ses besoins en termes de logement et d'accès à des services de base à travers la solidité des bâtiments.

Le site Internet de la Croix Rouge française comporte un moteur de recherche qui permet d'obtenir de détails sur les projets de l'organisation selon le type d'action, le pays d'intervention et le statut de l'action (« fini » ou « en cours »). Les résultats de la recherche comportent des listes d'actions menées. Pour Haïti, les interventions de l'organisation incluent : l'accès à l'eau et sensibilisation à l'hygiène, l'amélioration des conditions de vie des populations sinistrées, ainsi que des soins de santé primaire et le soutien psycho-social. L'image de l'Autre est strictement liée à ses besoins primaires et au fait qu'il manque de ces conditions de base de son existence.

Médecins du Monde organise l'information concernant ses interventions à l'international dans une rubrique à part, avec possibilité de consulter les actions pays par pays. Une mappe-monde permet un accès direct à l'aide de hyperliens. En Haïti, MDM assure la mise en place des cliniques mobiles, des activités de chirurgie, des consultations et campagnes de vaccination, des actions contre l'épidémie de choléra, mais également la formation du personnel médical local ou des activités psycho-sociales. Les interventions sont classées en quatre catégories, définies en termes d'objectifs : « apporter des soins médico-chirurgicaux à la suite su séisme », « réduire l'impact du séisme sur la santé physique et mentale », « réduire la mortalité materno-infantile » et « lutter contre l'épidémie de choléra ». Il est intéressant de remarquer la fait que pour chaque objectif, le discours est organisé selon trois axes : les actions, les résultats et les perspectives.

Déjà présente en Haïti entre 2005 et 2007, l'association Solidarités Internationales précise sur son site ses domaines d'intervention après le tremblement de terre : eau, assainissement et hygiène, sécurité alimentaire, projet de réinstallation des sinistrés. L'organisation participe également aux actions d'urgence face à l'épidémie de choléra, en collaboration avec des ONG médicales. Dans ce cas, l'image de l'Autre s'efface laissant place à l'intervention de secours. L'Autre est exclusivement représenté de manière quantitative : nombre de victimes, de réfugiés, de malades, etc. Le récit est majoritairement un discours d'accompagnement de l'action mise en place par l'association et un plaidoyer pour son efficacité.

Dans la communication des ONG, à travers une forme spécifique d'organisation du discours sur la nature des interventions, l'image de l'Autre est fragmentée, étant principalement tributaire à la manière dans laquelle les structures organisent et définissent leurs missions. « L'Autre-Victime » est ainsi en grande mesure intégré dans les dispositifs de communication des organisations et des entités discursives définissant l'action d'aide. Le dispositif de communication (ici, le site internet) est organisé en fonction de cette relation de subordination : dans tous les cas, les références à la population haïtienne se fait à partir de rubriques de type « Nos missions » ou « Nos actions ». De la même manière, la représentations de l'Autre dans le discours des ONG sur leurs missions comporte une dimension dominante : le besoin, le manque de services de base, la vulnérabilité. Dans la majorité de cas, cette dimension comporte également un discours quantitatif chiffré de type argumentatif (nombre de consultations assurées, de dispensaires réhabilités, d'interventions chirurgicales pratiquées, de vaccins administrés, etc.) qui assure une mise en scène favorable de l'efficacité de l'action de solidarité internationale.

2. DÉSIGNATION DE L'AUTRE COMME VICTIME D'UNE SITUATION DE CRISE

Dans cette partie de l'analyse nous nous sommes intéressées notamment à la manière dans laquelle les ONG désignent la population haïtienne bénéficiaire de leurs interventions de solidarité internationale d'urgence. Nous pouvons observer trois registres discursifs distincts :

un registre factuel où la dénomination se fait à l'aide de noms spécifiques à la qualité de victime, des chiffres ou des actions de secours
un registre émotionnel qui passe notamment par les témoignages qui, par l'identification des victimes, apportent une personnalisation de la souffrance.
un registre performatif qui incite le lecteur à l'action symbolique de soutien, à savoir au don.

Pour illustrer le registre factuel dans notre corpus, nous présenterons ici quelques exemples issus des discours présents sur les sites Internet des ONG.

- Dénomination *par des noms spécifiques*

Action contre la Faim : « populations affectées par les crises » ; « populations sinistrées » ; « familles déplacées » ; « enfants atteints de malnutrition aiguë sévère » ; « personnes en détresse»

Architectes de l'Urgence : « pour les plus défavorisés » ; « bénéficiaires » ; « la population traumatisée » ; « enfants en situation de risque »

Croix Rouge française : « les populations affectées par le séisme » ; « les populations sinistrées » ; « les personnes victimes du séisme » ;

Médecins du Monde : « victimes de la catastrophe du 12 janvier 2010 » ; « victimes de la catastrophe du 12 janvier 2010 » ; « patients atteints du choléra » ;

Solidarités International : « victimes », « déplacés », « populations sinistrées »

- Dénomination *par des chiffres*

Action contre la Faim : « plus de 220 000 morts, 300 à 400 000 blessés et 1 200 000 sans-abris » ; « près de la moitié de la ville de Port-au-Prince a été détruite et les principales agglomérations à hauteur de 50 à 90% » ; « Un an après le début de l'épidémie, la propagation du choléra s'élève à plus de 470 000 cas dans le pays, dont 6 331 décès. »

Architectes de l'Urgence : « Au total à ce jour, 574.500 personnes ont à nouveau accès à des soins dans des conditions sures et adaptées » ; « Avant le séisme, 30 000 personnes vivaient dans ce quartier. » ;

Croix Rouge française : « Environ 3 millions de personnes ont été affectées par le séisme et ses répliques. » ; « près de 2 millions de personnes se sont retrouvées sans-abris » ; « près de 50% des habitations de la ville de Port-au-Prince ont été détruites ou endommagées. »

Médecins du Monde : « un taux de mortalité maternelle atteignant 630/100 000 naissances et un taux de mortalité infantile de 87/ 100 000 » ; « Depuis le début de l'épidémie, en octobre 2010, plus d'un demi-million de Haïtiens ont été touchés par le choléra »

Solidarités International : « 2.000 morts à Petit-Goâve », « 50 sites pour plus de 50.000 personnes »

- Dénomination *par des actions* :

Action contre la Faim : « soutenir les personnes en déstresse psychologique » ; « répondre aux besoins primaires des populations (directement et indirectement) affectées par les crises » ; « sensibilisation à l'allaitement, à la diversification alimentaire et aux problématiques psychosociales »

Architectes de l'Urgence : « assistance des populations dans la reconstruction » ; « améliorer l'accès aux soins » ; « fournir un cadre éducatif adapté et sûr. » ; « améliorer leurs conditions de vies – alimentation, conditions sanitaires, vie sociale etc. »

Croix Rouge française : « réduction de la vulnérabilité des populations » ; « soutien psychosocial en situation d'urgence » ; « distribution de produits de première nécessité » ; « amélioration des conditions de vie des populations sinistrées »

Médecins du Monde : « améliorer l'accès aux soins » ; « distribuer des médicaments essentiels » ; « prise en charge des femmes victimes de violences » ;

Solidarités International : « retour des déplacées », « nettoyage des débris », « soutien des populations »

En ce qui concerne le registre émotionnel, il est présent dans des rubriques « Témoignages », qui mettent en scène des histoires personnelles à travers le récit des responsables de terrain des ONG ou à travers les victimes. Le récit est personnalisé, facilitant l'identification lecteur/victime selon le modèle du story telling spécifique au journalisme de fait divers. Les images sont fortes, réalistes, introduisant le lecteur dans l'ambiance de souffrance vécue par les Haïtiens après le tremblement de terre.

Quelques exemples :

Action contre la Faim : « Olivier est arrivé au bureau. Il a du finir le trajet à pied. Les rues ne sont pas praticables. Nos locaux sont éventrés. Nos voitures sont ensevelies sous les gravats, le premier étage s'est empilé sur le RDC… » ; « Problématique de la gestion des corps : il n'y a plus de morgues dans la ville. » ; « Traumatisme psychologique considérable pour la population : pertes de proches dans des conditions effroyables, cris des personnes, famille coincées sous les décombres, angoisse pour les personnes dont on reste sans nouvelles, vue et odeur des nombreux cadavres, blessures graves et au niveau matériel, beaucoup ont tout perdu. »

Architectes de l'Urgence : « Ayant tout perdu dans le tremblement de terre, les enfants de l'orphelinat Cœur Foyer de Pitié vivent dans le dénuement le plus total ne disposant d'aucun lit, mobilier ou matériel éducatif. La Directrice et 5 bénévoles s'occupent au quotidien des enfants s'efforçant de subvenir aux besoins alimentaires et sanitaires des orphelins bien qu'il n'y ait ni eau ni électricité. »

Croix Rouge française (les témoignages des responsables terrain sont présentées sous forme des vidéos sur le site de l'organisation) : Aaron Brendt, chef de la délégation en Haïti - « Une catastrophe sans précédent » ; « Dans la vie il y a la mort /Si tu meurs t'as tort / Prudence est mère de sûreté / Personne ne résiste à la mort » (paroles d'une chanson rap interprété par un jeune haïtien)

Médecins du Monde : « « Port-au-Prince n'est plus une ville, c'est un immense bidonville. Le séisme, les hommes politiques, le choléra, on vit à travers l'enfer ici. (Francis, un habitant du quartier de Carrefour-Feuille) » ;

Solidarités International : « Les gens tremblaient, pleuraient, criaient et appelaient au Seigneur à chaque réplique » ; « J'entendais les gens coincés sous les décombres appeler à l'aide » ; « Le lendemain, l'odeur de la mort est devenue très forte. Les corps gonflaient, se putréfiaient » ; «beaucoup de gens inhument leurs morts près de chez eux, dans un coin de ravine, là où ils peuvent. ».

Souvent, le récit est accompagné par des incitations à l'aide, dans un registre performatif :

Action contre la Faim : « Face à l'immobilisme grandissant des bailleurs de fonds, ACF appelle la communauté internationale et les donateurs privés à prolonger leurs efforts pour la population haïtienne afin que les efforts faits depuis deux ans puissent porter leurs fruits durablement. »

Architectes de l'Urgence : « Mais sans votre aide, rien n'est possible ! »

Croix Rouge française : « Sans don, pas d'action ! » ; « Vous n'imaginez pas la portée de votre action » ; « Tant qu'il y aura des personnes vivant dans des camps, ce qui risque de perdurer, ou dans les décombres d'un quartier détruit, la Croix-Rouge française ne pourra considérer sa mission comme accomplie. »

Médecins du Monde : « Oublier c'est humain, agir aussi ! »

Solidarités International : « En Haïti, le fléau du choléra s'abat sur un pays meurtri qui a déjà enterré ses morts à la va-vite il y a à peine 10 mois ! La situation est terrible. Il ne faut pas oublier Haïti. » ; « Alors qu'Haïti se prépare aux effets potentiellement dévastateurs d'un cyclone ou d'une tempête tropicale, la dépression de vendredi a mis en lumière les immenses défis qu'il reste à relever en termes de préparation à la gestion des désastres naturels. »

3. L'Autre dans les messages d'appel à don

Les appels au don comportent deux dimensions importantes en termes de communication des ONG : d'un côté la définition d'une cause de solidarité internationale afin de stimuler l'engagement du donateur et, de l'autre côté, la visibilité de l'utilisation des fonds collectés qui contribue à la notoriété et à la crédibilité de l'organisation. Ainsi, l'image de l'Autre, se construit dans ce cas dans l'articulation entre ces deux logiques : celle de l'engagement et celle d'efficience institutionnelle. Nous observerons ici notamment comment les ONG établissent une cohérence entre ces deux logiques, déclinés en rationalités communicationnelles.

La rubrique « Faire un don » est présente sur la page d'accueil de tous les sites analysés. Sa visibilité maximale est assurée par son emplacement, ainsi que par un code couleur différent de la charte graphique utilisée dans la réalisation du site. Elle permet un accès rapide et facile au formulaire de don, accompagnés par des éléments iconiques et linguistiques à rôle argumentatif.

Les arguments utilisés peuvent être groupés dans les catégories suivantes :

Des arguments concernant l'éthique de l'action et du financement

Médecins du Monde affirme son principe de « mutualisation de dons », qui permettrait

> « d'intervenir uniquement en fonction des besoins réels sur le terrain et non en fonction de considérations financières ou de la forte médiatisation de situations d'urgence ».

Une partie importante concerne la manière dans laquelle l'organisation utilise les fonds collectés : partie consacrée aux bénéficiaires, au fonctionnement de l'ONG, à la communication. La Croix Rouge insiste sur la transparence de l'association en termes de fonctionnement, de l'utilisation de ses ressources et met en avant son appartenance au Comité de la Charte de Déontologie des organisations sociales et humanitaires faisant appel à la générosité du public, « permettant de donner en confiance ». Des rapports détaillés sur les ressources et les dépenses des organisations sont systématiquement téléchargeables à partir des pages d'accueil des sites analysés.

Des arguments concernant l'efficacité de l'action

Les ONG mentionnent dans ce sens : le nombre de personnes bénéficiaires des actions d'aide, le nombre et la qualité des projets financés par les dons, les compétences des travailleurs humanitaires (salariés ou bénévoles) agissant pour ce compte de l'organisation.

Des arguments valorisant le donateur

Nous pouvons inclure ici l'avantage fiscal que l'acte de don ouvre au donateur, mais également les avantages symboliques (reconnaissance, dette accomplie, aide du prochain, etc.) liés à l'acte du don comme forme d'engagement.

Les ONG utilisent ces arguments de manière différente, en fonction de leurs valeurs et de leurs stratégies de communication. Malgré cela, de manière générale les arguments se trouvent articulés, voir en relation de cause à effet. Nous pouvons mentionner dans ce sens la rubrique « Faites un don » du site Internet de l'Action contre la Faim, qui précise que l'organisation affectera les dons en fonction des urgences et que « l'efficacité de nos missions repose également sur la confiance que vous nous faites quant à cette liberté d'affectation ».

De manière générale, la page concernant les appels à don représentent une mise en scène d'une triple articulation : l'implication du citoyen à travers le don - l'action efficiente et éthique de l'organisation - la solution à la souffrance de l'Autre lointain. La symbolique de cette articulation discursive réalise finalement le rapprochement, la relation entre les différents éléments, nécessaire à la réalisation de l'action de solidarité.

CONCLUSIONS

De manière générale, nous avons pu identifier dans le discours des organisations trois niveaux rhétoriques - mettant en évidence un regard spécifique, une logique esthétique et des logiques de communication d'organisation -, chacun comportant des dispositifs communs de mise en scène, déclinés de manière spécifique :

- Le niveau du discours lui-même qui met en scène une rhétorique du témoignage, notamment à travers le choix des éléments énonciatifs forts.
- Le niveau de la valorisation esthétique, par une récupération de la rhétorique du témoignage et son articulation aux rhétoriques de sensibilisation « grand public » mises en place par l'ONG.
- Le niveau de la valorisation pragmatique des discours qui rajoute un niveau rhétorique performatif intrinsèque aux pratiques de plaidoyer.

Pour synthétiser notre travail de cadrage, le tableau suivant met en évidence l'articulation entre, d'un côté, les pratiques et les discours spécifiques mis en place par les organisations de solidarité et, de l'autre côté, la représentation de l'Autre comme partie du projet de solidarité.

	PRATIQUES	**DISCOURS**	**FIGURE DE L'AUTRE dans la communication des ONG**
La dette/cause de solidarité internationale	Identification des besoins	Témoignage	L'Autre intégré dans une logique de souffrance collective : la cause
L'engagement	Planification des actions	Plaidoyer	Articulation entre l'Autre personnalisée et les missions de l'organisation
La responsabilité	Financement	Communication pour collecte de fonds	L'Autre inscrit dans l'articulation entre une responsabilité institutionnelle et une responsabilité individuelle
L'unité d'action	Déroulement des missions	Communication-projet	L'Autre définit comme bénéficiaire de l'action

Fig 32-1 – La figure de l'Autre dans le modèle de « communication de solidarité ».

Nous pensons que l'action institutionnelle de solidarité internationale implique une instrumentalisation de la figure de l'étranger dans la communication des ONG. La rationalité solidaire, qui comporte une dimension politique importante, place le paradigme de la solidarité dans l'articulation entre les logiques discursives et les logiques de l'action. L'Autre-victime est symboliquement rapproché, introduit dans notre quotidien, devient l'objet de nos responsabilités collectives et individuelles et déclenche les mécanismes du don. Dans les pratiques institutionnelles, cette relation victime-organisation-donateur est une expression de la spécificité de la communication solidaire, mais elle assure et exprime surtout la légitimité de l'action de solidarité.

BIBLIOGRAPHIE

Bertin, E (2007). *Penser la stratégie dans le champ de la communication*, Une approche sémiotique, Nouveaux actes sémiotiques n° 110, Presses Universitaires de Limoges.

Dornier, C & Dulong, R (dir.) (2005). *Esthétique du témoignage*, Paris : Ed. de la Maison des Sciences de l'homme.

Fontanille, J (2007). « Ethos, pathos et persuasion, le corps dans l'argumentation. Le cas du témoignage », In *Les configurations dynamiques des émotions,* Toronto : Sémiotica.

Gazendam, H W M (2003). Models as Coherent Sign Structure. In Gazendam, H W M, Jorna, R J & and Cijsouw, R S (2003). *Dynamics and change in organizations: Studies in organizational semiotics*, Dordrecht : Kluwer Academic Publishers.

Mauss, M (2007). *Essai sur le don. Forme et raison de l'échange dans les sociétés archaïques*, Paris : PUF, coll. « Quadrige Grands textes » (première publication 1923/1924, in *Année Sociologique*).

Meyer, M (2004). *La rhétorique*, Paris : PUF.

Robichaud, S (2003). *Le bénévolat, entre le cœur et la raison*, Québec : Les Editions JCL.

Sexton, J (dir.) (2005). *Éthique et dilemmes dans les organisations,* Laval : Les Presses de l'Université Laval.

Vanderdorpe, C (1990). « Paradigme et syntagme », in *Revue québécoise de linguistique théorique et appliquée*, 9, 169–193.

Wenger, E (2002). *Communities of Practice : Learning, Meaning, and Identity*, Cambridge, Cambridge University Press.

EXPLORATIVE PILOT STUDY REGARDING THE ROLE OF NEGATIVE AFFECT IN PERFORMING EMOTIONAL LABOUR

DAN FLORIN STANESCU AND ELENA MADALINA IORGA

Abstract

A recurring issue since the 1930s, the study of emotions in work settings continues to receive increased research attention in the field of organizational psychology. One of the most popular topics as part of this "affective revolution" is emotional labour. We chose to approach emotional labour using the conceptualization of Glomb and Tews (2003) as the behavioural expression or non-expression of felt or unfelt emotions in accordance with display rules. On the other hand, consistent with other organizational researches, we also used the dimensional approach of emotions as states of negatively toned affectivity in order to determine whether they influence emotional experiences at work, in the case of clerks. Therefore, the study was conducted using two standardized international tests – PANAS-X (Watson & Clark, 1994) and DEELS (Glomb & Tews, 2003) on a sample of 80 store clerks. The results confirmed that high scores at negative affectivity are significantly related, in the case of the sample, in discussion with the genuine expression of negative emotions – respectively the suppression of negative emotions when performing emotional labour. The foregoing supports the idea that, although the overall prevalence of negative emotions is lower than that of positive emotions, the more people report negative affect as the dominant emotional experience dimension, the more they tend to either genuinely express or suppress feelings of anger, fear, sadness or hate as part of the emotional work demands. In work involving customer interactions, such as that done by store clerks, individuals are required to display positive emotions, so the emotion regulation strategy of faking negative emotions was not related to the PANAS-X scales. Other affective states were also taken into account, of which shyness, fatigue, and surprise offered relevant insights.

Key words: negative affect, emotional labor, discrete emotions

INTRODUCTION

The concept of emotion is now "extremely fashionable", as noted by Scherer (2005, p. 696). And the interest in the phenomenon is considerable, especially in work settings, since "better than any other source of information, the emotions can reveal the dynamics of the struggle of employees to adapt to organizational life" (Lazarus & Cohen-Charash, 2001, p. 45). Lazarus and Cohen-Charash (2001) claim there are three main directions in studying emotions in the workplace: research on positive and negative affectivity as dispositions (aimed to determine the consequences of the two dimensions of emotional experience on work behaviour and attitudes), research on moods (with a focus on the relationship between positive moods and work behaviour), and research on emotional labour, which describes the ways in which role demands and organizational culture determine emotional display (thus, affectivity is assessed in terms of displayed emotions, rather than felt emotions which are subjectively experienced).

Glomb and Tews (2003) also emphasize the topicality of examining the role of emotions in organizational life, with focus on emotional labour. Coined by the American sociologist Arlie Hochschild in her seminal work *The Managed Heart* (1983), the term soon became a privileged topic, requiring conceptualization and operationalization. Emotional labour was initially described as "the management of feeling to create a publicly observable facial and bodily display" (Hochschild, 2003, p. 7).

Based on the dramaturgical perspective advanced by Goffman (1959), Hochschild acknowledged the importance of controlling emotions as part of an impression management dictated by display rules. Further on, the sociologist suggested different strategies of "acting". But, apart from the surface acting (performed when the employee changes only the outward appearance and behaviour in order to exhibit required emotions) that was also suggested by other emotional labour researchers, the unique contribution of Hochschild consisted in advancing the notion of deep acting. Borrowing the term from a theatrical director, she described deep acting as both active (when, although the employee's feelings do not fit the situation, one uses training or past experiences to alter what one feels in order to meet the organizational emotional demands) and passive (when the employee spontaneously feels what one is required to feel, an exertion involved in the display).

From this point forward, the emotional labour construct was subject to a series of extensions and interpretations. Wharton (1993), for example, preserving the original sense of the term as management of feelings, carried out a study to determine the variations of degree and types of emotion management. Moreover, she found that the concept of emotional labour is a multidimensional concept with different outcomes depending on the work settings where the employee "performs". The phenomenon was also approached with focus on the observable behaviour, as "the act of displaying appropriate emotions" (Ashforth & Humphrey, 1993). In order to better understand the concept, Ashforth and Humphrey used the social identity theory as a moderator.

Rafaeli and Sutton (1987), on the other hand, used the role expectations model to make sense of the emotional labour. Likewise, they referred to surface and deep acting as "faking mechanisms", stating a difference in "faith" (that is, intentionality) between the two processes: surface acting was seen as "faking in bad faith" (since what motivates the employee to display the required emotions is the personal goal of keeping the job), while deep acting was assimilated as "faking in good faith" (the intention of the employee is just to seem authentic).

As seen above, Wharton (1993) acknowledged the multidimensional structure of the emotional labour, but Morris and Feldman (1996) actually distinguished four such dimensions: the frequency of interactions, attentiveness (intensity of emotions and duration of interaction), variety of emotions required (the organizational expectations for employees in their interactions with clients), and emotional dissonance (an internal state of tension due to the difference between felt and feigned emotions). However, these findings were questioned both from a conceptual and methodological point of view by Kruml and Geddes (2000), who claimed that some dimensions, such as frequency or duration of service interactions, are not emotional labour but rather job characteristics that influence the way in which employees perform emotional labour.

Instead, Kruml and Geddes hold that emotional labour represents "what employees perform when they are required to feel, or at least project the appearance of, certain emotions as they engage in job-relevant interactions" (2000, p. 9). Their study supports a two-dimensional view of the emotional labour construct: emotive dissonance (which was stated before and thus further validated) and emotive effort (a new construct in the emotional labour literature).

Although the conceptual advancements regarding emotional labour are more often conflicting, Grandey (2000) noted that, regardless of the strategy used or the dimensions implied, each of them is based on the assumption that emotional labour involves regulating one's emotions and emotional expressions in order to act consistently with organizational display rules. On this basis, Grandey formulated an integrated model of emotional labour, building on Gross's emotion regulation strategies (1998b). Thereby, Hochschild's deep acting was assimilated to Gross's antecedent-focused emotion regulation, whereas response-focused emotion regulation, understood as modifying expression either by faking or by enhancing nonverbal signs of emotion, was seen as corresponding to surface acting.

Furthermore, Grandey introduced the idea that the more one perceives the emotional work requirements, the more one will adopt specific regulating strategies. From this point of view, Jones and Best (1995) and Wharton and Erickson (1993) identified integrative emotional work requirements (which imply being pleasant and affiliative, such as in customer service), differentiating emotional work requirements (demanding mainly negative emotions, which create social distance, as is the case of bill collectors or police officers), and masking work requirements (which refer to rather neutral demeanours that allow the employee to place himself in a reserved position – as is the case of judges or clinicians).

Up to this point, one can argue that emotional labour cannot be discussed as a dichotomous variable (in terms of presence or absence), but rather must be considered in its multiple dimensions. Diefendorff and Greguras also argue that "the simple express–suppress distinction does not fully represent how individuals manage their emotional expressions at work" (2009, p. 890). In their study, the authors contextualized emotional display rules, based on the assumption that these rules are more complex and nuanced than had been considered in prior research. In order to prove that, Difendorff and Greguras examined the role of discrete emotions and targets in shaping display rules perceptions. Their findings indicated that expression accounted for less than a third of the display rules, when considering the positive emotion of happiness, and that neutrality (equivalent to suppression) accounted for less than half of the display rules, when considering negative emotions. Thus, most employees characterized their display rules as involving something other than complete expression or suppression.

But Diefendorff and Greguras were not the first ones to introduce discrete emotions in the study of emotional labour. Glomb and Tews (2003) proposed a conceptualization of emotional labour and developed a scale (the Discrete Emotions Emotional Labor Scale) using the semantic classification of emotions proposed by Shaver et al. (1987). In it, they retained the love, joy, anger, sadness and fear categories (each containing two or three emotions of different intensities). In defining their emotional labour construct, Glomb and Tews discussed the commonality in different theoretical approaches regarding emotional labour: the internal state of dissonance, the internal processes involved in creating emotional displays (such as deep acting and surface acting), and the behavioural display (as the most proximal component of emotional labour).

Glomb and Tews defined emotional labour as the "behavioral expression and non-expression of felt or unfelt emotions in accordance with display rules" (2003, p. 4). Hence, they focused on the behaviour of emotional expression, consisting of genuine, faked and suppressed positive and negative emotional displays. Their framework addresses some important issues. First, Glomb and Tews acknowledge that conforming to display rules may mean expressing an appropriate emotion, as well as not expressing an inappropriate one. Second, they distinguish between genuine, faked and suppressed emotions – from this point of view, Hochschild stated from the very beginning a clear distinction between genuinely felt emotions and deep acting and surface acting ("feelings do not erupt spontaneously or automatically in either deep acting or surface acting. In both cases the actor has learned to intervene either in creating the inner shape of a feeling or in shaping the outward appearance of one") (2003, p. 36). The expression of naturally felt emotions as a distinct strategy for displaying emotions at work was also acknowledged in a subsequent study (Diefendorff, Croyle & Gosserand, 2005).

The most important aspect, considering the objectives of the current study, is the fact that Glomb and Tews introduced specific emotions beyond a broad positive-negative distinction in the study of emotional labour, removing the "guesswork" regarding what respondents consider positive and negative emotions (2003, p. 6). This is even more important since, as shown by Gibson (2006), despite the "affective revolution" in the study of organizational behaviour, emotions remain a partly taboo subject. Therefore, mindfulness (as heightened awareness) represents an important variable in acknowledging that emotions are a central, rather than a hidden, part of work life.

Moving forward, Glomb and Tews's focus on discrete emotions is consistent with a switch in perspective in recent developments regarding emotions, both in everyday life and organizational settings. Zelenski and Larsen (2000) examined emotions in daily life, using an experience sampling methodology in order to determine the distribution of basic emotions. Their findings supported the idea that positive emotions are more often experienced by individuals. Moreover, addressing the question concerning the discreteness (whether basic emotions are in fact uncorrelated or if they conform to a more dimensional model), the authors concluded that a discrete emotions model fits the data for emotions as states, whereas a dimensional model seems more appropriate when talking about emotions as traits.

On the other hand, Rafaeli, Semmer and Tschan (n.d.) reported that people generally seem to experience negative emotions more often at work than at home. In the same manner, Grandey, Tam, and Brauburger (2002) found that, when asked to report every event that elicited strong feelings at work, employees indicated more negative than positive emotions. They indicated frustration as the most intense negative emotion experienced and respectively liking as the most intense positive emotion. Some authors have pointed out the fact that people tend to recall negative experiences more easily than positive ones, terming this tendency as the negativity bias (Robins & Judge, 2009). Scherer, Wranick, Sangsue, Tran, and Scherer (2004) identified anger as one of the most frequently felt negative emotions at work, due to interactions with others (clients, colleagues, supervisors). Experience sampling studies also showed that activities related to work are among the least enjoyable, with the exception of commuting to and from one's work or household (Stone et al., 2006).

However, when it comes to the study of emotions in organizations, Lazarus and Cohen-Charash (2001) argue for using discrete emotions rather than the emotional dispositions approach. The main reason for this lies in the theory advanced by Izard (1993) regarding the adaptive functions of discrete emotions, as each basic emotion represents the primary motivational system for human behavior and each serves unique organizational and regulatory functions. Therefore, claim Lazarus and Cohen-Charash (2001), in terms of understanding and predicting what happens within the process of organizational adaptation and change, the use of discrete emotions allows an in-depth examination. In other words, knowing exactly which emotion is dominant in a specific situation, one gets to learn much more about the appraisal and the coping process.

Another critique advanced by Lazarus and Cohen-Charash (2001) against the dimensional approach of emotions refers to the exclusively dispositional emphasis that this perspective adopts, regardless of the environmental factors. Elfenbein (2007) admits that strong situations can overwhelm the impact of personality as some jobs were proven to be inherently more stressful than others (Motowildo, Packard & Manning, 1986). For example, frontline employees have to regulate their emotions more since they interact with individuals who are not under the control of the organization and whose needs are sometimes opposed to those of the organization (Wharton & Erickson, 1993). Therefore, because quality is a more subjective judgement of an experience, emotional labour is more relevant for the service sector than for other "more tangible areas", such as manufacturing (Wharton & Erickson, 1993, p. 475).

Despite the importance of situational issues highlighted by the authors mentioned above, Fineman (1996) found that organizational actors have a so-called "emotional history" that they use in responding to different stimuli, meaning they use their emotional experiences when encountering events repeatedly. One can imply, together with Elfenbein (2007), that emotional states and traits influence one another in that traits determine the likelihood of experiencing particular states (Fleeson as cited in Elfenbein, 2007). This aspect was also highlighted by Weiss and Cropanzano (1996), who acknowledged that affective traits represent predispositions, which influence the intensity of emotional responses, meaning a generally pessimistic and aversive person will exert more emotional labour in order to be consistent with the emotional work requirements.

Moving forward, as reported by Diener and Larson, Higginson or Larsen and Ketallar (as cited in Elfenbein, 2007), individuals high in positive affect are more focused externally on promoting positive outcomes whereas those high in negative affect are more focused internally on preventing negative outcomes. Hence, the prevalence of the positive or the negative affect determines the regulatory strategy used (promotion or prevention). Taking this into account, we developed the first research question of the current study: what emotional labour strategy do store clerks use, dependent on the dominant emotional experience dimension?

Miner, Glomb and Hulin (2005) examined the relationship event – mood – behaviour in work settings and found that the association between negative events and mood was approximately five times stronger than that between positive events and mood, even though positive events were reported three to five times more frequently than negative events. Based on these assumptions, we formulated our next research question: what is the relationship between the expression of either genuine or faked negative emotions, as well as the suppression of negative emotions and other emotional experiences, such as shyness, fatigue, serenity, or surprise, in the case of store clerks?

In a recent study, Judge, Wolf and Hirst (2009) found that there are intra-individual differences in terms of personal costs when performing emotional labour. This variation was explained via positive and negative state affect and extraversion. The results confirmed that those who experience negative moods more often tend to engage in surface acting, which leads them to increased emotional exhaustion and decreased job satisfaction. Deep acting was only associated with lower positive affect, meaning that in their efforts to reduce the experience of negative moods, individuals may, although unintentionally, reduce the intensity of the positive mood too. As for the influence of extraversion, Judge et al. (2009) noted that emotional labour is generally more difficult and less rewarding for introverts as compared to extraverts.

In the same manner, in a study regarding the dispositional antecedents and consequences of emotional labour at work, Schaubroeck and Jones (2000) supported, from an employee-focused approach of emotional labour, the positive association between negative affectivity and perceived emotional labour. Hence, the individual emotionality may affect the way one performs emotional labour in terms of intensity, which may further lead to experiencing more job-induced tension. These results are consistent with the findings of Diefendorff and Richard (2003), who reported neuroticism (a proxy measure of negative affectivity) to be a significant predictor of the employee's perceived demand to suppress negative emotions. This brought us to our last research question: what are the implications of the emotional labor strategies used to regulate anger, fear, sadness, and hate on other affective states, such as shyness, fatigue, serenity and surprise?

Mood was also long known as an antecedent of emotional labour (Totterdell & Holman, 2003), since there has to be an emotion present in order for the employee to engage in a regulation process. The emotion regulation strategy chosen can be influenced by the mood the employee is already experiencing. Furthermore, Ilies, Scott, and Judge (2006) observed that state affect contributes to daily variations in different indicators of employee well-being, beyond the effects of trait affect. Considering all this, the current research seeks to investigate whether the emotional experience at work is influenced by negative affect. Therefore, we evaluated the prevalence in the past four weeks of eight specific affects (fear, hostility, guilt and sadness as basic negative emotion categories and shyness, fatigue, serenity and surprise as other affective categories) in order to determine the extent to which they influence the emotional labour strategy used by a sample of Romanian store clerks.

METHODOLOGY

The objective of the present study was to determine the relationship between emotional labour – in terms of expression of genuine or faked negative emotions and of suppression of negative emotions – and the individual's emotionality.

Emotions appear to be important "facets of the products the service industry sells to clients" (Bakker & Heuven, 2006, p. 425). Since working in a customer service job requires conforming to display rules which mainly imply behaving in a positive manner, the study was conducted on a sample consisting of 80 store clerks. The average age of the sample was 32.4 years (SD=5.12) and the majority of the respondents were females (48 females, 32 men). The participants were employees of two supermarkets from Bucharest. They were randomly selected from all the store clerks of the two supermarkets, given the fact that they usually work in shifts. The questionnaires were paper and pencil and administered by a trained professional in groups consisting of 10 individuals each. In order to maintain the confidentiality of the respondents, they were not asked to sign the tests after completing them.

In order to reach the proposed objective and to answer the above research questions, two standardized instruments were administered: DEELS – the Discrete Emotions Emotional Labor Scale (Glomb & Tews, 2003) and PANAS-X – he Positive Affect and Negative Affect Schedule–Expanded Form (Watson & Clark, 1994).

The Discrete Emotions Emotional Labor Scale (Glomb & Tews, 2003) consists of three subscales: genuine expression, faking and suppression. For each subscale, the respondents are asked to assess on a five point Likert scale (e.g. 1 = I never genuinely express this to 5 = I genuinely express this many times a day) the extent to which they have experienced the indicated discrete emotions, in terms of frequency, over the last four weeks. Because of the socially undesirable connotations with the words "faked" and "suppressed", the terms are not used as such. Therefore, the respondents are asked, for example, "How often do you express feelings of (sadness) on the job when you really don't feel that way?" or "How often do you keep (sadness) to yourself when you really feel that way?" The questionnaire consists of 14 items describing both positive and negative discrete emotions. Because the focus of the present study was on negative emotions, we chose to report in the results section only the findings regarding the discrete negative emotions (9 items: the anger category – expressed through anger, aggravation and irritation; the sadness category –

expressed through distress and sadness; the fear category – fear and anxiety, respectively; and the hate category – hate and disliking).

Although the instrument directly addresses only the question of the frequency in performing emotional labour, the DEELS also provides an indirect means of determining the variety (as it includes different emotions families) and the intensity (as one emotion category consists of emotions with different intensities) as they have emerged in the literature as important dimensions of emotional labour.

The Positive Affect and Negative Affect Schedule–Expanded Form (Watson & Clark, 1994) comprises two higher order scales that describe the valence of the affective states (general positive and general negative), as well as 11 specific affects, which describe the content, the distinctive qualities of the individual affects and are grouped in three scales (basic negative emotions, basic positive emotions and other affective states). The respondents were asked to assess the extent to which they felt each of the 60 items representing different feelings and emotions (e.g. general positive – active, alert, enthusiastic, proud; general negative – afraid, nervous, upset; basic negative – afraid, disgusted, ashamed, sad; basic positive – happy, delighted, confident, determined; other – shy, tired, calm, astonished) in the past four weeks, using a five point Likert scale (1 = very slightly or not at all; 5 = extremely).

RESULTS

In order to explore the relationship between negative affect and emotional labour, we first calculated the means and standard deviations for both the scales and the respective subscales of the two constructs analyzed. The results are reported in Tables 33-1 and 33-2. We answered the research questions termed in the literature review by determining the bivariate correlations between the emotional labour scales and subscales and those describing affective states, as assessed by PANAS-X. The results are reported in Tables 33-3, 4, 5 and 6.

Descriptive Statistics

The mean values for the negative scales of emotional labour show that the store clerks from our sample generally either express the negative emotions that they actually feel (M=2.35, SD=.56) or suppress them in order to meet the organizational display rules (M=2.39, SD=.87). As we took into account a typical sample of customer service work, where people are asked to respond to integrative emotional work requirements (which imply displaying positive emotions), it is not surprising that faking emotion regulation in the case of negative emotions was reported merely a few times a month (since expressing negative emotions is not an organizational demand, participants have no reason to fake them).

Table 33-1. Means and standard deviations for emotional labor scales and subscales

DEELS scales and subscales	Mean	Standard deviation
Genuine -	2.35	.56
Faked -	1.52	.61
Suppressed -	2.39	.87
Anger genuine	2.46	.75
Anger faked	1.52	.84
Anger suppressed	2.45	.96
Fear genuine	2.08	.67
Fear faked	1.40	.65
Fear suppressed	2.33	1.12
Sadness genuine	2.88	.67
Sadness faked	1.75	.89
Sadness suppressed	2.45	.99
Hate genuine	1.93	.72
Hate faked	1.40	.66
Hate suppressed	2.30	.92

From the four negative emotion categories, sadness appears to be the most often expressed when actually felt (M=2.88, SD=.67). At the other end of the continuum in terms of frequency of the emotional expression are emotions from the hate category (M=1.93, SD=.72). Instead, participants from our sample report said they tend to keep feelings of anger to themselves (M=2.30, SD=.92), as well as feelings of fear (M=2.33, SD=1.12). Furthermore, the mean values for these two emotion families are similar to those of suppressed anger (M=2.45, SD=.96) and suppressed sadness (M=2.45, SD=.99).

At first look, one may observe that participants usually tend to keep negative emotions in work settings to themselves as part of the emotional work requirements (which encourage the display of positive emotions and the suppression of negative emotions in service encounters), but they also report genuinely expressing the respective emotions (the mean values for the two emotion regulation strategies are comparable in the case of all discrete negative emotions assessed through DEELS).

This trend can be better explained by taking a closer look at the participant results in terms of the intensity of feelings and emotions they felt in the last four weeks, irrespective of if at work or at home.

So, as shown in Table 33-2, participants experienced both general and basic positive emotions to a greater extent (M=3.29, SD=.49; M=3.52, SD=.55). But, despite the lower prevalence of negative emotions (finding consistent with other studies that confirmed individuals usually experience positive emotions more often in everyday life (Zelenski & Larsen, 2000) as well as in work settings, according to Fisher, 2002), the results of the basic negative subscales regarding the extent to which store clerks subjectively experience negative emotions should be considered taking into account the influence of this type of emotionality on individual behaviour, in terms of intensity (Miner et al., 2005).

Another aspect worth taking into consideration is that the other affects category mean (shyness, fatigue, serenity, surprise) (M=2.70, SD=.36) is slightly higher than that of general negative emotions (M=2.27, SD=.65), respective of basic negative emotions (M=2.18, SD=.65). From the four categories comprised of the other affective states scale, serenity is the most frequently and also the most intensely felt (M=3.49, SD=.82). Further on, the correlations matrix will determine the implications of these findings from the point of view of the relationship between using emotional labour in order to regulate negative emotions and the negative dimension of emotional experience in the case of the sample analyzed.

Table 33-2. Means and standard deviations for PANAS-X scales and subscales

PANAS-X scales and subscales	Mean	**Standard deviation**
General +	3.29	.49
General -	2.27	.65
Basic +	3.52	.55
Basic -	2.18	.65
Other	2.70	.36
Fear	2.46	.66
Hostility	2.26	.71
Guilt	1.76	.65
Sadness	2.19	.91
Shyness	2.12	.83
Fatigue	2.92	.59
Serenity	3.49	.82
Surprise	2.50	.93

Test of Research Questions

Although the descriptive statistics offer valuable insights regarding the relationship between emotional labour and negative affectivity in the case of a sample of store clerks, determining the bivariate correlations further tones the findings. It is important to state from the very beginning that the tables presented in this section include only the variables which showed significant correlations.

In order to answer our first research question, we calculated the correlations between the emotional labour scales and subscales as well as the overall scales of positive and negative affect schedule.

Table 33-3. Bivariate Pearson correlations between the emotional labour negative scales and subscales and the PANAS-X overall scales

	General +	General -	Basic +	Basic -	Other
Genuine -	-.039	.488**	-.099	.468**	.017
Suppressed -	.027	.422*	-.110	.414*	.467**
Anger genuine	-.079	.421*	-.127	.387*	.024
Fear genuine	.095	.438*	-.072	.444*	.167
Fear suppressed	.038	.431*	-.044	.405*	.390*
Sadness genuine	-.075	.503**	-.107	.487**	.026
Sadness suppressed	-.104	.381*	-.163	.452*	.546**
Hate suppressed	.063	.369*	-.086	.314	.368*

As can be seen from the correlation matrix reported in Table 33-3, expressing genuinely felt negative emotions is positively related with experiencing both general negative ($r=.488$, $p<0.01$) and basic negative emotions ($r=.468$, $p<0.01$) as dominant emotional dimensions. In the same manner, suppressing negative emotions positively correlates with usually feeling pessimistic and aversive ($r=.422$, $p<0.05$, $r=.414$, $p<0.01$), but it is also positively associated with other affective states ($r=.467$, $p<0.01$).

From the four negative discrete emotion categories taken into account when assessing emotional labour, only three support the foregoing relationship, of which sadness shows the strongest association with the scale of other affective states (fear suppressed, $r=.390$, $p<0.05$, sadness suppressed, $r=.546$, $p<0.01$, hate suppressed, $r=.368$, $p<0.05$). A possible explanation could be that sadness was identified as the most frequently experienced negative emotion, as shown previously.

On the other hand, suppressing feelings of fear, sadness and hate occurs when individuals experience, to a greater extent, both basic negative and general negative emotions. So, the more one feels sad and blue, for instance, the more one will not display bodily and facial signs of anxiety ($r=.431$, $p<0.05$, $r=.405$, $p<0.05$), distress ($r=.381$, $p<0.05$, $r=.452$, $p<0.05$) or dislike ($r=.369$, $p<0.05$). When it comes to regulating fear and sadness, it seems that store clerks from the research sample chose to keep their emotions to themselves when general or basic negative emotions were experienced together with other affective states (fear suppressed, $r=.390$, $p<0.01$; sadness suppressed, $r=.546$, $p<0.01$).

Another finding, as shown in Table 33-3, is that individuals who report high scores in negative affectivity on both general and basic scales tend to exclusively use the genuine expression of negative emotions when they experience anger as a dominant emotional dimension ($r=.421$, $p<0.05$, $r=.387$, $p<0.05$), but tend to suppress feelings of hate or disliking ($r=.369$, $p<0.05$). Meanwhile, when it comes to regulating fear and sadness this distinction is no longer supported, results show that they use both the genuine expression ($r=.438$, $p<0.05$, $r=.444$, $p<0.05$; $r=.503$, $p<0.01$, $r=.487$, $p<0.01$) and the suppression of these two families of negative emotions ($r=.431$, $p<0.05$, $r=.405$, $p<0.05$; $r=.381$, $p<0.05$, $r=.452$, $p<0.05$) when predisposed to feeling irritated or angry.

Moving forward, we focused on what happens in terms of performing emotional labour when specific, basic negative emotions are taken into consideration. In order to answer this question, we determined the correlations between the emotional labour negative scales and subscales and the basic negative emotions subscales of the PANAS-X. The results are reported in Table 33-4.

The results seem to indicate that the more one feels nervous, afraid, irritable, guilty, or ashamed, the more one will display the negative emotions felt in service encounters, since genuinely expressed negative emotions positively correlate with fear ($r=.489$, $p<0.01$), hostility ($r=.399$, $p<0.05$) and guilt ($r=.442$, $p<0.05$) as dominant emotional dimensions. When store clerks from our sample generally feel sad, downhearted, alone, or are shaky or scared, they tend to keep the negative emotions felt in work settings to themselves ($r=.462$, $p<0.01$; $r=.399$, $p<0.05$).

The prevalence of hostility and guilt (understood as ashamed, blameworthy, angry at self, disgusted with self, or dissatisfied with self) positively influences the expression of naturally felt anger ($r=.365$, $p<0.05$; $r=.396$, $p<0.05$), irrespective of the organizational display rules. That is because the two basic negative emotions can be eventually taken as two distinct forms of anger in terms of directionality – hostility refers to feelings of anger oriented towards others, whereas guilt can consist of feelings of anger oriented towards one's self. Regardless of the subject towards it is oriented, anger was found to mediate the relationship between the perception of injustice and retaliatory behaviour (Barclay, Skarlicki & Pugh, 2005).

Table 33-4. Bivariate Pearson correlations between the emotional labour negative scales and subscales and the basic negative affective states from PANAS-X

	Fear	Hostility	Guilt	Sadness
Genuine -	.489**	.399*	.442*	.310
Suppressed -	.462**	.334	.353	.399*
Anger genuine	.333	.365*	.396*	.233
Fear genuine	.514**	.267	.428*	.402*
Fear suppressed	.413*	.382*	.347	.354
Sadness genuine	.519**	.332	.510**	.347
Sadness suppressed	.521**	.312	.428*	.468**
Hate suppressed	.366*	.260	.255	.257

On the other hand, when people are scared, afraid, or nervous they tend to suppress feelings of hate or disliking ($r=.366$, $p<0.05$). Given the context of service interactions, store clerks prefer not to show their dislike to customers, for fear of losing their reinforcements.

Results also highlight that when store clerks from our sample are feeling sad and blue, they choose to keep it to themselves ($r=.468$, $p<0.01$) rather than express it. This relationship can be considered by taking into account the findings of Brief and Weiss (2002), who acknowledged that experiencing negative affect is usually determined by poor social interactions, reduced motivation and performance, lower creativity, and increased withdrawal behaviour.

As we noted earlier, the other affective states assessed through PANAS-X emerged as an important factor in suppressing negative emotions, such as fear, sadness or hate, when performing emotional labour. Based on that, we took a closer look at the possible associations between the three emotional labor strategies mentioned by Glomb and Tews (2003) (expressing naturally felt emotions, faking emotions and suppressing emotions) and the other affective states (shyness, fatigue, serenity and surprise).

Table 33-5. Bivariate Pearson correlations between the emotional labour negative scales and the other affective states from PANAS-X

	Shyness	Fatigue	Serenity	Surprise
Genuine -	-.084	.446*	-.310	.429*

At this first level, the analysis revealed that the more one feels sleepy, tired, drowsy (r=.446, p<0.05) or is amazed, astonished (r=.429, p<0.01), the more one will actually display the negative emotions induced by encounters in the workplace. That is because both fatigue and surprise imply (based on different reasons) a lack of control that enables the natural expression of emotions felt, although negative and thus inappropriate in people works such as store clerks.

In order to obtain more insight regarding the relationship between performing emotional labor in terms of expressing or non-expressing negative emotions and the emotionality of individuals, we carried on the above analysis by determining the correlations between the four discrete negative emotions categories from DEELS and the specific other affective states from PANAS-X.

As is shown in Table 33-6, fatigue and surprise account mainly for the genuine expression of sadness (r=.573, p<0.01; r=.425, p<0.05). Being amazed also influences keeping sadness to oneself (r=.368, p<0.05), but from this point of view shyness shows a stronger relationship with not displaying feelings of sadness (r=.404, p<0.05). Being shy, sheepish is negatively related with faking hate (r=-.400, p<0.05).

Table 33-6. Bivariate Pearson correlations between the emotional labour negative subscales and the other affective states from PANAS-X

	Shyness	Fatigue	Serenity	Surprise
Sadness genuine	-.049	.573**	-.254	.425*
Sadness suppressed	.404*	.322	-.220	.368*
Hate faked	-.400*	-.050	.000	.001

The results presented acknowledge the fact that, when it comes to regulating the behavior of emotional expression, either by genuinely expressing discrete negative emotions or by suppressing them, the dominant dimension of emotional experience has significant implications in the case of the sample under consideration. Hence, the more one is oriented towards experiencing negative emotions, the higher the tendency to either express them as such or to suppress them, since they are considered inappropriate in service encounters. Choosing one of the emotion regulation strategies mentioned above depends mainly on the other affective states experienced besides the general and/or basic negative emotions.

Conclusions

The current study offers relevant insights regarding the research of emotions in the workplace. Despite the fact that organizations lack the actual control over the employee emotions, they can reduce the difference between expected and felt emotions by encouraging employees to actually experience the required emotions. That is, because changes in affect are quite hard to accomplish, as shown by Hemenover (as cited in Judge et al., 2009), attempts to regulate affect do not always go as intended (Larsen as cited in Judge et al., 2009). By focusing on the discrete emotions approach of emotional labour, the effects of the dominant emotional dimension emerge more clearly, varying with the emotion being regulated or the mechanism/strategy used, along with the individual's regulatory skills (Côté, 2005).

Our findings suggest that sadness is the most frequently experienced negative emotion, in the case of store clerks. At the same time, consistent with other findings (Scherer et al., 2004), anger also emerged as an important negative emotion in work settings, especially when individuals experience hostility or guilt. Another critical finding is that store clerks from our sample tend to genuinely express the negative emotions that they feel, irrespective of the display rules and mainly when they feel tired or amazed. The suppressing emotion regulation strategy is used if there are other affective states experienced, besides the basic or general negative emotions. This relationship needs further support as a more detailed analysis (considering the four specific other affective states) did not reveal which specific affective state or states explain the association identified between the two overall scales.

Of course, the present results should also be discussed in terms of limitations of the study. As a first limitation, the current research is an explorative pilot study, hence the conclusions cannot be taken as generally valid in the Romanian work context – the results reported express only the relationship between emotional labour and positive affect in the case of a specific frontline workers sample, that of store clerks. Furthermore, the sample used in conducting the survey is limited. From the point of view of the analyses undergone, a mix of methods would have probably made possible a more in-depth examination.

As for the practical implications of the current findings, it is important for organizations to heighten their awareness regarding the central role of emotions in the workplace, as supported by Gibson (2006). Social relations in work settings (with customers, colleagues, supervisors) were frequently identified as triggers of emotions, both positive and negative, as shown by Rafaeli et al. (n.d.). Among the most important aspects in determining emotions, Weiss, Suckow and Cropanzano (1999) pointed out that a sense of justice and fairness is closely related to respect and appreciation (Semmer, McGrath & Beehr, 2005). The lack of these kind of reinforcements, together with dispositional factors (such as negative affectivity, as shown in the present study), may lead to consequences varying from withdrawal to other, more severe forms of counterproductive behaviours, such as reduced performance or health problems (Semmer et al., 2005). Therefore, by understanding the social relations in work settings, service-based companies can develop and implement policies that meet the needs of both internal and external customers, since emotional labour was proven a key determinant of quality of service and organizational performance, as termed by Hsieh and Guy (2008).

References

Ashforth, B & Humphrey, R (1993). Emotional Labor in Service Roles: The Influence of Identity. *Academy of Management Review,* 18(1), 88–115.

Bakker, A B & Heuven, E (2006). Emotional Dissonance, Burnout and In-role Performance among Nurses and Police Officers. *International Journal of Stress Management,* 13, 423–440.

Barclay, L. J., Skarlicki, D. P., & Pugh, S. D. (2005). Exploring the role of emotions in injustice perceptions and retaliation. Journal of Applied Psychology, 90, 629-643.

Brief, A P & Weiss, H (2002). Organizational Behavior: Affect in the Workplace. *Annual Review of Psychology,* 53, 279–307.

Côté, S (2005). A Social Interaction Model of the Effects of Emotion Regulation on Work Strain. *Academy of Management Review,* 30, 509–530.

Diefendorff, J M, Croyle, M & Gosserand, R (2005). The Dimensionality and Antecedents of Emotional Labor Strategies. *Journal of Vocational Behavior,* 66, 339–357.

Diefendorff, J M & Greguras, G J (2009). Contextualizing Emotional Display Rules: Examining the roles of Targets and Discrete Emotions in Shaping Display Rules. *Journal of Management,* 35, 880–898.

Diefendorff, J M & Richard, E M (2003). Antecedents and Consequences of Emotional Display Rule Perceptions. *Journal of Applied Psychology*. 88(2), 284–294.

Elfenbein, H A (2007). *Emotions in Organizations: A Review in Stages.* Working Paper Series, Institute for Research on Labor and Employment, Berkeley.

Fineman, S (1996). Emotion and Organizing. In S Clegg, C Hardy & W Nord (eds). *Handbook of Organization Studies*, London: Sage.

Fisher, C D (2002). Antecedents and Consequences of Real-time Affective Reactions to Work. *Motivation and Emotion,* 26(1), 3–30.

Gibson, D E (2006). Emotional Episodes at Work: An Experiential Exercise in Feeling and Expressing Emotions. *Journal of Management Education,* 30(3), 477–500.

Glomb, T M, & Tews, M J (2003). Emotional Labor: A Conceptualization and Scale Development. *Journal of Vocational Psychology,* 64, 1–23.

Grandey, A (2000). Emotion Regulation in the Workplace: A New Way to Conceptualize Emotional Labor. *Journal of Occupational Health Psychology,* 5(1), 95–110.

Grandey, A, Tam, A P & Brauburger, A L (2002). Affective States and Traits in the Workplace: Diary and Survey Data from Young Workers. *Motivation and Emotion,* 36, 31–55.

Gross, J (1998b). The Emerging Field of Emotion Regulation: An Integrative Review. *Review of General Psychology,* 2, 271–299.

Hochschild, A R (2003). *The Managed Hearth: Commercialization of Human Feeling* (2nd ed.), London: University of California Press.

Hsieh, C W & Guy, M (2009). Performance Outcomes: The Relationship Between Managing the "Heart" and Managing Client Satisfaction. *Review of Public Personnel Administration,* 291, 41–57.

Ilies, R, Scott, B A & Judge, T A (2006). The Interactive Effects of Personal Traits and Experienced States on Intraindividual Patterns of Citizenship Behavior. *Academy of Management Journal,* 49, 561–575.

Izard, C E (1993). Organizational and Motivational Functions of Discrete Emotions. In M Lewis & J M Haviland (ed.). *Handbook of Emotions* (pp. 631–641). New York: Guilford.

Jones, R G & Best, R G (1995). *An Examination of the Impact of Emotional Work Requirements on Individual and Organization*, Paper presented at the Annual Convention of the Academy of Management, Vancouver, British Columbia, Canada.

Judge, T A, Wolf, E F & Hurst, C (2009). Is Emotional Labor More Difficult for Some than for Others? A Multilevel, Experience-sampling Study. *In Personnel Psychology,* 62, 57–88.

Kruml, S M & Geddes, D (2000). Exploring the Dimensions of Emotional Labor: The Heart of Hochschild's Work. *Management Communication Quarterly,* 14, 8–49.

Lazarus, R S & Cohen-Charash, Y (2001). Discrete Emotions in Organizational Life. In R L Payne and G L Cooper (Eds.), *Emotions at Work: Theory, Research and Applications for Management* (pp. 45–48). Chichester: Wiley.

Miner, A G, Glomb & T M, Hulin, C (2005). Experience Sampling Mood and its Correlates at Work. *Journal of Occupational and Organizational Psychology,* 78, 171–193.

Morris, A & Feldman, D (1996). The Dimensions, Antecedents and Consequences of Emotional Labor. *Academy of Management Review,* 21(4), 906–1010.

Moskowitz, D S & Côté, S (1995). Do Interpersonal Traits Predict Affect? A Comparison of Three Models. *Journal of Personality and Social Psychology,* 69, 915–924.

Motowildo, S J, Packard, J S & Manning, M R (1986). Occupational Stress: Its Causes and Consequences on Job Performance. *Journal of Applied Psychology,* 71(4), 618–629.

Rafaeli, A, Semmer, N & Tschan, F (n.d.). Emotion in Work Settings. In *Oxford Companion to the Affective Sciences*, Oxford University Press.

Rafaeli, A & Sutton, R (1987). Expression of Emotion as Part of the Work Role. *Academy of Management Review,* 12(1), 23–37.

Robins, S P & Judge, T A (2009). *Organizational Behavior*, Upper Saddle River: Prentice-Hall.

Shaver, P, Schwartz, J, Kirson, D & O'Connor, C (1987). Emotion Knowledge: Further Exploration of a Prototype Approach. *Journal of Personality and Social Psychology,* 52(6), 1061–1086.

Schaubroeck, J & Jones, J R (2000). Antecedents of Workplace Emotional Labor Dimensions and Moderators of their Effects on Physical Symptoms. *Journal of Organizational Behavior,* 21(2), 163–183.

Scherer, K R (2005). What are Emotions? And how can they be Measured? *Social Science Information,* 44(4), 695–729.

Scherer, K R, Wranick, T, Sangsue, J, Tran, V & Scherer, U (2004). Emotions in Everyday Life: Probability of Occurrence, Risk Factors, Appraisal and Reaction Patterns. *Social Science Information.* 43(4), 499–570.

Semmer, N K, McGrath, J E & Beehr, T A (2005). Conceptual Issues in Research on Stress and Health. In C L Cooper (Eds.), *Handbook of Stress and Health* (pp. 1–43). New York: CRC Press.

Stone, A A, Schwartz, J E, Schwarz, N, Schkade, D, Krueger, A & Kahneman, D (2006). A Population Approach to the Study of Emotion: Diurnal Rhythms of a Working Day Examined with the Day Reconstruction Method. *Emotion,* 6(1), 139–149.

Totterdell, P & Holman, D (2003). Emotion Regulation in Customer Service Roles: Testing a Model of Emotional Labor. *Journal of Occupational Health Psychology,* 8, 55–73.

Watson, D & Clark, L A (1994). *The PANAS-X. Manual for the Positive and Negative Affect Schedule – Expanded Form,* University of Iowa.

Weiss, H M & Cropanzano, R (1996). Affective Events Theory: A theoretical discussion of the structure, causes, and consequences of affective experiences at work. In B. M. Staw and L. L. Cummings (Eds.), Research in Organizational Behavior, Vol. 18 (pp. 1-74). Greenwich, CT: JAI Press.

Weiss, H, Suckow, K & Cropanzano, R (1999). Effects of Justice Conditions on Discrete Emotions. *Journal of Applied Psychology,* 84(5), 786–794.

Wharton, A S (1993). The Affective Consequences of Service Work. *Work and Occupations,* 20, 205–232.

Wharton, A S & Erickson, R J (1993). Managing Emotions on the Job and at Home: Understanding the Consequences of Multiple Emotional Roles. *Academy of Management Review,* 18(3), 457–495.

Zelenski, J M & Larsen, R J (2000). The Distribution of Basic Emotions in Everyday Life: A State and Trait Perspective from Experience Sampling Data. *Journal of Research in Personality,* 34, 178-–197.

ICT, Migrant Networks and Transnational Identity

Rita Sever

Abstract

The global expansion of Information Communication Technology (ICT) widens access to information, enhances communication capacity and is expected to promote social inclusion and facilitate democratic participation. Among the most influential factors facilitating these phenomena is the effect of globalization on languages in cyberspace.

Global migration is turning many societies into culturally diverse societies, as immigrants settle down and their descendants become ethnic minorities in their host country. Migrants often leave behind not only physical capital but also much of their social capital. ICT – both global and glocal – plays a major role in nurturing "virtual" social capital. Global social networking sites encourage the development of bridging social capital, while local immigrant digital networks enable them to develop bonding social capital in their new country. Transnational networks enable them to maintain some of their former bonding social capital in their country of origin. The traditional image of the uprooted immigrant is being replaced by the image of a connected immigrant. Today's migrants are the actors of a culture of bonds, which they maintain even as they move about. This culture of bonds became visible and highly dynamic since migrants began using ICT massively. It is more and more common for migrants to maintain remote relations typical of relations of proximity and to activate them on a daily basis. From a Diaspora perspective, immigrants are also emigrants. ICT enables them to engage in transnational connections and maintain transnational and/or pluricultural identities.

Diaspora as an analytic term is relevant for investigations of media practices among contemporary immigrants, leaving room for questions of multiple belonging with implications for everyday life. In recent years, especially with the advent of Digital Broadcasting Satellite (DBS) technology, transnational media have become central in the consumption of news by immigrant populations, who tend to seek news very broadly. Extensive news media consumption, the desire for more international news than is found in the national television channels and a critical stance towards the news from these channels are also part of the picture.

Temporary and permanent immigrants use the internet as a "bridgespace", a virtual space that supports flows of people, goods, capital and ideas between the country of origin and the country of destination. "Matrimonial" sites are but one example. Migrant networks play important roles for immigrants and their descendants. Ethnic minority communities develop online portals in which major dilemmas emerge, such as essentialism vs fluidity of identities; universalism vs particularism; or recognition vs redistribution. Internet discussion forums are popular online meeting places for diaspora people. Here they articulate race and culture in the public cyberspaces. One of the recurring topics in these discussions is the nature of their identity and how this relates to living overseas. Participants exchange personal experiences, political opinions, emotional and intellectual expectations about the outer and inner limits of identity and/or culture in their everyday lives. On the web, second-generation immigrant youths orient themselves to the country where they live (bridging between cultures) as well as to their parents' country of origin (bonding of social capital).

Key words: ICT, Diaspora, migrant networks, transnational identity.

Migration, Social Capital and the Role of ICT

Migrants often leave behind not only physical capital (e.g. land, house etc.) but also much of the social capital which they used to possess in their country of origin.

Social capital is a concept that highlights the value of social relations and the role of cooperation and confidence to get collective or economic results. Since social contacts affect the productivity of individuals and groups, social consists of the expectative benefits derived from the preferential treatment and cooperation between individuals and groups. Putnam (2005) distinguished between bonding social capital and bridging social capital. The former (bonding social capital) refers to the value assigned to social networks within homogeneous groups of people (e.g. members of the extended family, friends, neighbours etc.) that are characterized by generalized reciprocity. [1] The latter (bridging social capital) refers to the value of socially heterogeneous networks. For immigrants, their homogeneous networks are a source of comfort, help and support in times of hardships and crises. The heterogeneous networks are a source of more diversified information and advice that could be essential in the process of resettlement.

ICT – both global and glocal – plays a major role in nurturing "virtual" social capital, which is still a new area of research. Global social networking sites (e.g. Facebook) encourage the development of bridging social capital, while local immigrant digital networks enable them to develop bonding social capital in their new country and transnational networks enable them to maintain some of their former social capital in their country of origin.

Migration, Ethnicity and the Culture of Bonds

"Individuals don't migrate; networks migrate."
—Sanchez, 1999

Huge waves of global migration are turning many information-technology societies into culturally diverse societies. First-generation immigrants are followed by second/ third/further generations in the host country and become part of the country's ethnic minorities (often beside native minorities such as the Aborigenes in Australia, the native Americans in the USA, the Palestinian citizens of Israel etc.), often part of ethnic divides.

The term "immigrants" is usually used for the foreign-born inhabitants of a country, and then replaced by the term "ethnic group/minority" to include also the second/third generation offsprings of these immigrants who have settled in the new country.

Black British, Indian/South Asian, Chinese and Muslim minority communities in the UK, (Siapera, 2006), Asians and Latinos in the USA (Harris, Jamison & Trujillo, 2008; Mossberger, Tolbert & Gilbert, 2006), NRI – temporary and permanent immigrants to the USA from India, typically called Non-Resident Indians (Adams & Ghose, 2003), people from the Pacific Islands who live in the USA, Australia and New Zealand (Franklin, 2003), Turkish or Moroccan minority groups in the Netherlands

[1] Generalized reciprocity in a network means that people operate benevolently within a large network of social transactions without expectations about getting specific benefits in return – other than, perhaps, the sort of social insurance provided by the continuance of the network itself.

and Flanders (D'Haenens, Koeman & Saeys, 2007), Ghanaian non-citizen immigrants in London (Herbert et al., 2008), Colombians in Chicago (Balcazar, Garcia-Iriarte & Suarez-Balcazar, 2009), Russian (Leshem & Lissak, 2000) or Ethiopian (Sever, 2007a) Israelis – all these are but a few examples.

Transnationalism refers to the multiple ties and interactions that link peoples across borders. It serves to challenge conventional assumptions regarding the importance of traditional borders and boundaries in defining who we are, how we think, and with whom we associate. It raises questions like "How does one's home define who one is?" Transnational identity refers to people who identify with more than one culture, more than one nation. In some cases it raises questions about divided loyalty.

Current trends in thinking on contemporary migration (in particular, theories on transnational networks) agree that today's migrants are the actors of a culture of bonds, which they themselves have founded and which they maintain even as they move about. Formerly a latent feature but typical of all groups on the move, this culture of bonds became visible and highly dynamic once migrants began massively to use modern information and communication technologies (ICT).

While various theories of globalization focus solely on the dimensions of economic and political transactions, Drori (2007) expands on the cultural and institutional dimensions of globalization and highlights five shared dimensions between globalization and ICT, networks being one of them (the other four are: economic transactions, political relations, globality, and world norms). It is becoming more and more common for migrants to maintain remote relations typical of relations of proximity and to activate them on a daily basis. Thus Diminescu (2008) states that the paradigmatic figure of the uprooted migrant is yielding to another figure: the connected migrant.

Globalization, Glocalization and the Role of Language in the Formation of Migrant Networks and Transnational Identity

Among the most influential factors facilitating – sometimes even just enabling – immigrants' networks is the effect of glocalization on languages in cyberspace.

At the beginning, most of the Web pages in the world were in English, and most of the early nationally-oriented Internet newsgroups conducted their discussion in English as well. This state of affairs caused great consternation for many people around the world. But it turns out that the fears of an English-dominated Internet were premature. The number of non-English websites is growing rapidly and many of the more newly active Internet newsgroups extensively use the national language.

Underlying this change of direction is a more general shift from globalization to glocalization (Sever, 2009). The first wave of globalization – whether in economics or in the media – witnessed vertical control from international centres, as witnessed for example by the rise of media giants such as CNN and MTV. But in more recent waves, a process of relocalization is occurring, as corporations seek to maximize their market share by shaping their products for local conditions. Thus, while CNN and MTV originally broadcast around the world in English, they are now producing editions in Hindi, Spanish and other languages in order to compete with other international and regional media outlets. A similar process is occurring with the Internet, although via a more spontaneous and bottom-up process. Whereas more than 90 per cent of the early users of the Internet were located in North America, the net is now growing fastest in developing countries such as China and India and many others. In response to this situation, web browsers are being adapted for an increasing number of languages and character sets. Thus, while Internet users around the world still use English for global communication, today they are increasingly turning to their own language to reach websites or join discussions in transnational immigrant networks. (Warschauer 2000).

Immigrants' mother tongue plays an important role in transnational identities. Fialkova (2005) claims that the Russian language and culture are more important factors than group consciousness for immigrants from the FSU. Massey & Magaly (2010) found that the use of Spanish played an important unifying role for Latino immigrants in the US, especially when reinforced through participation in language-specific social networks. They explored the formation and content of transnational identities among first and second generation Latino youths in three different urban sites in the northeastern United States: Philadelphia, New York City and the New Jersey urban corridor connecting these two poles. They found a solidification of a pan-national Latino identity in the second generation; this did not necessarily imply ghettoization, but defined an ideological space from which the second generation encountered American society and its diverse peoples: whites, blacks, Asians, and others. Latinidad was employed conceptually as a key distinction between themselves and the rest of American society. The use of Spanish played an important unifying role. Respondents spoke about feeling able to communicate in an "emotional way" with other Latinos in contrast with the "Nordic" way they talked to white Americans, an alienation heightened by their poverty and economic insecurity. Feelings of “Latinidad” were bound up with commonalities of experience, language, culture, social interaction, and emotional sensibilities.

DIASPORA, IMMIGRANT NETWORKS AND ICT

Diaspora as an analytic term is relevant for observations and empirical investigations of media practices among contemporary immigrants, leaving room for questions of multiple belonging and conflicting loyalties, with implications for everyday life.

Defining diasporas, scholars indicate the importance of their symbolic dimensions and the ethnic group consciousness. In the case of immigrants from the FSU the vision of “home”, loyalty and belonging are renegotiated both in the metropolis and in the diaspora. Virtual encounters of ex-Soviets enable emigrants residing in various countries to sort out memories of the past and new experiences in host countries relying on familiar cultural codes and symbols. Not all ex-Soviets involved in the activities of these sites consciously belong to the diaspora. Even if they do, this does not presuppose loyalty to the Russian Federation, and the discourse of return to the fatherland has only a marginal role. Other sites seem more oriented to the successful integration in the host country, but they also reflect immigrants’ attempts to reproduce familiar institutions, cultural practices, and loyalty to the Russian language (Fialkova & Yelenevskaya, 2005).

In recent years, especially with the advent Digital Broadcasting Satellite (DBS) technology, transnational media has become central in the consumption of news by immigrant populations. This has received some attention as a factor associated with the lack of integration into their new societies (Christiansen, 2004). Instead, a transnational-identity perspective could be useful here. People with migrant experience tend to seek news very broadly. Extensive news media consumption, the desire for more international news than is found in the national television channels and a critical stance towards the news from these channels are also part of the picture. A diaspora perspective transforms the prospect presented by observers and journalists, worried about integration processes and prompts considerations that immigrants are also emigrants (Christiansen, 2004).

The importance of diaspora groups and transnational links is illustrated, for example, in various coping strategies that Ghanaian migrant workers in London developed to overcome their difficulties, at the individual and collective levels (Herbert et al., 2008).

The rise of the diaspora concepts is strongly linked to ICT and its use by migrants. Succesful immigrants in affluent countries sometimes make use of ICT to assist development in their third-world country of origin. An interesting example is presented by Ndangam (2008) who studied how a media organization (*The Post* newspaper) located in Cameroon, namely within the "have not" side of the digital divide, was publishing online. A skills inadequacy in the newsroom and a relatively weak telecommunications infrastructure in the country have prompted the newspaper's online version not only to target a diasporic audience, but to rely on the expertise and resources of this audience in the development and administration of its website. Illustrating this mode of collaboration between the diasporic audience and the newspaper and detailing its implications for news production and editorial decision-making, Ndangam argues that this model of online news publishing, rarely evidenced in the literature, illustrates the nature and significance of transnational relationships in the diffusion and adoption of online publishing. It simultaneously reflects an alternative transnational practice through which African migrants engage with their home of origin.

Ethnic minority youths in the Netherlands orient themselves on the web to the country where they live (bridging between cultures) as well as to their parents' country of origin (bonding of social capital) (D'Haenens, Koeman & Saeys, 2007).

Temporary and permanent immigrants from India to the USA (typically called Non-Resident Indians or NRIs) use the internet as a "bridgespace", namely a virtual space that supports flows of people, goods, capital and ideas between South Asia and North America. "Matrimonial" sites, namely sites designed to support the identification of marriage partners, are one example (Adams & Ghose, 2003).

The Internet serves migrants as the meeting place of dispersed communities. In Israel, for instance, almost half (48.5%) of first-generation recent immigrants[2] participate in online forums – more than the general Jewish (38.9%) and Arab (34.1%) population (CBS, 2007).

Internet discussion forums are popular online meeting places for the Polynesian Diaspora – people from the Pacific Islands who live in the USA, Australia and New Zealand. Here they articulate race and culture in public cyberspaces. One of the most frequently recurring topics in the discussions is the nature of their identity and how this relates to living overseas. Participants, many of whom are of mixed race, exchange personal experiences, political opinions, emotional and intellectual

---

[2] Immigrated since 1990.

expectations about the outer and inner limits of race/ethnicity, and/or culture in their everyday lives (Franklin, 2003).

For Russian emigrants from FSU, two kinds of websites are created: one is institutional sites, the other grassroots sites. The former are web pages that have emerged at the initiative of various Russian government institutions and non-governmental organizations (NGO);[3] the latter are sites created by emigrants, both individuals and NGOs. Sites created by the Russian state organizations aim to promote ties with "compatriots abroad". Reflecting a new trend in Russian policies, proclaiming ties with the diaspora a high priority issue, these sites aim at increasing expatriates' involvement in economic, cultural and scientific life in the "old country" and encourage repatriation. Sites of the second kind, grassroots initiatives of the migrants, contribute to community building as forums for sharing useful information about institutions, laws and customs in the receiving society and building up a network of services rendered by immigrants to their co-ethnics. Many of these cater to the cultural needs of the newcomers and thus respond to challenges of integration and acculturation (Fialkova & Yelenevskaya, 2005).

Today's migrants are able to maintain strong economic, cultural, political and physical ties to their place of birth. Traditional immigrant issues such as citizenship, political incorporation and cultural assimilation are being rapidly transformed (Sanchez, 1999). The concept of transnationalism allows for individual diversity and collective similarity to co-exist (Green & Power, 2005).

Some of the research of transnational identities and networks focuses on immigrants to neighbor countries, such as New Zealanders in Australia (Green & Power, 2005) or Mexicans in the US (Velasco Ortiz, 2005). But globalization has made transnational connections to exist also between far-away countries, one well known example being Russian immigrants in Israel, Canada or the US.

The increasing volume of transnational practices foster identity construction across borders, thereby disjoining geographical space and social space in which identities are constructed and negotiated. Some of the recent studies focus on the linkage between transnationalism and transnational identity; namely on transnational identity formation among immigrant groups with high level of transnational organizing of economic and political activities (Green & Powers, 2005; Velasco Ortiz, 2005).

---

[3] Similarly, Israeli government and NGOs maintain websites for addressing the Jewish diaspora abroad.

Others pay increasing attention to transnational identity construction of immigrant groups without high levels of transnationalism (Han, 2010).

Here are a few examples.

Green & Power (2005) investigated how migration to Australia affects New Zealanders' sense of identity. New Zealanders living in Australia have both an enhanced sense of their New Zealand identity and a new transnational identity, created through their experiences and interactions within their new society together with their continued contact with their country of origin.

Velasco Ortiz (2005) investigated groups located on both sides of the Mexico–US border that have maintained strong links with towns and villages in the Mixteca region of Oaxaca. Her research brings to light the way in which the dispersion of members of different communities is offset by the formation of migrant networks with family and community ties, while the politicization of these networks enables the formation of both hometown associations and transnational pan-ethnic organizations. She documented and analysed the construction of novel identities formed within transnational contexts that may not conform to identities in either the "sending" or "receiving" societies. She described in detail the emergence of a wide range of transnational indigenous organizations and communities in the greater Mexico–US border region. She examined the formation of ethnic identity under the conditions of international migration, giving special attention to the emergence of organizations and their leaders as collective and individual ethnic agents of change. Three lines of development: the formation of organizations beyond the confines of home communities; the emergence of indigenous migrant leaders; and the shaping of ethnic consciousness that assimilates the experiences of a community straddling the border.

Han (2010) examined the identity dynamics among Korean military wives in the US who do not have high level of transnationalism but negotiate their identities transnationally by way of various identity practices to imagine themselves as members of multiple communities across national and cultural boundaries. His study reveals that the non-mobile immigrants created multilayered "imagined communities" which converts their identities to multiple identities. This effort is the part of the non-mobile immigrants' gradual adaptation to US society and resistance to assimilation.

The Impact of the Digital Divide between Migrants' Countries of Origin and Their Countries of Destination

The term "digital divide" is often used as an indicator of inequality between people and between countries and populations. It refers to gaps in future opportunities between those with different degrees of connectedness to information and communication technology (ICT). Originally, the term was used to address the assumed polarization between those who have and those who don't have access – first to computers, later on also to the Internet. Today however the digital divide notion is gradually widening. Digital awareness divide, infrastructure divide, unequal skills and unequal ability to use information technology as means of production – all these are different dimensions of the digital divide. It can take the form of inequality in various facets of digital accessibility: financial, cognitive, content and political (Mizrachi et al, 2005).

The digital divide discourse takes place on two different levels: one is an international level (i.e. inequality between countries), the other an intranational or individual level (i.e. inequality between people or sub-groups of a country's population).

Access to ICT in different countries is shaped by the interaction of socioeconomic, political, cultural, social, and technological factors. Fuchs (2009) identifies factors which influence Internet usage in 126 countries and shows that income inequality measured by the Gini coefficient is an important influencing factor besides per capita income, the degree of urbanization and the level of democratization. The results question reductionist digital divide approaches that analyse information inequality by focusing on a single variable such as technology or markets.

The adoption of mobile phones has been skyrocketing globally during the current decade, but present adoption levels are quite uneven across countries. Such disparities are also found over a range of other information and communications technologies. Stump, Wen & Zhan (2008) investigated the adoption of mobile phones at the country level of analysis across 170 nations, examining the effects of three country-level socioeconomic factors paralleling the individual-level demographic traits that in past studies have predominantly predicted early adoption of innovations. They found positive effects of populations' mean age and wealth measured by GNP (Gross National Product), but no impact of a nation's education level.

Drori & Jang (2003) attempted to find patterns of differentiation between countries worldwide and between blocs of countries in terms of IT connectedness. Their results indicate that the global digital divide is more a product of networking into global society than it is a mere reflection of local economic capabilities.

Many of the immigrants to the so-called first world, affluent countries, come from the so-called third-world, developing, poor countries. For immigrants coming from these countries, namely those on the "wrong side" of the digital divide, the proliferation of ICT in their country of destination might widen the gap between them and the local population. On the other hand, for immigrants coming from countries that are digitally advanced, the internet can be quite helpful in the processes of resettlement and transnational identity formation.

Diaspora, Transnationalism and Divided Loyalties

Rather than seeing migration as the loss of one national identity, it could be seen as the platform of building a transnational identity that derives from both the country of origin and the host country. But transnational identities are in danger of being suspected to carry divided loyalties – to the country they came from and to the country they settled in. When the two countries are in conflict with each other, this danger is very real. Israel supplies an interesting example of how two different kinds of transnational identities are being treated.

In Israel, diaspora and transnationalism play different roles for Jews and non-Jews, and for the two large minority groups: Russian immigrants and native Palestinian citizens of the Israeli state.

For Israeli Jews the concept diaspora encompasses not only contemporary emigrants from Israel, but all Jews that do not live in Israel. The Jewish diaspora is believed to be two thousand years old.

For the Palestinian citizens of Israel, native for many generations, diaspora means relatives, neighbours and friends who have migrated from Israel to Western or Arab countries, many of the latter being enemy states for the Israeli state. Thus Palestinian citizens in Israel who maintain transnational connections with their diaspora, especially in Arab countries, are looked upon suspiciously by the Jewish public and officials; such connections are often defined as "forbidden association with enemy agencies". Transnational identity is perceived as reflecting disloyalty to the Israeli state, and public identification with people in surrounding Arab countries, are addressed as bordering on national betrayal.

The Russian immigrants are in a different position. They see themselves as part of a wide ex-Soviet Russian speaking diaspora residing in various parts of the western world. The Israeli public accepts this half-heartedly. Their transnational connections are accepted as financially beneficial but their transnational identity is resented as reluctance to assimilate and as a barrier to their absorption in Jewish society, as betrayal of the Zionist ideology and – as elsewhere (Christiansen, 2004) – as a factor associated with lack of integration into their new society. ICT facilitates their transnational ties, which in turn contribute to the maintenance of cultural diversity in Israel and help redefine the notion of integration in non-assimilative terms.

CONCLUSION

Migrants often have to leave behind physical capital, as well as much of their social capital. ICT – both global and glocal – plays a major role in nurturing new "virtual" social capital. Global social networking sites encourage the development of bridging social capital, while local immigrant digital networks enable them to develop bonding social capital in their new country and transnational networks enable them to maintain some of their former bonding social capital in their country of origin.

The traditional image of the uprooted immigrant is being replaced by the image of a connected immigrant. Today's migrants are the actors of a culture of bonds, which they themselves have founded and which they maintain even as they move about. This culture of bonds became visible and highly dynamic since migrants began using ICT massively. It is more and more common for migrants to maintain remote relations typical of relations of proximity and to activate them on a daily basis.

Temporary and permanent immigrants use the internet as a "bridgespace", a virtual space that supports flows of people, goods, capital and ideas between the country of origin and the country of destination. "Matrimonial" sites, those sites designed to support the identification of marriage partners, are one example. Migrant networks play important roles for immigrants and their descendants. Ethnic minority communities develop online portals in which major dilemmas emerge, such as essentialism vs fluidity of identities; universalism vs particularism; or recognition vs redistribution. Internet discussion forums are popular online meeting places for diaspora people. Here they are articulating race and culture in the public cyberspaces of the worldwide web. One of the recurring topics in these discussions is the nature of their identity and how this relates to living overseas. Participants exchange personal experiences, political opinions, emotional and intellectual expectations about the outer and inner limits of identity and/or culture in their everyday lives. On the web, second-generation immigrant youths orient themselves to the country where they live (bridging cultures) as well as to their parents' country of origin (bonding of social capital).

Some of the research of transnational identities and networks focuses on immigrants to neighboring countries, but globalization and ICT have enabled transnational connections to exist also between people in far-away countries. The increasing volume of transnational practices foster identity construction across borders, thereby disjoining geographical space and social space in which identities are constructed and negotiated. Transnational identity formation is found among immigrant groups with high level of transnational organizing of economic and political activities, but transnational identity construction is also found in immigrant groups without high levels of transnationalism.

In the case of immigrants who do not have high levels of actual transnation activity, their resistance to assimilation while gradually adapting to their new society, may involve various identity practices to imagine themselves as members of multiple communities across national and cultural boundaries.

Immigrants sometimes employ a transnational identity conceptually as a key distinction between themselves and the rest of the host society. The solidification of a pan-national identity in second-generation immigrants does not necessarily imply ghettoization; it may define an ideological space from which the second generation encounters the host society and its diverse peoples. The use of mother-tongue also plays an important unifying role, especially when it is reinforced through participation in language-specific social networks. Transnational identities are bound up with commonalities of experience, language, culture, social interaction, and emotional sensibilities. Immigrants have both an enhanced sense of their original identity and a new transnational identity, created through their experiences and interactions within their new society together with their continued contact with their country of origin. The construction of novel identities formed within transnational contexts may not conform to identities in either the "sending" or "receiving" societies.

The formation of ethnic identity under the conditions of international migration, may go hand in hand with the emergence of organizations and their leaders as collective and individual ethnic agents of change. Concepts such as diaspora, transnational relations and transnational identities are gradually gaining attention among researchers of migration. After all, immigrants (to one country) are also emigrants (from another one). ICT enables them to engage in transnational connections, develop their bonding and bridging social capital, develop and maintain transnational and/or pluricultural identities.

Diaspora as an analytic term is relevant for observations and empirical investigations of media practices among contemporary immigrants, leaving room for questions of multiple belonging and conflict of loyalties, with implications for everyday life.

The concept of transnationalism allows for individual diversity and collective similarity to co-exist. Rather than seeing migration as the loss of one national identity, it could be seen as the building of a transnational identity that derives from both the country of origin and the host country. But transnational identities are in danger of being suspected to carry divided loyalties – to the country they came from and to the country they settled in. When the two countries are in conflict with each other, this danger is quite conspicuous.

REFERENCES

Adams, P C & Ghose, R (2003). India.com: the construction of a space between. *Progress in Human Geography,* 27 (August), 414–437.

Balcazar, F E, Garcia-Iriarte, E & Suarez-Balcazar, Y (2009). Participatory Action Research With Colombian Immigrants. *Hispanic Journal of Behavioral Sciences*, 31, 112–127.

CBS – The Israeli Central Bureau of Statistics http://www.cbs.gov.il/reader 2004, 2005,2007, 2008, 2009.

Christiansen, C C (2004). News Media Consumption among Immigrants in Europe: The Relevance of Diaspora. *Ethnicities*, 4(June): 185–207.

D'Haenens, L, Koeman J & F Saeys (2007). Digital Citizenship among Ethnic Minority Youths in the Netherlands and Flanders. *New Media & Society,* 9(2), 278–299.

Diminescu, D (2008). The Connected Migrant: An Epistemological Manifesto. *Social Science Information,* 47(4), 565–579.

Drori, G (2007). Information Society as a Global Policy Agenda: What Does It Tell Us About the Age of Globalization? *International Journal of Comparative Sociology,* 48, 297–316.

Drori, G & Jang, Y S (2003). The Global Digital Divide: A Sociological Assessment of Trends and Causes. *Social Science Computer Review* 21(2), 144–161.

Fialkova, L (2005). Emigrants from the FSU and the Russian-language Internet. *Toronto Slavic Quarterly*, 12. http://www.utoronto.ca/tsq/12/fialkova12.shtml

Fialkova, L & Yelenevskaya, M (2005). Incipient Soviet Diaspora: Encounters in Cyberspace. *Narodna Umjetnost: Croatian Journal of Ethnology and Folklore Research*, 42(1), 83–101.

Franklin, M I (2003). I Define My Own Identity: Pacific Articulations of "Race" and "Culture" on the Internet. *Ethnicities,* 3 (December), 465–490.

Fuchs C (2009). The Role of Income Inequality in a Multivariate Cross-National Analysis of the Digital Divide. *Social Science Computer Review,* 27, 41–58.

Green, A, & Power, M R (2005). *Social Construction of Transnational Identity*, Annual Conference of the Australian and New Zealand Communication Association, Christchurch, New Zealand.

Han, D (2010). The Formation of Transnational Identities by Non-Traditional Transnationals: The Case of Korean Military Wives and their Transnational Identitity Formation. *Global Studies Journal,* 3(2), 249–260. Available at http://gsj.cgpublisher.com/product/pub.184/prod.159

Harris, A L, Jamison, K M & Trujillo, M H (2008). Disparities in the Educational Success of Immigrants: An Assessment of the Immigrant Effect for Asians and Latinos. *Annals of the American Academy of Political and Social Science,* 620(November), 90–114.

Herbert, J, May, J, Wills, K, Datta, K, Evans, Y & McIlwaine, C (2008). Multicultural Living? Experiences of Everyday Racism Among Ghanaian Migrants in London. *European Urban and Regional Studies,* 15, 103–117.

Leshem, E & Lissak, M (2000). Formation of "Russian" Community in Israel. In L Dymerskaya-Tsigelman (ed.), *The Jews of the Soviet Union in Transition*, 4(19), 47–66.

Massey, D S & Magaly, S R (2010). *Brokered Boundaries: Creating Immigrant Identity in Anti-Immigrant Times.* New York: Russell Sage Foundation.

Mizrachi, Y Bar, N, Katsermov, I & Oron, N (eds) (2005). *e-Readiness and Digital Divide survey, Israel 2005*. Jerusalem, Israel: Ministry of Finance (Hebrew) www.maor.gov.il

Mossberger, K, Tolbert, C J, & Gilbert, M (2006). Race, Place, and Information Technology. *Urban Affairs Revie,* 41(May), 583–620.

Ndangam, L N (2008). Free lunch? Cameroon's Diaspora and Online News Publishing. *New Media Society,* 10(August), 585–604.

Putnam, R D (2005). *Is Society Taking Care of the Marginalized Citizen?* Paper presented at the World Leisure European Conference in Malmo, Sweden, 23–27 May.

Sanchez, A (1999). *Transnationalism not assimilation.* Available at http://www.plannersnetwork.org/publications/1999_136/sanchez.htm

Sever, R (2007a). *Ethiopian Youth in Israel – Status Report*, Jerusalem: SHATIL (Hebrew)

—. (2007b). The Language of Integration: Promoting Immigrant Integration by Active Encouragement of Mother-tongue Maintenance and Inter-cultural Bridgemaking in Education. In Perry, P (ed), *Education in a Multi-cultural Society*. Tel Aviv: Carmel. (Hebrew) pp. 67–104.

—. (2009). *Evaluation of "Glocalized" Multi-level Interventions.* Paper presented at the 39th World Congress of IIS in Yerevan, Armenia, June 11–14.

Siapera, E (2006). Multiculturalism Online :The Internet and the Dilemmas of Multicultural Politics. *European Journal of Cultural Studies,* 9(1), 5–24.

Stump, R L, Wen G & Zhan, L (2008). Exploring the Digital Divide in Mobile-phone Adoption Levels across Countries: Do Population Socioeconomic Traits Operate in the Same Manner as Their Individual-level Demographic Counterparts?" *Journal of Macromarketing,* 28(December), 397–412.

Velasco Ortiz, L (2005). *Mixtec Transnational Identity*, Tucson Arizona: University of Arizona Press.

Warschauer, M (2000). Language, Identity, and the Internet. In B Kolko, L Nakamura & G Rodman (eds), *Race in Cyberspace*. New York: Routledge.